NATIONAL UNDERWRITER
a division of ALM Media, LLC

THE TOOLS & TECHNIQUES OF INCOME TAX PLANNING, 7TH EDITION

Stephan R. Leimberg, Esq., Michael S. Jackson, CPA/PFS, M.T., Jay Katz, J.D., LL.M., John J. Scroggin, J.D., LL.M., AEP, and Robert S. Keebler, CPA/PFS, MST, AEP (Distinguished), CGMA

With the passage of the SECURE Act in late 2019 and the recent COVID-19 legislation, financial advisors, planners, and insurance professionals are in need of up-to-date, reliable tools and expert insights into income tax planning techniques.

Every area of tax planning covered in this book is accompanied by the tools and techniques you can use to:

- Help your clients successfully navigate the latest income tax rules and regulations;
- Quickly simplify the tax aspects of complex planning strategies; and
- Confidently advise your individual clients as well as small- and medium-size business owners.

This 7th edition of *The Tools & Techniques of Income Tax Planning* provides all of that in abundance. All chapters have been completely updated to reflect the many changes brought about by the new pieces of legislation and the rules changes that have accompanied them. New and revised material includes:

- New chapters on the SECURE Act and COVID-19 legislation
- Details on IRS and DOL regulatory changes
- Updated advice on retirement planning issues, including COVID-19 hardship distributions, changing RMD requirements, and new contribution rules
- Coverage of new rules eliminating the "stretch IRA" and planning advice to help clients meet their estate planning goals
- Litigation updates
- And more!

Consistent with the first several editions of this valuable resource, readers benefit from:

- Detailed explanations of complex real-world tax issues
- Easy-to-read explanations of how various tax strategies work and when they should and should not be employed
- Clear, thorough examples that show exactly when certain tax rules apply and how planners can help their clients avoid "tax traps" that can lead to unexpected and unnecessary tax liability

- Comprehensive explanation of investment-related tax concepts, which help investors and planners devise tax-efficient strategies
- Thoughtful, independent advice about the best strategies for specific situations

As with all the resources in the highly acclaimed Leimberg Library, every area covered in this book is accompanied by the tools, techniques, practice tips, and examples you can use to help your clients successfully navigate the complex course of income tax planning and confidently meet their needs.

Related Titles Also Available:

- *Tax Facts on Investments*
- *Tax Facts on Individuals & Small Business*
- *The Tools & Techniques of Financial Planning*
- *The Tools & Techniques of Estate Planning*
- *The Tools & Techniques of Employee Benefit and Retirement Planning*

7TH EDITION

The Tools & Techniques of

Income Tax Planning

LEIMBERG LIBRARY

Stephan R. Leimberg

Michael S. Jackson • Jay Katz
John J. Scroggin • Robert S. Keebler

ISBN 978-1-949506-57-0

Library of Congress Control Number: 2020938817

This publication is designed to provide accurate and authoritative information in regard to the subject matter covered. It is sold with the understanding that the publisher is not engaged in rendering legal, accounting or other professional service. If legal advice or other expert assistance is required, the services of a competent professional person should be sought. – From a Declaration of Principles jointly adapted by a Committee of The American Bar Association and a Committee of Publishers and Associations.

THE NATIONAL UNDERWRITER COMPANY

The National Underwriter Company
A division of ALM Media, LLC
4157 Olympic Blvd., Suite 225
Erlanger, KY 41018

Seventh Edition

Printed in the United States of America

ABOUT THE NATIONAL UNDERWRITER COMPANY
a division of ALM Media, LLC

For over 120 years, The National Underwriter Company, *a division of ALM Media, LLC* has been the first in line with the targeted tax, insurance, and financial planning information you need to make critical business decisions. Boasting nearly a century of expert experience, our reputable editors are dedicated to putting accurate and relevant information right at your fingertips. With *Tax Facts, FC&S® Expert Coverage Interpretation, Tools & Techniques, Field Guide, Insurance Coverage Law Center, Property & Casualty Coverage Guides* and other resources available in print, eBook, or online, you can be assured that as the industry evolves National Underwriter will be at the forefront with the thorough and easy-to-use resources you rely on for success.

Update Service Notification

This National Underwriter Company publication is regularly updated to include coverage of developments and changes that affect the content. If you did not purchase this publication directly from The National Underwriter Company, *a division of ALM Media, LLC* and you want to receive these important updates sent on a 30-day review basis and billed separately, please contact us at (800) 543-0874. Or you can mail your request with your name, company, address, and the title of the book to:

The National Underwriter Company
a division of ALM Media, LLC
4157 Olympic Boulevard
Suite 225
Erlanger, KY 41018

If you purchased this publication from The National Underwriter Company, *a division of ALM Media, LLC,* directly, you have already been registered for the update service.

Contact Information

To order any National Underwriter Company title, please

- call 1-800-543-0874, 8-6 ET Monday – Thursday and 8 to 5 ET Friday
- online bookstore at www.nationalunderwriter.com, or
- mail to Orders Department, The National Underwriter Company, *a division of ALM Media, LLC,* 4157 Olympic Blvd., Ste. 225, Erlanger, KY 41018

DEDICATIONS

Stephan R. Leimberg

To My Best Friend in All The World, my Wife Jo-Ann,
To My Daughters, Charlee and Lara,
and To My Grandsons, Max and Aaron

Michael S. Jackson

To my extraordinary wife, Maria,
for her constant love, support and encouragement.
To my wonderful children, Jared and Rebecca,
who make me so proud day after day.

Jay Katz

Dedicated to the memory of my son, Asher Katz.
Although way too short, his life will be forever celebrated
and remembered in the lifetimes of those who knew him.
Also, dedicated to my wife, Peggy and my other
son, Braum who also celebrate the memory of Asher.

John J. Scroggin

To Lynn who continues to amaze me after 37 years

Robert S. Keebler

To my wife Bonnie and my children Grant, Emily, Mitchell, and Spencer

ABOUT THE AUTHORS

Stephan R. Leimberg

Stephan R. Leimberg is CEO of Leimberg and LeClair, Inc., an estate and financial planning software company, CEO of LISI, Leimberg Information Services, Inc., an email newsletter service, and President of Leimberg Associates, Inc., a publishing and software company. He is an Adjunct Professor in the Masters of Taxation Program of Villanova University School of Law and former adjunct at Temple University School of Law. He holds a B.A. from Temple University, and a J.D. from Temple University School of Law. Leimberg is the Editor of the American Society of Financial Service Professionals audio publication, *Keeping Current*.

Leimberg is the author or co-author of numerous books on estate, financial, and employee benefit and retirement planning and a nationally known speaker. Leimberg is the creator and principal author of the entire nine book *Tools & Techniques* series including *The Tools & Techniques of Estate Planning, The Tools & Techniques of Financial Planning, The Tools & Techniques of Employee Benefit and Retirement Planning, The Tools & Techniques of Life Insurance Planning, The Tools & Techniques of Charitable Planning, The Tools & Techniques of Investment Planning, The Tools & Techniques of Risk Management, The Tools & Techniques of Practice Management*, and *The Tools & Techniques of Retirement Income Planning*. Leimberg is co-author of *Tax Planning with Life Insurance* with noted attorney Howard Zaritsky, *The Book of Trusts* with attorneys Charles K. Plotnick and Daniel Evans, and *How to Settle an Estate* with Charles K. Plotnick. He was also a contributing author of the American Bar Association's *The Lawyer's Guide to Retirement*.

Leimberg is co-creator of many software packages for the financial services professional including Estate and Financial Planning *NumberCruncher* (estate planning), *DeCoupleCruncher* (estate planning), *Financial Analyzer II* (financial calculations), *Estate Planning Quickview* (Estate Planning Flow Charts), *Life Settlement NumberCruncher* (life settlement buy-hold analysis), *Planning Ahead for a Secure Retirement* (PowerPoint Client Seminar) and *Toward a Zero Estate Tax* (PowerPoint Client Estate Planning Seminar).

A nationally known speaker, Professor Leimberg has addressed the Miami Tax Institute, the NYU Tax Institute, the Federal Tax Bar, the Notre Dame Law School and Duke University Law School's Estate Planning Conference, the National Association of Estate Planners and Councils, the AICPA's National Estate Planning Forum, the ABA Section on Taxation, and The Annual Meeting of the American Society of Financial Service Professionals. Leimberg has also spoken to the Federal Bureau of Investigation, and the National Aeronautics and Space Administration.

Leimberg was awarded the Excellence in Writing Award of the American Bar Association's Probate and Property Section. He has been honored as Estate Planner of the Year by the Montgomery County Estate Planning Council and as Distinguished Estate Planner by the Philadelphia Estate Planning Council. He is also a recipient of the President's Cup of the Philadelphia Life Underwriters, a two time Boris Todorovitch Lecturer, and the First Ben Feldman Lecturer.

Leimberg was named Edward N. Polisher Lecturer of the Dickinson School of Law and 2004 recipient of the National Association of Estate Planners and Councils Distinguished Accredited Estate Planner award.

Leimberg's LISI email newsletter/data base at www.leimbergservices.com is used daily by thousands of estate, financial, employee benefit, charitable, and retirement planning practitioners.

Michael S. Jackson

Michael S. Jackson, CPA/PFS, M.T., is a Tax Partner with Grant Thornton and leads the Philadelphia Private Wealth Services Practice. He has over twenty years of experience providing a wide range of tax compliance and consulting, financial planning and wealth transfer strategies for closely held businesses, private and publicly held company executives and affluent families. He began his career with Ernst & Young, LLP in their Entrepreneurial Services Group, specializing in S corporation, partnership, and individual tax consulting and compliance. Prior to joining Grant Thornton, Mike was a partner at SMART and Associates, LLP and held a senior management position in their tax and financial planning division.

Mike is a frequent lecturer of tax and financial planning topics for various organizations, including the American Institute of Certified Public Accountants, Lehigh University, Institute for International Research, and the Skybridge Alternative Conference. In addition to *The Tools & Techniques of Income Tax Planning* he is a co-author of *The Tools & Techniques of Financial Planning*, which is widely used as educational and editorial resource material by the financial planning profession. In addition, Mike has authored articles for Bloomberg/BNA's *Tax Management Memorandum and Estates, Gifts and Trusts Journal*, and is regularly interviewed by national, regional, and local news organizations.

Mike is a Certified Public Accountant in Pennsylvania and a member of the American Institute of Certified Public Accountants and Pennsylvania Institute of Certified Public Accountants. In 1998, he received his certification as a Personal Financial Specialist by the American Institute of Certified Public Accountants. He holds a Masters in Taxation from Villanova University School of Law and graduated magna cum laude from Drexel University with a Bachelor of Science in Business Administration, with majors in accounting and finance.

Jay Katz

Jay Katz is the executive editor of the 5th Edition of *The Tools & Techniques of Income Tax Planning* as well as the author of several new chapters. He is also a tax attorney concentrating on litigating tax cases, handling examination audits and collection matters, as well as submitting offers in compromise for corporate and individual clients. Jay has the distinction of earning two LLMs in taxation from the NYU and University of Florida graduate tax programs. During twelve years as a professor at Widener University Law School and Beasley School of Law at Temple University, Jay has taught virtually every tax and estate planning course on the curriculum and was the director of the Widener tax clinic.

Also a prolific author, Jay is a contributing editor and member of the Tax Facts Advisory Board at the National Underwriter Company, a co-author of the 17th Edition of *The Tools & Techniques of Estate Planning*, as well as a freelance editor for the *CPA Journal*. Additional writing credentials include seven published law review tax articles, including "An Offer in Compromise You Can't Confuse: It is not the Opening Bid of a Delinquent Taxpayer to Play Let's Make a Tax Deal with the Internal Revenue Service," 81 *Miss. L. J.* 1673 (2012) (lead article); "The William O. Douglas Tax Factor: Where Did the Spin Stop and Who Was He Looking Out For?" 3 *Charlotte Law Review* 133 (2012) (lead article); and "The Untold Story of Crane v. Commissioner Reveals an Inconvenient Tax Truth: Useless Depreciation Deductions Cause Global Basis Erosion to Bait A Hazardous Tax Trap For Unwitting Taxpayers," 30 Va. Tax Rev. 559 (2011).

John J. Scroggin

John J. "Jeff" Scroggin has been married for 37 years to Lynn Geiger Scroggin and has three children. His oldest son is a professional blacksmith, his daughter works as a charitable event planner & fundraiser and his youngest son is an Iraq war veteran. Jeff has practiced as a CPA and then as a business, tax and estate planning attorney for over 40 years. He is co-creator of the "Family Incentive Trust" and creator of the "The Family Love Letter" which has had over a million copies printed. Jeff practices out of an 1883 house in the historic district of Roswell, Georgia. The building contains one of the largest collections of tax memorabilia in the US. The tax collection was featured in a front page article in the Wall Street Journal on April 15, 2015.

Jeff served as a Member of the University of Florida Levin College of Law Board of Trustees from 2011 to 2016. Jeff received the following degrees from the University of Florida: B.S.B.A. (Accounting), 1974; Juris Doctorate, 1977; Master of Laws in Taxation (LL.M.), 1979. Jeff has taught tax law at the University of Florida College of Law and College of Business. Jeff is a Founding Board member of the University of Florida College of Law Tax Institute and a Founding member of the University of Florida Advisor Network. He was a CPA with Arthur Andersen's nationwide estate planning group. He is a Nationally Accredited Estate Planner (NAEPC), is rated "AV" by Martindale Hubbell (since 1990) and has been named as a Georgia "Super-Lawyer" for every year since 2009. Jeff was Founding Editor-in-Chief of the

NAEPC Journal of Estate and Tax Planning (2006-2010) and was Co-Editor of Commerce Clearing House's *Journal of Practical Estate Planning* (2004-2006). Jeff was Chairman of the North Fulton Community Foundation (2007-2009) and a member of the Board of Directors of the National Association of Estate Planners and Councils (2002-2010). He was a member of the Board of Directors of the Historic Roswell Convention and Visitors Bureau (2004-2015). He served as Founding Chairman of the Friends of Barrington Hall (2008-2012) and was President of the North Georgia Estate Planning Council (2002-2005).

Jeff is the author of over 250 published articles and columns. Among the publications are: *Estate Planning, Taxes, Financial and Estate Planning, Practical Tax Strategies, Leimberg Information Services, NAEPC Journal of Estate and Tax Planning, ABA Property and Probate, ABA Practical Tax Lawyer, ABA Practical Lawyer, AICPA Tax Advisor, Journal of Estates and Trusts, Trusts and Estates, Zaristky's Estate Planning Alert, Journal of Financial Services Professionals, Journal of Financial Planning, Financial Services Professionals Newsletter, CCH Journal of Practical Estate Planning, Advisor Today, RIA Tax Watch, Financial Planning, the Atlanta Bar Journal* and the *Georgia Bar Journal*. He was an Estate Planning Columnist for Advisor Today Magazine (1997-2010).

Jeff is a frequent speaker on business, tax and estate planning issues. Among the groups he has spoken for are: The University of Florida College of Law Graduate Tax Program (2004, 2008, 2009, 2010, 2012, 2013, 2015), the Florida Tax Institute (2014, 2015, 2016), the Million Dollar Roundtable, the State Bar of Georgia (1992, 1996, 1997, 1998, 1999, 2000, 2001, 2002, 2003, 2005, 2006, 2009, 2013), The National Convention of the Financial Planning Association (1997, 1998, 2003, 2004, 2005, 2006, 2007, 2008, 2011, 2014, 2016), the Financial Planning Association Annual Retreat(2000, 2002, 2014, 2015), the Atlanta Bar Association (2005, 2013), Georgia Society of CPAs Annual Estate Planning Conference (2007, 2010, 2011, 2012, 2016), the Annual Convention of the National Association of Estate Planners and Councils (1995, 2016), the Georgia Federal Tax Conference (2012, 2013, 2014), the Columbus Ohio Community Foundation, the Dallas Foundation, The International Forum (2009, 2010), and the Annual Convention of National Beer Wholesalers Association (2003, 2005, 2006, 2007, 2008 & 2009).

Jeff has been extensively quoted in a number of media sources, including: the Wall Street Journal (1999, 2004, 2005, 2006, 2007, 2009, March 2010, August 2010, April 2015), CNN Headline News (on the Terri Schavio case), The New York Times (2005, 2013, 2014), USA Today, Atlanta Journal/Constitution(1999, 2002, 2005, 2010), National Public Radio Marketplace Radio, National Public Radio Talk of the Town, Forbes Magazine (1999, 2001, 2012, 2014), Fortune Magazine (1998, 2000, 2001), Bloomberg Wealth Management, New York Times International Herald Tribune, Money Magazine, Smart Money Magazine, South China Post, The LA Times, BNA Estates Gifts & Trusts Journal, Newsday, Chicago Sun-Times, Miami Herald, and MSN (2010, 2013, 2015).

Robert S. Keebler

Robert S. Keebler, CPA/PFS, MST, AEP (Distinguished), CGMA is a partner with Keebler & Associates, LLP and is a 2007 recipient of the prestigious Accredited Estate Planners (Distinguished) award from the National Association of Estate Planners & Councils. He has been named by CPA Magazine as one of the *Top 100 Most Influential Practitioners in the United States* and one of the *Top 40 Tax Advisors to Know During a Recession*. Mr. Keebler is the past Editor-in-Chief of CCH's magazine, *Journal of Retirement Planning*, and a member of CCH's Financial and Estate Planning Advisory Board. His practice includes family wealth transfer and preservation planning, charitable giving, retirement distribution planning, and estate administration. Mr. Keebler frequently represents clients before the National Office of the Internal Revenue Service (IRS) in the private letter ruling process and in estate, gift and income tax examinations and appeals.

In the past 20 years, he has received over 150 favorable private letter rulings including several key rulings of "first impression." Mr. Keebler is nationally recognized as an expert in estate and retirement planning and works collaboratively with other experts on academic reviews and papers, and client matters. Mr. Keebler is the author of over 75 articles and columns and editor, author, or co-author of many books and treatises on wealth transfer and taxation, including the Warren, Gorham & Lamont of RIA treatise Esperti, Peterson and Keebler/Irrevocable Trusts: Analysis with Forms.

Mr. Keebler is a member of the editorial board of the Society of Financial Service Professionals "Keeping Current" series. He is a featured columnist for CCH's *Taxes Magazine* – "Family Tax Planning Forum," Steve Leimberg's "News of the Week Newsletter" and the Bureau of National Affairs Tax Division. Bob is also a contributing author to the American Bar Association's *The ABA Practical Guide to Estate Planning*. He also had his article "Is That Your 'Final' Answer?" published in *Tax Management Compensation Planning Journal*. Bob frequently is quoted in national publications such as *New York Times, Chicago Tribune, Baltimore Sun, Barrons, Bloomberg Wealth Manager, Financial Advisor, Forbes, Kiplinger, Lawyer's Weekly, On Wall Street, The Wall Street Journal, USA Today, Wealth Manager*, and *Worth* in addition to many local and regional newspapers.

He is a frequent speaker for legal, accounting, insurance and financial planning groups throughout the United States at seminars and conferences on advanced IRA distribution strategies, estate planning and trust administration topics including the AICPA's Advanced Estate Planning, Personal Financial Planning Conference and Tax Strategies for the High Income Individual Conference.

Mr. Keebler graduated (cum laude) from Lakeland College with a degree in Accountancy and the University of Wisconsin - Milwaukee with a Masters in Taxation. Before practicing in Northeastern Wisconsin, he practiced with Price Waterhouse where he concentrated in taxation.

ABOUT THE EDITOR

Jason Gilbert, J.D., M.A., is the Senior Editor with the Practical Insights Division of The National Underwriter Company, a division of ALM Media, LLC. He edits and develops publications related to tax and insurance products, including titles in the *Advisor's Guide* and the *Tools & Techniques* series of investment and planning products. He also develops content for National Underwriter's other financial services publications and online products. He has worked on insurance and tax publications for more than nine years.

Jason has been a practicing attorney for more than a dozen years in the areas of criminal defense, products liability, and regulatory enforcement actions. Prior to joining National Underwriter, his experience in the insurance and tax fields has included work as a Westlaw contributor for Thomson Reuters and a tax advisor and social media contributor for Intuit. He is an honors graduate from Wright State University and holds a J.D. from the University of Cincinnati College of Law as well as a master's degree in Economics from Miami University in Ohio.

EDITORIAL SERVICES

Connie L. Jump, Senior Manager, Editorial Operations

Patti O'Leary, Senior Editorial Assistant

CONTENTS

Tools of Income Tax Planning

Techniques of Income Tax Planning

Appendices

SOURCES OF INCOME TAX LAW FUNDAMENTALS

CHAPTER 1

Clearly anyone who has prepared a tax return or dealt with tax issues realizes that the federal income tax laws can be hard to comprehend and difficult to apply. The sheer number of tax provisions and their complexity can be somewhat daunting. Even the IRS, the nation's tax collection agency, acknowledges that "for anyone not familiar with the inner workings of tax administration, the array of IRS guidance may seem, well, a little puzzling at first glance."[1] Since Albert Einstein expressed his concern that tax laws were among the most complex of all human tasks, this statement by the IRS could be one of the great understatements of all time!

Yet, all tax professionals as well as financial planners must have a good general working knowledge of the tax laws in order to effectively assist clients. This chapter identifies the sources of federal tax law, the relative importance of each federal tax law source, and how to identify a source by its citation.

Obviously, federal tax law begins with the Internal Revenue Code (Code), a codification of tax statutes enacted by Congress. As discussed later in the chapter, the IRS and the Treasury Department promulgate regulations interpreting the Code providing guidance to taxpayers who are required to comply with the tax law. Regulations generally have the force of law. Disputes between the IRS and taxpayers are often litigated. Although the binding effect of judicial decisions varies with the level of the court, judicial interpretation of tax law is often impactful. Finally, on a less formal basis, the IRS issues revenue ruling, revenue procedures and other pronouncements that provide additional guidance for taxpayers. Although this type of guidance lacks the force and effect of law, it provides useful help to taxpayers.

Additionally, legislative history and tax publications are also helpful secondary authorities that offer explanations and interpretations of the tax law. Although these sources are not binding, they are helpful tools to assist the taxpayer.

In addition to a working knowledge of the Code, regulations, IRS rulings (and other IRS authored guidance), and court decisions, tax professionals and financial planners should be tuned into potential changes in tax law. Pending legislation, newly issued regulations and pending tax litigation awaiting court resolution are key examples of potential "game changers." In recent years, most of the focus has been on whether Congress would enact "extenders" of provisions scheduled to expire as opposed to substantive changes of tax law. However, in the evolving world of tax law, substantive changes are inevitable.

THE INTERNAL REVENUE CODE

Congress derives its power to tax from the United States Constitution. Congress exercises this power by enacting tax statutes that are codified in the Code. Currently, the Code is more formally referred to as the Internal Revenue Code of 1986. Thus, all new provisions, amendments or repeals of tax provisions are to the 1986 Code. More broadly, the Code in its entirety is codified as Title 26 of the *United States Code*.[2]

Because the Code is the law, the IRS and all courts are required to follow it. Keep in mind, however, that even though the Code is voluminous, the meaning of each provision is far from clear. Unanswered questions arise daily as taxpayers attempt to apply the general provisions of the Code to many different factual situations. Thus, the role of the IRS is to administer and interpret the Code provisions enacted by promulgating regulations and other forms of guidance.

The Code is divided into subtitles, chapters, parts, sections, subsections, paragraphs, and subparagraphs. However, *citations* to provisions of the Code refer only to sections, subsections, paragraphs, and subparagraphs.[3] A Code section may be referred to generally as "IRC Section 101." However, when referring to a more specific part, the section should be cited as "IRC §101(a)(2)(B)." Separated into its essential components, this citation refers to:

- Internal Revenue Code Section 101;
- subsection (a);
- paragraph (2);
- subparagraph (B).

TREASURY REGULATIONS

Treasury regulations are issued by the IRS and the Treasury Department to: (1) provide guidance for new tax legislation (usually adding or amending provisions of the Code), and (2) address issues that arise with respect to existing Code sections. Through examples and exploratory material, the regulations reflect the IRS interpretation of the Code sections and direction to taxpayers as to how they must comply with those sections.

The Internal Revenue Regulations (Title 26) is one of 50 titles in the *Code of Federal Regulations* (CFR).[4] Regulations are initially published in proposed form in the *Federal Register*[5] in what is known as a "Notice of Proposed Rule Making" (NPRM). After public input has been fully considered by the IRS, through written comments and comments made in person at a public hearing, a final or temporary regulation is published as a "Treasury Decision" (TD) in the *Federal Register*.

Regulations are referred to by section numbers that roughly correspond to the sections of the Code. For example, the citation, "26 CFR §1.170-1(a)(3)" refers to a regulation that explains some aspect of Code Section 170.

Relative Weight of Regulations

There are two types of regulations, *legislative* and *interpretative*. Although both types are generally given the force and effect of law by the courts, *legislative* regulations carry the greater weight. In fact, they carry the same weight as the underlying Code. This is because, by specific mandate written into the text of the applicable Code section, Congress has authorized the Secretary of the Treasury to issue specific regulations.

For example, IRC section 469(l) (a *legislative* regulation dealing with the passive activity loss rules) provides: "The Secretary [of the Treasury] shall prescribe such regulations as may be necessary or appropriate to carry out provisions of this section . . ." The courts have interpreted this to mean that *legislative* regulations are entitled to "controlling weight unless they are arbitrary, capricious, or manifestly contrary to the statute."[6]

Conversely, pursuant to IRC section 7805(a), interpretative regulations are issued under the general rule making authority of the Treasury Department. Because *interpretative* regulations are not promulgated with specific Congressional authority, they are subject to challenge if they do not implement the underlying Code section in a reasonable manner.[7]

A regulation (*legislative* or *interpretative*) promulgated by the Treasury may be in one of three forms: *Proposed, Temporary* or *Final*.

Proposed Regulation: As the name implies, a *proposed* regulation is simply insight provided by the IRS as to how it interprets (at least at that moment) a specific Code section(s). Similar to all regulations, they are published in the Federal Register. After the regulations are issued, the public is invited to submit comments and concerns. Based upon those comments, the IRS may or may not modify the regulations prior to their finalization. Although *proposed* regulations are not at the level of *temporary* or *final* regulations, according to the Internal Revenue Manual, a taxpayer may rely on them and examiners (revenue agents who audit taxpayer income tax returns) should follow them unless they are contrary to existing *temporary* or *final* regulations.[8]

Temporary Regulations: Following the enactment of tax legislation (amendments or additions to the Code), *temporary* regulations are sometimes promulgated to provide taxpayers with guidance with respect to "procedural and computation matters" in regard to the new tax law pending the issuance of *final* regulations.[9]

Final Regulations: As the name implies, *final* regulations set forth the IRS final interpretation of new or existing tax law. They supersede both *proposed* and *temporary* regulations.[10]

IRS RULING AND GUIDANCE

Revenue Rulings

A *revenue ruling* is an IRS interpretation of tax law as applied to a specific fact pattern set forth in the ruling. Published in the *Internal Revenue Bulletin*, revenue rulings are generally based on fact patterns that have recurred in a number of private letter rulings and/or technical advice memoranda (both discussed below) in which the IRS reached a similar conclusion. Although revenue rulings do not have the binding effect of regulations, assuming facts substantially the same as the one presented in a revenue ruling, a taxpayer may rely on the IRS holding in planning or in litigation against the IRS.[11] Finally, even though courts are not bound to follow revenue rulings (particularly when cited by the IRS as an expression of its opinion of the tax law), they are more likely to follow them if relied upon by a taxpayer.[12]

An example of a citation of a revenue ruling is "Rev. Rul. 2003-99, 2003-34 IRB 388," which separated into components means:

- the 99th revenue ruling issued by the IRS in 2003;
- published in the 34th issue of the *Internal Revenue Bulletin;*
- beginning on page 388.

Revenue Procedures

Unlike a revenue ruling that deals with the interpretation of tax law, a *revenue procedure* (also published in the *Internal Revenue Bulletin*) provides guidance to assist taxpayers with procedural issues relevant to tax return preparation and other actions (such as making elections).[13] For example, a revenue procedure might explain how a taxpayer entitled to deduct automobile expenses may use a mileage rate allowance in lieu of actual expenses. Similar to a revenue ruling, a revenue procedure does not have the binding effect of regulations, but may be relied upon by taxpayers.

An example of a citation of a revenue procedure is "Rev. Proc. 2003-60, 2003-31 IRB 274," which separated into components means:

- the 60th revenue ruling issued by the IRS in 2003;
- published in the 31st issue of the *Internal Revenue Bulletin;*
- beginning on page 274.

Private Letter Rulings

A *private letter ruling* (PLR) is a written statement of interpretation and application of tax laws issued by the IRS to a taxpayer in response to the taxpayer's request for the IRS position with respect to the tax consequences of a proposed transaction. Typically, a taxpayer will request a PLR prior to consummating a transaction with potentially significant tax consequences (positive or negative). Thus, forewarned of an IRS interpretation that would result in negative tax consequences, the taxpayer might decide not to consummate and/or modify the transaction to avoid that result. On the other hand, if the taxpayer receives a favorable ruling, he or she may rely on it provided the taxpayer accurately described the proposed transaction and carried it out as described. Importantly, the holding of a PLR may not be relied on by anyone other than the taxpayer requesting the ruling or IRS personnel.[14]

Significantly, at the beginning of each calendar year, the IRS issues a revenue procedure stating the issues on which it will not issue private letter rulings.[15] So a taxpayer contemplating a transaction involving a no-ruling issue with significant potential tax consequences has no means of seeking an advance interpretation from the IRS.

PLRs are made available to the public after all identifying information regarding the requesting taxpayers have been redacted. An example of a citation of a PLR is "Priv. Ltr. Rul. 201417023," which separated into components means – working backwards:

- the 23rd private letter ruling;
- issued in the published in the 17th week;
- of 2014.

In spite of the fact that PLRs may not be relied upon by any person other than the requesting taxpayer, tax professionals often look to IRS rulings (particularly PLRs related to the same issue in which the IRS reaches the same result) in projecting the IRS's likely position on a given issue. Recognizing the non-binding effect of PLRs, tax professionals advise their clients to proceed with caution.

Technical Advice Memoranda

A technical advice memorandum (TAM) is furnished by the Office of Chief Counsel upon the request of an IRS director (or an area director) in response to technical or procedural questions that develop from an examination of a taxpayer's return, a consideration of a taxpayer's claim for a refund or credit, or any other matter involving a specific taxpayer under the jurisdiction of the territory manager (or the area director).

TAMs are issued for closed transactions, only. They provide the Service's interpretation of the proper application of tax laws, regulations, revenue rulings or other precedents. The advice rendered represents a final determination of the position of the IRS, but only with respect to the specific issue in the specific case in which the advice is issued.

TAMs are generally made public after all information has been removed that could identify the taxpayer whose circumstances triggered the specific memorandum. An example of a citation for a TAM is "TAM 200335032," which when separated into its components (2003 – 35 – 032) means:

- the 32nd technical advice memorandum;
- issued during the 35th week;
- of 2003.

Announcements

An announcement is a public pronouncement issued by the IRS that has immediate or short-term value. For example, announcements can be used to summarize some new tax law or regulations without making any substantive interpretation; to state what regulations likely to be published in the immediate future will say; or to notify taxpayers of the existence of an approaching deadline. Announcements are published in the *Internal Revenue Bulletin*. Announcements have the same binding effect as revenue rulings do.[16]

An example of an announcement citation is "Ann. 2012-37, 2012-45 IRB 543 ___," which when separated into its components means:

- the 37th announcement issued by the IRS in 2012;
- published in the 45th issue of the *Internal Revenue Bulletin*;
- published on page 543___ (the blank space for the page number means that the final page numbering has not been set).

Notices

A notice is also a public pronouncement that may contain guidance that involves substantive interpretations of the Internal Revenue Code or other provisions of the law. For example, notices may indicate what regulations that may not be published in the immediate future will say. Notices are also published in the *Internal Revenue Bulletin* and have the same binding effect as revenue rulings do. An example of a citation is "Notice 2003-33, 2003-23 IRB 990," which when separated into its components means:

- the 33rd revenue ruling issued by the IRS in 2003;
- published in the 23rd issue of the *Internal Revenue Bulletin;*
- beginning on page 990.

THE COURTS

United States Tax Court

The United States Tax Court is a national court (no jury) hearing cases of taxpayers from all fifty states. For a case to be heard by the Tax Court, the IRS must have sent the taxpayer a Notice of Deficiency, also referred to as a Ninety Day Letter (a letter stating that the IRS has determined that the taxpayer owes more tax than reported by the taxpayer). In turn, within ninety days (there are no extensions), the taxpayer must file a petition with Tax Court to challenge the proposed tax assessment. For the convenience of taxpayers who live throughout the country, Tax Court judges travel to locations close to the taxpayers to hear their cases.[17]

Most Tax Court cases are decided by the judge who hears the case. These cases usually concerning factual disputes resolved by settled tax law are referred to as memorandum decisions. However, in cases in which a novel tax law issue is decided, the entire Tax Court bench (nineteen judges) reviews and decides the case. Those decisions are officially reported and are referred to as regular reported decisions.

The primary advantage of litigating a tax case in Tax Court is to challenge the IRS position without first paying the assessed tax. Conversely, if the taxpayer desires to litigate the case in a United States District Court or the U.S. Court of Federal Claims, the taxpayer must pay the tax first and file a claim for refund to the IRS that results in a denial or no response from the IRS within six months of making the claim.[18]

Because the Tax Court is on the same level as a United States District Court, Tax Court decisions that are appealed (by the IRS or the taxpayer) are reviewed by the Circuit Court of Appeals in which the taxpayer resides. For that reason, if the issue in a case before the Tax Court has been decided in a certain way by that circuit court (the taxpayer's "home" circuit), the Tax Court is bound by that precedence (this is known as the *Golsen* rule). So, if on a similar issue, the taxpayer's home circuit has ruled in favor of the taxpayer, the Tax Court is bound to rule in the same way. On the other hand, if the taxpayer's home circuit has not ruled on the issue, the Tax Court may follow its own rule. Other than the Tax Court itself, Tax Court decisions on any given issue do not bind other courts or the IRS.

There are three types of Tax Court decisions: (1) regular decisions that are officially reported; (2) memorandum decisions; and (3) summary opinions. For obvious reasons, regular officially reported decisions published in the U.S. Tax Court Reports carry greater weight than the other two types of decisions. Conversely, memorandum decisions are unofficially published by commercial publishers (CCH and Thomson Reuters). Finally, summary opinions issued in "small tax" cases (discussed in more detail later in the chapter) have no precedential value, are not officially published and cannot be appealed.

An example of a citation of an officially published Tax Court reported decision is *Mayo v. Commissioner*, 136 TC 81 (2011) which means:

- Mayo is the name of the taxpayer who brought a petition contesting the proposed assessment of the IRS Commissioner (sometimes abbreviated as "Comm'r.");
- Published in volume 136, page 81 of the Tax Court Reports;
- Decided by the Tax Court in 2011.

An example of a citation of a Tax Court memorandum decision is *George B. Douglas and Pearl J. Douglas*, TC Memo 2014-14 which means:

- George and Pearl Douglas were the taxpayers/ petitioners;
- The 14th memorandum decision decided by the Tax Court in 2014.

SMALL TAX CASES

To litigate a tax dispute in Tax Court, the taxpayer must file a petition within ninety days of receiving a Notice of Deficiency from the IRS. The fee for filing a petition, payable upon filing, is $60. A Tax Court case may be treated as a *small tax case* if: (1) the amount of the deficiency that the taxpayer disputes *and* (2) the amount he claims was overpaid do not exceed $50,000 (including any additions to the tax and certain penalties) of income taxes for any one tax year.[19]

Unless the taxpayer checks the box on the petition requesting the case to be treated as a small tax case, it will be tried under the Tax Court's regular procedures. The IRS may object to small tax case treatment because the case involves an important tax question that should be heard under normal procedures and be subject to appeal, or that the decision should serve as a precedent for other similar matters. At any time before trial, the Tax Court or the taxpayer may remove the small tax case designation and direct that the case be handled as a regular case. After trial, but before the court enters a decision, the Tax Court may order that the small tax case proceeding be discontinued if: (1) the disputed amount or claimed overpayment will exceed $50,000 per year; and (2) the amount of the excess is large enough to justify granting the request.

Generally, small tax case proceedings are less formal and result in speedier dispositions than regular trials. Trials are conducted by one judge, without a jury. Taxpayers may be represented by practitioners admitted to practice before the Tax Court bar, or they may represent themselves if they wish.

The Tax Court judge's decision is issued in a Summary Opinion. A Summary Opinion cannot be relied on as precedent, and the decision cannot be appealed by the taxpayer or the IRS.

Finally, an example of a citation of a Tax Court summary opinion is TC Summary Opinion 2013-44.

As noted above, Tax Court opinions are not binding on the IRS (beyond the specific decision). For that reason, if the IRS acquiesces to the decision (reported or memorandum), it means the IRS will not appeal the case (indicating the IRS will follow the decision at least for the time being). Conversely, if the IRS does not acquiesce to the decision, it means the IRS will not follow that decision in other taxpayer disputes. It does not necessarily mean, however, that the IRS will appeal the decision.

Finally, as noted above, the losing party of a reported decision or memorandum decision (but not a summary opinion) may appeal the decision to the court of appeals for the circuit in which the taxpayer lives.

United States District Court

There are many federal district courts throughout the United States. To contest a tax deficiency in a district court, a taxpayer must:

(1) pay the tax first;

(2) file a claim for a refund with the IRS;

(3) wait six months during which the taxpayer's claim is denied by the IRS or the IRS does not respond one way or the other within that period; and then

(4) sue for a refund.

The taxpayer or the government may request a jury trial. Otherwise, one judge will hear the taxpayer's case.

Unless a decision involving a similar issue had been reversed on appeal, a district court should follow its prior decision in subsequent cases involving the same issue. A district court decision is not binding on the IRS in its dealings with other taxpayers, nor does it bind any other court. However, federal courts are inclined to follow the decisions of other federal courts.

The losing party in a district court may appeal to the court of appeals for the circuit in which the district court is located. If the decision is reversed on appeal, all the district courts in that circuit (as well as the Tax Court) must follow the decision of the court of appeals in deciding future cases.

When the Service loses a case in a district court, and decides *not* to appeal the decision, it can announce its "acq." (acquiescence) or its "nonacq." (nonacquiescence) in the decision. The meaning of these terms is the same as when used in Tax Court decisions (see above).

District court decisions are published in the *Federal Supplement* ("F. Supp."). An example of a district court citation is "*May v. McGowan*, 97 F. Supp. 326 (W.D. N.Y. 1950)," which when broken into its components means:

- the taxpayer May sued IRS District Director McGowan;
- the decision may be found in volume 97 of the *Federal Supplement*, on page 326; and
- the case was decided by the district court for the Western District of New York in 1950.

United States Courts of Appeals

There are thirteen United States courts of appeals—one for each of eleven regional circuits, one for the District of Columbia, and one for the Federal Circuit. (See Figure 1.1 for the location of each court and the states and territories in the respective circuits.[20]) In most tax cases, the appeals court usually renders the final word. This is because circuit court decisions are appealable to the United States Supreme Court which hears very few tax cases.

Figure 1.1

1st Cir	Boston, Mass. (Me., Mass., N.H., R.I., Puerto Rico)
2nd Cir	New York City, N.Y. (Conn., N.Y., Vt.)
3rd Cir	Philadelphia, Pa. (Del., N.J., Pa., Virgin Islands)
4th Cir.	Richmond, Va. (Md., N.C., S.C., Va., W. Va.)
5th Cir	New Orleans, La. (La., Miss., Texas)
6th Cir	Cincinnati, Ohio (Ky., Mich., Ohio, Tenn.)
7th Cir	Chicago, Ill. (Ill., Ind., Wis.)
8th Cir	St. Louis, Mo. (Ark., Iowa, Minn., Mo., Neb., N. Dak., S. Dak.)
9th Cir	San Francisco, Calif. (Alaska, Ariz., Calif., Hawaii, Idaho, Mont., Nevada, Oregon, Washington, Guam)
10th Cir	Denver, Colo. (Colo., Kans., N. Mex., Okla., Utah, Wyo.)
11th Cir	Atlanta, Ga. (Ala., Fla., Ga.)
D.C. Cir	Washington, D.C. (District of Columbia)
Federal Circuit	Wash., D.C. (nationwide jurisdiction)

A decision by a circuit court of appeals binds all district courts in that circuit. However, the decision of a court of appeals for one circuit does not bind the court of appeals, or the district courts, of another circuit. The Tax Court is bound by a court of appeals decision *only if* an appeal from the Tax Court decision could only be made to that particular court of appeals (*Golsen* rule). A court of appeals decision does not bind the IRS in dealing with other cases. In fact, the IRS has often forced (and may continue to force) taxpayers to litigate an issue, even after having been defeated in several circuits.

The IRS may announce its "acq." (acquiescence) or "nonacq." (nonacquiescence) to decisions of the courts of appeals. The meaning of these terms is generally the same with respect to a court of appeals decision as with a Tax Court or a district court decision (see above).[21]

However, decisions of the Court of Appeals for the Federal Circuit (see below) have nationwide *precedence* – that is, all courts, including the Court of Federal Claims, whose appeals are heard by the Court of Appeals for the Federal Circuit are bound by its decisions. Decisions of the courts of appeals are published in the *Federal Reporter* ("F.2d.," or "F.3d"). An example of a citation for a circuit court of appeals decision is "*Scott v. United States*, 328 F.3d 132 (4th Cir. 2003)," which when broken down into its parts means:

- the taxpayer Scott versus the United States;
- reported in volume 328, on page 132 of the third series of the *Federal Reporter*;
- decided by the Fourth Circuit Court of Appeals in 2003.

United States Court of Federal Claims

The court now referred to as the United States Court of Federal Claims (formerly known as the United States Court of Claims before 1982, and as the United States Claims Court from 1982 – 1992) is located in Washington, D.C. The judges of the Federal Claims Court travel anywhere in the United States and hear cases at times and places established to minimize the citizens' inconvenience and expense.

A taxpayer who wants to challenge a tax deficiency in the Court of Federal Claims must:

(1) pay the tax first;

(2) file a claim for a refund with the IRS;

(3) wait six months during which the taxpayer's claim is denied by the IRS or the IRS does not respond one way or the other within that period; and then

(4) sue for a refund.

A Court of Federal Claims decision does *not* bind the IRS in disposing of other cases. Furthermore, other courts are not bound by a Court of Federal Claims decision (but they may be influenced by it). If the Service announces its "acq." (acquiescence) in a decision of the Court of Federal Claims, it will follow the decision in disposing of cases with the same controlling facts. On the other hand, if the Service announces its "nonacq." (nonacquiescence) in a decision, it generally will not follow the decision in cases involving other taxpayers.

A taxpayer who receives an unfavorable decision in the Court of Federal Claims may appeal to the United States Court of Appeals for the Federal Circuit. (This appellate court is headquartered in Washington, but it is authorized to hear cases at other designated places throughout the United States.) As noted above, decisions of the Court of Appeals for the Federal Circuit have nationwide *precedence* – that is, all courts, including the Court of Federal Claims, whose appeals are heard by the Court of Appeals for the Federal Circuit are bound by its decisions.

Citations to the Court of Federal Claims may appear in one of the following forms, depending on when the case was decided:

Pre-1982:

Mississippi River Fuel Co. v. U. S., 314 F.2d 953 (Ct.Cl. 1963), which tells us that the case was decided by the Court of Claims in 1963, and is located in volume 314 of the *Federal Reporter*, 2nd series, starting at page 953.

1982 – 1992:

Wm. T. Thompson Co. v. U.S., 26 Cl.Ct. 17 (Cl.Ct. 1992), which tells us that the case was decided by the United States Claims Court in 1992, and is located in volume 26 of the *United States Claims Court Reporter* starting at page 17.

Transpac Drilling Venture v. U.S., 1992-2 USTC ¶50,486 (Cl.Ct. 1992), which tells us that the case was decided by the United States Claims Court in 1992 and is located in the second of the 1992 volumes of the *U.S. Tax Cases Reporter*, at paragraph 50,486.

Post-1992:

Alexander v. U.S., 28 Fed.Cl. 475 (Fed.Cl. 1993), which tells us that the case was decided by the United States Court of Federal Claims in 1993 and can be found in the 28th volume of the *Federal Claims Reporter* starting at page 475.

Gustafson v. U.S., 1993-1 USTC ¶50,071 (Fed.Cl. 1993), which tells us that the case was decided by the United States Court of Federal Claims in 1993 and can be found in the first of the 1993 volumes of the *U.S. Tax Cases Reporter* at paragraph 50,071.

The Supreme Court of the United States

Very few of the thousands of tax cases arising every year are appealed all the way to the Supreme Court. Even fewer are actually reviewed by the Court. However, if the Supreme Court renders a decision on an issue, the IRS and every court in the United States must follow the decision in dealing with future cases.

The first step in attempting to appeal a tax case to the Supreme Court is to file a "writ of certiorari"—which is essentially a petition that is a request to be heard. Whether the Court will hear the case is entirely within the Court's discretion. The Supreme Court normally denies over 1,000 petitions every year.

Significantly, the Supreme Court's denial of a writ is not an indication of its view on the merits of the case. The denial of a writ simply means that fewer than four Supreme Court justices deemed it desirable to review a decision of the lower court as a matter "of sound judicial discretion."[22] Those few tax cases the Court actually consents to review usually involve: (1) a question as to the constitutionality of a provision of the Code; (2) a conflict between decisions of courts of appeals; or (3) an issue of wide public import.

United States Supreme Court decisions are published in the *United States Supreme Court Reports* ("U.S."). An example of a Supreme Court citation is "*Commissioner v. Tufts*, 461 U.S. 300 (1983)," which when separated into its components means:

- the case involving the taxpayer Tufts;
- reported in volume 471 of the *United States Reports*;
- beginning on page 300; and
- decided by the Supreme Court in 1983.

Legislative History and Other Secondary Authority

Frequently, there are tax problems that are not specifically covered in the Code, the regulations, the rulings, or court decisions. In many instances, the tax professional will make an educated guess, based on knowledge of the tax law, as to the probable tax consequences of the transaction. However, another potential source of guidance can be found in the reports of the Congressional tax committees. Although the reports of the Congressional tax committees are not the tax law, they can be helpful in interpreting a particular piece of legislation.[23]

The Staff of the Joint Committee on Taxation of the Senate and the House publish a *General Explanation* of the provisions of each new major tax act. Each *General Explanation* is referred to as a *Blue Book*. A "blue book" is generally written within several months after a new piece of legislation has passed. The purpose of the *General Explanation* is to amplify skimpy legislative history of hastily enacted compromise provisions. This information is based on the knowledge of the staff members who generally participated in drafting the provisions of the history of the legislation.

The Blue Book is considered "authority" only for the purposes of avoiding the penalty on the substantial understatement of income tax.[24] The *General Explanation* does not technically rise to the level of legislative history because it is authored by a congressional staff and not by Congress. But even the Tax Court has acknowledged that the *General Explanation* can serve as a helpful aid in interpreting tax statutes.[25]

In addition to legislative history and the *Blue Book*, there are also books, tax services, tax magazines,

HOW TAX LAWS ARE MADE

Tax bills originate in the Ways and Means Committee of the House of Representatives. This committee drafts the bill and a report explaining the bill to the members of the House. If the bill passes the House, it is sent to the Senate Finance Committee, which may reject the bill, approve it in its entirety, or amend it. If the Senate Finance Committee sends the bill to the Senate for vote, it will also write a committee report explaining its version of the bill.

If the versions of the bills passed by the House and the Senate are different, both versions must be sent to a *conference committee*, which is comprised of a few members from the House and the Senate. The conference committee "irons out" the disputed points, and drafts a conference bill and a conference committee report. The conference committee's version of the bill then goes back to the House and the Senate for a vote. If passed by both houses, the tax bill is sent to the President for approval. When the President signs the bill, it becomes a Public Law and part of the Internal Revenue Code.

proceedings of tax institutes and articles published in the law reviews of the various law schools. Although these publications represent only the authors' personal opinions, the tax adviser may benefit from the research and opinions of other practitioners and legal scholars. Obviously, tax publications do not bind courts or the IRS.

WHERE CAN I FIND OUT MORE?

1. The Internal Revenue Code can be viewed at www.findlaw.com/casecode/uscodes/, and at uscode.house.gov/usc.htm.

2. Treasury regulations can be viewed at www.irs.gov/.

3. Revenue rulings, revenue procedures, announcements, and bulletins are published in the *Internal Revenue Bulletin* (IRB) at www.irs.gov/.

4. Selected cases, rulings, and legislation of importance to tax practitioners are available at www.leimberg-services.com.

FREQUENTLY ASKED QUESTIONS

Question – What is the primary difference between a *revenue ruling* and a *revenue procedure*?

Answer – A revenue ruling generally reflects the IRS interpretation of the application of certain tax law provisions to a specific set of facts. On the hand, a revenue procedure provides procedural guidance with respect to return filing or other tax procedural actions and elections.

Question – What types of tax disputes are best suited for the Tax Court? A District Court?

Answer – In general, complex tax issues may be better suited for the Tax Court because the Tax Court only hears tax cases (often involving complex tax issues) so Tax Court judges have a wealth of tax law knowledge and experience. On the other hand, district courts hear cases in all areas of law. It is also likely that district court judges may not have tax expertise. Because in district court, the taxpayer can opt for a jury trial if he or she believes his or her case would receive a more sympathetic review from a jury, the district court might be preferable.

Ultimately, the choice of forum may rest on pure economics. To litigate a case in district court, the taxpayer must have sufficient funds to pay the tax up front and sue for a refund. If not, the taxpayer's only alternative is to litigate his or her case in Tax Court that does not require the upfront payment of tax. However, it may take a significant amount of time to litigate the case. During that time, interest and penalties on the disputed tax liability continue to accrue. If the taxpayer wins, he or she would owe nothing. Conversely, if the taxpayer loses, all the accrued interest and penalty in addition to the tax assessment that the taxpayer now owes may be substantial.

Question – In addition to the forms of guidance discussed in this chapter, what other forms of guidance from the IRS is available?

Answer – *Chief Counsel Advice* is written advice or instructions prepared by a national office component of the IRS' Office of Chief Counsel. It is issued to the field (i.e., revenue agents) or to service center employees of the IRS to (1) convey the IRS' legal interpretation, or (2) the IRS's position or policy relating to a revenue provision, or (3) the assessment of any liability under a revenue provision.

Through *Service Center Advice*, the Office of Chief Counsel provides legal advice to the IRS service centers and related IRS functions with regard to their tax administration responsibilities. This advice is distributed and published to provide consistent legal advice to all affected IRS functions and Counsel Office on matters raised by the IRS's various functions.

Information letters provide general statements of well-defined law without applying them to a specific set of facts. They are furnished by the IRS National Office in response to requests for general information by taxpayers, by congresspersons on behalf of constituents, or by congresspersons on their own behalf. Information letters are merely advisory and have no binding effect on the IRS. The release of information letters is intended to increase public confidence that the tax system operates fairly and in an even-handed manner with respect to all taxpayers. All three types of guidance can be viewed online at www.irs.gov.

Question – Are any of the Service's internal training materials available for review online by taxpayers and their advisers?

Answer – Yes. *The Internal Revenue Manual* contains the policies, procedures, instructions, guidelines, and delegations of authority, which direct the operation, and administration of the IRS. One of many topics include tax administration. The IRS also makes its *Market Segment Specialization Programs* available online. These programs focus on developing examiners for a particular market segment. A market segment may be an industry such as construction, entertainment, or a particular profession (e.g., attorneys, real estate agents), or an issue like passive activity losses. In addition, the IRS makes its Continuing Professional Education manuals available annually. The information in these manuals can provide some insight into the issues that revenue agents are being trained to focus on in future audits.

Question – Can a taxpayer rely on the information in an IRS Publication to support his position concerning a particular tax issue?

Answer – Publications provide taxpayers with detailed information on key topics that will assist in the preparation of their tax return. They are designed to supplement forms and instructions by answering typical tax questions and providing helpful examples for a particular topic. They are published as explanations that reflect the Service's interpretation of the law, but are not intended to replace the law or change its meaning. So for that reason, even if the publication incorrectly states the tax law, the taxpayer may not rely on it as authority.

Question – What is Fast Track Mediation?

Answer – Fast Track Mediation allows taxpayers to resolve collection disputes with the IRS at the earliest possible stage in the collection process. Once the FTM application is accepted, the goal is resolution within forty days. With FTM, a trained mediator from the IRS Office of Appeals is assigned to help the taxpayer and IRS Collection reach an agreement on the disputed issue(s). No one can impose a decision on either the taxpayer or the IRS.[26]

CHAPTER ENDNOTES

1. "Understanding IRS Guidance – A Brief Primer," Available at: http://www.irs.gov/uac/Understanding-IRS-Guidance-A-Brief-Primer.
2. A code is a compilation of individual statutes arranged in a particular order.
3. A citation is a reference to where the law can be found in a reporter (i.e., a book containing court decisions issued by a particular court or group of courts).
4. The Code of Federal Regulations is a compilation of all regulations issued by the executive departments and agencies of the federal government.
5. The Federal Register is an official government publication.
6. *Rite Aid Corporation v. United States*, 255 F. 3d 1357 (Fed. Cir. 2001); IRM 4.10.7.2.3.2 (01-01-2006).
7. *National Muffler Dealers Association, Inc. v. United States*, 440 U.S. 472, 146 (1979).
8. IRM 4.10.7.2.3.3 1 A. (01-01-2006).
9. IRM 4.10.7.2.3.3 1 B. (01-01-2006).
10. IRM 4.10.7.2.3.3 1 C. (01-01-2006).
11. IRM 4.10.7.2.6 (01-01-2006).
12. In *Estate of McClendon v. Commissioner*, 135 F.3d 1517 (5th Cir. 1998), the Fifth Circuit held that the IRS and the Tax Court were bound to follow revenue rulings.
13. IRM 4.10.7.2.6 2 (01-01-2006).
14. However, in the absence of other definitive authority, tax advisors often rely on the holdings of PLRs to project the likely IRS interpretation of the tax outcome of transactions with similar facts.

15. *See*, e.g., Rev. Proc. 2015-1, 2015 IRB 1.
16. IRM 4.10.7.2.4.1.
17. The list of cities in which the Tax Court travels to hear cases can be found at www.ustaxcourt.gov/faq.htm.
18. *Flora v. U.S.*, 362 U.S. 145 (1960).
19. IRC Secs. 7463(a), 7463(e).
20. The types of cases heard by the Court of Appeals for the Federal Circuit are determined by subject matter. Appeals from decisions made by the United States Court of Federal Claims are heard by the Court of Appeals for the Federal Circuit.
21. There is one exception—if he Service does not acquiesce in a court of appeals case, it will recognize the impact on cases that arise within the deciding circuit.
22. Rule 10, Supreme Court Rules; *Maryland v. Baltimore Radio Show, Inc.*, 338 U.S. 912 (1950).
23. In fact, the Treasury Department sometimes takes material from committee reports to include in its regulations.
24. See Treas. Reg. §1.6662-4(d)(3)(iii).
25. See, e.g., *Maria Rivera v. Comm'r.*, 89 TC 343 (1987).
26. See Rev. Proc. 2003-41, 2003-25 IRB 1047.

INCOME TAX RETURN FILING REQUIREMENTS

CHAPTER 2

INTRODUCTION

Most individual taxpayers pay a large portion of their income tax *during* the tax year through employer withholding or by making estimated tax payments. On April 15 of the following year, an income tax return must be filed to determine the exact amount of tax liability. With the tax return, the taxpayer is required to pay the balance due or is entitled to request a refund for overpayment of tax or refundable credit. This chapter explains the filing requirements of an income tax return, when the return is due, what an income tax return audit entails, and what to do if the taxpayer disagrees with the amount of tax the IRS claims is due.

INCOME TAX FILING REQUIREMENTS

The amount of gross income, filing status, and age generally determine whether an individual must file an income tax return. Ultimately, the determinative factor in whether a return must be filed is the amount of an individual's *gross* income rather than taxable income.[1] Then, depending on the taxpayer's filing status and age, if a taxpayer's gross income exceeds a predetermined amount, a return is required even if the taxpayer's liability is zero due to deductions and exemptions exceeding gross income.

The Tax Reform Act of 2017 changed the filing requirements for the tax years ending in 2018 and beyond. Both 2017 and the new filing requirements are discussed below.

Tax Years up to 2017

For 2017, based on filing status and age, an income tax return must be filed if *gross income* (i.e., all income received in the form of money, goods, property, and services that is not exempt from tax—see Chapter 3) exceeds the following gross income thresholds listed below. These amounts are the sum of the applicable personal exemption(s) and standard deduction amount.

(1) **Married filing jointly**—$20,800 (if one spouse is blind or elderly—$22,050; if both spouses are blind *or* elderly—$23,300 if both spouses are blind *and* elderly—$25,700).

(2) **Qualifying Widow(er) with qualifying child**—$16,750 (if elderly or blind—$18,000; if elderly and blind—$19,150).

(3) **Head-of-household**—$13,400 (if blind or elderly—$14,950; if elderly and blind—$16,640).

(4) **Single persons**—$10,400 (if blind or elderly—$11,950; if blind and elderly—$13,340).

(5) **Married filing separately**—if neither spouse itemizes, each spouse must file a return if his or her gross income equals or exceeds $10,400 (if blind or elderly—$11,600; if blind and elderly—$12,850). If either spouse itemizes—$4,050.

(6) **Dependents**—for 2017, an individual who may be claimed as a dependent of another must file a return if gross income exceeds the following amounts:

- **Earned Income Only**

Single	
Under 65 and not blind	$6,300
Either 65 or blind	$7,850
65 and blind	$9,400
Married	
Under 65 and not blind	$6,300
Either 65 or blind	$7,550
65 and blind	$8,800

- **Unearned Income Only**

Single	
Under 65 and not blind	$1,050
Either 65 or blind	$2,600
65 and blind	$4,150
Married	
Under 65 and not blind	$1,050
Either 65 or blind	$2,300
65 and blind	$3,550

- **Earned and Unearned Income**

Single

If single, under age sixty-five and not blind, a dependent must file an income tax return if any of the following apply:

- o Unearned income exceeds $1,050
- o Earned income exceeds $6,350
- o Gross income exceeds the greater of (a) $1,050 or (b) earned income up to $6,000 plus $350.

If single, age sixty-five or blind, a dependent must file an income tax return if any of the following apply:

- o Unearned income exceeds $2,600 ($4,150 if sixty-five or older and blind).
- o Earned income exceeds $7,900 ($9,450 if sixty-five or older and blind).
- o Gross income exceeds the greater of (a) $2,600 ($4,150 if sixty-five or older and blind) or (b) earned income up to $5,950 plus $1,900 ($3,450 if sixty-five or older and blind).

Married

If married, under age sixty-five and not blind, a dependent must file an income tax return if any of the following apply:

- o The dependent's gross income is at least $5 and the dependent's spouse files a separate return and itemizes deductions.
- o Unearned income exceeds $1,050
- o Earned income exceeds $6,350
- o Gross income exceeds the greater of (a) $1,050 or (b) earned income up to $6,000 plus $350.

If married age sixty-five or blind, a dependent must file an income tax return if any of the following apply:

- o The dependent's gross income is at least $5 and the dependent's spouse files a separate trust and itemizes deductions
- o Unearned income exceeds $2,300 ($3,550 if sixty-five or older and blind)
- o Earned income exceeds $7,600 ($8,850 if sixty-five or older and blind)
- o Gross income exceeds the greater of (a) $2,300 ($3,550 if sixty-five or older and blind) or (b) earned income up to $6,000 plus $1,600 ($2,850 if sixty-five or older and blind).

(7) Taxpayers who are **non-resident aliens** or who are filing a **short year return** because of a change in their annual accounting period—$4,050.[2]

(8) If a taxpayer dies, his or her executor, administrator, or legal representative must file a final return for the decedent on or before the regular due date for that year regardless of when the decedent died during the year.[3]

Example: Ashley, a single taxpayer, died on May 4, 2018. Even though Ashley's final tax year ended before December 31, 2018, her final return is not due until April 15, 2019.

---

(9) A self-employed taxpayer must file a return if he has net earnings from self-employment of $400 or more.[4]

Filing in 2018 and Beyond

The 2017 Tax Act modified the rules governing who is required to file a tax return for tax years beginning in 2018 through 2025. Because of the suspension of the personal exemption, unmarried individuals whose gross income exceeds the applicable standard deduction are now required to file a tax return for the year.

Married individuals are required to file a tax return if the individual's gross income, when combined with his or her spouse's gross income, is more than the standard deduction that applies to a joint return and:

1. the individual and his or her spouse, at the close of the tax year, shared the same household;

2. the individual's spouse does not file a separate return; and

3. neither the individual nor his or her spouse is a dependent of another taxpayer who has income (other than earned income) in excess of $500.

Therefore, a return must generally be filed for taxable year 2020 by every individual whose gross income exceeds the following limits:

- Married persons filing jointly—$24,400 (if one spouse is sixty-five or older—$25,700; if both spouses are sixty-five or older—$27,000).

- Surviving spouse–$24,400 (if sixty-five or older—$25,700).

- Head-of-household—$18,350 (if sixty-five or older—$20,000).

- Single persons—$12,200 (if sixty-five or older—$13,850).[5]

Note that the new law also imposes a due diligence requirement for tax preparers in determining whether head of household filing status is appropriate. A $500 penalty will now apply for each failure of a tax preparer to satisfy due diligence requirements (to be released in the future) with respect to determining head of household status. This penalty also applies with respect to eligibility for the child tax credit, the Hope and Lifetime Learning tax credits and the earned income tax credit.[6]

OTHER REASONS TO FILE EVEN IF NOT REQUIRED TO DO SO

Claiming a Refund or Refundable Credit

Some taxpayers who are not required to file a return may nonetheless be entitled to a refund. For example, a taxpayer with wage income below the gross income filing requirement threshold may nonetheless have federal income tax withheld from wages. However, the only way a taxpayer can obtain a refund from the IRS is to file a return on which the refund is claimed. Similarly, low-income taxpayers not required to file a return who are eligible for the *refundable* Earned Income Credit should file a return in order to obtain the appropriate refund. This is because a refundable credit is payable to an eligible taxpayer regardless of whether or to what extent the taxpayer paid or is subject to tax. Any individual who receives advance payments of the earned income credits should also file a return to verify his or her entitlement to the credit in addition to claiming any additional credit that may be available.

Example: Asher is a single taxpayer over age sixty-five and has a part-time job from which he earned $5,000. Asher's W-2 form indicates that his employer withheld $500 of federal income tax from Asher's wages. Because Asher's gross income is well below the applicable gross income threshold, he is not required to file a return. However, to recoup the $500 of taxes withheld by his employer, Asher must file a return showing zero tax due and request a refund.

Starting the Running of the Statute of Limitations

Another reason to file a return is to begin the running of the statute of limitations on assessment of tax. During that time, the IRS can challenge the taxpayer's tax return as filed and propose an assessment of additional tax. Generally, the statute of limitations for the assessment is three years. However, the statute of limitations for a tax year in which a tax return was not filed does not begin to run until it is filed. So by filing a return (even if not required to do so) will start the running of the statute of limitations.

Documenting an NOL

It is possible for a taxpayer to generate a loss in a year in which he or she was not required to file a tax return. If such a loss qualifies as a Net Operation Loss (NOL), such loss may be carried back and/or carried back as a deduction to reduce or eliminate taxable income from another tax year. In order to establish the existence and the amount of a NOL, the taxpayer must file a return.

FILING STATUS

Taxpayers file returns based on their filing status. In this section, the various filing status categories are discussed.

Single. An unmarried person who is not a head of household (see below) files as a single, unmarried taxpayer.

Married filing jointly. Married persons (including same-sex spouses) may elect to file a joint return upon which they report their combined income and deductions even though one spouse has no income.[7] Married persons may not, however, file a joint return if (1) either spouse is a nonresident alien, or (2) they have different taxable years (unless the difference is due solely as the result of the death of the other spouse).[8] Subject to certain exceptions, spouses who file a joint return are liable for the entire amount of the tax including the tax attributable to the other spouse.[9]

The taxable income thresholds of the various rate brackets are more favorable for married couples filing jointly than the combined taxable income thresholds for married couples filing separately. (See Appendix E.) For this reason as well as for many other reasons, married taxpayers are generally subject to less overall tax if they file jointly rather than separately. Fortunately, after the due date of the return (but within the applicable statute of limitations), subject to certain limitations, married taxpayers who initially file separately are allowed to amend their returns and file jointly.[10] However, a married couple who filed jointly are precluded, after the due date for the return, from amending their return to file separately.[11]

Married filing separately. Married persons may file two separate returns on which each spouse reports separate income and deductions. As noted above, generally, the overall tax liability of spouses filing separately is higher than spouses filing jointly. Nevertheless, depending on the circumstances, there may be scenarios in which filing separately is more beneficial than filing jointly.

In some cases, as noted above, some married couples do not qualify to file a joint return (as was the case prior to the Supreme Court's recent decisions with respect to same-sex couples). Often, married couples file separate returns for non-tax reasons, such as separation without a legal divorce or separation order or to avoid unknown tax exposure of the other spouse who may not have reported all of his or her income.

Qualifying widow(er) with dependent child. In the year of the decedent's death, the surviving spouse may file a joint return with the deceased spouse (claiming the deceased spouse's personal exemption). Although the widow or widower is legally single, for the first two years following the year of the decedent spouse's death, he or she may be able to use the beneficial married filing jointly tax rates. To take advantage of this tax benefit:

- a *dependent* child or stepchild must be living with the surviving spouse who contributes over one-half of the cost of maintaining the home;[12] *and*

- the surviving spouse is entitled to claim a dependency exemption for the child.[13]

Conversely, a surviving spouse will not be considered to be a qualifying widow(er) if either of the following applies:

- the surviving spouse remarries; or

- the surviving spouse could not have filed a joint return with the deceased spouse (e.g., because the deceased spouse was a nonresident alien).[14]

Head-of-household. Subject to the requirements detailed below, an unmarried taxpayer (other than a non-resident alien[15]) who maintains a home for a qualifying child may file as head-of-household. The taxable income thresholds of the tax brackets for a head-of-household are the most taxpayer favorable of any filing status (see Appendix E). In order to qualify for head of household filing status, the taxpayer must meet all of the following conditions.

The taxpayer must be:

(a) either

(i) unmarried;

(ii) legally separated from his or her spouse under a decree of divorce or of separate maintenance; or

(iii) married, living apart from his or her spouse during the last six months of the taxable year; *and*

(b) maintain as his or her home a household that constitutes the principal place of abode for *a qualifying child* (see below) with respect to whom the individual is entitled to claim a dependency exemption, and with respect to whom the individual furnishes over one-half the cost of maintaining such household during the taxable year.

Qualifying child means an individual who: (1) is the taxpayer's "child" (i.e., the taxpayer's son, daughter, stepson, stepdaughter, or eligible foster child); (2) has the same principal place of abode as the taxpayer for more than one-half of the year; (3) has not attained the age of nineteen by the close of the calendar year in which the tax year begins, *or* is a student who has not attained the age of twenty-four as of the close of the calendar year; *and* (4) has not provided over one-half of the individual's own support for the calendar year in which the taxpayer's taxable year begins.

Importantly, it is not necessary that the child have less than a certain amount of gross income or that the head-of-household furnish more than one-half of the child's support. If the child is married, he or she must qualify as a dependent of the parent claiming head-of-household status or would qualify except for the waiver of the exemption by the custodial parent *or* any other person for whom the taxpayer can claim a dependency exemption except a cousin or unrelated person living in the household. An exception to this rule is made with respect to a taxpayer's dependent mother or father; so long as the taxpayer maintains the household in which the dependent parent lives, it need not be the taxpayer's home.

WHEN TO FILE

Income tax liability is computed annually, i.e., *the taxable year*.[16] For most taxpayers, the *calendar year* is their taxable year.[17] The filing due date for taxpayer's using the calendar tax year is on or before April 15 of the following year.[18]

Rather than the calendar year, some taxpayers, however, may use a *fiscal year* as their tax year. (A *fiscal year* is a period of twelve months ending on the last day of a month *other than* December.)[19] The filing due date for taxpayer's using a fiscal tax year is on or before the fifteenth day of the fourth month after the close of the fiscal year.[20]

Example: Asher is a single taxpayer reporting income based on a fiscal year ending October 31st. Therefore, his fiscal year beginning on November 1, 2019 ends on October 31, 2020. Asher's income tax return for such fiscal year is due on or before February 15, 2021.

WHAT CONSTITUTES TIMELY FILING

A timely filed return must be sent or transmitted to the IRS on or before the due date. For this reason, it is important that taxpayers who paper file their returns on or around the due date are able to verify that the return was sent no later than April 15. If the due date for filing a return falls on a weekend (Saturday or Sunday), or on a legal holiday, the due date is delayed until the next business day.[21] In any event, the postmark date is the verification of filing.

Paper Filing: If a return is paper filed (rather than filed electronically), it is considered to be timely filed, if the envelope in which it is mailed is:

- properly addressed, and
- postmarked no later than the due date.[22]

Assuming the taxpayer sends the return by US Mail, the postmark date will be stamped on the envelope by the postal service. For that reason, it behooves a taxpayer who paper files the return on April 15 to drop the return at the post office (rather than in a free standing mail box that may or may not be postmarked that day). If a taxpayer sends the income tax return via one of the private delivery services designated by the IRS (i.e., DHL Express, Federal Express, United Parcel Service), the postmark date is generally the date recorded in the private delivery service database or marked on the mailing label.

Electronic Filing: An electronically filed return (IRS e-file) is considered filed on time if the authorized electronic return transmitter postmarks the transmission by the due date.[23] With the advent of electronic filing, paper filing has become increasingly less common. However, because electronic filing involves transmission over the internet, paper filing remains viable for taxpayers concerned with tax-related identity theft.

Filing extensions—automatic six-month filing extension: If for some reason, a taxpayer is unable to file a return by the due date (April 15), it is possible to file an automatic six-month extension (October 15). There are two ways to file for an automatic six-month extension:

(1) By the due date for filing the income tax return (see What Constitutes Timely Filing, above), file a paper Form 4868 (Application for Automatic Extension of Time to File U.S. Individual Income Tax Return) and mail it to the appropriate address

(2) By the due date, file an e-file extension request

It is important to note that the taxpayer must qualify to file the automatic extension. According to the Form 4868, there are three requirements: (1) estimate the tax liability using the information available to the taxpayer; (2) enter the total tax liability (i.e., the estimated amount) on the form; and (3) file the form by the regular due date of the income tax return. Even if the extension is filed by the regular due date of the income tax return, the IRS could reject the extension (deem it invalid), if the taxpayer fails to make a good faith estimate of his or her income tax liability.[24] As a result, the taxpayer would be subject to the failure to file penalty (5 percent of the unpaid tax for each month or part of month that the tax is unpaid, not to exceed 25 percent[25]). For that reason, it behooves the taxpayer to make a good faith estimate of his or her tax liability and enter that amount as instructed. (See Frequently Asked Questions, below for more analysis).

Finally, the automatic extension is not an extension to pay. So even if the taxpayer successfully files an automatic extension to file, any tax not paid by the regular due date is subject to interest and the failure to pay penalty (0.5 percent of the unpaid tax for each month or part of month that the tax is unpaid, not to exceed 25 percent[26]). If the taxpayer files a timely extension, however, and has paid at least 90 percent of his actual tax liability on or before the due date of the return, and pays the balance on or before the extension due date, there would not be a failure-to-pay penalty imposed.

Individuals serving in combat zones and U.S. citizens living outside the United States are also eligible for automatic extensions. Service personnel serving in combat zones are generally eligible for extensions for the period of service in the zone plus 180 days.

Paying the tax. If, after reducing the tax owing by amounts of withheld tax as well as any estimated tax payments (see Chapter 14), there is a balance due, that amount should be paid with the individual's return or automatic extension. Online payment of taxes have become more common, using a withdrawal from a bank account or a credit card (for a fee).

If the taxpayer is unable to pay the full amount owing, the taxpayer can request a monthly installment payment arrangement. The request is made on Form 9465 that can be filed with the Form 1040 or separately. On that form, the taxpayer proposes to make monthly payments in a specified amount. If accepted by the IRS, there is a small fee that the taxpayer can pay or roll into the amount owing. Finally, if the taxpayer enters into a monthly installment payment arrangement, the failure-to-pay penalty is reduced from 0.5 percent to 0.25 percent provided the taxpayer filed a timely return.[27]

FREQUENTLY ASKED QUESTIONS

Question – What is the statute of limitations period for individual taxpayers to file a claim for a refund (or credit)?

Answer – An individual must file a claim for a refund (or credit) within the later of the following periods:

- three years from the date the taxpayer filed the original return; or
- two years from the date he paid the tax.[28]

If the individual does not file a claim within this period, he generally is no longer entitled to a refund or credit.[29]

Example: On April 15, 2019, Asher filed his 2018 Form 1040 income tax return. On May 1, 2021, Asher made a tax payment of $2,500 with respect to his 2018 income tax return. Determining that he overpaid, Asher decides to file a claim for refund. In terms of a deadline, Asher has until April 30, 2023 to file a claim for refund with respect to that tax payment. This is because it is later than three years from the date he filed the original return (April 14, 2022).

Question – What penalties might apply to a taxpayer who fails to file a return or pay taxes on time?

Answer – **Failure-to-file penalty.** If the taxpayer fails to file his or her return by the due date (including extensions), the penalty is 5 percent of the amount of tax not paid by the due date (without regard to extensions) for each month, or part of a month, that the return is late. However, the aggregate amount of the penalty cannot exceed 25 percent of the unpaid tax.[30] If the taxpayer is able to demonstrate that the failure to timely file was due to reasonable cause and not neglect, the IRS has the authority to abate the penalty. For returns that are at least sixty days late, there is a minimum penalty of the lesser of $135 or 100 percent of the amount of tax required to be shown as tax on the return that was not timely paid.[31]

Failure-to-pay penalty. The penalty for failure to timely pay tax on is 0.50 percent of the unpaid taxes for each month, or part of a month, after the due date that the tax is not paid.[32] If the taxpayer files a timely extension, however, and has paid at least 90 percent of his actual tax liability on or before the due date of his return, and pays the balance on or before the extension due date, there would not be failure-to-pay penalty imposed. With respect to estimated tax payments, there is no failure-to-penalty imposed. However, the underpayment of estimated tax results in imposition of an interest penalty (compounded daily) at an annual rate that is adjusted quarterly to three percentage points over the short-term applicable federal rate (see Chapter 14 for more details).[33]

Question – What penalties might apply to a taxpayer who underpays his taxes or understates his income?

Answer – **Accuracy-related penalty.** If the taxpayer underpays his tax due to negligence or disregard of the rules, he will generally have to pay a penalty equal to 20 percent of the underpayment.[34]

Substantial understatement of income tax penalty. An understatement occurs when the amount shown on the return is less than the correct tax. The understatement is considered to be *substantial* if it is more than the larger of the following: (1) 10 percent of the correct tax, or (2) $5,000.[35] The amount of the understatement will be reduced to the extent that it is due to: (1) substantial authority for the position (e.g., Treasury regulations, revenue rulings, revenue procedures, notice and announcements issued by the IRS), or (2) adequate disclosure on the tax return and a reasonable basis.[36]

Question – What criminal penalties can be pursued against a noncompliant taxpayer?

Answer – A taxpayer or return preparer may be subject to criminal prosecution for such actions as: tax evasion; willful failure to file a return, supply information, or pay any tax due; fraud and false statements; or preparing and filing a fraudulent return.[37]

Question – How does the Bankruptcy Abuse Prevention and Consumer Protection Act of 2005 add tax filings to a debtor's responsibilities in a bankruptcy proceeding?

Answer – The Bankruptcy Abuse Prevention and Consumer Protection Act of 2005 (BAPCPA 2005) amended the United States Bankruptcy Code by adding new responsibilities for debtors. Under the BAPCPA, if a debtor fails to file a return that becomes due after the date of their bankruptcy petition, or fail to file an extension, the IRS may request the Bankruptcy Court to order a conversion (change from Chapter 7 to Chapter 11 or from Chapter 11 to Chapter 13, for example) or dismissal of the case.

In order to have a plan confirmed, a Chapter 13 debtor must also file all tax returns with the IRS for the four-year period prior to the filing of the bankruptcy petition. The debtor must establish filing by the first meeting of creditors.

Seven days before the first meeting of creditors, a debtor must provide trustees a copy of the most recently filed federal tax return or a transcript of the return. Similarly, copies of amendments to such returns, and any past due returns filed while the case is pending, must also be filed with the court if requested. The returns or transcripts must be provided to the court at the same time they are filed with the IRS. If the returns or transcripts are not filed, a Chapter 7 discharge will not be granted, or a Chapter 11 or 13 plan will not be confirmed. In addition, debtors must also provide a copy of the tax return or transcript to requesting creditors.

Guidance released by the Service in 2006 clarifies that under the Bankruptcy Code, the bankruptcy estate—rather than the debtor—must include in its gross income: (1) the debtor's "gross earnings" from his performance of services after the commencement of the case, and (2) the gross income from property acquired by the debtor after the commencement of the case. "Gross earnings" includes wages and other compensation earned by a debtor who is an employee, as well as self-employment income earned by an individual who is self-employed.[38]

CHAPTER ENDNOTES

1. IRC Sec. 6012(a)(1)(A).
2. IRC Sec. §6012(a), 63(c), 151; Rev. Proc. 2013-35 IRB 537.
3. IRC Secs. 6012(a), 6012(b).
4. IRC Sec. 6017.
5. IRC Sec. 6012(f).
6. IRC Sec. 6695(g).
7. IRC Sec. 6013(a).
8. IRC Sec. 6013(a).
9. IRC Sec. 6015. However, under the "innocent spouse" rules, a spouse may be relieved of the liability under certain circumstances. See Chapter 22.
10. IRC Sec. 6013(b)(1).
11. Treas. Reg. §1.6013-1(a)(1). This means a married couple who filed a joint return prior to the filing deadline may amend the return prior to the due date of the return.
12. IRC Sec. 2(a).
13. IRC Sec. 2(a)(1).
14. IRC Sec. 2(a)(2).
15. See IRC Sec. §2, 152.
16. IRC Sec. 441(a).
17. See IRC Sec. 441(g).
18. IRC Sec. 6072(a).
19. If the taxpayer keeps his book on a fiscal year basis, he *must* also determine his tax liability on a fiscal year basis.
20. IRC Sec. 6072(a).
21. IRC Sec. 7503.
22. IRC Sec. 6072(a); Notice 2004-83, 2004-2 CB 1030.
23. An authorized electronic return transmitter is a participant in the IRS e-file program that transmits electronic tax information directly to the IRS.
24. IRM 8.17.7.3.
25. IRC Sec. 6651(a)(1).
26. IRC Sec. 6651(a)(2).
27. IRC Sec. 6651(h).
28. IRC 6511(a).
29. IRC Sec. 6511(a). For the detailed explanation of when a refund claim must be filed if the time for filing such refund claim falls on a weekend or a legal holiday, see Rev. Rul. 2003-41, 2003-17 IRB 814.
30. IRC Sec. 6651(a).
31. IRC Sec. 6651(a).
32. IRC Sec. 6651(a).
33. IRC Sec. 6621(a)(2).
34. IRC Sec. 6662(a).
35. IRC Sec. 6662(d).
36. IRC Sec. 6662(d)(2)(B).
37. IRC Secs. 7201, 7202, 7203, 7206, 7207.
38. Notice 2006-83, 2006-40 IRB 596.

GROSS INCOME

CHAPTER 3

WHAT IS GROSS INCOME?

Gross income is the starting point in the computation of taxable income. Simply stated, taxable income is gross income minus deductions and personal exemptions for individuals. More fundamentally, taxable income is the difference between inflows of economic benefits and outflows expense items. As defined in Code section 61(a) of the Internal Revenue Code, gross income is essentially any economic benefit "from whatever source"[1] received—or deemed to be received—by the taxpayer. Although fifteen types of gross income are specifically listed, any item that confers an economic benefit to the taxpayer (whether listed or not) is presumed to be included in gross income.[2] Only items specifically excluded from gross income pursuant to other Code sections escape taxation.

At first glance, many of the fifteen types of gross income listed under section 61(a) appear to be self-explanatory. However, in some cases, further refinement can be found in other Code sections and Treasury Regulations. Specifically, the fifteen listed types of gross income are as follows:

1. **Compensation for services rendered** includes wages, salaries, fees, commissions, fringe benefits, and similar items that are usually paid to employees. For the most part, this is W-2 income classified as earned income discussed below. In addition, there are special rules that apply to transfers of property from an employer to an employee that are subject to substantial risk of forfeiture, employer retirement plan contributions, and certain stock options discussed later in this chapter.

2. **Gross income derived from business** is generally defined as the gross receipts from sales or services less business expenses, including cost of goods sold.[3] This category also includes payments received as "independent contractors" for those individuals who are not treated as employees and receive a Form 1099 reporting earnings rather than a Form W-2. This type of income is often referred to as "self-employment income," and is classified as earned income, as discussed below.

3. **Gains derived from dealings in property** includes the taxpayer's profit from the sale or exchange of property. In computing the profit, the amount included in gross income is the difference between the economic benefit received (the amount realized from the sale or exchange of the property) and "adjusted basis," which is the cost of the property to the taxpayer, adjusted as appropriate.[4] Moreover, in order for income to be characterized as a capital gain (discussed below), there must be a sale or exchange of a capital asset.[5]

4. **Interest earned from bonds or bond funds** is set forth on a Form 1099-INT that is usually issued by a brokerage company or the like. Banks also issue Forms 1099-INT on interest earned by CDs and other interest-bearing accounts. It also includes interest received or imputed from private loans.[6]

5. **Rents** received.

6. **Royalties** received.

7. **Dividends declared on publicly traded stock** are set forth on a Form 1099 DIV that is usually issued by a brokerage company. Closely held corporations can also make dividend distributions.[7]

8. **Alimony** (and separate maintenance payments) is included in gross income of the payee spouse. Taxable alimony is defined in Code section 71.

9. **Annuities** provide a stream of income payable over a term of years or for life, and their income is subject to special taxation rules set forth in Code section 72.

10. **Income from life insurance (and endowment) contracts** generally does not include death benefits received by the beneficiary of life insurance. However, there are circumstances in which "income" from life insurance may be includible in gross income.[8]

11. **Pensions** cover a broad range of distributions to retirees from a variety of retirement plans such as 401(k) plans, defined benefit plans, and IRAs.[9]

12. **Income from discharge of indebtedness** is a taxable economic benefit to the taxpayer that occurs when a debtor discharges the taxpayer's debt without receiving compensation from the taxpayer. As discussed below, some or all of the discharged debt may be excluded from gross income pursuant to Code section 108, depending on the circumstances of the discharge.

13. **Distributive share of partnership gross income** is included in the gross income of each partner. A partnership is a pass-through entity, so for income tax purposes, all partnership income flows through to the partners.[10]

14. **Income in respect of a decedent** is gross income that the decedent was entitled to, but had not yet received at the time of death. Because the decedent had not received the income prior to death, the decedent's last tax return (for a short tax year assuming he or she died sometime during the calendar year) would not include such income. Thus, the taxpayer who ultimately receives the income (the estate or beneficiary of the decedent) after the decedent's death must include it in gross income in the tax year it was received.[11]

15. **Income from an interest in an estate or trust.** Under rather complicated rules, income generated from an estate or trust may be taxable to the estate, trust and/or beneficiaries.[12]

In addition to the items listed under section 61(a), other sections of the Code specifically identify certain other items as being included in gross income. The reason these items are set forth in their own Code sections is because of special rules that affect their implementation. Those other specifically included gross income items are:

- **Services of a child.** A child's wages (from a part-time job, for example) are included in the gross income of the child rather than the parent. This is to distinguish a child's earned income from a child's investment income. In contrast, a child's investment income in excess of a certain amount ($2,100 in 2020) is treated as if it was the parents' income taxable at the parents' highest tax rate and is often referred to as the Kiddie Tax, as discussed below.[13]

- **Prizes and awards** are included in gross income and include "amounts received from radio and television giveaway shows, door prizes and awards in contests of all types." Employee achievement awards are also included.[14] There is, however, an exception for awards or prizes made in recognition of past achievements in religious, charitable, scientific, educational, artistic, literary or civic fields. Notable examples of this exception are the Nobel Peace Prize and the Pulitzer Prize for journalism.[15]

- **Premiums paid by an employer for group term life insurance** purchased for employees are partially excluded from gross income. The cost of the first $50,000 of group term life insurance paid by an employer on behalf of an employee is excluded from the gross income of the employee.[16] The incremental cost of insurance in excess of the $50,000 threshold is included in the employee's gross income (see Appendix D).

- **Reimbursement for moving expenses** merits further explanation. Certain moving expenses paid by a taxpayer in connection with a job change or transfer are deductible under Code section 217. In lieu of a deduction, if those deductible expenses were paid or reimbursed by the employer, the reimbursement would be excluded from gross income under Code section 132(a)(6), and the employee would not be able to deduct those expenses. An employer's reimbursement for moving expenses that *would not* have been deductible under section 217 must be included in the gross income of the reimbursed employee.[17]

- **Property transferred in connection with performance of services** is includible in gross income under Code section 61(a)(1), just like any other form of compensation. However, this inclusion under Code section 83 has a twist because it provides that the employee does not have to include the property in gross income if it is subject to a substantial risk of forfeiture, i.e., the employee must return the property back to the employee if the employee fails to meet certain conditions such as remaining in the employ of the employer for a number of years. The availability of a "section 83(b) election" presents tax planning opportunities for the employee that will be discussed below.

- **Transfer of appreciated property to a political organization** can be included in gross income. This is a provision that effectively prevents a taxpayer from receiving a tax benefit by making such a contribution to a political organization that is otherwise non-deductible. To illustrate this point, assume a taxpayer has land bought for $10,000, but is now worth $100,000. The taxpayer could sell the land, pay tax on the $90,000 gain and contribute the net proceeds to a political organization. Alternatively, the taxpayer could simply contribute the land to the political organization. Without this rule, there would be no taxable gain for the taxpayer in the latter instance, and the political organization would receive $100,000 of land. By avoiding the gain, the taxpayer would have effectively enjoyed a $90,000 deduction for a political contribution. To prevent such back-door deductions, the taxpayer is deemed to have sold the property to the political organization for the fair market value of the property. As a result, the contributing taxpayer must include the difference between the fair market value of the property and the cost basis of the property in gross income.[18]

- **Unemployment compensation** in excess of $2,400 is includible in gross income.[19]

- **Social Security and Tier 1 railroad retirement benefits** can be included in gross income. Depending on the income and filing status of the taxpayer, either 50 or 85 percent of such benefits may be included.[20]

WHAT ARE EXCLUSIONS FROM GROSS INCOME?

As stated above, any economic benefit is presumed to be included in gross income. The only way to overcome that presumption is to find a Code section that specifically excludes an economic benefit from gross income. Because the computation of taxable income begins with a determination of gross income, excluded items are not part of the tax base. Essentially, any item excluded from gross income is tax-free income for the taxpayer.

Items that are specifically *excluded* from gross income under the Code are as follows:

- **Certain death benefits**. In general, life insurance proceeds paid to the beneficiary of the underlying policy are fully excludable from gross income regardless of the amount of the death benefit. So assume that in 2016, brother purchases a $1,000,000 life insurance policy naming his sister as beneficiary. Upon brother's death in 2020, none of the $1,000,000 death benefit would be included in sister's gross income.[21] However, if brother were to transfer the policy to sister for *"any valuable consideration,"* it would essentially convert the $1,000,000 tax-free exclusion from gross income into a highly taxable inclusion in gross income. Known as the so called "transfer for value rule," sister would include in gross income the difference between the gross proceeds ($1,000,000) less the consideration paid including subsequent premiums. So, if the total amount of consideration and subsequent premiums was $50,000, sister would include $950,000 in gross income ($1,000,000 minus $50,000). Moreover, the character of the income would be ordinary meaning that the lion's share of the death

MUNICIPAL BONDS

Municipal bonds (often referred to as "munis" or "tax-exempts") have traditionally been among the safest investments and, thus, a favorite with conservative, income-seeking investors. The creditworthiness of bond issuers is evaluated and rated (e.g., AAA) by professional rating agencies, such as Moody's or Standard & Poor's.

Higher-income individuals have also favored municipal bonds because they tend to provide a higher "taxable equivalent yield"—meaning that if an investor's tax bracket (including state and local taxes) is high enough, the lower yield of a tax-exempt bond will most likely result in a higher after-tax return than would be produced by a comparable taxable instrument. For example, assuming an investor is in the 28 percent tax bracket, a tax-exempt yield of 6 percent is equivalent to a taxable yield of 8.33 percent. The chart in Appendix A shows the relationship between taxable and tax-free income for individuals in various brackets.

Some municipal bonds are "double" tax-exempt—that is, they are exempt from both federal and state taxes. Others are "triple" tax-exempt—meaning that they are exempt from federal, state, and local taxes (i.e., city, county, etc.). Generally, the income is exempt from taxation only within the state where the bond was issued.

Interest from "private activity" municipal bonds may—or may not—be exempt from federal income taxation. Private activity bonds are bonds used for nongovernmental purposes, including: industrial development bonds; and bonds for which the proceeds are used in the trade or business of persons other than a state or local government (e.g., student loans, qualified mortgages, and qualified waste disposal facilities).[22] Receipt of private activity bond interest may trigger alternative minimum tax for some individuals (see Chapter 11).[23]

benefit would be taxed at the highest ordinary income tax rate (39.6 percent).[24] For a more complete discussion of the "transfer for value rule," including significant exceptions to its application, see Chapter 25 of *The Tools & Techniques of Life Insurance Planning*.

- **Gifts and inheritances**. A gift, bequest, devise, or inheritance of money or property are excluded from gross income.[25] Conversely, *income* generated from gifts, bequests, devises, or inheritances are included in gross income of the recipient. Similarly, gifts, bequests, devise or inheritances of income from property (i.e., income distributed from a trust) is also included in the gross income of the recipient.[26]

- **Municipal bond interest**. Interest on bonds issued by state and local governments is usually *excluded* from gross income. If an individual receives tax-exempt interest, and that person is required to file an income tax return (see Chapter 2 and Chapter 8), he must report the amount of tax-exempt interest received during the tax year on his return even though tax-exempt interest is not subject to income tax.[27] Furthermore, even though municipal bond interest may be excluded from gross income, it must be taken into account in the calculation when determining whether Social Security payments are includible in gross income.[28] For more information on municipal bonds, see the sidebar, "Municipal Bonds."

- **Compensation for injuries and sickness.** Amounts received on account of personal physical injuries or physical sickness is generally excludable from gross income.[29] For example, a jury award for injuries sustained in an automobile accident would be excludable from gross income. But payments received as compensation for lost income and/or other economic damages must be included in the recipient's gross income. Payments awarded in an emotional distress suit are generally *not* treated as a physical injury or physical sickness and, therefore, are not excludable.[30] Furthermore, punitive damages—where the court is penalizing the wrongdoer for egregious behavior—must generally be included in the injured party's income.[31]

- **Contributions made by employers to health and accident plans.** Pursuant to section 106(a) of the Code, premiums paid through an employer-provided accident or health insurance plan are excluded from the gross income of the employee. Under those circumstances, however, the employee must include in gross income any amount received by virtue of being covered by such plan for personal injury or sickness (i.e., disability payments) that would have been otherwise excluded from gross income.[32] In other words, if the employee receives the tax-free benefit of not including employer-paid accident or health insurance premiums in gross income, there is no tax-free double dipping with regard to the receipt of what would have otherwise been excludible personal injury or sickness payments received through that coverage. On the other hand, an employer's *reimbursement* of an employee under a MERP (Medical Expense Reimbursement Plan) for expenses incurred by the employee for medical care of himself, his spouse, or his dependents may be fully excludable from gross income.[33]

- **Amounts received under health or accident plans.** If an individual has purchased a health insurance policy and paid premiums with the individual's own funds, the benefits received under that policy are excludable from gross income.[34] If both the employer and the employee share the premium cost, only the amount received by the employee attributable to the employer's premium payments is includible in the employee's gross income.[35]

- **Rental value of a parsonage.** A member of the clergy is permitted to exclude from income the fair rental value of a home (including utilities) or a housing allowance provided as part of compensation. This applies only to ordained, licensed, or commissioned clergy.[36]

- **Income from the discharge of indebtedness.** Although discharge of indebtedness is includible in gross income,[37] under certain circumstances, all or part of the amount discharged may be excluded from gross income. Those circumstances and the extent of the exclusion are as follows:

  (1) A discharge received in a bankruptcy proceeding.[38]

  (2) The discharge of all or part of a student loan specifically providing for such discharge in exchange for the debtor "work[ing] for a certain period of time in certain professions for any of a broad class of employers" (e.g., a doctor who commits to work for a rural hospital or clinic).[39]

  (3) The discharge of any debt where the payment would have been deductible had it actually been made by the debtor. Stated differently, the discharge of debt income and the lost deduction are treated as offsetting resulting in no taxable income. For example, the discharge of interest on a business related loan would be excluded from gross income because had the taxpayer actually made the payment, it would have been deductible in exactly the same amount.[40]

  (4) If a seller of property financed through purchase money debt reduces a portion of the debt for no consideration, that reduction is treated as a decrease in the purchase price rather than a discharge of the purchase money debt.[41]

  (5) A discharge that occurs when a taxpayer is insolvent, but only to the extent of the taxpayer's insolvency. To illustrate, assume that at the time of the discharge of $120,000 of debt, the taxpayer had assets of $20,000 and no other debt beyond what was discharged. After the discharge, the taxpayer's net worth would be $20,000. In this instance, $100,000 (the amount by which the taxpayer was insolvent) of the $120,000 of discharged debt would be excluded from gross income. The remaining $20,000—the amount of the taxpayer's resulting solvency—would be includible in gross income.[42]

  (6) The discharge of qualified farm indebtedness, which is defined as debt incurred directly in a farming business in which 50 percent or more of the gross receipts for the three preceding tax years prior to the tax year of discharge is attributable to the farming business, subject to certain limitations.[43]

  (7) The discharge of qualified real property business indebtedness, which is defined as secured debt incurred or assumed to acquire, construct, reconstruct, or substantially improve property used in a trade or business, subject to certain limitations.[44]

  (8) The discharge of qualified principal residence indebtedness of up to $2 million pursuant to a short sale or foreclosure.[45]

- **Recovery of "tax benefit" items.** Pursuant to the "tax benefit rule," a taxpayer who recovers by refund, reimbursement or collection an amount that in a prior tax year provided a tax benefit in the form of a deduction, refund or credit must essentially pay back that tax benefit by including that amount in gross income in the tax year of recovery. For example, assume in 2019, the taxpayer claimed a bad debt deduction for a loan default. Then, in 2020, the debtor unexpectedly repaid the loan to the taxpayer. Under the tax benefit rule, because the taxpayer recovered the amount of the loan previously deducted as a bad debt, the taxpayer would have to include the amount of the loan repayment. However, the amount included in gross income is limited to the amount by which the deduction or credit taken for the recovered amount resulted in tax savings in the earlier year. To illustrate this point, assume in 2020, the taxpayer received a state income tax refund for taxes paid in the 2019 tax year. If the taxpayer had itemized, the state income tax paid in 2019 could have been claimed as a deduction for Federal income tax purposes, and, thus reduced the taxpayer's tax liability. However, if the taxpayer did not itemize in 2019, the payment of the state income tax would not have conferred any tax benefit to the taxpayer. Thus, the recovery of the state income tax via refund in 2020 would not be included in gross income.[46]

- **Qualified scholarships.** Amounts received as a "qualified scholarship or fellowship" are not includible in gross income. A "qualified scholarship or fellowship" is any amount the individual receives that is for tuition and fees to enroll at or attend an education institution; *or* fees, books, supplies, and equipment required for courses at the educational institution.[47]

- **Meals or lodging furnished for the convenience of the employer.** The value of meals and lodging provided to an employee (and his family) by the individual's employer at no cost to the employee are not includible in gross income if the following conditions are met:

  - Meals must be furnished on the business premises of the employer, *and* must be furnished for the employer's convenience.

  - Lodging must be furnished on the business premises of the employer, for the convenience of the employer, *and* must be a condition of the individual's employment.[48]

- **Gain from the sale of a principal residence.** Unmarried taxpayers may exclude up to $250,000 of gain from the sale of a principal residence. Married taxpayers filing jointly may exclude up to $500,000. The full exclusion is available if the taxpayer:

  (1) has used and owned the home as a principal residence for two of the five years preceding the date of the sale; *and*

  (2) has *not* claimed the exclusion in the past two years.

  However, even if the taxpayer does not meet the above requirements, a partial exclusion may still be permitted. If the sale of the home is due to a change in place of employment, health problems, or unforeseen circumstances, then a reduced maximum exclusion may be available to the individual. The maximum exclusion is multiplied by the ratio that the "qualifying period" bears to the two-year period.[49]

- **Educational assistance programs.** An individual may exclude up to $5,250 of employer-provided educational assistance from gross income. The exclusion applies to undergraduate and graduate level courses.[50]

- **Dependent care assistance programs.** Dependent care benefits are generally excludable from gross income. Such benefits include amounts the employer pays directly to the employee for the care of certain individuals *and* the fair market value of care in a day care facility provided or sponsored by the individual's employer.

  The amount that can be excluded is limited to the lesser of: (1) the total amount of dependent care benefits the individual received during the year; (2) the total amount of qualified expenses the individual incurred during the year; (3) the individual's earned income; (4) the income of the individual's spouse; or (5) $5,000, or $2,500 if married filing separately.[51]

- **Certain personal injury liability assignments.** This exclusion relates to structured settlements of damages payable in periodic payments that would have otherwise been excluded from the gross income of the injured party (i.e., on account of physical injury or sickness). In operation, the obligation to make future periodic payments to the injured party is assigned by the wrongdoer to a "qualified assignment company." Using funds received from the wrongdoer, the qualified assignment company acquires a "qualified funding asset" such as an annuity or a US treasury obligation held by a trustee. Subsequently, the company issuing the annuity or the trustee makes the periodic payments to the injured party. Under such an arrangement, none of the amounts received by the injured party would be included in gross income.[52]

- **Certain fringe benefits.** Pursuant to Code section 61(a)(1), fringe benefits, a form of compensation, are included in gross income. (See Figure 3.1 for a more comprehensive list.) However, the fringe benefits listed below are specifically excluded from gross income:

  (1) No-additional-cost services

  (2) Qualified employee discounts

  (3) Working condition fringe benefits

  (4) De minimis fringe benefits

  (5) Qualified transportation fringe benefits

  (6) Qualified moving expense reimbursement

  (7) Qualified retirement planning services

  (8) Qualified military base realignment and closure benefits[53]

- **Income from United States savings bonds used to pay higher education expenses.** A taxpayer may exclude interest on United States savings bonds if the bonds are Series EE or Series I savings bonds, and the proceeds must be used to pay *qualified higher education expenses* (i.e., tuition and fees) required for enrollment at an eligible higher education institution for the bond owner or his/her dependents.

  In addition, for taxable years beginning in 2020, for all filers other than married filing jointly, the amount of the exclusion begins to phase out for modified adjusted gross income in excess of $82,350, with a complete phase out at $97,350. For married individuals filing jointly, the exclusion begins to phase out for modified adjusted gross income in excess of $123,550, with a complete phase out at $153,550.[54]

- **Adoption assistance programs.** For taxable years beginning in 2020, an employee may exclude $14,080 of expenses paid and then reimbursed by his employer under an adoption assistance program in connection with the employee's adoption of an eligible child. The amount of the exclusion phases out for modified adjusted gross income in excess of $211,160 with a complete phase out at $251,160.[55]

- **Medicare Advantage MSA.** Distributions for "qualified medical expenses" from "Medicare Advantage MSAs" (Medical Savings Accounts) generally are not includible in gross income. Qualified medical expenses are medical and dental expenses that would be deductible under Code section 213.[56] A "Medicare Advantage MSA" is available only to taxpayers who are entitled to benefits under Medicare Part A, and are enrolled under Part B.[57]

- **Disaster relief payments.** Gross income does not include disaster relief payments intended to help victims of natural disasters.[58] Payments made to victims of a "qualified disaster" on or after September 11, 2001 are also excludable from income. "Qualified disaster" generally means a disaster resulting from a terrorist or military action or a catastrophic airline accident.[59]

Other specifically excluded items include: improvements made by a lessee (i.e., tenant) on the lessor's (i.e., landlord's) property;[60] certain types of combat zone compensation for Armed Forces members;[61] capital contributions to a corporation;[62] amounts received under group legal services plans;[63] certain reduced uniformed services retirement pay;[64] amounts received under insurance contracts for certain living expenses;[65] and cafeteria plans.[66]

Figure 3.1

FRINGE BENEFITS*	
Type of fringe benefit	**Includable in gross income?**
Accident or health plan provided by employer	No
Athletic facilities	No
De minimis (minimal value gifts, such as holiday gifts)	No
Cash (bonus check, gift certificate)	Yes
Non-cash (holiday ham)	No
Dependent care benefits	No, if less than applicable limit
Educational assistance: - Cost is $5,250 or less - Cost exceeds $5,250	 No Yes
Employee discounts	No, unless discount "not qualified"
Financial counseling fees	Yes, but a limited deduction may be available
Group-term life insurance - Cost is $50,000 or less - Cost is greater than $50,000	 No Yes
Meals and lodging	No
Moving expense reimbursement	No
No-additional cost service (i.e., services received for free, or at reduced cost to employee that employer offers for sale to the public and that does not have a substantial additional cost)	No
Retirement planning services	No
Transportation	No, if less than applicable limit
Working condition fringe benefit (i.e., an employer provided product or service that the employer would have been able to deduct had he paid for it himself)	No

* The information in this table is based on the general rule governing each type of compensation. It is not intended to cover all exceptions and/or contingencies.

Other Non-Income Items

Return of capital. Under our income tax system, economic benefits are taxed only once. Thus, the "return of capital" or recovery of after-tax dollars is *not* an economic benefit includible in gross income. Money used to buy property is presumed to be after-tax dollars. So, if an individual buys stock for $10,000 and sells it for $10,000, there is no income because the seller merely recovered the after-tax purchase price. Conversely, if the individual sells the stock for $10,500, there is a profit or $500 that would be includible in gross income pursuant to Code section 61(a)(3).[67]

Loans. The proceeds from a loan are not gross income to the borrower because the economic benefit of the use of the borrowed funds is offset by a corresponding obligation to repay the loan. Similarly, the repayment of the principal amount of the loan is not gross income to the lender because the lender is merely recouping the after-tax dollars loaned to the borrower. Interest income is included in gross income pursuant to Code section 61(a)(4).

Income Characterization Has Tax Significance

Once it is determined that an item is included in gross income, and, no exclusion applies, the next step is to determine the character of the income. The character of the income has two significant roles in income taxation. First, the character of the income determines the tax rates at which the income is to be taxed. Second, the deductibility of certain expenses or losses may be limited based upon characterization. Income is characterized as either *ordinary income* or *capital gain*. Ordinary income is essentially any type of gross income with the exception of gain from the sale or exchange of a capital asset or property described in Code section 1231(b).[68] Capital gain is gain from the sale or exchange of a capital asset, and can be short-term (the asset was owned ty the tax payer for no more than one year) or long-term (the asset was owned for more than one year).[69] The tax rates for ordinary income and short-term capital gain are the same, and range from 10 percent to 39.6 percent.[70] The tax rates for long-term capital gain and qualified dividends[71] (ordinary income taxed at the same tax rates as long-term capital gain) are either 0, 15 or 20 percent, depending on the taxpayer's income level.[72]

Long- and Short-term capital losses can be deducted to offset the amount of long- and short-term capital gains plus $3,000 of ordinary income. Any non-deductible capital loss is carried forward indefinitely, subject to the same restriction.[73] In other words, if a taxpayer has a *net* capital loss in any given tax year, no more than $3,000 of that loss would be deductible against other ordinary income. Without any capital gains to be offset, a taxpayer with a net capital loss of $100,000 would need thirty-four years to fully deduct the entire loss at the rate of $3,000 per year.

For a more detailed explanation of capital gains and qualified dividends, see Chapter 4.

Income Classifications Have Tax Significance

In addition to determining the character of taxable gross income, the *classification* of certain types of gross income can have tax significance. As discussed below, the classification of gross income can be relevant to the allowance of a tax credit, an exclusion from gross income, a limitation on certain deductions, and can be the basis for an additional tax.

Earned Income

The classification of certain types of gross income as *earned income* is a prerequisite for qualifying for the earned income tax credit. The earned income tax credit is a refundable credit meaning that even if the amount of the credit exceeds the amount of tax withheld by the taxpayer's employer or otherwise paid by the taxpayer, the taxpayer would nonetheless be entitled to a refund.[74] The credit is available to those taxpayers who have low or moderate earned income. For purposes of this tax credit, earned income includes:

1. wages, salaries, tips, bonuses, and other employee compensation to the extent it is included in gross income;[75]

2. net earnings from self-employment;[76] and

3. gross income received as a "statutory employee" (agent or commission drivers; certain full-time life insurance salespeople; full-time traveling salespeople; and home workers).[77]

In addition to the earned income credit, there is a foreign earned income exclusion available to U.S. citizens and U.S. resident aliens who work in a foreign country. This credit allows taxpayers who are employed overseas to exclude a relatively large amount of their foreign earned income from gross income. The amount of the foreign earned income subject to the exclusion is indexed for inflation. For the 2016 tax year, the exclusion amount was $101,300.[78]

Investment Income

Investment income (sometimes referred to as "unearned income") is another classification of gross income with tax significance. For example, investment interest (interest paid on a loan that was used to purchase investment property) is deductible only to the extent of net investment income.[79] Any excess "loss" is carried over to subsequent years subject to the same rules, and is only deductible to extent of net investment income in those subsequent years. For this purpose, investment income is income from property held for investment, such as stocks, bonds, and investment property. It includes dividends and royalties as well as the gain from the sale of investment property.[80]

In addition to being a limitation on the deductibility of investment interest, net investment income is also subject to the 3.8 percent net investment income tax imposed on high income taxpayers.[81] For this purpose, investment interest also includes annuity payments, rent generated from investment type property, and passive activity income (described below).[82]

A child's investment income in excess of $2,100 is subject to the "kiddie tax." The purpose of the kiddie tax is to prevent parents from shifting investment income taxed at their higher tax rate to their children to be taxed at their much lower tax rate. For example, parents may be tempted to transfer a substantial investment portfolio to a child so that the income generated therefrom would be taxed to the child rather than the parents. When the kiddie tax applies, the child's investment or unearned income is treated as if it was earned by the parents, and, thus, taxed at the parents' highest tax rate. For this purpose, investment income includes interest, dividends and capital gain distributions. The kiddie tax applies:

1. until the year in which child attains the age of eighteen regardless of the amount of the child's earned income;

2. in the year the child attains the age of eighteen, unless the child's earned income is more than half of his or her overall support; or

3. in any year from the ages of nineteen to twenty-three, if the child is a full-time student during any part of at least five months and earned income is less than half of the child's overall support.[83]

Passive Activity Income

Passive activity income is income generated from any trade or business activity in which the taxpayer does not "materially participate."[84] Generally, a taxpayer is considered to *materially participate* in an activity if he is involved in the operations of the activity on a regular, continuous, and substantial basis. Note that rental activities are considered to be a passive activity even if the taxpayer materially participates in the activity.[85] This classification is important because if a taxpayer has positive non-passive income from Venture A and substantial non-passive business deductions from Venture B, the Venture B business deductions can offset the taxable income from Venture A. This is not the case with passive activity deductions that are only deductible to the extent of passive activity income.[86] So if the income generated in Venture A was non-passive and the business deductions generated in Venture B were passive, the Venture B deductions could not be applied to reduce the Venture A income. However, if the taxpayer generated passive income in subsequent tax years, the leftover Venture B passive deductions from this year could be deducted against such income. For a more detailed explanation of passive activity income, see Chapter 23.[87]

INCOME DEFERAL AND TIMING ISSUES

There is a distinction between an *exclusion* of income and a *deferral* of income. An exclusion provision means that an item that would otherwise be included in gross income is never taxed. A deferral excludes certain economic benefits from gross income based on the taxpayer meeting the qualifications of the relevant Code section. However, the income may be taxable in the future depending on the qualifications of the deferral. For example, although the gain realized by the taxpayer with regard to like-kind exchanges,[88] involuntary conversions[89] and certain exchanges of insurance policies[90] would be excluded from gross income, the inherent gain remains preserved in the replacement property and would be included in gross income if the taxpayer disposed of the property in a taxable transaction at a later date.[91] In addition to those provisions, as discussed below, there are a number of gross income deferrals available to employees.

Selected Employee Compensation Deferrals

Retirement plan contributions. Employer contributions to a qualified retirement plan (such as a pension, profit-sharing, or stock-bonus plan) for an employee are generally not included in the employee's gross income at the time of the contribution. Over time, the income generated by the invested contributions grows tax-free. When the employee retires, the distributions to the employee would be included in gross income. The tax treatment of retirement plan contributions and distributions is discussed in greater detail in Chapter 31 and Appendix A, as well as the companion resource to this volume, *Tools & Techniques of Employee Benefit and Retirement Planning*.

Stock options. Stock options generally come in two varieties: (1) qualified incentive stock options (ISOs); and (2) nonqualified stock options (NQSOs).[92] The tax treatment and timing for each type of option differs significantly and is based on several different factors. For details on the tax treatment of ISOs and NQSOs, see Chapter 27, and our companion resource, *Tools & Techniques of Employee Benefit and Retirement Planning*.

Section 83(b) election. Pursuant to Code section 83(a), the value of property transferred to an employee is not includible in the employee's gross income until it becomes totally vested and not subject to a substantial risk of forfeiture. An example of a substantial risk of forfeiture would the requirement that the employee must return the property if the employee fails to remain employed with the employer for a number of years. Only in the tax year in which the property vests due to the employee satisfying the condition would the value of the property be included in gross income.

The election provided by Code section 83(b) can provide significant planning opportunities for the employee by allowing the employee the option of including the value of the stock as income in the year he or she receives it, even if it has not vested. For example, assume that in 2016, the employer transfers stock worth $10,000 to the employee, subject to forfeiture if the employee does not remain in the employ of the employer for the next five years. Further, assume that at the time of vesting in 2019, the stock is worth $25,000. In the absence of a section 83(b) election, the employee would have no income to report in 2016, but be required to include $25,000 (the value of the stock) as compensation income in 2019, taxable at ordinary income rates.[93] In the alternative, if the employee made a section 83(b) election in 2016, he or she would be required to include the stock's value of $10,000 as compensation income, taxable at ordinary income rates. When ownership of the stock vests in 2019, there would be no reportable gross income, even though the stock had appreciated by $15,000. Moreover, as long as the employee simply held the stock, there would be no further income. When the employee sells the stock, the gain (proceeds from the sale minus the initial $10,000 that was included in gross income in 2016) would be treated as a long-term capital gain rather than ordinary income.

The difference between the two options can be significant for the taxpayer. Without a section 83(b) election, although the employee would not report any of the income until 2019, the $25,000 then included in gross income as compensation would be subject to ordinary income rates. With a section 83(b) election, although the employee would report $10,000 of ordinary income in 2016, none of the appreciation would be taxed until the stock was sold. If the stock was sold in 2019 or anytime thereafter, the gain ($15,000 if sold in 2019) would be taxed at the preferential capital gain rates. Under the latter scenario, the employee would effectively convert what would otherwise be ordinary income into a long-term capital gain, and would be able to control when the gain was taxed by deciding when to sell the stock

Advance payment for services. Most taxpayers report income and deductions under the cash method of accounting, meaning that they report compensation in the year it is received without regard to when it was actually earned. For example, if a taxpayer receives a 2019 bonus in 2020, it would be includible in gross income in 2020 even though it was earned in 2019. Similarly, if the taxpayer receives part of 2020 compensation in 2019, that amount would be includible in gross income in 2015 even though it was not earned until 2020.[94] Conversely, under the accrual method of accounting, income is reported in the year it is earned without regard to when it is received. An accrual method taxpayer who did not receive a 2019 bonus until 2020 would include it in gross income in 2019, the year in which it was earned. In spite of this general rule, an accrual method taxpayer is often treated as a cash method taxpayer with regard to the receipt of income. An accrual method taxpayer must include compensation in gross income on the earliest of:

1. when the payment is received;
2. when the income is due to the taxpayer;
3. when the income is earned; or
4. with respect to property, when title has passed.[95]

For that reason, it would appear that even under the accrual method of accounting, advance payment for services must be included in gross income in the tax year in which it was paid. There is, however, an exception for an advance payment of services to be performed by the end of the following tax year. For example, in 2019, if an accrual method taxpayer receives an advance for services to be performed by the end of 2020, the taxpayer can elect to defer the inclusion of that income until 2020. However, the taxpayer may only extend the deferral one tax year beyond the year of payment. If the taxpayer received an advance payment in 2019 for services to be performed by the end of 2021, the exception would not apply and he or she would be required to include the advance payment in gross income in 2019.[96]

BEWARE OF SEVERAL TAX TRAPS

Constructive Receipt of Income

In order to defer income from one tax year to another, a cash method taxpayer may be tempted to delay the deposit of the last paycheck of the year to the following tax year. In the alternative, he or she might ask the employer to hold the check until January. Likewise, knowing that the postal service will attempt to deliver the taxpayer's last payroll check on the last day of the year, the taxpayer might choose not to be home to accept delivery. By doing so, he or she is attempting to delay the receipt of income and, thus, the inclusion of that income until the following tax year. Under the doctrine of *constructive receipt of income*, none of these ploys would work. Under this doctrine, the taxpayer must include all income that is available to him (credited, set apart, or otherwise available), even though it may not actually be in his possession.[97] So in any of the scenarios described above, the taxpayer would have to include those amounts in gross income in the tax year they were constructively received rather than the later tax year.

Imputed Income From a Below Market Loan

Taxpayers with a close relationship (employer/employee, corporation/shareholder or parent/child) are often tempted to make below market or even interest free loans. By doing so, both the lender and the borrower would enjoy substantial economic and tax benefits. For example, in the case of an interest-free loan, the borrower would enjoy the economic benefit of having the use of the borrowed funds without the economic burden of paying interest. In turn, the lender would be able to provide the economic benefit of the use of the loaned money to the borrower without having to include interest payments from the borrower in gross income. Because the scope of gross income is so broad and is designed to capture any economic benefit as taxable income, Code section 7872 treats such "below-market" loans in a way that would trigger "imputed income" and possibly result in adverse tax consequences to the lender and the borrower. For this purpose, a "below-market" loan is a loan on which either no interest is charged, *or* the interest charged is at a rate below the applicable federal rate (AFR), and thus considered as not charging adequate interest.[98] (A complete history and current AFR rates can be found at http://www.leimberg.com).

In the case of a below market loan, section 7872 effectively rewrites the transaction by imputing that the lender:

- made a loan to the borrower in exchange for a note (even though no such note really exists) that requires the payment of interest at the AFR; and

- transferred the amount of foregone interest to the borrower (even though nothing was actually transferred). The amount of the foregone interest is the difference between the AFR and the amount actually paid by the borrower. For example, if the lender made an interest-free loan, the entire amount of the AFR would be an imputed transfer to the borrower.

What would the tax consequences be to the borrower who is deemed to have received an amount equal to the foregone interest from the lender? From the borrower's perspective, the classification of the income from the foregone interest is predicated on the borrower's relationship with the lender. For example, if the lender was the employer of the borrower, the phantom payment is deemed to be a form of compensation includible in the borrower/employee's gross income. If the lender was a corporation and the borrower was a shareholder, the phantom payment is deemed be a dividend distribution, also includible in the borrower/shareholder's gross income. Finally, if the lender was a parent and the borrower was a child, the phantom payment would be treated as a gift to the borrower/child, and, thus not included in the gross income.

From the lender's perspective, Code section 7872(a) specifically states that "the forgone interest shall be treated as . . . retransferred by the borrower to the lender as interest"—even though no such interest payment was actually made. The lender will have to include the phantom payment as interest income, although under many circumstances the lender will have an offsetting deduction for the income provided to the borrower.

Consider the following example, in which an employer provides an employee with a no-interest loan of $100,000. Assume that the AFR is 6 percent, providing $6,000 in interest. If the employer had simply paid the employee a bonus of $6,000, the employee would have $6,000 of compensation income and the employer would be entitled to a $6,000 compensation deduction. Then, if the employee paid the employer $6,000 of interest, the employer would have $6,000 of interest income. The employee may or may not be entitled to an interest deduction depending on how he or she used the borrowed funds. Code section 7872 simply recasts a below market loan in just that way. When the employer makes an interest free loan of $100,000 to the employee, the Code treats the employer as if it had paid the employee compensation in the amount of the foregone interest ($6,000). Then, it treats the employee as using the phantom compensation to pay the employer the interest that should have been charged on that loan. In both scenarios, the employee has compensation income and the employer has interest income. Here, the employer also gets a deduction for the phantom compensation and the transaction is a wash. From the employee's perspective, whether he or she would be entitled to a deduction depends on how the borrowed funds are used, just as it would in any regular loan.

Although the tax consequences of below market loans can be onerous, there are several de minimis exceptions that may apply.[99] For example, compensation-related loans (often considered wage advances), corporate-shareholder loans, and loans between individuals for non-business and non-investment purposes are generally exempt so long as the balance owed never exceeds $10,000. Finally—as can be seen in the example above—the deduction consequences with respect to such below market loans are complicated, and many of them are beyond the scope of this chapter.

Restoration of Income Previously Taxed

The *claim of right* doctrine applies to the receipt of income that the taxpayer may have a contingent obligation to repay at a later date. In spite of a potential obligation to repay, the taxpayer must nonetheless include it in gross income unless "the individual recognizes his liability under an existing and fixed obligation and makes provisions for repayment."[100] For example, assume an employee receives a bonus that the employer could possibly dispute and compel the employee to repay at some later date. At the time the bonus was received, there was no fixed obligation for repayment, nor had the employee made any provision for its repayment. Under the claim of right doctrine, the taxpayer would be compelled to include the bonus in gross income. However, in the event the taxpayer was subsequently required to repay all or part of such bonus, the taxpayer would be entitled to "a deduction for the amount of the repayment and, in effect, a credit for the amount of tax that would have been saved in the year of inclusion if the repaid amount had been excluded from that year's gross income."[101]

WHERE CAN I FIND OUT MORE?

1. *Tax Facts on Insurance & Employee Benefits* (National Underwriter Company; published annually).

2. *Tools and Techniques of Employee Benefit and Retirement Planning* (National Underwriter Company).

FREQUENTLY ASKED QUESTIONS

Question – What are installment sales? How are installment payments taxed?

Answer – An installment sale is a sale of property in which the seller makes a gain, and provides credit to the buyer under terms that require at least one payment to be made after the close of the taxable year in which the property was sold. There is usually a promissory note that requires the buyer to pay principal and interest over the payment term of the arrangement. As each payment is received, the seller includes the entire interest portion of the payment in gross income. As to the principal portion of the payment, with each yearly installment, a ratable amount of the gain is included in gross income. This allows the selling taxpayer to spread his or her gain over the payment term.[102]

Example: Mary Worth owns land which she purchased four years ago for $20,000. In 2020, Mary sells the land to Betty Buyer for $100,000, payable in five $20,000 annual installments. The sale is evidenced with a promissory note bearing market rate interest and specifying the interest payments to be made in addition to the $20,000 annual payments toward the purchase price.

Viewing the transaction as a whole, Mary would have a total gain of $80,000 (the selling price of $100,000 less her cost basis of $20,000). Thus, under the installment method of reporting, Mary would ratably include her overall gain in gross income over the five-year term. Since each payment is $20,000 (exclusive of interest), Mary would determine her ratable yearly gain by multiplying the payment by the *gross profit ratio*, which is defined as the total gain as a percentage of the selling price. In this case, the gross profit ratio is 80 percent ($80,000 total gain/$100,000 selling price). For each of the five years, Mary would include $16,000

(80 percent) of the annual payment as gross income. The remaining $4,000 of each principal payment is a tax-free recovery of her cost basis over the same five-year period. So, at the end of the five-year term, Mary would have ratably included $80,000 of income ($16,000 each year) and $20,000 of tax-free recovery of her cost basis ($4,000 each year). The interest payment(s) she received each year would be separately included as gross income in the years in which they are received.

Question – Are attorneys' fees includible in the gross income of an injured party?

Answer – It depends. To the extent that the injured party is awarded a non-taxable judgment for physical injuries, attorneys' fees are not included in the gross income of the injured party. For all other taxable judgment awards the winning litigant must include the entire amount of the judgment including the contingent attorneys' fees in gross income according to a 2005 decision by the United States Supreme Court in *Commissioner v. Banks*.[103]

In the years leading up to the Supreme Court's pronouncement, the number of lawsuits filed in this country had steadily increased. It was not surprising that the tax issues triggered by the large judgments being awarded to injured individuals would also attract increased attention from the IRS. With respect to the judgment awards received by an injured party for personal injuries or sickness, there has never been a dispute since none of it is ever included in the injured party's gross income.[104] For that reason, the portion of the settlement paid in attorneys' fees was inconsequential since the entire award would be non-taxable.

But many lawsuits other than personal injury are also handled on a *contingency basis* – meaning that the plaintiff's attorney gets paid only if the case is won. Consequently, until *Banks* was decided in 2005, a major point of contention was whether the injured party must include the attorneys' contingency fees in gross income or simply include the net amount of the judgment actually received in gross income. In *Banks*, the Supreme Court resolved the dispute by holding that the winning litigant must include the entire amount of the judgment in gross income. As discussed below, the aftermath of the decision has created a substantial tax hardship for the winning litigant.

Attorneys' fees are deductible under Code section 212 as an expense incurred in connection with the production of income, and treated as a miscellaneous itemized deduction subject to a 2 percent adjusted gross income floor.[105] To see why this is important, assume that a court awarded the taxpayer $300,000 in taxable economic damages. Of that amount, $100,000 is payable to her attorney as a contingent fee and deductible pursuant to section 212. Assuming the taxpayer had no other deductions and the award was the taxpayer's only income, 2 percent of $300,000 is $6,000, so the itemized deduction would be limited to $94,000. In addition, by virtue of the section 68 phase-out (overall limitation on itemized deductions), the itemized deduction would be further reduced to $92,500. Thus, even though the taxpayer received $200,000, she would be essentially taxed on $207,500 or $7,500 more than she had received. Compounding the taxpayer's tax woes would be the imposition of the alternative minimum tax that is triggered by the large miscellaneous itemized deduction of the attorneys' fees. As a result, the taxpayer's overall tax liability on the net $200,000 award would be $78,800 ($51,834 regular tax plus $26,966 of alternative minimum tax).

Conversely, if the $100,000 of attorneys' fees were simply taken out of the equation since the taxpayer was only entitled to receive an amount equal to two-thirds of the judgment, or $200,000, the tax consequences would be dramatically different, and arguably much fairer. Assuming the $200,000 was the taxpayer's only income, in the absence of adverse tax consequences caused by the miscellaneous itemized deduction of attorneys' fees that were not fully deductible and triggered alternative minimum tax, there would only be a regular tax of $46,831. So in spite of the fact that in both scenarios, the taxpayer's net share of the judgment was $200,000, under current law, the tax difference resulting from the inclusion of the attorneys' fees in gross income would be over $40,000. Ultimately, it will take an act of Congress to change this result.

Question – Are damages received for certain nonphysical personal injuries includible in the gross income of an injured party?

Answer – Marrita Murphy sued in district court to recover income taxes paid on compensatory damages she had been awarded for emotional distress and loss of reputation in an administrative action brought against her former employer. Murphy contended that under Code section 104(a)(2), her award should have been excluded from her gross income because it was compensation received "on account of personal physical injuries or physical sickness." Alternatively, Murphy maintained that section 104(a)(2) is unconstitutional because it fails to exclude from gross income revenue that is not "income" within the meaning of the Sixteenth Amendment to the Constitution of the United States. The district court rejected all of Murphy's claims on the merits and granted summary judgment for the government and the IRS.[106]

The United States Court of Appeals for the District of Columbia concluded (on rehearing) that Murphy's compensatory award was not received on account of personal physical injuries, was not exempt from taxation pursuant to section 104(a)(2), and was therefore part of Murphy's "gross income," as defined by Code section 61. It also decided that the tax was constitutional because it was an excise tax rather than a direct tax and was uniform throughout the United States. Accordingly, the appeals court affirmed the judgment of the district court.[107]

Question – What are the individual income tax rates under the 2017 Tax Act?

Answer – The 2017 Tax Act changed the ordinary income tax rates that will apply to individuals beginning in 2018.[108] For 2020, the applicable inflation-adjusted tax rates and income thresholds are outlined in the chart below:

	Taxable Income			
Tax Rate	**Single**	**Married Filing Jointly Including Qualifying Widow(er) with Dependent Child**	**Married Filing Separately**	**Head of Household**
10%	$0 to $9,875	$0 to $19,750	$0 to $9,875	$0 to $14,100
12%	$9,875-$40,100	$19,750-$80,200	$9,875 -$40,100	$14,100-$53,700
22%	$40,100-$85,525	$80,200-$171,050	$40,100-$85,525	$53,700-$85,500
24%	$85,525-$163,300	$171,050-$326,600	$85,525-$163,300	$85,500-$163,300
32%	$163,300-$207,350	$326,600-$414,700	$163,300-$207,350	$163,300-$207,350
35%	$207,350-$518,400	$414,700-$622,050	$207,230-$311,025	$207,350-$518,400
37%	Over $518,400	Over $622,050	Over $311,025	Over $518,400

The 2018 income thresholds are as stated in the above table, and will not be adjusted for inflation until 2019.

Under prior law, the income tax rates and brackets for 2017 were as follows:[109]

	Taxable Income			
Tax Rate	**Single**	**Married Filing Jointly Including Qualifying Widow(er) with Dependent Child**	**Married Filing Separately**	**Head of Household**
10%	$0 to $9,325	$0 to $18,650	$0 to $9,325	$0 to $13,350
15%	$9,325-$37,950	$18,650-$75,900	$9,325-$37,950	$13,350-$50,800
25%	$37,950-$91,900	$75,900-$153,100	$37,950-$76,550	$50,800-$131,200
28%	$91,900-$191,650	$153,100-$233,350	$76,550-$116,675	$131,200-$212,500
33%	$191,650-$416,700	$233,350-$416,700	$116,675-$208,350	$212,500-$416,700
35%	$416,700-$418,400	$416,700-$470,700	$208,350-$235,350	$416,700-$444,550
39.6%	Over $418,400	Over $470,700	Over $235,350	Over $444,550

The applicable tax rates and income thresholds imposed by the 2017 Tax Act are set to expire for tax years beginning after December 31, 2025.

Question – How does tax reform impact the treatment of unearned income of minors, or the so-called "kiddie tax"?

Answer – Under prior law, children under the age of nineteen (age twenty-four for students) were required to pay tax on their unearned income above a certain amount at their parents' marginal rate.[110]

The so-called "kiddie tax" applies to children who have not attained certain ages before the close of the taxable year, who have at least one parent alive at the close of the taxable year, and who have over $2,100 (in 2015-2020) of unearned income.[111]

The kiddie tax applies to:

1. a child under age eighteen; *or*

2. a child who has attained the age of eighteen if: (a) the child has not attained the age of nineteen (twenty-four in the case of a full-time student) before the close of the taxable year; and (b) the earned income of the child does not exceed one-half of the amount of the child's support for the year.[112]

The tax applies only to "net unearned income." "Net unearned income" is defined as adjusted gross income that is not attributable to earned income, and that exceeds $2,100.[113]

The 2017 Tax Act aims to simplify the treatment of unearned income of minors by applying the tax rates that apply to trusts and estates to this income. Therefore, earned income of minors will be taxed according to the individual income tax rates prescribed for single filers,[114] and unearned income of minors will be taxed according to the applicable tax bracket that would apply if the income was that of a trust or estate (for both income that is subject to ordinary income tax rates and in determining the capital gains rate that will apply if long-term capital gains treatment is appropriate).[115]

The rates that will apply to trusts and estates under the 2017 Tax Act are as follows:

Tax Rate	Trusts and Estate Income
10%	$0 to $2,600
$260 plus 24% of the excess over $2,600	$2,600-$9,450
$1,868 plus 35% of the excess over $9,300	$9,450-$12,950
$3,075.50 plus 37% of the excess over $12,750	Over $12,950

This provision does not apply to tax years beginning after December 31, 2025.

Planning Point: Because the unearned income of minors was previously taxed at a parent's tax rate, this means that a child with a relatively small level of unearned income may pay less on this income (a child can essentially have up to $4,650 in unearned income before he or she moves out of the lowest 10 percent tax bracket—$2,100 that is exempt and $2,550 taxed at the 10 percent rate).

However, the minor will also jump into the highest tax bracket more quickly under the new law. While the minor's parents will not be taxed at the 37 percent rate until their combined income for the year exceeds $600,000 (assuming a joint return), the child will be taxed at that rate once he or she has unearned income in excess of only $12,500. As a result, some parents may wish to consider taking steps to reduce the child's taxable income (i.e., by keeping any funds invested until the child is no longer subject to the kiddie tax rules).

Question – Does tax reform impact the tax treatment of self-created intellectual property?

Answer – The 2017 Tax Act provides that gain or loss from the disposition of a self-created patent, invention, model or design, or secret formula or process will be taxed as ordinary income or loss. The election to treat musical compositions and copyrights in music as capital assets was not changed.[116]

These provisions are effective for tax years beginning after December 31, 2017.

CHAPTER ENDNOTES

1. IRC Sec. 61(a).
2. Treas. Reg. §1.61-1(a).
3. *See* Treas. Reg. §1.61-1(c) referencing "manufacturing, merchandising, or mining business," but obviously applicable to all businesses.
4. IRC Sec. 1001(a).
5. IRC Sec. 1222.
6. For example, §7872 imputes interest on certain below market loans discussed below.

7. See IRC Secs. 301 and 316 for the rules determining whether distributions from a corporation to shareholders are deemed to be taxable dividends.
8. See IRC Sec. 101 and Treasury Regulations, thereunder.
9. See IRC Secs. 72, 402 and 403.
10. IRC Sec. 702(c).
11. IRC Sec. 691(a) and discussed in more detail in Chapter 27.
12. Part 1 (§641 and following), Subchapter J, Chapter 1 of the Code.
13. IRC Sec. 73.
14. Treas. Reg. §1.74(a)(1). Also see IRC Sec. 74.
15. Treas. Reg. §1.74(b).
16. IRC Sec. 79.
17. IRC Sec. 82.
18. IRC Sec. 84.
19. IRC Sec. 85.
20. IRC Sec. 86. Rounding out other items specifically included in gross income are as follows: IRC Sec. 75 - dealers in tax-exempt securities (adjustment for bond premiums); IRC Sec. 77 - commodity credit loans; IRC Sec. 78 - dividends received from certain foreign corporations by domestic corporations choosing the foreign tax credit; IRC Sec. 80 - restoration of the value of certain securities; IRC Sec. 87 - the alcohol fuel credit; IRC Sec. 88 - certain amounts with respect to nuclear decommissioning costs; and IRC Sec. 89 - illegal federal irrigation subsidies.
21. IRC Sec. 101(a).
22. IRC Sec. 141.
23. IRC Sec. 57(a)(5).
24. IRC Secs. 61(a)(10) and 101(a)(2); Treas. Reg. §1.101-1. The amount included in gross income may also be deemed to be "investment income" for purposes of the 3.8 percent net investment income tax.
25. IRC Sec. 102(a); Treas. Reg. §1.102-1(a).
26. IRC Sec. 102(b); Treas. Reg. §1.102-1(b) and (c).
27. IRC Sec. 6012(d).
28. IRC Sec. 86(b)(2)(B).
29. IRC Sec. 104(a)(2). This is true whether the damages are received by the injured plaintiff in a lump sum, as periodic payments, or from a lawsuit or a settlement agreement.
30. IRC Sec. 104(a).
31. IRC Sec. 104(c). However, if punitive damages are awarded in a wrongful death action, and the applicable state law provides that punitive damages, only, may be awarded, then such damages would be excludable from income.
32. IRC Sec. 105(a).
33. IRC Sec. 105(b). But if an accident or health plan has reimbursed an employee for medical expenses he deducted in an earlier year, the employee may have to include some of the reimbursed amount in the year in which the reimbursement was received.
34. IRC Sec. 104(a)(3).
35. IRC Sec. 105.
36. IRC Sec. 107.
37. IRC Sec. 61(a)(12).
38. IRC Secs. 108(a)(1)(A) and (d)(2).
39. IRC Sec. 108(f).
40. IRC Sec. 108(e)(2).
41. IRC Sec. 108(e)(5).
42. IRC Secs. 108(a)(1)(b) and (d)(3).
43. IRC Secs. 108(a)(1)(C) and (g).
44. IRC Sec. 108(a)(1)(D) and (c)(1) and (2).
45. IRC Sec. 108(a)(1)(E) and (h).
46. IRC Sec. 111.
47. IRC Sec. 117.
48. IRC Sec. 119.
49. IRC Sec. 121.
50. IRC Sec. 127.
51. IRC Sec. 129.
52. IRC Sec. 130.
53. IRC Sec. 132(a)(1)-(8).
54. IRC Sec. 135. Rev. Proc. 2013-35, 2008-47 IRB 167.
55. IRC Secs. 137(a)(2) and (b)(1). Rev. Proc. 2013-35, 2008-45 IRB 167, Rev. Proc. 2015-53.
56. IRS Publication 969.
57. IRC Sec. 138(b). "Medicare Advantage MSA" was formerly known as "Medicare+Choice MSA."
58. Disaster Relief Act of 1974 (P.L. 98-233); 42 USC 408; Rev. Rul. 76-144, 1976-1 CB 144.
59. Victims of Terrorism Tax Relief Act of 2001 (P.L. 107-134); IRC Sec. 139.
60. IRC Sec. 109.
61. IRC Sec. 112.
62. IRC Sec. 118.
63. IRC Sec. 120.
64. IRC Sec. 122.
65. IRC Sec. 123.
66. IRC Sec. 125.
67. See IRC Sec. 1001(a).
68. IRC Sec. 1.
69. IRC Sec. 1222.
70. IRC Sec. 1.
71. IRC Sec. 1(h)(11). A qualified dividend is a dividend received from a domestic corporation or a qualified foreign corporation.
72. IRC Sec. 1(h). The 20 percent rate kicks in for single taxpayers with taxable income over $400,000 and married taxpayers filing jointly with taxable income over $450,000.
73. IRC Sec. 1211(b)(1).
74. I.R.C. Sec 32.
75. IRC Sec. 32(2)(A)(i).
76. Ministers are also considered to be self-employed.
77. IRC Sec. 32(c)(2). Statutory employees receive Form W-2s on which the "Statutory Employee" box is checked. They report their income and expenses on Schedule C (or Schedule C-EZ).
78. IRC Secs. 911(a), 922(b)(2)(A). See also Rev. Proc. 2013-35, IRB 167, Rev. Proc. 2015-53.
79. IRC Sec. 163(d)(1).
80. See IRS Publication 550.

81. IRC Sec. 1411.
82. IRC Sec. 1411(c)(2).
83. IRC Sec. 1(g).
84. IRC Sec. 469(c).
85. IRC Sec. 469(c)(2).
86. IRC Sec. 469(d)(1). It would also be considered "investment income" subject to the 3.8 percent net income tax. See IRC Sec. 1411(c).
87. IRC Sec. 469(h)(1).
88. IRC Sec. 1031. See Chapter 29 for a more extended discussion of like-kind exchanges.
89. IRC Sec. 1033.
90. IRC Sec. 1035.
91. For example, although a taxpayer does not have to include the gain realized from a like-kind exchange or involuntary conversion in gross income, upon the subsequent sale of the replacement property, any realized gain would be included in gross income.
92. IRC Sec. 422.
93. IRC Sec. 61(a)(1).
94. Treas. Reg. §1.451-1(a).
95. IRS Publication 538.
96. IRS Publication 538.
97. Treas. Reg. §1.451-1(a).
98. IRC Sec. 7872.
99. IRC Sec. 7872(c)(2), (c)(1)(B) and (c)(1)(C).
100. IRC Sec. 1341(a).
101. *Hamlett v. Comm'r*, T.C.M. (RIA) 2004-78 at 7 n.8.
102. IRC Sec. 453.
103. *Comm. v. Banks and Comm. v. Banaitis*, 125 S. Ct. 826, rev'g, 345 F.3d 373 (2003).
104. IRC Sec. 104(a)(2). See *Comm. v. Schleir*, 515 US 323 (1995). This exclusion from gross income is based on the theory that the injured party has already "suffered enough" without having to pay tax on the amounts intended to compensate him for his injuries.
105. IRC Sec. 67(a).
106. *Murphy v. Comm.*, 362 F.Supp.2d 206 (2005); see note 72 and note 74, below, for subsequent appellate case history.
107. *Murphy v. Comm.*, 493 F.3d 170 (D.C. Cir. 2007).
108. P.L. 115-97; IRC Sec. 1(j)(2). See also *Tax Facts* Q 738, Q 8509 and Appendices.
109. Rev. Proc. 2016-55, 2016-45 IRB 707.
110. See *Tax Facts* Q 677 and Q 8562. See also *Tax Facts* Q 738 for the current tax rates.
111. Rev. Proc. 2015-53, above.
112. IRC Sec. 1(g)(2).
113. IRC Sec. 1(g)(4); Rev. Proc. 2016-55, Rev. Proc. 2017-58.
114. IRC Sec. 1(j)(4)(B).
115. IRC Sec. 1(j)(4).
116. IRC Sec. 1221(a)(3). See also *Tax Facts* Q 8127.01.

CAPITAL GAINS AND LOSSES, RECAPTURE INCOME AND QUALIFIED DIVIDENDS

CHAPTER 4

INTRODUCTION TO CAPITAL GAINS AND LOSSES

Long term capital gain triggered by the sale or exchange of a capital asset is subject to lower maximum tax rates than ordinary income. The "gain" represents appreciation of the asset over the time in which the taxpayer held the asset. During the taxpayer's holding period, the appreciation in value of the asset is not taxed. Subsequently, in the tax year of sale, the taxpayer recognizes the taxable gain in one lump sum. Without the benefit of a lower tax rate, the inclusion of a lump sum all in one tax year might propel the taxpayer into a higher marginal tax bracket. Therefore, the tax imposed is likely to be much higher than it would have been had the gain been taxed incrementally on an annual basis. Conversely, short term capital gain is taxed at the same rates as any other type of ordinary income.

Capital losses of all kinds, long term or short term, are subject to special rules—none of which are particularly beneficial to the taxpayer. First, capital losses are only deductible to the extent of capital gains. Of small consolation is the fact that non-corporate taxpayers, i.e., individuals may use up to $3,000 of excess capital losses to offset ordinary income.[1] Capital losses in excess of $3,000 are carried forward to future tax years subject to the same limitations.

Example: This year, through various sales of capital assets, Asher realized a net capital loss of $103,000. After offsetting $3,000 of such capital loss against other ordinary income, the excess capital loss of $100,000 is carried forward to future tax years. Assuming that in those years, Asher lacks any capital gain to offset such capital loss, at the rate of $3,000 per year, it would take thirty-four years to deduct the entire capital loss against his other ordinary income.

With respect to corporate taxpayers, capital gains are taxed like any other income with no preferential tax rate. Although as is the case with non-corporate taxpayers, capital losses are deductible to the extent of capital losses, no amount of excess capital loss is deductible against ordinary income.[2] Excess capital loss may be carried back three years and forward up to five years.[3]

In determining whether income or loss is capital, long or short term, there four requirements: There must be:

1. a sale or exchange;
2. of a capital asset;
3. includible in gross income; and
4. held or owned by the taxpayer for more than one year (long term) or one year or less (short term).[4]

WHAT IS AND WHAT IS NOT A CAPITAL ASSET?

As indicated above, capital gain or loss is generated by the sale or exchange of a capital asset. IRS Section 1221 defines "capital asset" by listing types of property that are *not* capital assets. Property that is not a capital asset includes:

1. Inventory broadly defined to include property held by customers in the ordinary course of a trade or business.

2. Depreciable property or real estate used in a trade or business.

3. Copyright, a literary, musical or artistic composition, or a letter or memorandum or similar property held by the creator of such work or certain subsequent owners.[5] By election of the taxpayer, however, the sale or exchange of musical compositions or copyrights in musical works created by the taxpayer's personal efforts are treated as the sale or exchange of a capital asset.[6]

4. Accounts or notes receivable acquired in a trade or business in exchange for services provided or from the sale of inventory.

5. A publication of the U.S. Government received from the U.S. Government or its agency at a price that is less than what it is offered to the general public.

6. Any commodities derivative financial instrument held by a commodities derivative dealer.

7. Any hedging transaction which is identified as such before the close of the day on which it was acquired, originated, or entered into.

8. Supplies of the type regularly used or consumed by the taxpayer in the ordinary course of business of the taxpayer.

Although the determination of what is and what is not a capital asset might seem straightforward, it is often a contentious issue between the IRS and the taxpayer.

Example: In 2017, Asher purchased a house in a foreclosure sale. In 2019, after fixing it up, he sold the house at a profit. Additionally, in 2020, Asher purchased five additional houses that he fixed up. Subsequently, in 2020 he sold all the houses at a profit. To qualify for the preferential capital gain rate, Asher would contend that the houses were capital assets he purchased as investments. Conversely, the IRS might argue that Asher's gain should be characterized as ordinary income (subject to the highest marginal tax rates). In taking this position, the IRS would contend that the houses (similar to inventory) were sold by Asher in carrying on the trade or business of flipping then selling houses.

WHAT IS A SALE OR EXCHANGE?

A "sale" is a transfer of property for money or a promise to pay money.[7] An "exchange" is a transfer of property for other property.[8]

Example: Asher transfers stock he owns in a closely held corporation to Ashley in exchange for land. This transaction would be characterized as an exchange rather than a sale because Asher received property instead of money.

Deemed Sales or Exchanges. In addition to actual sales or exchanges, in some instances, the Code will deem a transaction to be a sale or exchange of property with capital gain or loss ramifications. In other words, even though a particular transaction did not constitute an actual sale or exchange, the Code will treat the transaction as if it did. For example:

1. A nonbusiness bad debt of a noncorporate taxpayer that becomes worthless during the taxable year is treated as a taxable loss from the sale or exchange of a capital asset held for a year or less (i.e., a short term capital loss).[9]

2. A security[10] (that is a capital asset in the hands of the taxpayer) that becomes worthless during the taxable year is treated as a sale or exchange.

3. Distributions from a corporation to a shareholder to the extent the distribution exceeds the corporation's earnings and profits and the shareholder's adjusted basis in the stock is treated as a sale or exchange of the underlying stock.[11]

Example 1: Three years ago, Bruce Rosen purchased 500 shares of Bellyup, Inc., a publicly traded corporation for $6,000. During the current year, Bellyup, Inc. ceased operations, filed for bankruptcy and was delisted from the securities and exchange markets. Because Bellyup stock became worthless, Bruce may claim a $6,000 loss from the sale or exchange of the stock deemed to have occurred on the last day of the taxable year.

Example 2: In 2020, Asher a shareholder in IT, Inc. receives a $1,000 distribution from the corporation. Asher acquired the shares for $100 in 2013. At the time of the distribution, IT, Inc. has earnings and profits of $200. In characterizing the distribution, Asher is deemed to have received a dividend of $200 (to the extent of IT's earnings and profits), a tax-free return of the basis of $100 in his stock and a capital gain of $700 from the deemed sale or exchange of Asher's underling stock.

Total distribution	$1,000
Dividend Distribution	$200
Return of basis	$100
Capital gain	$700

GAIN OR LOSS MUST BE INCLUDIBLE IN GROSS INCOME

Only gain or loss *recognized* in taxable transactions can qualify as capital gain. The amount of gain realized by the selling or exchanging taxpayer is the difference between the money and/or fair market value of the property received over the taxpayer's adjusted basis in the property sold or exchanged.[12] Conversely, the amount of loss realized by the selling or exchanging taxpayer is the difference between taxpayer's adjusted basis in the property sold or exchanged and the money and/or fair market value of the property received.

So to be characterized as capital gain or loss, the gain or loss realized must be includible in gross income (sometimes referred to as being recognized). Due to various exclusion or deferral sections not all realized gain is recognized. For example, gain or loss realized with respect to the transfer of property held for the productive use in a trade or business or for investment in exchange for like-kind property is not recognized. Often referred to as a tax-free like-kind exchange, the realized gain or loss is not realized (but deferred until it is sold or exchanged in a taxable transaction).[13] Therefore, such unrecognized gain remains dormant and is not counted as capital gain or loss.

Example: In 2013, Asher purchased land for $10,000 as an investment. In 2020, he exchanges the land for a different tract of land (also as an investment) worth $100,000. On the exchange, Asher realizes a gain of $90.000 ($100,000 minus $10,000). However, because the transaction qualifies as a like-kind exchange (see Chapter 29), Asher would not recognize the gain. Unrecognized gain is not considered capital gain.

HOLDING PERIOD

Depending on the taxpayer's holding period, the character of taxable gain or loss from a sale or exchange of a capital asset is either short term or long term. Essentially, the "holding period" is the duration of the taxpayer's ownership of the capital asset. The long term holding period is more than a year (i.e., at least a year and a day).[14] The short term holding period is a year or less.[15] Only long term capital gain is taxed at the preferential capital gain tax rates.

When a holding period begins and when it ends is not always clear. As a result, the holding periods of a number of common capital assets have been specified by the IRS (through regulation, pronouncement, etc.) and case law. For example, the holding period for stocks and bonds traded over the counter or through an exchange begins and ends on the trade date (rather than the settlement date)– i.e., the trade date is the date on which the taxpayer is contractually obligated to buy or sell the stock or bond.[16]

Example: John Hatch purchased 200 shares of Webster's, Inc. stock. Although the trade date for the transaction was July 31, 2019, the settlement date was August 3, 2019. On August 1, 2020 (the trade date for this transaction), John sold the stock for a profit. John's brokerage statement shows the transaction as If August 3, 2019 was the date used to measure the beginning of John's holding period, the recognized gain would be short term (because the end of the holding period, August 1, 2020 would be less than a year). However, since the holding period is deemed to begin on the trade date of the original purchase, July 31, 2019, the holding period is more than a year; and, thus, the gain is treated as long term capital gain.

Other Special Holding Period Rules: Under certain circumstances, property is not acquired by purchase or exchange. For that reason, there are special holding period rules that apply.

1. Section 83 Property – As a work or performance incentive, some employers will transfer company stock to an employee subject to forfeiture in the event the employee does not remain with the employer for a specified amount of time. Due to the risk of forfeiture, the taxpayer is not treated as the owner as long as the restrictions are in place. Specifically, the holding period of the taxpayer/employee begins "at the first time his rights in such property are transferable or are not subject to a substantial risk of forfeiture, whichever comes first."[17]

2. Property acquired from a decedent – Obviously, the actual ownership period of a beneficiary who acquires property from a decedent begins no earlier than the date of death. The Code, however, sets the beneficiary's holding period as more than one year (the long term period) regardless of the time the property was actually held.[18]

3. Tacked holding period – In some instances, the holding period of the transferor of an asset tacks or passes on to the transferee of the asset. This occurs when the transferee's basis in the property is the same basis in whole or in part as the transferor's basis.[19] For example, in the case of a gift of appreciated property (i.e., the date of gift fair market value is greater than the donor's basis in the gifted property), the donee's basis for determining gain or loss (should the donee sell or exchange the property) is the same as the transferor's basis in such property.[20]

Example: On January 2, Asher gave 1,000 shares of Stickershock.com, Inc. to his cousin, Ashley. Asher purchased the stock on October 31, 2017 (the trade date) for $6,000. On the date of the gift, the stock was worth $7,000. On November 7 of the same year Ashley sells the stock to a third party for $7,000. Since Ashley's basis in the stock is $6,000 (the same as Asher's basis), Asher's holding period is tacked on to her actual holding period. Therefore, she would recognize $1,000 of long term capital gain even though she did not acquire the stock more than one year after the date of the gift.

Another instance of a tacked holding period is with respect to property received in a tax-free or partially tax-free exchange. For example, in a tax-free like-kind exchange, the basis of the property received in the exchange is determined in whole or in part on the transferee's basis in the exchanged property.[21] Per IRC Section 1223(a)(1), the holding period with respect to the exchanged property tacks on to the property received in the exchange.

Example: On January 2, 2015, Asher purchased land for $10,000. On January 4, 2020, Asher exchanges the land for another track of land with a fair market value of $100,000. Because the transaction was a like-kind exchange, Asher did not recognize any of the $90,000 realized gain ($100,000 minus $10,000). On October 1, 2018, Asher sold the land he received in the exchange to a third party for $110,000. Because of the tacked holding period (beginning on January 2, 2015), Asher's recognized gain of $100,000 ($110,000 minus $10,000) is long term capital gain.

NETTING CAPITAL GAINS AND CAPITAL LOSSES AND CAPITAL GAINS TAX RATES

Determining the tax consequences of capital gain or loss begins with netting capital gains and capital losses. As explained below, there are three different maximum gain rates that are applicable to the net capital gain of different types of assets (referred to as "rate gain baskets"). Before detailing the netting process, the discussion begins with an explanation of the various maximum capital gains rates.

MAXIMUM CAPITAL GAINS RATES

The maximum capital gains rate with respect to *net capital gain* within each rate gain basket is different.[22] As discussed in more detail below, depending on the taxpayer's ordinary income tax bracket, for most capital assets (with the exception of the types of capital assets discussed below), the maximum capital gain rate is 0, 15, or 20 percent. Finally, although real property subject to depreciation is not a capital asset,[23] under certain circumstances the gain recognized with respect to the sale of such property (Section 1250 gain) is subject to a preferential capital gains rate of 25 percent. As to gain recognized with respect to collectibles and gain that is not excluded from the sale of qualified small business stock, the maximum capital gains rate is 28 percent. Finally, under certain circumstances the recognized gain from the sale of a "Section 1231 asset" may be treated as capital gain.

Maximum Capital Gains Rates with Respect to the Recognized Gain on the Sale or Exchange of Most Capital Assets

Depending on the taxpayer's ordinary income bracket, the maximum capital gains rate with respect to the gain recognized upon the sale of most capital assets is 0, 15 or 20 percent. Taxpayers in the two lowest ordinary income tax brackets (10 and 15 percent) are subject to a 0 percent maximum capital gains tax rate (meaning capital gain within this bracket is tax-free).[24] The maximum capital gains rate for all tax ordinary income brackets (other than the 10, 15 or 39.6 percent ordinary income tax rate) is 15 percent.[25] The maximum capital gains rate with respect to the 39.6 percent tax bracket is 20 percent.[26]

Example: This year, Christopher and Jennifer White have taxable income of $150,000 including $50,000 of net capital gain from the sale of stock. Because their income is less that $425,800, the tax on the net capital gain will be $7,500 (15 percent times $50,000). The tax on the ordinary income of $100,000 will be computed by applying the ordinary income rates.

Section 1250 Gains Subject to Maximum Capital Gains Rate of 25 Percent

Section 1250 property is real property (buildings and structural components) subject to depreciation.[27] Under prior tax law, the gain recognized upon the sale of Section 1250 was "recaptured" and taxed as ordinary income to the extent the depreciation claimed with respect to the property (a form of accelerated depreciation) exceeded the amount of depreciation that would have been claimed by using straight line depreciation. Since under current tax law, straight line depreciation is the only type of depreciation allowed with respect to real estate,[28] however, there is no depreciation to be recaptured.

Simply stated, under current tax law, upon the sale of Section 1250 property, the amount of recognized gain to the extent of straight line depreciation claimed (referred to as "unrecaptured 1250 gain") is taxed at a maximum capital gain rate of 25 percent.[29]

Maximum Capital Gains Rate of 28 Percent with Respect to the Recognized Gain on the Sale or Exchange of Collectibles and the Gain Not Excluded from the Sale of Qualified Small Business Stock

The maximum rate with respect to the gain recognized upon the sale of collectibles and gain that is not excluded from the sale of small business stock is 28 percent. According to the IRS, collectibles include a work of art, rug, antique, metal (such as gold, silver, and platinum bullion), gem, stamp, coin, or alcoholic beverage held more than 1 year. Additionally, collectibles gain includes gain from sale of an interest in a partnership, S corporation, or trust attributable to unrealized appreciation of collectibles.[30]

With respect to the sale of "qualified small business stock" held for more than five years, some or all of the recognized gain may be excluded from gross income under IRC Section 1202. To the extent that some of the gain is not excluded, the maximum capital gains rate is 28 percent.[31]

Potential Capital Gain Treatment from the Sale or Exchange of Section 1231 Property

Although as mentioned earlier in this chapter, depreciable or real property used in a trade or business are not capital assets, IRC Section 1231 may characterize the recognized gain on the sale or exchange of such assets as capital gain. In fact, Section 1231 property is defined as depreciable property or real property used in a trade or business held for more than one year (i.e., the same duration as the long term capital gain or loss holding period).[32]

Simply stated, Section 1231 gain is any recognized gain with respect to Section 1231 property that is not attributable to IRC Section 1245 recapture (discussed below).[33]

Example: In 2013, Asher purchased a machine for $100,000 to be used in his construction business. In 2020, after taking depreciation deductions during the intervening tax years, Asher sold the machine (with an adjusted basis of $60,000) for $110,000. Thus, Asher would recognize a total gain of $50,000 ($110,000 minus $60,000). Of that gain, $40,000 is attributable to depreciation recapture (the difference between Asher's original basis of $100,000 as reduced by the aggregate amount of depreciation deductions). The balance of the gain, $10,000, is treated as Section 1231 gain.

Conversely, Section 1231 loss is any recognized loss with respect to Section 1231 property.[34]

Example: In 2016, Asher purchased a computer for $10,000 to be used in his business. In 2020, after taking $4,500 of depreciation deductions during the intervening tax years, the adjusted basis in the computer was $5,500. At that time, Asher sold the computer for $5,000 and recognize a loss of $500 ($5,500 adjusted basis minus $5,000). The entire loss is treated as a Section 1231 loss.

Operationally, IRC Section 1231 always favors the taxpayer. If in the taxable year, Section 1231 gains exceed Section 1231 losses, the gains and losses are treated as capital. Therefore, the *net* gain would be taxed at the preferential capital gains tax rate.[35] Conversely, if in the taxable year, Section 1231 losses exceed Section 1231 gains, the gains and losses are treated as ordinary. Thus, the *net* loss would be treated as ordinary loss meaning unlike capital loss, it would be deductible from any type of income.[36]

Example: In 2018, Asher recognized a Section 1231 gain of $10,000 and a Section 1231 loss of $5,000. Because Section 1231 gains exceed Section 1231 losses by $5,000, Asher's net gain of $5,000 would be taxable at the applicable capital gains rate.

Section 1245 Recapture Always Treated as Ordinary Income

Property used by a taxpayer in a trade or business that is subject to wear and tear over its useful life is depreciable. In each tax year of use, the taxpayer deducts a portion of the original cost or basis as an ordinary deduction (meaning it offsets income of any kind). Essentially, the depreciation deduction presumes that the underlying asset will be "used up" to the extent of the depreciation deduction. As depreciation is claimed, the taxpayer's basis is reduced by the amount of the deduction. So, it is presumed that a depreciable asset with an original basis of $10,000 that was reduced by $4,000 of depreciation deductions would then be worth $6,000 the same amount as the taxpayer's adjusted basis in the asset. If, however, the taxpayer were to sell that depreciable asset for $7,000, the aggregate amount of depreciation deductions overstated the actual decline in value by $1,000. Therefore, pursuant to IRC Section 1245, that amount of "over claimed" depreciation must be recaptured as ordinary income.

In summary, pursuant to IRC Section 1245, recognized gain attributable to depreciation claimed with respect to Section 1245 property must be recaptured as ordinary income. Section 1245 property includes tangible and intangible property (with the exclusion with some exceptions of buildings and their structural components).[37] As discussed earlier in this chapter, recognized gain in excess of the aggregate amount of depreciation is treated as Section 1231 gain potentially subject to capital gains tax rates.

Example: Multimedia, Inc. purchased a conference table for $2,000. Over the next two tax years, the company claimed $1,000 of depreciation reducing the basis in the table to $1,000. At that time, the company sells the table for $3,500 resulting in a total gain of $2,500 ($3,500 minus $1,000). Of the $2,500 gain, $1,000 reflects the depreciation deductions claimed with respect to the table. Pursuant to IRC Section 1245, that amount is recaptured and taxed as ordinary income. The balance of the gain, $1,500 is treated as Section 1231 gain. Depending on whether the company has other Section 1231 gains and losses, the character of that gain could be long term capital gain.

NETTING CAPITAL GAIN AND LOSSES BY RATE GAIN BASKETS

As mentioned above, the tax consequences of capital gain and losses begins with netting. Because there are three "rate gain baskets", netting of gains and losses first occurs within in each basket. Then, once each rate gain basket has been netted, the gains and losses of the rate gain baskets are re-netted.

First Netting

In each rate gain basket, there are four types of capital gain or loss:

1. Short term capital gain – gain from the sale or exchange of property held for one year or less[38]
2. Short term capital loss – loss from the sale or exchange of property held for more than one year[39]
3. Long term capital gain – gain from a sale or exchange of property held for more than one year[40]
4. Long term capital loss – loss from a sale or exchange of property held for more than one year[41]

In this netting, short term capital gain and short term capital loss are netted. The result is either net short term capital gain or net short term capital loss.[42] Similarly, long term capital gain and long term capital loss are netted. The result is either net long term capital gain or net long term capital loss.[43] If the result of one netting is a net gain and the other is a net loss, the net gain and net loss are then netted. If the net loss exceeds the net gain, the result would be a net capital loss.[44] If the net gain exceeds the net loss, the result would be capital gain net income.[45] If the net long term capital gains exceed net short term capital losses, the result would be net capital gain.[46] This is significant because only net capital gain is taxed at the preferential capital gains tax rates.

Netting capital losses against capital gains serves the useful purpose of deducting capital losses by offsetting otherwise taxable capital gain. As mentioned earlier in the chapter, excess capital losses are only deductible to the extent of $3,000 (against ordinary income). The balance must be carried forward to future tax years subject to the same limitations.

Second Netting

After capital gains and losses have been netted in each of the rate gain baskets, the net gains and losses are netted against gains and losses in the other rate gain baskets. If one rate gain basket has a net loss, that loss is netted against the net gain in the rate gain basket with the highest rate, then the next highest rate gain basket, etc. Short term capital losses (including short term loss carryovers from other tax years) are first applied to reduce short term capital gains.

Example: In a single tax year, Ryan Alcott has the following capital gains and losses:

- $5,000 short term capital loss from the sale of stock;
- $6,000 long term capital loss from the sale of stock;
- $10,000 unrecaptured Section 1250 gain from the sale of real property; and
- $4,000 long term capital gain from the sale of collectibles.

Since Ryan has one amount from each rate gain basket, the netting process is as follows:

- The $6,000 of long term capital loss from the sale of stock offsets the $4,000 of long term capital gain from the sale of collectibles (28 percent the highest capital gain rate). After offsetting the collectible gain in full, the balance of the long term capital loss, $2,000 offsets a like amount of the $10,000 of unrecaptured 1250 gain (25 percent the next highest capital gain rate).
- The $5,000 of short term capital loss from the sale of stock offsets a like amount of the remaining $8,000 of unrecaptured 1250 gain.
- The result of the second netting is $3,000 of unrecaptured 1250 gain taxed at the maximum capital gains rate of 25 percent.

In the end, the netting process is favorable to the taxpayer because capital losses first offset the capital gains taxed at the highest capital gains rate. Therefore, the remaining taxable capital gain would be subject to the lowest possible capital gains rate.

QUALIFIED DIVIDENDS

Until recently, the taxation of dividends has not been favorable to the distributing corporation or the recipient shareholder. This is because dividend distributions are non-deductible to the distributing corporation. So, without a preferential divided tax rate, it was possible for a dividend distribution to be taxed at the highest corporate income tax rate as well as the shareholder's highest individual income tax rate.

Since 2003, however, dividends meeting the following three requirements are treated as "qualified dividends" taxable at the more favorable capital gains rate.[47]

The three requirements are:

1. The dividends are distributed by a domestic corporation or a qualified foreign corporation.

2. The taxpayer held the stock on which the dividend was paid for more than sixty days during the 121-day period beginning sixty days before the ex-dividend date.[48] The ex-dividend date is generally the first day following the declaration of a dividend that a buyer of the stock is not entitled to a dividend payment. Note that the rules are different for preferred stock, which requires a taxpayer hold the stock for ninety days during the 181-day period that begins ninety days before the ex-dividend date.[49]

3. The dividends are not one of the several "special" types of dividends as stated under IRC Section 1(h)(11), including, but not limited to, amounts:

   a. paid on deposits with mutual savings banks, cooperative banks, credit unions, savings and loan associations, building and loan associations and similar financial institutions;

   b. paid by a corporation on employer securities that are held on the date of record by an employee stock ownership plan (ESOP) maintained by that corporation;

   c. to the extent the taxpayer is obligated (under a short sale or otherwise) to make related payments for positions in substantially similar property; or

   d. paid on restricted stock, which should be treated as wage income unless the individual made an election IRC Section 83(b).

CAPITAL GAINS AND QUALIFIED DIVIDEND TAX RATES UNDER THE 2017 TAX REFORM ACT

Generally, the 2017 tax reform legislation retained the current tax rates that apply to long-term capital gains and qualified dividend income. However, the income thresholds that determine to whom those rates will apply have changed along with the changes to the individual income tax rates, as outlined below.[50]

2020 Capital Gains Tax Rates

	Single Filers	*Joint Filers*	*Heads of Household*	*Trusts and Estates*
0%	Less than $40,000	Less than $80,000	Less than $5316,700	Less than $2,650
15%	$40,600-$441,450	$80,200-$496,600	$53,600-$469,450	$2,650-$13,150
20%	More than $441,450	More than $496,000	More than $469,050	More than $13,150

As is the case under previously existing law, unrecaptured section 1250 gain will continue to be taxed at a maximum rate of 25 percent, and 28 percent rate gain will continue to be taxed at a maximum rate of 28 percent.[51] Short-term capital gains continue to be taxed according to the taxpayer's ordinary income tax rate, as under prior law.

The 3.8 percent tax on net investment income tax that applies in addition to the capital gains tax rates for certain high income taxpayers was also maintained under the new tax law.

OPPORTUNITY ZONES

The 2017 Tax Act created new rules governing the taxation of capital gains stemming from investments in qualified opportunity zones. Qualified opportunity zones are essentially low-income communities that are designated as opportunity zones for investment.

The 2017 Tax Act created new rules governing the taxation of capital gains stemming from investments in opportunity zones. Generally, the new rules allow a taxpayer to elect to defer recognizing any gains from a sale or exchange of any property held by the taxpayer to the extent that the gains do not exceed the aggregate amount that the taxpayer has invested in a qualified opportunity fund during the 180-day period beginning on the date of the sale or exchange.[52] The sale must not be to a related party.

Instead, the gain will be included in income in the year that includes the earlier of the date the investment is sold or exchanged or December 31, 2026.[53] The amount included is the excess of (1) the lesser of the amount excluded or the fair market value of the investment as of the date of the sale or exchange or December 31, 2026 over (2) the taxpayer's basis in the investment.[54]

The basis in the investment begins at zero and is increased as gain is recognized. If the investment is held for at least five years, the basis is increased by 10 percent of the gain deferred. If the investment is held for at least seven years, the basis is increased by an additional 5 percent of the gain deferred. If the taxpayer so elects and the investment is held for at least ten years, the basis is equal to the fair market value of the investment on the date the investment is sold or exchanged.[55]

A "qualified opportunity fund" means an investment vehicle organized as a corporation or partnership for the purpose of investing in qualified opportunity zone property where at least 90 percent of its assets are qualified opportunity zone property.[56]

Qualified opportunity zone property means property that is:

- qualified opportunity zone stock (generally, stock in a qualified opportunity zone acquired for cash after December 31, 2017);
- qualified opportunity zone partnership interests (generally, interests in a qualified opportunity zone partnership acquired for cash after December 31, 2017); and
- qualified opportunity zone business property

"Qualified opportunity business zone property" is defined as tangible property used in a trade or business of the qualified opportunity fund where substantially all of the property's use is in a qualified opportunity zone. The property must be acquired by purchase after December 31, 2017 and the original use begins with the qualified opportunity fund or the fund substantially improves the property.

"Qualified opportunity zone business" means a trade or business that meets the following requirements:

- substantially all of the property owned by the business is qualified opportunity zone business property
- at least 50 percent of the gross income of the entity is derived from the active conduct of business
- a substantial portion of the intangible property of the entity is used in the active conduct of any such business
- less than 5 percent of the average of the aggregate unadjusted bases of the property of the entity is attributable to nonqualified financial property
- the business is not used to provide facilities such as a golf course, country club, massage parlor, sun tanning salon, racetrack or other gambling facility, or store that primarily sells alcohol.[57]

If tangible property ceases to be qualified opportunity zone business property, it will continue to be treated as such for the lesser of (1) five years after the date it ceases to be qualified or (2) the date when the property is no longer held by a qualified opportunity zone business.[58]

Designation of Opportunity Zones

Opportunity zones are to be designated by the states during a "determination period," which is the ninety-day period beginning on the date of enactment of the 2017 Tax Act (a thirty-day extension period is specifically permitted).[59]

The number of opportunity zones may not exceed 25 percent of the number of low-income communities in the state (although if the number of low income communities in the state is less than one hundred, a total of twenty-five may be designated as opportunity zones).[60] "Low income community" has the same definition as under the rules governing the new markets tax credit (Code section 45D), meaning:

1. for communities located within a metropolitan area the poverty rate for the community is at least 20 percent;

2. if the community is not located within a metropolitan area, the median family income for the community does not exceed 80 percent of statewide median family income; or

3. if the community is located within a metropolitan area, the median family income for the community does not exceed 80 percent of the greater of:

    a. statewide median family income; or

    b. the metropolitan area median family income.

Communities are determined based upon census tracts,[61] and the designation as a qualified opportunity zone remains in effect for a ten-year period.[62]

MISCELLANEOUS ISSUES

Election to Treat Net Capital Gain and Qualified Dividends as Investment Income. Investment interest (i.e., interest on borrowing to fund investments) is deductible only to the extent of investment income.[63] The excess of investment interest over investment income must be carried over to future tax years subject to the same limitation. In order to increase the amount of investment income (so as to be able to deduct a greater amount of investment interest), the taxpayer may elect to treat net capital gain and qualified dividends as investment income.[64] However, if the taxpayer elects to do so, the capital gain and/or dividend income would be taxed in the same way as ordinary income.[65]

Alternative Minimum Tax. The capital gains tax rates apply to both regular income tax and the alternative minimum tax.[66] However, the net capital gain for alternative minimum tax purposes must be recomputed using any adjustments or preferences attributable to the gain.

Net Investment Income Tax. Assuming the taxpayer's adjusted gross income is above the applicable thresholds, certain capital gains may be included as net investment income subject to the 3.8 percent net investment income tax.[67]

FREQUENTLY ASKED QUESTIONS

Question – Can capital losses offset Section 1231 gains?

Answer – Yes. If Section 1231 gains exceed Section 1231 losses, all gains and losses are treated as long term capital gain and loss. Moreover, to the extent not totally offset by the Section 1231 losses, there would be excess Section 1231 gain. As a result, if the taxpayer has other capital losses, those losses can be used to offset the net Section 1231 gain.

Question – During the tax year, Buckshot, Inc. sold a truck used in business (Section 1245 property) it had purchased and fully depreciated for $10,000. In an attempt to offset the $10,000 gain, Buckshot sold investments at a loss of $10,000. Can the $10,000 loss offset the $10,000 gain?

Answer – No. The $10,000 gain on the sale of the truck is ordinary income recaptured pursuant to IRC Section 1245. Conversely, the $10,000 capital loss on the sale of the investments is deductible only to the extent of capital gain. Moreover, a corporation, unlike an individual may, not deduct $3,000 of excess capital loss against ordinary income. Therefore, Buckshot would have to carry back the capital loss three years and forward up to five years to be deducted only against capital gains recognized in those tax years.

Question – Where on Form 1040 are capital gains and losses reported?

Answer – Capital gains and losses from the sale or exchange of capital assets are reported on Schedule D. Gains or losses on the sale of Section 1231 property and properties subject to potential Section 1245 recapture are reported on Form 4797.

Question – Can a partnership carry forward disallowed business interest?

Answer – The 2017 Tax Act created a special rule to allow partnerships to carry forward certain disallowed business interest (the rule does not apply to S corporations or other pass-through entities, although the new law specifies that similar rules will apply). The general rules governing carrying forward disallowed business interest do not apply to partnerships.

Instead, disallowed business interest is allocated to each partner in the same manner as non-separately stated taxable income or loss of the partnership.[68] The partner is entitled to deduct his or her share of excess business interest in any future year, but only against excess taxable income attributed to the partner by the partnership, and when the excess taxable income is related to the activities that created the excess business interest carryforward.[69]

Such a deduction also requires a corresponding reduction in excess taxable income. Further, if excess business interest is attributed to a partner, his or her basis in the partnership interest is reduced (not below zero) by the amount of the allocation even though the carryforward does not permit a partner's deduction in the year of the basis reduction. The partner's deduction in a future year for the carried forward interest will not require another basis adjustment.

If the partner disposes of the partnership interest after a basis adjustment occurred, immediately before the disposition the partner's basis will be increased by the amount that any basis reduction exceeds the amount of excess interest expense that has been deducted by the partner.[70]

CHAPTER ENDNOTES

1. IRC Sec. 1211(b).
2. IRC Sec. 1211(a).
3. IRC Sec. 1212(a)(1).
4. IRC Sec. 1222.
5. IRC Sec. 1221(a)(3)
6. IRC Sec. 1221(b)(3).
7. *Rogers v Comm'r*, 103 F.2d 790 (9th Cir. 1939).
8. *Helvering v. William Flaccus Oak Leather Co.*, 313 U.S. 247 (1941).
9. IRC 166(d).
10. A "security" includes a share of stock in a corporation, a right to subscribe for or to receive a share of stock in a corporation or a bond, debenture, note or certificate, or other evidence of indebtedness issued by a corporation or government, with interest coupons or in registered form. IRC Sec. 165(g).
11. IRC Sec. 301(c).
12. IRC Sec. 1001(a).
13. IRC Sec. 1031(a).
14. IRC Secs. 1222(3)-(4).
15. IRC Secs. 1222(1)-(2).
16. Rev. Rul. 66-97, 1966-1 C.B. 190.
17. IRC Sec. 83(f).
18. IRC Sec. 1223(11). For the rule to apply, the beneficiary's basis of the property acquired from the decedent must have been stepped up or down to date of death fair market value per IRC Sec. 1014.
19. IRC Sec. 1223(a)(2).
20. IRC Sec. 1015(a). However, if at the time of the gift, the donor's basis in the property is less than the date of gift fair market value, the donee's basis for computing loss, is the lesser fair market value of the property. Since in that instance, the donee's basis is not the donor's basis, the holding period for purposes of computing loss begins on the date of the gift.
21. IRC Sec. 1031(b).
22. IRC Sec. 1(h).
23. IRC Sec. 1221(2).
24. IRC Sec. 1(h)(B).
25. IRC Sec. 1(h)(1)(C).
26. IRC Sec. 1(h)(1)(D).
27. IRC Sec. 1250(c).
28. IRC Sec. 168(b)(3).
29. IRC Sec. 1(h)(1)(D).
30. IRS Publication 17, page 118.
31. IRC Sec. 1(h)(4).
32. IRC Sec. 1231(a)(3)(A)(i).
33. IRC Sec. 1231(a)(3)(A).
34. IRC Sec. 1231(a)(3)(B).
35. IRC Sec. 1231(a)(1).
36. IRC Sec. 1231(a)(2).
37. IRC Sec. 1245(a)(3).
38. IRC Sec. 1221(1).
39. IRC Sec. 1221(2).
40. IRC Sec. 1221(3).
41. IRC Sec. 1221(4)
42. IRC Secs. 1221(5) and (6).
43. IRC Secs. 1221(7) and (8).
44. IRC Sec. 1221(10).
45. IRC Sec. 1221(9).
46. IRC Sec. 1221(11),
47. IRC Sec. 1(h)(11).
48. IRC Sec. 1(h)(11)(B)(iii)(I).
49. IRC Sec. 1(h)(11)(B)(iii)(I).
50. IRC Sec. 1(h)-(j).
51. IRC Secs. 1(h)(4), 1(h)(6).
52. IRC Sec. 1400Z-2(a).
53. IRC Sec. 1400Z-2(b)(1).
54. IRC Sec. 1400Z-2(b)(2).

55. IRC Sec. 1400Z-2(c).
56. IRC Sec. 1400Z-2(d)(1).
57. IRC Sec. 1400Z-2(d)(3).
58. IRC Sec. 1400Z-2(d)(3)(B).
59. IRC Sec. 1400Z-1.
60. IRC Sec. 1400Z-1 (d).
61. IRC Secs. 45D(e), 1400Z-1(c)(1).
62. IRC Sec. 1400Z-1(f).
63. IRC Sec. 163(d).
64. IRC Sec. 163(d)(4)(B).
65. IRC Sec. 1(h)(2).
66. IRC Sec. 55(b)(3).
67. IRC Sec. 1411(c)(1)(A)(iii).
68. IRC Sec. 163(j)(4).
69. IRC Sec. 163(j)(4)(B).
70. IRC Sec. 163(j)(4)(B)(iii).

QUALIFIED BUSINESS INCOME DEDUCTION[1]

CHAPTER 5

INTRODUCTION

On December 22, 2017, President Trump signed into law the Tax Cuts and Jobs Act (TCJA). One of the key provisions in the Act is a 20 percent deduction for the qualified business income (QBI) of non-corporate taxpayers under new code section 199A. This section is effective for tax years after 2017 and, unless lawmakers act, it sunsets on December 31, 2025.

Rationale

The most important goal of the TCJA was to reduce the tax rates on C corporations to make them more competitive in world markets. Reducing the top C corporation rate from 35 percent to 21 percent, however, put pass-through businesses at a disadvantage relative to C corporations. Thus, the 20 percent deduction was added to the Act to give pass-through entities a comparable tax break. The 20 percent deduction, in theory, reduces the tax rate from a maximum of 37 percent to a maximum of 29.6 percent.

Eligible Taxpayers

The deduction applies to non-corporate taxpayers, including sole proprietorships, partnerships, LLCs,[2] S corporations, trusts, estates, qualified cooperatives and real estate investment trusts (REITs).[3] It is calculated on an annual basis and will be reported as a line item on Form 1040. For partnerships or S corporations, the deduction applies at the partner or shareholder level, and each partner or shareholder takes into account his or her allocable share of the deduction.[4] The section 199A deduction is not available to C corporations that own pass-through businesses.[5]

Application of the Deduction

The 20 percent deduction applies only for income tax purposes and does not reduce the net investment income tax, Medicare tax or the self-employment tax.[6] The deduction is not allowed in computing adjusted gross income (AGI), but rather is applied against **taxable** income.[7] Although it is an itemized deduction, it is not subject to any of the limitations on such deductions.[8]

MECHANICS OF THE DEDUCTION

The statute begins with a basic, relatively straightforward computation of the deduction. It is complicated, however by two important limitations, a W-2 wage/unadjusted basis limitation and a specified service trade or business (SSTB) limitation.

Basic Calculation

The statute gives eligible taxpayers a deduction equal to the lesser of:

- 20 percent of the combined qualified business income (QBI) of the taxpayer; or
- 20 percent of taxable ordinary income[9]

For purposes of this calculation, combined qualified business income is (1) the ordinary income from each qualified trade or business[10] plus (2) 20 percent of the qualified real estate investment trust (REIT) dividends and qualified publicly traded partnership (QPTP) income.[11]

Example 1. Larry, a single taxpayer, is the sole proprietor of an ice cream parlor. The store building is leased. Larry's profit from the store is $90,000 and he has no capital gains, REIT, QPTP or other income. Larry claims the new $12,000 standard deduction,[12] making his taxable income $78,000. Larry's section 199A deduction is the lesser of:

(1) 20 percent of his business income from the store (.2 × $90,000 = $18,000); or

(2) 20 percent of his taxable ordinary income (.2 × $78,000 = $15,600).

Because Larry's tentative deduction ($18,000) exceeds 20 percent of his taxable income ($15,600), his deduction is limited to $15,600, reducing his taxable income from $78,000 to $62,400. Because Larry is in the 22 percent marginal income tax bracket, he saves $3,432 in taxes (.22 × $15,600).

Example 2. Cindy is an architect with income of $280,000 from the business. She has no other income. Cindy's husband, Ned, is a student with no income. Cindy and Ned claim the $24,000 standard deduction for married taxpayers filing jointly, giving them $256,000 of taxable income. Cindy's tentative section 199A deduction is $56,000 (.2 × $280,000). However, her deduction cannot exceed 20 percent of taxable income over net capital gains. 20 percent of Cindy's taxable income is $51,200 (.2 × $256,000), so her section 199A deduction is reduced from $56,000 to $51,200.

W-2/UNADJUSTED BASIS LIMITATION

Under this limitation, the portion of the deduction attributable to the taxpayer's QBI from the trade or business[13] cannot exceed the greater of

- 50 percent of the taxpayer's allocable share of the wages paid by the business with respect to QBI; or
- 25 percent of the taxpayer's allocable share of wages plus 2.5 percent of the unadjusted basis of qualified property owned by the business.[14]

The W-2 wage/unadjusted basis limitation does not begin to apply until taxable income reaches $326,600 for married taxpayers filing jointly and $163,300 (in 2020) for all other eligible taxpayers. In 2020, the phase-in is complete for married taxpayers filing jointly (MFJ) at $426,600 and for all other taxpayers at $213,300.[15] The following chart shows how the limitation applies to taxpayers based on filing status and level of taxable income.

	MFJ	ALL OTHERS
No limitation	$0 - $326,600	$0 - $163,300
Phase-In	$326,600 - $426,600	$163,300 - $213,300
Full Limitation	$426,600+	$213,300+

The examples below illustrate how the Code section 199A deduction is calculated for taxpayers subject to the full limitation.

Example 3. Jake, a married taxpayer filing jointly with his wife, Julie, runs a restaurant that produces $110,000 of pass-through income. Julie is a teacher who earns $64,000. The couple claims the standard deduction of $24,000, making their taxable income $150,000 ($174,000 – $24,000). Because Jake and Julie have taxable income of less than $326,600, the W-2 wage/unadjusted basis limitation does not apply. The 20 percent of taxable income over capital gains limitation does not apply either because the tentative QBI deduction (.2 × $110,000 = $22,000) is less than 20 percent of taxable income (.2 × $150,000 = $30,000). Thus, they receive the full 20 percent section 199A deduction (.2 × $110,000 = $22,000).

Example 4. Curtis and Shannon own a restaurant that produces $500,000 of taxable income. The restaurant building is leased. The couple has another $100,000 of taxable income from investments and claims the standard deduction of $24,000. Curtis and Shannon perform most of the work at the restaurant and pay $80,000 of W-2 wages to part-time help. Because their taxable income exceeds $426,600, the W-2/

unadjusted basis limitation applies in full. The QBI deduction for Curtis and Shannon is:

(1) the lesser of 20 percent of pass-through income (.2 × $500,000 = $100,000);

OR

(2) the greater of 50 percent of W-2 wages (.5 × $80,000 = $40,000) or 25 percent of Curtis and Shannon's allocable share of W-2 wages ($20,000) + 2.5 percent of the unadjusted basis in the restaurant building ($0) = $20,000.

Thus, the deduction is the lesser of $100,000 or $40,000 = $40,000.

This $40,000 deduction is substantially less than 20 percent of the couple's taxable income (.2 × $576,000 = $115,200) so the taxable income limitation does not apply.

Example 5. Assume the same facts as in Example 4, except that Curtis and Shannon buy the restaurant building for $1,000,000. Their deduction is now:

(1) the lesser of 20 percent of QBI (.2 × $500,000 = $100,000);

OR

(2) the greater of 50 percent of wages (.5 × $80,000 = $40,000), or 25 percent of wages ($20,000) + 2.5 percent of unadjusted basis ($25,000) = $45,000.

The taxable income limitation does not apply because 20 percent of their taxable income ($115,200) exceeds 20 percent of QBI ($100,000) so their deduction is increased from $40,000 to $45,000.[16]

Example 6. Grandpa Mark and Grandma Linda own an apartment building that was purchased for $500,000 and hasn't been fully depreciated. The building generates $100,000 of pass-through income, producing a tentative section 199A deduction of $20,000 (.2 × $100,000). They pay a company to manage and maintain the building. Their section 199A deduction is:

(1) the lesser of 20 percent of pass-through income (.2 × $100,000 = $20,000);

OR

(2) the greater of 50 percent of W-2 wages (.5 × $0 = $0), or 25 percent of Grandpa Mark and Grandma Linda's allocable share of W-2 wages ($0) + 2.5 percent of unadjusted basis (.025 × $500,000) = $12,500.

Thus, Grandpa Mark and Grandma Linda get a deduction of $12,500.

Example 7. Assume the same facts as in Example 6 except that Grandpa Mark and Grandma Linda hire Charles to manage the building and pay him a salary of $45,000 a year. Their section 199A deduction is now:

(1) the lesser of 20 percent of pass-through income (.2 × $100,000 = $20,000);

OR

(2) the greater of 50 percent of W-2 wages (.5 × $45,000 = $22,500), or 25 percent of Grandpa Mark and Grandma Linda's allocable share of W-2 wages ($11,250) + 2.5 percent of unadjusted basis ($12,500) = $23,750

Grandpa Mark and Grandma Linda can now claim the full $20,000 section 199A deduction each year.

Phase-in of the W-2 Wage/ Unadjusted Basis Limitation

As taxable income rises from $326,600 to $426,600 for married taxpayers filing jointly and from $163,300 to $213,300 (in 2020) for all other taxpayers, the W-2 wages/unadjusted basis limitation is gradually phased in as illustrated in the following examples.

Example 8. Lisa is the sole proprietor of a profitable candy store who files a joint return with her husband, Chuck. The store produces $375,000 of business income. It paid wages of $120,000 and has no depreciable property.

Lisa and Chuck's taxable income is $395,000. The QBI deduction is calculated as follows.

Tentative QBI (.2 × $375,000)	$75,000
W-2/unadjusted basis limitation (.5 × $120,000)	$60,000
Tentative deduction minus full W-2 limitation amount ($75,000 - $60,000)	$15,000
Phase-in % [($395,000 -$326,600)/$100,000]	= 68.4%
Phase-in amount (.684 × $15,000)	$10,260
Tentative deduction minus phase-in amount ($75,000 - $10,260)	$64,740
20% of taxable income (.2 × $395,000)	$79,000
Section 199A deduction	$64,740

Example 9. Herb, a single taxpayer, is the sole proprietor of a profitable flower store. The store produces $160,000 of business income. It paid wages of $40,000 and had no depreciable property. Herb's taxable income is $177,500. His QBI deduction is calculated as follows.

Tentative QBI (.2 × $160,000)	$32,000
W-2/unadjusted basis limitation (.5 × $40,000)	$20,000
Tentative deduction minus W-2 limitation amount ($32,000 - $20,000)	$12,000
Phase-out % [($177,500 -$163,300)/$50,000]	= 28.4%
Phase-out amount (.4 × $12,000)	$3,408
Tentative deduction minus phase-out amount ($32,000 - $4,800)	$28,592
20% of taxable income (.2 × $177,500)	$35,500
Section 199A deduction	$28,592

Specified Service Trade or Business (SSTB) Limitation

Under the general rule, the section 199A deduction does not apply to specified service businesses.[17] These businesses include any business involving the performance of services in the fields of health, law, accounting, actuarial science, performing arts, consulting, athletics, financial services, brokerage services, or any trade or business where the principal asset of the trade or business is the reputation or skill of one or more owners or employees.[18]

Also included are businesses that involve the performance of services that consist of investing and investment management, trading, or dealing in securities.[19]

Phase-out of the Deduction

However, taxpayers in these businesses can still claim a 20 percent deduction if their income is below certain threshold levels. For married taxpayers filing jointly, the threshold level is $326,600 and for all other taxpayers, $163,300.[20] As income rises above these levels, the deduction is gradually phased out. For married taxpayers filing jointly, the phase-out is complete at income of $426,600 and for all other taxpayers at income of $213,300.

Example 10. Brad is a married lawyer with a solo practice that generates $450,000 of pass-through income. Because taxable income exceeds $426,600, the section 199A deduction is completely phased out and Brad gets no 20 percent deduction.

Example 11. Jim is a single taxpayer and the sole owner of an accounting business. His income from the business is $189,500 and he has no other income. Jim claims a $12,000 standard deduction, making his taxable income $177,500. Jim's tentative Code section 199A deduction is $37,900 (.2 × $189,500). Because his taxable income exceeds $163,300, this deduction is phased out.

Jim's $177,500 of taxable income is 40 percent of the way through the phase-out range ($20,000/$50,000) so he loses 40 percent of the QBI deduction. Thus, Jim's deduction is reduced by $15,160 (.4 × $37,900). This leaves him with a $22,740 QBI deduction ($37,900 tentative deduction - $15,160 phase-out amount). The taxable income limitation does not apply because 20 percent of taxable income (.2×177,500= $35,500) exceeds $22,740.

Note that for every increase of $5,000 in taxable income for specified service businesses above $163,300 for single taxpayers and every increase of $10,000 in taxable income above $326,600 for married taxpayers, the QBI deduction is reduced by 10 percent. In other words, each 10 percent increase in income above the threshold amount produces a 10 percent reduction in the QBI deduction. Thus, for example, for married taxpayers filing jointly the taxpayers keep 90 percent of the deduction at $325,000 of taxable income, 80 percent of the deduction at $335,000 of taxable income and so on.

DEFINITIONS

To perform the calculations shown above, it is necessary to understand the terms in the calculation formula. These terms include:

- Qualified business income (QBI)
- Qualified trade or business
- Specified service trade or business (SSTB)
- W-2 wages
- Qualified property
- Unadjusted tax basis
- Taxable income
- REIT dividends
- Qualified publicly traded partnership (QPTP) income

Most of the terms are adequately defined in the statute, but the scope of others is uncertain and further guidance will be required.

Qualified Business Income (QBI)

The term "qualified business income" means, for any taxable year, the net amount of qualified items of income, gain, deduction, and loss with respect to any qualified trade or business of the taxpayer.[21] It refers to the taxpayer's net income after payment of wages, business expenses and other deductions for the business and includes rental income.

Example 12. A qualified business has $100 of ordinary income from inventory sales, and makes a $25 expenditure that must be capitalized and amortized over five years. The business income is $95 ($100 minus $5 current-year ordinary amortization deduction).[22]

The income must be effectively connected with the conduct of a U.S. trade or business within the meaning of Code section 864(c) and must be included or allowed in determining taxable income for the tax year.[23] The term "trade or business" is discussed in the next section.

QBI does *not* include:

- Any qualified REIT dividends, qualified cooperative dividends, or qualified publicly traded partnership income[24]
- Reasonable compensation paid to the taxpayer by any qualified trade or business for services rendered with respect to the trade or business[25]
- Any guaranteed payment to a partner for services to the business under Code section 707(c)[26]
- Any payment to a partner for services rendered with respect to the trade or business[27]
- Capital gains and losses[28]
- Dividends or dividend equivalents[29]
- Any interest income other than interest income properly allocable to a trade or business[30]
- Certain foreign personal holding company income[31]
- Any amount received from an annuity which is not received in connection with the trade or business[32]
- Any item of deduction or loss properly allocable to an amount described in any of the preceding clauses[33]

Note that the statute favors business owners and self-employed individuals over wage earners. To obtain a deduction, employees must either become independent contractors or own or invest in a business.

Example 13. Mabel has $90,000 of wages, $25,000 of capital gains and $20,000 of interest income. None of the income is QBI, so Mabel gets no deduction.

Example 14. Assume the same facts as in the previous example except that Mabel also tutors high school students in mathematics, earning an additional $10,000/year. Mabel can now claim a Code section 199A deduction of $2,000 (.2 × $10,000).

Income from sources within Puerto Rico is included in the calculation of QBI if all such income is taxable under Code section 1.[34] It is not clear whether amounts treated as ordinary income under Code section 751 (unrealized receivables and inventory items are included in QBI). Finally, there is no requirement that qualified business income must be "active" income.

Section 1231 Gain

It is not clear whether Code section 1231 gain is qualified business income. Code section 1231 gain is generally gain on real property used in the trade or business or depreciable personal property used in the trade or business.[35] Certain property is excluded from the definition, however. Excluded items include:

1. inventory;[36]
2. property primarily held for sale to customers in the ordinary course of business;[37]
3. copyrights, literary works, musical or artistic compositions, letter memorandums or similar property;[38]
4. timber, coal, or domestic iron ore with respect to which Code section 631 applies;
5. certain livestock;[39] and
6. unharvested crops sold in conjunction with a sale of land that qualifies as Code section 1231 property.[40]

Code section 199A(c)(3)(B) provides that no deduction is allowed for short-term capital gains, long-term capital gains, short-term capital losses or long-term capital losses. Code section 1221 provides that depreciable property or real property used in the trade or business (i.e., Code section 1231 property) is excluded from the definition of a capital asset.[41] Thus, it would appear to follow, that gain on the sale of section 1231 assets should qualify as QBI. On the other hand, Code section 1231(a)(1) states that if the section 1231 gains for any taxable year exceed the section 1231 losses for the year, such gains and losses shall be treated as long-term capital gains or long-term capital losses, as the case may be.[42] Thus, the IRS will have to issue guidance on whether section 1231 income qualifies as QBI.

S Corporations and Reasonable Compensation

S corporation profits qualify as QBI, but salaries paid to shareholders who perform services for the S corporation don't qualify. To increase the 199A deduction, S corporations may reduce the salaries of shareholders who perform services for the company and make a corresponding increase in profits. If the IRS believes the shareholder is not being paid reasonable compensation, however, it may re-characterize a portion of a profits distribution as compensation,[43] possibly reducing the 199A deduction.

Partnerships and LLCs and Reasonable Compensation

The Committee Report states that "*qualified business income does not include any amount paid by an S corporation as reasonable compensation of the taxpayer.*" It says nothing about reasonable compensation paid to a sole proprietor, partner or LLC member, though. The reason for excluding only reasonable compensation paid to an S corporation shareholder is presumably that compensation paid to an S corporation shareholder is treated as W-2 wages subject to self-employment taxes. By converting reasonable compensation into pass-through income, S corporations can avoid self-employment tax and the IRS has long tried to prevent this by imposing a reasonable compensation requirement. Other pass-through entities cannot pay W-2 wages to their owners, so there was no reason for the IRS to try to re-characterize income passed through to owners of these businesses as compensation.

Following enactment of Code section 199A, however, pass-through income will be taxed more favorably than compensation income for all pass-through entities. Unlike, the Committee Report, Code section 199A(c)(4) does not limit application of the reasonable compensation restriction to S corporations, stating that "*Qualified business income shall not include reasonable compensation paid to the taxpayer by any qualified trade or business of the taxpayer for services rendered with respect to the trade or business.*" Thus, the IRS might take the position based on the Code section that the pass-through income of sole proprietorships, partnerships and LLCs should be reduced by a reasonable amount of compensation for the owners just like the income of an S corporation.

If the IRS did this, it would create an important advantage for S corporations over other pass-through entities, however. Under current law, S corporations are subject to the reasonable compensation requirement, but this disadvantage is offset by the S corporation's ability to use wages paid to owners in calculating the W-2/unadjusted basis limitation. If the reasonable compensation requirement was extended to sole proprietorships, partnerships and LLCs, it would seem only fair that these entities should also be able to count salaries paid to owners as W-2 income for purposes of the W-2/unadjusted basis limitation.[44]

Note that although guaranteed payments are excluded from QBI, there is no requirement to make guaranteed payments to partners like there is for paying reasonable compensation to an S corporation shareholder. Thus, partnerships and LLCs could effectively convert what would ordinarily be non-qualified guaranteed payments into pass-through income by reducing or eliminating guaranteed payments and treating these amounts as pass-through income qualifying as QBI. Nothing would be lost under Code section 199A by doing so because guaranteed payments don't count as W-2 wages for purposes of the W-2 wage/unadjusted basis limitation. If a partnership interest is received by gift, however, Code section 704(e) requires that the partnership must provide an allowance of reasonable compensation for the services of the donor partner.[45] The IRS may argue that the allocation of compensation to the donor partner is unreasonably low and convert what would otherwise be QBI into salary income.

QUALIFIED TRADE OR BUSINESS

A *qualified* trade or business is any trade or business other than (1) a specified service trade or business, or (2) the trade or business of performing services as an employee.[46] Although the phrase "trade or business" appears in over fifty Code sections and 800 subsections, neither the Code nor the regulations has ever provided an all-purpose definition. Thus, the definition has been left to the courts. The case law could be summarized as follows.

- Determining whether an individual is carrying on a trade or business requires an examination of the facts involved in each case.[47]
- To be engaged in a trade or business, an individual must be involved in an activity with continuity and regularity, and the primary purpose for engaging in the activity must be to produce income or profit.[48]
- A sporadic activity, a hobby, or an amusement diversion does not qualify.[49]
- Expenses incident to caring for one's own investments, even on a large enough scale to require an office and staff, are not deductible as paid or incurred in carrying on a trade or business.[50]
- Holding one's self out to others as engaged in the selling of goods or services is not required.[51]

Rental Real Estate

Determining whether an activity rises to the level of a trade or business is particularly important in the context of rental real estate. Renting or managing rental property could be either a business activity or as an investment activity depending on the facts of the case.

The Tax Court has repeatedly held that the rental of even a single piece of real property can constitute a trade or business.[52] According to the IRS, ownership and management of real property does not constitute a trade or business as a matter of law, however.[53] The question of whether there is a trade or business is ultimately one of fact and depends on the scope of ownership and management activities. Owning rental property qualifies as a business if it is engaged in to earn a profit and the activity is sufficiently systematic and continuous.[54] If not, rental ownership will be treated as an investment rather than as a trade or business.[55]

Grouping Trades or Businesses

The computation of the Code section 199A deduction is done separately for each qualified trade or business[56] but, as noted above, the statute does not explain what is meant by a trade or business. Thus, it is unclear whether activities of separate entities can be grouped together for purposes of doing the calculations. Regulations under Code section 469, dealing with identifying and grouping activities for purposes of the passive loss rules might be used as a starting point for determining when two or more trades or businesses could be grouped together.[57] Regulations under Code section 448(d), might also be helpful.[58] These regulations address when trades or businesses are separate and distinct and, thus, eligible to use different accounting methods for the businesses.

Specified Service Trade or Business (SSTB)

A specified service trade or business is (1) any trade or business listed in Code section 1202(e)(3)(A) other than engineering or architecture,59 and (2) any business which involves the performance of services that consist of investing and investment management, trading, or dealing in securities, partnership interests, or commodities.60 The trades or businesses listed in Code section 1202(e)(3)(A) are trades or businesses involving performance of services in the fields of:

- Health
- Law
- Accounting
- Actuarial science
- Performing arts
- Consulting
- Athletics
- Financial services
- Brokerage services
- Any trade or business where the principal asset of the trade or business is the reputation or skill of one of its employees[61]

Section 1202 Guidance

For purposes of section 199A, the last category applies to the reputation or skill of business owners as well as to the reputation or skill of one or more employees.[62] This category may be very difficult to define because, arguably, most successful small businesses owe much of their success to the reputation or skill of their owners and/or employees. It remains to be seen how broadly this category will be defined.[63] One possible way for the IRS to address this issue would be to formulate a list of safe harbor businesses.

Example 15. Amy is a nationally known pastry chef who owns a bakery. Although the bakery produces products rather than services, the reputation or skill category may apply.

Note that although Code section 199A uses Code section 1202(e)(3) to identify service businesses, it does not mention the businesses listed in Code sections 1202(e)(3)(B), 1202(e)(3)(C), and 1202(e)(3)(D). These include:

- Any banking, insurance, financing, leasing, investing or similar business[64]
- Any farming business (including the business of raising or harvesting trees)[65]
- Any business involving the production or extraction of products of a character with respect to which a deduction is allowable under section 613 or 613(A).[66]

Inclusion of the businesses listed in Code section 1202(e)(3)(A) but not the businesses listed in the other sections of 1202(e)(3), would seem to indicate that Congress intended to exclude these businesses from the definition of specified service business. An argument might be made that these businesses might still be treated as specified service trades or businesses under the catch-all category relating to the reputation or skill of one or more owners or employees. This appears to be unlikely, however, at least for mining and most farming businesses, because they produce undifferentiated commodities.

Until recently, qualifying as a small business corporation under Code section 1202 produced little tax benefit.[67] The lack of interest in the exclusion and the difficulty of defining the term qualified trade or business, deterred the IRS from issuing regulations and taxpayers from seeking rulings. As a result, there is very little law on the scope of service businesses under section 1202. The only guidance appears to be two private letter rulings on the health care category.[68]

It is not clear how to treat an entity that combines a specified service trade or business and a qualified business. For example, there is no guidance on whether the specified service trade or business taints the qualified business, causing the entire entity to be treated as an SSTB.

Fortunately, as noted in the Committee Report, additional guidance is available on some of the categories under Code section 448(d)(2). This section prohibits use of the cash method of accounting for most C corporations, but allows an exception for personal service corporations.[69] Thus, guidance under section 448(d)(2) may be helpful in determining the scope of some of the service businesses listed under Code section 1202(e)(1)(A).

W-2 Wages

The term "W-2 wages" means, with respect to any person for any taxable year of such person, the amounts described in paragraphs (3) and (8) of section 6051(a) paid by such person with respect to employment of employees by such person during the calendar year ending during such taxable year.[70] Thus, it includes:

- wages paid to an employee as defined in Code section 3401(a);
- elective deferrals (within the meaning of Code section 402(g)(3);
- deferred compensation under Code section 457; and
- Roth IRA contributions as defined in Code section 402A.

These amounts only count, however, if they are properly allocable to QBI.[71] They are also excluded if they aren't properly included in a return filed with the Social Security Administration on or before the sixtieth day after the due date (including extensions) for such return.[72] Elective deferrals include elective contributions made to SIMPLE IRAs, 401(k) plans, SARSEPs, and 403(b) plans.[73]

The term W-2 wages does not include payments to independent contractors or management fees.[74] Note that an S corporation can pay W-2 wages to the entity's owners but partnerships and LLCs cannot.[75] This might be an important advantage for S corporations that pay most of the wages to the business owners.

Code section 199A does not address the question of whether amounts paid to leased employees from a professional employer organization (PEO)[76] are W-2 wages for purposes of the QBI and W-2 wage/unadjusted basis limitation. It appears, however, that whether amounts paid to leased employees or clients of PEOs would be W-2 wages would depend on who the worker's employer was under the common law.[77] Under common law rules, a worker is an employee if the employer has the right to control what work will be done and how it will be done. This is true even if the employee is given freedom of action. What counts is that the employer has the right to control not that the employer actually exerts control. The IRS has listed twenty factors that can be used in determining whether a worker is a common law employee.[78]

Qualified Property

The 2.5 percent of the unadjusted basis component of the W-2 wages/capital limitation applies to any property that is:

- tangible;
- depreciable;
- held by, and available for use in, the qualified business at the close of the year;
- used at any time during the taxable year for production of QBI; and
- for which the depreciable period hasn't ended before the end of the taxable year.[79]

The depreciable period for the property cannot end prior to the last day of the year for which the deduction is claimed. For this purpose, the end of the depreciable period is the later of ten years after the property was placed in service or the last day of the last full year in the asset's regular depreciation period under Code section 168 (not the period under the alternative depreciation system (ADS)).[80]

Example 16. In 2018, Tom acquires machinery for use in his business. The depreciation period for the machinery is five years. The unadjusted basis of the machinery can be counted for the longer of five or ten years. Thus, its basis can be used for the W-2 wage/unadjusted basis calculation from 2018 through 2027.

The basis of property generally cannot be counted for the W-2/unadjusted basis limitation if it was fully depreciated before 2018. It appears, however, that property placed in service after 2008 might still be counted under the ten-year rule even if its normal depreciation period has expired.[81]

An S corporation shareholder or partner's portion of an entity's unadjusted basis is allocated based on the shareholder or partner's share of the entity's unadjusted basis immediately after acquisition of the qualified property.[82] It is not clear how these percentages change if a new owner joins the entity. Nor is it clear how improvements to tangible property are treated under the unadjusted basis rules.

Example 17. Carol and Karen are equal partners in the CK Partnership. Depreciation expense is allocated 40 percent to Carol and 60 percent to Karen. CK partnership owns depreciable property with an unadjusted basis of $100,000. Carol can use $40,000 for her W-2 wages/unadjusted basis limitation and Karen can use $60,000.

Code section 199A(h) directs the IRS to prescribe rules similar to those under Code section 179(d)(2) to prevent manipulation of the depreciable period of qualified property using transactions between related parties.[83]

Code section 199A(h) also directs the IRS to prescribe rules for determining the unadjusted basis immediately after acquisition of qualified property acquired in like-kind exchanges or involuntary conversions.[84] This guidance may also apply to sale-leaseback transactions.[85]

The Committee Report does not address the acquisition date of property acquired from a decedent. It appears that the acquisition date should be the date of death. Thus, it may be possible to increase the unadjusted basis by the amount of the step-up under Code section 1014 or, in the case of a partnership, with a Code section 754 basis step-up. Using the date of death as the acquisition date would also extend the depreciable period for the property. These questions may be covered in the anti-abuse guidance to be provided pursuant to Code section 199A(h).

Unadjusted Tax Basis

The "unadjusted basis" in qualified property is the property's basis immediately after acquisition, unreduced by any depreciation deductions.[86]

Taxable Income

Taxable income is computed in the usual manner, without regard to the 20 percent 199A deduction.[87]

Qualified REIT Dividend

A qualified REIT dividend is any dividend received from a real estate investment trust that is not (1) a capital asset, or (2) qualified dividend income subject to tax at long term capital gain rates.[88]

Qualified Publicly Traded Partnership Income

Qualified publicly traded partnership income means, with respect to any qualified trade or business of the taxpayer, the sum of:

1. The net amount of the taxpayer's allocable share of each item of qualified item of income, gain, deduction or loss from a publicly traded partnership not treated as a corporation; and

2. Any gain recognized by such taxpayer upon disposition of its interest in such partnership to the extent such gain is treated as an amount realized from the sale or exchange of property other than a capital asset under Code section 751(a) (i.e., gain on the sale of hot assets).[89]

SPECIAL RULES AND UNANSWERED QUESTIONS

Code section 199A includes a number of special rules. These include rules on:

- The application of Code section 199A to partnerships and S corporations

- The application of Code section 199A to trusts and estates

- The coordination of Code section 199A with the alternative minimum tax (AMT)
- The carryover of losses
- The treatment of NOLs under Code section 199A
- The effect of the Code section 199A deduction on tax basis
- The extension of the accuracy related penalty to taxpayers who claim the deduction

These issues are discussed in detail below.

Application to Partnerships and S Corporations

In the case of a partnership or S corporation, Code section 199A is applied at the partner or shareholder level.[90] The following rules apply for purposes of calculating the 20 percent deduction:

1. Each partner or shareholder takes into account such person's allocable share of each qualified item of income, gain, deduction, and loss
2. Each partner or shareholder is treated as having W-2 wages and unadjusted basis in an amount equal to such person's allocable share immediately after acquisition of qualified property for the taxable year in an amount equal to such person's allocable share of the W-2 wages and the unadjusted basis immediately after acquisition of qualified property of the partnership or S corporation for the taxable year (as determined under regulations prescribed by the Secretary)
3. For purposes of (2) above, a partner's or shareholder's allocable share of W-2 wages shall be determined in the same manner as the partner's or shareholder's allocable share of wage expenses
4. For purposes of (2) above, a partner's or shareholder's allocable share of the unadjusted basis immediately after acquisition of qualified property shall be determined in the same manner as the partner's or shareholder's allocable share of depreciation
5. In the case of an S corporation, an allocable share shall be the shareholder's pro rata share of an item[91]

Calculating an S corporation shareholder's allocable share of an item should be relatively straightforward. Each shareholder's pro rata share of any item would be determined by assigning an equal portion of such item to each day of the taxable year and then dividing that portion pro rata among the shares outstanding on such day.[92]

Example 18. On January 6 of this year, X incorporates as a calendar year corporation, issues 100 shares of common stock to each of A and B, and files an election to be an S corporation. On July 24 B sells 25 shares of X stock to C. Thus, for this year, A owned 50 percent of the outstanding shares of X on each day of the year, B owned 50 percent on each day from January 6, 2017 to July 24, 2017 (200 days), and 25 percent from July 25 to December 31 (160 days), and C owned 25 percent from July 25 to December 31. During this taxable year, X pays $720,000 of wages.

For each day in X's taxable year, the shareholders' pro rata shares are as follows.

A	$720,000/360 days × 50% ownership = $1,000/day	
B	first 200 days	$720,000/360 days × 50% ownership = $1,000/day
	last 160 days	$720,000/360 days × 25% ownership = $500/day
C	$720,000/360 days × 25% ownership = $500/day	

The allocation of wages then looks like this:

A $1,000/day × $360/day = $360,000

B ($1,000/day × 200 days) + ($500/day × 160 days) = $280,000

C $500/day × 160 days = $80,000[93]

Determining a partner's allocable share might be much more difficult, particularly if there are special allocations. The determination would presumably be made under Code section 704 and the section 704 regulations. Regulations issued under former Code section 199 might be helpful in this regard. Prior to its repeal by the TCJA, this section provided a deduction for income attributable to domestic production activities.[94] Like the new section 199A, former section 199 limited the deduction to 50 percent of wages paid and allocated wages at the partner or shareholder level.[95] Apparently acknowledging this complexity in this area, Code section 199A(f)(4) provides that the IRS will issue regulations on the allocation of items of wages and on applying Code section 199A to tiered entities.

Example 19. Partner X has a 40 percent ownership interest in non-service Partnership XYZ. In Year 1, the partnership had $2,500,000 of ordinary income, $900,000 of wage expense and held depreciable property with a basis of $250,000. There are no special allocations, so X is allocated 40 percent of all partnership items. Thus, X's allocable share of each item in the QBI calculation is as follows.

Income	$1,000,000
W-2 wages	$360,000
Unadjusted basis	$100,000

X's section 199A deduction is then

The lesser of:

1. 20% of X's allocable share of flow-through income ($200,000); or

2. the greater of:

   a. 50% of X's allocable share of W-2 wages ($180,000); or

   b. 25% of X's allocable share of W-2 wages ($90,000) + 2.5% of X's allocable share of basis ($2,500) = $92,500

Thus, the deduction is the lesser of $200,000 or $180,000 = $180,000.

Because the taxable income limitation is applied at the partner or shareholder level, some owners might benefit more from the 20 percent deduction than others. Thus, it may be possible to maximize deductions by making special allocations of W-2 wages and depreciation deductions.

Application to Trusts and Estates

The Committee Report makes it clear that trusts and estates are eligible for the 20 percent QBI deduction.[96] Rules similar to the rules under section 199(d)(1)(B)(i) (as in effect on December 1, 2017) apply to the apportionment of W-2 wages and the apportionment of unadjusted basis immediately after acquisition of qualified property under this section.

Example 20. In the ABC Trust, 75 percent of the DNI is distributed to the beneficiaries and 25 percent is retained in the trust. It appears that the beneficiaries will get 75 percent of the QBI deduction and the trust will get 25 percent.

Coordination with the AMT

The alternative minimum tax (AMT) was designed to make sure high income taxpayers who could reduce regular income tax to very low levels by taking advantage of certain deductions and tax benefit items still paid a significant amount of tax. The AMT accomplishes this by adding to regular taxable income the amount of tax preference items in Code section 57 and making certain adjustments to income under Code sections 56 and 58. There are also some special rules under Code section 59. The AMT income is generally taxed at a rate of 26 or 28 percent.[97] For purposes of determining qualified business income under Code section 199A, the adjustments under Code sections 56 to 59 are ignored.[98]

Carryover of Losses

If the net amount of qualified income, gain, deduction, and loss of a qualified trade or business of the taxpayer is less than zero for any tax year, the amount is carried over as a loss from a qualified trade or business in the next tax year.[99]

Example 21. Cathy has qualified business income of $30,000 from qualified business A and a business loss of $50,000 from qualified business B in Year 1. Cathy does not get a section 199A deduction for Year 1 and has a carryover qualified business loss of $20,000 to Year 2. Assume that in Year 2 she has qualified business income of $30,000 from qualified business A and qualified business income of $40,000 from qualified business B. To determine the deduction for Year 2, Cathy reduces the 20 percent deductible amount determined for the qualified business income of $70,000 from qualified businesses A and B by 20 percent of the $20,000 carryover qualified business loss. Thus, the Year 2 deduction is $10,000 (.2 × $50,000).[100]

Treatment of Net Operating Losses (NOLs)

The section 199A deduction cannot be used to create an NOL. It must be removed from the NOL calculation.[101]

Effect of the Deduction on the Tax Basis of an S Corporation Shareholder

An S corporation shareholder's basis in stock of the corporation is increased by the shareholder's share of the entity's income.[102] Although the TCJA does not address how this rule applies when a shareholder's S corporation income is reduced by the 20 percent section 199A deduction, it appears that the deduction shouldn't be taken into account in calculating a partner's basis increase.

Example 22. Ray is a shareholder in the ABC S corporation with a basis of $15,000 in his stock. ABC was never a C corporation and has no earnings and profits. Ray's share of S corporation income for this year is $100,000 and he qualifies for the full 20 percent deduction under Code section 199A, reducing his taxable income to $80,000. ABC distributes $100,000 to Ray. If Ray's basis of $15,000 was increased only by the $80,000 of taxable income, he would recognize $5,000 of income on the distribution ($100,000 distribution - $95,000 basis).[103] If this was the correct result, it would seem to eliminate part of the benefit of the section 199A deduction. Thus, it appears that Ray's basis in his S corporation stock should be increased by $100,000.

Extension of Accuracy-related Penalties

Prior to enactment of the TCJA, there was a substantial understatement of income tax for purposes of imposing the 20 percent accuracy-related penalty if the amount of an understatement exceeded the greater of 10 percent of the tax required to be shown or $5,000.[104] Apparently expecting taxpayers to aggressively claim deductions under Code section 199A, Congress reduced the threshold amount for application of the penalty to the greater of 5 percent of the correct tax or $5,000.[105]

It is important to note that the lower threshold does not just apply to understatements arising out of the Code section 199A deduction. Instead, it applies to any taxpayer who claims the section 199A deduction on a return regardless of whether the understatement resulted from an excess deduction under section 199A or because of understatements resulted from any other reporting error. It also applies regardless of the amount of the Code section 199A deduction claimed.

The term understatement for purposes of the substantial understatement penalty means the excess of:

- The amount of tax required to be shown on the return, over
- The amount of tax imposed which is actually shown on the return[106]

To the extent that a taxpayer (1) has substantial authority for the reported tax treatment of a position, or (2) has a reasonable basis for the position and makes adequate disclosure, the amount of the understatement is reduced.[107]

Example 23. In 2016, Jane, a calendar year taxpayer files a return for 2015 which shows tax payable of $64,000. Subsequent adjustments on audit increase Jane's tax liability to $70,000. There is a substantial understatement of tax if the $6,000 underpayment exceeds the greater of (1) 10 percent of the correct tax ($7,000), or (2) $5,000. Since $6,000 does not exceed $7,000, there is no substantial understatement.

Example 24. Assume the same facts as in Example 23 except that the return is filed in 2019 for the 2018 tax year and the new 5 percent rule has gone into effect. Also assume that Jane has claimed a QBI deduction under Code section 199A. Now there is a substantial understatement of tax if the underpayment ($6,000) exceeds the greater of 5 percent of the correct tax ($3,500) or $5,000. Since $6,000 exceeds $5,000, there is a substantial understatement.

Example 25. Assume the same facts as in Example 24 except that Jane had substantial authority for an item resulting in an adjustment that increased her tax liability by $2,000. The item is not a tax shelter.[108] The amount of tax treated as shown on Jane's return is increased by this $2,000 amount to $66,000. This reduces the underpayment to $4,000. Since this amount is less than the greater of $3,300 or $5,000, there is no substantial understatement of tax.[109]

UNANSWERED QUESTIONS

Code section 199A and the Committee Report left a number of important questions unanswered. In a letter to the Department of the Treasury, the AICPA requested guidance on the following issues:[110]

- The meaning of specified service trade or business.
- The calculation of QBI when flowing through multiple tiered entities.
- The netting computation of losses from one business against gains from another business.
- The effect of an existing grouping of trades or businesses (e.g., under section 469) for purposes of the limitations based on W-2 wages, adjusted basis of assets and specified service business. If grouping is allowed, will taxpayers have an opportunity to regroup their trades or businesses to take advantage of the deduction?
- Whether wages are determined in a manner similar to the concepts provided in Reg. section 1.199-2(a)(2). In other words, by considering the wages of common law employees regardless of who is responsible for paying the wages.
- Whether a trade or business is defined as an activity within an entity. For example, what if an entity has two clearly separate trades or businesses?
- Whether all similar qualified businesses are aggregated for purposes of the calculation or if each business is evaluated separately. For taxpayers with non-qualified business activities, there is a *de minimis* percentage at which the activity is not excluded. Does the taxpayer make separate computations for the personal service activity versus the non-personal service activity?
- Whether the taxpayer may consider a management company an integral part of the operating trade or business (and thus, not a specified business activity) if substantially all of the management company's income is from that other trade or business.
- The qualification of real property rental income as qualified business income (or loss).
- If grouping is allowed, whether taxpayers may treat the rental of real estate to their related C corporation (e.g., a self-rental) as trade or business income.
- The determination of items effectively connected with a business, e.g., section 1245 gains and losses, retirement plan contributions of partners and sole proprietors, the section 162(l) deduction and one-half of self-employment tax.
- The unadjusted basis of assets expensed under section 179 or subject to bonus depreciation.
- The unadjusted basis of assets held as of January 1, 2018.
- The unadjusted basis of property subject to 743(b) basis adjustments.
- The effect, if any, of the 20 percent deduction on net investment income tax calculations.

TAX PLANNING UNDER SECTION 199A

Tax planning under Code section 199A involves the following topics.

1. Managing limitation amounts by Increasing or decreasing W-2 wages, increasing unadjusted

basis, reducing taxable income to avoid limitation amounts, or increasing ordinary income to avoid the 20 percent of net income over capital gains limitation

2. Employee vs. independent contractor status

3. Planning for marital status

4. Promoting employees to partner status

5. Choice of entity decision, including choosing between a pass-through entity vs. C corporation and a sole proprietorship vs. partnership/LLC vs. S corporation

6. Tax planning for service businesses

Managing Limitation Amounts

The limitations on the QBI deduction can be managed by:

- increasing or decreasing W-2 wages
- increasing adjusted basis
- reducing taxable income to avoid the W-2 wage/unadjusted basis and SSTB limitations
- increasing ordinary income to avoid the 20 percent of net income over capital gains limitation.

Increasing or Decreasing W-2 Wages

Depending on the facts of the case, either increasing or decreasing W-2 wages may increase the Code section 199A deduction. Disregarding unadjusted basis for the time being, if 20 percent of QBI exceeds 50 percent of W-2 wages it may be possible to increase the limitation amount by increasing wages. The following examples illustrate various ways in which this might be done.

Example 26. John and his wife, Melissa, have taxable income of $426,600. They own a small coffee roasting business. The business:

- Is structured as a sole proprietorship
- Generates $100,000 of QBI
- Has no employees
- Has no qualified property because it leases its space and equipment

A sole proprietorship cannot pay W-2 wages to its owners. This means that John and Melissa's 199A deduction is the lesser of:

(1) 20 percent of QBI ($20,000), or

(2) the greater of 50 percent of W-2 wages ($0) or unadjusted basis in qualified property ($0).

Thus, John and Melissa have a section 199A deduction of $0.

Example 27. Assume the same facts as in Example 26, except that John & Melissa convert the business to a partnership and pay Melissa a guaranteed payment of $50,000/year. The section 199A deduction would still be zero because guaranteed payments aren't W-2 wages.[111] To create W-2 wages the business would have to pay wages to employees.

Example 28. Assume the same facts as in Example 27 except that John and Melissa convert the business to an S corporation. An S corporation can pay W-2 wages to its owners as well as to employees. If the business pays Melissa $50,000 in W-2 wages, the Code section 199A deduction is the lesser of:

(1) 20 percent of QBI (.2 × $50,000 = $10,000);[112] or

(2) 50 percent of W-2 wages (.5 × $50,000) = $25,000.

Thus, the section 199A deduction is $10,000.

Note that the optimal amount of income to be paid is achieved by setting 50 percent of wages equal to 20 percent of QBI. This is illustrated in the next example.

Example 29. Assume the same facts as in Example 28 except that John and Melissa realize that their section 199A deduction might be larger if Melissa was paid less because W-2 wages don't count as QBI. They determine that the optimal deduction would be achieved if Melissa was paid 28.5714 percent of the pass-through income ($28,571.40) and the remaining $71,428.60 was treated as QBI.[113] Note that 28.5714 percent equals 2/7 of the income. The amount of the QBI deduction would be the lesser of:

(1) 20 percent of QBI (.2 × $71,428.60 = $14,285.70); or

(2) 50 percent of wages (.5 × $28,571.40 = $14,285.70).

Note that if Melissa is paid either more or less than this amount, the deduction will go down.[114]

Unfortunately, if the business does not pay Melissa reasonable compensation for the work she does, the IRS will re-characterize a portion of the profits interest passing through to her as wages.[115] If $50,000 was reasonable compensation for running the coffee roasting business in the previous example and Melissa's pay was reduced to $28,571.40, the IRS might try to re-characterize some or all of the income as wages.

Wages can also be increased by converting independent contractors to employees.

Example 30. Ted, a single taxpayer, is the sole proprietor of the TR trucking company. He pays his two drivers $50,000/year each, but they work as independent contractors so there are no W-2 wages. Ted has no depreciable property because the trucks are leased. His pass-through income from the business is $225,000 per year and his taxable income is $250,000. Ted's section 199A deduction is the lesser of.

(1) QBI (.2 × $225,000 = $45,000); or

(2) the greater of W-2 wages or unadjusted basis, both of which are $0.

Thus, Ted gets no section 199A deduction.

Suppose, however, that he converts the drivers into employees. His section 199A deduction would then be the lesser of $45,000 or 50% × $100,000 of W-2 wages = $50,000. Thus, the conversion would increase Ted's QBI deduction to $45,000. The downside would be that the drivers would each lose a $10,000 QBI deduction (.2 × $50,000) because, while independent contractors qualify for the section 199A deduction, employees don't.[116]

Finally, the section 199A deduction can be increased by simply paying employees higher wages.

Example 31. Linda, a single taxpayer, is the sole proprietor of a bakery. Linda's net income from the bakery is $130,000/year and her taxable income is $240,000. Linda has one part-time employee, Marge, who Linda pays $20,000/year. The bakery has no depreciable property.

Linda's section 199A deduction is the lesser of (1) .2 × $130,000 QBI = $26,000 or (2) .5 × $20,000 W-2 wages = $10,000. Marge has been doing excellent work and Linda has been thinking of giving her a substantial raise. If Linda increases Marge's salary to $30,000 (reducing net income to $120,000), she can increase her section 199A deduction to $15,000. This is the lesser of (1) .2 × $120,000 = $24,000 or, (2) .5 × $30,000 = $15,000. Decreasing QBI does not reduce the section 199A deduction because 20 percent of QBI still exceeds the 50 percent of W-2 wages limitation. Because Linda is in the 24 percent marginal tax bracket, the additional $5,000 deduction is worth $1,200 (.24 × $5,000). In effect, the Treasury pays for part of Marge's raise.

Decreasing W-2 Wages

In the previous examples, 20 percent of QBI exceeded 50 percent of W-2 wages so it was advantageous to increase W-2 wages.[117] If, on the other hand, 20 percent of QBI is less than the 50 percent W-2 wage limitation, it may be advantageous to reduce wages. Because wages aren't included in QBI, this will increase pass-through income and the amount of QBI.

Example 32. Tim and his wife, Dora, are the sole owners of an S corporation. The business produces $150,000 of profit and pays Dora a salary of $120,000 for operating the business. The business owns no depreciable property. If Tim and Dora do no planning, their section 199A is the lesser of:

(1) 20 percent of QBI ($30,000);

OR

(2) the greater of 50 percent of W-2 wages ($60,000) or unadjusted basis ($0).

This makes the section 199A deduction $30,000. To increase the deduction, they decide to reduce Dora's W-2 wages by $40,000. This increases QBI by $40,000 and increases their section 199A deduction to the lesser of:

(1) 20 percent of QBI ($200,000);

OR

(2) the greater of 50 percent of W-2 wages ($40,000) or unadjusted basis, both of which are $0.

By reducing Dora's wages by $40,000, the section 199A deduction is increased by $8,000 to $38,000. This is a good result, but the deduction could be made slightly higher by paying Dora 2/7 of the sum of Dora's wages + company profit. This amount would be 2/7 × $270,000 = $77,142.86, leaving the $192,857.14 of pass-through income ($270,000 - $77,142.86). Then, the section 199A deduction would be the lesser of:

(1) 20 percent of QBI ($38,571);

OR

(2) the greater of 50 percent of W-2 wages ($77,143) or unadjusted basis ($0).

Again, the IRS might question whether the business was paying reasonable compensation.

Increasing Unadjusted Basis

Up to this point we have been assuming that unadjusted basis was zero and showing how changes in W-2 wages could increase the section 199A deduction. We now turn to the unadjusted basis component of the W-2 wage/unadjusted basis limitation. Unadjusted basis can be increased by either acquiring depreciable property or by owning property instead of leasing it.

Example 33. Bill and Kelly own a small unincorporated widget manufacturing business that produces $1,000,000 of net income per year. Bill and Kelly do all the work so there are no W-2 wages. They rent a building and lease the machinery used to make the widgets. If Bill and Kelly do no planning, their section 199A deduction will be $0, the lesser of:

(1) 20 percent of QBI ($200,000);

OR

(2) the greater of 50 percent of W-2 wages or unadjusted basis, both of which are $0.

Now suppose that instead of leasing, Bill and Kelly decide to buy the building for $1,000,000. Their section 199A deduction amount is now the lesser of:

(1) 20 percent of QBI ($200,000);

OR

(2) the greater of 50 percent of W-2 wages ($0) or 25 percent of wages plus 2.5 percent of basis ($0 + $25,000).

Example 34. Beth owns a trucking company with $800,000 of QBI so her tentative QBI deduction is $160,000. Beth's taxable income is $700,000 so the W-2/unadjusted basis limitation applies in full. All the company's trucks are leased, the company owns no depreciable real property and the drivers are all independent contractors so the W-2/unadjusted basis limitation is $0 and Beth gets no section 199A deduction.

Example 35. Assume the same facts as in Example 34 except that the company buys the trucks for $1,000,000. This increases the W-2 wage/unadjusted basis limitation to $25,000, giving Beth a $25,000 deduction.

Reducing Taxable Income to Avoid the W-2 Wage/Unadjusted Basis and SSTB Limitations

The W-2 wage and SSTB limitations are phased in as taxable income increases from $163,300 to $213,300 for single taxpayers and from $326,600 to $426,600 for married taxpayers filing jointly. It may be possible to avoid, or at least diminish the effect of these limitations by decreasing taxable income.

Charitable Deductions and Qualified Plan Contributions

Two easy ways to reduce taxable income to avoid or minimize application of the W-2 wage/unadjusted basis and SSTB limitations are making charitable contributions and making contributions to qualified plans.

Example 36. Tom is a married lawyer with a solo practice. He pays $80,000 in wages to his employees. The building that houses the practice is leased. The law practice generates $500,000 of QBI and Tom's taxable income in 2020 will be $355,000. Without planning, his tentative QBI deduction is 20 percent of $500,000 = $100,000. Because the law practice is a service business and Tom's taxable income exceeds $326,600, however, part of the deduction is phased out. Tom's income is 40 percent of the way through the phase-out range ($40,000/$100,000) so he loses 40 percent of the deduction (.4 × $100,000 = $40,000). This leaves Tom with a section 199A deduction of $60,000.

Example 37. Assume the same facts as in Example 36 except that Tom makes a $30,000 charitable contribution to the American Cancer Society. This reduces his taxable below the $326,600 phase-out threshold and eliminates any phase-out. Thus, Tom gets the full $80,000 deduction.

Gifts of Business Interests

Taxpayers might also consider gifting shares of a business to family members. This would spread income from the business among several taxpayers, making it easier to stay below the phase-in or phase-out threshold amounts.

Example 38. Al and Paula are married taxpayers filing jointly with $400,000 of QBI from AP Partnership and taxable income of $500,000. The AP Partnership pays no wages. Because Al and Paula have taxable income over $426,600, the W-2 wage limitation applies in full and they get no Code section 199A deduction.

Al and Paula have two children, Ted and Susan, both married taxpayers in their late twenties, each with taxable MFJ income of $100,000. Al and Paula gift a 25 percent interest in AP to Ted and a 25 percent interest in AP to Susan, shifting $100,000 of qualified business income to each of them. Following the transfer, Al and Paula have taxable income of $300,000 and Ted and Susan have taxable income of $200,000 each. Thus, all of them qualify for the full 20 percent deduction on AP income.

Avoiding the 20 Percent of Taxable Income Over Capital Gain Limitation—Increasing Taxable Income

Even if QBI is not limited by the W-2 wages/unadjusted basis limitation, it may be limited by the 20 percent of taxable income over capital gains limitation. In this situation, an owner of a non-service business may wish to earn additional income outside the pass-through business.

Example 39. Gary is a single farmer with income of $100,000 and no capital gains. Gary claims $15,000 of itemized deductions, reducing his taxable income to $85,000. Although his tentative QBI deduction is $20,000 (.2 × $100,000), the deduction is limited to $17,500 (.2 × $85,000) because of the taxable income limitation (20 percent of taxable income over capital gains). During the winter, Gary works at a store in a nearby town and earns $15,000 of additional income. This increases his taxable income over capital gain to $100,000 and his

20 percent of taxable income limitation to $20,000, so he can use the full amount of his tentative QBI. If Gary had instead sold a small parcel of land and recognized a gain of $15,000, this income wouldn't have increased his limitation amount.

Employee vs. Independent Contractor Status

Classification of a worker as an independent contractor or as an employee makes a big difference both for workers and for employers under Code section 199A. Payments for work done by an independent contractor are QBI and can qualify for the 20 percent QBI deduction, but payments for similar work done by an employee cannot.[118] Thus, workers receive more favorable tax treatment if they are treated as independent contractors. On the other hand, payments to employees for work done count as W-2 wages for an employer, enabling the employer to increase its W-2 wage/unadjusted basis limitation amount but payments to independent contractors don't. Thus, employers and workers have conflicting objectives under Code section 199A. Workers want to be treated as independent contractors, but employers would rather treat them as employees.

This oversimplifies the decision for two reasons, however. First, an employer cannot just decide that a worker will be treated as an employee and a worker cannot just decide that he wants to be treated as an independent contractor. The worker actually has to qualify for the desired status. The IRS takes the position that in determining whether a worker is an employee or an independent contractor it is necessary to consider all evidence of the degree of control and independence in the work relationship. The facts that provide this evidence fall into three categories: Behavioral Control, Financial Control, and Relationship of the Parties.

Behavioral Control covers facts that show if the business has a right to direct and control what work is accomplished and how the work is done, through instructions, training, or other means.

Financial Control covers facts that show if the business has a right to direct or control the financial and business aspects of the worker's job. This includes:

- The extent to which the worker has unreimbursed business expense
- The extent of the worker's investment in the facilities or tools used in performing services
- The extent to which the worker makes his or her services available to the relevant market
- How the business pays the worker
- The extent to which the worker can realize a profit or incur a loss

Relationship of the Parties covers facts that show the type of relationship the parties have. This includes:

- Written contracts describing the relationship the parties intended to create
- Whether the business provides the worker with employee-type benefits, such as insurance, a pension plan, vacation pay, or sick pay
- The permanency of the relationship
- The extent to which services performed by the worker are a key aspect of the regular business of the company[119]

In addition, even if the worker qualifies for the desired status, there may be important trade-offs. If workers are treated as employees, the employer would have to pay payroll taxes, comply with wage and hour requirements, reimburse workers for business expenses, cover the employees under worker's compensation insurance and perhaps provide other benefits. There are also downsides for workers who choose to be independent contractors. They would have to pay both halves of the Medicare and Social Security taxes up to the Social Security wage base ($137,700 in 2020) and might give up important fringe benefits like health insurance.

Increasing QBI

One way to increase QBI would be to convert guaranteed payments in a partnership into pass-through income. While guaranteed payments don't count as QBI, distributive shares are included. Unlike S corporations, partnerships aren't required to pay reasonable compensation.

Example 40. Paul and his brother Al, single taxpayers, are 50 percent partners in a non-service business that owns no depreciable property. The net income of the business is $600,000, of which $300,000 is distributed to the partners in the form of guaranteed payments. Paul and Al both have income in excess of $213,300 so the W-2/unadjusted basis limitation applies in full. The business has no depreciable property, but pays $400,000 in wages to its employees. The total section 199A deduction, split evenly between the partners is the lesser of:

(1) 20 percent of QBI ($60,000);

OR

(2) the greater of 50 percent of W-2 wages ($200,000) or unadjusted basis ($100,000).

Since 20 percent of QBI ($60,000) is less than the partners' W-2 wage/unadjusted basis limitation amount ($200,000), their section 199A deduction could be augmented by increasing QBI.

Suppose that Paul and Al each reduces his guaranteed payment by $100,000. This would increase total QBI by $200,000 to $500,000. The amount of the QBI deduction would be the lesser of:

(1) 20 percent of QBI ($100,000);

OR

(2) the greater of 50 percent of W-2 wages ($200,000) or unadjusted basis ($100,000).

This would increase the brothers total section 199A deduction from $60,000 to $100,000.

Business income could also be increased by purchasing leased equipment and real estate. This would also increase the unadjusted basis component of the W-2/unadjusted basis limitation.

Planning for Marital Status

Getting married could either improve the tax consequences under Code section 199A or make them worse.

Example 41. Dawn is a single doctor making $282,000 per year. Her boyfriend, Sam, makes $52,000 per year as a teacher. Neither Dawn nor Sam qualifies for any section 199A deduction, Dawn because she works in an SSTB and Sam because he is an employee. Both of them claim a $12,000 standard deduction. If they get married, their taxable income will be $310,000 ($334,000 – $24,000 standard deduction). Because their income is below the $326,600 threshold amount, they will get a deduction for the full amount of their QBI (.2 × $282,000 = $56,400).

Example 42. Larry and his girlfriend, Robin, are both consultants. Larry's annual pay is $500,000/year and Robin's annual pay is $150,000. Larry currently receives no deduction under section 199A because his income exceeds the $213,300 threshold amount. On the other hand, Dawn receives the full 20 percent QBI deduction because her income is below $163,300. This deduction will be $30,000 (.2 × $150,000). If they get married and file joint returns, their income will be $650,000. Because this amount exceeds $426,600, they would receive no section 199A deduction. It appears, however, that Robin could retain her deduction if the spouses filed separately. The threshold amount for the phase-out of the deduction is $163,300 for all taxpayers other than married taxpayers filing jointly,[120] so it appears that Robin could still get $30,000 deduction if she filed a separate return.

Promoting Partnership Employees to Partner Status

Partners can qualify for the section 199A deduction, but employees of the partnership cannot. In a close case, this might tip the scales in favor of promoting a given employee.[121]

CHOICE OF ENTITY DECISION

The enactment of Code section 199A may cause taxpayers to re-evaluate the choice of entity decisions: (1) the choice between a C corporation and a pass-through entity, and (2) the choice among the various types of pass-through entities (sole proprietorships, partnerships, LLCs and S corporations).

Choice of Entity—C Corporation vs. Pass-Through Entity

Historically, pass-through entities generally had more favorable tax consequences for closely-held businesses than C corporations. The top initial tax rates on operating income were similar: 35 percent for corporations and 39.6 percent for pass-through entities.

However, when the income was distributed to owners or the business was sold, there was a second level of tax for C corporations but not for pass-through entities. Dividends were generally subject to a second level of tax at 23.8 percent. This was the 20 percent capital gains rate on qualified dividends[122] plus an additional 3.8 percent net investment income tax (NIIT).[123] The same rate applied to sales of the C corporation stock.[124] This brought the effective tax rate on C corporation income up to 50.47 percent [(.35) + (.65 × .238) = .35 + .1547 = 50.47%].

By contrast, distributions from S corporations are tax-free to shareholders unless the distribution exceeds the shareholder's basis in the stock[125] or the S corporation is a former C corporation and the distribution exceeds the S corporation's accumulated adjustment account (AAA).[126] Moreover, S corporation shareholders increase the basis of their stock by their share of corporate income, in effect eliminating the second level of tax when the stock is sold.[127] Thus, the difference in rates between C corporations and pass-through entities was generally 10.87 percentage points for taxpayers in the highest tax bracket (50.47% - 39.6%).

There are several reasons why this calculation may have overstated the tax advantage of the pass-through entities, however. First, the second level of tax may not be paid for a long time after the income is earned because it is deferred until the income is distributed as a dividend or until the stock is sold.[128] Second, there may never be a second level of tax at all. If dividends aren't paid and the shareholder dies with the stock, the heirs will receive a step-up in basis, eliminating the increase in the stock's value due to the retained earnings. Third, C corporations can deduct shareholder distributions made in the form of wages, fringe benefits and deferred compensation.[129]

Changed Tax Rates–Nominal

The most important goal of the TCJA was to lower C corporation tax rates to make American corporations more competitive. This was accomplished by reducing the corporate tax rate from 35 percent to 21 percent. If this had been the only rate change, however, it would have made C corporations far more favorable relative to S corporations, partnerships, LLCs and sole proprietorships. This presumably would have led to mass conversion of these latter businesses into C corporations. To prevent this, the TCJA made a comparable reduction in the tax rate for pass through entities by enacting the 20 percent 199A deduction. The following chart shows how the two changes left the spread between the top tax rates for C corporations and S corporations nearly the same when the second level of tax on C corporation income is taken into account.

	BEFORE TCJA	AFTER TCJA
C Corporation total tax rate	50.47%[130]	39.80%[131]
S Corporation tax rate	39.60%	29.60%[132]
Spread	10.87%	10.20%

This chart oversimplifies the difference between the C corporation and the S corporation tax rates, however. As a practical matter, the actual C corporation rate will often be significantly lower and the actual S corporation rate will often be significantly higher.

Effective C Corporation Rate

The highest initial C corporation tax rate on operating income is far lower than the S corporation rate (21 percent vs. 37 percent) and the initial C corporation rate continues to be lower than the top tax rate on pass-through income even if the owner of the pass-through entity can claim the full 20 percent Code section 199A deduction (21 percent vs. 29.6 percent). The effective C corporation rate only becomes higher when the second level of tax is taken into account. Dividends are generally taxed at 23.8 percent for affluent shareholders and the same rate applies to sales of the C corporation stock.[133] This brings the effective tax rate on C corporation income up to 39.8 percent (.21 + [.79 × .238]) following enactment of the TCJA.

But, as noted above, the second level of tax is not payable until the income is distributed as a dividend or until the stock is sold. If the shareholders don't need the income, payment of dividends could be substantially deferred, reducing the present value of the second level of tax.[134] If dividends were never paid at all, the retained income would stay in the company and increase the value of the shareholders' stock. This increase in the value of the stock wouldn't be taxed until the shares were sold, again producing tax deferral. In fact, if dividends weren't paid and the shareholders died with the stock, their heirs would receive a stepped-up basis and there would never be a second level of tax. In that case, the maximum tax rate on C corporation stock would be 21 percent compared with a top rate of tax of 29.6 percent on the income from pass-through entities.

C corporations may also be able to claim larger deductions for state and local taxes. The TCJA limits the deduction for state and local taxes to $10,000 for individuals ($5,000 for married individuals filing separately).[135] Thus, state or local taxes paid by an individual on income received from a pass-through entity are subject to the $10,000 limitation. The $10,000 limitation does not apply to C corporations so the state and local taxes paid by a C corporation are fully deductible, reducing the effective tax rate on C corporation income. In high tax states, this might be a significant advantage for C corporations relative to pass-through entities.

Effective Pass-Through Rate

In many cases, owners of pass-through entities will not receive the full benefit of the 20 percent section 199A deduction because of the phase-in and phase-out rules. Some entities will lack the W-2 wages or basis in property necessary to provide a significant benefit from the new deduction for their owners. Others will be specified service businesses. These limitations might substantially increase the rate of tax paid on pass-through income, perhaps to as high as 37 percent.

As the preceding discussion suggests, the effect of section 199A on entity choice will depend on the facts for a given business. The key variables will be the extent to which the entity could mitigate the second level of tax if it is a C corporation and the extent to which it could take advantage of the 20 percent section 199A deduction if it is a pass-through entity. Of course, all the relevant pre-TCJA choice of entity factors would also have to be taken into account.

Sunset Provision

Another factor that must be considered is that while the change in the C corporation rate is permanent, the 20 percent Code section 199A deduction is scheduled to be eliminated at the end of 2025. This may make C corporation owners reluctant to convert their business to a pass-through entity. On the other hand, some businesses might wish to start as a pass-through entity to take advantage of the deduction through 2025 and then convert to a C corporation to take advantage of the low 21 percent rate if the 199A deduction sunsets.

Finally, even if a conversion would produce somewhat better tax consequences, it might not be worth the trouble. This is particularly true if gain would have to be recognized on the conversion.[136]

Entity Choice and Qualified Small Business Stock (Code section 1202)

By converting a partnership or LLC to a C corporation, taxpayers may be able to get the low 21 percent corporate tax rate without a second level of tax. Under Code section 1202, non-corporate taxpayers can exclude 100 percent of the gain realized on the sale of qualified small business stock.[137] Qualified small business stock is stock in a C corporation that meets the following requirements.[138]

1. The stock was issued after August 10, 1993[139]
2. The issuer of the stock was a "qualified small business" when the stock was issued[140]
3. The taxpayer acquired the stock at original issue in exchange for money or property other than stock or as compensation for services to the corporation (other than as underwriter of the stock)[141]
4. The corporation met an active business requirement and was a C corporation during substantially all of the taxpayer's holding period for the stock[142]
5. The value of the corporation's aggregate gross assets does not exceed $50 million[143]

Finally, to qualify for the exclusion, the qualified small business stock must be held for at least five years.[144]

On the surface, it might appear that the conversion of a partnership or LLC to a C corporation would fail to meet the original issuance requirement because the stock would first be issued to the partnership or LLC before being distributed to the individual owners. However, under a special rule, a partner (or LLC member) who receives stock from a partnership or LLC is treated as receiving the stock at its original issuance.[145] Finally, note that only the gain accruing after the conversion date is eligible for the exclusion.[146]

The IRS provided guidance on how to convert a partnership to a corporation in Revenue Ruling 84-111.[147] The ruling allows taxpayers to use any of three methods.

One potential downside of making the conversion is that buyers generally prefer to buy assets rather than stock so they can amortize or depreciate the purchase price. As a result, they are willing to pay more for assets than for stock. While an asset sale is possible with a pass-through entity, Code section 1202 only applies to a sale of stock.

Sole Proprietorship vs. S Corporation vs. Partnership/LLC

The new Code section 199A deduction also affects the sole proprietorship, S corporation, partnership/LLC decision. It appears that S corporations may be more favorable for higher income entities while sole proprietorships and partnerships/LLCs may be more favorable for lower income entities for purposes of the Code section 199A deduction. This is illustrated in the following examples.

Example 43. Assume that a business could operate as a sole proprietorship, S corporation or partnership. The owner is a married taxpayer filing jointly with no other taxable income. His share of operating income is $800,000 and, in the case of an S corporation or partnership, he receives $200,000 as W-2 wages or as a guaranteed payment. None of the entities pays any wages to non-owner employees or has any depreciable property. The following chart shows that with relatively high income (above the applicable W-2/unadjusted basis threshold amount), the S corporation is more favorable than the sole proprietorship or partnership because of its ability to pay W-2 wages.

	Sole Proprietorship	S Corp	Partnership
Business income	$800,000	$800,000	$800,000
W-2 wages	N/A[148]	$200,000	N/A[149]
Guaranteed payments	N/A	N/A	$200,000
Net income	$800,000	$600,000	$600,000
QBI	$800,000	$600,000	$600,000
Tentative deduction	$160,000	$120,000	$120,000
50% of W-2 wages	$0	$100,000	$0
Final 199A deduction	$0	$100,000	$0

Example 44. Assume the same facts as in Example 43, except that the business has only $250,000 of operating income. The relative tax benefits of the different entities are now reversed. The payment of W-2 wages becomes a disadvantage for the S corporation because it reduces QBI without producing any offsetting benefit. There is no advantage to paying the W-2 wages because the W-2/unadjusted basis limitation does not begin to apply until taxable income reaches $326,600 for married taxpayers filing jointly. Thus, the QBI deduction for the S corporation is reduced by 20 percent of the $100,000 paid in wages and there is no corresponding reduction for the other entities, giving the sole proprietorship or partnership a QBI deduction $20,000 greater than the QBI deduction for the S corporation.

	Sole Proprietorship	S Corp	Partnership
Business income	$250,000	$250,000	$250,000
W-2 wages	N/A	$100,000[150]	N/A
Guaranteed payments	N/A	N/A	$0[151]
Net income	$250,000	$150,000	$250,000
QBI	$250,000	$150,000	$250,000
Tentative deduction	$50,000	$30,000	$50,000
50% of W-2 wages	N/A	N/A	N/A
Final deduction	$50,000	$30,000	$50,000

The best choice of entity decision will vary depending on a number of variables. Thus, extensive modeling will be necessary to determine the best option based on the client's particular fact situation.[152]

Figure 5.1

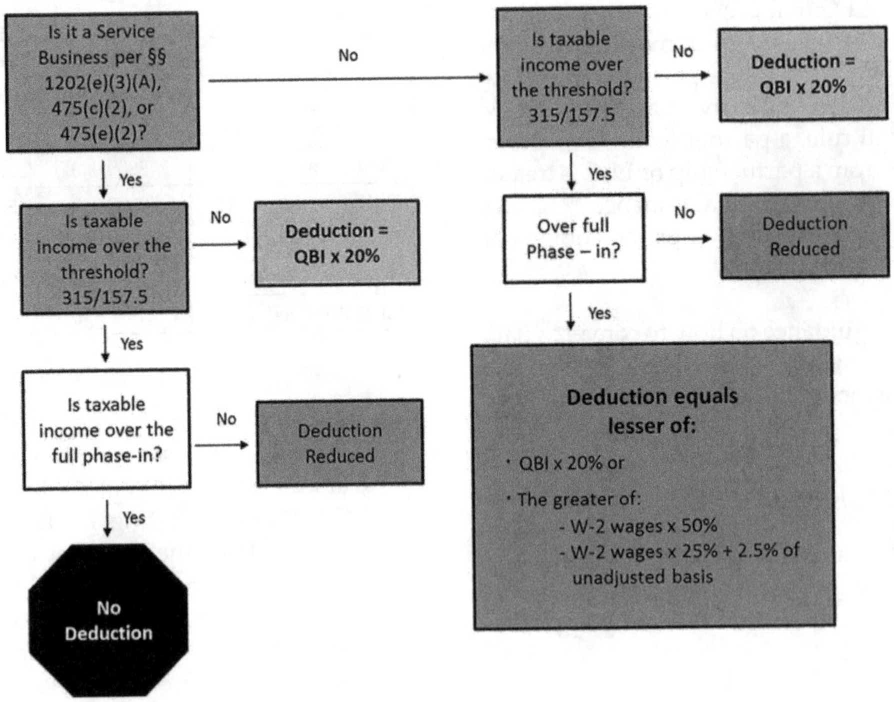

CHAPTER ENDNOTES

1. This chapter is excerpted from the *Qualified Business Income Deduction* book by Bob Keebler and Peter Melcher, available online through Leimberg Information Services (LISI) at https://leimbergservices.com/wdev/bkbooks.cfm.
2. Includes single member LLCs and any other LLC that does not elect to be taxed as a corporation.
3. A REIT is a company that invests in property or property loans and sells shares in those investments in a manner similar to mutual funds. They must pass on to shareholders at least 90% of their income.
4. I.R.C. § 199A(f).
5. I.R.C. § 199A(a).
6. I.R.C. §199A(f)(3).
7. New I.R.C. § 62(a), as added, by Act Sec. 11011(b).
8. I.R.C. §section 62(a) and 63(b).
9. I.R.C. § 199A(a).
10. Capital gains aren't included because they are already subject to a reduced rate of tax.
11. I.R.C. § 199A(b).
12. Note that personal exemptions were eliminated by the TCJA.
13. Note that the REIT and QPTP portion of combined QBI is not subject to this limitation. Combined QBI is still subject to the 20 percent of taxable income limitation, however.
14. I.R.C. § 199A(b).
15. I.R.C. § 199A(b)(3).
16. Note that 25 percent of W-2 wages + 2.5 percent of unadjusted basis will exceed 50% of wages whenever the unadjusted basis of qualified property exceeds 10 times W-2 wages. Here, unadjusted basis ($1,000,000) is more than 10 × wages (10 × 80,000 = $800,000), so 2.5 percent of unadjusted basis will be greater than 50% of wages.
17. I.R.C. § 199A(d)(2).
18. I.R.C. § 199A(d)(2)(A) and 1202(e)(3)(A). Note that under I.R.C. § 1202(e)(3)(A), the reputation or skill category applies only to employees and not to owners. Thus, I.R.C. § 199A expands the scope of this category.
19. I.R.C. § 199A(d)(2)(B); 475(c)(2); 475(e)(2). The definition of an SSTB is discussed in further detail in Chapter 2 below.
20. These threshold amounts will be indexed for inflation in taxable years beginning after 2018 (IRC section 199A(e)(2)(B)).
21. I.R.C. § 199A(c)(1)(A).
22. Joint Conference Committee Explanation.
23. I.R.C. § 199A(c)(3)(A)(i). Qualification is determined by substituting "qualified trade or business" (within the meaning of section 199A) for "non-resident alien individual" or a foreign corporation every place it appears.
24. I.R.C. § 199A(c)(1).
25. I.R.C. § 199A(c)(4)(A).
26. I.R.C. § 199A(c)(4)(B).
27. I.R.C. § 199A(c)(3)(C).
28. I.R.C. § 199A(c)(3)(B)(i).
29. I.R.C. § 199A(c)(3)(B)(ii).

30. I.R.C. § 199A(c)(3)(B)(iii). This would include, for example, bank accounts.
31. I.R.C. § 199A(c)(3)(B)(iv) and I.R.C. § 199A(c)(3)(B)(v).
32. I.R.C. § 199A(c)(3)(B)(vi).
33. I.R.C. § 199A(c)(3)(vii).
34. I.R.C. § 199A(f)(1)(C).
35. I.R.C. § 1231(b)(1).
36. I.R.C. § 1231(b)(1)(A).
37. I.R.C. § 1231(b)(1)(B).
38. I.R.C. § 1231(b)(1)(C).
39. I.R.C. §1231(b)(3).
40. I.R.C. § 1231(b)(4).
41. I.R.C. § 1221(a)(2).
42. I.R.C. § 1231(a)(1).
43. See, for example, *Radke*, 895 F.2d 1196 (7th Cir. 1990); *Grey*, 119 TC 121 (2002), aff'd 93 AFTR 2nd 2004-1626 (3rd Cir. 2004).
44. This would be consistent with Congress's intention in enacting I.R.C. § 199A of not favoring one type of entity over others.
45. I.R.C. § 704(e)(2).
46. I.R.C. § 199A(d).
47. *Higgins v. Commissioner*, 312 U.S. 212 (1941).
48. *Commissioner v. Groetzinger*, 480 US 23 (1987).
49. *Id.*
50. *Commissioner v. Groetzinger*, 480 US 23 (1987).
51. *Id.* For example, gambling could be a trade or business.
52. Fegan *v. Commissioner*, 71 T.C. 791, 814 (1979); *Elek v. Commissioner*, 30 T.C. 731 (1958), acq. 1958-2 C.B. 5; *Lagreide v. Commissioner*, 23 T.C. 508 (1954); *Hazard v. Commissioner*, 7 T.C. 372 (1946), acq. 1946-2 C.B.
53. The IRS recently reiterated this point in the preamble to final regulations for I.R.C. § 1411.
54. *Alvary v. United States*, 302 F.2d 790 (2d Cir. 1962); (*Curphey v. Commissioner*, 73 T.C. 766 (1980)). *Fackler v. Commissioner*, 133 F.2d 509 (6th Cir. 1943), affg. 45 B.T.A. 708 (1941); *Bauer v. United States*, 144 Ct. Cl. 308, (1958); (*Curphey v. Commissioner*, 73 T.C. 766 (1980)).
55. *Curphey v. Commissioner*, 73 T.C. 766 (1980).
56. I.R.C. § 199A(b)(1)(A).
57. Reg. section 1.469-4. It remains to be seen what approach the IRS will take, however.
58. Reg. section 1.446-1(d).
59. I.R.C. § 199(d)(2)(A). I.R.C. § 1202 provides an exclusion on the gain of qualified small business stock, which is generally stock in a corporation that operates a business other than a service business. Thus, the statute defines what is meant by a service business.
60. I.R.C. § 199A(d)(2)(B).
61. It is not clear whether engineering and architecture are automatically excluded from the definition of specified service business or if they could be included as trades or businesses in which the principal asset of the trade or business is the reputation or skill of one of its employees. In some cases, it appears that the skill or reputation of an owner or employee would clearly be the principal assets of a business (e.g., an architecture business owned by Frank Lloyd Wright).
62. I.R.C. § 199(d)(2)(A).
63. Some businesses would clearly fall into this category, like self-employed artists, sculptors or authors. At the other extreme would be a business that produces commodity type products that are very basic and undifferentiated.
64. I.R.C. § 1202(e)(3)(B).
65. I.R.C. § 1202(e)(3)(C).
66. I.R.C. § 1202(e)(3)(D). I.R.C. § 613 applies to percentage depletion on mines and certain other natural deposits. IRC section 613A applies to percentage depletion on oil and gas.
67. For qualified small business stock purchased before February 18, 2009, the I.R.C. § 1202 gain exclusion was only 50 percent and the remaining portion was taxed at capital gains rates. Moreover, a portion of the excluded gain was an unfavorable adjustment in computing the AMT. The exclusion rate was briefly increased to 75 percent and then to 100% in 2010.
68. In PLR 201717010, the IRS ruled that a company providing laboratory reports to health care professionals was a qualified small business under I.R.C. § 1202. In PLR 201436001, the IRS ruled that a pharmaceutical company that specialized in commercialization of experimental drugs was engaged in a qualified trade or business under I.R.C. § 1202 despite the proximity of its business activities to the field of health. These activities included (1) research on drug formulation effectiveness, (2) pre-commercial testing procedures such as clinical testing, and (3) manufacturing of drugs. In addition, the company worked with clients to solve problems in the pharmaceutical industry, such as developing successful drug manufacturing processes.
69. I.R.C. § 448(d)(2)(A).
70. I.R.C. § 199A.
71. I.R.C. § 199A(b)(4)(A).
72. I.R.C. § 199A(b)(4)(B).
73. 402(g)(3).
74. I.R.C. § 3401.
75. Revenue Ruling 69-184.
76. PEOs are used by small businesses to outsource employee management functions.
77. This was the result under repealed I.R.C. § 199, which used a similar definition of W-2 wages. *U.S. v. Total Employment Co Inc*, 93 AFTR 2d 2004-1036 (DC FL 2004; Chief Counsel Advice 200415008; PLR 20134702; *U.S. v. Garami, Imre*, 95-2 USTC ¶50520 (DC FL 1995)).
78. Revenue Ruling 87-41. See also Rev. Proc. 2006-22.
79. I.R.C. § 199A(b)(6)(A).
80. I.R.C. § 199A.
81. I.R.C. § 199A(b)(6). This may have to be clarified in IRS guidance.
82. I.R.C. § 199A(f)(1)(A)(iii).
83. I.R.C. § 199(h)(1). I.R.C. § 179 allows taxpayers to elect to expense certain depreciable business assets. IRC section 179(d)(1) provides that the expensing election applies to property acquired by purchase for use in the active conduct of a trade or business. I.R.C. § 179(d)(2) then states that the term "purchase" applies to an acquisition of property only if: (1) The property is not acquired from a related party within the meaning of I.R.C. § 267(b) or 707(a), (2) the property is not acquired by one component member of a controlled group from another component member of

the same controlled group, and (3) the basis of the property in the hands of the person acquiring it is not determined in whole or in part by reference to the adjusted basis in the hands of the person from whom it was acquired or under I.R.C. § 1014 (basis of property received from a decedent).

84. I.R.C. § 199(h)(2).
85. Joint Explanatory Statement of the Conference Committee.
86. This would generally be the taxpayer's original cost basis under I.R.C. § 1011(a).
87. I.R.C. § 199A(e)(1).
88. I.R.C. § 199A(e)(3).
89. I.R.C. § 199A(e)(5).
90. I.R.C. § 199A(f)(1).
91. I.R.C. § 199A(f)(2).
92. I.R.C. § 1377(a)(1).
93. Reg. section 1.1377-1(c), Example 1.
94. The Domestic Production Activities Deduction, or DPAD.
95. I.R.C. § 199(b) and Reg. section 1.199-5(b).
96. Joint Explanatory Statement of the Committee of Conference at page 48. See also, I.R.C. § 199A stating that the deduction applies to all taxpayers other than C corporations and I.R.C. § 199(A)(f)(1)(B), providing a reference to I.R.C. § 199(f)(1)(B) for rules for apportioning W-2 wages and unadjusted basis to trusts and estates.
97. I.R.C. § 55.
98. I.R.C. § 199(f)(2).
99. I.R.C. § 199A(c)(2).
100. Joint Conference Committee Explanation.
101. I.R.C. § 172(d)(8).
102. I.R.C. § 1367(a)(1)(A).
103. I.R.C. § 1368(b)(2).
104. I.R.C. § 6662(d)(1)(A).
105. New I.R.C. § 6662(d)(1)(C).
106. I.R.C. § 6662(d)(2).
107. I.R.C. § 6662(d)(2)(B). A taxpayer is generally considered to have a reasonable basis for a position if the chance of prevailing on the merits is at least 20 percent. Substantial authority is defined as a probability of success that is more than a reasonable basis but less than more likely than not. Thus, it is generally thought of as a probability of success of approximately 35 percent [(.2 + .5)/2)].
108. The substantial basis/reasonable basis + disclosure reduction does not apply to any item attributable to a tax shelter (I.R.C. § 6662(d)(2)(C)).
109. Reg. section 1.6662-4(b)(6).
110. Request for Immediate Guidance Regarding Section 199A, February 21, 2018, section 14.
111. A partnership can't pay W-2 wages to a partner (Revenue Ruling 69-184).
112. Recall that wages don't count as QBI, reducing QBI to $50,000.
113. Let X = optimal wage payment. Assume income of $100,000.
    - .5X = .2($100,000 -X)
    - .5X = $20,000 -.2x
    - X = $40,000 -.4X
    - 1.4X = $40,000
    - X = $40,000/1.4 = $28,571.40
114. For example, if Melissa is paid $40,000, the deduction would be $12,000 (the lesser of .2 × $60,000 QBI = $12,000 or .5 × $40,000 = $20,000). If Melissa was paid $20,000, the deduction would be $10,000 (the lesser of .2 × $80,000 QBI = $16,000 or .5 × $20,000 = $10,000).
115. This is done to prevent avoidance of self-employment tax.
116. See the section later in this Chapter on the tradeoffs between employee status and independent contractor status.
117. With the caveat that wages paid to S corporation owners reduce the section 199A deduction when wage payments exceed 2/7 of QBI.
118. I.R.C. § 199A(d)(1)(B).
119. IRS Topic #762.
120. I.R.C. § 199(e)(2)(A).
121. Of course many other factors would be involved in making the decision.
122. I.R.C. § 1(h)(11)(A). Qualified dividend income means dividends received during the tax year from domestic corporations and qualified foreign corporations.
123. See I.R.C. § 1411.
124. H. Rep. No. 108-94 (P.L. 108-27) p. 31.
125. I.R.C. § 1368(b). The excess amount is treated as a dividend to the extent of earnings and profits.
126. I.R.C. section 1368(c) and 1368(e).
127. I.R.C. § 1367(a)(1).
128. Note that many closely-held C corporations never pay dividends.
129. The IRS may try to re-characterize these payments as dividends under I.R.C. § 316.
130. 35 percent corporate level tax + 28 percent tax at individual level on qualified dividends, corporate liquidation or sale of the stock by the shareholder. Then, .35 + (.238 × .65) = .5047 = 50.47%.
131. .21 + (.238 × .79) = .398 = 39.8%.
132. 37% top rate × .8 = 29.6%.
133. H. Rep. No. 108-94 (P.L. 108-27) p. 31.
134. The benefit of this tax deferral would be that the shareholder could obtain a return on the money that would otherwise be used to pay the tax for the period during which the tax was deferred.
135. New I.R.C. § 164(b)(6)(B).
136. For example, when a C corporation is converted into an LLC, the transaction is treated as a liquidation of the corporation under I.R.C. §section 336 and 331, followed by a liquidating distribution of the net proceeds to the shareholders. I.R.C. § 336 provides that gain or loss is recognized on a liquidating distribution of property as if the property was sold to the distributee at its fair market value.
137. I.R.C. § 1202(a). Note that this 100% exclusion applied only to qualified small business stock acquired after September 27, 2010. For stock acquired between February 17, 2009 and before September 28, 2010, the exclusion rate is 75%. For stock acquired before February 17, 2009, the exclusion rate is 50 percent.
138. I.R.C. § 1202(c)(1).
139. I.R.C. § 1202(c)(1).
140. I.R.C. § 1202(c)(1)(A).

141. I.R.C. § 1202(c)(1)(B).
142. I.R.C. § 1202(c)(2)(A).
143. I.R.C. § 1202(d)(1)(A).
144. I.R.C. § 1202(a)(1). When a taxpayer receives stock in an I.R.C. § 351 exchange, the taxpayer's holding period in the stock generally includes the holding period for the property exchanged for the stock (I.R.C. § 1223(1)). Notwithstanding this general rule, however, the five-year holding period requirement for the I.R.C. § 1202 gain exclusion begins on the date of incorporation (I.R.C. § 1202(i)(1)(A)). Thus, taxpayers must wait at least five years after the date of the conversion before selling the stock.
145. I.R.C. §section 1202(g) and 1202(h).
146. I.R.C. § 1202(i)(1)(B).
147. 1984-2 C.B. 88.
148. A sole proprietorship can't pay W-2 wages to its owner.
149. A partnership can't pay W-2 wages to partners (PLR 69-184).
150. An S corporation must pay reasonable compensation to its shareholders. See, for example, *Radke*, 895 F.2d 1196 (7th Cir. 1990); *Grey*, 119 TC 121 (2002), aff'd 93 AFTR 2nd 2004-1626 (3rd Cir. 2004).
151. A partnership has no obligation to make guaranteed payments.
152. Concept and charts adapted from Nitti, T., *Tax Geek Tuesday: Making Sense of the New 20% Qualified Business Income Deduction*, *Forbes*, December 26, 2017.

BUSINESS AND NONBUSINESS LOSSES

CHAPTER 6

INTRODUCTION

A loss is a reduction in the value of property that is owned by a taxpayer. The Code provides that certain types of losses are deductible against taxable income. Like all deductions, loss deductions can only be taken if a Code section specifically allows for it.[1] Deductions that arise from losses can be related to a taxpayer's business or trade, or they can be personal losses that affect the value of a taxpayer's property. Business losses and personal losses are treated differently by the Code, and some losses that seem quite similar may result in very different deductions depending on the specific circumstances of the loss.

WHAT KINDS OF BUSINESS LOSSES CAN BE DEDUCTED?

Business losses can occur in a variety of circumstances. The sale of property at a price that does not recover the owner's investment can result in a loss. Businesses can sustain losses from their operations or find that debt that is owed to them has become uncollectable. And like individuals, businesses can suffer unexpected casualty losses from theft and natural disasters. While unfortunate, all of these types of losses can be taken as deductions that reduce the amount of tax owed by the taxpayer.

Loss from a Sale of Property

A loss can occur when a taxpayer sells or exchanges property for an amount less than the basis in such property. Basis (or cost) is an accounting concept that represents a taxpayer's after-tax investment in the acquired property.[2] In a business context, basis is often adjusted over time for various factors (such as depreciation) that are beyond the scope of this chapter.

Basis is important because it is half of the equation that determines whether a property owner realizes a gain or loss from a sale, which may then result in a corresponding item of income or deduction. If a property sells for less than its basis, the seller may be entitled to a deduction for the loss (the difference between the basis and the sale price) under Code section 165.

Example: Several years ago, Ira Investor purchased raw land as an investment for $100,000. After the fair market value of the land decreases to $80,000, Ira sells the land for that amount to Debby Developer. Because Ira recovers only $80,000 of his initial $100,000 original cost, he realizes a $20,000 loss on that investment[3] that is potentially deductible pursuant to section 165.

NET OPERATING LOSS

The net operating loss deduction (NOL) is one of the most favorable deductions available to a taxpayer engaged in a trade or business. In a given tax year, an NOL occurs when business deductions exceed business income. Under Code section 172, the deduction from this type of loss may be taken as a deduction for a prior tax year (carried back) or a subsequent tax year (carried forward). The NOL is only available for net business losses—losses attributable to personal or investment deductions can never be part of an NOL.

The NOL deduction essentially "permit[s] a taxpayer to set off its lean years against its lush years, and to strike something like an average taxable income computed over a period longer than one year."[4] Stated differently, carrying an NOL forward or back provides the taxpayer with an opportunity to take advantage of what was otherwise—in the year in which it was generated—a useless deduction.

In order to have an NOL, a taxpayer with business income and deductions must have negative taxable income. Once the negative taxable income is calculated, all net nonbusiness capital loss and net nonbusiness ordinary loss (the extent to which nonbusiness deductions exceed nonbusiness income) are subtracted from that amount. If taxable income is still negative after making those adjustments, the amount of negative taxable income is the NOL.

Using NOL to Reduce Tax in Other Years

If a taxpayer has an unused portion of an NOL deduction, he or she may apply that unused portion to other tax years. The default rule for applying the NOL is first to carry it back to the second year preceding the NOL year and then to the tax year immediately preceding the NOL year. Thereafter, any remaining NOL is carried forward to subsequent years following the NOL year until it is used up.[5]

Because the NOL is comprised exclusively of business expenses, it is considered an above-the-line deduction.[6] An above-the-line deduction is subtracted from gross income before calculating adjusted gross income, and is generally more favorable to the taxpayer than a below-the-line deduction. (See Chapter 7 for a more detailed discussion of the differences between the two types of deductions.)

Example: This year, Barry, a self-employed engineer reporting income and deductions on Schedule C had gross fees of $100,000 and business expenses of $150,000. Other than his engineering fees, Barry had no other income. The entire $150,000 of business expenses are above-the-line deductions,[7] leaving Barry with no taxable income for this year and an unused $50,000 NOL. This unused amount of the deduction can be carried forward or back to other tax years and used as an above-the-line deduction against business income in those years.

A decision to carry an NOL back to prior years can be complex and often has more significant consequences than simply reducing the taxpayer's income for that year. Many types of credits and deductions are subject to income-based limitations and reductions. Carrying back unused NOL to reduce income in past years' returns can have significant impacts on those limitations.

For example, up to 85 percent of the amount of a taxpayer's social security payments is potentially taxable depending on the taxpayer's total adjusted gross income. If a carried-back NOL deduction reduces that income on an amended return, the amount of taxable social security payments would also be reduced.

As mentioned above, the default rule for deducting an NOL is to carry it back two years, then one. Thereafter, any remaining unused NOL is carried forward in successive years until it is used up. However, Code section 172(b)(3) allows the taxpayer to waive the carry back period and simply carried the NOL forward for up to twenty years. Figure 6.1 sets forth the pros and the cons for electing or not electing to waive the NOL carry-back.

Figure 6.1

REASONS TO CARRY BACK NOL	REASONS TO NOT CARRY BACK NOL
• Immediate refund (the amended returns can be filed along with the current year's return) • Large tax liability in prior two years • Expectation of lower income and/or tax rates in future years	• Lack of tax liability in prior tax years • State does not allow NOL carry-back to reduce state income tax • Expectation of higher future income and/or tax rates • Potential audit issues in prior two years

IMPACT OF THE 2017 TAX REFORM ACT ON CORPORATIONS

The 2017 Tax Reform Act impacts corporate taxpayers in several important ways, including changes in the NOL carry forward/carryback rules and the deduction for interest on indebtedness.

NOL Carry Forward and Carry Back Rules

Under the 2017 Tax Act, net operating loss (NOL) deductions for corporations are limited to 80 percent of taxable income.[8] Further, amounts carried into other years must be adjusted to account for the limitation on losses that applies to tax years beginning after December 31, 2017. Property and casualty insurance companies are excluded from this limitation.[9]

The provisions providing for two-year NOL carrybacks and special carrybacks are eliminated under tax reform (with the exception of the trade or business of farming, where a two-year carryback is permitted).[10] A two-year carryback and twenty-year carryforward for property and casualty insurance companies is permitted. Unused NOLs may be carried forward indefinitely.[11]

Interest on Indebtedness

Under prior law, business owners were typically permitted to deduct interest expenses incurred in carrying on a trade or business (subject to limitations).[12] The 2017 Tax Act generally limits the interest expense deduction to the sum of:

- business interest income;
- 30 percent of the business' adjusted taxable income; and
- floor plan financing interest (see below).[13]

Businesses with average annual gross receipts of $25 million or less for the three-taxable year period that ends with the previous tax year are exempt from this new limitation (i.e., businesses that meet the gross receipts test of IRC Section 448(c)).[14]

Generally, the limit applies at the taxpayer level, but in the case of a group of affiliated corporations that file a consolidated return, it applies at the consolidated tax return filing level.

"Business interest" generally excludes investment interest. It includes any interest paid or accrued on indebtedness properly allocable to carrying on a trade or business. "Business interest income" means the amount of interest that is included in the taxpayer's gross income for the tax year that is properly allocable to carrying on a trade or business.

"Adjusted taxable income" means taxable income computed without regard to:

1. items of income, gain, deduction or loss not allocable to carrying on a trade or business;
2. business interest or business interest income;
3. any net operating loss deduction (NOL);
4. the deduction for pass-through income under Section 199A; or
5. for years before 2022, any deduction for depreciation, amortization or depletion.[15]

For the purpose of the business interest deduction, adjusted taxable income is computed without regard for the deductions that are allowed for depreciation, amortization or depletion for tax years beginning after December 31, 2017 and before January 1, 2022.

"Floor plan financing interest" is interest paid or accrued on floor plan financing indebtedness, which is indebtedness incurred to finance the purchase of motor vehicles held for sale or lease to retail customers (and secured by the inventory that is acquired).[16]

As a result of these rules, business interest income and floor plan financing interest are fully deductible, with the limitation applying to 30 percent of the business' adjusted taxable income.

Unused interest expense deductions may be carried forward indefinitely.[17]

IMPACT OF THE 2017 TAX REFORM ACT ON NONCORPORATE TAXPAYERS

The 2017 Tax Reform Act also impacted noncorporate taxpayers in several ways, including new rules on excess business losses, built-in losses of a partnership, and the basis limitation on the deductibility of a partner's losses.

Excess Business Losses

Under the 2017 Tax Act, excess business losses (see below) of a non-corporate taxpayer are not allowed for the taxable year. These losses are carried forward and treated as part of the taxpayer's net operating loss ("NOL") carryforward in subsequent taxable years.[18]

NOL carryovers generally are allowed for a taxable year up to the lesser of the carryover amount or 90 percent (80 percent for taxable years beginning after December 31, 2022) of taxable income determined without regard to the deduction for NOLs.

An "excess business loss" is the excess of aggregate deductions of the taxpayer attributable to trades or businesses of the taxpayer (determined without regard to the limitation of the provision), over the sum of aggregate gross income or gain of the taxpayer plus a threshold amount. The annual threshold amount is $250,000 (or twice the otherwise applicable threshold amount for married taxpayers filing a joint return). This amount is indexed for inflation.[19]

In the case of a pass-through entity (such as a partnership or S corporation), these rules apply at the partner or shareholder level. Each partner's distributive share and each S corporation shareholder's pro rata share of items of income, gain, deduction, or loss of the partnership or S corporation are taken into account in applying the limitation for the taxable year of the partner or S corporation shareholder.[20] These rules apply after the application of the passive loss rules.[21]

These provisions are effective for tax years beginning after December 31, 2017 and before January 1, 2026. Further, for taxable years beginning after December 31, 2017 and before January 1, 2026, the limitation relating to excess farm losses does not apply.

Substantial Built-in Loss of a Partnership

Generally, a partnership must adjust the basis of partnership property following a transfer of a partnership interest if the partnership has suffered a substantial built-in loss immediately following the transfer. Under prior law, a substantial built-in loss existed if the adjusted basis in the partnership's property exceeded the fair market value of the property by more than $250,000.

The 2017 Tax Act expanded the definition of substantial built-in loss to include situations where, immediately after the transfer, the transferee would be allocated a net loss of more than $250,000 upon a hypothetical disposition by the partnership of all the partnership's assets in a taxable transaction for cash equal to the fair market value of the assets.[22]

Basis Limitation on a Partner's Losses

For tax years beginning after 2017, the basis limitation on the deductibility of a partner's losses applies to a partner's distributive share of charitable contributions and foreign taxes. Under prior law, those items were exempt from the limitation. This does not apply to the excess of fair market value over adjusted basis on charitable contributions of appreciated property.[23]

BAD BUSINESS DEBTS

In the normal course of operating a business, it is not uncommon for a taxpayer to loan out funds or extend credit to a third party. If such a debt becomes wholly or partially worthless, the taxpayer may be entitled to a business bad debt deduction.[24] Moreover, because a business bad debt deduction is treated as an ordinary business deduction[25] rather than a capital loss, it is an above-the-line deduction with no limitation of its deductibility.

In order for a bad debt to qualify as a business loss, it must meet three conditions:

First, it must be related to the taxpayer's business. This can happen in one of two ways: (1) the debt was made or acquired in the course of the business, or (2) the loss from the debt becoming worthless was incurred in the course of the taxpayer's business.[26]

Example: In 2017, Mary Mover, a sole proprietor, loaned a vendor $10,000 to pay for the delivery of a truck she had purchased as an addition to her moving business fleet. In 2019, Mary sold the moving business to Frederick Express but retained the debt owed by the vendor. In 2020, after Mary was no longer engaged in the moving business, the debt became worthless. Even though Mary was not then engaged in the moving business, Mary would be entitled to a full $10,000 ordinary business bad deduction because it was incurred by her at a time when she was so engaged.[27]

Second, the money that was to be received had the debt been paid must be "after-tax dollars."[28] In the context of bad business debts, this requirement is conceptually identical to cost basis. The deduction may only be taken for the value of the after-tax assets that were actually transferred to the borrower when the loan was made. For instance, the portion of uncollectable accounts receivable that are attributable to "lost profit' would not qualify for the business bad debt deduction.[29]

Example: Connie Contractor (a cash method taxpayer) installed windows on a restaurant owned by Barry Businessman. The total amount billed to Barry was $15,000. Of that amount, Connie's profit would have been $2,500. After the installation, Barry closes the restaurant and files for bankruptcy and the entire $15,000 bill is discharged. Because $2,500 of the loan represented pre-tax lost profit (i.e. Connie has no basis in that amount), the business bad debt deduction for Barry's account is only $12,500.

Third, in order to qualify for the bad business debt deduction, the debt must be worthless or partially worthless. Unfortunately, the Code does not define "worthless." Although the regulations use the term "evidence of worthlessness," the only specific example of worthlessness provided is bankruptcy.[30] More generally, the regulations state that a determination of worthlessness is based on circumstances indicating that a debt is worthless and uncollectable. Pursuing a legal collection action is not required as a prerequisite for the deduction if such action would be unlikely to satisfy the debt.[31] Examples of "evidence of worthlessness" include:

- The debtor goes out of business.
- The debtor cannot be located.
- The debtor dies and leaves an insolvent estate.
- The debtor goes into receivership.
- The taxpayer determines that a monetary judgment is non-collectable.

Loans to a Taxpayer's Own Corporation

In some instances, a taxpayer may loan money to a corporation in which the taxpayer is both a shareholder and an employee. In that case, the determination of whether the debt qualifies as a business debt depends on whether the dominant motivation for the loan was to protect the taxpayer's investment as a shareholder, or to protect his job as an employee.[32] If the purpose was to protect the investment, then he is participating as a shareholder, and the debt is not a business debt. If taxpayer is trying to protect his job, it is a business debt. In determining the taxpayer's dominant motivation, three factors are considered:

1. The size of the taxpayer's investment in the corporation.
2. The size of the taxpayer's salary as an employee.
3. The other sources of income available to the taxpayer at the time of the loan.

A large investment and ample other sources of income would likely indicate that the taxpayer's dominant motivation for the loan was protection of an investment rather than preservation of a job. As discussed in more detail below, a bad debt that does not qualify as a business bad debt may be deductible as a "nonbusiness bad debt." However, a nonbusiness bad debt is deducted as a short-term capital loss, which is much less favorable to the taxpayer.

Example: Barry Businessman invested $1,000,000 in a corporation that owns a hotel. Many key employees of the hotel earn more than $100,000. On the other hand, although included in the payroll, Barry rarely takes a paycheck. Additionally, Barry has always maintained ample personal financial resources. In 2015, Barry loaned the hotel $100,000. In 2020, due to adverse economic circumstances, the corporation filed for Chapter 7 bankruptcy in which all of its debts—including Barry's loan—were discharged. Based on the three factors listed above, it is clear that Barry's dominant motivation in making the loan was to protect his investment in the corporation. His investment in the corporation was significant when compared to his wages, and at the time of the loan Barry had ample financial resources. Thus, Barry's dominant motivation was to protect his investment as a shareholder and the worthless bad debt would not qualify for the business bad debt deduction.

Guarantors

In a direct loan, the taxpayer transfers available assets to the debtor, and the debtor is supposed to repay the taxpayer. Under certain circumstances, rather than loaning money directly, the taxpayer will be the guarantor of a debt. This means that the taxpayer guarantees that a loan made by a third party to the debtor will be repaid. If the debtor is unable to pay, the taxpayer, as guarantor of the loan, can be legally compelled to pay the debt. If a guarantor is forced to pay the loan (and is not reimbursed by the original debtor), he or she may be entitled to a business bad debt deduction.

The rules governing whether a worthless debt is a business bad debt are similar to rules that govern loans made to a taxpayer's own corporation. If the guaranty arose out of the guarantor's *business* interest, the underlying debt is considered a business debt. On the other hand, if the guarantor's dominant motivation was to protect his *investment* in the debtor entity, or was a transaction entered into for profit (independent of his trade or business), the underlying debt would not be a business debt.[33]

In addition to the dominant motivation test, there are three other requirements for the allowance of a guarantor business bad debt deduction:

1. The guarantor must be legally obligated to make the payment (although actual legal action against the guarantor is not required).

2. The guarantor must have entered into the guaranty agreement before the obligation became worthless.

3. The guarantor must have received reasonable consideration for entering into the agreement.[34]

"Reasonable consideration" is defined broadly, and need not be explicit or direct compensation. If the guarantor entered into the agreement in circumstances that are customary for the industry or the guarantor's position within the company, this is considered to be "reasonable consideration."

Example 1: Amy is a shareholder in a corporation that provides a telephone answering service to professionals. Amy is also the CEO of the corporation, and depends on her salary as her primary source of income. In 2014, the corporation borrows $100,000 from a bank to purchase equipment. The bank insists that Amy personally guaranty the loan. In 2020, the corporation ceases to operate and the bank compels Amy to repay the balance of the loan. Here, Amy would be entitled to a business bad debt deduction because:

- Amy's dominant motivation for the guaranty was to protect her job.
- Amy signed a legally enforceable guaranty agreement.
- Amy executed the guaranty agreement prior to the debt becoming worthless.
- Amy's consideration was the preservation of the corporation so as to maintain her salary as CEO.

Example 2: Assume the same facts as the example above, except Amy is a major shareholder in the corporation with no involvement in its operations. Since Amy's dominant motivation was to preserve her investment in the corporation, she would not be entitled to a business bad deduction with regard to the repayment of the loan.

Finally, guarantors may only take a deduction for money that they actually paid toward the guaranteed debt. If the lender agrees to let the guarantor make payments for a period that covers more than one tax year, the deduction for the bad business debt is limited in each of those years to the amount actually paid toward the guaranteed debt.

CASUALTY LOSSES

Subject to certain limitations discussed below, a casualty loss of property used in a trade or business (that is not compensated by insurance) can be taken as an ordinary deduction.[35] A "casualty loss" is damage or destruction of property from a sudden, unexpected, or unusual event, including natural disasters, theft, and vandalism.

The amount of the loss is the difference in the fair market value of the property before and after the casualty event.[36] To prevent taxpayers from enjoying a "tax windfall" from a casualty loss, Treasury Regulation section 1.165-7(b)(1) limits the loss to the lesser of:

- the decrease in value of the damaged property (the difference between the FMV of the property before and after the casualty); or
- the adjusted basis of the property before the casualty.

Additionally, if insurance coverage is available, no casualty loss is allowed for any damage that was reimbursed by insurance. Moreover, the deduction is not allowed if insurance coverage is available but the taxpayer fails to file a timely claim.[37] Finally, in the event the damaged property is "totaled," a reduction for salvage value is also required.

Example: Larry Laundry, a sole proprietor, owns and operates a dry cleaning business. As the result of a fire, a cleaning press with a fair market value of $20,000 and an adjusted basis of $10,000 was damaged. The cleaning press was unusable after the fire, but has a salvage value of $1,000. Larry's insurance covered $6,000 of his loss. Despite sustaining an economic casualty loss of $14,000, Larry's deduction would be limited to his adjusted basis of $10,000, and further reduced by his insurance payout and the salvage value of the press.

Decrease in FMV	$20,000
Adjusted basis	$10,000
Tentative deductible casualty loss (lesser of the two)	$10,000
Less insurance reimbursement	– $6,000
Less salvage value	– $1,000
Resulting casualty deduction	**$3,000**

EMPLOYEE BENEFIT EXPENSES

The 2017 Tax Act changed many of the deduction rules for entertainment and meal expenses as well as several types of employee benefits described below.

Business-related Entertainment Expenses

Under the 2017 Tax Act, the previously existing 50 percent deduction for entertainment expenses that are directly connected with a business activity is eliminated. This applies to any activity considered entertainment, recreation or amusement, including membership dues with respect to any club organized for business, pleasure, recreational or social purposes.[38]

The 50 percent deduction for meal expenses remains in effect (including meals consumed while travelling for business). The 2017 Tax Act also would provide that the 50 percent deduction for meals would be expanded to include expenses associated with providing meals through an eating facility meeting de minimis fringe benefit requirements.[39] The deduction for meals provided at the convenience of the employer expires after December 31, 2025.[40]

Qualified Transportation Benefits

The 2017 Tax Act eliminated the ability of taxpayers to exclude qualified bicycle commuting expense reimbursements from gross income and wages from December 31, 2017 to January 1, 2026. Further, employers are no longer permitted to provide these benefits on a tax-free basis.[41]

The 2017 Tax Act eliminated deductions for expenses associated with providing any qualified transportation fringe to employees, and except for ensuring employee safety, any expense incurred for providing transportation (or any payment or reimbursement) for commuting between the employee's residence and place of employment. Employees can continue to pay for mass transit and parking benefits using pre-tax dollars through employer-sponsored salary reduction programs. These rules are effective for tax years beginning after December 31, 2017.[42]

Credit for Paid Family and Medical Leave

The 2017 Tax Act created a new temporary tax credit for employers that provide paid family and medical leave to employees.[43] The credit is an amount equal to 12.5 percent of the wages that are paid to qualifying employees during a period where the employee was on family and medical leave if the employee is paid 50 percent of the normal wages that he or she would receive from the employer. The credit increases by 0.25 percentage points (but can never exceed 25 percent) for each percentage point by which the rate of payment exceeds 50 percent of wages. Only twelve weeks of family and medical leave can be taken into account for any one employee.

In order to qualify, employers must have a written policy in place to allow all qualifying full-time employees no less than two weeks of paid family and medical leave each year. Further, all part-time employees must be allowed a pro-rated amount of paid family and medical leave.[44] Any leave paid for by the state or local government is not taken into account.[45]

"Qualifying employees" are those who have been employed by the employer for one year or more and who had compensation that did not exceed 60 percent of the compensation threshold for highly compensated employees[46] in the previous year.[47]

"Family and medical leave" is as defined under Section 102(a)(1)(a)-(e) or Section 102(a)(3) of the Family and Medical Leave Act of 1993. Paid leave that is vacation leave, personal leave or other medical or sick leave does not qualify for the new tax credit.[48]

This credit is only available for tax years beginning after December 31, 2017 and before December 31, 2019, and is a part of the general business tax credit.[49] The credit is allowed against the alternative minimum tax (AMT).

Although the credit is allowed to be taken against the AMT, because of the increased AMT exemption amounts and compensation limits that apply to the credit itself, many clients will be unable to use the credit against the AMT.

Employee Achievement Awards

Generally, certain employee achievement awards granted by an employer to recognize the employee's length of service or safety achievements are not taxable to the employee and are deductible by the employer.

Under the 2017 Tax Act, certain awards are excluded from this treatment, including cash, cash equivalents, gift certificates, vacations, meals, lodging, tickets to sports or theater events, stocks, bonds, securities and other similar items.[50]

This essentially means that employee achievement awards must be received in the form of tangible personal property in order to receive favorable tax treatment. These provisions are effective for tax years beginning after December 31, 2017.

Moving Expenses

Under the 2017 Tax Act, employers are no longer able to reimburse employees on a tax-free basis for certain moving expenses. The suspension of this provision is effective for tax years beginning after December 31, 2017 and before January 1, 2026.

Although the employer deduction for moving expenses is suspended from 2018 through 2025, an exception exists for members of the armed forces (and their spouses and dependents) who are on active duty.[51]

The deduction for moving expenses under IRC Section 217 is also suspended for tax years beginning after December 31, 2017 and before January 1, 2026.[52]

Service Awards for Bona Fide Volunteers

The 2017 Tax Act increased the aggregate amount of length of service awards that may accrue for a bona fide volunteer with respect to any year of service to $6,000 (from $3,000) for tax years beginning after December 31, 2017.[53] The $6,000 amount will be adjusted for inflation in $500 increments.

WHAT KINDS OF PERSONAL LOSSES CAN BE DEDUCTED?

Several of the business loss deductions—bad debt and casualty losses—have personal loss equivalents that may also result in a deduction for the taxpayer. In addition, the Code includes deductions for several types of personal losses that are unavailable for businesses, such as gambling and hobby losses. Finally, the type of loss that individual tax payers are most likely to experience—loss on investments—is covered in detail in Chapter 4.

Nonbusiness Bad Debt Deduction

There are two significant differences between the deductibility of nonbusiness bad debts and business bad debts: First, a nonbusiness bad debt must be totally worthless for it to be deductible.[54] Second, the deduction is characterized as a short-term capital loss rather than an ordinary deduction.[55] As discussed in Chapter 7, capital losses are deductible only to the extent of capital gains, plus $3,000.[56] Examples of nonbusiness bad debt include:

- Any debt that does not qualify as a business bad debt because the taxpayer's dominant motivation for making the loan was to protect an investment rather than related to a trade or business.
- A loan to a relative or friend with reasonable anticipation that loan would be repaid.
- A lost deposit, such as with a building contractor who later becomes insolvent.
- Funds deposited in a failed bank that does not have deposit insurance.

Example: In 2016, Larry Loser loans his son $10,000 for the purchase of a car, which is documented by a promissory note signed by his son. In 2020, Larry Jr. files for bankruptcy and discharges the debt, which has a balance of $8,000. Larry Sr. has a $1,000 capital gain from the sale of a stock in 2020. Here, Larry's nonbusiness bad debt deduction is limited to $4,000—the extent of his capital gain for 2020, plus $3,000.

Personal Casualty Losses

In addition to business casualty losses, Code section 165(c)(3) also allows a deduction for a personal casualty loss. Although the method in determining the amount of the casualty loss is generally the same as for business casualty losses, there are a few key differences.

First, each personal casualty loss is subject to a $100 floor. This means that right off the top, a personal casualty loss must be reduced by $100.[57] Second, personal casualty losses are only deductible to the extent that they exceed 10 percent of adjusted gross income.[58] Effectively, this means that the casualty loss is reduced by 10 percent of a taxpayer's AGI. Finally, casualty losses are limited to the adjusted basis of the property, though typically the bases for personal property are not subject to scheduled depreciation as they are for business property.

Example: Harry Homeowner purchased a house in 2014 for $200,000. In 2020, when the FMV value of Harry's house was $250,000, a flood caused a significant amount of damage to the house and reduced its FMV to $125,000. Harry filed a timely insurance claim and received $50,000, the maximum amount of his coverage. For 2020, Harry's adjusted gross income is $200,000.

Decrease in FMV	$125,000
Adjusted basis (original cost)	$200,000
Tentative personal casualty loss (lesser of the two)	$125,000
Less Insurance Reimbursement	– $50,000
Less $100 floor	– $100
Less 10% of AGI	– $20,000
Personal casualty loss deduction	**$54,900**

Finally, the personal casualty loss deduction is a regular itemized deduction not subject to the 2 percent of adjusted gross income floor.[59] There are additional rules that apply when a taxpayer has "insurance gain" (which can occur when the insurance reimbursement exceeds the value of the property), but they are complex and beyond the scope of this chapter.

Ponzi Scheme Losses

A *Ponzi scheme* is a fraudulent investment technique employed to recruit investors with promises of above-market-rate returns. The scheme is fraudulent because instead of actually investing an investor's funds, the perpetrator fulfills the promise of high returns by using money it receives from other investors. As long as the flow of funds from new investors continues, the scheme can run indefinitely. Ponzi scheme losses blur the line between investment losses and casualty losses from theft.

The most recent prominent Ponzi scheme was perpetrated by Bernie Madoff. In Rev. Rul. 2009-9,[60] the IRS provided guidance with respect to the deductibility of losses suffered by those who invested with Madoff, as well as in other Ponzi schemes:

- Ponzi scheme losses are theft losses because the perpetrator intended to deprive the investors of money through criminal acts. Thus, the character of the loss is ordinary, not capital.
- In opening up an investment account with a Ponzi perpetrator, investors enter into a transaction for profit. Therefore, none of the section 165(h) deduction limitations apply.[61]
- Although Ponzi scheme losses are itemized deductions, they are not miscellaneous itemized deductions subject to the 2 percent of adjusted gross income floor.[62] The loss would is deductible in the year the theft was discovered.
- The amount of the deduction is the sum of all investments plus any "earnings" reported by the taxpayer as gross income over the period of the scheme, less any distributions received.[63]
- If a business suffered Ponzi scheme losses and is computing an NOL, the Ponzi loss deduction is included in the computation.[64]
- If the investor has a claim for reimbursement that has a reasonable prospect of recovery, the amount of the deduction must be reduced by the actual or anticipated recovery. If the amount recovered is more than anticipated, the additional recovery is included as income for the year in which it is received.

Example: In 2011, Iris Investor opened an account with Charles & Bernie Investment Advisors (C&B) with an initial deposit of $1000. Unbeknownst to her, C&B was running a Ponzi scheme. Iris maintained her account with C&B through 2019 without incident. During that time she continued to invest more money with C&B, reported income from her investment, and occasionally received distributions from the account. At the beginning of 2020, C&B's Ponzi scheme was revealed, resulting in criminal charges. Iris estimates that she will receive $200 in court-ordered restitution from C&B. Iris receives no restitution in 2018, but receives $250 in restitution in 2021.

	Iris' C&B investments	False C&B earnings included in Iris' gross income	Distributions to Iris
2011	$1000	$0	None
2012	None	$100	None
2013	$200	$100	None
2014	None	$100	None
2015	None	$100	None
2016	None	$100	None
2017	None	$100	None
2018	None	$100	None
2019	None	$100	$300
2020	None	None	None
Total	**$1,200**	**$600**	**$300**

Iris' 2018 deductible loss is computed as follows:

Total investment	$1,200
False earnings reported as income	$ 600
Subtotal	$1,800
Less distributions	– $300
Less anticipated restitution	– $200
Total deductible loss	**$1,300**

Finally, because the restitution that Iris received in 2021 was $50 more than she had estimated in her 2018 loss deduction, Iris must report the $50 as income in 2021.

Gambling Losses

Although for the most part gambling is viewed as a recreational (and therefore nonbusiness) activity, there are a significant number of professional gamblers. Unlike a casual gambler, a professional gambler is recognized as being engaged in a trade or business.[65] Whether casual or professional, however, section 165(d) limits the deductibility of wagering losses to the amount of wagering gains. This means that *net* wagering losses are not deductible from any other income. In spite of this uniform rule, however, professional gamblers enjoy much more favorable treatment of their losses than casual gamblers in many respects.

Casual Gamblers

A casual gambler is not considered to be engaged in wagering as a trade or business. Therefore, a casual gambler's non-wagering expenses (such as travel to casinos, books, seminars, etc.) are nondeductible personal expenses.[66] Depending on the game and the amount of winnings, gambling establishments may be required to furnish a Form W-2G to the gambler.

Although a casual gambler may deduct gambling losses to the extent of gambling winnings, they are not actually netted. The gambling winnings are reported as other income on Line 21 of Form 1040, but gambling losses are reported on Schedule A as below-the-line (or itemized) deductions. If a taxpayer's itemized deductions do not exceed the amount of the standard deduction, the gambling losses are essentially nondeductible. Thus, a taxpayer may end up paying tax on the entire amount of gambling winnings unreduced by what might be a substantial amount of gambling losses.

Example: In 2020, Gary and Grace Gamble, married taxpayers, filing jointly, have $12,000 of gambling winnings and $35,000 of gambling losses. The taxpayers' only itemized deduction is the gambling losses.

Because gambling losses are deductible only to the extent of gambling winnings, the excess of Gary and Grace's gambling losses ($23,000) are totally nondeductible. The remaining $12,000 of gambling losses qualifies as an itemized deduction. However, the standard deduction for a married couple filing jointly in 2020 is $24,000. Since, their gambling losses (the taxpayers' only itemized deduction) do not exceed their standard deduction, Gary and Grace should take the standard deduction for the extra $1,000. However, doing so means that none of the gambling losses are deductible. Despite the fact that the Gambles lost almost three times as much as they won, they will nonetheless pay tax on their $12,000 of gambling winnings.

Professional Gamblers

As mentioned above, the rule limiting the deductibility of gambling losses to gambling gains applies to both casual and professional gamblers. However, because a professional gambler is in the trade or business of gambling, the gambling losses (to the extent deductible) are deducted on Schedule C as an above-the-line deduction. Consequently, those losses are deductible dollar-for-dollar even if the taxpayer does not itemize.

Additionally, under a 2008 IRS memorandum[67] and a 2011 Tax Court case,[68] the non-wagering expenses of a professional gambler (such as seminars, books, transportation, meals and lodging) incurred to engage in gambling activities are now considered "ordinary and necessary" business expenses, and the deduction of those expenses is not limited by gambling winnings.

The significance of this new method of reporting gambling income and deductions is invaluable to professional gamblers. Under the new more liberal rules, they may now first offset their winnings with their losses, and then use other business expenses to create an NOL.

Example: Gary Gamble is a professional poker player. Throughout the year, Gary traveled to various casinos and other venues to participate in poker tournaments. For that year, Gary had gambling winnings of $75,000, gambling losses of $100,000, and $15,000 of business expenses for transportation, meals and lodging.

On a Schedule C, Gary reports his gambling income and deductions as follows:

Wagering gains	$75,000
Wagering losses	$100,000
Deductible wagering losses	$75,000
Wagering income	-$0-
Deductible non-wagering expenses	$15,000
Business loss (Potentially NOL)	($15,000)

Hobby Losses

Similar to the gambling loss limitation, deductions with respect to hobby activities are deductible only to the extent of income from such activities.[69] However, with regard to the deductibility of hobby losses, there is one significant negative tax difference. Although the deductible gambling losses of a casual gambler are below-the-line itemized deductions, hobby losses are miscellaneous itemized deductions[70] which are deductible only to the extent that they exceed 2 percent of adjusted gross income. Moreover, if that amount plus the taxpayer's other itemized deductions do not exceed the amount of the standard deduction; the hobby loss deduction provides no benefit to the taxpayer.

Example: This year, Fred and Francine Farmer, married taxpayers, filing jointly, have combined wage income of $150,000. Fred is employed as a newspaper reporter and Francine is an executive chef. On the side, they grow flowers that they sell to their neighbors and others. From that activity, they generated $10,000 of income and $25,000 of deductions. Their itemized deductions include $6,500 of mortgage interest and $3,000 of property taxes. If the flower activity is treated as a hobby, the hobby deductions do not exceed the Farmers' standard deduction and provide no tax benefit. Despite having a net loss of $15,000, they nonetheless pay tax on $10,000 of flower sale income and have a total income of $160,000.

Flower Sale Income	$10,000
Flower sale expenses	$25,000
Tentative hobby deduction	$10,000
Less 2% of AGI	– $7,500
Total hobby deduction	$2,500
Other Itemized deduction (mortgage interest and property taxes)	$9,500
Total itemized deductions	$12,000
Standard deduction	$24,000

If the Farmers' flower activity was treated as a trade or business, the income would be reported on Schedule C and all of the relevant expenses would be deductible without limitation. As a result, the $15,000 business loss would be deductible from the Farmers' $150,000 wage income regardless of the level of the standard deduction, leaving them with a total income of $135,000.

Here, the same set of income and expenses yields a net difference in $25,000 income, depending on whether it is treated as hobby or business.

Is an Activity a Hobby or a Business?

Whether an activity should be treated as a hobby or trade or business is a question of fact, and the IRS and the taxpayer may come to different conclusions on this issue. Often, activities that have a pleasure element are susceptible to classification by the IRS as hobby activities. Code section 183(d) provides a rebuttable presumption that an activity is a business if it produced a profit for at least three of the last five tax years.[71] Additionally, the regulations list the following factors that may be considered to resolve this issue:[72]

1. *The manner in which the taxpayer carries on the activity.* Does the taxpayer participate in the activity with a businesslike approach, including keeping complete and accurate books and records? If so, it is more likely to be perceived as a business, rather than a hobby.

2. *The expertise of the taxpayers or their advisors.* If the skill and techniques employed in the activity are on par with other professionals in that field, it may indicate that the activity should be classified as a trade or business.

3. *The time and effort expended by the taxpayers on the activity.* If a taxpayer devotes a substantial amount of time on a regular basis to the activity, it would strengthen the arguments for treating it as a business.

4. *Expectation that assets used in the activity may appreciate in value.* This factor encompasses the possibility that in addition to the profit from the activity, one of the taxpayer's motives is the appreciation in the value of assets associated with the activity.

5. *The success of the taxpayer in other similar activities.* This factor focuses on a taxpayer's prior track record with respect to operating profitable businesses. Someone who has started profitable businesses before (particularly in similar fields) is more likely to be running a business.

6. *The taxpayer's history of income or losses with respect to the business.* It is common for a legitimate trade or business to sustain a loss in the first few years. However, sustained long-term losses indicate that the activity may be a hobby, rather than a business.

7. *The amount of profits earned.* An activity in which over a number of years, a taxpayer generates a small amount of profits in relation to a large investment is probably not indicative of an activity engaged in for profit.

8. *The financial status of the taxpayer.* If the taxpayer has a significant amount of income from other sources, it is more likely that activity is not engaged in for profit—especially if there are personal and recreational elements involved in that activity.

9. *Elements of personal pleasure or recreation inherent in the activity.* The greater the potential personal pleasure or recreation that an activity involves, the less likely the taxpayer is engaged in it for profit.

Taxpayers who believe that their activity is a trade or business have the option of using Form 5213 to postpone the determination of whether the activity is a hobby or a business. Making this election ensures that the IRS will not challenge the treatment of the activity as a business until the end of the first four years in which the taxpayer is engaged in the activity,[73] and the deduction of all activity-related expenses is allowed. However, if the IRS determines that the activity was not engaged in for profit after the expiration of the presumption period, the hobby loss rules would be applied retroactively, potentially subjecting the taxpayer to a significant disallowance of deductions as well as accuracy-related penalties.[74]

In the end, even after evaluating all the above factors, it may remain unclear whether the activity is a legitimate business or a mere hobby. Moreover, if the taxpayer and IRS disagree, it may be up to the Tax Court to ultimately decide the issue.

Figure 6.2

DRAWBACKS OF (CASUAL) GAMBLING AND HOBBY LOSSES

	Gambling Loss	Hobby Loss
Deductions limited to income?	Yes	Yes
Allowable deductions save taxes only if itemized deductions exceed the standard deduction?	Yes	Yes
Associated income increases AGI, resulting in limitation of other credits and deductions?	Yes	Yes
Miscellaneous itemized deduction potentially triggering or increasing AMT?	No	Yes
Excess losses cannot be carried over to other tax years?	Yes	Yes

FREQUENTLY ASKED QUESTIONS

Question – Does an NOL that is carried back or forward to other years offset self-employment income; and, thus, reduce self-employment tax in those years?

Answer – No. Section 1402(a)(4) specifically excludes the NOL as a deductible item in the computation of self-employment income.

Example: In 2018, Allison Accountant a self-employed CPA generated net fees of $150,000 (self-employment income). Assume for purposes of this example that Allison's adjusted gross income and taxable income was also $150,000. Self-employment income is subject to both regular income tax and self-employment tax.

In 2020, Allison sustained a net operating loss of $70,000 that she carried back to the 2018 tax year. For income tax purposes, the $70,000 NOL reduces her 2018 taxable income to $80,000. On the other hand, pursuant to section 1402(a)(4), there would be no similar adjustment to Allison's $150,000 self-employment income. As a result, the NOL would reduce Allison's 2018 taxable income; and, thus, her income tax liability. However, it would not reduce Allison's 2018 self-employment income, and her self-employment tax liability would remain the same.[75]

Question – If an NOL is carried back to a prior tax year, should the taxpayer file for a refund with a Form 1040X (amended income tax return) or Form 1045 (application for tentative refund)?

Answer – Either form is acceptable. However, there are different rules that apply depending on which form is filed.

Form 1045

- Must be filed within one year after the year in which the NOL arose.
- Must be filed separately and not attached to the Form 1040 for the year in which the NOL was generated.
- The IRS will process the Form 1045 within ninety days of the later of 1) the date it is filed; or 2) the last day of the month that includes the due date (including extensions) for filing the Form 1040 for the year the NOL was generated.

Form 1040X

- Must be filed no later than three years after the due date of the return for the applicable tax year.
- The IRS is not required to process the amended return within ninety days. However, if the amended return is not processed within six months from the date it is filed, the taxpayer may file a suit for a refund.

Assuming the taxpayer decides to file within one year after the year in which the NOL arose, Form 1045 would be the better option because unlike Form 1040X, the IRS must process it within a ninety-day period. However, if the taxpayer fails to file a Form 1045 within the one year filing period, her only option would be to file a Form 1040X.

Question – In determining the decrease in the FMV of property as a result of a casualty loss, can the costs of repairs be used as the measure of the decrease in value?

Answer – Yes, subject to the following conditions:

- The repairs are necessary to restore the property to its condition immediately prior to the casualty.
- The cost of the repairs is not excessive.
- The repairs are limited to the damage caused by the casualty.
- The repairs do not cause the FMV of the property to exceed the value of the property prior to the casualty.

Question – How does the 2017 Tax Reform Legislation modify the treatment of research, development and experimental expenditures?

Answer – The research and development credit under IRC Section 41 was retained by the 2017 Tax Act.

However, with respect to amounts paid or incurred in tax years beginning after December 31, 2021, certain research and experimental expenses must be capitalized or amortized over a five-year period (fifteen years if the research is conducted outside of the U.S.).[76] This provision specifically applies to software development expenditures.[77]

Land acquisition costs, mining costs (including oil and gas exploration) are not subject to the new requirement.[78]

Once the property is abandoned, retired or otherwise disposed of, the remaining basis in the property must continue to be amortized over the remaining time period.[79]

The credit for clinical testing expenses was limited to 25 percent (reduced from 50 percent) of qualified clinical testing expenses for the year. Taxpayers are also entitled to elect a reduced credit instead of a reduction in other allowable deductions for the year.[80]

Question – What are the new rules governing deductions for settlements paid in connection with sexual harassment claims?

Answer – Under the 2017 Tax Act, no deduction is permitted for settlements, payments or attorney's fees paid in connection with sexual harassment or sexual abuse claims if the payments are subject to a nondisclosure agreement.[81]

CHAPTER ENDNOTES

1. The Supreme Court has described deductions as a matter of "legislative grace." *INDOPCO, Inc. v. Comm.*, 503 US 79, 84 (1992).
2. IRC Sec. 1012.
3. IRC Sec. 1001(a)
4. *Libson Shops v. Koehler*, 353 U.S. 382 (1957).
5. IRC Sec. 172(b). NOL may be carried forward for a maximum of twenty years.
6. IRC Sec. 62(a).
7. IRC Sec. 62(a).
8. IRC Sec. 172(a).
9. IRC Sec. 172(b)(1)(C).
10. IRC Sec. 172(b)(1)(A).
11. IRC Sec. 172.
12. IRC Sec. 163(j).
13. IRC Sec. 163(j)(1).
14. IRC Secs. 163(j)(2), 448(c).
15. IRC Sec. 163(j)(8).
16. IRC Sec. 163(j)(9).
17. IRC Sec. 163(j)(2).
18. IRC Sec. 461(l).
19. IRC Sec. 461(l)(3).
20. IRC Sec. 461(l)(4).
21. IRC Sec. 461(l)(6).
22. IRC Sec. 743(d)(1).
23. IRC Sec. 704.
24. IRC Sec. 166(a).
25. IRC Sec. 166(a).
26. Treas. Reg. §1.166-5(b).
27. Treas. Reg. §1.166-5(1)(d), Example 1.
28. IRC Sec. 166(b).
29. Calculating the deduction allowed by this requirement is straightforward for cash method taxpayers. The issue becomes more complex for businesses that use an accrual method.
30. Treas. Reg. §1.166-2.
31. Treas. Reg. §1.166-2(b).
32. *Generes v. Comm'r.*, 405 U.S. 93 (1972).
33. Joint Comm. On Taxation, *General Explanation of the Tax Reform Act of 1976 Rep. No. JCS-33-76*, at 158 (1976); Treas. Reg. §1.166-9(a).
34. Treas. Reg. §1.166-9.
35. IRC Sec. 166(d).
36. Treas. Reg. §1.165-7(b)(1)(i).
37. IRC Sec. 165(h)(4)(E).
38. IRC Sec. 274(a).
39. IRC Sec. 274(n).
40. IRC Sec. 274(o).
41. IRC Secs. 132(f)(8), 274(l).
42. IRC Sec. 274(a)(4).
43. IRC Sec. 45S (added by the 2017 Tax Act).
44. IRC Sec. 45S(c)(1).
45. IRC Sec. 45S(c)(4).
46. Under IRC Sec. 414(g)(1)(B).
47. IRC Sec. 45S(d).
48. IRC Sec. 45S(e).
49. IRC Sec. 45S(a)(1).
50. IRC Secs. 74, 274(j)(3).
51. IRC Sec. 132(g).
52. IRC Sec. 217(k).
53. IRC Sec. 457(e)(11)(B).
54. IRC Sec. 166. This means partially worthless nonbusiness loans are not deductible unless and until they become totally worthless.
55. IRC Sec. 166(d).
56. IRC Sec. 1211(b)(1).
57. IRC Sec. 165(h)(1).
58. IRC Sec. 165(h)(2).

59. IRC Sec. 67(b)(3).
60. IRB 2009-14 (April 6, 2009).
61. Pursuant to IRC sec. 165(h)(1), a deduction for a theft loss is allowable only to the extent it exceeds $100. Pursuant to IRC sec. 165(h)(2), a personal theft loss is deductible only to the extent that it exceeds the sum of all casualty gains (including thefts), plus so much of the excess that exceeds 10 percent of the taxpayer's adjusted gross income.
62. IRC Sec. 67(b)(3).
63. IRC Sec. 67(b)(3).
64. IRC Sec. 172(d)(4). Although nonbusiness deductions are excluded from the NOL, casualty losses—including theft—with respect to a transaction entered into for profit are allowable as part of the NOL deduction.
65. *Comm'r. v. Groetzinger*, 480 U.S. 23 (1987).
66. IRC Sec. 262.
67. Office of Chief Counsel Internal Revenue Service Memorandum AM2008-013 (December 19, 2008).
68. *Mayo v. Comm'r.*, 136 T.C. 81 (2011).
69. IRC Sec. 183(b).
70. IRC Sec. 67.
71. In case of an activity which consists in major part of the breeding, training, showing or racing horses, the safe harbor presumption period is two or more tax years in a consecutive seven year period. IRC Sec. 183(d).
72. Treas. Reg. §1.183-2(b)(1)-(9).
73. IRC Sec. 183(e)(1). If the 7 year period applies, the IRS will not challenge the validity of the business, if at all, until the end of the 6th year in which the taxpayer first engaged in the activity.
74. IRC Sec. 6662.
75. *Decrescenzo v. Comm'r.*, T.C. Memo. 2012-51 (2012).
76. IRC Sec. 174(a)(2).
77. IRC Sec. 174(c)(3).
78. IRC Sec. 174(c).
79. IRC Sec. 174(d).
80. IRC Sec. 45C(a), 280C(b)(3).
81. IRC Sec. 162(q).

DEDUCTIONS

CHAPTER 7

INTRODUCTION

The purpose of income taxation is to tax the inflows of economic benefits, so it is only fair that the taxpayer should be entitled to deduct the outflows of money necessary to generate those economic benefits. In a perfect world, the difference between economic inflows and monetary outflows should be the amount subject to income tax, and taxpayers often take the availability of deductions for granted. However, in sharp contrast to the Internal Revenue Code's broad presumption to include any economic benefit in gross income, there is a narrow presumption with regard to allowing deductions for monetary outflows. In fact, no deduction can ever be taken unless a Code section specifically allows for it.[1]

Simply stated, a deduction is an outlay, usually of money, that reduces the taxable income and therefore also lowers tax liability. The actual tax savings of a deduction is directly correlated with the taxpayer's tax rate. For example, assume that Sam Smith has taxable income of $10,000, a tax rate of 15 percent, and a $200 potential deduction. With no deductions, Sam's tax liability would be $1,500 (15 percent of $10,000). With the $200 deduction, Sam's taxable income would be reduced to $9,800 and, thus, his tax liability would be $1,470 (15 percent of $9,800). The tax savings to Sam from a $200 deduction is $30 (15 percent of $200).

Next, assume the same facts, except now Sam's tax rate is 20 percent. Without the deduction, Sam's tax liability would be $2,000 (20 percent of $10,000). As in the prior fact pattern, the $200 deduction would reduce his taxable income to $9,800. However, due to the higher tax rate, his tax liability would be $1,960 (20 percent of $9,800), resulting in a tax savings of $40. Comparing the two examples, Sam's tax savings were $10 more when his tax rate was twenty percent instead of fifteen percent.

One important conclusion from the above examples is that spending money just to create tax deductions does not make economic sense. No matter how high the tax rate, each dollar of deduction only saves a percentage of that dollar. Even if the taxpayer's tax rate is 39.6 percent, a $1 deduction only saves approximately 40 cents of that dollar. For this reason, many taxpayers fund deductions by using borrowed money (including credit cards) to pay for deductible items. Although in the long run, the taxpayer will ultimately have to repay the loan, in the short run, the deductible items paid with the borrowed funds reduce the current tax year's tax liability.

Importantly, not all allowable deductions find their way onto the taxpayer's Form 1040. This is because each specifically identified allowable deduction must survive a gauntlet of other Code sections that, depending on the circumstances, could limit or even completely eliminate the amount of the deduction. Even those deductions that survive are not treated alike; some are designated as "above-the-line" deductions and some as "below-the-line" deductions. Above-the-line deductions are not usually subject to further reduction and, in some cases, may enhance other tax benefits. Below-the-line deductions are often subject to further reduction and may trigger the alternative minimum tax.[2] The differences are discussed in detail below.

HOW DO DEDUCTIONS WORK?

Generally, a taxpayer generates income other than wages through operating a business or investments. The Code allows certain deductions for expenses related to each of these types of income as well as deductions for certain personal expenses that effectively "reward" the taxpayer for engaging in certain activities.

The Code is far more generous in allowing deductions related to trade or business income and designates them, for the most part, to the much more beneficial above-the-line deductions. Conversely, deductions related to investment income are much harder to come by. The Code imposes a more extensive array of limitations or elimination provisions, and, for the most part, those deductions that are allowable are the much less beneficial below-the-line deductions. Finally, the Code is the least generous with personal deductions, with many of them subject to limitations, phase-outs and floors (discussed in detail below) that effectively eliminate their availability to high-income taxpayers. Although some personal deductions are designated as above-the-line deductions, the more common ones are below-the-line deductions.

The steps necessary to determine whether—and to what extent—an expense item will ultimately be deductible and whether it will be an above-the-line or below-the-line deduction are as follows:

Step 1 – Is the item deductible as a business, investment, or personal expense?

Step 2 – What limits apply to the deduction?

Step 3 – Is the deduction to an above-the-line or below-the-line deduction?

Step 1 – Is the Item Deductible as a Business, Investment, or Personal Expense?

Trade or Business Deductions

The term "trade or business" is actually a single term that is interchangeable with the term "business." Although the term appears in many Code sections, it is not defined in the Code or Treasury Regulations. However, in its publications, the IRS has defined "trade or business" to mean "any activity conducted for the production of income from selling goods or performing services."[3] Several trade or business expenses such as interest,[4] the payment of local and state taxes,[5] and unrecoverable bad debts owed by customers[6] are specifically identified as being deductible. However, it would be impractical to enact a separate Code section for every possible business expense. For that reason, Code section 162 serves as a "catch-all" provision by which all other trade or business expenses (office supplies, utilities, repairs, etc.) that meet broad requirements are deductible.[7] Helpfully, Schedule C (a common attachment to Form 1040 used to report business deductions) lists common items deductible under section 162 including rent, insurance, supplies, utilities, and advertising. When considering what types of expenses may qualify as a business deduction, Schedule C can be a good place to start.

In order for an item to be deductible under section 162(a), it must meet the following requirements:

1. It must be "ordinary"

2. It must be "necessary"

3. It must be an "expense," rather than an "expenditure"

4. It must be used to carry out a trade or business

The first two requirements, "ordinary" and "necessary," are questions of fact that require a case-by-case analysis. The term "ordinary" means the item is not unusual in the type of business the taxpayer is conducting. For example, newspaper or internet advertising would be an ordinary expense item for an accountant or tax lawyer. On the other hand, buying and maintaining a yacht to display a banner with the words "Form 1040" would not be considered ordinary advertising. For that reason, the cost of the yacht expenses would not be deductible.[8] Next, the term "necessary" means the item is appropriate and helpful to the business and its cost is reasonable. So, although transportation to and from a meeting would be appropriate and helpful to most businesses, with the availability of much less expensive commercial flights, the cost of chartering a private plane would probably not be reasonable.

The third requirement is the item must be an "expense" rather than an "expenditure." An expense is an item of short duration (used up in a year or less)[9] such as labor, rent, supplies, incidental repairs and advertising.[10] The common denominator of expense items is a relatively short shelf life that requires constant replenishment. Conversely, the cost of heavy manufacturing machinery and buildings that have long periods of usefulness spanning many tax years are expenditures. Even though the cost of office supplies and a warehouse are ordinary and necessary, only the former is deductible under section 162(a).

The fourth and fifth requirements of "carrying out" a "trade or business" must be considered together. First, the taxpayer must be actually operating the business in order to deduct any ordinary and necessary expense. For example, when operating a franchise restaurant, the cost of renting a building and utilities would certainly be deductible under section 162(a). However, if a taxpayer had just acquired a franchise and was preparing to open the restaurant and was not yet serving patrons, the taxpayer would not at that time be carrying on a restaurant business. As a result, the rent and utility expenses would not be deductible under section 162(a).[11]

However, all is not lost with respect to the deductibility of expenditures or pre-opening expenses. In the case of an expenditure, if all the other requirements of section 162(a) are otherwise met, instead of being currently deductible, the expenditure would be *depreciable* pursuant to Code sections 167 and 168. An expenditure generates taxable income throughout a useful life that covers multiple tax years. Depreciation matches a portion of the cost of the expenditure with each tax year's income over a recovery period that approximates the expenditure's useful life.[12] For example, the cost of a warehouse would be depreciable over a recovery period of thirty-nine years, so that a portion of its cost would match each tax year's income over that same period.[13]

In the case of the pre-opening costs (referred to as "start-up expenditures"), the taxpayer may elect to amortize those costs over a period of at least sixty months, beginning in the month in which the trade or business actually commenced.[14] So, beginning in the month in which the restaurant opened for business, a pro-rata share of start-up expenditures would be deductible over the tax years spanning the sixty-month amortization period pursuant to Code section 195 rather than section 162. In other words, instead of deducting start-up expenditures all in the year they were incurred, they must instead be amortized over time.

Investment Deductions

Similar to section 162, Code section 212 is the catch-all provision for the deductibility of investment type items—investment counsel fees, clerical help, office rent, etc.[15]—not specifically deductible under some other Code section. The first three requirements of section 212—"ordinary," "necessary," and "expense"—are identical to the section 162 requirements and require no further explanation.[16] Beyond those requirements, investment expenses must be incurred in one of two contexts:

1. The production or collection of income[17]
2. The management, conservation or maintenance of property held for the production of income[18]

These contexts are very broad and may often overlap. Examples of investment expenses include the costs associated with buying and selling investment property, the occasional rental of real property (such as a vacation home), and projects undertaken for profit that do not rise to the level of a trade or business, such as a joint venture. Investment activity is more passive than the grinding intensity of a trade or business. Finally, the fees of tax professionals including tax preparation fees or accounting and legal fees related to a Tax Court litigation, audits, or tax collection actions are also deductible under section 212.[19]

Personal Deductions

Although generally deductions are not allowed for personal, living and family expenses, the Code does allow deductions for certain personal expenses. These deductions are designed to provide tax relief for certain situations and encourage taxpayers to engage in certain activities. Those deductible items include the following:

- Alimony payments[20] are deductible as an accounting adjustment for the payor spouse. In a marriage, each spouse's income is taxed one time, either on a joint return or on married-filing-separately returns. For a divorced couple, the alimony payment deduction simply reflects the transfer of income from one ex-spouse to another. Consistent with taxing the income only once, the payee spouse includes the alimony in gross income and the payor spouse deducts it. As a result of the Tax Cuts and Jobs Act of 2017 (TCJA), alimony deductions will be discontinued for payments pursuant to divorce and separation agreements that are executed after December 31, 2018. Payments made pursuant to agreements executed before that date will continue to be deductible under the old rules, even if those payments are made well after the 2018 tax year. See Chapter 24 for a more detailed discussion of the tax consequences of marriage and divorce

- The IRA deduction[21] encourages taxpayers to save for retirement by allowing them to deduct contributions to a retirement plan.

- Deductions for student loan interest[22] and college tuition and fees paid reward taxpayers for pursuing education.

- The deduction for one-half of self-employment taxes paid[23] is an attempt to equalize the tax treatment of W-2 employees with those who are self-employed. For W-2 employees, one-half of the FICA tax imposed on the wages of a W-2 employee (7.65 percent) is paid by the employer. Even though that payment is an economic benefit to the employee, it is considered an obligation of the employer, and that amount is not included in the employee's taxable wages. On the other hand, a self-employed taxpayer must pay the entire amount of the FICA (referred to as self-employment tax when paid by a self-employed taxpayer), or 15.3 percent of self-employment income up to a certain limit, which includes the amount that a W-2 employer would be obligated to pay. In an attempt to equalize the tax treatment of a self-employed taxpayer with the W-2 taxpayer, the self-employed taxpayer is allowed a deduction for one-half of the self-employment taxes paid.

- Self-employed health insurance deduction[24] is another attempt to equalize tax treatment of W-2 employees with self-employed taxpayers. Since employer-provided health insurance is excluded from a W-2 employee's gross income, a self-employed taxpayer may deduct health insurance premiums as an equalizer.

- The deduction for contributions to self-employed retirement plans[25] is another equalizer with W-2 employees covered under an employer-sponsored plan.

- The deduction for contributions to Health Savings Accounts encourages taxpayers to use HSAs to pay for health care expenses. [26]

- The deduction for penalties on early withdrawals of retirement savings[27] provides a small measure of assistance to those taxpayers who are compelled to dip into savings prematurely.

- The medical and dental expenses deduction[28] can provide a tax break to those who pay significant out-of-pocket medical and dental expenses. However, the deduction is subject to a 7.5 percent adjusted gross income floor (in 2018, 10 percent for 2019 and beyond) and is a below-the-line deduction (discussed below), so its benefit is often illusory. Only taxpayers with high medical expenses in a single tax year would ever be likely to take advantage of this deduction.

- The state income and property tax deduction[29] gives some relief to taxpayers who are taxed by multiple jurisdictions.

- The mortgage interest deduction[30] helps homeowners by allowing them to deduct the interest (not principal) paid on their mortgages.

- The charitable contribution deduction[31] rewards taxpayers for giving donation to charitable causes.

Step 2 – What Limits Apply to the Deduction?

Finding a Code section allowing for the deduction of a certain item is just the first step on the road to using the deduction to reduce tax liability. There is a variety of instances in which another Code section may derail the process by limiting or even eliminating an otherwise allowable deduction.

Trade or Business Deductions

As discussed above, trade or business deductions are by far the most generous allowed by the Code. In fact, as a general rule, "[t]he full amount of the allowable deduction for ordinary and necessary expenses in carrying on a trade or business is deductible, even though such expenses exceed the gross income derived during the taxable year from such business."[32] This means that the net loss from a trade or business (the excess amount of deductions over income) is deductible and can be applied to reduce income from other sources.

However, the Code imposes some limits on common business expenses. For example, in many businesses, it is common practice to take a client out for a meal to discuss business. In an attempt to prevent the taxpayer from disguising personal expenses as deductible business expenses, Code section 274 sets forth strict substantiation rules requiring the taxpayer to document the specific business purpose of any such meals or entertainment. If the taxpayer fails to meet these requirements, the deduction would be totally disallowed. Even if the taxpayer adequately meets the substantiation requirements, the deduction for meals is limited to 50 percent of the cost.[33]

Perhaps one of the most significant limitations of trade or business deductions relates to *passive activity loss,* which was discussed in Chapter 3. Passive activity losses are restricted such that they may only be deducted to offset passive activity income, not any other types of income (investment, business, or otherwise) that a taxpayer may have. This restriction can significantly impact the amount of tax liability faced by a taxpayer with passive activity loss deductions.

Example. Assume the taxpayer was a general partner in a music publishing business partnership but had no actual involvement in the operation of the business. A partnership is a pass-through entity from which all income and deductions flow through to the individual partners as "distributive shares." If the passive general partner's distributive share of partnership income was $10,000 and the distributive share of partnership deductions was $20,000, only $10,000 of the $20,000 in expenses would actually be deductible because he or she did not materially participate in the partnership business. Unless the partner had passive activity income from some other activity, the other $10,000 would be not be deductible.[34]

For a more detailed explanation of the tax nuances of passive activities, see Chapter 23.

Investment Deductions

The Code does not particularly favor investment deductions, and often imposes restrictions that limit and sometimes eliminate what would otherwise be a deductible expense. For example, Code Section 163(d)(1) limits the deductibility of investment interest to net investment income (defined as investment income less investment related expenses other than interest). Generally, investment income includes interest, dividends, royalties as well as the gain from the sale of investment property. Similar to passive activity losses, discussed above, investment interest is deductible only to the extent of a like amount of net investment income.

Example. Assume in the current year, the taxpayer pays investment interest of $15,000. If net investment income is $7,000, the current year's investment interest deduction would be limited to $7,000, leaving $8,000 of investment interest that is not deductible in the current tax year. The excess non-deductible investment interest must be carried over to subsequent years and remains deductible only to the extent of net investment income in those years.

Perhaps, the most significant limitation of investment type deductions relates to capital loss. A capital loss is the loss from the sale or exchange of a capital asset usually held for investment.

Example. If a taxpayer purchased ten shares of stock (a capital asset) for $5,000 and then sells the stock for $2,000, there would be a $3,000 capital loss. The deductibility of capital loss is limited to an offsetting amount of capital gain, plus $3,000 that would be deductible against any other type of income. To illustrate the application of these rules, assume that in the current tax year, the taxpayer has $80,000 of capital gain and $150,000 of capital loss. Of the $150,000 of capital loss, $80,000 would be deductible as an offset against the $80,000 of capital gain. As to the remaining $70,000 of net capital loss, only $3,000 would be deductible against other current tax year income. The remaining $67,000 of capital loss would be carried forward to subsequent tax years subject to the same rules. Assuming the taxpayer did not have any capital gains in any subsequent tax year to offset the capital loss carried forward, it would take twenty-three years, at the rate of $3,000 per year, for the taxpayer to fully deduct the remaining $67,000 of capital loss.

Some restrictions completely eliminate the use of an investment expense as a deduction. For example, a taxpayer may borrow funds to finance the purchase of an investment security to generate investment income and/or to hold for potential sale at a gain. The investment interest payable on such borrowing is deductible pursuant to Code section 163(d). However, if the loan proceeds were used to purchase a tax-exempt bond (generating tax-exempt interest), the investment interest payable on the borrowed funds would be disallowed under Code section 265.[35] In fact, section 265 disallows any type of otherwise deductible section 212 expense that is directly related to the acquisition or maintenance of a tax-exempt security.

Another example of potential deductions that are completely eliminated relates to the attendance of investment-themed seminars that cover various investment opportunities and strategies. While these expenses may be directly relevant to a taxpayer's income-generating investment activities, the deduction is specifically disallowed under Code section 274(h)(7).

Personal Deductions

Unlike business and investment deductions that are related to the generation of income, most personal deductions provide taxpayers with a measure of tax relief or encourage them to engage in certain activities. Thus, the Code often limits or eliminates these deductions for high income taxpayers through the use of "phase-outs," "floors" or "ceilings" that are based on a taxpayer's adjusted gross income.

Phase-outs

A "phase-out" of a deduction is a gradual pro-rata reduction of a deduction over a range of adjusted gross income. For example, if the phase-out range is between $70,000 and $80,000 of adjusted gross income, it means that beginning at the threshold adjusted gross income amount of $70,000, the taxpayer will only be able to take a percentage of the deduction. The percentage of the deduction that is available will decrease as the taxpayer's adjusted gross income rises toward the top of the phase-out range ($80,000). The deduction is completely unavailable for taxpayers with adjusted gross incomes above the top of the phase-out range.

An example of a phased-out deduction is found in Code section 219, which allows taxpayers making contributions to traditional IRAs to deduct contributions of $6,000 (plus a $1,000 catch-up amount for taxpayers older than fifty). In 2020, the deduction for single and head of household taxpayers who are covered by a work-place plan begins phasing out at the adjusted gross income threshold amount of $65,000 and is completely phased out at $75,000. For married spouses filing jointly where the spouse covered by a work place plan is the one making the IRA contribution, the deduction phases out between adjusted gross incomes of $103,000 and $123,000. For married taxpayers filing jointly where the non-covered spouse is the one making the distribution, the deduction phases out between adjusted gross incomes of $196,000 and $206,000. Taxpayers with adjusted gross incomes between the two phase-out values for their respective filing status may only deduct a percentage of their IRA contributions. If their adjusted gross incomes are above the top level of the phase-out, they may not deduct any of their contributions.

Floors

An adjusted gross income "floor" means that a deduction is not allowed until the amount of the potential deduction exceeds the floor. For example, assume the deduction for a certain expense is subject to a 7.5 percent adjusted gross income floor. If the taxpayer's adjusted gross income is $100,000, the "floor" would be $7,500. Thus, any amount of the deductible expense that is $7,500 or less would be under the floor and non-deductible. If the amount of the expense was $8,000, only $500—the amount by which the expense exceeds the floor—would be deductible.

Ceilings

A "ceiling" is the opposite of a floor and means that a deduction is limited to a certain percentage of adjusted gross income. The resulting amount is a ceiling beyond which no deduction would be allowed. For example, assume a taxpayer incurred $45,000 of a potentially deductible expense, and, that the deduction is limited to 15 percent of adjusted gross income. If the taxpayer's adjusted gross income was $200,000, the "ceiling," or the maximum amount deductible for that particular deduction would be $30,000 (15 percent of $200,000). The remaining $15,000 would not be deductible because it exceeds the ceiling. If the taxpayer's adjusted income was $300,000, the entire $45,000 would be deductible, as it would be the exact amount of the ceiling (15 percent of $300,000).

Charitable contribution deductions are subject to two different ceilings depending on the type of charitable organization receiving the contribution. In the case of a contribution of money to a public charity, the amount of the deductible contribution is limited to 60 percent of the taxpayer's "contribution base," which is essentially adjusted gross income. To the extent that the charitable contribution exceeds 60 percent of the taxpayer's contribution base, such amount is not deductible, and must be carried over to the next tax year (with a five-year maximum carry-over period) subject to the same limitation. Charitable contributions to private foundations are limited to 30 percent of the taxpayer's contribution base. Similarly, to the extent the contribution exceeds 30 percent of the taxpayer's contribution base, such amount is carried over to the next year (again, with a five-year maximum carry over-period subject to the same limitation). For a more detailed discussion of charitable contribution planning, see Chapter 28.

With phase-outs and floors, a taxpayer's adjusted gross income is inversely proportionate to the amount of the deduction; the higher the adjusted gross income, the lower the deduction amount. Conversely (although a ceiling essentially establishes a limitation for a deduction), the higher adjusted gross incomes have higher ceilings, and the amount of the deduction increases as gross adjusted income goes up.

Step 3 – Is the Deduction an "Above-the-Line" or "Below-the-Line Deduction?"

After determining which deductions have survived the hurdles of step 2, the final step is to determine which of those deductions are "above-the-line" deductions, and which are "below-the-line" deductions. As discussed below, that designation will be a significant factor in the ultimate tax benefit the taxpayer receives from those deductions.

Above-the-Line Deductions

"Above-the-line" deductions are deducted directly from gross income to compute adjusted gross income. Generally, if a deduction is specifically listed in Code section 62(a), it is an above-the-line deduction. If not, by default, it is a below-the-line deduction. An above-the-line business or investment deduction is always more beneficial to the taxpayer than a below the line deductions, because it is subject to no further limitations so that it reduces gross income dollar-for-dollar.[36]

Business Deductions

Consistent with the Code's preference for business-related deductions, section 62(a)(1) is a catch-all section by which all trade or business deductions, with the exception of certain unreimbursed employee business expenses, are designated as above-the-line deductions.[37] This means that all deductions allowable by Code section 162, as well as all other trade or business-related deductions (business interest, depreciation, start-up expenditures, depreciation, etc.) are above-the-line deductions.

Investment Deductions

As a general rule, investment deductions are below-the-line deductions. There are, however, three exceptions. One is for all deductions attributable to rent and royalty income not generated in the context of a trade or business.[38] For example, a taxpayer who occasionally rents a room in his or her home or a vacation home is probably not in a rental trade or business. Notwithstanding this fact, the section 212 deductions related to such rentals (utilities, repairs, commissions, advertising, etc.) are designated as above-the-line deductions.

Another exception relates to capital losses. As discussed above, capital losses are deductible to the extent of capital gains, plus $3,000 that is deductible against any other type of income.[39] Allowable capital loss deductions are designated as above-the-line deductions.[40]

Finally, Code section 165 designates the penalty for an early withdrawal of funds from a retirement savings account as an above-the-line deduction.[41]

Personal Deductions

While many items that taxpayers think of as "personal" deductions are often designated as below-the-line, some are not. The following personal deductions are designated as above-the-line deductions:

- Alimony payments (pre-2019 agreements only)[42]
- IRA contribution[43]

- Student loan interest[44]
- Qualified tuition and fees[45]
- One-half of self-employment tax[46]
- Self-employed health insurance[47]
- Contributions to self-employed retirement plans[48]
- Contributions to Health Savings Accounts[49]

Below-the-Line Deductions

As discussed above, above-the-line deductions are deducted from gross income in the computation of adjusted gross income. Therefore, all remaining deductions are by default "below-the-line" deductions (often referred to as "itemized deductions"). For the most part, itemized deductions are comprised of investment and personal deductions. Below-the-line deductions are often subject to phase-outs and floors that limit—and sometimes entirely eliminate—their value to the taxpayer. Once the amount of deductible below-the-line deductions is determined, that amount is deducted from adjusted gross income as the next-to-last step in the computation of taxable income.

Regular vs. Miscellaneous Below-the-Line Deductions

Within the realm of below-the-line deductions or itemized deductions, there are "miscellaneous" and "regular" itemized deductions. Miscellaneous itemize deductions are subject to a 2 percent adjusted gross income floor, and are often the least tax beneficial of all below-the-line deductions. Any itemized deduction not listed under section 67(b) is a miscellaneous itemized deduction. Conversely, any below-the-line deduction that *is* listed under Code section 67(b) is referred to as a "regular itemized deduction." The following are the most common "regular itemized deductions":

- Medical and dental expenses
- Taxes
- Interest
- Charitable contributions

USING ABOVE-THE-LINE AND BELOW-THE-LINE DEDUCTIONS TO COMPUTE TAXABLE INCOME

Once all the steps in the identification of above-the-line and below-the-line deductions have been completed, it is then possible to employ them in the computation of taxable income. The computation can be broken into three parts:

1. Determination of adjusted gross income
2. Deciding whether to use the standard or itemized deductions
3. Calculation of personal and dependent exemptions

Determining Adjusted Gross Income

The best way to explain how to compute adjusted gross income is to use the 2017 Form 1040 as a model. The bottom of the first page of the form—line 37—contains the entry "adjusted gross income." This means that all items of gross income minus above-the-line deductions are entered above line 37 (hence the term "above-the-line"). What tends to be confusing is that lines 7 through 21 appear to be items of gross income, the total of which is entered on line 22 (total income). The entries for lines 23 through 35 are above-the-line deductions that are specifically identified, but only include personal deductions. So where are the other above-the-line deductions, including business and investment deductions? They are included in the various forms and schedules that are used to calculate the taxpayer's gross income, as explained in Figure 7.1.

As demonstrated by Figure 7.1, various types of non-personal above-the-line deductions are netted against their respective income as computed on separate schedules and forms. The net numbers, positive or negative, are brought over to the first page of Form 1040. Consequently, the net income or loss numbers account for the above-the-line deductions. Next, the personal above-the-line deductions are totaled and subtracted from adjusted gross income.

Figure 7.1

ADJUSTED GROSS INCOME: GROSS INCOME MINUS "ABOVE-THE-LINE" DEDUCTIONS	
Gross income received by the taxpayer.	7. Wages and Salaries 8. Taxable Interest 9. Dividends 10.Taxable Refunds 11. Alimony Received (pre-2019 agreements only) 15. IRA Distributions 16. Pensions and Annuities 19. Unemployment Compensation 20. Social Security Benefits 21. Other Income
Items of gross income that are reduced by above-the-line deductions as computed on a separate schedule to be attached to the return.	12. Business income – Schedule C includes gross business income and above-the-line trade or business expenses deductions. The net amount income or loss is brought over to line 12 on Form 1040. 13. Capital Gain – Schedule D includes capital gain offset by capital losses. On the same schedule, the capital losses are netted with capital gains. A net capital gain is brought over to line 13 in its entirety. Alternatively, up to $3,000 of a net capital loss is brought over to line 13. 14. Other Gains or Losses includes Form 4797 entries, in which all losses from sales of property not listed on Schedule D are netted from gains from such sales. The net amount—either a positive or negative number—is brought over to line 14. 17. Rental Real Estate Income – Schedule E includes rental income offset by rental-related expenses (above-the-line deductions). The net amount is brought over to line 17. 18. Farm Income – Schedule F calculates net farm income. The net amount is brought over to line 18.
Total Income – Line 22	Total Income is the sum of lines 7 through 21 and incorporates the above-the-line deductions described above.
Other Above-the-line Deductions – Totaled on Line 36	23. Educator expense (expired at the end of 2013) 24. Certain business expenses of reservists, performing artists, and fee based officials 25. Health savings account deduction 26. Deductible part of self-employment tax 27. Self-employed SEP, SIMPLE and qualified plans 28. Self-employed health insurance deduction 29. Penalty on early withdrawal of retirement savings 30. Alimony paid (pre-2019 agreements only) 31. IRA deduction 32. Student loan deduction 33. Tuition and fees 34. Domestic production activities deduction
Adjusted Gross Income – Line 37	Total Income Minus Line 36.

The Standard Deduction vs. Itemized Deductions

After computing adjusted gross income, the next step is to subtract below-the-line deductions from adjusted gross income. However, in lieu of claiming below-the-line itemized deductions, taxpayers have the option of deducting the standard deduction. For tax year 2018, the standard deductions are as follows: single taxpayer - $12,200; head of household - $18,350; married filing jointly - $24,400; and married filing separately - $12,200.[50] The standard deduction reflects the minimum amount of an unconditional below-the-line deduction allowed to taxpayers based on filing status. This means that the taxpayer may deduct the greater of the standard deduction or the total amount of itemized deductions. If a single taxpayer had $10,000 of itemized deductions, he or she would deduct the higher standard deduction of $12,000. Conversely, if the single taxpayer had $15,000 of itemized deductions, he or she would deduct that amount.

In order to determine whether to claim the standard deduction or itemized deductions, the taxpayer must compute itemized deductions to ascertain which of the two is higher. Itemized deductions are entered on Schedule A of Form 1040. Using the 2018 Schedule A as a model, if the total amount of itemized deductions exceed the standard deduction, such amount is brought over to Form 1040, where it is deducted from adjusted gross income.

To illustrate the computation of itemized deductions, assume that for tax year 2020, a single taxpayer under the age of sixty-five has adjusted gross income of $80,000, medical expenses of $8,100, state income taxes of $430 and home mortgage interest of $8,500. Figure 7.2 sets forth an analysis of the deductibility of these items.

Based on the computations in Figure 7.2, it is clear that the taxpayer would deduct the higher of the sum of his or her itemized deductions ($14,300) rather than the lower standard deduction ($12,200). However, due to the application of the 7.5 percent AGI medical expense floor the taxpayer's otherwise allowable itemized deductions are reduced from $20,300 to $14,300, eliminating $6,000 of otherwise deductible expenses.

THE BOTTOM LINE COMPUTATION OF TAXABLE INCOME

The computation of taxable income follows a number of steps:

1. Begin by determining gross income.

2. After determining which allowable deductions are designated as above-the-line deductions and whether or not phase-outs apply, subtract the aggregate amount of the above-the-line deductions from gross income to arrive at adjusted gross income.

3. Last, determine whether to use the standard deduction or the aggregate amount of itemized deductions. To do so, ascertain which itemized deductions are regular and which are miscellaneous. Apply the applicable adjusted gross income floors to determine the bottom-line amount of itemized deductions. Then, determine and use the higher of the standard deduction or the total amount of itemized deductions. Subtract itemized deductions from adjusted gross income.

WHERE CAN I FIND OUT MORE?

Tax Facts on Insurance & Employee Benefits (National Underwriter Company; published annually).

Figure 7.2

BELOW-THE-LINE ITEMIZED DEDUCTIONS

For a single taxpayer with an adjusted gross income of $80,000 (Standard deduction: $12,000)

Expense Type	Amount Paid	Floor	Amount Deductible
Medical	$ 8,100	7.5% of AGI	$ 2,100
State Income Tax	$ 3,700	N/A	$ 3,700
Home Mortgage Interest	$ 8,500	N/A	$ 8,500
Total	$20,300		$14,300

FREQUENTLY ASKED QUESTIONS

Question – How can a taxpayer maximize deductions in the tax year in which taxpayer starts a new business?

Answer – Code Section 162(a) allows taxpayer to deduct business expenses provided they are incurred when the taxpayer is actually operating the business. Thus, pre-opening start-up expenditures are not deductible. However, once the taxpayer actually begins operating a trade or business, Code section 195 allows the taxpayer to amortize (deduct over time) the cost of all start-up expenditures over a period of not less than sixty months beginning in the month in which the taxpayer commences the business.

Assume that between January 1 and June 30 of the tax year, the taxpayer incurred the cost of rent, utilities and labor in the aggregate amount of $6,000 in preparing to open an accounting business. On July 1, the taxpayer opened for business, and through the end of the year incurred an additional cost of rent, utilities and labor also in the aggregate amount of $6,000. Although the taxpayer may deduct the entire $6,000 of the post-opening rent expenses under Code section 162(a), the $6,000 "start-up expenditures" would have to be amortized over a sixty-month period beginning in July, the month the business opened. As a result, only $600 of the $6,000 of start-up expenditures may be deducted in the first year (one-tenth of $6,000). So in the first year, despite spending $12,000 on rent, utilities and labor, her deduction would be limited to $6,600.

Obviously, the taxpayer would prefer to maximize the deductible amount of the calendar year costs. In order to do so, the taxpayer should consider opening for business as soon as possible even if it is in a makeshift office and even if not as fully equipped to begin operations as the taxpayer might desire. If opened for business on March 1, the section 162(a) deduction would be $10,000 (assuming expenses were $1,000 per month). Thus, only $2,000, the aggregate amount of start-up expenditures for January and February would be required to be amortized over a sixty month period.

Question – Is a tax credit or deduction more beneficial to the taxpayer?

Answer – Without question, a tax credit is more beneficial to the taxpayer. This is because each dollar of a tax credit saves one dollar of tax. In monetary terms, a taxpayer in the 37 percent tax bracket or the 22 percent tax bracket saves an equivalent amount of tax. Conversely, a tax deduction only saves the taxpayer the amount of tax that would have been owed without the deduction. If a taxpayer is in the 22 percent tax bracket, each dollar of a deduction would save the taxpayer 22 cents in tax. On the other hand, if the taxpayer was in the 37 percent tax bracket, each dollar of a deduction would save that taxpayer 37 cents in tax.

CHAPTER ENDNOTES

1. The Supreme Court has described deductions as a matter of "legislative grace." *INDOPCO, Inc. v. Comm'r*, 503 US 79, 84 (1992).
2. IRC Sec. 56(b). For purposes of computing the alternative minimum tax, many below-the-deductions are essentially disallowed.
3. IRS Publication 598.
4. IRC Sec. 163.
5. IRC Sec. 164.
6. IRC Sec. 165.
7. In addition to being a catch-all section for deductible business expenses, IRC Sec. 162(a) also identifies three specific deductible expenses, i.e., compensation (§162(a)(1)), travel expenses while away from home (§162(a)(2)) and rental expenses (§162(a)(3)).
8. See *Henry v. Comm'r*, 36 T.C. 879 (1961).
9. See *United States v. Akin*, 248 F.2d 742 (10th Cir. 1957).
10. Treas. Reg. §1.162-1(a).
11. See IRC Sec. 195.
12. See *Liddle v. Comm'r*, 103 T.C. 285 (1994).
13. IRC Sec. 168(c). However, as an exception, by taxpayer election, IRC Sec. 179 allows a generous deduction of the cost of certain depreciable property in year such property is placed in service. In 2013, the section 179 deduction limit was $500,000. However, for 2014, the deduction limit is to be reduced to $25,000. Additionally, a special 50 percent bonus depreciation deduction expired at the end of 2013. See H.R. 8 "The American Taxpayer Relief Act of 2012," 113th Cong. 2d Sess. (2014).
14. IRC Sec. 195(b).
15. *See* Treas. Reg. §1.212-1(g).
16. Treas. Reg. §1.212-1(d).
17. IRC Sec. 212(1).
18. IRC Sec. 212(2).
19. IRC Sec. 212(3).
20. IRC Sec. 215.
21. IRC Sec. 219.
22. IRC Secs. 221 and 222.

23. IRC Sec. 164(f).
24. IRC Sec. 162(l).
25. IRC Sec. 401(c)(2).
26. IRC Sec. 223.
27. IRC Sec. 165.
28. IRC Sec. 213.
29. IRC Sec. 164.
30. IRC Sec. 163.
31. IRC Sec. 170.
32. Treas. Reg. §1.162-1(a).
33. IRC Secs. 274(k), 274(n).
34. However, the disallowed loss carries over into subsequent tax years subject to the same rules. So, if in year one, the taxpayer has a $1,000 disallowed passive activity loss, but in year two has $1,000 of passive activity income, the loss would be deductible in year two. IRC Sec. 469(b).
35. If only a portion of the borrowed funds were used to purchase a tax-exempt bond, then an allocable portion of the investment income would be disallowed pursuant to section 265. The other portion of the borrowed funds used to purchase securities yielding taxable income would be deductible.
36. Conversely, some personal above-the-line deductions such as contributions to a traditional IRA are subject to phase-out.
37. IRC Sec. 62(a)(1) and (2). Unreimbursed employee business expenses are out of pocket business expenses paid for by an employee but not reimbursed by the employer. However, there is an exception for unreimbursed educator expenses paid by elementary and secondary school teachers not in excess of $250. This exception was scheduled to expire on December 31, 2013.
38. IRC Sec. 62(a)(4).
39. IRC Sec. 1211(b).
40. IRC Sec. 62(a)(3).
41. IRC Sec. 62(a)(9).
42. IRC Sec. 62(a)(10).
43. IRC Sec. 62(a)(7).
44. IRC Sec. 62(a)(17).
45. IRC Sec. 62(a)(18).
46. IRC Secs. 62(a)(1), 164(f).
47. IRS Publication 535. *See also* Gen. Couns. Mem. 200524001 (May 17, 2005).
48. IRC Sec. 62(a)(6).
49. IRC Sec. 62(a)(19).
50. IRC Sec. 63. There is an additional standard deduction for taxpayers who are blind or age sixty-five or older. For 2018, the additional standard deduction is $1,300. If such taxpayer is unmarried and not a surviving spouse, the additional standard deduction is $1,600 rather than $1,300. Certain taxpayers have a zero standard deduction, including: (1) married taxpayers filing separately, if either spouse itemizes; (2) non-resident aliens; (3) taxpayers filing a short year return (because of a change in their annual accounting period); *and* (4) estates or trusts, common trust funds, or partnerships.

CALCULATION OF TAX

CHAPTER 8

INTRODUCTION

The determination of a taxpayer's exact income tax liabilities is complex, but has three primary components. First a taxpayer must determine his or her filing status, which can vary based on a number of different factors related to the taxpayer's personal circumstances. The choice of filing status can have significant effects on the taxpayer's liability.

Second, the taxpayer must report all income received for the year. See Chapter 3 for a discussion of ordinary income reporting, and Chapter 4 for details about reporting capital gains and dividends. More details on the taxability of particular types of income are included below. A series of calculations are used to incorporate allowable deductions and exemptions (see Chapter 7) and arrive at taxable income.

Finally, a taxpayer's taxable income is used to determine liability. Liability for ordinary income taxes is determined by using the tax tables published by the IRS annually. Once the tax liability is calculated, tax credits (See Chapter 9) and prepayments (from withholding and/or quarterly payments) are applied against the liability to determine the amount of money that is either owed to the IRS or due to the taxpayer as a refund.

In addition to ordinary income taxes, certain taxpayers may face several types of additional tax liabilities:

- *AMT.* Taxpayers with relatively high incomes may also have to calculate their liabilities under the Alternative Minimum Tax (AMT) See Chapter 11 for details on the AMT.
- *Self-employment taxes.* Self-employment taxes are levied on earned income to cover social security and Medicare taxes. For wage earners, these liabilities are satisfied through employer withholding, and calculation of the liability by the taxpayer is generally not necessary. Self-employed individuals must calculate and pay (indeed, often pre-pay) these amounts themselves. These tax liabilities are collectively known as the "self-employment tax." See Chapter 12 for details on self-employment taxes.
- *Additional Medicare surtax.* Taxpayers with earned income above certain thresholds are subject to an additional 0.9 percent Medicare surtax on income above the relevant threshold. See Chapter 13.
- *Net investment income tax.* The net investment income tax (NIIT) is also an additional surtax that is imposed on investment income that exceeds certain thresholds. See Chapter 13.

DETERMINATION OF FILING STATUS

The first step to filing a federal income tax return is the determination of the taxpayer's correct filing status. In addition to the proper amount of tax, filing status is used to determine a taxpayer's filing requirements, standard deduction, and eligibility for certain credits and deductions. Generally, filing status is determined by marital status on the last day of the year.[1] A tax payer must file under one of five statuses:

Single. Taxpayers are single if they are unmarried and do not qualify for another filing status. Taxpayers are considered unmarried for the whole year if, on the last day of the tax year, they were unmarried or legally separated from a spouse under a divorce or separate maintenance decree.

Married Filing Jointly. A married couple may file a return together using the married filing jointly status. The couple can choose this status if they are considered married (state law governs whether a couple is married) and both agree to file a joint return. On a joint return, both spouses report their combined income and deduct their combined allowable expenses. A couple can file a joint return even if one of the spouses had no income or deductions.

Married Filing Separately. A couple can choose married filing separately as their filing status if they are married. This filing status may benefit a couple if they want to be responsible only for their own tax, or if this status results in less tax than filing a joint return. If both spouses do not agree to file a joint return, they must use the married filing separately status unless one of the spouses qualifies for head of household status.

If a taxpayer qualifies to file as head of household, instead of as married filing separately, the tax may be lower, they may be able to claim the earned income credit and certain other credits, and their standard deduction will be higher as well.

Head of Household. This status generally applies if the taxpayer is not married, or is considered unmarried at the end of the year, and has paid more than half the cost of maintaining a home for him or herself and a qualifying person. A married taxpayer may file as head of household if he or she files a separate return and the spouse did not live in the home during the last six months of the tax year. A qualifying person is either:

- a "qualifying child" for the purposes of the child tax credit; or
- a "qualifying individual" for the purposes of child and dependent tax credit.

See Chapter 9 for detailed discussion of which individuals can be a "qualifying child" or "qualifying individual."

Qualifying Widow(er) with Dependent Child. A taxpayer with one or more dependents may be eligible to use qualifying widow(er) with dependent child as their filing status for two years following the death of a spouse. For example, if a taxpayer's spouse died in 2018, and the taxpayer has not remarried, he or she may be able to use this filing status for 2019 and 2020. This status is beneficial because the tax brackets and standard deduction amounts are the same as the status for those married filing a joint return.[2]

Note that if the taxpayer has a same-sex spouse whom the taxpayer legally married in a state (or foreign country) that recognizes same-sex marriage, the taxpayer and spouse generally must use the married filing jointly or married filing separately filing status on their return, even if they now live in a state (or foreign country) that does not recognize same-sex marriage.[3]

WHAT TYPES OF INCOME CALCULATIONS ARE REQUIRED?

Gross income is the total of all amounts of taxable income from all sources. (See below for types of taxable income.) *Adjusted gross income* (AGI) is determined by subtracting any above-the-line deductions from gross income. "Above-the-the" line deductions include the following:[4]

- Business expense deductions attributable to a trade, business, or profession carried on by the individual taxpayer as a self-employed person, not as an employee[5]
- Deductions related to investment property held for the production of rents and royalties[6]
- Losses from the sale or exchange of property[7]
- Educator expenses[8]
- IRA deductions[9]
- Student loan interest[10]
- Tuition and fees (see Chapter 9 for details on education credits)[11]
- One-half of the self-employment tax (as calculated on Schedule SE)[12]
- Self-employed medical savings account contributions[13]
- Self-employed retirement plans[14]

- Contributions to Health Savings Accounts[15]
- Penalties on early withdrawal of savings[16]
- Alimony payments (discontinued for payments pursuant to divorce and separation agreements executed after December 31, 2018)[17]

See Chapter 3 for a more detailed discussion of the rules governing income calculations.

After calculating AGI, the final income calculation is *taxable income*, which is then used to determine tax liability. "Taxable income" is AGI, less personal exemptions and any below-the-line deductions. Below-the-line deductions vary widely, and are often subject to restrictions and limitations on their use that may be based on a taxpayer's income level and/or filing status. When determining below-the-line deductions, taxpayers may use one of two methods:

1. *Standard deduction.* Individuals may subtract from adjusted gross income an amount for each personal exemption allowable to the individual and the standard deduction (which varies with filing status).

2. *Itemized deductions.* Individuals may subtract from adjusted gross income an amount for each personal exemption allowable to the individual and the total of their itemized deductions.

Using either method, the resulting figure is "taxable income." The actual amount of tax due is then determined by referring to the tax rate tables.[18] See Chapter 7 for a discussion of the types of above- and below-the-line deductions that are available.

TAXATION OF PARTICULAR TYPES OF INCOME

Code section 61 defines the types of income that may be taxable, subject to certain deductions and credits. These income types are discussed in detail below.

Compensation for Services

This category includes fees, commissions, fringe benefits, and similar items. This category of income includes retirement plan contributions, stock options, restricted property (for example, stock with restrictions that affect its value), sick pay, advance commissions, bonuses and back pay awards, as well as tips. In most cases, a taxpayer must also report as income any amount received for personal injury or sickness through an employer-paid accident or health plan.[19]

Gross Income Derived from Business

In a manufacturing, merchandising, or mining business, "gross income" means the total sales, less the cost of goods sold, plus any income from investments and from incidental or outside operations or sources.[20]

Gains Derived from Dealings in Property

Gain realized on the sale or exchange of property is included in gross income, unless otherwise excluded. For this purpose, property includes tangible items (such as a building) and intangible items (such as goodwill). Generally, the gain is the excess of the amount realized over the unrecovered cost or other basis for the property sold or exchanged.[21] The specific rules for computing the amount of gain or loss are contained in Code section 1001 and related regulations.

Interest

Most interest that a taxpayer receives (interest on bank accounts, money market accounts, certificates of deposit, and deposited insurance dividends) is taxable income. Interest from treasury bonds is subject to federal income tax, but is exempt from all state and local income taxes. However, interest on some bonds used to finance government operations and issued by a state or territory, as well as interest in certain municipal bonds, is not taxable at the federal level.[22] Additionally, exempt-interest dividends received from a mutual fund or other regulated investment company, including those received from a qualified fund of funds in any tax year beginning after December 22, 2010, are not included in taxable income. Interest income is generally not subject to regular withholding. However, it may be subject to backup withholding to ensure that income tax is collected on the income.[23]

Rents

Rental income, defined as any payment that a taxpayer receives for the use or occupation of property, is includable in gross income. Rental income also includes amounts paid by a tenant to cancel a lease, any expenses of the taxpayer paid by the tenant, and the fair market value of property or services that the taxpayer receives instead of money.[24]

Royalties

Royalties from copyrights, patents, oil, gas, and mineral properties are taxable as ordinary income. Royalties from copyrights on literary, musical, or artistic works and similar property, or from patents on inventions, are amounts paid to a taxpayer for the right to use the work over a specified period of time. Royalties generally are based on the number of units sold, such as the number of books, tickets to a performance, or machines sold. Royalty income from oil, gas, and mineral properties is the amount a taxpayer receives when natural resources are extracted from the property. The royalties are based on units, such as barrels, tons, etc., and are paid to the taxpayer by a person or company who leases the property.[25]

Dividends

Dividends—the most common type of distribution from a corporation—are distributions from a corporation to its shareholders. Most dividends are paid in cash but may be paid as stock of another corporation or any other property. A taxpayer might also receive dividends through interest in a partnership, an estate, a trust, a subchapter S corporation, or from an association that is taxable as a corporation. A shareholder of a corporation may be deemed to receive a dividend if the corporation pays the debt of its shareholder, the shareholder receives services from the corporation, or the shareholder is allowed the use of the corporation's property. Additionally, a shareholder that provides services to a corporation may be deemed to receive a dividend if the corporation pays the shareholder service-provider in excess of what it would pay a third party for the same services. A shareholder may also receive distributions such as additional stock or stock rights in the distributing corporation; such distributions may or may not qualify as dividends. Dividends can either be classified as ordinary or qualified. Whereas ordinary dividends are taxable as ordinary income, qualified dividends that meet certain requirements are taxed at lower capital gain rates.[26]

Alimony and Separate Maintenance Payments

Alimony is a payment to or for a spouse or former spouse under a divorce or separation order. Alimony must be included in the spouse's or former spouse's income. Amounts paid under divorce or separate maintenance decrees or written separation agreements entered into between the taxpayer and his or her present or former spouse will be considered alimony for federal tax purposes if:

- The taxpayer and spouse or former spouse do not file a joint return with each other.
- The payor of the alimony makes payment in cash (including checks or money orders).
- The payment is received by (or on behalf of) the spouse or former spouse.
- The divorce or separate maintenance decree or written separation agreement does not say that the payment is not alimony.
- If legally separated under a decree of divorce or separate maintenance, the spouses or former spouses are not members of the same household when the alimony payment is made.
- The taxpayer has no liability to make the payment (in cash or property) after the death of their spouse or former spouse.
- The payment is not treated as child support or a property settlement.[27]

The Tax Cuts and Jobs Act of 2017 eliminated the deduction for alimony paid pursuant to divorce agreements entered into after 2018. See Chapter 24 for a more detailed discussion of the tax consequences of marriage and divorce.

Pensions and Annuities

If a taxpayer receives retirement benefits in the form of pension or annuity payments from a qualified employer retirement plan, all or some portion of the amounts received may be taxable. Even for payments that are taxable at the federal level, some states have special rules that reduce or eliminate state income taxes on pension payments. The payments that the taxpayer receives are fully taxable if the taxpayer has no investment in the contract because any of the following situations apply:

- The taxpayer did not contribute anything—or is not considered to have contributed anything—for the pension or annuity.
- The taxpayer's employer did not withhold contributions from the taxpayer's salary.
- The taxpayer received all of the contributions (the investment in the contract) tax-free in prior years.

If the taxpayer contributed after-tax dollars to a pension or annuity, the pension payments are partially taxable. No tax is payable on the part of the payment that represents a return of the after-tax amount the taxpayer paid. This amount is the investment in the contract, and includes the amounts the employer contributed that were taxable to the taxpayer when contributed.[28]

Income from Life Insurance and Endowment Contracts

Life insurance proceeds paid to a taxpayer beneficiary by reason of the death of the insured person are not taxable unless the policy was turned over to the taxpayer for a price. This is true even if the proceeds were paid under an accident or health insurance policy or an endowment contract. However, interest income received as a result of life insurance proceeds may be taxable. If death benefits are paid to the taxpayer in a lump sum or other than at regular intervals, only the benefits that are more than the amount payable to you at the time of the insured person's death are includable in income. If the benefit payable at death is not specified, benefit payments that are more than the present value of the premium payments at the time of death are included in income.

Life insurance proceeds that are received in installments are partly excludable from the taxpayer beneficiary's income. To determine the excluded part, the total lump sum payable at the death of the insured person is divided by the number of installments to be paid. Anything in excess of this excluded part is includable in income as interest.

If a life insurance policy is surrendered for cash, any proceeds that are more than the cost of the life insurance policy are includable in income. In most cases, the cost of the policy is the total of premiums paid, less any refunded premiums, rebates, dividends, or unrepaid loans that were not included in income.

Proceeds of an endowment contract that are paid in a lump sum on the contract's maturity are taxable only if the proceeds are more than the cost of the policy. The taxable amount is determined by subtracting any untaxed amount previously received under the contract from the total premiums (or other consideration) paid.[29]

Income from Discharge of Indebtedness

In general, a taxpayer is liable for a debt that is cancelled, forgiven, or discharged, and must include the canceled amount in gross income. Certain types of cancelled debt outlined in Code section 108 qualify for an exclusion from the taxpayer's income. Cancellation of all or part of a debt that is secured by property may occur because of a foreclosure, repossession, voluntary return of the property to the lender, abandonment of the property, or a loan modification. If the debt is secured by property and that property is taken by the lender in full or partial satisfaction of the debt, the taxpayer is treated as having sold that property and may have a taxable gain or loss.[30] See Chapter 34 for a detailed discussion of cancellation of debt issues.

Distributive Share of Partnership Gross Income

A partner's gross income includes his or her distributive share of the partnership's gross income. Generally, the partnership agreement determines a partner's distributive share of any item or class of items of income, gain, loss, deduction, or credit. However, the allocations provided for in the partnership agreement or any modification will be disregarded if they do not have substantial economic effect. If the partnership agreement does not provide for an allocation, or an allocation does not have substantial economic effect, the partner's distributive share of the partnership items is generally determined by the partner's interest in the partnership.[31]

Income in Respect of a Decedent

All income a decedent would have received had death not occurred and that was not properly includible on the final return, filed by the decedent's personal representative for the year of death, is income in respect of a decedent. Such income must be included in the income of one of the following:

- The decedent's estate, if the estate receives it.
- The beneficiary, if the right to income is passed directly to the beneficiary and the beneficiary receives it.
- Any person to whom the estate properly distributes the right to receive it.[32]

Income from an Interest in an Estate or Trust.

Interest received as a beneficiary of an estate or trust is generally taxable income. The beneficiary should receive a Schedule K-1 (Form 1041) from the fiduciary with information that needs to be reported on a Form 1040.[33]

Social Security Benefits

Social Security benefit income includes monthly retirement, survivor, and disability benefits. They do not include supplemental security income (SSI) payments, which are not taxable. Equivalent tier 1 railroad retirement benefits are the part of tier 1 benefits that a railroad employee or beneficiary would have been entitled to receive under the social security system. They are commonly called the "social security equivalent benefit" (SSEB) portion of tier 1 benefits.

If the taxpayer is married and files a joint return for the year, the taxpayer and spouse must combine their incomes and benefits to figure whether any of their combined benefits are taxable. Even if the spouse did not receive any benefits, the taxpayer must add the spouse's income to figure whether any of the benefits are taxable. If the only income the taxpayer received during the year was social security or the SSEB portion of tier 1 railroad retirement benefits, the benefits received generally are not taxable and the taxpayer probably does not have to file a return. If the taxpayer has income in addition to the social security (or railroad retirement) benefits, the taxpayer may have to file a return even if none of the benefits are taxable.

To determine whether any of a taxpayer's benefits may be taxable, compare the base amount for the filing status (explained below) with the total of: (1) One-half of the benefits, plus (2) All other income, including tax-exempt interest. When making this comparison, the taxpayer's other income is not reduced by any exclusions for: Interest from qualified U.S. savings bonds, Employer-provided adoption benefits, Foreign earned income or foreign housing, or Income earned by bona fide residents of American Samoa or Puerto Rico.

As described above, the base amount is:

- $25,000 if the taxpayer is single, head of household, or qualifying widow(er);
- $25,000 if the taxpayer is married filing separately and lived apart from the spouse for all of the year;
- $32,000 if the taxpayer is married filing jointly; or
- $0 if the taxpayer is married filing separately and lived with his or her spouse at any time during the year.[34]

Other Income

Income not otherwise described above may include such items as income received in barter exchanges, income received at sales parties, certain repayments, etc. For a discussion of other and miscellaneous income, see Chapter 12 of IRS Publication 17, *Your Income Tax.*

WHERE CAN I FIND OUT MORE?

Tax Facts on Insurance & Employee Benefits (National Underwriter Company, published annually and available online at search.taxfactsonline.com).

CHAPTER ENDNOTES

1. IRS Publication 17 (2013), Chap. 2; Internal Revenue Manual §21.6.1.1-6.
2. IRC Sec. 1; IRS Publication 17 (2013), IRS Tax Tip 2013-13 (Feb. 13, 2013).
3. IRS Publication 17 (2013).
4. IRC Sec. 62(a).
5. IRC Sec. 162.

6. IRC Sec. 212.
7. IRC Secs. 1211, 1222.
8. IRC Sec. 62(a)(2)(D).
9. IRC Sec. 219.
10. IRC Sec. 221.
11. IRC Sec. 222.
12. IRC Sec. 164(f).
13. IRC Sec. 220.
14. IRC Sec. 404.
15. IRC Sec. 223.
16. IRC Sec. 62(a)(9).
17. IRC Sec. 215.
18. Tax tables for individual taxpayers can be found in the instructions for IRS Form 1040.
19. IRC Sec. 61(a)(1).
20. IRC Sec. 61(a)(2); Treas. Reg. §1.61-3(a).
21. IRC Sec. 61(a)(3); Treas. Reg. §1.61-6(a).
22. IRS Tax Topic 403.
23. IRC Sec. 61(a)(4); IRS Publication 17, chap. 17.
24. IRC Sec. 61(a)(5); IRS Tax Topic 414.
25. IRC Sec. 61(a)(6); Treas. Reg. §1.512(b)-1; IRS Fact Sheet 2013-6 (April 2013).
26. IRC Sec. 61(a)(7); IRS Tax Topic 404. See IRS Publication 550 for a definition of qualified dividends.
27. IRC Sec. 61(a)(8); IRS Tax Topic 452.
28. IRC Secs. 61(a)(9), (a)(11); IRS Tax Topic 410.
29. IRC Sec. 61(a)(10); IRS Publication 17 (2013), Chap. 12.
30. IRC Secs. 61(a)(12), 108; Treas. Reg. §1.108-2; IRS Tax Topic 431.
31. IRC Secs. 61(a)(13), 704; Treas. Reg. §§1.61-13, 1.704-1(b)(2)(ii).
32. IRC Sec. 61(a)(14); IRS Publication 559 (2013).
33. IRC Sec. 61(a)(15); IRS Publication 17 (2013).
34. IRS Publication 17 (2013).

CREDITS

CHAPTER 9

INTRODUCTION

After the income tax has been computed by applying the tax rates to taxable income, certain credits and prepayments may be used to reduce the tax that is otherwise due. A *credit* represents a dollar-for dollar reduction of tax.

All tax credits are either *refundable* or *nonrefundable*. *Refundable* credits are recoverable regardless of the amount of the taxpayer's tax liability for the taxable year. In other words, the taxpayer might get money back (a "refund") if the amount of the credit is more than the amount of tax due. On the other hand, *nonrefundable* credits may be used only to reduce the taxpayer's tax liability, and are subject to certain other limitations. The *refundable* credits and prepayments include:

- Taxes withheld on wages
- Payments of estimated tax
- The Earned Income Credit[1]
- The child tax credit (which is only partially refundable)
- A credit for health insurance premiums paid by uninsured workers who were displaced by trade competition[2]

The first two refundable credits are simply refunds of money paid in advance by the taxpayer that was not required to meet his or her tax obligations. The earned income credit is discussed below. Additionally, some nonrefundable credits may become partially refundable under certain circumstances.

EARNED INCOME TAX CREDIT

The Earned Income Tax Credit (EITC) is a refundable tax credit that is designed to help the working poor. Because it targets household income, it has been called a "remarkably effective anti-poverty program."[3]

To qualify for the EITC, the taxpayer (and spouse if married filing jointly), must meet all of the following requirements:[4]

1. Have a Social Security number that is valid for employment.
2. Have earned income from wages, self-employment, or some other source.
3. Must file jointly if married.
4. Must be either:
   a. a U.S. citizen or resident alien all year, or
   b. a nonresident alien married to a U.S. citizen or resident alien who files a joint return and chooses to be treated as a resident alien.
5. Cannot be the qualifying child of another person.
6. Cannot file Form 2555 or 2555-EZ (related to foreign earned income).
7. Investment income must not exceed $3,350 for the year.

8. For 2020, earned income and adjusted gross income (AGI) must each be less than:

   a. $50,594 ($56,844 married filing jointly) with three or more qualifying children;

   b. $47,440 ($53,330 married filing jointly) with two qualifying children;

   c. $41,756 ($47,646 married filing jointly) with one qualifying child; or

   d. $15,820 ($21,710 married filing jointly) with no qualifying child.

If all of the preceding rules are satisfied, the IRS sets out the maximum credit that may be included on a taxpayer's return. These amounts are based on the number of qualifying children in the taxpayer's household. The amounts change every year. For 2020, the maximum credit is:[5]

Three or more qualifying children	$6,600
Two qualifying children	$5,920
One qualifying child	$3,584
No qualifying children	$538

For purposes of the EITC, a qualifying child must have a valid Social Security Number and meet certain relationship, age, residency, and joint return tests[6] outlined in Figure 9.1.

When a child is a qualifying child for more than one person, "tie breaker" rules apply. These rules do not apply to a spouse filing a joint tax return. Under the tie-breaker rules, the child is treated as a qualifying child only by:

- the parents if they file a joint return;

- the parent, if only one of the persons is the child's parent;

Figure 9.1

REQUIREMENTS FOR QUALIFYING CHILDREN UNDER THE EITC	
Relationship Test	• Must be a son, daughter, adopted child, stepchild, foster child, brother, sister, half-brother, half-sister, stepbrother, stepsister or descendant of any of them (i.e. grandchild, niece or nephew). • "Adopted children" include children lawfully placed with the taxpayer who is filing for adoption. • "Foster children" include children placed with the taxpayer by an authorized placement agency or court. • Relationships formed by marriage (stepdaughter, stepson, etc.), do not end when the marriage that formed the relationship ends.
Age Test	• Must be younger than 19 at the end of the year (or 24 if a full-time student), and younger than the taxpayer (or their spouse if filing a joint return); or • Any age if permanently and totally disabled.
Residency Test	• Must live with the taxpayer (or their spouse if filing a joint tax return) for more than half of the year. Time spent temporarily away from home due to special circumstances (school, illness, military service, etc.) is counted as time the child lived with the taxpayer.
Joint Return Test	• The child cannot file a joint return for the tax year unless the child and the child's spouse did not have a separate filing requirement and filed the joint return to claim a refund only. • A taxpayer cannot claim the EITC credit for a child who was married at the end of the year unless the child can be claimed as a dependent. Exceptions are available for children who could have been claimed as a dependent, but for an agreement to not claim the child contained in a Form 8332 or similar statement.

- the parent with whom the child lived the longest during the tax year, if two of the persons are the child's parent and they do not file a joint return together;
- the parent with the highest AGI if the child lived with each parent for the same amount of time during the tax year and they do not file a joint return together;
- the person with the highest AGI if no parent can claim the child as a qualifying child; or
- the person with the higher AGI than any parent who can also claim the child as a qualifying child but does not.

Additionally, IRS Publication 501 outlines special rules for children of divorced or separated parents.

Child Tax Credit

Eligible taxpayers who meet certain requirements may claim a child tax credit for each "qualifying child." While this credit is generally nonrefundable, a portion of it may be refundable under certain circumstances discussed below.

Through 2017, the amount of the child tax credit is $1,000.[7] Beginning in 2018, the child tax credit will increase to $2,000, $1,400 of which is refundable.[8]A qualifying child is an individual who:

- is the taxpayer's son, daughter, stepchild, foster child, brother, sister, stepbrother, or stepsister (or a descendant of any of them);
- is less than seventeen years old;
- has the same principal place of abode as the taxpayer for more than one-half of the taxable year; *and*
- has not provided over one-half of such individual's own support for the calendar year in which the taxpayer's taxable year begins.[9]

A qualifying child must also be a citizen or resident of the United States.[10] Any adopted children are treated the same as natural born children.[11] The taxpayer's return must identify the individual for whom the credit is being claimed by stating the child's name *and* taxpayer identification number (i.e., Social Security number). The child tax credit must generally be claimed for a full taxable year.[12]

For 2018 and beyond, the basic child tax credit is "phased out" (i.e., reduced) for taxpayers with AGIs in excess of $400,000 (join returns, $200,000 for all other types of filers). The phase-out amounts are not indexed for inflation.[13] These provisions are set to expire after 2025. More information about the impact of the 2017 Tax Reform Act is available in the Frequently Asked Questions below.

NONREFUNDABLE CREDITS

As mentioned above, nonrefundable credits can only be used to reduce a tax obligation from reported income. If a taxpayer has reduced income to zero and still has nonrefundable credits available, those excess credits cannot be used. Nonrefundable credits generally fall into two different categories: business and personal. Business credits are complex and technical, and are available in a wide variety of circumstances that are beyond the scope of this chapter.[14]

Personal credits include allowing a taxpayer to reduce tax obligations for a variety of reasons, including credits for children and other dependents who reside with the taxpayer, college-related expenses, and a "saver's credit"[15] available for contributions towards retirement savings that are made under certain circumstances. The foreign tax credit is also a personal credit that is available for taxes that were paid to foreign countries, and may apply to both businesses and individual taxpayers.[16]

Child and Dependent Care Credit

An individual may claim a credit for certain employment-related child and dependent care expenses.[17] The amount of the credit is up to 35 percent of expenses incurred for the care of a "qualifying individual" who is:

- a qualifying child of the taxpayer who is under age thirteen, and for whom the taxpayer is entitled to take a dependency exemption (see Chapter 4);
- a physically or mentally incapacitated dependent (including a spouse);[18] or

- a person who would have been the taxpayer's dependent but for the fact that income was more than $3,900 or the person filed a joint return.[19]

Payments for dependent care services are "employment-related" *if* they are incurred to enable the taxpayer to be employed or to seek employment (full or part-time).[20] Expenses for service outside the taxpayer's household qualify if they are for a qualifying child or a qualifying individual who regularly spends at least eight hours each day in the taxpayer's household.[21] However, no amount of any expenses for an overnight camp will be considered "employment-related."[22] Payments for child or dependent care to a close relative qualify for the credit if:

- neither the taxpayer nor his spouse is entitled to claim the relative as a dependent; *and*

- the relative is not a child of the taxpayer who is younger than age nineteen at the close of the taxable year.[23]

The name, address, and taxpayer identification number of the childcare provider must be stated on the taxpayer's return in order to claim the credit.[24] The Social Security number of the qualifying individual must also be included on the return in order to claim the credit.

Married couples must file a joint return in order to claim the credit. If the child's parents are divorced, and between them they (1) provide more than one-half of the child's support for the calendar year, *and* (2) have custody of the child for more than one-half of the calendar year, the child will be treated as a qualifying individual for the *custodial parent* (i.e., the one having custody for the greater portion of the year).[25]

Limitations

If the individual's adjusted gross income exceeds $15,000, the individual must reduce the 35 percent credit by one percentage point for each $2,000 (or fraction thereof) by which his adjusted gross income for the taxable year exceeds that amount. However, the reduction cannot exceed fifteen percentage points.[26] Consequently, for taxpayers with adjusted gross incomes of more than $43,000, the credit is 20 percent of qualifying expenses. The credit is also limited by the number of qualifying individuals. The credit taken may not exceed $3,000 for one qualifying individual or $6,000 for two or more qualifying individuals.

Finally, eligible expenses may not exceed the taxpayer's earned income (or the spouse's earned income, if smaller).[27] If an individual's employer provides a dependent care assistance program, the individual must reduce the amount of the allowable credit by any amounts excluded from income under the dependent care assistance program exclusion.[28] In the case of a spouse who is a full time student, the spouse is deemed to earn $250 per month in the case of one individual ($500 per month in the case of two or more individuals).[29]

Generally, the credit for employment-related expenses is allowable only for expenses which are both incurred and actually paid during the taxable year, regardless of the taxpayer's method of accounting.[30]

CREDIT FOR THE ELDERLY AND DISABLED

A nonrefundable credit for the elderly and disabled is available to individuals who are at least sixty-five years old or permanently and totally disabled.[31] An individual may be required to furnish proof of continuing disability.[32] The credit that can be applied is 15 percent of a qualified individual's "section 22 base amount" for the taxable year.[33] The section 22 base amount is:

- $5,000 for a single taxpayer (or married taxpayers filing jointly if only one spouse qualifies for the credit);

- $7,500 for married taxpayers filing jointly if both qualify; and

- $3,750 for married taxpayers filing separately.[34]

Married persons must generally file a joint return in order to claim the credit.[35]

Limitations

The section 22 base amount is subject to limitations. For individuals under age sixty-five, the base figure cannot exceed the amount of disability income received during the taxable year. "Disability income" is the taxable amount an individual receives under an employer plan as wages or payments in lieu of wages for the period he is absent from work on account of permanent and total disability.[36]

If benefits are received under a plan to which the employee has contributed, the portion of the disability income attributable to the *employer's* contribution is taxable, but the portion attributable to the *employee's* contribution is tax-free, and therefore would not limit the section 22 base amount.[37]

For married taxpayers filing jointly, if both are under age sixty-five, the base figure cannot exceed the amount of both spouses' disability income combined. However, if only one spouse is under age sixty-five, the base amount is limited to the sum of $5,000 *plus* the disability income of the spouse who is under age sixty-five for the taxable year.

In addition, the base figure (or the amount of disability income in the case of individuals under age sixty-five if that is less) is reduced by one-half of adjusted gross income in excess of the following amounts:

- $7,500 for single taxpayers
- $10,000 for married taxpayers filing joint returns
- $5,000 for married taxpayers filing separately[38]

A reduction is also made dollar-for-dollar for tax-exempt Social Security and railroad retirement benefits, as well as certain tax-exempt income.[39]

EDUCATION CREDITS

Two types of credits are available if a taxpayer or dependents incurred college expenses: the American Opportunity Tax Credit (which replaced the Hope Scholarship Credit) and the Lifetime Learning Credit.[40] While the credits are generally nonrefundable, under certain circumstances a portion of them may be refundable. These credits, and the applicable limitations and phase-outs, are described below and summarized in Figure 9.2.

American Opportunity Tax Credit

The American Recovery and Reinvestment Act of 2009[41] included the partially refundable American Opportunity Tax Credit (AOTC) to pay for higher education expenses. The AOTC renamed the existing HOPE education tax credit and modified it by making the credit available to a broader range of taxpayers, including many with higher incomes. It also added required course materials to the list of qualifying expenses and allows the credit to be claimed for four post-secondary education years instead of two.

The amount of the American opportunity credit (per eligible student) is the sum of:

(1) 100 percent of the first $2,000 of qualified education expenses paid for the eligible student; and

(2) 25 percent of the next $2,000 of qualified education expenses paid for that student.

The maximum credit amount is $2,500 per eligible student. Additionally, 40 percent of the credit is refundable.[42] To be eligible for the AOTC, a student must:

- be enrolled in a program leading toward a degree, certificate or other recognized post-secondary educational credential;
- have not completed the first four years of post-secondary education as of the beginning of the taxable year;
- carry at least half of the normal full-time work load for the course of study the student is pursuing for at least one academic period; and
- have not been convicted of a felony drug offense.[43]

Figure 9.2

	AOTC	LLC
Limit	$2,500 per student	$2,000
Covers	First 4 years of post-secondary ed.	Unlimited number of years
AGI Phase-out	$80,000-$90,000 single $160,000-$180,000 married	$55,000-$65,000 single $111,000-$131,000 married

Limitations

The full credit is available to individuals whose MAGI is $80,000 or less ($160,000 for married couples filing a joint return). The credit is gradually phased out for taxpayers with incomes above these levels, and taxpayers with MAGI exceeding $90,000 ($180,000 for joint filers) cannot claim the credit.

Lifetime Learning Credit

The Lifetime Learning Credit (LLC) provides a non-refundable tax credit equal to 20 percent of up to $10,000 of qualified tuition and related expenses paid during the taxable year for education furnished to the taxpayer, the taxpayer's spouse, and any claimed dependent. The expenses must be incurred for an academic period beginning in the taxable year (or treated as beginning in the taxable year).[44]

The LLC is a completely nonrefundable credit, meaning that it can reduce tax obligations to zero, but any excess will not be refunded to the taxpayer. Unlike the American Opportunity Tax Credit, there is no limit on the number of years the lifetime learning credit can be claimed for each student. The credit is available for all years of postsecondary education and for courses to acquire or improve job skills.[45]

Generally, the lifetime credit may be claimed by the taxpayer if the taxpayer pays qualified higher education expenses, such expenses are paid for an eligible student, and the eligible student is either the taxpayer, the taxpayer's spouse, or a dependent for whom the taxpayer claims an exemption on the taxpayer's tax return.

An academic period includes a semester, trimester, quarter, or other period of study (such as a summer school session) as reasonably determined by an educational institution. In the case of an educational institution that uses credit hours or clock hours and does not have academic terms, each payment period can be treated as an academic period.[46]

Limitations

The amount of the credit is phased out if the taxpayer's modified adjusted gross income (MAGI) is between $55,000 and $65,000 ($111,000 and $131,000 for joint returns).[47] Additionally, the LLC is unavailable if any of the following apply:

- The taxpayer's filing status is married filing separately.
- The taxpayer is listed as a dependent on another person's tax return (such as the taxpayer's parents').
- The taxpayer (or his or her spouse) was a nonresident alien for any part of the year and did not elect to be treated as a resident alien for tax purposes.
- The taxpayer claims the American Opportunity Credit or a Tuition and Fees Deduction for the same student.[48]

Prohibition on Double Benefits

The Code contains several restrictions on using the education credits in combination with one another. First, the LLC cannot be claimed on education expenses that are paid for with funds from a Coverdell education savings account (ESA), qualified tuition program (QTP), or any type of tax-free educational assistance (such as a scholarship, grant, or assistance provided by an employer).[49]

Additionally, if a taxpayer claims the LLC for particular education expenses, those same expenses cannot be used to claim the following education-related credits and deductions in addition to the LLC:

- A general deduction for higher education expenses (as, for example, a business expense)
- A tuition and fees deduction under Code section 222
- The AOTC

Other Personal Credits

Adoption credit. The adoption credit is available to individuals who pay or incur qualified adoption expenses in connection with the adoption of a child.[50] The maximum amount of the qualified adoption credit is $14,300 in 2020 per child for qualified adoption expenses paid. For 2020, the credit is phased out for taxpayers with MAGI between $214,520 and $254,520.[51]

Energy credits. For an overview of the energy-related credits for homeowners and car buyers, see Appendix C.

Foreign credit. The taxpayer is allowed a credit (or a deduction) for foreign income taxes paid or accrued.[52] The credit is subject to limitations.[53] Essentially the credit is limited to the United States rate of tax applied to the ratio of the foreign income compared to the taxpayer's worldwide income. In addition, income must be classified into "baskets" based on the type of income generated (passive, general).[54] For most individuals who are not employed overseas, their only foreign income will be from international investments generally included in the passive basket and the taxes will have been withheld in the foreign jurisdiction. Foreign credits not used in the current year are not refundable, but are instead carried back two years and then forward five years.

AMT CREDITS

Under conventional tax law, a taxpayer can use exclusions of certain kinds of income, and deductions and credits for certain expenses to significantly reduce tax liabilities. The alternative minimum tax (AMT) attempts to ensure that individuals and corporations that benefit from certain exclusions, deductions, or credits pay at least a minimum amount of tax. The AMT does so by establishing a completely separate set of calculations from the regular tax. These calculations do not contain a personal exemption, standard deduction, or many itemized deductions. If the tax benefits would reduce total tax below the AMT limit, the taxpayer must pay the higher AMT amount.[55]

To calculate the AMT for an individual, various tax preference items are added back into taxable income. This "grossed up" amount then becomes the tax base for the AMT. Next, the amount of the basic exemption is subtracted from the AMT tax base. For 2020, the exemption amounts amount are increased to $113,400 for married taxpayers filing joint returns (half this amount if separate returns are filed, $56,700) and $72,900 for all other taxpayers (other than estates and trusts). The AMT exemption amount for trusts and estates remains unchanged $25,400 in 2020.[56]

A two-tiered tax rate structure of 26 percent and 28 percent is then assessed against the remaining AMT tax base to determine AMT tax liability. The taxpayer then pays whichever is greater: his regular income tax liability or the AMT tax liability.[57] Importantly, many of the tax credits normally used to lower taxable income are reduced or eliminated when calculating the AMT (see Figure 9.3).

Figure 9.3

CREDITS THAT ARE REDUCED OR ELIMINATED FOR AMT INCOME CALCULATIONS

Eliminated Credits	Reduced Credits
Any general business credit (listed in Code section Sec. 38(b) and the instructions to IRS Form 3800, General Business Credit)	Child credit (up to $1,000 per child)[58]
Qualified electric vehicle credit	Energy credit (30% of the cost of certain fuel cell and energy property)[59]
The personal use part of the alternative fuel vehicle refueling property credit	Credit for foreign taxes[60]
The credit for prior year minimum tax[61]	Specified credits under IRC Sec. 38(c)(4) (i.e., alcohol fuel credit)[62]
	Alternative motor vehicle credit, including the tax credit for purchasing hybrid vehicles[63]

In addition to the preceding credits, a special minimum tax credit is allowed if a taxpayer is not liable for AMT in the current year, but paid AMT in one or more previous years. In this case, the taxpayer may be eligible to take the special minimum credit against his or her regular tax in the current year.[64]

Techniques for Reducing or Eliminating the AMT

The best way to reduce the AMT liability is to shift income or deductions in ways that facilitate reduction in regular and AMT taxes. For instance, because real estate and personal property taxes are not deductible for AMT if they are included in itemized deductions, a taxpayer who otherwise qualifies for the home office deduction can deduct part of these taxes on his or her 1040 Schedule C (Profit or Loss from Business), and such taxes will then be allowed to offset the AMT. The same is true for taxes deductible on rental schedule (Schedule E), or farm schedule (Schedule F or Form 4835).

Additionally, pre-tax 401(k) contributions and charitable donations reduce both taxable income and AMT. Cafeteria plans and flexible savings accounts—if offered by a taxpayer's employer and used to pay eligible medical or child-care expenses—will also reduce the taxpayer's reportable income.

When these strategies are used in combination with available tax credits the additional tax bite imposed by the AMT can be reduced or eliminated.

WHERE CAN I FIND OUT MORE?

Tax Facts on Life Insurance & Employee Benefits (National Underwriter Company).[65]

FREQUENTLY ASKED QUESTIONS

Question – Does tax reform expand the child tax credit? What is the new family tax credit?

Answer – The 2017 Tax Act eliminated the personal exemption (and the dependency exemption) and expanded the previously available child tax credit. Under the Act, the child tax credit is increased to $2,000 (from $1,000) per child under age seventeen. $1,400 of this per-child credit is refundable. The taxpayer must include the Social Security number for each child for which the refundable portion of the child tax credit is claimed.[66] The $1,400 refundable amount will be indexed for inflation and rounded to the next multiple of $100.[67]

A new family tax credit was created to allow for a $500 nonrefundable credit for dependent parents and other non-child dependents (the requirement for furnishing a Social Security number does not apply to this family tax credit).[68]

The credit will phase out for taxpayers with AGI of $400,000 (joint returns) or $200,000 (all other filers). The phase out amounts are not indexed for inflation.[69] As is the case with the suspension of the personal exemption, these provisions are set to expire after 2025.

Question – Does tax reform impact any personal tax credits other than the child tax credit?

Answer – Most of the personal tax credits were not impacted by tax reform. This includes the credit for the elderly and permanently disabled,[70] adoption credit,[71] the American Opportunity tax credit, Lifetime Learning tax credit,[72] and the saver's credit.[73]

CHAPTER ENDNOTES

1. IRC Sec. 32.
2. IRC Sec. 35.
3. Michael R. Strain, resident scholar in economic policy studies, American Enterprise Institute.
4. IRS Publication 596 (2013).
5. IRS Preview of 2014 EITC Income Limits, Maximum Credit Amounts and Tax Law Updates.
6. IRS Publication 3211 (Rev. Jan. 2014).
7. Economic Growth and Tax Relief Reconciliation Act, the Tax Relief, Unemployment Insurance Reauthorization and Job Creation Act of 2010, and the American Tax Relief Act.
8. EGTRRA 2001, §901.
9. IRC Secs. 24(c)(1), 152(a), 152(c).
10. IRC Sec. 24(c)(2).
11. IRC Sec. 152(f)(1)(B).
12. IRC Secs. 24(e), 24(f). An exception applies if the taxable year is cut short by the death of the taxpayer.
13. IRC Sec. 24(h)(3).
14. IRC Sec. 38(b). The general business credit also includes the portion of the alternative motor vehicle credit to which 30B(g)(1)

applies and the portion of the alternative fuel vehicle refueling property credit to which I.R.C. Section 30C(d)(1) applies. The general business credits are listed in IRC Sec. 38(b) and in the instructions to Form 3800 ("General Business Credits").

15. IRC Secs. 21, 22, 23, 24, 25A, and 25B.
16. IRC Sec. 901.
17. IRC Sec. 21(a)(1).
18. IRC Secs. 21(a)(2), 21(b)(1).
19. IRS Publication 503 (2013), p. 3.
20. IRC Sec. 21(b)(2); Treas. Reg. §1.44A-1(c).
21. IRC Sec. 21(b)(2).
22. IRC Sec. 21(b)(2).
23. IRC Sec. 21(e)(6).
24. IRC Sec. 21(e)(9).
25. IRC Sec. 21(e)(5); Treas. Reg. §1.21-1(b)(5). This rule applies even if the noncustodial parent claims the dependency exemption.
26. IRC Sec. 21(a)(2).
27. IRC Sec. 21(d).
28. IRC Sec. 21(c).
29. IRC Sec. 21(d)(2).
30. Treas. Reg. §1.44A-1(a)(3).
31. IRC Sec. 22(b).
32. See, e.g., Let. Rul. 8034008; Gen. Couns. Mem. 39269; S. Rep. No. 94938, 94th Cong., 2d Sess. 137 (1976), 1976-3 CB 175. Per IRC Sec. 22(e)(3), "Permanent and total disability" means the inability "to engage in any substantial gainful activity by reason of any medically determinable physical or mental impairment which can be expected to result in death or which has lasted or can be expected to last for a continuous period of not less than twelve months."
33. IRC Secs. 22(a), 26.
34. IRC Secs. 22(c)(2)(A), 22(e)(1).
35. IRC Sec. 22(e). An exception to the general rule applies if they live apart at all times during the taxable year.
36. IRC Sec. 22(c)(2)(B)(iii).
37. IRC Sec. 105(a).
38. IRC Sec. 22(d).
39. IRC Sec. 22(c)(3).
40. IRC Sec. 25A.
41. IRC Sec. 25A(b). The American Taxpayer Relief Act of 2012 extended the AOTC through December 2017.
42. IRC Sec. 25A(h)(5).
43. Treas. Reg. §1.25A-3(d).
44. IRC Sec. 25A(c); Treas. Reg. §1.25A-4(a). The credit is allowed for qualified education expenses paid for an academic period beginning in the tax year or in the first three months of the following tax year (e.g. a "spring" semester beginning in January, which may have expenses that are paid either before or after December 31).
45. IRS Publication 970 "Tax Benefits for Education" (2013).
46. Treas. Reg. §1.25A-2(c).
47. IRS Publication 970 "Tax Benefits for Education" (2013).
48. *Ibid.*
49. *Ibid.*, p. 21.
50. IRC Sec. 23(a)(1).
51. IRC Sec. 23(b)(1); Rev. Proc. 2008-66, 2008-45 IRB 1107.
52. IRC Sec. 901(a).
53. IRC Sec. 904(a).
54. IRC Sec. 904(d). The two "baskets" (passive category income and general category income) are effective for tax years beginning after December 31, 2006. Prior to January 1, 2007, there were nine baskets of income.
55. IRS Tax Topic 556 – Alternative Minimum Tax.
56. IRC Sec. 55(d)(4).
57. IRC Sec. 55(b). See also Congressional Research Service Report 7-5700 "The Alternative Minimum Tax for Individuals" by Steven Maguire (Sept. 20, 2012).
58. IRC Sec. 24.
59. IRC Sec. 48.
60. IRC Sec. 59.
61. Instructions to Form 6251, "Alternative Minimum Tax – Individuals."
62. IRC Sec. 40.
63. IRC Sec. 30.
64. IRC Sec. 53. Form 8801 determines the amount of the AMT related to deferral items, which generate credit for future years. This credit is available for individuals, trusts, and estates.
65. To order, call 1-800-543-0874, or visit: www.nationalunderwriter.com.
66. IRC Sec. 24(h)(7).
67. IRC Sec. 24(h).
68. IRC Sec. 24(h)(4).
69. IRC Sec. 24(h)(3).
70. IRC Sec. 22.
71. IRC Sec. 23.
72. IRC Sec. 25A.
73. IRC Sec. 25B.

ALTERNATIVE MINIMUM TAX

CHAPTER 10

INTRODUCTION

In essence, the alternative minimum tax (AMT) is an income system that runs parallel to the "regular" income tax system. Its intended purpose is to make sure that taxpayers with the financial wherewithal to take advantage of tax preferences to reduce or eliminate their regular income tax actually pay their fair share of tax. AMT applies to individuals, corporations and trusts and estates.

To determine whether AMT applies, the taxpayer's regular income tax liability is compared to tax liability computed under the AMT rules. For individual taxpayers, AMT is computed on Form 6251 attached to Form 1040. For corporations, AMT is computed on Form 4626 attached to Form 1120. If the AMT computed tax liability is greater than the regular income tax, the difference is the AMT owing.

In spite of being intended to ensure high-end taxpayers pay their fair share of tax, it is possible that much less affluent taxpayers may be subject to the tax. This is because AMT is strictly computational and in any given tax year a taxpayer may have certain tax preferences that trigger the tax. In an attempt to prevent AMT to impact unintended taxpayers, Congress permanently indexed AMT exemptions, brackets and phase-outs in 2012 and significantly increased the exemption and phase-out thresholds in the Tax Cuts and Jobs Act of 2017 (TCJA).

HOW AMT IS COMPUTED FOR INDIVIDUALS

For individuals, there are two AMT tax rates—26 percent and 28 percent. In 2018, the 26 percent rate is applied to alternative minimum taxable income (AMTI) of up to $197,900 ($98,950 for married taxpayers filing separately) and 28 percent pf AMTI exceeding that amount.[1] Because the maximum AMT rate is 28 percent, many taxpayers assume that being in the regular income tax 28 percent bracket or above means the AMT does not apply to them. Unfortunately, that is not the way AMT works. In other words, by virtue of adjustments and add backs of preference items, the amount of AMTI may be significantly higher than regular taxable income. Therefore, even if a taxpayer's regular income tax rate exceeds 28 percent, it is possible that applying the 28 percent AMT rate to a higher tax base may result in a greater amount of tax.

There are seven steps to determine an individual taxpayer's AMT:

Step 1: Compute regular taxable income on Form 1040.[2]

Step 2: Next, compute AMTI by adding or subtracting certain adjustments to taxable income.

Adjustments for individuals include:

- *Miscellaneous Itemized Deductions:* For regular income tax purposes, a taxpayer may deduct the aggregate amount of miscellaneous itemized deductions (as defined in IRC Section 67(b)) to the extent they exceed 2 percent of adjusted gross income. Examples of miscellaneous itemized deductions include investment expenses, tax preparation fees and unreimbursed employee business expenses. The amount exceeding 2 percent of adjusted gross income is added to the taxpayer's other itemized deductions. Then, if the aggregate amount of itemized deductions exceed the taxpayer's standard deduction, the higher amount is claimed as a below the line deduction. In computing AMTI, however, the amount of miscellaneous itemized deductions is added back to taxable income.[3]

Example. This year, Asher claimed a total of $15,000 of itemized deductions and his taxable income was $100,000. Of that amount, $2,000 was attributable to miscellaneous itemized deductions. In computing AMTI, the $2,000 of miscellaneous itemized deductions must be added to his taxable income. So, at this point Asher's AMTI would be $102,000.

- *Taxes claimed as itemized deductions:* Pursuant to IRC Section 164 there are a slew of tax deductible taxes including state, local and federal real estate taxes, personal property taxes, income taxes, and by election, in lieu of state and local income taxes, sales tax. To the extent that these taxes are personal and not business related, they may be claimed as an itemized deductions. In computing AMTI, these itemized deductions must be added back to taxable income.[4]

Example: Asher claimed a total of $15,000 of itemized deductions and his taxable income was $100,000. His itemized deductions included state income and property taxes in the total amount of $10,000. When computing AMTI, the $10,000 of taxes must be added to his taxable income. Therefore Asher's AMTI would be $110,000.

- *Medical Expenses:* Medical expenses are itemized deductions that are deductible to the extent that they exceed 7.5 percent of adjusted gross income.[5] For purposes of computing AMTI, medical expenses are allowed (meaning they are not added to taxable income) to the extent they exceed 7.5 percent of adjusted gross income.[6]

- *Investment Interest Expense:* Investment interest expenses (interest paid on borrowing to finance the purchase of investments, i.e., stock, etc.) is deductible (as an itemized deduction) only to the extent of investment income.[7] However, there are certain adjustments and/or preference items that affects what is treated as investment income or expense.[8] Once these are taking into account, it is possible that the deductible amount of investment interest expense may be reduced. The difference between the amount deducted for regular income tax purposes and the lesser AMT deductible amount would be added to taxable income.

- *Mortgage Interest:* The taxpayer is allowed an itemized deduction with respect to the interest on indebtedness incurred to acquire, construct or substantially improve the taxpayer's principal residence or second home ("qualifying indebtedness").[9] For 208, the AMT adjustment for the interest deduction on qualifying indebtedness as well as interest on refinanced indebtedness, but only to the extent of the outstanding balance of qualifying indebtedness has been eliminated.[10] Prior to 2018, interest paid on home equity indebtedness (i.e. debt secured by a mortgage on the taxpayer's residence, but not used to construct or improve it) was generally deductible, but not deductible for the purposes of computing AMTI.

- *Refunds of state income taxes.* As discussed above, for purposes of computing AMTI, deductible state income taxes are added to taxable income.[11] However, for regular income tax purposes, the refund of state income taxes deducted in a prior tax year is included in gross income in the tax year it is received. Since in computing AMTI, the state income tax deduction added to taxable income, a refund included in taxable income must be subtracted from taxable income.

Example. This year, Asher's taxable income was $100,000. Included in that amount is a $2,000 state income tax refund. To this point, with all the additions to taxable income, ATMI (including this tax year's state income tax deduction) is $110,000. Reducing that amount by the state refund includible in this tax year's regular taxable income, AMTI would be $108,000.

- *Standard deduction:* If the taxpayer claimed the standard deduction, it is added to taxable income in the computation of AMTI.[12]

- *Incentive Stock Options (ISOs):* Generally, a stock option, either an ISO or a nonqualified stock option allows an employee to acquire company stock for an exercise cost that is below the market value of the stock. With respect to a nonqualified stock option, the employee is taxed to the extent the market value of the stock exceeds the exercise cost. On the other hand, with respect to an ISO, the employee is taxed only when the stock acquired by the exercise of the option is sold.

However, for AMT purposes, an ISO is treated in the same way as a nonqualified stock option is treated for income tax purposes.[13] Therefore, in the computation of AMTI, taxable income is increased by the difference between the value of the stock and the "basis" of the stock. For this purpose, basis includes the exercise cost plus any transactional costs. Subsequently, in the tax year the stock is ultimately sold, the taxpayer is entitled to a reduction of ATMI to the extent of the difference between the amount recognized for regular income tax purposes over the amount of "gain" the taxpayer previously included in AMTI.

Example. Ron Gardner exercised 1,000 ISOs of his employer, WWW, Inc. for $10 an option when the stock was trading for $75 per share, or a total of $10,000 in exchange for stock valued at $75,000. Since the options are ISOs, Ron does not include the spread in gross income. Assuming no transactional costs, the difference between the market value of the stock, $75,000 and the exercise cost, or his basis, $10,000, Ron's AMTI is increased by the spread, or $65,000.

Three years later, when the stock is trading at $500 per share, Ron sells 500 shares for $50,000. Ron's basis in those shares is $5,000 (500 shares times a $10 per share exercise cost). For regular income tax purposes, Ron will report a long term capital gain of $45,000 ($50,000 minus $5,000).

For AMT purposes, the amount of his gain on the sale of half his option shares is not $45,000. This is because three years earlier $32,500 (the AMT gain on half of the option shares) was included in AMTI. So to prevent double AMT taxation, in computing AMTI, taxable income is reduced by the amount of the gain that was previously included in a prior year's AMTI. Therefore, the net "gain" included in AMTI would be $12,500 (or $45,000 regular taxable income gain minus $32,500 previously reported AMT gain).

- *Separately Stated AMT Adjustments from Pass-Through Entities:* Generally, pass-through entities are not subject to regular income tax. Instead, items of income and deduction are passed through to the shareholders, members, partners, etc. The character of the income, deductions, etc., in the hands of the entity passes through to their owners. For this reason, the Form K-1 issued to those individuals will include separately stated items with AMT significance.

- *Passive Activity Income or Loss:* The passive activity rules are applied separately for AMT purposes. So, if net passive activity income or loss for regular income tax purposes is different for AMT purposes, the difference is reported as an adjustment to AMTI.[14]

- *Depreciation:* For depreciable property placed in service after 1998, if the 200 percent declining balance method is used for regular income tax purposes, depreciation must be recalculated using the 150 percent declining balance method.[15] In computing AMTI, the difference between the deductible amounts of the two methods is added to taxable income as an adjustment. Any other depreciation method used for regular income tax purposes is also used for AMT purposes (meaning there would not be an AMTI adjustment).

- *NOL Adjustments:* The net operating loss (NOL) computed for regular income tax purposes is added to taxable income to be replaced with the ATM net operating loss (ATNOL). The computation of the ATNOL begins with the regular income tax NOL and increasing or decreasing it by AMT adjustments and preferences in the year of loss.[16] The maximum amount of ATMI that can be reduced by the ATNOL is 90 percent of ATMI computed without regard to the ATNOL.[17]

Example. In the current year, Jack has an NOL of $175,000 for regular income tax purposes. In that year of loss, there was an addition to ATMI of $15,000 attributable to a depreciation adjustment. Therefore, the ATNOL for the current year is $160,000 ($175,000 minus $15,000).

Step 3: Add tax preferences to AMTI.

- *Depletion:* The excess of the depletion deduction over the adjusted basis of the property at the end of the taxable year.[18]

- *Intangible Drilling Costs:* The amount by which excess intangible drilling costs are greater than 65 percent of the net income of the taxpayer's oil, gas and geothermal properties for the tax year.[19]

- *Tax-exempt interest on private activity bonds.* In computing AMTI, tax-exempt interest earned on specified private activity bonds must be added to taxable income. However, the amount included is reduced by deductions that would have been allowed if the tax-exempt interest was included in regular taxable income.[20]

Example. Asher earned $5,000 interest from several private activity bonds. For regular income tax purposes, the interest is excluded from gross income. To purchase those bonds, Asher borrowed $100,000 upon which he paid $3,000 of interest. Because the interest earned on the bonds is tax-free, the interest paid on the loan to purchase the bonds is not deductible for regular income tax purposes. However, because for AMT purposes, Asher must include the tax-free interest in AMTI, the otherwise nondeductible interest is deductible for AMTI purposes.

Investors in mutual funds that earn tax-exempt interest from private activity bonds must include the proportionate share of such tax-exempt interest in AMTI.[21]

- *Gains on small business stock.* Gains triggered by the sale of certain small business stock held for more than five years qualify for a 50 to 100 percent (depending on the year acquired) exclusion from gross income (see Chapter 30 for more details).[22] To qualify for this regular income tax treatment, small business stock must meet the following requirements:

  a. It must have been issued after August 10, 1993.[23]

  b. The taxpayer must be the original holder of the stock and the stock must have been acquired in exchange for money or other property (not including stock) or as compensation for services performed.[24]

  c. The corporation must be an active business.[25]

  d. The corporation must be a qualified small business, i.e., a domestic corporation with aggregate gross assets of less than $50,000.[26]

  If acquired before September 27, 2010, 7 percent of the amount of excluded gain that must be added to AMTI.[27]

Example. On June 30 of this year, Jack Armstrong realized a gain of $300,000 on the sale of qualified small business stock acquired in 1999. Of that amount, Jack excludes $150,000 for regular income tax purposes. In computing AMTI, Jack must add $10,500 (7 percent of $150,000) to taxable income.

Step 4: Compute the applicable exemption amount and subtract it from AMTI.

At this point, the computation of gross AMTI is complete. The next step is to subtract the exemption amount. The exemption amounts are based on the taxpayer's filing status. The AMTI exemptions are phased-out for AMTI above certain thresholds.

For 2020, the exemption amounts are as follows:[28]

AMT EXEMPTIONS

Filing Status	Exemption	Exemption Phase-Out
Single or Head of Household	$72,900	$518,400
Married Filing Jointly	$113,400	$1,036,800
Married Filing Separately	$56,700	$518,400
Trusts and Estates	$25,400	$84,800

Once a taxpayer reaches the amount of AMTI at which the phase-out begins, the exemption is reduced by 25 percent of the amount by which AMTI exceeds that beginning phase-out amount.

Step 5: Compute the AMT on AMTI as reduced by the appropriate exemption. There are two AMT rates for 2018: 26 percent for AMTI up to $197,900 ($97,400 for an individual filing married separately) and 28 percent for AMTI above that amount. The AMT tax rates are applied to AMTI minus the applicable exemption amount to determine the "tentative minimum tax."

If the tentative minimum tax does not exceed the taxpayer's regular income tax, there is no AMT. However, if the tentative minimum tax exceeds the taxpayer's regular income tax, the difference is AMT to be added to the regular income tax. AMT is reported on Form 1040 payable in the normal manner.

Step 6:

Example. In 2020, the Ashers, a married couple with two dependents, filed a joint return. Based on $151,900 of taxable income, their regular income tax was $25,297. The computation of AMT is as follows:

Taxable Income	$151,900
AMT adjustments	$40,000
Total tax preference items	$65,000
Subtotal	$256,900
Tentative AMT Exemption	$113,400
Reduction of AMT Exemption	$0
AMT Exemption as reduced	$113,400
AMTI	$143,500
Tentative minimum tax	$37,310
Regular Income tax	$25,297
AMT	$12,013

Step 7: Reduce AMT Liability by available credits.

Of the number of tax credits that are available to reduce a taxpayer's liability, only a few are also available to reduce a taxpayer's AMT liability. Those credits are: the adoption credit, the child tax credit, the retirement contribution credit and certain energy efficiency credits.

SPECIAL RULE FOR THE GENERAL BUSINESS TAX CREDIT

The business tax credit available to reduce regular income tax may not be used to reduce AMT. As applied to regular income tax, however, the amount of the allowed general business tax credit is limited by a special formula. Pursuant to the formula, the general business credit is limited to the taxpayer's net regular income tax (net of nonrefundable personal credits, foreign tax credit and certain other rarely used credits) minus the greater of (1) tentative minimum tax or (2) 25 percent of the amount by which the net regular income tax exceeds $25,000.[29]

Example: Jessica's net regular income tax was $50,000 and her tentative minimum tax was $47,000. In addition, Jessica was entitled to a $5,000 general business credit from one of her partnership investments. Because Jessica's tentative minimum tax ($47,000) is greater than 25 percent of the amount by which her regular income tax ($50,000) exceeds $25,000 (or 25 percent of $25,000, or $6,250), the general business credit is limited to $3,000 ($50,000 minus $47,000). The balance, $2,000, would be carried forward to future years subject to carry forward limitations.

AVAILABILITY OF THE MINIMUM TAX CREDIT

Through the minimum tax credit (MTC), a taxpayer subject to AMT in a given tax year(s) may have the opportunity to recoup some of the AMT as a credit offsetting regular income tax in a future tax year(s).[30] The MTC is the amount of AMT attributable to *deferral* adjustments or preferences. In computing AMT, "deferral adjustments and preferences" are adjustments made merely because of the timing of a particular tax item. Conversely, "*exclusion* adjustments and preferences" are adjustments in the AMT computation that would have been made regardless of timing. These adjustments and preferences are not taken into account in computing the MTC.

Examples of exclusion adjustments and preferences include the following items:[31]

- Taxes
- Medical Expenses

- Certain Residential Interest Expense (returns prior to 2018)
- Miscellaneous Itemized Deductions (returns prior to 2018)
- Personal Exemptions (returns prior to 2018)
- Excess Depletion
- Tax-exempt Interest from Private Activity Bonds
- Applicable Add-Back of Excluded Section 1202 Gain From Sale of Small Business Stock

The MTC is the difference between the taxpayer's actual AMT and the AMT computed only considering the exclusion adjustments and preferences.[32] Thus, the MTC is a credit only with respect to timing items that were included in the computation of AMT. In application, the MTC (computed on Form 8801) only reduces the taxpayer's regular income tax liability in a year in which the taxpayer is not subject to AMT. Any unused MTC is carried forward to future years. In any given tax year, the reduction of regular income tax by the MTC is limited to the amount of what the AMT would have been in that tax year. Therefore, it may take many tax years to completely use a MTC.

Example. In 2015, Jerry exercised a number of ISOs. Although the exercise did not trigger income tax, because the deferred regular taxable gain with respect to ISOs is a deferral (timing) adjustment, Jerry was subject to AMT. In addition to the ISO adjustment to taxable income in the computation of AMTI, the only other adjustments to taxable income were the standard deduction and personal exemption. In preparing his 2016 income tax return to claim the MTC with respect to 2015, on Form 8801, Jerry re-computes his AMT for 2015 considering only the two exclusion adjustments (standard deduction and personal exemption). As a result, the amount of AMT related to the ISO deferral adjustment was $22,000. Therefore, the entire $22,000 MTC carried forward to subsequent tax years will be available to reduce regular income tax liability in those years. However, the credit is available to offset regular income tax only in tax years in which Jerry is *not* subject to AMT. Figure 10.1 illustrates how the MTC would be applied as a credit against regular income tax in subsequent tax years.

Beginning in 2015, Jerry's $22,000 MTC created in 2014 was available to offset his regular income tax liability in subsequent years. In each of those ensuing tax years, because his regular income tax liability was greater than AMT, there was no AMT imposed. In applying the MTC year by year, however, the available credit was limited to the excess between Jerry's regular income tax liability and the amount of AMT computed for that year. Thus, the unused remaining MTC was carried forward to subsequent years subject to the same limitations. Finally, in 2019, the MTC was totally used up.

Figure 10.1

Year	MTC Available	Regular Income Tax Liability	Computed AMT	Amount of MTC offsetting regular Tax Liability	Remaining MTC Available
2016	$22,000	$25,000	$20,000	$5,000	$17,000
2017	$17,000	$25,000	$24,000	$1,000	$16,000
2018	$16,000	$30,000	$22,000	$8,000	$8,000
2019	$8,000	$30,000	$24,000	$6,000	$2,000
2020	$3,000	$32,000	$25,000	$2,000	$-0-

THE AMT AND CORPORATIONS

Prior to enactment of the Tax Cuts and Jobs Act of 2017 (TCJA) there was also an AMT for corporations. The Act repealed the AMT for corporations for tax years beginning after 2017.

CHAPTER ENDNOTES

1. Rev. Proc. 2015-53.
2. IRC Sec. 55(b)(2).
3. IRC Sec. 56(b)(1)(A)(I).
4. IRC Sec. 56(b)(1)(A)(ii).
5. IRC Sec. 213(a).
6. IRC Sec. 56(b)(1)(B)
7. IRC Sec. 163(d).
8. IRC Sec. 56(b)(1)(C).
9. IRC Sec. 163(h).
10. IRC Sec. 56(e)(1)(B).
11. IRC Sec. 56(b)(1)(D).
12. IRC Sec. 56(b)(1)(E).
13. IRC Sec. 56(b)(3).
14. IRC Sec. 58(b).
15. IRC Sec. 56(a)(1)(A).
16. IRC Sec. 56(d)(2).
17. IRC Sec. 56(d)(1)(A).
18. IRC Sec. 57(a)(1).
19. IRC Sec. 57(a)(2)(A).
20. IRC Sec. 57(a)(5)(A).
21. IRC Sec. 57(a)(5)(B).
22. IRC Sec. 1202(a)(1).
23. IRC Sec. 1202(c)(1).
24. IRC Sec. 1202(c)(1)(B).
25. IRC Sec. 1202(c)(2).
26. IRC Sec. 1202(c)(1)(A).
27. IRC Sec. 57(a)(7).
28. Rev. Proc. 2015-53.
29. IRC Sec. 38(c).
30. IRC Sec. 53(a).
31. IRC Sec. 53(d)(1)(B)(ii).
32. IRC Sec. 53(d)(1)(B)(i).

ALTERNATIVE MINIMUM TAX PLANNING FOR INDIVIDUALS

CHAPTER 11

As discussed in Chapter 10, the alternative minimum tax (AMT) is a second income tax system intended to ensure that high income taxpayers who are able to take advantage of favorable tax preferences that could reduce or eliminate their income tax liability pay their fair share of tax. So, if a taxpayer's AMT exceeds income tax, the taxpayer must pay the higher amount.

Unfortunately, because the AMT is purely computational, it is possible that many taxpayers with modest income may also be subject to AMT. In either case, AMT planning is essential.

IDENTIFYING THE AMT TRAPS

AMT planning begins with a basic understanding of what items of AMT adjustment or preference might trigger AMT. As discussed in Chapter 10, individual taxpayers who itemize deductions are required to eliminate some of those deductions in the computation of AMTI (the AMT tax base). In other words, the computation of AMTI begins with the taxpayer's regular taxable income increased by certain adjustments (as well as preferences) including adding certain regular tax deductible items. Essentially, for AMT purposes, those deductions are eliminated by adding them to taxable income. Itemized deductions unaffected by AMT (meaning they remain intact) are charitable deductions, casualty losses and allowable gambling losses. All other itemized deductions are either eliminated or modified for AMT purposes. Figure 11.1 details those special rules.

Additionally, there are other income-based adjustments and preference items that must be considered. Those items are detailed in Figure 11.2. Certain other deductions are also impacted by AMT. To minimize the impact, there are planning opportunities that involve making elections to lessen the deduction that created the problem. See Figure 11.3.

Finally, some credits that reduce a taxpayer's regular income tax liability may not be available to reduce AMT. For example, an individual's nonrefundable tax credits are allowed to offset regular income tax against AMT.

Figure 11.1

ITEMIZED DEDUCTION-BASED AMT TRAPS AND ESCAPES		
Itemized Deduction	**AMT Treatment (Trap)**	**Planning Idea (Escape)**
Medical Expenses	Deductible only to the extent they exceed 10 percent of AGI	Employer provided pre-tax medical deduction or Cafeteria Plan. In these plans, pre-tax funds are set aside for medical related expenses and are not impacted by AMT.
State, local, etc. Income, Real Estate, Sales Tax	Eliminated by AMT and disallowed amounts added to taxable income in the computation of AMTI.	If the taxpayer has a home office, the portion of real estate taxes allocable to the home office can be claimed as a business home office deduction.

Figure 11.2

INCOME-BASED AMT TRAPS AND ESCAPES		
Income	**AMT Treatment (Trap)**	**Planning Idea (Escape)**
State/Local Tax Refunds	State and local refunds received by taxpayers who itemized those taxes when paid must include the corresponding refund in gross income. Because state and local taxes are eliminated and added to taxable income in the computation of AMTI, in the year received, the refunds are subtracted from taxable income in the computation of AMTI.	Not really an issue. The adding of the state and local income deduction to taxable income in the computation of AMTI is offset by subtracting the corresponding refund from taxable income in the computation of AMTI in the year of receipt.
Tax-Exempt Interest	Tax-exempt interest from private activity bonds (excluded from regular taxable income) must be added to taxable income in the computation of AMTI.	Be aware of deductions incurred to acquire or carry private activity bonds that are disallowed for regular income tax purposes but are allowable as an investment interest expense for purposes of AMT.
Section 1202 Gain	7 percent of the excluded gain on qualified small business stock must be included in AMTI (applies to stock acquired before 9/27/2010).	Usually not a particularly damaging adjustment that in of itself may not trigger AMT.
Incentive Stock Options (ISOs)	For AMT purposes, the excess of the fair market value of the stock over the exercise cost of the option is added to taxable income in the computation of AMTI.	The timing of the exercise of an ISO is essential in maximizing the after-tax return to the taxpayer. This AMT adjustment can single-handedly create a taxpayer's AMT liability. On the other hand, it will create a MTC to be applied to reduce regular income tax in future tax year(s).
Adjusted Gain or Loss	Because in some cases there is a difference between an asset's regular income tax and AMT basis, there may be a significant difference between the regular income tax gain or loss as compared to the AMT gain or loss. In some cases, the adjustment for AMT purposes may be significant.	Maintain records detailing the regular income tax basis as well of the AMT basis of the assets. In the case of an ISO, the basis differential can be significant in the size of the MTC in reducing regular income tax in future year(s).
Capital Gains	Although the preferential treatment of capital gain is the same for regular income tax as well as for AMT purposes, a large amount of capital gain that increases overall taxable income may result in the imposition of AMT.	Consider the impact of a large amount of capital gain potentially triggering AMT in a particular tax year. For that reason, it may prudent to recognize all or a portion of capital gain into a non-AMT year(s).

Figure 11.3

DEDUCTION-BASED AMT TRAPS AND ESCAPES		
Deductions	**AMT Treatment (Trap)**	**Planning Idea (Escape)**
Standard Deduction	A taxpayer who does not itemize deductions claims the standard deduction for regular income tax purposes. For AMT purposes, the standard deduction is added to taxable income in the computation of AMTI.	Usually a non-issue. Most taxpayers who claim the standard deduction are not likely to be subject to AMT. Moreover, if the standard deduction is the only adjustment, there would not be any AMT.

Figure 11.3 (cont'd)

DEDUCTION-BASED AMT TRAPS AND ESCAPES		
Deductions	**AMT Treatment (Trap)**	**Planning Idea (Escape)**
Depletion, Depreciation, Passive Activities, Circulation and Research and Development Expenditures	All these items are business related deductions that in many cases are more accelerated for regular income tax purposes than for AMT.	Each item has a corresponding election which may be made to slow down the deduction and eliminate a potential AMT adjustment.
Alternative Tax Net Operating Loss (ATNOL)	In most cases, the ATNOL will not be same as the NOL for regular income tax purposes. Generally, the ATNOL is likely to be less than the NOL and is deductible only to the extent of 90 percent of a taxpayer's ATMI.	In the year an ATNOL is created, it may be more beneficial to carry an NOL for regular income tax purposes back to previous years rather than forward to future years. Even though carrying the NOL back may save more regular income tax (than if it was carried forward), more AMT savings (and thus more total tax savings) may be realized by carrying it forward.

AMT PLANNING TECHNIQUES

Generally, the impact of AMT on the taxpayer cannot be determined by analyzing only one particular year. For example, if a taxpayer is anticipating an unusually high amount of income in one year that will likely create AMT for that year, prudent planning should include an analysis of considering accelerating or deferring income or deductions over multiple years.

General planning strategies to be considered include:

1. moving income into an AMT year;
2. moving deductions into a non-AMT year;
3. timing the recognition of adjustment or preference items;
4. making elections to minimize the AMT; and
5. utilizing alternative minimum tax net operating loss (ATNOL).

MOVING INCOME INTO AN AMT YEAR

Timing the recognition of income from one tax year to another is a means of reducing or eliminating AMT. Accelerating income into a tax year in which AMT will be imposed works best for a taxpayer when the following conditions exist:

1. The taxpayer's marginal tax bracket in the current year is 28 percent or less but in future years will exceed 28 percent, the top bracket of AMT.
2. The AMT is primarily due to the adding exclusion adjustments or preferences to taxable income in the computation of AMTI.

In either of those scenarios, the taxpayer's AMT is not attributable to a high amount of income. Most likely, it was the addition of exclusion adjustments or preferences that increased AMTI to the level that ultimately triggered AMT. Therefore, to the extent AMT is generated by exclusion type adjustments, moving additional income into such a tax year would be prudent provided that it does not cause the taxpayer to be placed in a marginal regular income tax bracket greater than 28 percent.

MOVING DEDUCTIONS INTO A NON-AMT YEAR

Since itemized deductions such as state and local taxes, medical expenses in excess of 7.5 percent and investment interest expenses increase a taxpayer's exposure to AMT and do not create a MTC, if possible, it may be prudent for a taxpayer to pay those expenses in a tax year in which there would not be AMT.

Example: Each year, Nicolas and Amanda Wright, a married couple with no children earn a total of $100,000 in compensation. They make charitable contributions of $5,000, pay $6,000 in property taxes and $20,000 of mortgage interest. Five percent of their compensation is withheld for state income tax. In 2019, the Wrights recognized a long-term capital gain of $400,000 on the sale of stock. From that amount, they set aside $20,000 to pay the state income tax imposed on such gain. From an overall regular income tax and AMT perspective, would it be better for the Wrights to pay the state income tax in 2019 or on April 15, 2020, the due date of the state income tax return? Assume for purposes of this example that for 2020, the Wrights income, deductions and state withholding is the same as it normally is (without the 2019 capital gain). A multiple year analysis indicates a net overall tax savings of $1,000 if the state income tax was paid in 2016.

	Pay State Tax in 2019		Pay State Tax in 2020	
	2019	2020	2019	2020
Regular	$63,236	$7,508	$70,236	$4,508
AMT	$12,753	-0-	$9,753	-0-
Total Tax	$75,989	$7,508	$79,989	$4,508

As illustrated by the above multiple-year analysis, if the Wrights pay the state income tax in 2019, the total tax including AMT would be $75,989. In 2020, the total tax (no AMT) would be $7,508. Therefore, the total amount of tax paid over that two year period would be $83,497 ($75,989 plus $7,508). On the other hand, if the Wrights pay the state income tax in 2020, in 2019, the total tax including AMT would be $79,989 (or $4,000 more total tax than if the state income tax was paid in 2019). In 2020, however, the total tax (no AMT) would be $4,508 (or $3.000 less than the total tax than if the state income tax was paid in 2019). So, netting the total tax paid over the two year period, the Wrights would save $1,000 in total tax by paying the state income in 2019.

AMT PLANNING THROUGH THE TIMING OF ADJUSTMENTS AND PREFERENCES

Effective AMT planning can be accomplished by the timing of certain adjustments and preferences that are under the complete control of the taxpayer. To this point, this section will address ISOs and tax-exempt interest from private activity bonds.

Incentive Stock Options

One of the more common adjustments that has caused anguish for taxpayers is the ISO AMT adjustment. As discussed in more detail in Chapter 27, in the case of the exercise of an ISO, the difference between the fair market value of the company stock at the time of exercise (to be acquired by the employee) and the exercise cost is not subject to regular income tax. In the computation of AMTI, however, that spread is added to taxable income subjecting such "gain" to AMT.

Because the AMT ISO adjustment is a timing item, it creates a MTC that is available to reduce regular income tax in a subsequent non-ATM tax year. To be able to calculate the MTC, it is necessary to keep track of the taxpayer's AMT basis and regular income tax basis. For regular income tax purposes, the basis in the acquired stock is the exercise price plus any transaction costs. For AMT purposes, the basis in the acquired stock is the fair market value on the date of exercise plus any transaction costs. In the year in which the acquired stock is ultimately sold, the difference between the AMT basis and the regular income tax basis of the stock will reduce AMTI.

As a planning technique, the following timing strategies should be considered:

1. Exercising only the amount of ISOs that would not trigger AMT in a given tax year.

2. Coordinating the timing of the sale or exchange of ISO acquired stock with the exercise of newer ISOs.

3. Accelerating the exercise of NQSOs (non-qualified stock options) to a year in which the AMT applies to benefit from lower marginal tax rates.

Each of these planning techniques is discussed fully in Chapter 27.

Example 1: Kevin Peterson, a resident of Florida (with no state income tax) is an unmarried executive with a major corporation living in a rented apartment. In 2020, Kevin's compensation is likely to be $500,000. Otherwise, Kevin has no other income and does not itemize. Also, Kevin has 10,000 shares of ISOs with an exercise cost of $10 per share. Currently, the underlying stock has a fair market value of $30 per share. Because Kevin plans to hold the stock for a significant period of time and expects to receive more ISOs in the future, in 2020, his plan is to exercise as many ISOs as possible without triggering AMT. Doing the math, Kevin can exercise 1,596 ISOs without triggering AMT.

	No ISOs Exercised	2,900 ISOs Exercised
Taxable Income	$487,800	$487,800
Standard Deduction	$12,200	$12,200
ISO AMT Adjustment	-0-	$31,920
AMTI	$500,000	$531,920
Tentative Minimum Tax	$136,584	$145,522
Regular Income Tax	$145,525	$145,525
Total Tax	$145,525	$145,522

By exercising 1,596 ISOs, the spread between the fair market value of the underlying stock $31,920 (1,596 shares sold multiplied by the gain of $20 per share) is added to Kevin's taxable income in the computation of AMTI. However, even with this positive adjustment, the AMT would be equal to the regular income tax. Therefore, Kevin's overall tax liability is unaffected by the exercise of the 2,900 ISOs.

Example 2: Kevin exercises all 10,000 ISOs:

	No ISOs Exercised	10,000 ISOs Exercised
Taxable Income	$487,800	$487,800
Standard Deduction/ Personal Exemption	$12,200	$12,200
ISO AMT Adjustment -0-	$200,000	
AMTI	$500,000	$700,000
Tentative Minimum Tax	$136,584	$192,584
Regular Income Tax	$145,525	$145,525
AMT	-0-	$47,059
Total Tax	$145,525	$192,584

By exercising all 10,000 ISOs $200,000 is added to Kevin's taxable income in the computation of AMTI. However, this positive adjustment to AMTI would generate AMT of $47,059. So, if Kevin decides to exercise all 10,000 ISOs, it would cost him $47,059 of additional overall tax.

On the other hand, because the AMT is generated by a deferral or timing adjustment, the entire amount of AMT generated is also a MTC credit available to offset regular income tax in future non-AMT tax years.

Example 3: In 2021, Kevin's income is the same as it was in 2020 and he does not exercise any ISOs or sell any stock he acquired by exercise of ISOs in 2020. Because the AMT of $39,759 of AMT was generated by virtue of a deferral item, a MTC in that amount is available to reduce regular income tax in future years. Assuming that in 2021, his regular income tax is $145,525 and his tentative minimum tax liability is $136,584, so 2021 is a non-AMT year. Therefore, Kevin may reduce his regular income tax by $8,941 (the difference between his regular income tax liability and tentative minimum tax).

The balance of the MTC, $38,118 would be available to reduce regular income tax in future non-AMT tax years.

Interest from Private Activity Bonds

Although the interest earned on municipal bonds (state and local) is tax-free for regular income tax and AMT, interest earned on "specified private activity bonds" is added to taxable income in the computation of AMTI. The amount added to taxable income is reduced by any deductions (e.g., investment interest or investment expenses attributable to the acquisition or carrying of such private activity bonds) that would have been deductible for regular income tax purposes had such interest been taxable.

A bond is identified as being a "private activity bond" at the time of issue. Because private activity bond interest is subject to AMT, it is a less desirable investment. As a result, there is a smaller market for these bonds and the issuers must offer a slightly higher yield to successfully issue the bonds. In most cases, the higher yield is not sufficient to create an after-tax yield equal to the after-tax yield of tax-exempt bonds not subject to AMT. For an individual not subject to AMT, however, the higher yield offered by private activity bonds is attractive.

Doing the math by running the numbers is the best way to determine whether a municipal bond or a private activity bond with a higher yield results in the greater after-tax return.

MAKING ELECTIONS TO MINIMIZE THE AMT

Certain deductions that trigger AMT adjustments may be eliminated by making elections that spread deductions over a greater number of tax years, and, thus, mitigate or eliminate AMT. On the other hand, because the spread out deductions are lower than they would have been without the election, the taxpayer's regular taxable income is increased. Therefore, to assess the full impact of making or not making the elections, it is prudent to make multiple year projections to evaluate the potential costs and benefits.

Depreciation

Under MACRS, business property other than real estate is depreciated under the 200 percent declining balance method. For AMT purposes, however, the depreciation method can be no faster than the 150 percent declining balance method. To mitigate impact of AMT, there are two alternative elections available:

- *Straight line depreciation.*[1] In lieu of a 200 percent declining balance, the taxpayer elects the straight line depreciation method over the same recovery period. If this election is made, there is no AMT adjustment required. Other than saving potential AMT, for regular income tax purposes, the depreciation deduction is spread evenly over the recovery period. Therefore, unlike accelerated depreciation, the taxpayer loses the benefit of larger depreciation deductions in the earlier years of the recovery period. On the other hand, the straight line depreciation deductions in the later years of the recovery period would be greater than smaller depreciation deductions allowed in the later years of the accelerated depreciation recovery period.

- *150 percent declining balance.*[2] By making this election, the regular income tax and AMT depreciation method would be the same. Therefore, there would be no AMT adjustment.

Research and Experimental Expenditures

Pursuant to IRC Section 174(a), a taxpayer may deduct research and experimental expenses incurred in connection with a trade or business or elect to capitalize and amortize such costs over sixty months.[3] For AMT purposes, if an individual deducts research and experimental expenses, an adjustment must be made. The difference between the current year deduction for regular income tax purposes and the amount that would have been deducted had the expenses been capitalized and amortized over ten years is added to taxable income in computing AMTI.[4]

To avoid the above described AMT adjustment, the taxpayer may elect to capitalize and amortize research and experimental costs over ten years for regular income tax purposes.[5] The election can be made in any year such costs are incurred. In making the election, the taxpayer may elect to capitalize all or any portion of the costs. Because the election is not all or nothing with respect to the deductibility of such costs, there are planning opportunities. Another factor to consider is that as a deferral adjustment that would be made in the absence of an election, a MTC would be created available to reduce regular income tax in a non-ATM year.

However, if the taxpayer materially participates (as defined with respect to the private activity rules) in the business activities of the entity that incurred the costs, no such AMT adjustment would be made.[6]

Intangible Drilling Costs

For most taxpayers, intangible drilling costs are deductible due to investment in an oil or gas venture. IRC Section 263(c) provides the taxpayer with the option of capitalizing intangible drilling and development costs or deducting all costs in the year they were paid or incurred. If the taxpayer elects to expense those costs, it results in an AMT preference item equal to the amount by which "excess intangible drilling costs" exceeds 65 percent of the taxpayer's net income from oil, gas and geothermal properties for the year.[7] Excess intangible drilling costs is defined as the intangible drilling cost deduction amount from productive wells less the amount that would have been deductible if the productive intangible drilling costs were capitalized and either (a) amortized over ten years beginning in the first month of production; or (b) depleted using cost depletion.

In order to eliminate this AMT adjustment, pursuant to IRC Section 59(e), the taxpayer may elect to capitalize and amortize the intangible drilling costs over 60 months beginning in the month such costs were paid or incurred. Similar to the election for research and experimental expenditures, the election can be made for all or part of the intangible drilling costs. Because the election is not all or nothing with respect to the deductibility of such costs, there are planning opportunities. Another factor to consider is that as a deferral adjustment that would be made in the absence of an election, a MTC would be created available to reduce regular income tax in a non-ATM year.

The decision to make either of the elections described above merits due consideration. If the cause of the AMT is the result of deferral or timing adjustments, making an election may not yield a better result. For example, if the election is not made, the imposition of AMT will create a corresponding MTC that may be used to reduce regular income tax in future non-AMT years. On the other hand, if the election is made, current income will be increased as a result of lower current year deductions. If that occurs, regular income tax will likely be higher than it would have been without making the election. So, the ultimate decision may turn on which scenario yields the lowest overall tax.

Conversely, if the cause of the AMT is mainly attributable to exclusion adjustments that would have been made under any circumstances, by spreading out the deductions over more years, making an election could preserve a portion of the deduction to be used in future years when there is no AMT. In any event, in determining whether to make an election, the taxpayer should consider multiple year projections to assess which path would result in the lowest overall tax liability.

Finally, another reason to make the election that would result in an increase of current income would be to take advantage of NOLs that are about to expire. By doing so, the taxpayer may enjoy the double tax benefit of eliminating or substantially reducing AMT while offsetting the extra income with the NOLs.

UTILIZING ALTERNATIVE TAX NET OPERATING LOSS

It is possible that a taxpayer in any given tax year may have a NOL for regular income tax purposes as well as an alternative tax net operating loss (ATNOL) for AMT purposes. As discussed in Chapter 10 the ATNOL is computed by increasing or decreasing the regular income tax NOL by AMT adjustments and preferences in the year of loss.[8]

In using the ATNOL, it must be carried back or forward to the same tax year as the NOL. So the election to forego the NOL carryback (carrying it forward rather than carrying it back and then forward) also applies to the ATNOL.[9] Additionally, an ATNOL offsets AMTI in the carryback or carryforward year even if the taxpayer did not incur AMT in that year. So, in making the decision whether to forego the NOL carryback, the taxpayer should consider the AMT consequences of such an election. In other words, if a carryback of the NOL and ATNOL would save more overall tax than foregoing the carryback, the taxpayer should not make the election to forego the carryback.

Importantly, the amount of AMTI that can be reduced by an ATNOL in a carryback or carryforward year is limited to 90 percent of that year's AMTI determined without regard to the ATNOL.[10]

Example: Asher has an ATNOL of $160,000. Asher carries the ATNOL back two years in which his AMTI was $100,000. Even though Asher did not have any AMT in that year, he must offset the AMTI by an amount of the ATNOL equal to 90 percent of the AMTI. Therefore, the $100,000 of AMTI from the carryback year is reduced by $90,000. This leaves $70,000 of remaining ATNOL ($160,000 minus $90,000) to be used to offset AMTI in the subsequent carryback year.

FREQUENTLY ASKED QUESTIONS

Question – Are there states that impose AMT with respect to state income taxation?

Answer – With respect to individual state income taxation there are seven states that impose some form of AMT. These states are California, Colorado, Connecticut, Iowa, Maryland, Minnesota and Wisconsin. Recently, New York repealed its version of AMT. The mechanics of state AMT varies from state to state. Most are not indexed for inflation meaning that in those states, state AMT will affect more and more taxpayers in future tax years.

CHAPTER ENDNOTES

1. IRC Sec. 168(b)(3).
2. IRC Sec. 168(b)(2).
3. IRC Sec. 174(b).
4. IRC Sec. 56(b)(2).
5. IRC Sec. 59(e).
6. IRC Sec. 56(b)(2)(D).
7. IRC Sec. 57(a)(2).
8. IRC Sec. 56(d)(2).
9. Rev. Rul. 87-44, 1987-1 C.B. 3.
10. IRC Sec. 56(d)(1)(A).

SOCIAL SECURITY/ MEDICARE TAXES: WAGE EARNERS AND SELF-EMPLOYED INDIVIDUALS

CHAPTER 12

INTRODUCTION

In addition to regular income tax, the Internal Revenue Code imposes a flat social security tax and a flat Medicare tax on the *earned income* of wage earners (generally defined as taxpayers who work for someone else) and self-employed individuals. While the term "earned income" broadly describes the types of income that are subject to these two flat taxes, the actual calculation of their respective tax bases is significantly different.

Although the tax rate is the same for wage income and self-employment income, the tax base, tax liability computations, payment requirements for the taxes are different. The economic impact of these taxes on a self-employed individual is typically much greater than on a wage earner.

HOW DO THE SOCIAL SECURITY AND MEDICARE TAXES WORK?

The respective social security and the Medicare tax rates are 12.4 percent and 2.9 percent, for a total of 15.3 percent of earned income. The social security tax and the Medicare tax are often referred to as the "payroll tax" for wage earners and the "self-employment tax" for self-employed individuals. Employees are only obligated to pay half of the payroll tax, or 7.65 percent of the 15.3 percent total tax liability. Employers are required to withhold the employees' half of the payroll tax, as well as pay the other half directly. Because the payroll tax is a flat tax paid entirely through withholding, a wage earner will never have an outstanding payroll tax liability to pay out of pocket. Moreover, there is no line item on Form 1040 for employee payroll tax. Because employees do not actually pay the tax directly and do not see it on their regular income tax returns, they often do not realize its full impact.

Conversely, subject to some offsetting tax relief discussed below, self-employed taxpayers are obligated to pay the entire amount of self-employment tax directly to the IRS. Self-employed individuals report the tax on Form 1040 using a Schedule SE. In addition, to avoid penalties, they are obligated to make quarterly payments of estimated tax directly to the IRS to avoid a significant balance owed to the IRS on April 15.

SOCIAL SECURITY AND MEDICARE TAXES FOR WAGE EARNERS

As mentioned above, the social security tax and Medicare tax rates are the same on the wage income of a wage earner and as they are on the self-employment income of a self-employed individual. However, the operative statute for the imposition of payroll taxes on wage earners is the Federal Insurance Contributions Act, and collectively payroll taxes are referred to as the "FICA tax."[1]

Tax Base

Obviously, the tax base of a wage earner is wages (with certain exclusions). "Wages" is defined as compensation for employment in any form, including money, benefits, or property.[2] "Employment" is any service performed by an employee for the person employing him.[3] The term "service performed" goes beyond work actually done and encompasses the entire employee-employer relationship.[4]

Under this broad concept of employee compensation, sick pay, back pay, or vacation pay are treated as wages subject to the FICA tax. Additionally, a recent Supreme Court decision has expanded the definition of wages to include severance pay. In *U.S. v. Quality Stores, Inc.*,[5] the employer—in the midst of a Chapter 11 bankruptcy—made severance payments to 3,100 terminated employees. Reversing a decision by the Sixth Circuit Court of Appeals, the Supreme Court held that severance payments were paid in the realm of an employer-employee relationship, and thus were unquestionably wages. Under this ruling, severance payments—like any other type of wages—are subject to the FICA tax.

There are, however, certain types of employee compensation that are specifically exempted from the FICA tax. Figure 12.1 is a non-exclusive list of some of the excluded compensation.[6]

Figure 12.1

Type of Compensation Excluded	Requirements for FICA Exclusion
Employee business expense reimbursements	The reimbursements must be part of an "accountable plan," in which: • The deductible expense must be incurred by employee while performing employee-type services; • The reimbursement or advance must match actual amount of expense; • Expenses must be substantiated within reasonable period of time; and • Any amounts in excess of substantiated expenses must be returned to employer.
Noncash payments for household work, agricultural labor and services not in the employer's trade or business	• Wages are paid "in-kind" (i.e., goods, lodging, food, clothing and services); and • The services provided are not related to the employer's trade or business.
Reimbursed and employer-paid moving expenses	• Must be an expense that is otherwise deductible by the employee; and • Must be paid under an accountable plan.
Meals and lodging	• Meals must be furnished on employer's premises for the convenience of employer, (e.g., so employee is available during lunch for emergency. • Lodging must be furnished for the convenience of the employer on employer's premises as condition of employment.
Health insurance plans	Includes employer-paid accident or health insurance for employee, employee's spouse and dependents.
Health savings accounts and medical savings accounts	Includes contributions to Health Savings Accounts (HSAs) and Archer Medical Savings Accounts (MSAs).
Medical care reimbursements	Must be paid for employee under the employer's self-insured medical reimbursement plan.
Military differential pay	• Employee is on active duty for more than 30 days. • Payments must represent wages the employee would have received if performing services for the employer.

Figure 12.1 (cont'd)

Fringe benefits	Must be nontaxable (i.e., excluded from the gross income of the employee).
Family employees	Wages for a child under 18 who works for a parent in a trade or business.
Payments after an employee death or disability retirement	Amounts must be paid under a definite plan or system (i.e. sick pay plan).
Post-mortem sick pay payments	Paid to employee's estate or survivor after calendar year of employee's death.
Payments to employee entitled to disability insurance benefits	Includes payments made when an employee is entitled to disability insurance benefits pursuant to Section 223(a) of the Social Security Act.
Certain types of sick pay	Applies to sick pay payments made more than six calendar months after the last calendar month the employee worked.

Computation and Payment of FICA Tax

As mentioned above, the liability for the FICA tax is split equally between the employee and the employer.[7] Although the social security tax rate is much higher than the Medicare tax rate, it is capped at a certain (inflation-adjusted) amount of wages. For 2020, the social security tax caps at wages of $137,700.[8] Thus, the maximum amount of social security tax liability for the employee and employee shares would be $17,075 (12.4 percent of $128,700), or $8,537 each.

On the other hand, there is no cap on the Medicare tax. This means the combined employer/employee 2.9 percent tax rate will be imposed on all wages without limit. So, for 2020, although the imposition of social security tax ceases on wages in excess of $137,700, the Medicare tax is imposed on all wages. Moreover, starting 2013 an Additional Medicare Surtax of 0.9 percent is added to the 1.45 percent employee portion of the Medicare tax for wages above certain threshold levels. (For a more detailed discussion of the Additional Medicare Surtax, see Chapter 13.)

Each year, all wage items—including withholding of the employee's portion of the FICA tax—are reported on a Form W-2 that is provided to the employee and the Social Security Administration. However, the employer is actually responsible for the payment of the FICA tax. Essentially, on an ongoing basis, the employer remits both its share of FICA and the employee's share of FICA that was withheld from his or her wages in the form of a payroll tax deposit. Additionally, all FICA payments are reported quarterly to the IRS on Form 941.

Refunds or Tax Credits for Overpayment of Social Security Tax

Although the FICA tax withheld from an employee's paycheck is reported on Form W-2, there is no line item for it on Form 1040. A wage earner who never actually makes a FICA tax payment may be oblivious to FICA tax liability—much less its payment through wage withholding. Moreover, a wage earner with two or more jobs who is unaware of the social security wage cap may miss an opportunity to receive a tax credit or refund for an overpayment.

This could occur for a taxpayer with multiple jobs. Each employer only knows the amount that it has paid the employee. If an employee has aggregate wages from multiple jobs that exceed the social security tax cap for the year, it is quite possible that the employer may have paid more in social security taxes than was required. In that instance, the amount of social security tax withheld on wage income above the cap would be an overpayment, and the taxpayer can either apply the overpayment as a credit against income tax liability on Form 1040, or apply for a refund by filing Form 843.

Example. In 2020, William Widget was a salaried IT technician earning $100,000. In addition, William earned $60,000 in wages working evenings and weekends as a manager of a computer store. The 2018 social security wage cap was $137,700. Thus, while neither of the jobs paid wages in excess of the cap, the aggregate amount of William's wages exceeded the social security wage cap by $22,300.

William's two employers collectively withheld $9,920 in social security taxes (6.2 percent of $160,000), but his maximum amount of social security tax liability was only $8,537 (6.2 percent of $137,700). Here, William has a $1,383 social security tax overpayment.

SOCIAL SECURITY AND MEDICARE TAXES FOR SELF-EMPLOYED INDIVIDUALS

Analogous to the FICA tax imposed on wage income, social security and Medicare taxes are imposed on self-employment income through the Self-Employment Contributions Act of 1954 (SECA).[9] Unlike the FICA tax which has no line item on Form 1040, the SECA tax is computed on Schedule SE and entered on line 56 of Form 1040.

Tax Base

The SECA tax base (commonly referred to as *self-employment income*) is defined as "net earnings from self-employment,"[10] and includes income generated by:

1. a sole proprietor;
2. a single-member LLC that is treated as a disregarded entity and taxed as a sole proprietor;[11] and
3. a general partner's distributive share of ordinary income from the partnership.[12]

As the word "net" implies, gross self-employment income from the taxpayer's business is reduced by deductible expenses attributable to the business. (See Chapters 6 and 7 for a more detailed discussion of the types of deductions that may be used to reduce business income.)

For a sole proprietor or a single-member LLC, self-employment income is calculated on Schedule C. Specifically, a self-employed individual reports gross receipts less all allowable deductions. In this way, Schedule C serves the dual purpose of determining both business income for regular income tax purposes and net self-employment income for SECA purposes.

Similarly, ordinary income and deductions for a partnership are netted on the partnership level. The distributive share of that net income is allocated to each general partner[13] and recorded on a Schedule K-1 that is provided to each partner. That amount is then used on Schedule SE for SECA tax purposes.

Computation of SECA Tax

Unlike a wage earner whose liability is limited to half of the FICA tax, a self-employed individual is obligated to pay the entire amount of the 15.3 percent SECA tax. Similar to FICA, the social security tax cap for self-employment income is the same dollar amount as the social security wage cap ($137,700 in 2018 and indexed for inflation).[14]

Also like FICA, there is no cap on the amount of self-employment income subject to the Medicare tax, and the 0.9 percent Additional Medicare Surtax is added to the 2.9 percent Medicare tax rate for self-employment income that exceeds certain thresholds.

The first step in the computation of the SECA tax is to determine the amount of net self-employment income from all potential sources. If a taxpayer has more than one source of self-employment income, such as income from multiple Schedules C and/or K-1s, net income and loss from those sources are combined. Obviously, if the combined amount is negative, no SECA tax is owed.

Because a self-employed individual is compelled to pay the entire amount of the SECA tax, the following two types of tax relief are provided to ease the burden:

1. The SECA tax base is only 92.35 percent of net self-employment income earnings.[15]
2. The self-employed individual is entitled to an above-the-line *income tax deduction* equal to one half of the SECA tax.[16]

The first type of tax relief reduces the SECA tax base by 7.65 percent to lessen the amount of SECA tax a self-employed individual would otherwise owe. The above-the-line income tax deduction of one half of the SECA tax reduces taxable income; and, thus, lessens the amount of regular income tax a self-employed individual would otherwise owe. The purpose of this deduction is to level the playing field with wage earners. For wage earners, the employer is responsible for paying half of FICA taxes, and that amount is not included in the wage earner's taxable income.

Example: In 2020, Betty Business, an unmarried taxpayer, operated an IT business as a sole proprietor. In addition, she was a general partner in a partnership that owned and operated a computer store. Finally, she sold refurbished computers through a single-member LLC that was treated as a disregarded entity. Betty is a single taxpayer with no dependents and does not itemize deductions.

On a Schedule C reporting her IT income and expenses, Betty showed net income of $20,000. On a separate Schedule C reporting her refurbished computer income and expenses, Betty showed a net loss of $40,000. Finally, her income from the LLC—recorded on Schedule K-1—was $80,000.

Betty's net self-employment income and tax liabilities are computed as follows:

Net self-employment income	
IT business net income	$20,000
Refurbished computer business net loss	– $40,000
LLC income	$80,000
Net self-employment income	**$60,000**
SECA tax	
SECA tax base	$60,000 × 92.35% = $55,410
SECA tax owed	$55,410 × 15.3% = $8,478
Above-the line deduction for half of SECA tax	$4,239
Income tax	
Total income	**$60,000**
Less above-the-line SECA deduction	– $4,329
AGI	**$55,761**
Less standard deduction ($12,200)	– $12,200
Taxable Income	**$43,561**
Total tax liability	
Income tax (from tax tables)	$5,373
SECA tax	$8,478
Total tax liability	**$13,851**

Figure 12.2

COMPARISON OF TAXES ON EARNED INCOME: WAGES vs. SELF-EMPLOYMENT INCOME

	Wages (FICA)	**Self-Employment Income (SECA)**
Tax Rate	15.30%	15.30%
Amount Subject to Tax	100% of includible wage income	92.35% of self-employment income and/or general partner's distributive share of ordinary income
Who Is Responsible for Tax?	7.65% employee; 7.65% employer	100% Self-employed individual
Income Tax Deduction	None for the employee	Above the line deduction of half of the SECA Tax
Reporting on Form 1040	None for the employee	On Schedule SE and on line 56 on Form 1040
Social Security Earned Income Cap	$136,700 of wages for 2020 Adjusted annually for inflation	$137,700 (or $149,107 multiplied by 92.35%) Adjusted annually for inflation
Medicare Earned Income Cap	None	None
Subject to Additional Medicare Surtax	Yes	Yes

Are Wages and Self-Employment Income Taxed Equivalently?

If a wage earner and a self-employed individual have exactly the same amount of income, would they face the same tax liability? This is a hard question to answer with complete certainty. The 7.65 percent reduction of the SECA tax base provides only moderate tax relief. In the example from the previous section, the SECA tax on the entire amount of Betty's self-employment income ($60,000) would have been $9,180. With the 7.65 percent reduction of her self-employment income ($55,410), the SECA tax was $8,478. The tax savings of $702 does not appear to be that significant.[17]

On the other hand, the above-the-line deduction of one-half of the SECA tax provides more potent tax relief because it is available to all self-employed individuals, even those who do not itemize. The benefit of this deduction depends on the amount of the deduction and the self-employed individual's marginal tax rate. Obviously, higher deductions and higher marginal rates will increase the tax savings.

Above-the-line deductions that reduce adjusted gross income can potentially save tax in other ways because other tax benefits tend to phase out (and tax detriments tend to phase in) with higher amounts of adjusted gross income. Consequently, this deduction could provide even more benefits to a self-employed individual with tax items that are sensitive to the level of adjusted gross income.

For instance, such a deduction would be helpful to a self-employed individual with a substantial amount of miscellaneous itemized deductions, which are subject to a floor of 2 percent of adjusted gross income.[18] An above-the-line deduction that reduces adjusted gross income lowers the floor, and allows a greater amount of deductions.

Similarly, higher amounts of adjusted gross income increase the amount of social security benefits that are taxable.[19] For a self-employed individual receiving social security benefit payments, an above-the-line deduction that reduces adjusted gross income would also reduce the taxable amount of those payments.

Because of variations in the amount of the above-the-line SECA tax deduction, the marginal tax rate, and types of income-sensitive tax items that any given self-employed individual may have, there is no easy answer to the question above. What is clear (as illustrated in Figure 12.3), is that a self-employed individual who does not itemize will always pay a substantial greater amount of overall tax than a similarly situated wage earner.

Figure 12.3

SIDE-BY-SIDE COMPARISON OF A WAGE EARNER AND A SELF-EMPLOYED INDIVIDUAL

Both are single with no dependents or itemized deductions in tax year 2020.			
Wages	$110,000	Self-employment income	$110,000
Employee's share of the FICA tax:	$8,415 ($110,000 × 7.65%)	SECA tax:	$15,543 ($100,000 × 92.35% × 15.3%)
Wages $100,000	$100,000	Self-employment income	$110,000
Less standard deduction ($12,000)	– $12,200	Less half of SECA tax	– $7,772
		Less standard deduction ($12,000)	– $12,200
Taxable income	**$97,800**	**Taxable income**	**$90,028**
Regular income tax	$13,096	Regular income tax	$11,386
FICA tax	$8,415	SECA tax	$15,543
Total FICA and regular income tax	**$21,511**	**Total SECA and regular income tax:**	**$26,929**
Excess amount of total tax paid by self-employed individual as compared to wage earner: $26,929 – $21,511 = $5,418			

USING AN S CORPORATION TO REDUCE SOCIAL SECURITY AND MEDICARE TAXES

Individuals inclined to go into business for themselves should consider forming an S corporation to lessen the tax burden of being self-employed. S corporations do this by providing three important benefits.

1. *Shareholders can become employees.* In an S corporation, the individuals who would otherwise be sole proprietors or partners can be employed by the entity and be subject to the FICA rules rather than the SECA rules. As an employee, only half of the 15.3 percent FICA tax would be withheld from the individual's wages. While the full FICA tax is still paid, the half that is paid by the S corporation is a deductible business expense, and is never realized by the shareholder as income.

2. *Shareholders can take dividend distributions.* In lieu of taking strictly wage income, shareholders can take some of their compensation as "dividend distributions." Dividend distributions are considered capital gains rather than wages. This has two advantages: (a) they are not subject to the FICA tax;[20] and (b) they are often taxed at a lower rate than ordinary income. A shareholder/employee who is compensated with a combination of wages and dividend distributions could potentially realize a significant savings of FICA tax.

3. *Shareholders may be eligible for an additional Section 199A deduction on income from the S corporation (see Chapter 5).*

However, the IRS considers disproportionately large dividend distributions to be an inappropriate way to avoid FICA tax. In Revenue Ruling 74-44, two shareholders of an S corporation who provided services to the corporation received dividend distributions but no compensation. Under those circumstances, the IRS recharacterized the amount of the distributions that would have been reasonable compensation for the services provided as wages subject to FICA.[21]

Obviously, the facts of the revenue ruling were egregious because the shareholder/employees received no compensation. If the wages of a shareholder/employee are "reasonable compensation" for the services that were performed, he or she may legitimately receive some compensation in the form of dividend distributions. When determining whether the amount of wages paid constitutes "reasonable compensation" for a shareholder/employee, the IRS will consider a number of factors:[22]

- The shareholder/employee's training and experience;
- The duties and responsibilities of the shareholder/employee;
- The amount of time and effort devoted to the business;
- Compensation of similar employees who are not shareholders;
- What comparable businesses pay for similar services; and
- The use of a formula to determine compensation.

These factors are particularly relevant to a professional service corporation. Obviously, a shareholder/employee who provides substantial specialized professional services to the business should command a relatively high salary. On the other hand, a shareholder/employee who, with age, decides to assume a reduced role may be able to justify a lower amount of compensation, and, perhaps a significant amount as a dividend distribution.

An obvious lack of reasonable compensation is evidenced when the salary of a high qualified shareholder/employee is less than the salary of a lesser qualified non-shareholder/employee. Attempts to make up the difference through dividend distributions would not likely pass IRS scrutiny.

Another indication of reasonable compensation is what a comparable business would pay an employee for providing similar services. If the going compensation for a specific type of professional is $250,000, paying a shareholder/employee a salary of $50,000 to perform those same services would likely not be considered reasonable compensation. When deciding on how to distribute compensation between wages and dividend distributions, shareholders should consult independent salary surveys for their specific industries.

Finally, published, businesses can use industry-specific compensation formulas to determine the wages of a shareholder/employee as a percentage of sales or profits. The use of these formulas should allow the compensation decisions to withstand IRS scrutiny.

Example: Kristi is a veterinarian who owns a two-doctor practice. She sees patients five days per week in addition to her management duties. After realizing a $40,000 profit in 2019, in 2020 she incorporates her two-doctor veterinary practice as an S Corporation, Veterinary Medical Center, Inc. (VMC). VMC compensates her with monthly wages in the amount of 23 percent of her billings. Using this formula, her 2020 wages were $100,000, and she paid herself a total of $25,000 in quarterly dividend distributions. She also pays a less-experienced associate veterinarian wages in the amount of 20 percent of his billings, which resulted in $80,000 in wage compensation for 2020.

Although Kristi's wages are subject to both FICA tax and ordinary income tax, the dividend distribution would be subject only to income tax. As a result, Kristi would save a total of $3,825 of FICA tax (15.3 percent of $25,000). Note also that this does not include any analysis of potential savings under Section 199A (see Chapter 5 for more details)

Additionally, she can justify the dividend distributions by clearly showing that her wages were "reasonable compensation" for the services performed:

- She is an experienced and licensed veterinarian.
- Her duties included full-time clinical hours in addition to her management responsibilities.
- She worked in her practice five days per week.
- Her non-shareholder associate was paid similar wages (after accounting for his lower level of experience).
- Her wages were based on a formula that can be reconciled with the accounting records of the business.
- Her dividend distributions are similar to the profit earned by the business the year before.

FREQUENTLY ASKED QUESTIONS

Question – Are below-market or interest-free loans between an employer and employee subject to the FICA tax?

Answer – Yes, for loans greater than $10,000.[23] The amount of imputed "wages" subject to the FICA tax from such a loan is the difference between the interest that would have been payable to the employer using the applicable federal rate, and the amount actually that was paid by the employee.[24]

Example: Gary Gizmo borrows $100,000 from his employer. The loan is an interest-free demand loan. Assuming the applicable federal rate is 3 percent, the amount of Gary's imputed compensation is the foregone interest of $3,000. As a result, $3,000 of imputed wage income is subject to FICA tax.[25]

Question – Are there any additional filing requirements for individuals who form an S corporation rather than operate as sole proprietors or partners?

Answer – Yes. First, the S corporation must file an income tax return using Form 1120S. Unlike Form 1040, the filing deadline for a Form 1120S is March 15. Also, the S corporation must report wages quarterly using Form 941 and make periodic payroll tax deposits.

Question – Are there any other above-the-line deductions available for self-employed individuals?

Answer – Yes, a self-employed individual may be entitled to an above-the-line deduction for premiums paid on medical, dental or long-term care insurance policies that cover himself, his spouse, and his dependents. The deduction is available to sole proprietors, single-member LLCs treated as a disregarded entities, general partners, or a shareholders of an S corporation who own more than

2 percent of the outstanding stock. Since the deduction is personal (not business), it is not entered on Schedule C. Instead, it is taken as an above-the-line deduction on Form 1040.

CHAPTER ENDNOTES

1. Codified as Chapter 21 of the Internal Revenue Code (IRC Secs. 3101-3128).
2. IRC Sec. 3121(a).
3. IRC Sec. 3121(b).
4. *Social Security Bd. v. Nierotko*, 327 U.S. 358 (1946).
5. *U.S. v. Quality Stores, Inc.*, 572 U.S. __ (2014).
6. IRS Publication 15 (2014), "Wages and Other Compensation."
7. IRC Secs. 3101(a), 3111(a), 3101(b) and 3111(b).
8. Press Release, Social Security Administration (October 13, 2013).
9. SECA is codified as Chapter 2 of the Internal Revenue Code.
10. IRC Sec. 1402(a).
11. Treas. Reg. §301.7702-2(c)(2)(iv)(D), "Example (iii)."
12. IRC Sec. 1402(a).
13. IRC Sec. 702(a)(8).
14. IRS Publication 517 (2013).
15. Social Security Handbook, "Net Earnings from Self-Employment." Available at http://www.ssa.gov/OP_Home/handbook/handbook.html.
16. IRC Sec. 164(f).
17. Expressed as a percentage, the tax savings seem minimal. Based on self-employment income of $60,000, the lesser SECA tax of $8,478 would reduce the overall tax rate to 14.13 percent ($8,478/$60,000), or a savings of 1.17 percent.
18. IRC Sec. 67.
19. IRC Sec. 86.
20. Rev. Rul. 59-221, 1959-1 C.B. 225.
21. Rev. Rul. 74-44, 1974-1 C.B. 287.
22. IRS Fact Sheet 2008-25 (August 2008).
23. IRC Sec. 7872(c)(3). Below-market loans between employers and employees are subject to a $10,000 *de minimis* exception for the purposes taxation.
24. IRC Sec. 7872.
25. IRS Publication 15-A (2014).

ADDITIONAL MEDICARE SURTAX ON EARNED INCOME AND NET INVESTMENT INCOME TAX

CHAPTER 13

INTRODUCTION

There are two basic ways to increase taxes. The most obvious way is to raise the rate brackets. The other way is to impose a surtax. A *surtax* is a "tax levied on top of another tax,"[1] and is generally triggered when certain income levels are exceeded. The Health Care and Education Reconciliation Act of 2010[2] enacted two "flat" surtaxes. The "Additional Medicare Surtax" is a 0.9 percent tax on earned income, and the "Net Investment Income Tax" (NIIT) is a 3.8 percent tax on net investment income.

WHAT IS THE MEDICARE SURTAX?

As the name suggests, the Additional Medicare Surtax is not a new surtax, but instead increases the surtax rate and extends the tax base of the Health Insurance tax. The Health Insurance tax—itself a previously existing surtax—is also known as the Medicare tax, and is part of the Federal Insurance Contributions Act and Railroad Retirement Tax Act Taxes ("FICA").[3] FICA is imposed on all *earned income*, including wage-type income (salaries, commissions, etc.) that are typically reported on a W-2, as well as self-employment income (including income from self-proprietors, single-member LLCs taxed as sole proprietors, and general partners' distributive shares of partnership ordinary income).[4]

Effective for tax years 2013 and later, there is an Additional Medicare Surtax of 0.9 percent added to the FICA wages and/or self-employment income in excess of the applicable thresholds.[5] Once earned income exceeds the applicable threshold, the imposition of the Additional Medicare Surtax increases the overall Medicare tax rate to 3.8 percent (the same percentage as the flat NIIT rate, discussed below). The applicable thresholds for the Medicare surtax are defined in terms of earned income, and vary by filing status:

- $250,000 for a married couple filing jointly
- $125,000 for a married individual filing separately
- $200,000 for all other filing statuses[6]

Although the Additional Medicare Tax is not imposed on the employer share of the Medicare tax, the employer is nonetheless obligated to withhold 0.9 percent of an employee's wages in excess of $200,000 - without regard to whether such employee is actually subject to the tax.[7]

WHAT IS THE NET INVESTMENT INCOME TAX?

The Net Investment Income Tax ("NIIT") is the other surtax enacted pursuant to The Health Care and Education Reconciliation Act of 2010.[8] Unlike the Additional Medicare Surtax that is limited to individuals, estates and many trusts are also subject to the tax.[9] For individual taxpayers, the NIIT is a 3.8 percent surtax that is imposed on the lesser of:

- a taxpayer's net investment income; or
- the amount by which the taxpayer's adjusted gross income[10] exceeds the applicable

threshold amounts (which are the same as the Medicare surtax threshold amounts discussed above).[11]

The threshold amounts for the NIIT are the same as the Additional Medicare Tax thresholds. But these thresholds are based on the taxpayer's adjusted gross income, not earned income. Additionally, as discussed in more detail later in this chapter, the threshold amount for trusts and estates is much lower than the thresholds of the individual taxpayers subject to the tax.[12]

In essence, NIIT is a surtax on net investment income that has already been subject to regular federal income tax. In operation, the computation of net investment income is comparable to the computation of taxable income. With regard to regular taxation, items of gross income comprise the tax base. As discussed in Chapter 3, taxable income equals gross income minus deductions for the expenses necessary for generating that income. Similarly, with regard to NIIT, items of investment income that have already been taxed (i.e., were included in gross income) comprise the NIIT tax base. Thus, similar to the computation of taxable income, net *investment* income is gross investment income minus deductible expenses properly allocable to such income.

However, the devil is in the details, and the complexity of NIIT calculations cannot be underestimated.

The process of computing the NIIT obligation requires several steps:

1. First, identify items included in gross income that fit the Code definition of "investment income."

2. Second, identify deductions properly allocable to that income to determine the amount of "net investment income."

3. The final step—assuming the applicable threshold for the imposition of the tax has been crossed—is to multiply the NIIT rate of 3.8 percent by the lesser of:

   a. net investment income (as calculated in the second step), or

   b. the difference between the taxpayer's adjusted gross income and the applicable threshold.

Important caveat: Any item of income that is Medicare wage income or self-employment income is never considered net investment income, even if it would otherwise meet the Code definition. In that case, such income may be subject to the Additional Medicare Surtax.[13]

WHAT TYPES OF INCOMES ARE SUBJECT TO THE SURTAXES?

Each surtax has its own threshold (listed above) and tax base. The *threshold* is the triggering point of the surtax, and the *tax base* specifies the type of income that is subject to the surtax. The Additional Medicare Surtax threshold is based on the taxpayer's total amount of *earned income* (defined to include Medicare wages and/or self-employment income) in excess of the applicable threshold amount, and its tax base is the taxpayer's earned income.

The NIIT has the same threshold amounts, but it has a different tax base. It is applied to the lesser of either *adjusted gross income*—not earned income as is the case for the Medicare surtax.[14]—or net investment income. In other words, if the amount of net investment income is greater than the excess of adjusted gross income over the threshold amount, the NIIT would be imposed on the excess amount of adjusted gross income, rather than net investment income.

Example: Iris, a single taxpayer has adjusted gross income of $208,000, including a net investment income of $10,000. As a single taxpayer she has a threshold amount of $200,000. In Iris' case, the NIIT would be imposed on the $8,000 in AGI that is beyond the threshold amount—rather than her $10,000 of net investment income—because that is the lesser of the two amounts.

Significantly, any income subject to the Additional Medicare Tax is not also subject to the NIIT.[15] This means that wages and self-employment income are *never* included in the NIIT tax base, and thus are not subject to the NIIT. On the other hand, if the taxpayer has wages and/or self-employment income as well as net investment income, it is possible to be subject to both surtaxes. The Additional Medicare Tax could be imposed on the wage and self-employment income, while the NIIT could be imposed on the investment income. The example below illustrates the following fact pattern in which a taxpayer is subject to the Additional Medicare Surtax and the NIIT on top of the regular income tax.

Example: In 2020, Ira, a single taxpayer has $410,000 of taxable income which includes wages of $300,000 and net investment income of $110,000. After some preliminary calculations, Ira's adjusted gross income is determined to be $350,000.

Ira's regular tax without regard to the surtaxes is $94,879.[16] The Additional Medicare Surtax is also imposed because the taxpayer's earned income of $300,000 exceeds the threshold of $200,000 for a single individual,[17] resulting in $900 of Additional Medicare Surtax on the excess $100,000. Finally, the NIIT is also imposed because Ira's adjusted gross income exceeds the NIIT threshold of $200,000 for a single individual.[18]

Once the threshold is triggered, the tax would be computed on:

- the lesser of net investment income ($110,000); or
- the excess of adjusted gross income over the threshold amount ($150,000).

In Ira's case, the NIIT would be $4,180 (3.8 percent of $110,000).

Taxable Income $410,000 Including: Wages $300,000 Net Investment Income $110,000 Adjusted Gross Income $350,000	
Step 1: Compute Regular Income Tax on $410,000 of taxable income	**$58,020**
Step 2: Compute Additional Medicare Surtax on wages in excess of $200,000.	**0.9% of $100,000 = $900**
Step 3: Compute NIIT on $110,000 (the lesser of NII or AGI in excess of the threshold amount)	**$4,180**

This example demonstrates that the two surtaxes are subject to their own thresholds and their own tax rates that are levied on top of the regular income tax. Based on this illustration, the total tax liability with respect to the three taxes would be $63,100—of which $5,080 would be attributable to the two new surtaxes.

HOW DOES THE ADDITIONAL MEDICARE SURTAX WORK?

Although perhaps not the norm, it is possible for a taxpayer to have W-2 wage income as well as self-employment income from a business outside of employment. As stated above, the Additional Medicare Surtax is imposed on any combination of Medicare wages and self-employment income in excess of the applicable threshold. This is a relatively simple calculation, as demonstrated in the example below.

Example: A single taxpayer has Medicare wages of $275,000 and self-employment income of $100,000. Based on the single filing status, the applicable threshold is $200,000, and the total of Medicare wages and self-employment income exceeds the threshold by $175,000. To compute the Additional Medicare Surtax, multiply that amount by the surtax rate of 0.9 percent.

Medicare wages	$275,000
Self-employment income	$100,000
Total income subject to Additional Medicare Surtax	$275,000 + $100,000 = $375,000
Threshold for single taxpayer	$200,000
Income subject to Additional Medicare Surtax (amount by which Medicare and SE income exceeds threshold)	$375,000 – $200,000 = $175,000
Additional Medicare Surtax rate	0.9%
Additional Medicare Surtax obligation	$175,000 × 0.9% = $1,575

HOW DOES THE NIIT SURTAX WORK?

As stated above, the 3.8 percent NIIT surtax is imposed on "net investment income." In order to compute "net investment income," it is necessary to determine which items of regular gross income are considered "investment income." In the most general terms, Code section 1411(c) defines "investment income" as what would commonly be considered investment income. Beyond that, what else is considered investment income is more complicated. In essence, investment income also includes any passive activity income derived from a trade or business. As discussed in Chapter 3, a passive activity is any trade or business activity in which the taxpayer does not "materially participate."[19] Generally, a taxpayer materially participates in an activity if he is involved in the operations of the activity on a regular, continuous, and substantial basis. By implication, income derived from a trade or business in which a taxpayer materially participates would not be "investment income" for the purposes of the NIIT.

Important caveat: All income of any type generated by a business trading financial instruments or commodities is always treated as investment income, without exception.[20]

WHAT IS INCLUDED IN NET INVESTMENT INCOME?

Net investment income includes items that are specifically enumerated by the Internal Revenue Code, as well as other items that arise from a taxpayer's business activities or ownership of interests in corporate entities. These items are discussed in detail below.

Specifically Enumerated Investment Income Items

Section 1411(c)(1)(A)(i) specifically enumerates what most would consider the "traditional" types of investment income: interest, dividends, annuities, royalties and rents. However, there are exceptions. Such income would *not* be considered investment income if:

1. the income was generated in a trade or business;
2. the income was derived in the ordinary course of that trade or business; and
3. the trade or business activity generating the income is non-passive with respect to the taxpayer.

The term "trade or business" is defined the same way for net investment income as it is for regular income in Code section 162.[21] With regard to the second requirement, income "derived in the ordinary course of a trade or business" means the type of income the trade or business was designed to generate. Finally, the third requirement requires the taxpayer to materially participate in the trade or business that generates such income so that the activity is non-passive with respect to the taxpayer. In addition to this general exception, there are other exceptions set forth in the Code and regulations.

Figure 13.1 sets forth each of the five enumerated items of investment income with examples of circumstances in which they are either included or excluded from the scope of the NIIT. These examples assume that the income is not included in a general partner's distributive share of ordinary income or reportable on Schedule C for a sole proprietor or single-member LLC that is treated as a disregarded entity.

Income from Passive Business Activity

As discussed above, Code section 1411(c)(1)(A)(i) specifically enumerates five types of income treated as investment income. Conversely, Code section 1411(c)(1)(A)(ii) broadly includes all passive activity business income as net investment income.

However, there are exceptions. Passive activity income would *not* be considered investment income if:

1. the income was generated in a trade or business;
2. the income was "earned" in the ordinary course of that trade or business; and
3. the trade or business activity generating the income is non-passive *with respect to the taxpayer*.

An important issue is whether a shareholder of an S corporation must treat a distributive share of ordinary income (Line 1 of Schedule K-1 of Form 1120S) as investment income. The exception above can give a curious result. It is possible that the distributive share of the ordinary income of one shareholder may be treated as net investment income whereas the distributive share of another shareholder may be excluded from net investment income because, for an S corporation, the determination of whether an activity

Figure 13.1

SECTION 1411(c)(1)(A)(i) ITEMS	
Interest	
Included: Interest derived from the investment of working capital set aside for future use by a non-passive trade or business is nonetheless considered investment income.[22] *Included:* Interest distributed to a beneficiary from a trust or estate to the extent that character of the income would be net investment income.[23]	*Excluded:* Tax-exempt interest from a state or local bond is not investment income. (Because NIIT is a surtax on top of the regular income tax, any item excluded from gross income is also excluded from gross investment income.)[24] *Excluded:* "Self-charged interest" is interest charged by a taxpayer for lending money to a business that he or she owns and/or where he or she works. Because such taxpayers are generally not be in the trade or business of loaning money, without a specific exception, such interest income would be investment income. However, the regulations provide an exception if the lending taxpayer materially participates in the business. In that case, the interest income would not be considered investment income.[25] *Excluded:* Interest earned by a banking business with respect to which the taxpayer materially participates (so it is a non-passive activity) would not be investment income because it is derived in the ordinary course of business. (Interest is the type of income that a bank is designed to generate.)[26]
Dividends	
Included: All items defined as "dividends" in the Code.[27] *Included:* Dividends derived from the investment of working capital set aside for future use by a non-passive trade or business are nonetheless considered investment income.[28] *Included:* Dividends distributed to a beneficiary from a trust or estate to the extent that character of the income would be net investment income.[29]	*None excluded.* Dividends are always considered net investment income.
Annuities	
Included: Generally,gross income from annuities as defined by Code sections 72(a), (b) and (e) is considered investment income.[30]	*Excluded:* Gross income from annuities paid by an employer as compensation is not considered investment income.[31] *Excluded:* All distributions from retirement plans, including: qualified pension, profit-sharing and stock bonus plans; qualified annuity plans; annuities for employees of tax-exempt organizations or public schools; IRAs (regular and Roth); and deferred compensation plans of governments and tax-exempt organizations.[32]

Figure 13.1 (cont'd)

SECTION 1411(c)(1)(A)(i) ITEMS	
Royalties	
Included: Gross income from royalties—including mineral, oil, and gas royalties—as well as amounts received for the privilege of using patents, copyrights, secret processes and formulas, goodwill, trademarks, tradebrands, franchises and other like property.[33]	*None excluded.* Royalties are always considered net investment income.
Rents	
Included: Rents distributed to a beneficiary from a trust or estate to the extent that character of the income would be net investment income.[34]	*Excluded:* Rental income from a rental activity of a real estate professional. Generally, all rental income is considered passive, and is treated as investment income even if it was derived in the ordinary course of business. There is a safe harbor for "real estate professionals"[35] who participated in that rental activity for more than 500 hours during that year or more than five of any of the ten years immediately preceding that year.[36] *Excluded:* "Self-charged rent." Similar to self-charged interest, self-charged rent is rental income derived from renting property to a trade or business in which the taxpayer materially participates. According to the passive loss regulations, such income is treated as non-passive.[37] The final regulations extend the same treatment of self-charged rent as being non-passive if it would be treated as non-passive pursuant to the passive loss regulations, or if the taxpayer elects to group such rental activity with other rental trades or business (which is another way to convert rental income from passive to non-passive income).[38]

is non-passive is made at the shareholder level rather than the entity level.[39]

Example: Hugh Haule and Frederica Expresso are equal shareholders in an S corporation that delivers packages. Whereas Hugh works in the business on a fulltime basis, Frederick has no involvement in the business. In the current year, their S corporation earns $100,000 of ordinary income allocated $50,000 to each shareholder.

Hugh's distributive share of ordinary income is not treated as net investment income because it was earned in the ordinary course of business (meeting the first two requirements listed above), and—because Hugh actively works as a material participant in the business—it is a non-passive activity with respect to him (meeting the third requirement listed above). Conversely, Frederica's distributive share of ordinary income is net investment income to her. Although the income meets the first two requirements of being earned in a trade or business, as a non-participant in the business, it is a passive activity with respect to her because she does not actively work in the business (and thus it fails the third requirement of the exception).

Income from a Pass-through Entity

As discussed earlier in this chapter, "self-employment income" is never treated as net investment income regardless of whether it would otherwise meet the definition for such under the NIIT.[40] What can cause some confusion is that a taxpayer can receive some items meeting the definition of "net investment income" via an interest in a pass-through entity such as a partnership, LLC, or S corporation.[41] In some instances, the nature of the taxpayer's interest in the pass-through entity would cause such income to be treated as self-employment income.

In addition to the income of a sole proprietor, self-employment income also includes a general partner's distributive share of ordinary income and any item of income reported on Schedule C for a single-member LLC that is treated as a disregarded entity. For that reason, such income would be subject to the Additional Medicare Surtax even if it would otherwise meet the Code definition of net investment income.

On the other hand, with some exceptions, certain types of income, such as dividends, interest, gains from the disposition of property, and rent are generally not treated as self-employment income regardless of the taxpayer's interest in the entity.[42] Consequently, in most of those instances, such income would be subject to NIIT.

Figure 13.2 sets forth the various ownership interests in which the nature of the ownership interest may dictate whether the flow-through income would be characterized as self-employment income or potentially net investment income.

Gain from the Sale of Property Held by a Business

Unlike a general partner's distributive share of ordinary income or the income of a sole proprietor, gains from the disposition of property (other than inventory) are specifically excluded from self-employment income.[49] This provision applies across the board, and includes gains from the disposition of property that the taxpayer owns directly, as well as property that "flows through" to the taxpayer by virtue of an ownership interest in the entity disposing of the property.

Code section 1411(c)(1)(A)(iii) treats net gains from the disposition of property as net investment income if the property is held in a trade or business that is a passive activity with respect to the taxpayer. The word "disposition" is broadly defined as a "sale, exchange, transfer, conversion, cash settlement, cancellation, termination, lapse, expiration, or other disposition."[50] If the gain meets those requirements, it must be included in gross income under Code section 61(a)(3).[51]

Importantly, some "dispositions" can occur over long periods of time, leading to questions about when income from the gain of the disposition is realized by the taxpayer. Deferred or excluded gains such as gain from an installment sale,[52] like-kind exchanges,[53] involuntary conversions[54] and the sale of a principal residence[55] are not considered investment income *unless and until* they are included in regular gross income.[56]

In order for a gain from the disposition of property *not to be treated* as net investment income, the two following requirement must be met:

1. The gains were derived from property held in a trade or business.

2. The trade or business activity generating the gain is non-passive with respect to the taxpayer.

The following two examples demonstrate how gain from the sale of property held by a business may (or may not) be excluded from net investment income.

Figure 13.2

Ownership Interest	How the Income is Reported	Treated as Self-Employment Income?
General partner interest	Distributive share of partnership ordinary income.[43]	Always self-employment income.[44]
Sole proprietor (not a flow-through entity)	Reported on Schedule C.	Always self-employment income.[45]
Single-member LLC treated as a disregarded entity	Reported on Schedule C as if a sole proprietor.	Always self-employment income.[46]
Limited partner interest	Distributive share of ordinary Income.	Not self-employment income (potentially net investment income.)[47]
Shareholder of S corporation	Distributive share of any type of S corporation Income.	Not treated as self-employment income (potentially net investment income.)[48]

Example 1: Iris owns a boat in her own name and rents it to Ira for $100,000 per year. Iris' rental activity fails to meet both exclusion requirements because her rental activity does not reach the level of a trade or business, and because rental activities are always considered passive. Assume Iris sells the boat to Ira in a subsequent year and recognizes a taxable gain of $500,000. Having failed the requirements for exclusion in the prior year, Iris must include such gain as investment income.[57]

Example 2: Hugh Haule and Frederica Expresso are equal owners of a partnership engaged in the moving business. Hugh is involved in day-to-day operations, Frederica devotes all of her time to another endeavor. In 2020, the business sells a facility it had used to store furniture, recognizing a gain of $200,000 that is evenly allocated to both shareholders. Because the property was used in the S corporation's trade or business, and Hugh materially participates in the business, his share of the gain meets both exclusion requirements, and is not treated as investment income. Because Frederica does not materially participate in the business, she fails the second part of the test, and her allocable share of the gain would be treated as investment income for the purposes of the NIIT.

Gain from the Sale of an S Corporation or a Partnership

To this point in the discussion, the determination of whether income generated by pass-through entities such as S corporations and partnerships was treated as net investment income was based on the taxpayer's participation in the business. If the individual materially participated in the business, the income was not treated as net investment income. If the taxpayer's participation in the business was passive, the income was included as net investment income.

However, the sale of an interest in a pass-through entity to a third party does not generate any income or loss to the underlying entity. Similar to the sale of any individually-owned asset, the sale of an entity interest would generate gain or loss to the selling shareholder or partner. From the entity's perspective this is not a taxable event in and of itself, as one shareholder/partner is merely substituted for another shareholder/partner.

Code section 1411(c)(4) specifically addresses the extent to which the gain from the sale of an interest in a pass-through entity taxed as an S corporation (or a partnership) is to be treated as net investment income. In addition to "conventional" S corporations and partnerships, the section also addresses sales of interests in LLCs electing to be taxed as either one of those entities.[58]

First, section 1411(c)(4) creates a "fictional" pass-through scenario by recasting the transaction as if the entity had sold all of its assets for their fair market value, and the selling shareholder/partner was allocated his or her share of the gain or loss based on his or her ownership interest.

Second—in the same way as determining whether a shareholder/partner's distributive share of real gain from the sale of an entity asset would be excluded from net investment income—the two following requirements must be met in order to exclude the gain from net investment income:

- The gains were derived from property held in a trade or business.
- The trade or business activity generating the gain is non-passive with respect to the taxpayer.

The application of this test with regard to the sale of an interest in an S corporation or partnership can be problematic. The question of whether a shareholder/partner's distributive share of gain from the sale of a *single* entity asset is to be treated as net investment income depends on whether the asset was used in a trade or business activity that was passive or non-passive with respect to the taxpayer. What about a hypothetical sale of *all* the assets owned by the entity? Moreover, it is possible that any given entity may engage in more than one distinct business activity in which different assets are employed. It is equally possible that a shareholder/partner's participation in those distinct activities may vary.

For these reasons, the proposed regulations take an activity-by-activity approach. Based on the level of a shareholder/partner's participation in the distinct business activities, some of the gain from the hypothetical sale of entity assets may be characterized as net investment income and some may not. The proposed regulations also allow the use of two different formulas to determine a portion of the shareholder/partner's gain from the sale of his or interest would be similarly characterized.[59] Bear in mind that at the time of publication, these were only proposed regulations that were not final and are subject to change.

If the taxpayer does not materially participate in any of the business activities of the entity, the gain from the sale of the entity is all passive with respect to the taxpayer. Under these circumstances, there is no need to apply any formula, and the taxpayer's entire gain from the disposition of the interest would be treated as net investment income.

Equally obvious, if the taxpayer materially participates in all the business activities of the entity, they are all non-passive with respect to the taxpayer. In this instance, the taxpayer's entire gain from the disposition of the interest would not be treated as net investment income.[60]

Finally, if the taxpayer materially participates in only some of the business activities of the entity, one of the two formulas from the proposed regulations would be applied to determine how much of the taxpayer's gain on the sale of the entity interest would be treated as net investment income.

Problematically, the first formula requires the selling shareholder/partner to gather a significant amount of information regarding the underlying assets of the entity that may not be readily accessible. The second formula—the "optional simplified method"—requires much less information, all of which would be found on the taxpayer's Form K-1. However, it is only available to taxpayers who meet certain criteria.

The First Formula

The best way to understand the first formula is to walk through an example that shows the steps required and the information that needs to be gathered to follow those steps.

Example: Iris owns 50 percent of an S corporation engaged in two distinct business activities: a moving business and a telephone answering business. Iris works exclusively in the moving business and has no involvement in the telephone answering business. The S corporation has three assets:

Assets of Iris' S Corporation

Asset	Fair Market Value (FMV)	Basis (amount paid for the assets by Iris' S Corp)
Telephone Answering Equipment	$126,000	$136,000
Storage Warehouse	$150,000	$75,000
Marketable Securities	$50,000	$8,000

Assume that in 2020 Iris sells all of her stock in the S corporation to a third party and recognizes a capital gain of $200,000. The process of calculating Iris' net investment income from the sale using the first formula involves multiple steps.

Step 1 – Identify the different business activities within the entity. As stated above, the S corporation is engaged in a moving business and a telephone answering business.

Step 2 – Determine which business activities are passive and non-passive with respect to the selling taxpayer. Based on Iris' level of participation in the respective businesses, the moving business is non-passive and the telephone answering business is passive.

Step 3 – Identify what the proposed regulations define as "section 1411 property" with respect to the selling taxpayer. "Section 1411 property" includes:

- property that is associated with a business activity that was passive with respect to the taxpayer; and
- any marketable securities.[61]

By that definition, the telephone answering equipment and the marketable securities are section 1411 property. The storage warehouse is not section 1411 property because it is used in a business activity which is non-passive with respect to Iris.

Step 4 – Determine Iris' distributive share of gain from a hypothetical sale of the section 1411 property at FMV. The hypothetical sale of the telephone answering equipment would generate a $10,000 loss. Because Iris owns 50 percent of the S corporation, Iris' distributive share of the loss would be $5,000. The hypothetical sale of the marketable securities would yield a $42,000 gain, of which Iris' distributive share would be $21,000. Thus, Iris' net distributive share of the net gain would be $16,000 ($21,000 gain minus $5,000 loss).

Property	FMV	Basis	Gain/ Loss	Iris Share Gain/Loss
Telephone Answering Equipment	$126,000	$136,000	($10,000)	($5,000)
Marketable Securities	$50,000	$8,000	$42,000	$21,000
Total	**$176,000**	**$144,000**	**$32,000**	**$16,000**

Step 5–Determine the amount of gain treated as net investment income. This amount is the lesser of:

- the overall regular income tax gain ($200,000); or
- the shareholder's hypothetical distributive share of the entity gain as computed in Step 4 ($16,000).

Here, Iris' regular income tax gain was $200,000 and her hypothetical distributive share of S corporation gain from the sale of section 1411 assets was $16,000. As a result, Iris' net investment income from the sale using the first formula would be $16,000 with the balance of the gain, $184,000, excluded from net investment income.

Optional Simplified Method

The optional simplified method contained in the proposed regulations allows the taxpayer to compute net investment income from the sale or disposition of an S Corporation by multiplying the gain from the sale by a simple ratio.[62] One definition is key to understating the optional simplified method: the "section 1411 holding period," which is defined as the current year plus the last two years.

Importantly, not all taxpayers may use the optional simplified method. In order to do so, the taxpayer must qualify by satisfying one of two tests.

Test 1: The first test has two requirements:

1. The sum of net investment income, gain, loss and deduction (loss and deduction added as a positive numbers for purposes of this calculation) allocated to the selling taxpayer over the section 1411 holding period is less than 5 percent of the sum of all items of income, gain, loss and deduction (again, with loss and deduction added as positive numbers for purposes of this calculation), allocated to the selling taxpayer during the section 1411 holding period.
2. The total amount of gain recognized for regular income tax purposes with regard to the sale of the entity interest must be less than $5 million.

Test 2: Test 2 is simpler, and requires only that the total amount of gain recognized on the sale of the interest in the entity be less than $250,000.

Under the optional simplified method, the net investment income is computed by multiplying the gain from the sale of an interest in an S corporation or a partnership by a ratio that must be computed for each sale. The ratio is calculated by dividing the sum of *net* investment income, gain, deduction, or loss allocated to the seller by the sum of *all* items of income, gain, deduction, or loss allocated to the seller. Both values are calculated over the section 1411 holding period.

Multiplying the total gain from the sale by the ratio described above gives the amount of gain from the sale that is treated as net investment income. Stated differently, the amount of gain treated as net investment income is based on the percentage of the shareholder/partner's distributive share of net investment income over all income of the entity during the section 1411 holding period. Again, an example is helpful.

Example: Hugh Haule sells his S corporation stock to a third party and recognizes a gain of $500,000. The S corporation has two distinct businesses, a moving business in which Hugh materially participates, and a telephone answering business in which he does not materially participate.

Total Amounts over Section 1411 Holding Period	
Hugh's Distributive Share of Income Attributable from Non-Passive Moving Business	$2,000,000

Hugh's Distributive Share of Dividend Income	$50,000
Hugh's Distributive Share of Loss from Passive Telephone Answering Service	($15,000)

First, Hugh must determine whether he qualifies for the optional simplified method. Hugh's recognized gain of $500,000 clearly fails Test 2, so he must pass Test 1 in order to use the optional simplified method. To do so, the sum of his distributive share of *net* investment income, gain, loss and deduction (all added as a positive numbers) over the section 1411 holding period must be less than 5 percent of the sum of his distributive share of all income, gain, loss and deduction (all added as a positive numbers) over that same period.

Test 2		
Sum of net investment gain, loss, and deduction	Sum of all income, gain, loss, and deduction	Ratio of net investment income over all income must be less than 5%
$50,000 + $15,000 = $65,000	$2,000,000 + $50,000 + $15,000 = $2,065,000	$\frac{\$65{,}000}{\$2{,}065{,}000} = 3.15\%$

Here, Hugh passes Test 1 because $65,000 divided by $2,065,000 is approximately 3.15 percent, which is less than 5 percent required for the test. Therefore Hugh may use the optional simplified method.

Next, Hugh must determine the amount of gain that is treated as net investment income. To make that determination, he first calculates the ratio of the total distributive share of net income divided by the total distributive share of all items of income (again, all figures are for the section 1411 holding period). He then multiplies that ratio by the total gain from the sale to determine the amount of the gain that is included in net investment income.

Calculation of Net Investment Income from Sale	
Total distributive share of net income (net investment dividend income minus passive loss)	($50,000 – $15,000) = $35,000
Total distributive share of all income (non-passive income plus net investment dividend income, minus passive loss)	($2,000,000 + $50,000 – $15,000) = $2,035,000
Ratio	$\frac{\$35{,}000}{\$2{,}035{,}000} = 1.7\%$
Ratio multiplied by total gain from sale yields net investment income from sale	1.7% × $500,000 = $8,600

In this case, approximately 1.7 percent of all S corporation income allocated to Hugh over the section 1411 holding period was net investment income. Multiplying that percentage by the gain from the sale of his stock ($500,000), Hugh calculates that approximately $8,600 of the gain is *included* in net investment income, and the balance of $491,400 is *excluded* from net investment income.

How Is Net Gain Calculated?

Significantly, Code section 1411(c)(1)(A)(iii) refers to "net gain"—meaning that gains are netted against losses, as both terms are defined in the section. In a taxpayer-friendly provision, the final regulations provide for the treatment of capital gains and losses for net investment income purposes that parallels their treatment for regular income tax purposes. For regular income tax purposes, capital losses are deductible to the extent of capital gains plus $3,000 of any excess being deductible against other income. The unused excess loss is carried over to subsequent tax years subject to being netted against capital gains generated in such years. Similarly, a taxpayer may use the same netting rules to reduce investment income net gain to zero, with $3,000 of any excess reducing other investment income. Any unused excess capital loss is carried over to subsequent years to be re-employed in the same manner.[63]

Example: In 2020, Iris, a single taxpayer has the following items of income and loss: a $40,000 capital loss and a $10,000 capital gain from the sale of publicly traded stock, $300,000 of wage income and $5,000 of interest income. For regular income tax purposes, capital gain and loss are netted resulting in a net capital loss of $30,000, of which $3,000 can be used as a deduction against other income. The balance of the net capital loss, $27,000, would be carried over to subsequent tax years.

Viewing the example from a net investment income perspective, the two items of net investment income are:

1. the interest income of $5,000;[64] and

2. the gain generated from the stock sale of $10,000.[65]

The process of determining the "net gain" for investment income is the same as it is for regular income; the capital gain ($10,000) and capital loss ($40,000) are netted, but only to the extent of zeroing out the capital gain. Of the resulting $30,000 of net capital loss, $3,000 of it can be used reduce the $5,000 of interest income included as net investment income. Thus, Iris' 2019 net investment income would be $2,000, with a $27,000 capital loss to be carried over to subsequent tax years.

Now assume that Iris recognizes a capital gain of $30,000 in 2020 from the sale of publicly traded stock. For regular income tax purposes, the $27,000 capital loss carryover from 2019 is netted against the 2020 capital gain, resulting in a net capital gain of $3,000. Similarly, for purposes of computing net gain under Code section 1411(c)(1)(A)(iii), the same netting occurs to reduce the 2018 net gain included in net investment income to $3,000.[66]

Which Deductions Can Be Applied to Net Investment Income?

Up to this point the terms "net investment income" and "investment income" have been used interchangeably. Inherent in the term "net investment income," however, is the notion that certain deductions be allowed. Indeed, per Code section 1411(c)(1)(B), in arriving at "net investment income," investment income is reduced by "the deductions allowed by this subtitle which are properly allocable to such gross income or net gain." Figure 13.3 sets forth the list of deductions that are taken into account in determining net investment income.

It is important to note that deductions from investment income are subject to the same limitations as deductions for regular income tax. In other words, a taxpayer would not be entitled to a greater deduction from investment income than he or she would be entitled to for regular tax. For that reason, it is important to understand the hierarchy of deductions for regular income tax purposes.

Above-the-Line Investment Income Deductions

As discussed in Chapter 4, "above-the-line" deductions used to calculate adjusted gross income are usually the most beneficial deductions to the taxpayer. This is because they are not typically subject to restrictions that

Figure 13.3

AVAILABLE DEDUCTIONS AGAINST NET INVESTMENT INCOME
Deductions allocable to gross income from rents and royalties
Deductions allocable to gross income from trades or business to the extent not taken into account in determining self-employment income
Penalty on early withdrawal of savings
Net operating losses properly allocable to determining net investment income for any taxable year
Investment interest expenses as defined in Code section 163(d)(3)
Investment expenses as defined in Code section 163(d)(4)(c)
Taxes described in Code section 164(a)(3)
Investment expenses described in Code section 212(3)
Amortizable bond premium under Code section 171(a)(1)
In the case of a trust or estate, fiduciary expenses deductible under Code section 212
Losses allowed per Code section 165
Excess losses under Code section 642(h) upon termination of a trust or estate

would otherwise limit their deductibility. Taken "off the top," they reduce the amount of taxable income, dollar-per-dollar. For net investment income purposes, the above-the-line regular income tax deductions properly allocable to rent and royalty income, losses from the sale or exchange of property, net operating losses as well as the deduction for the penalty on early withdrawal of savings provide a similar tax benefit.[67]

Net Operating Losses

The final regulations allow a taxpayer to use a portion of net operating loss (NOL) to reduce net investment income as an above-the-line deduction.[68] This special net operating loss—referred to as a "section 1411 NOL" in the regulations—is the lesser of:

- a NOL for the loss year computed by including only items of investment income gross income less only properly allocable net investment income deductions; or
- the taxpayer's regular income tax NOL for the loss year.

Like regular NOLs, unused section 1411 NOLs can be carried over to subsequent tax years. The example in the final regulations—presented here in a simplified form—is helpful in understanding this technique.

Example: Assume that in 2020, the taxpayer's NOL for regular income tax purposes was \$1,000,000 and the section 1411 NOL (taking into account only net investment income and deductions) was \$200,000. Because the taxpayer had a net loss (and therefore no income) for 2018, the \$1,000,000 NOL and \$200,000 section 1411 NOL are available to be carried forward to subsequent tax years.

However, there is a bit of a twist. Although the taxpayer is entitled to an overall section 1411 NOL of \$200,000, in subsequent years, when applying the section 1411 NOL to from 2018 to later tax years the taxpayer must multiply regular income tax NOL carried over to that subsequent year by the ratio of the section 1411 NOL generated in 2020 divided by the regular income tax NOL generated in 2020. Here, that ratio is 0.2 (\$200,000 divided by \$1,000,000)

To illustrate this point, assume that in 2021 the taxpayer is has \$540,000 in income and elects to use \$540,000 of his 2020 NOL to reduce taxable income. For purposes of reducing the taxpayer's *net investment income* for that year, the carried over section 1411 NOL is limited to 20 percent of \$540,000, or \$108,000. Thus, going into 2022, the taxpayer has a remaining section 1411 NOL of \$92,000 (\$200,000 minus \$108,000).

Subsequently, in 2022, assume the taxpayer is able to use the balance of his 2020 NOL (\$460,000) to reduce that year's taxable income. Again, for purposes of reducing the taxpayer's net investment income for that year, the carried over section 1411 NOL is limited to 20 percent of \$460,000, or \$92,000.

Figure 13.4

2020: NO TAXABLE INCOME		
Regular income tax NOL available for subsequent years	Section 1411 NOL available for subsequent years	2020 ratio of regular NOL to section1411 NOL
\$1,000,000	\$200,000	$\left(\frac{\$2000{,}000}{\$1{,}000{,}000}\right) = 0.2$
2021: \$540,000 IN TAXABLE INCOME		
2020 regular taxable income NOL carried to 2021	Carried over 2020 NOL multiplied by 2020 ratio	2020 section 1411 NOL used to reduce 2021 net investment income
\$540,000	\$540,000 × 0.2	= \$108,000

Figure 13.4 (cont'd)

2022: TAXABLE INCOME GREATER THAN $460,000		
2020 regular taxable income NOL carried to 2022	Carried over 2020 NOL multiplied by 2020 ratio	2020 section 1411 NOL used to reduce 2022 net investment income
$460,000	$460,000 × 0.2	= $92,000
2021: 2020 REGULAR INCOME TAX NOL AND SECTION 1411 NOL EXHAUSTED		
		$\left(\frac{\$2000{,}000}{\$1{,}000{,}000}\right) = 0.2$
	$540,000 × 0.2	= $108,000
	$460,000 × 0.2	= $92,000

Below-the-Line Investment Income Deductions

Many of the deductions against investment income—such as state and local taxes, investment interest, professional fees and investment advisory fees—are treated for regular income tax as itemized deductions. These are known as "below-the-line" deductions. Unlike above-the-line deductions, below-the-line deductions are subject to limitations that often impact their ultimate deductibility.

For regular income tax purposes, some below-the-line deductions are treated as "miscellaneous itemized deductions"[69]—as opposed to "regular" itemized deductions—and are subject to a "floor" of 2 percent of adjusted gross income. This means that miscellaneous itemized deductions are deductible only to the extent they exceed 2 percent of a taxpayer's AGI.[70]

Both of these limitations apply to the computation of net investment income. The miscellaneous itemized deduction "floor" is applied to the miscellaneous itemized deductions first. The taxpayer must then determine if the section 68 phase-out will further reduce the miscellaneous itemized deductions that apply to the calculation of net investment income.[71]

With regard to the floor for net investment income miscellaneous itemized deductions, the regulations provide that the amount of miscellaneous itemized deductions tentatively deductible against net investment income is the lesser of:

- the amount of miscellaneous itemized deductions; or
- all miscellaneous itemized deductions (including those allocable to net investment income) that exceed the 2 percent of adjusted gross income floor.[72]

The following example illustrates how these rules work.

Example: Iris is a single taxpayer with the following items of income and miscellaneous itemized deductions:

Income	
Adjusted Gross Income	$500,000
Investment Income (included in adjusted gross income)	$150,000
Miscellaneous Itemized Deductions	
Investor Advisor Fees	$35,000
Other Non-Investment Income Miscellaneous Itemized Deductions	$15,000

Applying the special rule on net investment income miscellaneous itemized deduction rules to Iris, the amount deductible is the lesser of:

- her net investment income miscellaneous itemized deduction unreduced by the 2 percent floor ($35,000); or
- all miscellaneous itemized deduction after the applying the 2 percent floor ($20,000).

Thus, Iris' tentative miscellaneous itemized deduction against net investment income is the $20,000 of investor advisor fees.

After determining the tentative amount of allowable miscellaneous deductions, the next step is to apply the special rules for the section 68 phase-out of itemized deductions. The phase-out reduces *total* miscellaneous itemized deductions against *regular* income by 3 percent of the amount by which the taxpayer's adjusted gross income exceeds the threshold ($254,200 for single taxpayers).

- If the taxpayer's miscellaneous itemized deductions against net investment income (after applying the 2 percent AGI floor discussed in the previous step) are less than the total amount of miscellaneous itemized deductions against regular income permitted under the section 68 phase-out, then the net investment deductions remain unchanged.
- If the net investment income miscellaneous itemized deductions *exceed* what is permissible under the section 68 phase-out, the taxpayer may only take miscellaneous itemized deductions against net investment income up to the section 68 phase-out limit.

For purposes of this example, assume Iris has the following itemized deductions:

State income taxes properly allocable to net investment income (regular itemized deduction)	$40,000
Investment interest expense properly allocable to net investment income (regular itemized deduction)	$50,000
Deductible investor advisor fees (miscellaneous itemized deduction)	$20,000
Total itemized deductions against net investment income	**$110,000**
Additional miscellaneous itemized deductions against regular income	$90,000
Total Itemized Deductions Subject to the section 68 phase-out (including those not properly allocable to net investment income)	$200,000
Section 68 phase-out reduction (3% of difference between threshold and AGI)	($500,000 – $254,200 × 3% = $7,374
Total itemized deductions after section 68 phase-out	**$200,000 – $7,374 = $192,626**

Based on the foregoing itemized deduction scenario, the total of Iris' *net investment income* itemized deductions would be $110,000, and the total of *all* itemized deductions would be $200,000.

Using Excess Losses to Reduce Net Investment Income

In the discussion regarding the computation of "net gain" pursuant to Code section 1411(c)(1)(A)(iii), it was noted that the deductibility of loss was limited to the amount of gain, so a "net investment loss" would not be allowed for the purposes of the NIIT. In spite of that limitation, the final regulations allow those section 1411(c)(1)(A)(iii) losses to be used to reduce other net investment income provided those losses had been taken as a deduction in the computation of regular income tax.[73]

Example: Iris, a single taxpayer, has the following income sources:

Interest and dividends	$125,000
Ordinary losses from a trade or business trading in financial instruments or commodities	$60,000
Long-term capital gain from the sale of undeveloped land	$50,000

For regular income tax purposes, the $125,000 of interest and dividend income and the $50,000 of long-term capital gain are included in gross income. The $60,000 of ordinary loss is totally deductible without limitation—unlike capital loss, which is deductible to the extent of capital gain plus $3,000.) Ignoring itemized deductions and personal exemptions, Iris' *regular taxable income* would be $115,000 ($175,000 in interest, dividends, and long-term capital gain, minus $60,000 in business losses).

For the purposes of computing *net investment income,* recall that all income, gain, or loss from a business that trades in financial instruments or commodities is treated as net investment income regardless of whether the activity is non-passive with respect to the taxpayer. For Iris, the $125,000 of interest and dividend income and the $50,000 of long-term capital gain are clearly included in net investment income. However, the $60,000 loss is deductible only to the extent of the $50,000 gain. In other words, since the final regulations do not allow a "net" loss under Code section 1411(c)(1)(A)(iii), the regular income tax rule allowing such a loss would appear to be inapplicable. Thus, without further relief, the "net" $10,000 loss would not be allowed, resulting in $125,000 of interest and dividends included in net investment income rather than $115,000.

However, the final regulations allow Iris to use that otherwise useless loss to reduce her other net investment income. This is possible because the net $10,000 loss:

- was deductible for regular income tax purposes; and

- would have been allowed as reduction of net gain under Code section 1411(c)(1)(A)(iii) but for the net loss limitation.

Thus, Iris' investment income of $125,000 would be reduced by the $10,000 excess loss deduction resulting in $115,000 of net investment income.[74]

APPLICATION OF NIIT TO TRUSTS AND ESTATES

To this point in the chapter, the discussion of NIIT has focused exclusively on individual taxpayers. However, unless otherwise specifically excluded, all trusts and estates that are subject to the provisions Subchapter J of the Internal Revenue Code are also subject to NIIT.[75] The impact of NIIT on trusts and estates cannot be understated. Because trusts tend to remain in existence far longer than estates, the overall tax consequences of this surtax on trusts is likely to be even more profound, and the following discussion will focus mainly on trusts.

In operation, the 3.8 percent NIIT surtax is imposed on trusts and estates on the lesser of:

- "undistributed net investment income"; or

- the excess of adjusted gross income over the amount of the highest regular income tax bracket in effect for such taxable year.[76]

Compared to the thresholds for individual taxpayers that are based on adjusted gross income, the threshold for trusts and estates is based on the highest tax bracket of those entities. Though the threshold for trusts and estates is indexed for inflation (unlike the thresholds for individual taxpayers), that is of little comfort to fiduciaries and beneficiaries. The highest regular income tax bracket for trusts and estates (above which the NIIT surtax is imposed) begins at an amount that is significantly lower than the NIIT thresholds for individuals.[77]

For example, for tax year 2020, the highest regular income tax bracket for trusts and estates (37 percent) begins with taxable income in excess of $12,950. The unindexed thresholds for individual taxpayers (e.g. $250,000 for married taxpayers who are filing jointly) are much higher. Moreover, by their nature, most trusts and estates are likely to have *only* net investment income. This means that trusts and estates with relatively small amounts of net investment income may nonetheless be in the highest income tax bracket and be subject to the 3.8 percent NIIT.

As mentioned above, The NIIIT tax base of trusts and estates is "undistributed net investment income." In simple terms, undistributed net investment income is any net investment income—as defined by Code section 1411(c)(1)(A)—that is retained by a trust or an estate.[78] Distributions retain their characterization as net investment income when distributed to a beneficiary. If the trust has net investment income that is distributed to a beneficiary, it will be considered net investment income for beneficiary (as opposed to regular income).[79]

The two types of trusts most impacted by NIIT are "simple trusts" and "complex trusts." A simple trust is required to distribute all of its current fiduciary accounting income (FAI) to its beneficiaries.[80] FAI is income derived from principal such as interest and dividends (as opposed to capital gains derived from the sale or disposition of principal). Since a simple trust is required to distribute all of its FAI to its beneficiaries each year, its undistributed net investment income is limited to the capital gain it generates.

A complex trust is not required to make mandatory distributions to its beneficiaries.[81] Instead, complex trusts generally make discretionary distributions of FAI (and sometimes principal) to beneficiaries. A complex trust is likely to have a mix of net investment income that includes dividends, interest and capital gains. This income may or may not be retained by the trust.

In order to understand how to compute the undistributed net investment income of a trust, it is necessary to comprehend the meaning of distributable net income (DNI). Essentially, the DNI of a trust is the taxable income of a trust, with certain modifications.[82] Distributions to beneficiaries are not included in DNI,[83] effectively shifting the obligation to pay tax on the distributed income from the trust to the beneficiaries.

Similarly, for net investment income purposes, DNI that is distributed to a beneficiary is included in the beneficiary's net investment income, and is subject to the NIIT. Conversely, *undistributed* investment income included in DNI—as well undistributed investment income not included in DNI—is included in the net investment income tax base of the trust. The most notable exclusion of income from the computation of DNI is capital gain.

The following example from the regulations[84] demonstrates how to compute net investment income for a complex trust, including calculations of DNI.

Example: Assume that in 2020 the trustee of this complex trust makes a discretionary FAI distribution of $10,000 to Beneficiary A.

Trust Income 2020	
Dividend Income	$15,000
Interest Income	$10,000
Capital Gain	$5,000
IRA Distribution	$75,000
Total Trust Income	$105,000

Step 1: Determine the DNI of the trust. Code section 643(a) provides that the DNI of a trust is tentative taxable income ($105,000) minus capital gain. Excluding the $5,000 of capital gain, the DNI of the trust is $100,000.

Step 2: Determine the trust's distribution deduction. According to Code section 661(a), the distribution deduction of a complex trust is equal to the amount distributed (here, $10,000).

Step 3: Determine the extent to which the amount distributed is deemed to be net investment income. Code section 661(b) provides that the character of the amount distributed to the beneficiary "shall be treated as consisting of the same proportion of each class of income entering into the computation of distributable net income." In this example, the distribution of $10,000 is equal to 10 percent of $100,000, the total amount of DNI. Thus, the beneficiary is deemed to have received 10 percent of each type of income included in DNI.

Trust Income 2020		
Income in DNI	Retained by Trust	Distributed to Beneficiary
Dividend Income	$13,500	$1,500
Interest Income	$9,000	$1,000
IRA Distribution	$67,500	$7,500
Total	**$90,000**	**$10,000**

Step 4: Determine the amount of net investment income in DNI that is retained by the trust. In this case, most of the retained income is net investment income. The only exception is the IRA distribution. Pursuant to Code section 1411(c)(5), distributions from IRAs are excluded from net investment income.

Trust Income 2020		
Income in DNI	Retained by Trust	Net Investment Income
Dividend Income	$13,500	$13,500
Interest Income	$9,000	$9,000
IRA Distribution	$67,500	$0
Total	**$90,000**	**$22,500**

Step 5: Determine the total amount of net investment income retained by the trust. This should include any undistributed item of net investment income not included in DNI. Here, the $5,000 of capital gain excluded from DNI (clearly net investment income) is added to the $22,500 of net investment income retained by the trust. Thus, the total amount of undistributed net investment income is $27,500.

Step 6 – Compute the NIIT. The 3.8 percent NIIT surtax is imposed on the lesser of:

- undistributed Net Investment Income ($27,500): or
- $92,500, which is the excess of the adjusted gross income ($105,000) over the amount of the highest regular income tax bracket ($12,500).

In this example $27,500 is less than $92,500, so the NIIT would be 3.8 percent of $27,500, or $1,045.

HOW CAN INDIVIDUALS MINIMIZE THE NIIT?

1. *Create tax-exempt income.* Any investment type income that is excluded from gross income is also excluded from the NIIT base. Consequently, an investment in state and local bonds would yield income that is exempt from both regular and net investment taxes.

2. *Use life insurance.* A whole life insurance policy has an insurance component and an investment component. The growth of the investment component would depend on the amount of the premium and how it is invested. Investments earnings within the policy grow tax deferred and are therefore do have to be currently included in gross income. Moreover, some insurance policies allow the owner to borrow the "earnings" generated by the policy. Since borrowed funds are generally excluded from gross income, they would not be considered net investment income. Using life insurance in this way allows the owner to enjoy the benefit of policy earnings without being subject to regular income tax or NIIT.

3. *Materially participate in a business activity.* Income from a business in which the taxpayer materially participates (i.e. "non-passive") would not be included in net investment income. If a taxpayer was to materially participate in a business activity that was otherwise passive to him, he would effectively exclude the income from that business from the NIIT tax base. This strategy only works if materially participating in the business does not convert such income into self-employment income that is subject to the Additional Medicare Surtax. Although this technique would not work for a general partner, it would be effective for the shareholder of an S corporation.

4. *Increase voluntary contributions to a qualified retirement plan.* Many qualified retirement plans, such as a 401(k), allow for deductible voluntary contributions of a participant's wages. Although the amount of such contributions may vary from plan to plan, the regular income tax deductible limit for 2020 is $19,000 ($25,000 for taxpayers over forty-nine years old). Note that voluntary contributions are not deductible from Medicare wages subject to the Additional Medicare Surtax.[85] However, distributions from those plans (presumably upon the taxpayer's retirement) are excluded from net investment income,[86] and the earnings generated in the plan are tax-free until distributed. Compared to investing in vehicles that produce net investment income, investing additional amounts in a qualified retirement plan effectively converts future net investment income into excluded qualified plan distributions.

5. *Consider installment sales of property.* If a taxpayer sells property qualifying for reporting gain on the installment method, his or her gain is reportable on a ratable basis.[87]

Example: Assume in December 2020, Iris—a single taxpayer—has the opportunity to sell undeveloped land with a basis of $100,000 for $300,000. If Iris receives the entire selling price in 2018, her adjusted gross income would be increased by the total amount of the gain ($200,000). Assuming that her taxpayer's adjusted gross income for 2018 apart from the sale was $100,000; the additional $200,000 of adjusted gross income would increase her adjusted gross income to $300,000 and subject her to an additional $3,800 of NIIT (3.8 percent of $100,000).

On the other hand, if she received $150,000 of the sales price in December 2020 and $150,000 of the sales price in January 2021, her $200,000 gain would be spread equally over the two tax years (meaning her adjusted gross income would be increased by the $100,000 of gain reported in each tax year). Thus, in 2020, because her adjusted gross income would not exceed the $200,000 threshold (it would be exactly that amount), there would be no NIIT. Moreover, assuming the same adjusted gross income amount in 2021, she would avoid NIIT for that year as well. By converting an immediate sale into an installment sale that spans two "years," Iris could save $3,800 in NIIT obligations.

HOW CAN TRUSTS MINIMIZE THE NIIT?

1. *Allocate indirect expenses to undistributed net investment income.* The regulations allow for the allocation of the deduction of items indirectly attributable to any particular type of income to be allocated in any way, including the total allocation of the deduction to capital gain.[88] For example, by allocating all or part of trustee fees to capital gain not distributed by the trust, the amount of undistributed net income subject to NIIT would also be reduced.

2. *Make discretionary distributions of net investment income items to beneficiaries who are not subject to the NIIT.* Assuming a trustee is aware of the amounts of adjusted gross income of the trust beneficiaries, discretionary distributions of net investment net income could be made in amounts that would not cause the recipient beneficiary's adjusted gross income to exceed the applicable threshold and thus not be subject to NIIT. By doing so, the trustee could reduce NIIT within the trust without subjecting the beneficiary to the surtax.

However, the trustee must be mindful to not make distributions that would be contrary to the terms of the trust or otherwise be considered a breach of his or her fiduciary obligations. Moreover, even if the distribution would not cause the beneficiary's adjusted gross income to exceed the applicable NIIT threshold, the increase in income may deprive the taxpayer of some other tax benefits.

For example, a higher adjusted gross income would reduce or potentially eliminate the deductibility of miscellaneous itemized deductions subject to the 2 percent of adjusted gross income floor. Also, the taxation of social security benefits could be triggered by an increase in adjusted gross income.[89] There are many other examples of similar adverse tax consequences potentially triggered by an increase in adjusted gross income.[90]

FREQUENTLY ASKED QUESTIONS

Question – Do the regulations provide a means of allocating deductible state and local taxes between net investment income and non-net investment income?

Answer – The final regulations are very vague on this issue, providing that "in the case of a properly allocable deduction [such as state and local taxes] . . . that is allocable to both net investment income and excluded income, the portion of the deduction that is properly allocable to net investment income may be determined by using any reasonable method."[91]

Without endorsing any one method, the regulations provide examples of "reasonable methods." One method outlined is to allocate the state and local expense to net investment income based on the percentage of the taxpayer's net investment included in the taxpayer's total gross income.[92]

Example. In 2016, Hugh Haule has $600,000 of wages and $400,000 of interest income on which Hugh paid state income taxes of $100,000. Since 40 percent of Hugh's income is net investment income, Hugh could reasonably deduct $40,000 of the state income taxes paid against the $400,000 of net investment income. This results in a $16,000 NIIT deduction (40 percent of $400,000), leaving Hugh with $14,592 in NIIT liability (3.8 percent of $384,000 assuming no other NIIT deductions).

However, this strategy may be affected by some provisions of the 2017 Tax Reform Act. Consider the allocation of the state income tax deduction described in the example above, which is limited to $10,000 for tax years 2018 and beyond:

Example. In 2018 Hugh Haule once again has $600,000 of wages $400,000 of interest income, on which he paid $100,000 in state income taxes. Hugh can still allocate 40 percent of the deduction to net investment income, but the deduction itself is limited to $10,000 in 2018. Hugh's NIIT deduction is now just $4,000 (40 percent of $10,000), leaving him with $15,048 in NIIT liability for 2018 (3.8 percent of $396,000).

Question – Is there another alternative to decrease the undistributed net investment income of a trust other than a distribution of money to a beneficiary?

Answer – Yes. The trustee could make in in-kind distribution of trust assets.

Example: Assume a trust has appreciated stock with a fair market value of $30,000 and a basis of $10,000. If the trustee were to sell the stock for $30,000, there would be taxable capital gain of $20,000. Even if trustee distributed the entire $30,000 to the beneficiary, the $20,000 of gain deemed to be retained by the trust would be treated as undistributed net investment income subject to NIIT.[93]

In the alternative, the trustee could make a discretionary in-kind distribution of the stock. Such a distribution would not trigger taxable capital gain to the trust; and, thus, no undistributed investment income subject to NIIT.

The amount of the distribution to the beneficiary is the lesser of the stock's fair market value or basis in the hands of the trust.[94] In this example, the lesser number is the stock's $10,000 basis.

There is, however, an additional potential downside to the beneficiary. Because the beneficiary would take a carryover basis of $10,000 in the stock,[95] if the beneficiary were to sell the stock for $30,000, he or she would recognize a $20,000 capital gain that would be included as net investment income.

Question – Does the "sixty-five-day rule" apply with regard to a distribution of net investment income to a beneficiary?

Answer – Apparently, yes. Pursuant to Code section 663(b), by making an appropriate election, a trust can make a distribution to a beneficiary within sixty-five days after the end of the tax year and it will be considered to have been made on the last day of the preceding year. If the trustee makes this election, the deemed distribution would reduce the DNI remaining in the trust and shift the income tax consequences from the trust to the beneficiary. This rule allows the trustee to use the benefit of hindsight to determine whether a distribution would be in the best interest of the trust and/or beneficiary in the prior tax year.

Obviously, the use of the sixty-five-day rule would provide a similar benefit to a trustee in determining whether to make a distribution of net investment income effective for the preceding tax year. This would allow the trustee more time to evaluate the relative merits of making a distribution of net investment income to a beneficiary or retaining the income in the trust effective as of the end of the prior tax year.

Although, the final regulations do not directly acknowledge the application of the sixty-five-day rule with regard to distributions of net investment income, it was applied in Example 3 of Treasury Regulation section 1.1411-3(e). In that example, a section 663(b) election was effectively made by the executor of an estate. Since the sixty-five-day rule applies equally to trusts and estates, there is no reason to believe such an election would not be effective if made by a trustee of a trust.

Question – Does the 2017 Tax Reform Act Affect the calculation of NIIT or the Additional Medicare Surtax?

Answer – On its face, no. However, the 2017 Tax Reform Act changed the taxation of income for many pass through entities, including S corporations (see Chapter 5). While the new legislation does not change the calculation of the NIIT or the Additional Medicare Surtax, the regulations regarding the taxation of income from pass through entities have not been finalized at the time of publication, There is always a chance that any new regulations may make changes that will affect the calculation of the NIIT or Additional Medicare Surtax for shareholders of pass through entities.

CHAPTER ENDNOTES

1. "Definition of 'Surtax,'" Available at: www.investopedia.com/terms/s/surtax.asp.
2. P.L. 111-152, 124 Stat. 1029.
3. The other "FICA" tax is the old-age, survivors, and disability insurance tax (OASDI) also known as the social security tax.
4. Reported on Schedule SE of Form 1040.
5. Patient Protection and Affordable Care Act. P.L. No. 111-148.
6. IRC Secs. 3101(b)(2)(a), 1401(b)(2)(A).
7. IRC Sec. 3102(a).
8. P.L. 111-152, 124 Stat. 1029.
9. Not all trusts are subject to the NIIT. Those not subject to the tax include charitable trusts, qualified retirement plan trust, grantor trusts, real estate investment trusts and common trust funds. Treas. Reg. §1.1411-3(b); IRC Sec. 1411(e)(2).
10. The term used in Code section 1411(a)(1)(B) is "modified adjusted gross income" rather than "adjusted gross income." Throughout this chapter, the term "adjusted gross income" will be utilized because modified adjusted gross income is only relevant to the few taxpayers who claim the foreign earned income exclusion. Pursuant to Code section 1411(d), modified adjusted gross income is computed by adding the amount of the foreign earned income exclusion over the amount of any disallowed deductions or exclusions taken account in computing adjusted gross income pursuant to Code section 991(a)(1). For most taxpayers this modification would not be applicable, and the Code section1411(a)(1)(B) amount would be adjusted gross income.
11. IRC Sec. 1411(b)(1)-(3).
12. See IRC Sec. 1411(a)(2).
13. IRC Sec. 1411(c)(6).
14. IRC Sec. 1411(b).
15. See IRC Sec. 1411(c)(6).
16. For a single individual, the income tax on $410,000 of taxable income is computed as follows: $91,379 on taxable income of $400,000 plus 35% of $10,000 ($410,000 - $400,000), or $3,500, for a total tax of $94,879.
17. IRC Sec. 3101(b)(2)(C).
18. IRC Sec. 1411(b)(3).
19. IRC Sec. 469(c).
20. IRC Sec. 1411(c)(2).
21. Treas. Reg. §1.1411-1(d)(12). Although trade or business is not defined in Code section 162, it is commonly defined as offering goods or services to customers or clients on a regular basis.
22. IRC Sec. 1411(c)(3); Treas. Reg. §1.1411-6(a).
23. Treas. Reg. §1.1411-4(e)(1)(i).
24. Treas. Reg. §1.1411-1(d)(4)(i). All items of income excluded from gross income are also excluded from the investment income tax base. Interest on state or local bonds are excluded from gross income under Code section 103.
25. Treas. Reg. §1.1411-4(g)(5).
26. Treas. Reg. §1.1411-4(b)(3), Example 4.
27. Treas. Reg. §1.1411-1(d)(3).
28. Treas. Reg. §1.1411-6(a).
29. Treas. Reg. §1.1411-4(e)(1)(i).
30. Treas. Reg. §1.1411-1(d)(1). The regulation also provides that in case of a sale of annuity, the amount of gain no in excess of the surrender value would not be treated as investment income. If the sales price of the annuity exceeds its surrender value, the gain equal to the difference between the basis in the annuity and the surrender value would be treated as gross income from an annuity, and, thus, treated as investment income.
31. Treas. Reg. §1.1411-1(d)(1).
32. IRC Sec. 1411(c)(5).
33. Treas. Reg. §1.1411-1(d)(11).
34. Treas. Reg. §1.1411-4(e)(1)(i).
35. IRC Sec. 469(c)(7)(B) defines who is a "real estate professional."
36. Treas. Reg. §1.1411-4(g)(7).
37. Treas. Reg. §1.469-2(f)(6). As alluded numerous times in this chapter, with very limited exceptions, rental income is always treated as passive. The reason for recharacterizing self-charged interest as non-passive income is to prevent taxpayers from creating "passive income" to offset otherwise non-deductible passive loss.
38. Treas. Reg. §1.1411-4(g)(6).
39. Treas. Reg. §1.1411-4(b)(2)(i).
40. IRC Sec. 1411(c)(6).
41. See Treas. Reg. §1.1411-4(b)(3), Examples.
42. See generally I.R.C. Sec 1402 (listing certain income items that are excluded from the self-employment income tax base) and IRC Sec. 702(a) (listing certain income items that are "separately" listed on a partner's Form K-1 and, thus also excluded from the self-employment income tax base).
43. IRC Sec. 702(a)(8).
44. IRC Sec. 1402(a).
45. The net income from Schedule C flows to Schedule SE of Form 1040 upon which self-employment tax is calculated.
46. Treas. Reg. §301.7702-2(c)(2)(iv)(D), Example (iii).
47. IRC Sec. 1402(a)(13).
48. Rev. Rul. 59-221, 1959-1 C.B. 225 (undistributed S corporation income not considered self-employment income). However, Rev. Rul. 74-44, 1974-1 C.B. 287 provides that S corporation income distributed to a shareholder would be re-characterized as compensation subject to self-employment tax if paid in lieu of reasonable compensation for services performed for the corporation. However, "unrecharacterized" S corporation dividend distributions would not be treated as self-employment income per Code section 1402(a)(2).
49. IRC Sec. 1402(a)(3).
50. Treas. Reg. §1.1411-4(d)(1).
51. Treas. Reg. §1.1411-4(d)(3).
52. IRC Sec. 453.
53. IRC Sec. 1031.
54. IRC Sec. 1033.
55. IRC Sec. 121.
56. Part 2 of the preamble to the proposed regulations (REG-1030507-11, 77 Fed. Reg. 72612, at 72613 (12/05/2012); Treas. Reg. §1.1411-4(d)(3)(ii), Example 3, Example 4; Treas. Reg. §1.1411-4(d)(4)(i)(C), Example 2.

57. Treas. Reg. §1.1411-4(d)(4)(i)(C), Example 1.
58. Prop. Reg. §1.1411-7 (Dec. 2, 2013).
59. All of the discussion regarding the sale of an interest in an S corporation and partnership is based on Prop. Treas. Reg. §1.1411-7 (Dec. 2, 2013), replacing Prop. Treas. Reg. §1.1411-7 (2012).
60. This also assumes that the entity did not own any marketable securities otherwise known as section 1411 property. Obviously, marketable securities are investment assets not used in a trade or business.
61. The sale of marketable securities would always generate net investment income because they are not used in a trade or business.
62. Prop. Treas. Reg. §1.1411-7(c).
63. Treas. Reg. §1.1411-4(d)(2).
64. IRC Sec. 1411(c)(1)(A)(i).
65. IRC Sec. 1411(c)(1)(A)(iii).
66. Treas. Reg. §1.1411-4(d)(3)(ii), Example 1.
67. IRC Sec. IRC Secs. 62(a)(3),(4) and (9).
68. IRS Publication 536 (2013), Treas. Reg. §1.1411-4(h).
69. IRC Sec. 67.
70. See IRC Sec. 67(b) in which all below-the-line deductions *not* listed are considered miscellaneous itemized deductions.
71. Treas. Reg. §1.1411-4(f)(7).
72. Treas. Reg. §1.1411-4(f)(7)(i).
73. Treas. Reg. §1.1411-4(f)(i). Also, losses from the disposition of property are treated as above the line deductions for regular income tax purposes. IRC Sec. 62(a)(3).
74. Treas. Reg. §1.1411-4(h).
75. Treas. Reg. §1.1411-3.
76. IRC Sec. 1411(a)(2)(B)(ii).
77. The threshold for trusts and estates is indexed because the regular tax income tax brackets for trusts and estates are indexed for inflation.
78. Treas. Reg. §1.1411-3(a)(1). Subchapter J deals exclusively with the taxation of trusts and estates and their beneficiaries. Treas. Reg. §1.1411-3(b)(1) lists the types of trusts and estates specific excluded from NIIT.
79. IRC Secs. 652(b) and 662(b).
80. IRC Secs. 651(a).
81. IRC Sec. 662(a).
82. IRC Sec. 643(a).
83. IRC Secs. 651(a) (simple trust) and 661(a) (complex trust).
84. Treas. Reg. §1.1411-3(e)(5), Example 2.
85. IRC Sec. 3121(v)(1)(B).
86. IRC Sec. 1411(c)(5).
87. IRC Sec. 453.
88. Treas. Reg. §1.652(b)-3(c).
89. IRC Sec. 86.
90. IRC Sec. 219 (deductibility of a traditional IRA contribution).
91. Treas. Reg. §1.1411-4(g).
92. Treas. Reg. §1.1411-4(g).
93. IRC Sec. 643(e).
94. IRC Sec. 643(e)(2).
95. IRC Sec. 643(e)(1).

WITHHOLDING AND ESTIMATED TAX REQUIREMENTS

CHAPTER 14

INTRODUCTION

Federal income tax is collected on a "pay-as-you-go" system. This means that individuals must pay tax on their earned income at the time they receive it.

There are two methods for collecting individual income taxes in the year the income is earned:

1. *Withholding* on income earned during the year

2. *Estimated* tax payments

Employers are *required* to withhold a portion of each employee's wages. These amounts are subsequently applied toward the employee's tax liability when the employee files his income tax return.[1] After an individual determines tax liability, a credit may be taken against the tax for all amounts that have been withheld or paid as estimated taxes.[2] Any balance due must be paid, or a refund request must be filed for any overpayment.

Self-employed persons (and some employees) are generally required to file an estimated tax return and pay the estimated tax themselves, in either a lump sum or in installments. Actually, any taxpayer is required to make estimated tax payments if failure to pay would result in certain underpayments of tax.[3]

WAGE WITHHOLDING

Employers who pay wages to one or more employees *must* withhold a portion of each employee's wages and turn the withheld amount over to the government. The withheld amount is later applied toward the employee's tax liability on a federal income tax return.[4]

Note that only those payments that fall within the definition of "wages" are subject to withholding. "Wages" generally means pay for services rendered by an employee (e.g., salary, fees, bonuses, commissions, and vacation pay).[5]

Payments that are excludable from the employee's gross income (see Chapter 3) are generally not subject to withholding (e.g., employer-paid group term life insurance premiums).[6] Moving expenses are also exempt from withholding if the employer reasonably believes they will be deductible to the employee.[7]

Some types of employment are *specifically excluded* from withholding. For example, no withholding is required on payments made to ministers, priests, rabbis, or other clergypersons for performance of their regular duties. Likewise, no withholding is required on pay to a household worker, even a full-time worker. However, the household worker, even though classified as an employee, must still file an estimated tax return *and* pay the estimated tax currently.[8]

Withholding calculation. An employer may calculate the amount to be withheld by either the *percentage method* or the *wage-bracket table* method.[9] Both methods are based on graduated rates. Both the percentage and the wage-bracket methods take into account the employee's payroll period, marital status, and number of exemptions claimed.

The employee claims his exemptions and "standard deduction allowance" by filing Form W-4 with the employer. Usually, an employee may claim no more exemptions on Form W-4 than the number he is allowed on the return. Individuals may not claim the same exemption with more than one employer. In order to prevent over-withholding in some cases, the law permits an employee who has unusually large excess itemized deductions to claim one or more additional exemptions.[10]

Withholding on Pensions and Annuities

Unless a taxpayer elects otherwise, income tax will be withheld from benefits paid under pension or profit sharing plans and annuities.[11]

- If the payments are *periodic* (e.g., monthly), they are treated similarly to salaries and wages for the purpose of determining the amount of tax to be withheld. Form W-4P is used to indicate the individual's marital status and the number of allowances he is claiming. Individuals may also use Form W-4P to elect not to have any tax withheld.
- If the payments are *nonperiodic*, there is generally a flat withholding rate of 10 percent. Recipients of nonperiodic payments use Form W-4P only if they want to elect out of withholding.[12]

ESTIMATED TAX PAYMENTS

Who Must Estimate Tax Payments?

Taxpayers are generally required to pay estimated tax if failure to pay would result in an underpayment of federal income tax.[13] Specifically, taxpayers must make estimated tax payments if they expect to satisfy two criteria:

1. To owe at least $1,000 in tax after subtracting withholding and refundable credits
2. Their withholding and refundable credits to be less than the smaller of:
   a. 90 percent of the tax to be shown on the current year tax return; or
   b. 100 percent of the tax shown on the previous year's tax return (assuming the previous year's return covers a twelve-month period)[14]

In calculating the amount owed (or expected to be owed), taxpayers must include:

- the alternative minimum tax;
- self-employment tax;
- the Net Investment Income Tax (NIIT); and
- the Additional Medicare Surtax.[15]

An underpayment is the amount by which a required installment exceeds the amount, if any, paid on or before the due date of that installment. Taxpayers who anticipate an underpayment that would require estimated payments to be made have the option to increase their withholdings in such an amount that would reduce their underpayment to the point where they would no longer be required to make estimated payments. Obviously, the earlier in the tax year this adjustment is made, the easier it is to avoid estimated payments.

If estimated payments cannot be avoided through withholding adjustments, the due dates for the quarterly payments are April 15, June 15, September 15, and January 15 of the following year.[16]

Example 1: Jane files as head of household claiming her dependent son, takes the standard deduction, and expects no refundable credits for 2020.

Expected adjusted gross income (AGI) for 2020	$82,800
AGI for 2019	$73,700
Total tax on 2019 return (Form 1040, line 61)	$8,746
Total 2020 estimated tax	$11,015
Tax expected to be withheld in 2020	$10,000

Here, Jane expects to owe at least $1,000 for 2020 after subtracting her withholding from her expected total tax ($11,015 – $10,000 = $1,015). However, she expects her income tax withholding ($10,000) to be at least 90 percent of the tax to be shown on her 2020 return ($11,015 × 90 percent = $9,913.50). Jane does not need to pay estimated tax.

Example 2: The facts are the same as in Example 1, except that Jane expects only $8,700 tax to be withheld in 2020. This amount is less than 90 percent of the expected tax owed in 2020. Additionally, she does not expect her income tax withholding ($8,700) to be at least 100 percent of the total tax shown on her 2019 return ($8,746). Here, Jane must increase her withholding or pay estimated tax for 2020.

Example 3: The facts are the same as in Example 2, except that the total tax shown on Jane's 2019 return was $8,600. Because she expects to have more than $8,600 withheld in 2020 ($8,700), Jane does not need to pay estimated tax for 2020.[17]

How Are Additional Payments Calculated?

The required amount for each installment is 25 percent of the required annual payment.[18] Generally, the "required annual payment" is the lower of:

- 90 percent of the tax shown on the return for the taxable year (or, if no return is filed, 90 percent of the tax for the year); or
- 100 percent of the tax shown on the return for the preceding year (but only if the preceding taxable year consisted of twelve months and a return was filed for that year).[19]

However, for an individual whose adjusted gross income for the previous tax year exceeded $150,000 ($75,000 in the case of married individuals filing separately), the required annual payment is the lesser of:

- 90 percent of the current year's tax, as described above, or
- the *applicable percentage* (110 percent) of the tax shown on the return for the preceding year.[20]

Alternatively, individuals can pay estimated tax by paying a specified percentage of the current year's tax, computed by "annualizing" the taxable income for the months in the taxable year ending before the month in which the installment falls due. Under this method, the applicable percentages are as follows:

- 22.5 percent (1st quarter)
- 45 percent (2nd quarter)
- 67.5 percent (3rd quarter)
- 90 percent (4th quarter)[21]

If an individual underpays estimated taxes, an interest penalty (compounded daily) will be imposed at an annual rate, adjusted quarterly, to 3 percentage points over the short-term AFR (applicable federal rate).[22] However, no interest penalty will be imposed if *either* of the following applies:

- The tax shown on the return for the taxable year (or, if no return is filed, the tax) after reduction for withholdings is less than $1,000
- The taxpayer owed no tax for the preceding year (a taxable year consisting of twelve months) and the taxpayer was a U.S. citizen or resident for the entire taxable year.[23]

If the taxpayer elects to apply an overpayment to the succeeding year's estimated taxes, the overpayment will be applied to unpaid installments of estimated tax due on or after the date(s) the overpayment arose in the order in which they are required to be paid to avoid an interest penalty for failure to pay estimated income tax for that particular tax year.

SELF-EMPLOYMENT TAX

An individual whose net earnings from self-employment are $400 or more for the taxable year must pay the self-employment tax.[24] The rate for self-employment tax, as adjusted by an automatic cost-of-living increase in the earnings base, is 15.3 percent (12.4 percent OASDI and 2.9 percent hospital insurance). In 2020, the OASDI tax is imposed on up to $137,700 of self-employment income for a maximum OASDI tax of $21,068. The hospital insurance tax is imposed on all of a taxpayer's self-employment income. However, an above-the-line deduction is permitted for one-half of the self-employment tax paid by an individual and attributable to a trade or business carried on by the individual (not as an employee).[25] See Chapter 12 for more information about the calculation of self-employment taxes.

WHERE CAN I FIND OUT MORE?

Tax Facts on Insurance & Employee Benefits (National Underwriter Company).

CHAPTER ENDNOTES

1. IRC Sec. 3401(a).
2. IRC Sec. 31(a).
3. IRC Sec. 6017.
4. IRC Sec. 3402(a).
5. IRC Sec. 3401(a).
6. IRC Secs. 3401(a)(12), 3401(a)(14).
7. IRC Secs. 217 and 3401(a)(15); Treas. Reg. §31.3401(a)(15)-1.
8. IRC Secs. 3401(a) and 6017.
9. IRC Secs. 3402(b)-(c).
10. 1IRC Sec. 3402(m).
11. IRC Sec. 3405(a).
12. IRC Sec. 3405(b).
13. IRC Sec. 6654.
14. IRS Publication 505, "Who Must Pay Estimated Tax".
15. IRC Sec. 6654(d)(2)(B)(i). See also "Questions and Answers on the Net Investment Income Tax" at: www.irs.gov/uac/Newsroom/Net-Investment-Income-Tax-FAQs; and "Questions and Answers for the Additional Medicare Tax" at: www.irs.gov/Businesses/Small-Businesses-&-Self-Employed/Questions-and-Answers-for-the-Additional-Medicare-Tax. See Chapter 12 for more information on the NIIT and the Additional Medicare surtax.
16. IRC Secs. 6654(b)-(c).
17. IRS Publication 505, "Who Must Pay Estimated Tax," examples.
18. IRC Sec. 6654(d)(1)(A).
19. IRC Sec. 6654(d)(1)(B).
20. IRC Sec. 6654(d)(1)(C).
21. IRC Sec. 6654(d)(2).
22. IRC Sec. 6621(a)(2). A complete history of AFRs including the present rates can be found at www.leimberg.com.
23. IRC Sec. 6654(e).
24. IRC Sec. 6017.
25. IRC Sec. 164(f).

GRANTOR TRUSTS

CHAPTER 15

INTRODUCTION

A grantor trust is a trust in which the grantor and the trust are considered a single taxpayer by the income tax code. To put it simply, trust income and expenses are reported on the grantor's individual income tax return. Therefore, the grantor (not the trust) pays the income tax due on the grantor trust income. Most grantor trusts are revocable trusts and are included in the grantor's taxable estate; a common example is a revocable living trust. However, a common planning technique is to create an irrevocable grantor trust that is not included in the taxpayer's estate. Such a grantor trust is useful because payment of the trust's income tax liability by the grantor results in a tax-free gift to the trust beneficiaries and avoids the compressed trust tax brackets. These trusts are referred to as intentionally defective irrevocable trusts (IDITs) or intentionally defective grantor trusts (IDGTs) and are discussed later in this chapter.

TRUST POWERS THAT CREATE GRANTOR TRUST STATUS

Any trust can be a grantor trust. Specifically, IRC Sections 673 through 679 list trust powers which, if held by the grantor, cause the trust to be a grantor trust. The purpose of these rules, when added to the Tax Code in 1954, was to prevent high income taxpayers from creating multiple trusts and taking advantage of bracket ride in each while maintaining enjoyment or control of the income producing property. Compression of the trust tax brackets has largely eliminated this planning strategy, but the grantor trust rules remain in effect and can be used to create important tax benefits.

IRC Section 673 – Reversionary Interests

If the grantor of a trust has a reversionary interest in the trust exceeding five percent of the affected portion of the trust, the grantor is treated as the owner of the trust.[1] A reversionary interest means there is the possibility that the trust corpus could return to the grantor.

Example: Asher creates a trust for Ashley providing for discretionary income and/or principal distributions for her life. If upon Ashley's death the corpus returns to Asher (because there is no other successor beneficiary), Asher has a reversionary interest in the trust.

In order for grantor trust status to apply, the value of the reversion at the time the trust is created must be more than 5 percent of the trust corpus. Therefore, in the above example, if Ashley is relatively young and has a long life expectancy, it is possible that Asher's reversionary interest would be less than 5 percent.

There is an exception for reversionary interest taking effect at death of a minor lineal descendent beneficiary of the grantor.

Example: Asher creates a trust for his daughter Ashley providing income to her until she reaches the age of twenty-one at which time the trust will terminate and distribute the remaining trust corpus to her. However, if Ashley dies before attaining the age of twenty-one, the principal will return to Asher. Because of the exception noted above, Asher's reversion interest in the trust will not cause it to be a grantor trust even if the value of the reversion exceeds 5 percent.

IRC Section 674 – The Power to Control Beneficial Enjoyment

This is the power to control beneficial enjoyment of trust corpus or income held by the grantor, the grantor's spouse or nonadverse party.[2] Examples of control include the power to invade corpus, the power to accumulate income or the power to sprinkle income among beneficiaries.

Specifically listed in IRC Section 674 are exceptions of trust powers that do not cause a trust to be treated as a grantor trust. The exceptions are as follows:

- Power to hold or accumulate income for distribution for the benefit of a person the grantor is legally obligated to support (other than the grantor's spouse), i.e., a power that the Code specifically provides will not cause the income of a trust to be taxed to the grantor.[3]

- Power to affect the beneficial enjoyment of income that is effective only after the occurrence of an event does not cause the income to be taxable to the grantor prior to such occurrence. However, if such power was a 5 percent reversionary interest held by the grantor (that would have caused the trust to be a grantor trust pursuant to IRC 673), this exception does not apply and the income is taxable to the grantor. So from a planning perspective, the occurrence of the event should be far enough into the future so that the value of the reversionary interest is less than 5 percent. Finally, once the event occurs, the income is taxable to the grantor unless the grantor relinquishes the power.

- Power of disposition from a trust exercisable only by will other than the power to appoint income that was accumulated at the discretion of the grantor or a nonadverse party, or both, without the approval or consent of any adverse party.

- Power to allocate income or corpus among charitable beneficiaries does not cause the trust to be a grantor trust. For this exception to apply, the income or corpus (as the case may be) must be irrevocably allocated to charity.

- Power to distribute corpus subject to a reasonably definite standard set forth in the trust agreement. A common example of such a standard is health, education, maintenance or support (HEMS).

- Power to distribute corpus to a current income beneficiary provided the distribution is charged against the distributee beneficiary's proportionate share of trust principal.

- Power to withhold income temporarily to a beneficiary provided the income must be distributed at a later time to the beneficiary, the beneficiary's estate, as the beneficiary designates subject to limited or special power of appointment (i.e., to another person at the beneficiary's direction), termination of the trust, or with current principal distributions or to the current income beneficiaries in shares irrevocably specified in the trust agreement.

- Power to withhold income during the disability of a beneficiary or minority.

- Power to allocate receipts and disbursements between income and principal.

IRC Section 675 – Administrative Powers

Certain administrative powers held by the grantor or the grantor's spouse can also cause a trust to be treated as a grantor trust. These powers include:

1. Power to deal with trust property for less than adequate and full consideration. This power includes the ability to purchase or exchange property at a discount. If the grantor has this power, he or she could effectively terminate the trust by raiding it of its assets.

2. Power to borrow trust property without adequate interest or security. This means that if the trust document allows the grantor to borrow, the failure of the trust document to require the payment of adequate interest

or without adequate security will cause the trust (or portion of the trust) to be treated as a grantor trust.

3. Actual borrowing by the grantor or the grantor's spouse of corpus or income that has not been completely repaid by the beginning of the next taxable year. Failure to do so will cause the trust to be treated as a grantor trust. However, this does not include a loan authorized by a trust requiring the grantor to pay adequate interest with adequate security if the loan was made by a trustee other than the grantor or a related or subservient trustee.

4. General administrative powers exercised by a person in a nonfiduciary capacity without the approval of a person in a fiduciary capacity including:

   - The power to vote or direct the voting of stock or other securities of a corporation in which the holdings of the grantor and the trust are significant from the viewpoint of voting control.

   - The power to control the investment or reinvestment of trust funds or by vetoing proposed investments or reinvestments to the extent the trust funds consist of stock and securities of corporations in which the holdings of the grantor and the trust are significant from the viewpoint of voting control.

   - The power to reacquire trust corpus by substituting other property of equivalent value.

IRC Section 676 – Power to Revoke

This is the power to revoke a trust and re-vest title of the trust assets to the grantor. It applies to the assets (and corresponding income) of the trust subject to this power. This power includes the power to terminate, amend, alter or appoint. If this power cannot be exercised until the occurrence of an event, the trust is not considered a grantor trust until the occurrence of such event provided that if the power were a reversionary interest, the value of such interest must not have exceeded 5 percent of the trust principal on the date the trust was created. Once the event occurs, the trust would be treated as a grantor trust with respect to the portion of the trust subject to this power.

IRC Section 677 – Income Used for the Benefit of the Grantor or the Grantor's Spouse.

This involves the use of trust income for the benefit of the grantor or the grantor's spouse without the consent of an adverse party or in the discretion of the grantor, the grantor's spouse or nonadverse party. The specific scenarios resulting in grantor trust status include:

- Discretionary or actual distribution of trust income to grantor or grantor's spouse.

- Discretion to actual holding or accumulation of trust income for future distribution to the grantor or the grantor's spouse.

- Trust income applied to pay insurance premiums on the life of the grantor or the grantor's wife.

- To the extent distributed, the power to use trust income for the legal obligated support of the grantor's dependents.

Example: Grantor transfers $100,000 to an irrevocable life insurance trust for the benefit of the grantor's children. The income on the trust is used to buy life insurance (owned by the trust) on the grantor's life. The trust generates $8,000 of income of which $6,500 is used to pay the premiums. The amount applied to pay premiums, $6,500 is taxable to the grantor. The remaining $1,500 ($8,000 – $6,500) of income is taxable to the trust.

IRC Section 678 – Person Other than the Grantor treated as Owner of the Trust

Under certain circumstances, a person other than the original grantor of a trust may be deemed to be the owner of such trust. As a result, the trust would be a grantor trust as to that other person. This occurs when an individual has the power to appoint trust principal or income to himself or herself or if such individual had released such a power but maintained sufficient control that, if he or she had been the grantor, would have caused the trust to be a grantor trust.

Example: Asher creates a trust. The primary beneficiary is Ashley. Upon her death, the remainder will pass to her living issue. At any time during the term of the trust, Ashley has the power to withdraw any or all of the trust corpus. Due to her unfettered access to the trust, she is treated as the owner of the trust (i.e., it is deemed to be a grantor trust with respect to her) even if she never exercises that power.

However, if the original grantor is deemed to be the owner of the trust as to the income, there can be no other person deemed to be the owner of the trust. So, if the grantor is deemed to be the owner of the principal (but not the income), another person could be deemed to be the owner of the income (and, thus taxed on it). Finally, if a beneficiary has the discretion to apply principal or income to satisfy legal obligations, the beneficiary is treated as the owner of the trust. However, to the extent the power is to satisfy support obligations of dependents, the beneficiary is treated as the grantor/owner only when the income or principal is used to discharge that obligation.

TAX TREATMENT OF GRANTOR TRUSTS

For income tax purposes, to the extent a grantor is treated as the owner of a grantor trust, the grantor must include all trust income, deductions and credits with any other income, deductions and credits in computing taxable income.[4] Thus, for example, the grantor may deduct charitable contributions made by the trust and be taxed on the trust's foreign source income.[5]

A grantor may also be deemed to own only a portion of a trust. The portion of the trust income taxable to the grantor depends on the specific portion of the trust deemed owned by the grantor. The ways in which a grantor owns a portion of a trust include the following:

- Ownership of the ordinary income portion or only the principal portion;
- Ownership of a fractional or pecuniary share of all items of trust income and principal; or
- Ownership of all income attributable to certain assets.[6]

REPORTING TRUST INCOME AND PAYMENT OF TAXES

As stated above, the grantor reports all trust income, deductions and credits on a personal income tax return. A Form 1041 must also be filed on which the trust name, address and tax identification number is entered. Although the items of income, deduction and credit are not reported on the Form 1041, a separate statement (referred to as a grantor tax information letter) summarizing the items reported on the grantor's personal income tax return is attached to the blank Form 1041.[7]

There are other alternative methods of reporting. One method is for the trustee of the trust to file Forms 1099 in lieu of a Form 1041. Thus, the payor(s) files Forms 1099 listing the trust as the taxpayer which in turn shifts the income to the grantor with the second set of Forms 1099. However, this method may be problematic in situations in which the there are multiple taxable transactions and multiple payors. Moreover, the trustee must prepare a grantor tax information letter for the grantor to attach to the personal income tax return.[8]

Another alternative method eliminates the need for the trust to file a Form 1041 or Forms 1099. Here, the payor lists the grantor as the owner of the assets. The trustee provides the payor with the grantor's name, social security number and trust address. As a result, the grantor reports all of the income on Form 1040 without the need to file any other forms.[9]

WHY GRANTOR TRUSTS ARE USED

Avoiding Probate

Although revocable grantor trusts do not save estate tax (because they are included in the grantor's gross estate), they are commonly used to avoid probate because the property held in trust are not probate assets (even though they are attachable by creditors of the estate). Avoiding probate saves costs and delays the distribution of assets as well as the publicity inherent in the probate process.

Intentionally Defective Irrevocable Trust (IDIT)

High net worth taxpayers can save income tax and estate tax by creating an intentionally defective irrevocable trust (IDIT) (also known as an intentionally defective grantor trust or IDGT). An IDIT is a grantor trust that is not included in the grantor's estate. To make the trust defective, the trust provides one of the powers that causes it to be a grantor trust for income tax purposes but not included in the grantor's estate. As a result, the grantor is taxed on the income and the transferred property is removed from the grantor's estate. Although the transfer of the property to the trust would be subject to gift tax, the post-transfer appreciation would be estate tax-free.

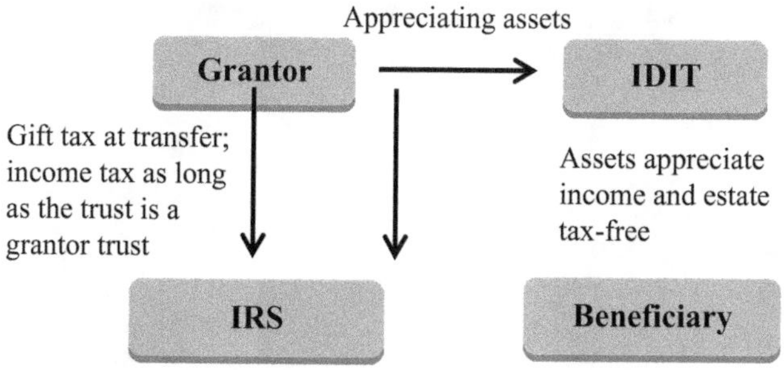

For example, an IDIT would be appropriate for a grantor who desires to accumulate income in a trust for a minor. For the duration of the trust, trust income is taxed to the grantor/parent rather than to the trust which might be subject to a higher marginal tax rate. The payment of income taxes by the grantor results in a gift and estate tax-free transfer to the beneficiary.[10] Payment of the trust's income tax liability by the grantor enables the IDIT's assets to grow at their pre-tax rate of return.

Example: Grantor funds an IDIT with $100,000 worth of corporate bonds with a yield of 6 percent gift tax-free using the applicable exclusion amount. The grantor's combined federal and state marginal income tax rate is 50 percent. The grantor lives for ten years after the trust is funded and the corporate bond portfolio then has a value of $179,085. The $79,085 therefore transfers free of the estate tax. A significant part of this tax-free transfer is attributable to grantor paying the income tax due on the bond yield.

Period	Beginning Balance	Yield 6%	Tax 0%	Ending Balance
1	$ 100,000	6000.000	0	$ 106,000
2	$ 106,000	6360.000	0	$ 112,360
3	$ 112,360	6741.600	0	$ 119,102
4	$ 119,102	7146.096	0	$ 126,248
5	$ 126,248	7574.862	0	$ 133,823
6	$ 133,823	8029.353	0	$ 141,852
7	$ 141,852	8511.115	0	$ 150,363
8	$ 150,363	9021.782	0	$ 159,385
9	$ 159,385	9563.088	0	$ 168,948
10	$ 168,948	10136.870	0	$ 179,085

Period	Beginning Balance	Yield 6%	Tax 50%	Ending Balance
1	$ 100,000	6,000	(3,000)	$ 103,000
2	$ 103,000	6,180	(3,090)	$ 106,090
3	$ 106,090	6,365	(3,183)	$ 109,273
4	$ 109,273	6,556	(3,278)	$ 112,551
5	$ 112,551	6,753	(3,377)	$ 115,927
6	$ 115,927	6,956	(3,478)	$ 119,405
7	$ 119,405	7,164	(3,582)	$ 122,987
8	$ 122,987	7,379	(3,690)	$ 126,677
9	$ 126,677	7,601	(3,800)	$ 130,477
10	$ 130,477	7,829	(3,914)	$ 134,392

An IDIT can also serve as a means of distributing income to beneficiaries with the tax paid by the grantor. So, in addition to removing assets from the estate, the grantor is able to provide gift-tax free income to beneficiaries.

In selecting a power to retain, the grantor must be mindful not to choose a power that will cause the assets of the trust to be included in the gross estate. The powers to avoid include:

- A more than 5 percent reversionary interest with respect to the trust corpus;
- Certain administrative powers, such as the power to vote stock;
- Power to retain the trust income.

FREQUENTLY ASKED QUESTIONS

Question – What is the benefit of creating a grantor trust that will be included in the grantor's gross estate?

Answer – Considering the large estate tax exemption ($11,580,000 in 2018) as well as the portability of a deceased spouse's unused exemption, there are few estates subject to estate tax. Moreover, at the death of the grantor, the basis of appreciated assets within such a trust are "stepped–up" to their date of death fair market value saving the beneficiaries income tax on a subsequent sale of such assets. So, for a grantor who is not likely to be subject to estate tax, capturing the income tax advantages discussed in this chapter and the basis "step-up" may be very advantageous to the grantor and beneficiaries.

CHAPTER ENDNOTES

1. IRC Sec. 673(a).
2. IRC Sec. 672(b). IRC Section 672(a) defines an "adverse party" as any person who has a substantial beneficial interest in a trust that would be adversely affected by the exercise or nonexercise of the power he or she possesses with respect to the trust. For example, a person with a general power of appointment over trust property has a beneficial interest in the trust. Thus, a "non-adverse party" is a person who does not possess those powers.
3. IRC Sec. 677(b). In other words, as long as the discretionary power is not exercised, the grantor is not taxed on the trust income. To the extent it is exercised to provide legal support, the grantor would be taxed on the distributed income.
4. Treas. Reg. §1.671-2(a).
5. Treas. Reg. §1.671-2(c).
6. Treas. Reg. §1.671-3.
7. Treas. Reg. §1.671-4(a).
8. Treas. Reg. §1.671-4(b)(2)(iii).
9. Treas. Reg. §1.671-2(b)(2)(i)(A).
10. Rev. Rul. 2004-64.

INCOME TAXATION OF TRUSTS AND ESTATES

CHAPTER 16

WHAT IS THE DIFFERENCE BETWEEN A SIMPLE AND COMPLEX TRUST?

The Tax Code categorizes trusts as either simple or complex. A simple trust has the following characteristics:

- It is required to distribute all trust income annually.
- Does not permit charitable contributions.
- Does not distribute corpus.[1]

Each year, beneficiaries of simple trusts are deemed to receive all trust income whether or not it is distributed. This means the beneficiaries, rather than the trust report, the income subject to income tax.[2] Generally, trust income or fiduciary accounting income includes dividends, interest, and rental income. Because capital gain is usually not considered to be fiduciary accounting income,[3] it is taxable to the trust rather than the beneficiary.[4]

A complex trust has some or all of the following characteristics:

- The trustee may have the discretion to accumulate or distribute income.
- Beneficiaries may receive mandatory or discretionary distributions.
- The trustee may have the discretion to distribute corpus or income accumulated in prior years.
- The trust may provide for charitable distributions.

Estates are subject to income tax in the same manner as a complex trust.

COMPUTATION OF TAXABLE INCOME OF TRUSTS

Subject to special rules, the taxable income of a trust (simple or complex) is computed in the same manner as for an individual. The gross income of a trust is reduced by deductions to arrive at taxable income. For complex trusts and estates this includes a deduction for certain income distributed to beneficiaries who in turn recognize the distribution as taxable income.

COMMON ITEMS OF GROSS INCOME

Similar to an individual, the types of gross income received by a trust may include interest, dividend, rental income and gains (or losses) from the sale of trust property.

DISTRIBUTABLE NET INCOME

As noted above, a complex trust or an estate is taxable on the income it retains and the beneficiaries are taxed on the trust income they receive (or are deemed to have received). For that reason, the trust is entitled to a deduction for amounts distributed to beneficiaries. The distribution deduction prevents trust income from being taxed twice, i.e., to the trust and the beneficiaries. The amount of trust income that can be included in the gross income of the beneficiaries and deducted from the gross income of the trust is called *distributable net income* (DNI). Importantly, the character of the income (e.g. whether income is taxed at ordinary or capital gain rates) carries out with the distribution.

COMPUTING THE TAXABLE INCOME OF A TRUST OR ESTATE

Computations

Step 1 – Determine the gross income (or loss) of the trust.

Step 2 – Determine the trust's deductions. Generally, these are "deductions for costs . . . in connection with the administration of an estate or a trust and which would not have been incurred if the property were not held in such trust or estate."[5]

Prior to a Supreme Court decision,[6] there was some controversy as to what types of deductible expenses are unique to a trust. In the aftermath of that decision, the IRS issued final regulations creating five categories of deductions including ownership costs, tax preparation fees, investment advisory fees, appraisal fees and "certain fiduciary expenses."[7] The rationale for ascertaining whether an expense is a miscellaneous itemized deduction or an above the line deduction is whether the expense is commonly incurred by individuals. If is unique to a trust or estate, then it is an above the line deduction. An example of this is the tax preparation fee of an estate tax return, a generation skipping transfer tax return, a fiduciary income tax return (Form 1041) and the decedent's final income tax return.[8]

Step 3 – Determine the personal exemption.[9] The personal exemptions are $300[10] for a simple trust, $100 for a complex trust,[11] and $600[12] for an estate.

Step 4 – Compute the tentative taxable income. The tentative taxable income of a trust (or estate) is gross income minus all deductions with the exception of the distribution deduction. The distribution deduction is the amount of trust income deemed to be distributed to beneficiaries who are required to report it on their individual income tax returns. As explained in Step 5, the starting point for the distribution deduction is tentative taxable income.

Step 5 – Compute the distribution deduction of a simple trust or complex trust.[13]

The distribution deduction is the lesser of the amount of income distributed (reduced by tax-exempt interest) or DNI (reduced by tax-exempt income).[14]

Sub-Step A – Compute the fiduciary accounting income. An important element of this analysis is whether the trust instrument (or applicable law) requires that trust expenses be paid from fiduciary accounting income or trust principal and whether capital gains are included in fiduciary accounting income. If trust expenses are paid out of fiduciary accounting income, it reduces the amount received by the income beneficiaries. If capital gains are included in fiduciary accounting income, it increases the amount received by beneficiaries.

Sub-Step B – Compute the DNI of the trust.

DNI is computed as follows:[15]

Taxable income

\+ Income distribution deduction

\+ Exemption ($300 for a simple trust)

\+ Net tax-exempt income

\+ Capital losses*

< Capital gains* >

< Extraordinary stock dividends >

= Distributable Net Income (DNI)

*These adjustments are not made in the year of termination or if capital gains are included in fiduciary accounting income.

Step 6 – Compare distributions with DNI. The distribution deduction is the lesser of the two.[16]

Step 7 – Deduct the distribution deduction from tentative taxable income. The difference is the taxable income of the trust.

Step 8 – Apply the rate table of IRC Section 1(e) to determine the tax of the trust.

INCOME TAX RATES FOR TRUSTS AND ESTATES

The income tax brackets for trusts and estates are much more compressed than those for individuals, reaching the maximum rate of 37 percent on income of just $12,951 in 2020.

Tax Rate	Trusts and Estate Income
10%	$0 to $2,600
$260 plus 24% of the excess over $2,600	$2,600-$9,450
$1,868 plus 35% of the excess over $9,300	$9,450-$12,950
$3,075.50 plus 37% of the excess over $12,950	Over $12,950

AMT

The alternative minimum tax (AMT) also applies to estates and trusts. For 2020, the AMT exemption deduction for estates and trusts is $25,400. This deduction is phased-out by $1 for every $4 the trust's or estate's income exceeds $84,800. The AMT tax rate applicable is 26 percent for taxable income less than or equal to $197,900 and 28 percent for taxable income which exceeds that amount.

Example (Simple Trust)

In 2020, the Jones Trust, a simple trust with one beneficiary, Asher, has the following items of income and administrative expenses (allocated to corpus meaning they are to be paid out of trust principal rather than from the income to be distributed to the beneficiaries):

Dividends	$6,000
Interest income	$8,000
Capital gains	$4,000
Trustee fees	$2,000

Step 1 – Determine the gross income of the trust.

$18,000 (dividends, interest and capital gains).

Step 2 – Determine deductions of the trust.

$2,000 (trustee fees).

Step 3 – Determine the trust's personal exemption.

$300 personal exemption for a simple trust.

Step 4 – Compute the tentative taxable income of the trust.

$18,000

($2,000)

($300)

$15,700 Tentative Taxable Income

Step 5 – Compute the distribution deduction of the trust.

Sub-Step A – Compute fiduciary accounting income.

Fiduciary accounting income is $14,000 (dividends and interest; capital gains are not included in this example). Since the trustee fees are allocated to corpus they do not reduce fiduciary accounting income. Therefore, the income beneficiaries receive the entire $14,000 of fiduciary accounting income.

Sub-Step B – Compute the DNI of the trust.

Tentative Taxable Income	$15,700
Add back personal exemption	$300
Deduct capital gains	($4,000)
DNI	$12,000

Step 6 – Compare fiduciary accounting income ($14,000) with DNI ($12,000). The distribution deduction is $12,000, the lesser of the two.

Step 7 – Deduct the distribution deduction from tentative taxable income. The distribution deduction is the lesser of the two:

Tentative Taxable Income	$15,700
Less Distribution Deduction	($12,000)
Taxable Income of Trust	$3,700

Step 8 – Apply the tax rate of IRC Section 1(e) to determine the tax of the trust.

Using 2020 tax rates, the total tax is $264 (0 percent of $2,600, plus 24 percent of $1,100). As to Asher, the beneficiary, the amount included in his gross income is the lesser of fiduciary accounting income ($14,000) or DNI ($12,000).[17] Thus, although Asher received $14,000 of fiduciary accounting income, the amount includible in his gross income is $12,000.

The character of the income is the same in the hands of the beneficiary as it is to the trust. In this example, there is a total of $8,000 of interest income and $6,000 of dividend income. The amount of each type of income is in proportion to the amount of that type of income included in DNI.[18] To determine the amount of interest income, In this case, Asher must include $6,857 in gross income:

$$\frac{\$8,000}{\$14,000} \times \$12,000 = \$6,857$$

Similarly, to determine the amount of dividend income Asher must include $5,143 in dividend income:

$$\frac{\$6,000}{\$14,000} \times \$12,000 = \$5,143$$

Additionally, the interest income and dividend income is included in Asher's net investment income and is potentially subject to the net investment income tax (discussed later in the chapter). The remaining $2,000 Asher received in excess of the amount of DNI is income tax-free.[19]

Example (Complex Trust)

In 2020, per the terms of the trust document, the Jones Trust, a complex trust with two beneficiaries, Asher and Ashley, is required to distribute one-half of fiduciary accounting income to Asher and is permitted to make discretionary distributions to Ashley. In addition to Asher's mandatory distribution, the trustee made a discretionary distribution of $3,000. The trust document allocates trustee fees and capital gains to corpus. The trust has the following items of income and administrative expenses:

Interest income	$14,000
Capital gains	$4,000
Trustee fees	$2,000

Step 1 – Determine the gross income of the trust.

$18,000 (interest and capital gains).

Step 2 – Determine deductions of the trust.

$2,000 (trustee fees).

Step 3 – Determine the trust's miscellaneous itemized deductions.

None.

Step 4 – Determine the trust's personal exemption.

$100 personal exemption for a simple trust.

Step 5 – Compute the tentative taxable income of the trust.

$18,000

($2,000)

($100)

$15,900 Tentative Taxable Income

Step 6 – Compute the distribution deduction of the trust.

Sub-Step A – Determine the total amount of trust distributions to beneficiaries.

Asher is to receive one-half of the fiduciary accounting income of the trust. The only item of fiduciary accounting income is $14,000 of interest income. Since the trustee fees are allocated to corpus, Asher who is to receive one-half of the fiduciary accounting income would receive $7,000. Ashley is to receive a discretionary distribution of $3,000. Therefore, total distributions are $10,000.

Sub-Step B – Compute the DNI of the trust.

Tentative Taxable Income	$15,900
Add back personal exemption	$100
Deduct capital gains	($4,000)
DNI	$12,000

Step 8 – Compare total distributions ($10,000) with DNI ($12,000). The distribution deduction is $10,000, the lesser of the two.

Step 9 – Deduct the distribution deduction from tentative taxable income. The distribution deduction is the lesser of the two.

Tentative Taxable Income	$15,900
Less Distribution Deduction	($10,000)
Taxable Income of Trust	$5,900

The trust retained $4,000 of capital gain and the balance of $1,900 is interest income.

Step 10 – Apply the tax rate of IRC Section 1(e) to determine the tax of the trust.

Assuming 2020 tax rates, the total tax is $685. When a trust has both ordinary income and capital gains, the ordinary income fills the tax brackets first. Thus, the $1,900 of ordinary income is taxed at 0 percent. The first $700 of capital gain (up to $2,600) falls into the 0 percent capital gains bracket. The remaining $3,300 ($4,000 - $700) is taxed at 15 percent and produces a tax of $495. This makes the total tax payable $685.

Asher, who received 70 percent of the total amount distributed to the beneficiaries ($7,000 of $10,000), must include $7,000 of interest income. Ashley, who received 30 percent of the total distribution ($3,000 of $10,000), must include $3,000 of interest income. Because interest income is considered net investment income, it must be taken into account by both beneficiaries in determining whether they would be subject to the net investment income tax (see below).

Application of Net Investment Income Tax to Trusts and Estates

The *3.8 percent net investment income tax* (NIIT) applies to trusts and estates that are subject to the provisions of Subchapter J of the Internal Revenue Code.[20] The impact of NIIT on trusts and estates cannot be understated. Because trusts tend to remain in existence far longer than estates, the overall tax consequences of this surtax on trusts is likely to be even more profound.

In operation, the 3.8 percent NIIT surtax is imposed on trusts and estates on the lesser of:

- "undistributed net investment income", or
- the excess of adjusted gross income over the amount of the highest regular income tax bracket in effect for such taxable year.[21]

Compared to individual taxpayers, the NIIT threshold for trusts and estates is very low. It begins at only $12,750 in 2020 (the beginning of the highest ordinary income bracket for trusts. Although this threshold is indexed for inflation; and, the NIIT thresholds are likewise indexed (unlike the thresholds for individual taxpayers), that is of little comfort to fiduciaries and beneficiaries.

More trusts and estates will be subject to NIIT compared to individual taxpayers. Moreover, because most trusts and estates are likely to have *only* net investment income, trusts and estates with relatively small amounts of net investment income may nonetheless be in the highest income tax bracket subject to the 3.8 percent NIIT.

As stated above, the NIIIT tax base of trusts and estates is "undistributed net investment income." In simple terms, undistributed net investment income is any net investment income—as defined by Code section 1411(c)(1)(A)—that is retained by a trust or an estate.[22] As to beneficiaries, distributions of net investment income retain their characterization. In other words, net investment income distributed by a trust is considered net investment income by the beneficiary.[23] From a planning perspective, to the extent authorized by the trust document, it may behoove a trustee of a trust to avoid NIIT by distributing net investment income to individual beneficiar(ies) with income levels below the applicable NIIT thresholds.

COMPUTATION OF NET INVESMENT INCOME OF A TRUST AND BENEFICIARY

For net investment income purposes, net investment income in DNI that is distributed to a beneficiary is included in the beneficiary's net investment income potentially subject to NIIT. Conversely, *undistributed* net investment income in DNI—as well as undistributed net investment income not in DNI—is included in the net investment income tax base of the trust. The most notable net investment income not in DNI is capital gain.

The following example from the regulations[24] demonstrates how to compute net investment income for a complex trust, including DNI calculations

Example

Assume that in 2020 the trustee of this complex trust makes a discretionary income distribution of $10,000 to Beneficiary A.

Trust Income 2020	
Dividend Income	$15,000
Interest Income	$10,000
Capital Gain	$5,000
IRA Distribution	$75,000
Total Trust Income	*$105,000*

Step 1: Determine the DNI of the trust. As explained earlier in this chapter (ignoring the personal exemption), the DNI of a trust is tentative taxable income ($105,000) minus capital gain. Excluding the $5,000 of capital gain, the DNI of the trust is $100,000.

Step 2: Determine the trust's distribution deduction. The distribution deduction of a complex trust is the lesser of DNI ($100,000) and the amount of all distributions (here, $10,000).

Step 3: Determine the extent to which the amount distributed is deemed to be net investment income. IRC Section 661(b) provides that the character of the amount distributed to the beneficiary "shall be treated as consisting of the same proportion of each class of income entering into the computation of distributable net income." In this example, the distribution of $10,000 is equal to 10 percent of $100,000, the total amount of DNI. Thus, the beneficiary is deemed to have received 10 percent of each type of income included in DNI.

Trust Income 2020		
Income in DNI	Retained by Trust	Distributed to Beneficiary
Dividend Income	$13,500	$1,500
Interest Income	$9,000	$1,000
IRA Distribution	$67,500	$7,500
Total	*$90,000*	*$10,000*

Step 4: Determine the amount of net investment income in DNI that is retained by the trust. In this case, only $22,500 of the retained income is net investment income. Per IRC Section 1411(c)(5), the $67,500 distribution from an IRA distribution is not net investment income (NII).

Trust Income 2020		
Income in DNI	Retained by Trust	Net Investment Income
Dividend Income	$13,500	$13,500
Interest Income	$9,000	$9,000
IRA Distribution	$67,500	$0
Total	*$90,000*	*$22,500*

Step 5: Determine the total amount of net investment income retained by the trust. This should include any undistributed item of net investment income not included in DNI. Here, the $5,000 of capital gain excluded from DNI (clearly net investment income) is added to the $22,500 of net investment income included in DNI retained by the trust. Thus, the total amount of trust undistributed net investment income is $27,500.

Step 6: Compute the NIIT. The 3.8 percent NIIT surtax is imposed on the lesser of:

- undistributed NII ($27,500), or
- $92,500, which is the excess of the adjusted gross income ($105,000) over the amount of the highest regular income tax bracket ($12,500).

In this example $27,500 is less than $92,850, so the NIIT would be 3.8 percent of $27,500, or $1,045.

As to the beneficiary, of the $10,000 distribution, $2,500 (dividend income $1,500 and interest income $1,000) is net investment income. The $7,500 IRA distribution is not NII.

TAX CONSEQUENSES OF TRUST DISTRIBUTIONS OF PROPERTY (OTHER THAN MONEY)

To create a trust, grantors transfer money and/or property into it. In most instances, such transfers do not result in income tax consequences to the grantor or the trust.

If a trustee distributes property (other than cash) to beneficiaries, there is no taxable gain or loss triggered to the trust. In other words, it is treated in the same way as a distribution of money for purposes of computing the distribution deduction for the trust and the amount includible in the gross income of the beneficiaries (subject to the DNI rules discussed above). The amount deemed to be distributed is the lesser of: the basis of the property; or its fair market value. The beneficiary receiving the property takes a carryover basis (the same basis as it was in the hands of the trustee).[25] So, if the beneficiary receives appreciated property, he or she will recognize the gain upon the subsequent sale of the property.

On the other hand, the trustee has the option (by election) to report the gain on the entity level. By making the election, the trust is deemed to have sold the property to the recipient beneficiary for fair market value. As a consequence of this election, the amount of the distribution deduction and the amount includible in the beneficiary's gross income is the fair market value of the property (subject to the DNI rules discussed above). The beneficiary's basis in the property is its fair market value.

The availability of this election provides an important planning opportunity or tax trap with respect to appreciated property held in trust. If the election is not made, by subsequent sale, the unrealized gain would be recognized by the beneficiary. Conversely, if the election is made, the unrealized gain would be recognized by the trust rather than the beneficiary. However, as discussed above, the threshold for the imposition of the NIIT is much lower for a trust than it is for an individual. So to the extent that the deemed sale by the trust would generate capital gain, the trust may be subject to the NIIT. On the other hand, if the property was sold by an individual beneficiary with income levels below the applicable threshold, there would not be any NIIT triggered by the sale.

Example: Jane Smith transferred stock with a fair market value of $100,000 and a basis of $25,000 to the newly created Smith Trust. The transfer had no income tax consequences to either Jane or the trust.

Ten years later, when the stock was worth $150,000 and the trust had DNI of $15,000, the trustee distributed the stock to the beneficiary. Since the amount distributed to the beneficiary is the lesser of the basis in the stock ($25,000) or its fair market value ($150,000), the beneficiary is deemed to have received $25,000. However, because DNI ($15,000) is less than the amount distributed, the beneficiary includes $15,000 in gross income (the remaining $10,000 of the distribution is considered to be an income tax-free gift). The beneficiary's basis in the stock is $25,000 (carried over from the trust). Correspondingly, the trust is entitled to a $15,000 distribution deduction. So, if the beneficiary were to sell the stock for its fair market value, the beneficiary would report $125,000 of long term capital gain. If the beneficiary were single and had additional income of $75,000 or less, the beneficiary would not be subject to NIIT.[26]

If, in the alternative, the trustee elects to report the gain (as if it sold the stock to the beneficiary), the beneficiary is deemed to receive a distribution of the fair market value of the stock ($150,000). However, because DNI ($15,000) is less than the amount distributed (DNI was not increased because capital gain is usually excluded from DNI), the beneficiary includes $15,000 in gross income (the remaining $135,000 is considered to be an income tax-free gift). The trust reports capital gain of $125,000 ($150,000 - $25,000) and is entitled to a distribution deduction of $15,000. In this scenario, the $125,000 of capital gain is net investment income. Since the threshold for the imposition of the NIIT is $12,500, most of the capital gain income would be taxed at 23.8 percent.

SIXTY-FIVE DAY RULE

As of the last day of the tax year, trustees who are required to distribute trust income to beneficiaries may not know how much trust income the trust generated. To provide additional time, there is a sixty-five day period beyond the close of the tax year to make the necessary determinations and make the appropriate distributions. By election made by the trustee on Form 1041 (trust income tax return), the amounts distributed during that period are deemed to be paid on the last day of the previous tax year.[27]

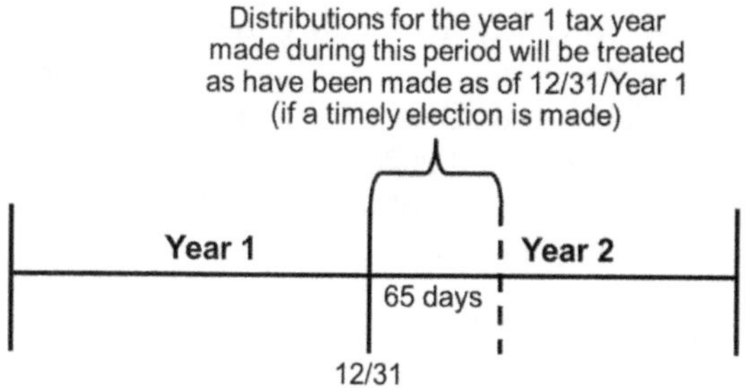

FILING TRUST INCOME TAX RETURNS

The trustee is responsible for filing the Form 1041 and paying the tax owed. If the tax is not paid by the trust, transferee liability may attach to the assets distributed to the beneficiaries (who may be ultimately responsible to pay the tax).[28] With the exception of wholly charitable trusts, a trust must use a calendar year as its tax year. Although most trusts are cash basis taxpayers, trusts with substantial business and real estate holdings sometimes use the accrual basis.

Because trusts are separate taxable entities (apart from their beneficiaries), the beneficiaries do not receive the benefits of trust losses until the trust is terminated. Similar to other taxpayers, trust net operating losses may be carried back two years and forward twenty years. Net capital losses may be carried forward indefinitely. When a trust is terminated, any unused losses are allocated to the beneficiaries in proportion to the amount of corpus each beneficiary receives when the trust is terminated.

INCOME TAX ISSUES UNIQUE TO AN ESTATE

Fiscal Tax Year

As discussed above, an estate is taxed in the same manner as a complex trust.[29] Unlike a trust, however, an estate can use a fiscal year rather than a calendar year as its taxable year. Thus, the executor's ability to elect a fiscal year provides an opportunity to defer the reporting of income by a beneficiary of the estate to a future year or otherwise create a favorable tax-year.

Example: Ashley died on November 26, 2019. Ashley's executor elected a fiscal year ending November 30th as the estate's tax year. As a result, the estate's first tax year was only five days. On December 4, 2019, the executor distributed interest income generated by the estate to the beneficiary, Asher. Because the estate's second tax year began on December 1 and does not end until November 30, 2020, the distribution Asher received in 2019 is not reportable by him until his 2020 tax year.

Qualified Revocable Trust

A qualified revocable trust is a trust treated as owned by a decedent by virtue of the power to revoke the trust during life. At election of the executor and trustee, the trust is treated as part of the estate for purposes of filing an income tax return.[30] The election is valid for two years from the earlier of the date of death or six months after the final determination of estate tax liability. There are several tax advantages in making this election. As discussed above, an estate may elect a fiscal year as its tax year. Because the trust is deemed to be part of the estate, the trustee can take advantage of that benefit. Thus, there is the possibility of deferring income distributable from the trust to a beneficiary to a future tax year. Another advantage is the charitable set aside deduction can be made by the trust.[31]

Estimated Payments

Unlike a trust, an estate is not required to make estimated quarterly tax payments until the third year following the decedent's death (assuming it is in existence that long).[32] Moreover, in the estate's final tax year, the executor may elect to treat any portion of an estimated payment made by the estate as an estimated payment made by a beneficiary. If this election is made, the payment is treated as a distribution (potentially taxable) to the beneficiary as if it were paid on the last day of the taxable year.[33]

WHERE CAN I FIND OUT MORE?

1. FDIC, *Trust Examination Manual,* available at: https://www.fdic.gov/regulations/examinations/trustmanual/index/html.

2. Keene, David, "A Primer on the Uniform Principal and Income Act: How Accounting Affects Trust and Estate Beneficiaries," from Leimberg & LeClair available at: http://www.leimberg.xom/freeresources/truarticles/primeronuniformprincipal.html.

FREQUENTLY ASKED QUESTIONS

Question – Considering that the trust tax brackets are far more compressed than individual tax brackets and that the 3.8 percent net investment income tax is triggered at a much lower threshold, how can trusts be used to save income tax?

Answer – There are several ways trusts can save tax. First, if a trust distributes all its income, the individual beneficiaries who may be in lower tax brackets would pay the tax on the income. Many trusts, including simple trusts and trusts that qualify for the estate and marital deduction (QTIPs) are required to distribute all income annually. Also, many complex trusts provide the trustee with the authority to make discretionary income distributions.

Second, if the trust is a grantor trust, the trust's income is taxed to the grantor rather than to the trust and the trust and estate tax brackets do not apply.

Third, by investing in tax-exempt securities or growth assets (that do not generate significant income), the taxable income of the trust will be limited.

Fourth, high income taxpayers can receive a small amount of "bracket-ride" by shifting income producing assets to complex trusts. For example, a taxpayer subject to the 37 percent federal tax bracket can shift $12,500 of income to a complex trust and save a small amount of income tax.

CHAPTER ENDNOTES

1. IRC Secs. 642(e) and 642(f).
2. IRC Sec. 652(a).
3. Selling an item of principal is replacing one principal asset for another and therefore the gain is not usually considered fiduciary accounting income. However, in certain instances, the trust document or state law can cause or allow capital gains to be included in fiduciary accounting income.
4. Some trust documents state that capital gain is to be considered as trust income distributable to the beneficiaries. In that case, similar to other trust income, the beneficiaries of a simple trust would report that income.
5. IRC Sec. 67(e).
6. *Knight v. Commissioner*, 128 S. Ct. 782 (2008).
7. Treas. Reg. §1.67-4(b).
8. Reg. §1.67-4(b)(3).
9. IRC Sec. 642(b).
10. IRC Sec. 642(b)(2)(B).
11. IRC Sec. 642(b)(2)(A). Note that a trust that distributes all of its income in a given year is entitled to the $300 personal exemption of a simple trust.
12. IRC Sec. 62(b)(1).
13. With certain nuances, the computation of the distribution deduction of a complex trust or estate is similar to the computation of the distribution deduction of a simple trust.
14. IRC Secs. 651(a) and (b).
15. IRC Sec. 643(a).
16. IRC Sec. 651(b).
17. IRC Sec. 652(a).
18. IRC Sec. 652(b).
19. IRC Sec. 102(a).
20. Treas. Reg. §1.1411-3.
21. IRC Sec. 1411(a)(2)(B)(ii).
22. Treas. Reg. §1.1411-3(a)(1). Subchapter J deals exclusively with the taxation of trusts and estates and their beneficiaries. Treas. Reg. §1.1411-3(b)(1) lists the types of trusts and estates specific excluded from NIIT.
23. IRC Secs. 652(b) and 662(b).
24. Treas. Reg. §1.1411-3(e)(5), Example 2.
25. Treas. Reg. §1.663(b)-2.
26. IRC Sec. 1411(b)(3).
27. IRC Sec. 644.
28. Treas. Reg. § 1.641(b)-2.
29. However, the personal exemption of an estate is $600 as compared to the $300 personal exemption for a complex trust.
30. IRC Sec. 645.
31. IRC Sec. 642(c).
32. IRC Sec. 6654(l).
33. IRC Sec. 643(g).

INCOME AND DEDUCTIONS IN RESPECT OF A DECEDENT

CHAPTER 17

OVERVIEW OF INCOME IN RESPECT OF A DECEDENT

Just as no good deed goes unpunished, essentially no taxable income goes untaxed. With respect to a decedent, the date of death is the last day of his or her final tax year.[1] Therefore, items of gross income of a cash basis taxpayer that are not received prior to the date of death would not be includible on his or her final income tax return.[2] Any such item is referred to as *income in respect of a decedent* (IRD). Since such an item would not be taxable to the decedent, to ensure IRD is taxed, the individual or entity (trust or estate) that receives it must include it in gross income.[3]

Example: Sam Stone, a cash basis taxpayer, was a long-term agent for XYZ Insurance. Several weeks prior to his death, Sam closed one of the largest sales of his career earning him a first year commission of $50,000. Two months after Sam's death, the commission was paid to his estate. Consequently, the commission is treated as IRD and was not includible of Sam's final income tax return. Therefore, Sam's estate must include the bonus in gross income in the taxable year of receipt.

COMMON TYPES OF IRD

As discussed above, any type of taxable income that is not includible on the final income tax return of a cash basis decedent is IRD. Common examples of IRD are:

Salary, bonuses, commissions and payments for work in progress earned but not received at the time of death: Amounts contractually due but not paid at the death of an employee or an independent contractor are clearly items of IRD.[4] Case law has expended the scope of compensation treated as IRD to include voluntary payments (non-contractual) to a deceased employee's estate or spouse. Due to the employer/employee relationship, courts have held that amounts so paid because of a moral obligation or custom or policy are nonetheless compensation that would have been taxable as such had it been received by the decedent during lifetime.[5]

Employee Stock Options: This is another form of compensation and is usually an: (1) Incentive Stock Option (ISO) or (2) a Nonqualified Stock Option (NQSO). Both types of stock options grant the employee (in some cases non-employee consultants or board members) the right to purchase company stock at a price established at the time the option is granted. If certain requirements are met, ISOs may receive advantageous tax treatment.

The critical dates and tax consequences applicable to both types of stock options are summarized in Figure 17.1 (See Chapter 27 for a complete discussion of employee stock options).

If the owner of either type of stock option dies prior to exercise and the options survive his or her death, there is no taxable income to the decedent. In addition, there is no IRD. However, most stock options permit the decedent's estate to exercise surviving options within a defined period (three months is the statutory maximum for ISOs). As summarized in Figure 17.2, the exercise or sale of employee stock options may be subject to IRD treatment.

Interest Income: Because interest income generally accrues on a daily basis, interest accruing (but not paid) to a cash basis taxpayer as of the date of death is IRD.

Figure 17.1

CRITICAL DATE	NQSOs	ISOs
Grant or issuance of option	Not taxable	Not taxable
Expiration of option date	Not taxable	Not taxable
Exercise of option	Taxable as compensation (ordinary income) to the extent the FMV of the stock exceeds the exercise or option price.	Not subject to regular income tax, but is included in Alternative Minimum Taxable Income (AMTI) for Alternative Minimum Tax (AMT) purposes to the extent the FMV of the stock exceeds the exercise or option price.
Sale of option shares	Capital gain or loss measured by the difference between the FMV at exercise (basis) and proceeds from the sale. To qualify as a long term capital gain, the stock must be held for more than a year from the exercise date.	Ordinary compensation income if sold within two years from the grant of the option and one year of exercise. To qualify as long term capital gain, the stock must be sold after the 2yr/1yr holding period. Amount of the gain is the excess of the proceeds of sale over the exercise or option price (basis). For AMT purposes, gain or loss on the sale is the difference between the FMV at the date of exercise and proceeds from the sale.

Figure 17.2

CRITICAL DATE	NQSOs	ISOs
Exercise of option	Taxable as IRD to the extent of the FMV of the stock at the date of death exceeds the exercise or option price. Any additional appreciation of the stock between the date of death and the exercise date is ordinary income, but not IRD.	Not IRD and not subject to regular income tax, but includible as AMTI for AMT purposes to the extent FMV of the stock exceeds the exercise or option price.
Sale of option shares - NQSOs	No IRD – Capital gain or loss measured by the difference between FMV at the exercise date and proceeds of sale. Must hold stock for over one year from date of exercise to qualify for long term capital gain.	
Sale of ISOs before the end of the 2yr/1yr holding period		Ordinary IRD income, at least in part, if sold within two years from grant of option and one year of exercise. IRD amount is the excess of the FMV at the date of death over the exercise or option price. Any additional appreciation between the date of death and the exercise date is ordinary income but not IRD.
Sale of ISOs after the 2yr/1yr holding period		No IRD for regular income tax purposes. Long term capital gain is sold after the 2yr/1yr holding period. Amount of gain is the excess of the proceeds of sale over the exercise or option price. For AMT purposes, gain or loss on the sale is difference between the FMV at the date of exercise and the sale proceeds.

Meriting separate discussion are the rules regarding "original issue discount" and U.S. Savings Bonds.

Original Issue Discount: The most common example of an "original issue discount" (OID) instrument is a "zero coupon" bond. The bond is purchased at a discount, i.e., an amount that is less than the face amount due at maturity. Between the time of issuance and maturity, no interest is paid to the bond holder. For tax purposes, the difference between the face amount and the discount price is treated as interest earned, but not payable until maturity. For example, the difference between a zero coupon bond with a face amount of $1,000 (due at maturity) and the discount purchase price of $800 is $200 of interest.

With regard to the inclusion of the interest income, all taxpayers (cash and accrual basis) must recognize the income as it is earned, on a daily basis, over the life of the bond.[6] Therefore, similar to an accrual basis taxpayer, a cash basis taxpayer would be required to include all interest accruing to the date of death on his or her final income tax return. As a result, OID interest can never be IRD.

U.S. Savings Bonds: Although many U.S. Savings bonds, such as Series EE bonds are similar to OID instruments because they pay no interest until maturity, they are not subject to the OID rules.[7] This means that the interest accrued as of the owner's date of death would be IRD. However, a cash basis taxpayer may elect to recognize income as it accrues.[8] From a planning perspective, if the decedent did not have a significant amount of income to report in his or her final tax year, it may be prudent for the executor make the election. This way the interest reportable by the decedent may trigger little or no tax rather than it being taxable to a beneficiary as IRD who may be in a higher tax bracket.

Dividend Income: Whether dividend income is considered to be IRD or is reportable on the decedent's final income tax returns depends on the interplay of (1) the date of death; (2) dividend declaration date; (3) record date (the date on which owners of record are legally entitled to dividends) ; and (4) dividend payment date.

- If decedent dies after the dividend declaration date but before the record date, ordinary income to the recipient, but not IRD (because on the record date, the decedent's successor in interest rather than the decedent was the owner of record).
- If the decedent dies after the record date but before the dividend payment date, the dividend is IRD.
- If the record date is not fixed, the declaration date is the decisive date. Therefore,
  - o If the decedent dies before the declaration date, ordinary income to the recipient, but not IRD.
  - o If the decedent dies after the declaration date but before the payment date, the dividend is IRD.

Retirement Distributions: With the exception of contributions made by the decedent with after-tax dollars, distributions received by an estate or beneficiary from a qualified retirement plan of the decedent is IRD. Qualified retirement plans include employer or union pension and profit sharing plans, 401(k) and 403(b) plans, self-employed Keogh plans and IRAs.

Unrealized appreciation in employer securities held in a retirement plan that are distributed as a lump sum to the original owner or at death to beneficiaries receive special tax treatment. Only the cost basis of the securities (the FMV of the securities as of the date placed into the account), plus the value of other assets or money received is taxable at the time of distribution. Any appreciation in the employer securities accruing after they were contributed to the plan is not taxable until the securities are sold or otherwise disposed of by the distributee.

The IRD element is the amount of unrealized appreciation of those securities as of the date of death that is taxable upon the sale or other disposition of the securities. Any post-date of death appreciation would not be treated as IRD and would generate capital gain when sold. Therefore, a subsequent sale of employer securities could result in both IRD income and capital gain.

Income from pass-through entities. Income from a pass-through entity is taxable to the owners or beneficiaries of the entity. Pass-through entities include partnerships, S Corporations, Limited Liability Companies (LLCs usually taxed as a partnership or S Corporation), estates and trusts. Pass-through income received by the decedent's estate or beneficiaries of the decedent vary among entity types.

Partnerships (including LLCs taxed as partnerships). At the death of a partner, the decedent's interest in the partnership effectively terminates. Accordingly, a partnership Form K-1 (reporting the decedent's distributive share of partnership income) will be issued in the name of the decedent for the portion of the tax year ending on the date of death to be included on the decedent's final return. As to the estate or other successor in interest, a separate Form K-1 will be issued for the balance of the tax year. None of the income is IRD.

With respect to distributions in liquidation of a decedent's partnership interest, whether they are treated as IRD to the successor in interest depends on the nature of the distribution.

- If the amount received is considered a distributive share of partnership income,[9] it is IRD.[10] For example, this would be the result if a partnership agreement stated that the estate or beneficiaries of the deceased partner are entitled to what would have been the deceased partner's distributive share of income for the next three years.

- The receipt of a guaranteed payment[11] due but not paid to the decedent prior to death would be IRD.[12]

- There is no IRD with respect to payments in exchange for a deceased partner's interest in partnership property[13] unless:

  - o the payments are attributed to "hot assets" such as unrealized receivables, or

  - o the payments are in exchange for goodwill, unless the partnership agreement provides for such payments, but only if:

    - ♦ capital is not a material income-producing factor (e.g., a law firm partnership or other personal service partnership); and

    - ♦ the deceased partner was a general partner.[14]

S Corporations. Similar to a partnership, the death of an S Corporation shareholder terminates the shareholder's interest in the corporation. A Form K-1 will be issued reporting the decedent's distributive share of the S Corporation income up to the date of death. As to the estate or other successor in interest, a separate Form K-1 will be issued for the balance of the tax year. None of the income is IRD.

However, a person obtaining a decedent's S Corporation stock must recognize as IRD the deceased shareholder's share of items that would have been IRD if such items were obtained directly from the decedent.[15] For example, the decedent shareholder's share of the income generated from the unrealized receivables of a cash basis S Corporation will result in IRD to the successor beneficiary just as if such person obtained the receivables directly from the decedent.

Estates and Trusts. In the year of death, even if the will or trust instrument requires all income to be distributed, a beneficiary of an estate or trust reports income only to the extent distributions are actually received. To the extent that income required to be distributed is distributed after the decedent beneficiary's death, the distribution received by the ultimate beneficiary is IRD.[16]

Installment Sale Notes. Installment reporting allows a taxpayer to ratably include in income the profit from the sale of property as the proceeds are received over a period of years. For example, assume that a taxpayer sells property with a $10,000 basis for $100,000 to be paid in $20,000 annual installments over five years. The taxpayer's gross profit ratio is 90 percent ($90,000 total gain divided by $100,000, which are the total proceeds). In each year, the taxpayer will include 90 percent of the payment ($18,000) in income and exclude 10 percent of the payment ($2,000) as a recovery of basis. Thus, over five years, the taxpayer would include $90,000 in income ($18,000 × 5) and recover $10,000 basis ($2,000 × 5).

The profit component of an unpaid installment obligation transmitted at death (the difference between the face amount of the obligation and the decedent's basis) is IRD.[17] So, as installment payments are paid, the recipient includes the profit component in gross income.

IRD issues with respect to insurance proceeds and the transfer of value rules. Generally, the death benefits received by the beneficiary of a life insurance policy are tax-free.[18] A major exception to the tax-free receipt of death benefits is a "transfer for value."[19] The transfer for value rules apply when a life insurance policy is transferred in exchange for consideration and none of the exceptions apply. The following is a simple example of the transfer for value rules.

Example: Mable Jacobs, the insured, age ninety-five, owned a $500,000 life insurance policy with a cash value of $275,000. To raise money to pay medical bills, Mabel sold the policy to Sally Jones, a friend, for $300,000. Upon the sale, Mable would recognize $40,000 of ordinary income (the difference between the sales price $300,000 and her basis, $260,000, i.e., the aggregate amount of insurance premium payments she made over the term of the policy).

Two months later, Mable died. Due to the transfer for value rules, the receipt of the death benefits are not totally tax-free to Sally. Having paid no additional insurance premiums after the sale, Sally would recognize $200,000 of income, the difference between the death benefits received ($500,000) and the amount she paid for the policy ($300,000).

If the purchaser of a life insurance policy dies before the insured's death, there may be an element of IRD.

Example: If Sally died one month after purchasing the policy from Mabel who in turn died one month later, Sally's estate would receive the $500,000 death benefit on Mabel's life. At the time of Sally's death (prior to Mabel's death), the value of the life insurance policy was $350,000. So the estate would have to report $200,000 of income, the difference between the death benefit and the purchase price. Of that amount, $50,000 would be IRD (representing the appreciation of the life insurance policy as of the date of Sally's death). The balance of $150,000 would be non-IRD income taxable to the estate.

CHARACTER OF IRD

Generally, the character of IRD income to the recipient is the same as the character of the income to the decedent had the decedent lived to receive it.[20] Therefore, qualified dividends and long term capital gain retain their character meaning they would be taxed to the recipient at the maximum capital gain/qualified dividend tax rate of 20 percent. Also, those items would be included in the recipient's net investment income potentially subject to the 3.8 percent net investment income tax rate.[21]

A notable exception to this rule, however, is self-employment income subject to self-employment tax. Self-employment tax is imposed on gross income derived from carrying on a trade or business. This means it is imposed on the individual who actually performed those services. So, the ultimate recipient of self-employment IRD income is not the one who performed those services. For that reason, although such income would be subject to regular income tax as IRD, it would not be subject to self-employment tax.[22]

Example: During life, Asher was an independent contractor providing IT services. Upon his death, he was entitled to receive $10,000 for services rendered. Ultimately, Asher's estate received the payment. As IRD, the estate must include it in gross income. However, because it was self-employment income earned by Asher in carrying on his trade or business, it would not be subject to self-employment tax.

Importantly, since by definition IRD are items of income that would have been included in the decedent's gross income had the decedent been alive to receive them, tax-exempt interest and other items specifically excluded from gross income are not IRD. Therefore, these items are not taxable to the recipient.

WHO PAYS INCOME TAX ON IRD AND WHEN IS IT TRIGGERED?

Generally, IRD is taxable to the individual or entity who receives it in the tax year it is received. In other words, IRD is not recognized as income until the underlying payment is actually or constructively received. So, whether the IRD recipient is a cash or accrual basis taxpayer, IRD income is not recognized until it is received. Similar to any property of a decedent, IRD passes to a beneficiary by will, inheritance, beneficiary designation or operation of law. Common recipients of IRD include the following:

1. Decedent's probate estate.

2. Inter vivos trust – A trust created during the decedent's lifetime to hold certain assets and to receive assets at the decedent's death (including the right to receive income). Such trusts

essentially serve as the decedent's probate estate with respect to such assets.

3. An individual beneficiary of the probate estate or testamentary trust that acquires the right to the IRD before payment had been made.

4. A named successor beneficiary of a qualified retirement plan or IRA.

5. A person who obtains the right to income by "operation of law." For example, an individual who was a joint owner with the decedent of a Series EE bond with the right of survivorship would become the sole owner of the bond at the decedent's death.

Because an estate can elect a fiscal taxable year, there is some flexibility with respect to reporting the IRD.

Example: Joe Miller died on November 28. 2017. In December 2019 his estate received a $20,000 bonus (IRD) from Joe's employer for services rendered prior to Joe's death. If the estate elects a calendar year, the IRD would be included in 2019. On the other hand, if the estate elects a fiscal year ending November 30, the first tax year of the estate would end on November 30, 2019 before the receipt of the bonus. Therefore, the IRD received by the estate in December would be taxable in the following tax year ending on November 30, 2020.

Distributee from Probate Estate: If the estate distributes the right to receive IRD to an individual, trust, etc. to satisfy an inheritance, devise, or devise, the recipient reports the income in the tax year of receipt.[23]

Distributee of IRD upon death of successor-in-interest. If an individual with the right to receive IRD dies prior to receipt of the IRD payment and that right passes to another individual, the IRD will not be includible in gross income until that individual receives it, provided

1. the right to receive the IRD was acquired from the original decedent by bequest, devise, or inheritance, and

2. the IRD was never included in the taxable income of the original decedent or first successor.[24]

Person acquiring right to IRD by reason of decedent's death (e.g., named beneficiary of IRA). This includes IRD that passes by beneficiary designation. For example, an individual named as the successor beneficiary of an IRA or retirement plan is taxed as he or she receives distributions.[25]

Person receiving IRD in satisfaction of a pecuniary (fixed dollar amount) bequest. If an item of IRD is distributed to an individual in satisfaction of a pecuniary bequest (i.e., a bequest of an amount of money that is satisfied via a transfer of a right to receive IRD), the transferor (usually the estate) recognizes income in an amount equal to the present value of the IRD. In other words, even though the IRD has not yet been paid, the use of the IRD to satisfy an unrelated bequest accelerates the income recognition.

Example: Per his will, Uncle Melvin left his nephew, Harry Henshaw, a specific bequest of $10,000. At Melvin's death, he was entitled to a $10,000 commission (IRD) payable within six months. In lieu of payment, the executor assigned Harry the right to receive the $10,000 commission. At the time of the assignment, the present value of the future payment of the commission was $9,750. As a result of transferring the IRD in satisfaction of Harry's pecuniary bequest, the estate must recognize $9,750 of ordinary income.

Transfer of IRD prior to receipt. If an item of IRD is transferred for any reason other than the consequence of the decedent's death, the transferor must recognize income in an amount equal to the fair market value of the IRD right.[26]

Example: At Ashley's death in 2018, Asher became entitled to receive her bonus check of $10,000 not due until January 1, 2020. In 2019, Asher transfers his right to receive it to Joel in order to repay a $10,000 loan. By virtue of the transfer, Asher must include the fair market value of the IRD in gross income reportable in 2019. Similarly, if Asher had transferred his right to receive Ashley's bonus check to Joel as a gift, the result would the same – Asher would include the fair market value of the IRD in gross income in the year it was gifted.

OVERVIEW OF DEDUCTIONS IN RESPECT OF A DECEDENT

Similar to IRD, a cash basis taxpayer may have incurred deductible expenses that were not paid by the decedent prior to death. Thus, those deductible expenses may not be claimed on the decedent's final income tax return. Such deductible expenses are referred to as *deductions in respect of a decedent* (DRD). Items of DRD are deductible by the payor of those expenses.[27]

Example: In earning the $50,000 commission, Sam incurred $6,000 of deductible business expenses that were not paid prior to his death. Subsequently, the estate paid those expenses, and, thus, were deductible on the estate's Form 1041 in the tax year in which they were paid.

Like IRD, DRD is generally deductible in the year of payment. As a result, even if the person ultimately making the payment is an accrual basis taxpayer, the DRD is deductible only when paid. Importantly, if property passing from the decedent is subject to a liability that is deductible DRD, the payment of the liability by the recipient of the property is deductible in the year paid,[28] even if there was no IRD received with respect to the property.

SPECIFIC DEDUCTIBLE ITEMS OF DRD

The expenses that may be deducted as DRD are specifically listed in IRC Section 691(b). These expenses include:

1. ordinary and necessary business expenses,[29]
2. interest expense,[30]
3. taxes,[31]
4. investment expenses,[32] and
5. depletion.[33]

DEDUCTION FOR IRD INCLUDED IN THE RECIPIENT'S GROSS INCOME TO MITIGATE DOUBLE TAXATION

In essence, an item of IRD is a decedent's right to receive a sum of money. Thus, in addition to IRD being taxable to the ultimate recipient, its value is includible in the decedent's gross estate potentially subject to estate tax. Similarly, a deductible item of DRD that is paid satisfies a debt of the decedent's estate. Therefore, the amount of the DRD is deductible from the decedent's gross estate.

Example: For estate tax purposes, Sam who was entitled but had not yet received a $50,000 commission must have the right to that commission included in his gross estate. Similarly, the $6,000 of business expenses incurred but unpaid prior to his death are a deductible claim from his gross estate. So, for income tax purposes, upon the receipt of the commission and the payment of expenses, the estate has net taxable income of $44,000. In addition, for estate tax purposes, there would be a net inclusion of $44,000 in Sam's gross estate.

As illustrated above, IRD is subject to income tax and potentially estate tax. The rationale for a double tax is sound. In the previous example, had Sam received the commissions and paid the expenses prior to his death, he would have included $44,000 in gross income. Additionally, the net amount would have been included in his gross estate. So in that sense, the concept of IRD and DRD achieves the same end result.

However, with the high estate exclusion as indexed for inflation ($11,580,000 in 2020) together with the portability of the unused exemption amount of a deceased spouse, the imposition of an estate tax is less likely. In any event, for those estates subject to estate tax, double taxation is mitigated by allowing an income tax deduction to the recipient of IRD (net of any DRD paid by the recipient) for the estate tax attributable to the inclusion of such IRD in the gross estate.[34]

To determine the amount of estate tax attributable to the IRD, the estate tax is computed with and without the IRD.

Example: The estate of Murray Lang included a $50,000 bonus (IRD) Murray was owed but had not received as of the date of his death. The bonus was ultimately paid to his son, Ron. The total estate tax paid by Murray's estate was $125,000. To compute the income tax deduction, the estate tax is recomputed without including the $50,000 bonus receivable. Since the estate was subject to a marginal estate tax bracket of 40 percent applicable to the entire $50,000 bonus, the recomputed estate tax was $105,000, or a difference of $20,000. Therefore, for the year in which Ron received the bonus, his income tax return would include IRD of $50,000 and a $20,000 deduction for estate tax attributable to the inclusion of IRD in the gross estate.

Importantly, for individuals, the deduction is an itemized deduction.[35] Therefore, if an individual does not itemize, the deduction will be wasted. Therefore, a taxpayer who anticipates such a deduction should manage income and other deductions so as to receive the maximum tax benefit from such deduction.

CHAPTER ENDNOTES

1. Treas. Reg. §1.443-1(a)(2).
2. Although date of death is the last day of a decedent's last income tax return, the income tax return is nonetheless due on the regular due date. For example, if a decedent died on January 2, 2015, his or her income tax return would be due on April 15, 2016. Treas. Reg. §1.443-1(a)(2).
3. IRC Sec. 691(a).
4. Treas. Reg. §1.691(a)-1(d).
5. See *e.g. Rollert v. Comm'r.*, 752 F.2d 1128 (6th Cir. 1985), *aff'g* 80 TC 619 (1983). Even in cases in which a voluntary discretionary payment was not included in the employee's gross estate (due to lack of an enforceable right), courts have held the payment to be IRD. See *e.g. Kramer v. U.S.*, 406 F.2d 1363 (6th Cir. 1969)
6. IRC Sec. 1272(a).
7. IRC Sec. 1272(a)(2)(B).
8. IRC Sec. 454(a).
9. IRC Sec. 736(a)(1).
10. IRC Sec. 753.
11. IRC Sec. 736(a)(2).
12. IRC Sec. 753.
13. IRC Sec. 736(b).
14. IRC Secs. 736(b)(2) and (b)(3).
15. IRC Sec. 1367(b)(4).F.
16. Treas. Reg. §1.691(c)-2.
17. IRC Sec. 691(a)(4).
18. IRC Sec. 101(a)(1).
19. IRC Sec. 101(a)(2).
20. IRC Sec. 691(a)(3).
21. Treas. Reg. §1.691(a)-1(d).
22. Rev. Rul. 59-162, 1959-1, CB. 224.
23. Treas. Reg. §1.691(a)(4)(b)(3).
24. Treas. Reg. §1.691(a)-1(c).
25. IRC Sec. 691(a)(1).
26. IRC Sec. 691(a)(2).
27. IRC Sec. 691(b).
28. IRC Sec. 691(b)(1)(B).
29. Trade or business expenses of the decedent deductible pursuant to IRC Sec. 162.
30. Interest expense incurred by the decedent deductible pursuant to IRC Sec. 163.
31. Taxes (such as property tax) deductible pursuant to IRC Sec. 164.
32. Investment expenses of the decedent deductible pursuant to IRC Sec. 212.
33. Depletion deductible pursuant to IRC Sec. 611.
34. IRC Sec. 691(c).
35. But not a miscellaneous deduction subject to the 2 percent adjusted gross income floor. IRC Sec. 67(b)(7).

ACCOUNTING METHODS AND TIMING ISSUES

CHAPTER 18

INTRODUCTION

For tax reporting purposes, an accounting method is a set of rules used to determine when and how income and expenses are reported. Although no single method is required of all taxpayers, each taxpayer must use a method that clearly reflects income and expenses and use that method consistently.

There are two basic accounting methods:

- **Cash Method:** Under the cash method, income is reported in the tax period during which it is received. Expenses are deducted in the tax period during which they are paid. The cash method is simple, and is used by most individual taxpayers. Under certain circumstances, some taxpayers may not use the cash method.

- **Accrual Method:** Under the accrual method, income is reported in the tax period during which it is earned, even if it is not received until a subsequent tax year. Expenses are deducted in the tax period during which they are incurred, whether or not they are paid that year. Although the accrual method more realistically matches income and expenses, it is more complicated.

Regardless of the taxpayer's method of accounting, there are certain transactions that require all taxpayers to use special and hybrid (combination) methods of accounting. For example, certain long-term contracts (see below) and installment sales (see Chapter 30) require special accounting methods that all taxpayers must use in reporting these transactions There are also special uniform capitalization methods of accounting for certain direct and indirect costs allocable to real and tangible personal property produced by the taxpayer. See the discussion of the UNICAP rules below.

WHAT ARE THE CONSIDERATIONS FOR A TAXPAYER TO USE ONE METHOD OF ACCOUNTING OR THE OTHER?

1. Because the cash method is relatively straightforward and easy to implement, it may be appropriate for any individual or a small business not precluded from using that method.

2. Generally, a business that produces, purchases, or sells merchandise is required to use the accrual method for sales and purchases of the business inventory. However, as discussed below, there are exceptions for certain *qualifying taxpayers* and *qualifying small business taxpayers.*

3. Generally, a C corporation or a partnership with a C corporation partner with *average annual gross receipts* exceeding $5 million is required to use the accrual method.

4. A *family corporation* engaged in farming with gross receipts of $25 million or less for each prior tax year after 1985 may use the cash method. This is discussed further below.

5. A *qualified personal service corporation* may use the cash method regardless of its gross receipts. This is discussed further below.

6. An entity classified as a *tax shelter* must use the accrual method of accounting.[1]

7. A taxpayer who spends money to acquire, produce, or improve tangible property that are otherwise deductible may have to capitalize all or some of

those costs under the Code section 263A uniform capitalization rules which require a special uniform capitalization method of accounting (see below).

TIMING OF INCOME AND DEDUCTIONS

Regardless of the taxpayer's method of accounting, being able to control the timing of income and deductions may result in tax savings or take advantage of the time value of money.

Saving Taxes. Taxes may be saved when income is shifted to a year in which tax rates are lower. Taxes may also be saved when deductions are shifted to a year in which tax rates are higher. Tax amounts are indexed for inflation and may be higher or lower based on changes in tax laws from year to year. Additionally, taxes can be saved by controlling the amount of income or deductions in a year so that certain tax benefits can be achieved. For example, medical deductions are generally limited to the amount of medical expenses in excess of 10 percent of adjusted gross income. So, to reduce taxable income, a taxpayer may shift relatively large medical expenses to a tax year in which adjusted gross income is lower to maximize the deductibility of those medical expenses.

Benefits of Deferring Due to Time Value of Money. If tax rates remain level, by accelerating deductions into an earlier year and shifting income into a later year effectively defers taxes to that later year. By doing so, the taxpayer can invest the tax money deferred to earn additional income. If tax rates are lower in later years, the shifting described above would save additional taxes. On the other hand, if tax rates are higher in the later year, the time value of the early year tax savings must be weighed against the cost of paying increased taxes in the later tax years.

WHEN IS THE TIMING OF INCOME AND DEDUCTIONS AN EFFECTIVE TAX SAVINGS STRATEGY?

1. If Congress increases tax rates prospectively, the taxpayer should consider accelerating income and deferring deductions before the changes take full effect. Conversely, if Congress decreases tax rates prospectively, the taxpayer should consider deferring income and accelerating deductions to the tax years in which those lower rated come into effect.

2. The income of some taxpayers is subject to fluctuation. Income might fluctuate due to a loss of a job or a job change, because of the nature of the job (e.g., commissions are not level), general economic conditions (e.g., an upturn or a downturn), when a spouse starts or stops working, on account of disability, or at retirement. If income is projected to be high in one particular year and lower in another year, the taxpayer should consider moving income out of and deductions into the higher income year. When income is low in a particular year, the taxpayer should consider moving income into and deductions out of that year.

3. As discussed above, even if the taxpayer's tax rates stay the same, the taxpayer should consider deferring income and accelerating deductions to take advantage of the time value of money.

4. There are a number of special provisions for deferring income discussed elsewhere in this book. Retirement plans, including individual retirement accounts and qualified plans are often used to defer income to later in life when taxable income and tax liability are less than it was in a taxpayer's younger more productive years. Installment sales may be used to spread out the gain derived from the sale of assets over the years in which payments are received. A like-kind exchange of property can be used to postpone recognition of gain until the replacement property is disposed of in a taxable transaction (such as a sale). Sale of property to a charity in return for a charitable annuity or contribution of appreciated property to a charitable remainder trust can be used to obtain a current income tax charitable deduction while deferring recognition of gain from the property until later years. Nonqualified deferred compensation, discussed in *The Tools & Techniques of Employee Benefit and Retirement Planning*, is another way to defer income until a later year. Annuities, discussed in *The Tools & Techniques of Life Insurance Planning*, allow income to be deferred until annuity payments are received.

THE CASH METHOD

Advantages

1. The cash method of accounting is relatively straightforward and easy to implement.

2. As discussed above, timing of both income and deductions is important. The cash method of

accounting provides a limited but useful amount of planning flexibility in postponing income or accelerating deductions. As discussed below, there are ways to postpone income by delaying receipt of income, including *constructive receipt* to a later tax period. Similarly, with some exceptions, deductible expenses attributable to a later tax period may be accelerated into the current tax period by paying expenses before the close of the tax period.

The Fundamentals of the Cash Method

1. **Income.** All items of income are included in the taxpayer's gross income during the tax year such income is actually or constructively received. Income is constructively received when it is credited to a taxpayer's account, set apart, or otherwise made available without restriction, even if the taxpayer does not actually take physical possession of the income until after the close of the tax year.

2. **Deductions.** Generally, expenses are deductible in the tax year in which they are actually paid. For example, for the 2019 tax year, a cash method taxpayer can deduct a January 2020 utility payment made in December 2019. But under some circumstances, to avoid a distortion of taxable income and for other reasons, the acceleration of deductions are restricted. For example, prepaid interest or rent generally cannot be deducted until the expense is accrued or incurred. Investment interest expense is not deductible unless there is investment income to offset the deduction (see Chapter 7). Passive losses may not be deducted until there is passive income. A taxpayer may deduct losses with respect to certain activities only to the extent the taxpayer is at risk (see Chapter 23). Only a limited amount of net capital losses are deductible in any year; otherwise such losses must be offset by capital gains or carried over to another year (see Chapter 4).

3. Any hybrid (combination) method of accounting which includes the cash method is treated as the cash method.

4. The following individuals and entities may generally use the cash method of accounting:

   - Individuals and sole proprietorships.

   - S corporations.

   - C corporations and partnerships, other than those engaged in the business of farming, that meets the *average annual gross receipts* test for every tax year after 1985 (1975 if engaged in the farming business).[2] A C corporation or partnership meets the test for a tax year if the average annual gross receipts from the three prior tax years do not exceed $5 million (or $1 million for those engaged in the business of farming).[3]

   - Partnerships, other than those engaged in the business of farming, without a C corporation as a partner, regardless of the gross receipts.

   - C corporations and partnerships engaged in the business of farming with *average annual gross receipts* not exceeding $1 million.

   - Family corporations, including those engaged in the business of farming, with gross receipts of $25 million or less for each prior tax year after 1985. A *family corporation* is a corporation of which at least 50 percent of the combined voting power of all voting stock and at least 50 percent of all classes of non-voting stock are owned directly or indirectly by members of the same family.[4] Members of a family include the taxpayer's siblings, parents' and grandparents' siblings, ancestors and lineal descendants, a spouse or estate of any of the foregoing.[5]

   - A qualified personal service corporation is a corporation in which at least 95 percent of the activities are performing services in the fields of health, veterinary services, law, engineering, surveying, architecture, accounting, actuarial science, performing arts, or consulting (the function test).[6] In addition, at least 95 percent of the stock must be owned directly or indirectly by employees performing services for the corporation in one of the fields described above, by retired employees who performed services in those fields, or by the estate of a former employee who performed services in those fields (the ownership test).[7] Ownership by any other person who acquired the stock by reason of the death of a former employee who performed services in one of the fields described above also counts toward the 95 percent, but only for the two-year period beginning on the date of death.

   - Qualifying taxpayer[8] or a qualifying small business taxpayer[9] engaged in an activity in which the production, purchase, or sale of merchandise is an income-producing factor in the taxpayer's business.[10] A taxpayer is a *qualifying taxpayer* if the taxpayer's *average annual gross receipts* do not exceed $1 million.[11] A taxpayer is a qualifying small business taxpayer if the taxpayer's *average annual gross receipts* do not exceed $10 million and the principal business activity for the prior tax year was not retailing, wholesaling, manufacturing, mining, publishing, or sound recording.[12]

Planning Strategies for a Cash Method Taxpayer: Accelerating or deferring income or deductions is often simply a matter of moving the income or deduction from one year to the next year, or vice versa. It can be as simple as shifting income or deductions from January of one year to December of the preceding year, or from December of one year to January of the following year. For example, stock could be sold in December 2019 or January 2020, depending on whether the taxpayer would pay less overall tax by reporting the capital gain in 2019 or 2020. Similarly, it may be advantageous for the taxpayer to receive a year-end bonus in either December of one year or January of the next year. Similarly, deductible real estate taxes or medical expenses could be paid in December 2019 or January 2020, depending on which year the deductions would be more advantageous. Similarly, charitable contributions could be made in either December of one year or January of the next year.

Example: Robin expects to be in the 25 percent marginal tax rate bracket in both 2019 and 2020. Therefore, the tax on her $10,000 bonus will be 2,500 whether it is paid on December 31, 2019 or January 2, 2020. However, by receiving the bonus in January 2020, the tax on her bonus will be deferred until she has to pay the tax on April 15, 2021. So, by deferring her bonus from one tax year to the next tax year, she will be able to invest the money and generate additional income. So from a time value of money perspective, postponing the tax disbursement on the deferred income is advantageous.

THE ACCRUAL METHOD

1. Because the purpose of the accrual method is to match income and expenses in the correct tax year, it better reflects the profitability of a business. For that reason, it may be preferable to the cash method that accounts for income and deductions based on receipts and payments (that may be unpredictable) so as to provide owners, suppliers, lenders, or potential buyers a meaningful picture of business operations.

2. Because the accrual method is generally required for non-tax reporting purposes, an accrual method taxpayer can use the same accounts for tax purposes. Conversely, a cash method business may have to keep two sets of accounts. Therefore, using the accrual method for tax purposes may result in some savings.

The Fundamentals of the Accrual Method

1. Generally, any taxpayer may use the accrual method of accounting.

2. **Income.** Generally, the taxpayer must include items of income in gross income in the tax year in which all events that fix the right to receive the income have occurred, provided the amount of income can be determined with reasonable accuracy. This is commonly referred to as the "all-events" test. If in one tax year, the taxpayer includes a reasonably estimated amount in gross income, but in a later tax year, the actual amount is determined to be different, the taxpayer must take the difference (plus or minus) into account in the later tax year.

Example: Joseph is a sole proprietor operating a small computer business. On December 30, 2019, Joseph sells one computer to Jill for $1,000 and a second computer to Jack for $1,500. Jill pays for the computer by check and takes it home immediately. Joseph deposits Jill's check for $1,000 on January 2, 2020.

On the other hand, Jack also takes his computer immediately, but asks Joseph to bill him. On January 2, 2020, Joseph bills Jack, receives payment back on January 29, 2020 and deposits the check on January 30, 2020.

If Joseph is a cash method taxpayer, he includes Jill's payment of $1,000 in gross income in 2019, the tax year of receipt even though he did not deposit her check until the next tax year. Because Joseph received the check in 2019, it does not matter when he deposited it. On the other hand, because of Jack's request not to be billed until 2020 and having received no payment from Jack in 2019, Joseph includes Jack's payment of $1,500 in gross income in 2020, the year of receipt.

Conversely, if Joseph is an accrual method taxpayer, Joseph includes both payments in gross income in 2019 because that is the year in which he sold and delivered the computers to Jack and Jill. Therefore, by virtue of delivering the two computers in sale transactions, 2019 is the tax year in which Joseph's right to the income was established.

---

3. **Deductions:** Generally, the taxpayer deducts expenses when the *all-events test* has been met and *economic performance* by the service or product provider has occurred. The all-events test is met when all events have occurred that fix the fact of liability, and the liability can be determined with reasonable accuracy.

Example: Asher is a sole proprietor who operates a bed and breakfast. On December 1, 2019, Asher hires Joel a plumber to fix a leaky pipe. Joel fixes the pipe on December 30, 2019. Asher pays Joel $1,000 for his services on January 4, 2020.

If Asher is an accrual method taxpayer, because his obligation to pay and economic performance occurred in 2019, Asher would deduct the $1,000 charge in 2019. On the other hand, if Asher was a cash method taxpayer, even though economic performance occurred in 2019, Asher did not actually pay the charge until 2020. For that reason, the $1,000 charge would not be deductible until 2020.

Limited Planning Opportunities. Because of the preciseness of the accrual method, the ability of a taxpayer to shift income and deductions from one tax year to another is very limited as compared to a taxpayer using the cash method of accounting.

ACCOUNTING METHODS UNDER THE 2017 TAX REFORM ACT

The 2017 Tax Reform Act created important changes for businesses that use both the cash basis and the accrual methods. Both are discussed below. Additionally, there are new options for dealing with long term contracts that are detailed in the FAQs at the end of this chapter. The new rules are effective for tax years beginning after December 31, 2017.

Businesses Using the Cash Basis Method

The 2017 Tax Act provides that the cash method of accounting can be used by taxpayers that satisfy the gross receipts test regardless of whether the purchase, production or sale of merchandise is an income producing factor. The gross receipts test allows taxpayers with annual average gross receipts that do not exceed $25 million for the three prior tax years (the "$25 million gross receipts test") to use the cash method. The $25 million amount is indexed for inflation beginning after 2018.[13]

As under prior law, qualified personal service corporations, partnerships without C corporation partners, S corporations, and other pass-through entities are allowed to use the cash method without regard to whether they meet the $25 million gross receipts test, so long as the use of such method clearly reflects income.

Taxpayers who meet the $25 million gross receipts test are also exempt from the application of IRC Section 263A uniform capitalization rules.[14] Previously existing exemptions that are not based on the taxpayer's gross receipts continue to apply.

These changes would be considered a change in accounting method that is made with the consent of the Treasury Secretary for IRC Section 481 purposes.[15]

Businesses Using the Accrual Method

Under the 2017 Tax Act, taxpayers that meet the $25 million gross receipts test (see above) are no longer required to account for inventory under IRC Section 471 and can instead use a method of accounting for inventory that either (1) treats inventory as non-incidental materials and supplies or (2) matches the taxpayer's method of inventory accounting as used for financial accounting purposes.[16] Under prior law, taxpayers were only permitted to account for inventory as materials and supplies that are non-incidental if they had average gross receipts of less than $10 million.[17]

Taxpayers that fail the $25 million gross receipts test are not eligible for the new rules governing inventory accounting. The $25 million threshold will be indexed annually for inflation.

UNIFORM CAPITALIZATION (UNICAP) RULES

The IRC Section 263A uniform capitalization, or UNICAP rules, were enacted by Congress as the result of the U.S. Supreme Court's decision in *Commissioner v. Idaho Power Company*.[18] To appreciate the impact of that case, it is necessary to understand that the depreciation recovery period of equipment is much shorter than the depreciation recovery period of a facility (i.e., a building). In other words, the annual depreciation deduction computed based on a short recovery period is greater than the annual depreciation deduction computed based on a much longer recovery period. As explained below, that was the issue of contention between the taxpayer and the IRS.

In *Idaho Power*, the taxpayer used its own equipment to construct its own facilities. For depreciation purposes, the taxpayer claimed annual depreciation deductions based on the relatively short recovery period of the equipment. Conversely, the IRS argued that the cost of such equipment should be added to the cost of the facilities. Effectively capitalized under IRC Section 263, the cost of the equipment would be depreciated over the much longer recovery period of facilities. Obviously, the annual depreciation deduction claimed by the taxpayer with respect to the equipment was greater than the annual depreciation deduction computed by capitalizing and adding the cost of the equipment to the building. The Supreme Court upheld the IRS position. By enacting IRC Section 263A, Congress codified the Supreme Court's holding and expanded it as discussed below.

Application of the UNICAP rules. The UNICAP rules are explained in a step by step analysis as follows:

Step 1 – Does the taxpayer produce or acquire any of the following in the course of a trade or business or an activity carried on for profit?

- Produce real or tangible personal property for use in the business or activity.
- Produce real or tangible personal property for sale to customers.
- Acquire property for resale. However, this rule does not apply to personal property if the taxpayer's average annual gross receipts are $10 million or less.

"Producing property" includes constructing, building, installing, manufacturing, developing, improving, creating, raising, or growing the property. Property produced for the taxpayer under a contract is treated as produced by the taxpayer to the extent the taxpayer makes payments or otherwise incurs costs in connection with the property.

"Tangible personal property" includes films, sound recordings, video tapes, books, artwork, photographs, or similar property containing words, ideas, concepts, images, or sounds.

Step 2 – Do any of the exceptions apply?

The UNICAP rules do not apply to:

- Resellers of personal property with average annual gross receipts of $10 million or less for the three prior tax years
- Property used for personal or non-business purposes or for purposes not connected with a trade or business or an activity conducted for profit
- Research and experimental expenditures deductible under Section 174
- Intangible drilling and development costs of oil and gas or geothermal wells or any amortization deduction allowable under Section 59(e) for intangible drilling, development, or mining exploration expenditures
- Property produced under a long-term contract, except for certain home construction contracts described in Section 460(e)(1)
- Timber and certain ornamental trees raised, harvested, or grown, and the underlying land
- Qualified creative expenses incurred as a freelance (self-employed) writer, photographer, or artist that are otherwise deductible
- Costs allocable to natural gas acquired for resale, to the extent these costs would otherwise be allocable to "cushion gas" stored underground
- Property produced if substantial construction occurred before March 1, 1986
- Property provided to customers in connection with providing services. It must be de minimis,

and not be inventory in the hands of the service provider

- Loan originations

- The costs of certain producers who use a simplified production method and whose total indirect costs are $200,000 or less

Step 3 – Identify the costs that must be capitalized and those that are currently deductible.

Importantly, only otherwise deductible items may be capitalized. So that determination must be made at the outset. In addition, any cost required to be capitalized under IRC Section 263A may not be included in inventory or charged to capital accounts or basis any earlier than the taxable year during which the amount is incurred within the meaning of Treasury regulation §1.446-1(c)(1)(ii).[19]

After meeting these threshold requirements, the resulting pool of costs are divided into three groups: (i) capitalizable costs, (ii) deductible costs, and (iii) indirect costs. IRC Section 263A requires the capitalization of direct and an allocable portion of the indirect costs that benefit or are incurred by reason of a production or resale activity. Deductible costs are currently deductible and are not capitalized.

Group 1. Capitalizable costs that are incurred for production and resale activities must be capitalized. Using inventory as an example, capitalizable costs include direct materials and direct labor used in production.[20]

Group 2. These are costs that are currently deductible and not allocated to inventory. Obviously, none of these costs are capitalized. Examples of these kinds of costs include:

- selling and distributing costs
- marketing
- advertising
- R&D expenses
- Section 179 costs
- Section 165 losses
- income taxes
- warranty and product liability costs

Also, costs associated with the following type of activities:

- overall management and policies
- strategic business planning
- general financial accounting
- personnel policy
- quality control policy
- internal audit[21]

Group 3. "Indirect costs" are costs that are indirectly attributable to inventory and must be capitalized. In other words, there may be a pool of costs that are indirectly related to various activities. A portion may be currently deductible and a portion must be capitalized.

The regulations list Group 3 type costs that must be bifurcated between capitalization and being currently deductible. Examples of such expenses are:

- indirect labor costs
- officer's compensation
- pension costs
- employee benefits
- rent
- depreciation
- real estate taxes
- utilities
- repairs and maintenance
- interest on debt
- quality control and inspection
- administrative costs
- insurance
- engineering and design[22]

Bifurcating Group 3 Indirect Costs

The regulations provide three different ways to bifurcate Group 3 indirect costs between capitalization and current deductibility. Those methods are:

- Burden rate and standard cost methods: Very complex methods that involve pre-established rates or standard allowances.

- Any reasonable allocation method. This method would appear to provide the taxpayer with some discretion in the allocation. According to the regulations, an allocation is reasonable if (a) the amount capitalized would not materially differ from the amount that would be capitalized using the burden rate or standard cost methods and (b) the method is applied consistently.

Example: Asher manufactures and sells widgets. He rents a huge building that he uses to manufacture the widgets and to provide office space for his employees. Of the total square footage of the building, Asher uses 45 percent for manufacturing and storage of the widgets. If Asher's rent and utility costs are $100,000 a year, the capitalization of 45 percent of those costs to Asher's inventory would be a reasonable method.

Allocating the Indirect Costs to Inventory

After completing the bifurcating process, the indirect costs allocated to inventory are referred to as "additional Section 263A costs." In filling out the cost of goods sold schedule attached to the tax return, there is a line item for additional Section 263A costs.

Allocate Additional Section 263A Costs to Ending Inventory

Since additional Section 263A costs are an increase in the cost of goods, a portion of those costs must be allocated to ending inventory. The formula to be used is (additional Section 263A costs)/ (cost of goods sold excluding beginning and ending inventory) * ending inventory.

Example: Asher is a sole proprietor manufacturing and selling widgets. In 2016, Asher incurred the following costs:

• Inventory Materials:	$1,000,000
• Inventory Direct: Labor	$500,000
• Warranty Costs:	$100,000
• Rent:	$100,000
• Utilities:	$30,000
• Advertising:	$10,000
• Officer Comp:	$250,000

Group 1: Capitalized costs of the widgets including materials and direct labor - $1,500,000. This is the amount of cost of goods without taking into account additional Section 263A costs.

Group 2: Costs that are totally deductible (do not have to be capitalized) include warranty costs and advertising.

Group 3: In this example, the indirect costs are the officer's compensation, rent and utilities. Using a reasonable method of allocation based on percentages, the officers spent 25 percent of their time on issues related to the production of widgets. So, based on that percentage, the amount of officer compensation (total $250,000) added to additional Section 263A costs would be $62,500. Of Asher's facility, 60 percent of it is used for the production and storage of the widgets. Therefore, based on that percentage, the amount of rent and utilities (total $130,000) added to additional section 263A costs would be $78,000. So, the total amount of additional Section 263A costs is $140,500.

The final step is to allocate a portion of additional Section 263A costs ($140,500) to ending inventory. In the current year, Asher's ending inventory (without taking into account additional Section 263A costs) is $800,000.

Based on the formula:

$140,500 (additional Section 263A costs)/ $1,500,000 (cost of goods excluding beginning and ending inventory) * $800,000 = $74,933 (additional Section 263A costs allocated to ending inventory. That amount will be added (capitalized) to ending inventory.

CHANGING ACCOUNTING METHODS

Procedurally, a taxpayer (such as a corporation) chooses any permitted accounting method on the taxpayer's first tax return. Although, the accounting method selected must clearly reflect the taxpayer's income and expenses, no specific IRS approval is required when making the initial choice. For each tax year thereafter, however, the taxpayer must consistently use the selected method.

Generally, to make an accounting change, the taxpayer must receive permission from the IRS. A change in accounting method includes not only a change in the taxpayer's overall accounting method, but also a change in the treatment of any material item.

When Is It Indicated?

If an existing method of accounting does not provide the most favorable tax treatment, a taxpayer should consider whether a change in accounting method is desirable. As indicated above, with the permission of the IRS, a taxpayer may potentially change to any acceptable accounting method.

What Are the Requirements?

1. A request to change accounting methods is made on Form 3115 filed in the tax year for which the change is requested. In some cases, the taxpayer must pay a user fee.[23] The application requires the taxpayer to account for all items that will be duplicated or omitted as a result of the proposed accounting change, and to calculate the adjustments necessary to prevent the duplications or omissions.[24]

2. The IRS has set up procedures and requirements for a number of specific changes that will be automatically granted by the IRS with the filing of Form 3115, but require no user fee. Revenue Procedure 2008-52[25] sets out the procedures for obtaining automatic consent, and lists, in the appendix, the areas in which a taxpayer can obtain automatic consent. The list is quite extensive and includes accounting method changes ranging from the commonplace to the obscure. The following are just a few examples of changes that will be granted with automatic consent.

   a. Changing the overall accounting method from cash or hybrid to accrual

   b. Certain small taxpayers changing to the overall cash method

   c. Changing from the reserve method to the specific charge-off method of accounting for bad debts

   d. A restaurant or tavern changing its method of accounting for the cost of restaurant smallwares

   e. Changing the treatment of timber fertilization costs from capital expenditures to ordinary and necessary business expenses

   f. Changing accounting methods to obtain the Liberty Zone bonus depreciation deduction

3. Taxpayers who have received approval from the IRS for an accounting change, or who have been ordered by the IRS to make an accounting change, must make adjustments to income to account for the net effect of the accounting change. Where the net effect of an accounting change is small, the adjustments must be accounted for in the year of the change. Where the net effect of an accounting change is greater than $3,000, either positive or negative, however, a taxpayer is entitled to use either of two alternative methods: the *three-year method* or the *reconstruction of income method.*[26]

Under the *three-year method,* the net amount of the adjustment is divided by three. This amount is then added to the taxable income for the current year and for each of the two prior years.[27] Where an accounting change is made voluntarily, the period can be extended to four years.[28]

Under the *reconstruction of income method,* the income for prior years is recomputed using the new method of accounting for all prior years during which the taxpayer used the former accounting method.[29] The adjustment for the current tax year is then limited to the combined net increase for the prior years. For a business that has been operating for a while, reconstructing income for prior years can be cumbersome. For that reason, this method is not often used.

Example: Joseph's small computer business is a limited liability company taxed as a sole proprietorship. After ten years in business, because his business has grown, Joseph decides to switch from the cash method to the accrual method of accounting.

Because the business had been using the cash method, the business has $50,000 in accounts receivable that were not reported in income last year. Similarly, the business has $15,000 in accounts payable that were not deductible because they were not paid.

Pursuant to Revenue Procedure 2008-52, Joseph files Form 3115 requesting a change for which the IRS has granted automatic approval. The netting of the $50,000 accounts receivable with the $15,000 of accounts payable results in a positive adjustment of $35,000. Joseph elects to include the $35,000 positive adjustment in income over four years, at the rate of $8,750 per year.

Change of Accounting Method to Implement UNICAP Rules

Any change from deducting to capitalizing an item of cost or expense (or from capitalizing to deducting the item) is deemed to be a change in the method of accounting.[30] Revenue Procedure 2014-16 provides rules for changing the accounting method used for costs that are required to be capitalized under UNICAP rules.[31] For example, the revenue procedure adds as automatic approval accounting method changes to include a change to adopt a reasonable method of indirect costs under Treasury regulation section 1.263A-1(f)(4)(a). Additionally, the rules waive certain limitations which precluded accounting method changes by taxpayers under IRS examination[32] if the accounting method changes are filed on a single Form 3115.

If the taxpayer is changing any unit(s) of property or the identification of any building structure(s) or system(s) for purposes of determining whether amounts are deducted as repair and maintenance costs, or capitalized as improvement costs, the taxpayer must include with Form 3115 a detailed description of the unit(s) of property, building structure(s), or buildings system(s) used under both its present and proposed method of accounting, together with a citation to the paragraph of the final regulation or temporary regulation under which the unit of property is permitted

WHERE CAN I FIND OUT MORE?

1. IRS Publication 538, Accounting Periods and Methods (Rev. December 2012).
2. IRS Publication 334, Tax Guide for Small Business (Revised Annually).
3. Revenue Procedure 2001-10, 2001-2 IRB 272.
4. Revenue Procedure 2002-9, 2002-1 CB 327.

FREQUENTLY ASKED QUESTIONS

Question – Can changing the method of accounting for inventory benefit a taxpayer?

Answer – For taxpayers who maintain inventories for their businesses, the method of accounting for the costs of inventory can have a major impact on taxable income. Inventory methods of accounting are used to match up costs between the purchase or manufacture of inventory and the subsequent sale of that inventory. If the taxpayer uses, the First-In-First-Out (FIFO) inventory method, the oldest item of inventory is deemed to be the inventory sold. Conversely if the taxpayer uses the Last-In-First-Out (LIFO) inventory method, the newest item of inventory is deeded to be the inventory sold.

In most industries, where inventory costs are inflationary, the last purchased inventory usually has a higher cost of goods sold amount. The higher the cost of goods sold, the lower the income. Therefore, if LIFO is used, the taxpayer can reduce income by matching up the latest – and more expensive – items in inventory with current sales, leaving older and less expensive items remaining in inventory. These taxpayers, if currently using the FIFO or another inventory method might benefit from a switch to LIFO. In certain industries, such as the computer industry, where costs are constantly declining, LIFO would achieve the opposite result of increasing taxable income.

Because inventories are so important, there are special requirements for taxpayers changing to the LIFO accounting method.[33] Advance approval is generally not required to change to the LIFO method, but Form 970 should be filed along with the taxpayer's tax return for the year of the change.

Form 970 includes an analysis of the beginning and ending inventories.

Question – Are taxpayers required to use any particular accounting period?

Answer – Taxpayers must use a "tax year" to report taxable income. A tax year is an annual accounting period for keeping records and reporting income and expenses. Depending on the taxpayer, a tax year may be a calendar year or a fiscal year (including a 52-53-week tax year). (Taxpayers who are not in existence for an entire year, or who change their tax year, may be required to report on a short tax year.)

A calendar year is a period of twelve consecutive months that begins on January 1 and runs through December 31. A calendar-year taxpayer must maintain books and record and report income and expenses for that period. Generally, anyone can adopt the calendar year as a tax year; moreover, certain taxpayers are required to use a calendar year by the Code or Treasury regulations (see below).

A fiscal year is a period of twelve consecutive months that ends on the last day of any month except December 31. Taxpayers who are allowed to adopt a fiscal year must maintain books and records and report income and expenses using that period.

Certain taxpayers may also adopt a 52-53-week tax year. A 52-53-week tax year always ends on the same day of the week. The tax year may end on either (1) the last time that the chosen day falls in a given month or (2) the closest time the chosen day falls to the end of the given month. This definition will result in a tax year that is fifty-two weeks long in most years, but that is fifty-three weeks long in certain years.

Taxpayers who wish to change their tax year must file Form 1128 (*Application To Adopt, Change, or Retain a Tax Year*) to request IRS approval. (S Corporations must use Form 2553 (*Election by a Small Business Corporation*) instead.)

Question – Which taxpayers are required to adopt a particular tax year?

Answer – Generally, individuals must adopt the calendar year as their tax year, but an individual may adopt a fiscal year if the individual maintains books and records on the basis of the adopted fiscal year.

Partnerships must generally conform its tax year to its partners' tax years (either the tax year used by a majority of partners, the tax year used by all the principal (5 percent) partners, or the year that results in the least aggregate deferral of income to the partners). A partnership may also use a 52-53-week tax year ending with reference to the required tax year. To use any other than the required tax year, a partnership must establish a business purpose for a different tax year or file an election under Code section 444 (see below).

S Corporations and Personal Service Corporations (PSCs) must generally use a calendar year or a 52-53-week tax year ending with reference to the calendar year or must establish a business purpose for a different tax year. An S Corporation may also file an election under section 444.

Question – What is a "section 444 election?"

Answer – Under Code section 444, a partnership, S Corporation, or PSC may elect to use a tax year other than its required tax year. Under a section 444 election, an electing entity must make certain required payments or distributions in exchange for adopting a tax year that begins no more than three months later than the required tax year.[34] (A tax year other than a required year that is used because of valid business purpose does not require a Section 444 election.)

Question – Are taxpayers required to use any particular method to account for long-term contracts?

Answer – Yes. Generally, the income from any "long-term contract" must be determined using the "percentage of completion" (POC) method of accounting.[35] A "long-term contract" means any contract for the manufacture, building, installation, or construction of property, if such contract is not completed within the taxable year in which such contract is entered into.[36]

Under the POC method, a taxpayer generally must include in income the portion of the total contract price that corresponds to the percentage of the entire contract that the taxpayer has completed during the taxable year. The percentage of completion is determined by comparing current contract costs incurred with estimated total contract costs. Thus, the taxpayer includes a portion of the total contract price in gross income as the taxpayer incurs allocable contract costs.[37]

The requirement to use the POC does not apply to home construction contracts or to other construction contracts estimated to be completed within the two-year period beginning on the contract commencement date, where the taxpayer's average annual gross receipts for the three taxable years preceding the taxable year in which such contract is entered into do not exceed $10,000,000.[38]

Question – Can a taxpayer operate two businesses using different accounting methods for each?

Answer – A taxpayer operating two or more separate and distinct businesses can use a different accounting method for each. In order to be distinct, each business must maintain a complete and separate set of books and records. Furthermore, a taxpayer may not shift profits or losses between businesses so that income is not clearly reflected.

Question – What happens if a business using the accrual method of accounting incurs a business expense with a related business using the cash method of accounting?

Answer – Where a taxpayer using the accrual method of accounting owes a debt to a *related person* using the cash method of accounting, the taxpayer may not deduct the expense until it is actually paid *and* that amount is includible in the recipient's gross income.[39]

Question – When calculating the present value of tax savings, what investment rate should be used?

Answer – Excellent question for which there is no single correct answer. The investment rate differs from taxpayer to taxpayer. Conceptually, the taxpayer would use the after-tax rate of return of investments the taxpayer is investing in because the tax savings represents money that may be added to, or at least not withdrawn from, those investments to pay taxes. For some investors, this rate may be the rate of return earned on risk-free investments, such as Treasury securities and certificates of deposit. For others, such as the owners of closely held businesses, the rate of return may far exceed investment returns available in the securities markets.

Question – Does tax reform change the accounting rules that govern businesses with long-term contracts? Does tax reform change the percentage of completion contract rules?

Answer – The 2017 Tax Act expands the exception for small construction contracts from the requirement to use the percentage-of-completion method. Under the new rules, contracts that fall within the exception include those contracts for the construction or improvement of real property if the contract:

(1) is expected (at the time the contract is entered into) to be completed within two years of commencement of the contract, and

(2) is performed by a taxpayer that (during the tax year in which the contract was entered into) meets the $25 million gross receipts test (see "Accounting Methods under the 2017 Tax Reform Act" above).[40]

Taxpayers that fail the $25 million gross receipts test are not eligible for the exception from using the percentage-of-completion method for the tax year. Further, under these rules there is no permitted adjustment under IRC Section 481(a) for contracts entered into before January 1, 2018.[41]

The $25 million threshold will be indexed annually for inflation. The new rules governing accounting for long-term contracts are effective for tax years beginning after December 31, 2017.

CHAPTER ENDNOTES

1. Treas. Reg. §1446-1(e)(3).
2. IRC Sec. 481; Treas. Reg. §1.446-1(e)(3).
3. 2008-36 I.R.B. 587.
4. IRC Sec. 481.
5. IRC Sec. 481(b)(1).
6. IRC Sec. 481(c); Rev. Proc. 97-27, 1997-1 CB 680.
7. IRC Sec. 481(b)(2).
8. IRC Sec. 448(a)(3).
9. IRC Secs. 448(c), 447(d).
10. IRC Sec. 472.
11. IRC Secs. 448(c), 447(d).
12. IRC Sec. 447(d)(2)(C).
13. IRC Sec. 448(c).
14. IRC Sec. 263A(i).
15. IRC Sec. 448(d)(7).
16. IRC Sec. 471(c)(1).
17. IRC Sec. 471.
18. 418 U.S. 1 (1974).
19. See Treas. Reg. §1.263A-1(c)(2)(ii).
20. Treas, Reg. §1.263A-1(e)(2)(i) and (ii)

21. Treas, Reg. §1.263A-1(e).
22. Treas, Reg. §1.263A-1(e)(3)(ii)
23. IRC Sec. 447(e).
24. IRC Sec. 448(d)(2)(A).
25. IRC Sec. 448(d)(2)(B).
26. IRC Secs. 446, 471.
27. Rev. Proc. 2001-10, 2001-2 I.R.B. 272.
28. Notice 2001-76, 2001-52 I.R.B. 613.
29. Rev. Proc. 2001-10, 2001-2 I.R.B. 272.
30. Internal Revenue Manual §4.11.6.2 (05-13-2005).
31. 2014-9 I.R.B. 606.
32. 2011-4 I.R.B. 330.
33. Notice 2001-76, 2001-52 I.R.B. 613.
34. IRC Secs. 280H, 444, 7519.
35. IRC Sec. 460(a).
36. IRC Sec. 460(f).
37. Treas. Reg. §1.460-4(b)(1).
38. IRC Sec. 460(e)(1).
39. IRC Sec. 267(a)(2). For the definition of "related person," see IRC Sec. 267(b).
40. IRC Secs. 460(e)(1)(B)(ii), 448(c).
41. IRC Sec. 460(e)(2)(B).

CHOICE OF ENTITY

CHAPTER 19

INTRODUCTION

When establishing a new business, the first step is to choose the business entity in which to operate. In choosing the appropriate entity, the owner(s) must decide which business entity type best supports the objectives of the business. Other considerations include tax implications, protection from liability, flexibility in ownership, and state business laws. Given the multitude of the factors to be considered by a new business owner, this chapter provides a general overview of those factors with the main focus on the federal tax implications of such a decision.

The following is a list of common business entities:

1. Sole Proprietorship
2. Partnerships
   a. General Partnership
   b. Limited Partnership
   c. Limited Liability Partnership
   d. Limited Liability Limited Partnership
3. Limited Liability Companies
4. Corporations
   a. C Corporation
   b. S Corporation

SOLE PROPRIETORSHIP

Simply stated, a sole proprietorship is a one-person business operation. Other than obtaining a business license and perhaps a trade name, the sole proprietor and the sole proprietorship are a single legal entity. Therefore, a sole proprietorship does not provide the owner any protection from liability. This means sole proprietors are personally liable for all debts, liabilities and obligations of the business.

Similarly, for income tax purposes, there is no distinction between the owner and the business. Although the sole proprietorship may apply for its own tax identification number (sometimes referred to as a TIN or EIN), the sole proprietor is the "taxpayer." Thus, there is no separate sole proprietor tax form. All income and deductions are reported on Schedule C of the sole proprietor's Form 1040. The net income or loss is carried over to line 12 on the first page of the Form 1040.

Advantages of a Sole Proprietorship as an Entity Choice

Non-Tax Implications

Because a sole proprietorship is not a separate legal entity, there are no formalities of creation other than obtaining a business license and a DBA application (to do business under a certain name). Additionally, unlike a corporation, there are no required meetings. From a management perspective, a sole proprietorship is also easy to operate as the sole proprietor makes all management decisions.

Tax Implications

From an income tax perspective, although a sole proprietor must keep separate business records, income and deductions are reported on the owner's Schedule C of Form 1040. Thus, the taxpayer is required to file only one single return. Generally, any loss reported on Schedule C (deductions exceed income) can be deducted from the owner's or owner's spouse's (if a joint return is filed) other income.

Disadvantages of a Sole Proprietorship as an Entity Choice

Non-Tax Implications

A sole proprietorship provides no liability protection for the owner. Therefore, the owner has unlimited liability for all business debt, liabilities and obligations. These obligations may include damages caused by acts of sole proprietorship employees. A judgment against the business is a judgement against the owner so that personal assets may be attachable by the creditor. Because of a sole proprietor's overall vulnerability to claims against the business, few investors are likely to invest significant funds in a sole proprietorship.

The existence of sole proprietorship ends at the death (or disability) of its owner. Thus, in most cases, very little of the value of a sole proprietorship can be transferred upon the owner's death. Additionally, the sole proprietorship is a poor estate planning tool since it is impossible to fractionalize or create layers of interests that can be transferred during the owner's life or upon death to others.

Tax Implications

From a tax perspective, all net income reported on Schedule C is treated as *self-employment income* subject to self-employment tax. Essentially, self-employment tax is social security and Medicare tax imposed on sole proprietors in addition to income tax. Unlike an employee who pays half of the tax (the employer pays the other half), a sole proprietor is obligated to pay the entire amount of the tax. In 2020, the self-employment income tax rate is 15.3 percent (12.4 percent for social security tax and 2.9 percent for Medicare tax). Although the social security portion of the tax (12.4 percent) caps at $137,700 of self-employment income, the Medicare tax portion (2.9 percent) continues indefinitely. For a detailed discussion of the tax implications of self-employment income, see Chapter 14.

Caution: Sole Proprietorship with Employees. A sole proprietorship with employees must withhold from their wages a) federal income tax and b) the employee's share of FICA and Medicare tax (7.65 percent) (collectively referred to as the "Trust Fund Taxes"). In addition, the sole proprietorship/employer is responsible for its share of FICA and Medicare tax (7.65 percent) (referred to as the "Employer's Tax Share"). Trust Fund Taxes and Employer's Tax Share must be paid over to the IRS. In the event the sole proprietorship does not pay these taxes to the IRS, unlike a corporation or LLC, the sole proprietor is responsible for the entire unpaid balance of the Trust Fund Taxes and the *Employer's Tax Share* including interest and penalties.

Example: For several years, Asher operated an IT business as a sole proprietorship with three employees. This year, Asher goes out of business. At that time, there are outstanding payroll tax liabilities including $13,500 of Trust Fund Taxes and $3,500 of Employer's Tax Share. Even though Asher's sole proprietorship went out of business, Asher is responsible for the total outstanding payroll tax liability ($17,000) plus interest and penalties.

Conversely, if Asher had formed a corporation or LLC to operate his business, he as the shareholder/owner would be responsible only for the Trust Fund Taxes.

PARTNERSHIP

For tax purposes, a partnership comprised of two or more persons includes a syndicate, group, pool, joint venture, or other unincorporated organization through or by means of which any business, financial operation, or venture is carried on, and which is not, within the meaning of federal tax laws, a corporation or a trust or estate.[1]

Although there are various types of partnerships, they are essentially taxed in the same way. For federal income tax purposes, a partnership is not subject to entity level income tax. In essence, a partnership is a pass-through entity so that partnership income, deductions, capital gains and losses, charitable contributions, stock dividends, etc. flow through to the partners to be reported on their separate income tax returns.

The four main types of partnerships are:

1. *General Partnerships:* The traditional type of partnership in which each partner with a share of profits is a fully active principal with a voice in its management. The partners are jointly and severally obligated with respect to partnership debts, liabilities and obligations. Importantly, each partner has full legal authority to act on behalf of the partnership within the scope of its business activities.

2. *Limited Partnerships:* Generally, operating on the authority of the Uniform Limited Partnership Act (as adopted by most states), it is a partnership with one or more general partners and one or more limited partners. Unlike a general partnership, a limited partner's liability is limited to his or her investment in the partnership. A limited partnership must have at least one general partner with unlimited personal liability.

3. *Limited Liability Partnerships (LLP):* Similar to a general partnership, in an LLP, the partners enjoy partial liability. Although partners are liable for their own wrongful acts, they are not liable for the wrongdoing of other partners. LLPs are a function of state law and some states limit what types of business can function as an LLP.

4. *Limited Liability Limited Partnerships (LLLP):* In this version of a limited partnership, the LLLP general partners are afforded limited liability. Importantly, LLLPs are not available in all states so general partners in a state that recognizes LLLPs may be subject to liability in a jurisdiction that does not recognize LLLPs.

Fundamentals of a Partnership

Although partnerships may be created orally, most partnerships are governed by an executed written partnership agreement. Unless the partnership agreement provides otherwise, most state statutes provide that:

- All partners share equally in profits and losses irrespective of the proportionate value of the capital or services each has contributed.

- All partners have equal rights in the management and conduct of the partnership business.

- No partner is entitled to remuneration for acting in the partnership business, except that a surviving partner is entitled to reasonable compensation for winding up the partnership affairs.

- No person can become a member of a partnership without the consent of all the partners.

Typically, a well drafted partnership agreement is not just boilerplate but specific to that partnership. For example, the partnership agreement should document the initial property contributed to the partnership by each partner. It should also set forth the allocation of partnership profits or losses among the individual partners.

The partnership agreement should also include a provision dealing with the buyout of a partner who dies or withdraws from the partnership. Usually, such a provision grants the remaining partners the right to purchase such partner's interest pursuant to a set price or a buyout formula set forth in the partnership agreement.

As to partnership affairs, provided a given transaction is within the scope of the partnership business and not otherwise restricted by the partnership agreement, any general partner can conduct partnership business and bind the other partners. Subject to the exceptions listed below, each general partner is bound by all manners of partnership business even fraudulent acts of other partners.

However, the following are examples of the acts of individual partners that cannot bind the other partners:

1. Confession of judgments

2. Disposition of the goodwill of the business

3. Assignment of partnership property to a creditor, or to a trustee, for the benefit of a creditor, or of all creditors

4. Performance of any act that would make it impossible to carry on the ordinary business of the partnership

5. Submission of partnership claims to arbitration

All partners are co-owners of property held in the name of the partnership, and all have the right to possess the property for partnership purposes. No partner has the right, without the consent of the other partners, to possess partnership property for any non-partnership purpose, or to assign rights in specific partnership property.

Taxation of Partners

As mentioned above, partnership items of income, deduction, etc. pass through from the partnership level to the partners. In turn, each partner reports the proportionate share of those items on each partner's individual personal income tax return. The character of the income and deduction determined at the partnership level also passes through to the partners.

Procedurally, even though a partnership is not subject to income tax, it files a Form 1065 (essentially an informational return) on which it reports all income and deductions. Pursuant to IRC Section 702(a), each partner's share of specific items of income and deduction are "separately stated" and recorded on a Schedule K-1 (one for each partner). The separately stated items are:

- Long-term capital gains and losses
- Short-term capital gains and losses
- Section 1231 gains and losses
- Charitable contributions
- Dividends
- Foreign taxes
- Other items as to be determined by Treasury Regulations
- All other income or deductions ("Catchall Income" or "Catchall Deduction")

In conjunction with the partnership filing of Form 1065, the partnership provides each partner with a Schedule K-1 to be used in the preparation of the individual Form 1040. Based on the type of the separately stated income or deduction, the partner enters those items on the appropriate Form 1040 schedule. Unless a special allocation is made (discussed below), each item of income and deduction is allocated to partners in proportion to their interests in the partnership.

Example: Max, Aaron, Charlene, and Kevin each contribute $25,000 to form the new 4J General Partnership. At the end of the first year, the partnership has Catchall Income of $1,000,000; ordinary business expenses (Catchall Deductions) of $500,000; capital gains of $25,000; charitable contributions of $5,000; and $10,000 in dividends from partnership stock holdings.

The partnership files Form 1065 and on a Schedule K-1 for each partner separately listing the Catchall Income, Catchall Deductions, capital gains, charitable contributions, and stock dividends. Each Schedule K-1 (provided to each partner) as follows:

- $125,000 (one-quarter of the net Catchall Income of $500,000);
- capital gains of $6,250 (25 percent of $25,000);
- charitable contributions of $1,250 (25 percent of $5,000); and
- stock dividends of $2,500 (25 percent of $10,000).

Each partner will report those items on the appropriate schedule on his or her individual Form 1040.

Capital Accounts

Simply stated, partner capital accounts represent each partner's share of the equity of the partnership. So, when partners form a partnership, each partner has a beginning capital account that included the amount of money and the fair market value of any property contributed to the partnership. Thereafter, a partner's capital account can be:

- increased by additional contributions;
- decreased by distributions;
- increased by income; or
- decreased by deductions and expenses.

The following chart illustrates the changes in the capital accounts of each partner in the above example:

Partner	Beginning Capital Account – Initial Contribution	Increase to Capital Account	Decrease to Capital Account	Ending Capital Account
Max	$25,000	$125,000 Net Catchall Income $6,250 Capital Gain $2,500 Stock Dividend or Total of $133,750	$1,250 Charitable Contribution	$157,500($25,000 plus $133,750 minus $1,250)
Aaron	$25,000	$125,000 Net Catchall Income $6,500 Capital Gain $2,500 Stock Dividend or Total of $133,750	$1,250 Charitable Contribution	$157,500 ($25,000 plus $133,750 minus $1,250)
Charlene	$25,000	$125,000 Net Catchall Income $6,500 Capital Gain $2,500 Stock Dividend or Total of $133,750	$1,250 Charitable Contribution	$157,500 ($25,000 plus $133,750 minus $1,250)
Kevin	$25,000	$125,000 Net Catchall Income $6,250 Capital Gain $2,500 Stock Dividend or Total of $133,750	$1,250 Charitable Contribution	$157,500 ($25,000 plus $133,750 minus $1,250)

Special Allocations

Subject to special and complicated rules, a partnership is permitted to deviate from the proportionate allocation of income and deductions described above. Referred to as *special allocations*, the IRC Section 704(b) regulations require that any special allocation must have *substantial economic effect*. There is a two-part test to determine if an allocation has substantial economic effect.[2]

First, an allocation must have "economic effect." The economic effect of any allocation must be properly documented. To do so, the regulations require that proper partnership accounting must include the following:

- A capital account for each partner that accurately reflects increases and decreases to the equity interest in the partnership.
- Upon the liquidation of the partnership, each partner must receive an amount equal to the positive capital account balance.
- If a partner's capital account falls below zero, the partner must be unconditionally obligated to restore the amount of the deficit.

Stated differently, for an allocation to have economic effect, the tax consequences must be consistent with the economic consequences to the partner. In another words, a partner who receives a special allocation of income must derive the economic benefit of an increase to the equity interest in the partnership. Similarly, a partner who receives a special allocation of a deduction must suffer the economic detriment of a decrease in equity interest in the partnership. Finally, if the allocation of a deduction causes a partner's capital account to fall below zero (because the deduction is greater than the capital account balance), the partner must have the obligation to restore the deficit. Otherwise, the partner would receive the tax benefit of the deduction with no corresponding adverse economic consequences.

Example: Asher, a general partner in BRASH, has a positive capital account of $5,000. That year, Asher receives a special allocation of a $10,000 depreciation deduction. To have economic effect, Asher's capital account must be reduced from positive $5,000 to negative $5,000. Upon the liquidation of the partnership, Asher would be obligated to restore his negative $5,000 capital account by injecting $5,000 into the partnership.

Second, an allocation that passes the economic effect test must also be substantial. Generally, as illustrated in the example below, substantiality means that that the allocation changes the economic sharing arrangement of the partners in some meaningful The rationale for substantiality is to prevent partners from making special allocations for purely tax motivated reasons so as to prevent tax abusive allocations. The regulations list the following three types of allocations that are not considered substantial:

- Shifting allocations
- Transitory allocations
- "Some Help, No Hurt" allocations

Shifting Allocation Example. Asher and Miranda Wright are equal partners in a partnership. From another business, Asher has a substantial net operating loss. From other business ventures and investments, Miranda has a substantial amount of income taxable in the highest income tax bracket. This year, the partnership earns tax-free municipal bond interest on its investments as well as operating income from its business. The partnership allocates all tax-free municipal bond interest to Miranda and an equal amount of operating income to Asher. The remaining operating income is allocated equally between them.

Assuming these allocations have economic effect, they do not meet the substantiality test. This is because Miranda, as a partner in the highest income tax bracket, benefits from the allocation of tax-free interest. On the other hand, Asher, who has a substantial net operating loss, uses it to offset the allocation of business operating income. In the end, because equal overall dollar amounts were allocated to the partners, the allocations did not alter their equal economic sharing arrangement. In fact, the only consequence of the allocation was tax savings to both partners. For this reason, the allocation is not substantial.

Distributive Shares of Partnership Income and Loss

As discussed above, for tax purposes, partnership income and loss passes through to the partners to be reported on their individual income tax returns. This is true whether any of a partner's distributive share of income is actually distributed to the partner. The deductibility of a partner's distributive share of partnership loss is limited to the partner's basis in the partnership (referred to as "outside basis").

Sale of Partnership Interests

A partner's interest in a partnership is treated as a capital asset. Generally, the gain recognized on the sale of a partnership interest is capital (long or short-term depending on the partner's holding period). Any gain attributable to activities in which the selling partner did not materially participate is characterized as net investment income. Therefore, it may be subject to the 3.8 percent net investment income tax (NIIT). (See Chapter 13 for an extensive discussion on the NIIT).

Finally, to the extent that IRC Section 751 applies, some of the recognized gain on the sale of a partnership interest will be treated as ordinary income.[3] A more detailed discussion of this topic is beyond the scope of this chapter.

Advantages of a Partnership as an Entity Choice

Non-Tax Implications

Generally, partnerships are easy to set up and are much less regulated than corporations. Because there are multiple owners in a partnership, there are more sources from which to raise capital. In terms of income or profits, there is great flexibility to split those among partners in a manner that is not necessarily proportionate to the underlying partnership interests.

Caution: For a disproportionate allocation (a special allocation) to be respected for tax purposes, the allocation must have substantial economic effect. See discussion of special allocations, above.

Tax Implications

Unlike S corporations, partnerships are permitted to make special allocations of income and profits among the partners. However, as discussed throughout this part of the chapter, to be respected for tax purposes, the allocation must have substantial economic effect.

For individuals likely to have an estate subject to estate tax, creating family limited partnership may be a useful planning technique. Gifting or devising family limited partnership interests (subject to valuation discounts) to the younger generation can be an effective way to leverage the estate and gift tax exemption; and, thus, reduce gift and estate tax. Additionally, shifting income from the older generation to a younger generation can be accomplished by gifting a family limited partnership interest to a child or grandchild.

Disadvantages of a Partnership as an Entity Choice

Non-Tax Implications

General partners are jointly and severally liable for the debts, liabilities and obligations of the partnership. In fact, the risk is not limited to a partner's interest in the partnership. So, if only a single general partner is solvent (regardless of the interest in the partnership), that partner would be personally liable for the entire amount of partnership debt.

Without proper planning, including a carefully drafted partnership agreement, basic partnership occurrences such as withdrawal of a partner or termination of the partnership may be problematic. For example, if not specifically addressed in a partnership agreement, by operation of applicable state law, a partnership may automatically terminate if a partner dies, becomes incompetent, or withdraws. Additionally, resolving personal or management conflicts between partners can be difficult in the absence of a clear management structure governed by a partnership agreement with comprehensive provisions addressing such matters.

Tax Implications

As illustrated throughout this part of the chapter, partnership taxation and accounting can be very complex. The failure to comply with the variety of special rules may result in unintended harsh tax consequences. Moreover, hiring a tax attorney and/or a CPA for assistance could be expensive.

Similar to a sole proprietorship, a partner's distributive share of partnership business income is treated as self-employment income. Therefore, in addition to income tax, each partner must pay 15.3 percent (12.4 percent for social security tax and 2.9 percent for Medicare tax) on the partner's derivative share of business income. Although the social security portion of the tax (12.4 percent) caps at $118,000 of self- employment income, the Medicare tax portion (2.9 percent) continues indefinitely. For a detailed discussion of the tax implications of self-employment income, see Chapter 12.

Caution: Partnership with Employees. A partnership with employees must withhold from their wages a) federal income tax and b) the employee's share of FICA and Medicare tax (7.65 percent) (collectively referred to as the "Trust Fund Taxes"). In addition, the partnership/employer is responsible for its share of FICA and Medicare tax (7.65 percent) (referred to as the "Employer's Tax Share"). The Trust Fund Taxes and the Employer's Tax Share must be paid over to the IRS. In the event the partnership fails to pay these taxes to the IRS, unlike a corporation or LLC, the general partners are jointly and severally responsible for the entire unpaid balance of the Trust Fund Taxes and the *Employer's Tax Share* including interest and penalties.

Example: For several years, Asher and Miranda Wright operated an IT business as a partnership with three employees. This year, the partnership dissolves. At that time, there are outstanding payroll tax liabilities including $13,500 of Trust Fund Taxes and $3,500 of Employer's Tax Share. Even though the partnership no longer exists, Asher and Miranda are jointly and severally responsible for the total outstanding payroll tax liability ($17,000) plus interest and penalties.

Conversely, if Asher and Miranda had formed a corporation or LLC, they as the shareholders/owners would be responsible only for the Trust Fund Taxes.

LIMITED LIABILITY COMPANY

Limited Liability Companies (LLCs) are hybrid business entities created under state law. Although, as discussed below, they may be taxed as a sole proprietorship or partnership, they are afforded the limited liability normally associated with corporations. LLCs are available in all states, but the requirements, operating rules, and tax treatment vary widely among the states. For instance, some states impose a state income tax on LLCs as an entity while others do not. The best source of information with regard to forming an LLC is likely the Secretary of State website of the state of formation.

Taxation of LLCs and Its Members

By election on Form 8832, depending on the owner composition, an LLC can choose to be taxed as a sole proprietorship, partnership, S corporation or C corporation. If an election is not made, there are certain default rules that apply. For example, an LLC with two or more members will be treated as a partnership for federal income tax purposes (partnerships are discussed in more detail above).

Example: John, Jane, James, and Jill each contribute $25,000 in forming 4J Enterprises, LLC. They file articles of organization with the secretary of state and execute an operating agreement. Under the operating agreement, each member has defined management responsibilities and is entitled to one-quarter of the business profits.

If the LLC does not file a Form 8832 electing to be taxed as a particular entity, the LLC will be treated as a partnership for federal income tax purposes. This means the LLC will file a Form 1065 (partnership income tax return) and issue a Schedule K-1 to each member. On the other hand, if the members want to be taxed as a C corporation or an S corporation, the LLC must file Form 8832 to elect that treatment.

There is also a default designation with respect to a single-member LLC. If a Form 8832 is not filed, a single-member LLC will be taxed as a sole proprietorship. A single member LLC is often referred to as a "disregarded entity" because the income and deductions are reported by the member on Schedule C just like a sole proprietor. On the other hand, by filing a Form 8832, however, a single-member LLC can elect to be taxed as a C corporation or an S corporation.

An LLC classified as a partnership becomes a sole proprietorship if the LLC's membership is reduced to one member. A single-member LLC taxed as a sole proprietorship becomes a partnership when the LLC gains a second member. If an elective classification change under the "Check-the-Box" regulations becomes effective at the same time as a membership change, the elective change takes precedence over the change in membership.[4]

An LLC may change a classification election by filing Form 8832 with the IRS. The change may be from a prior election or the LLC's default tax treatment. A change may be effective no more than seventy-five days before, or no more than twelve months after the election is filed. Once a change of classification election has been filed, another change may not be made for sixty months.[5] An initial election for a newly-formed entity does not count as a change; therefore, a change of election may be filed within sixty months of the initial election.

Federal tax laws automatically classify and tax certain LLC business entities as corporations:[6]

- A business entity formed under a federal or state statute or under a statute of a federally recognized Indian tribe if the statute describes or refers to the entity as incorporated or as a corporation, body corporate, or body politic.
- A business entity formed under a federal or state statute if the statute describes or refers to the entity as a joint stock association.
- A state-chartered business entity conducting banking activities, if any of its deposits are insured by the FDIC.
- A business entity wholly owned by a state of political subdivision thereof, or a business entity wholly owned by a foreign government.
- An insurance company
- A business entity taxable as a corporation under a provision of the code other than Code section 7701(a)(3).
- Certain named foreign entities equivalent to corporations.

Advantages of an LLC as an Entity Choice

Non-Tax Implications

From a liability protection perspective, doing business as an LLC is a sound choice for a single individual or multiple individuals. In the case of a single-member LLC, the individual can operate in the manner of a sole proprietor with limited liability. Multiple individuals can operate their business in the manner of a partnership with limited liability. In either case, if the LLC goes out of business, is unable to pay its creditors or is sued, the personal assets of the members (held outside of the LLC) would be protected.

An LLC has fewer required formalities under state law than a corporation. For example, a corporation is generally required to have a board of directors and to hold annual meetings, whereas, LLCs are usually not subject to these formalities.

An LLC has a great deal of flexibility in ownership and management structure. Other than an LLC electing to be taxed as an S Corporation, there is no minimum or maximum number of members. LLC members can be individuals (including non-resident aliens), partnerships, trusts, corporations, or other LLCs. Members may collectively manage an LLC or elect or hire a management group to do so. Unlike a limited partnership, members may be actively involved in managing the business without jeopardizing limited liability.

Tax Implications

The main tax advantage of forming an LLC as a business entity is the ability of the members to elect to be taxed in the manner of an entity of the members choosing. By making an election on Form 8832, the members of an LLC (other than certain entities that are automatically classified as corporation) choose the tax regime under which the entity (or its owners) will be taxed.

Another tax advantage relates to delinquent employment taxes. Although a single-member LLC is a disregarded entity for income tax purposes (the member reports income and deductions on Schedule C of the individual income tax return), it is a separate entity with respect to state law creditor liability. For that reason, although the single member would likely be obligated to pay the Trust Fund Taxes as a responsible person, the single member would not be obligated to pay the delinquent Employer's Tax Share.[7] Likewise, members of an LLC taxed as a partnership are also not obligated to pay delinquent Employer's Tax Share.[8]

Disadvantages of an LLC as an Entity Choice

Non-Tax Implications

Because LLC requirements vary from state to state, if there are state law conflicts, multi-state transactions can be complicated.

Some states tax LLCs treated as partnerships for federal income tax purposes as separate tax paying entities, or assess a fee for conducting business in this form. As a result, they would be subject to an additional tax and/or fees in addition to the tax paid by the members.

Tax Implications

The tax disadvantages of an LLC are the same as they would be if instead of creating an LLC, the owners had formed a sole proprietorship, partnership, C corporation or S corporation.

C CORPORATION

Generally, a subchapter "C" corporation is a corporation or an entity treated as a corporation (where the owners do not elect to be taxed as an S corporation, discussed below). Legally, a corporation is a separate entity so that its owners/shareholders are not personally liable with respect to corporate debt. Almost all states require a corporation to file articles of incorporation or certificates of formation. These documents will usually include the corporation's legal name, purpose, and the name and address of an agent located in the state to be served if the corporation be sued. Some states may also require a corporate charter and/or the corporate bylaws to be filed.

Depending on the law of a particular state, a corporation is required to hold an annual shareholder meeting as well as periodic meetings of the board of directors. Generally, there must be formal elections of directors and recorded minutes of shareholder and board of director meetings.

Unlike a sole proprietorship and any other pass through entity, a corporation is a separate taxpayer so that it reports its income and deductions (Form 1120) and pays its own tax. Generally, the taxable income of a corporation is computed in the same way as for an individual. However, personal deductions, standard deduction and personal exemptions available to an individual are not allowed for a corporation. As to charitable contributions, they are deductible to the extent of 10 percent of taxable income (with certain adjustments). Generally, charitable contributions in excess of the 10 percent limit may be carried forward for five years.[9]

Similar to individuals, capital gains and losses are netted. As of the date of this publication, however, there is no special tax rate for capital gains generated by a C corporation. Therefore, all capital gains (short or long-term) are taxed at the corporation's regular tax rates. This means like any other income, the maximum capital gains rate of a C corporation, is 35 percent.

The separate corporate tax rates are as follows:[10]

Taxable Income	Tax	Tax Rate on Excess
0	0	15%
$50,000	$7,500	25%
$75,000	$13,750	34%
$100,000	$22,250	39%
$335,000	$113,900	34%
$10,000,000	$3,400,000	35%
$15,000,000	$5,150,000	38%
$18,333,333	$6,416,667	35%

The purpose of the 39 percent and the 38 percent rate inserted in the middle of the tax rate table is to phase out the graduated tax rates available at lower income levels. Fully phased out, 35 percent is the highest tax rate a corporation will pay on its total income.

Advantages of a C Corporation as an Entity Choice

Non-Tax Implications

A corporation offers limited liability to the owners of the business. This means corporate shareholders are not personally responsible for the corporation's debt, liabilities and obligations.

Shares in a corporation can be easily transferred by sale, gift, or bequest. Unlike, a sole proprietorship or partnership that go out of existence upon the death of an owner, a corporation has continuity of life. Thus, a corporation will continue to exist even if a shareholder dies or its shares change hands.

Tax Implications

As indicated by the corporate income tax table, above, the tax rates on the first $75,000 of income are very taxpayer favorable. So for a small business with ongoing capital needs, the tax on income retained by the corporation is relatively low. As a result, such low tax rates encourage corporate growth.

Unlike sole proprietorships and partnerships, a C corporation is allowed to use a fiscal tax year rather than a calendar year. Depending on the circumstances, there may be certain tax advantages in using a fiscal year as the corporation's tax year.

As to delinquent employment taxes, although an owner/officer/shareholder may be obligated to pay delinquent Trust Fund Taxes, they are not obligated to pay delinquent the Employer's Tax Share.

Unlike other entity types, C corporations can offer a wide array of tax-free benefits such as an IRC Section 105 health reimbursement plan to its shareholders/employees.

Disadvantages of a C Corporation as an Entity Choice

Non-Tax Implications

Of all the business entities discussed in this chapter, more formalities are usually required in the operation of a corporation. In many instances, the creation of a corporation requires the filing of multiple documents. In operation, formalities include formal elections of directors, meetings of the board of directors, and shareholder meetings. Many owners of small corporations may view these requirements as a waste of time and unimportant—being inclined to ignore them. However, if these formalities are not observed and the entity is sued by a creditor, local courts may disregard the corporate existence. As a result, the owners may not receive the limited liability protection afforded to shareholders. In that case, the shareholders would likely be treated as partners or a sole proprietor and personally obligated to satisfy the entity's liabilities.

Tax Implications

One of the primary disadvantages of a corporation is the double taxation of corporate profits in the form of a dividend. As previously discussed, a corporation is a separate entity subject to entity level tax on its profits. However, unlike compensation paid to a shareholder/employee, dividend distributions are not deductible by the corporation. Moreover, the recipient shareholder is taxed on the dividend. So, in essence, by denying a corporate level deduction for a dividend distribution, those earnings, when distributed to a shareholder, are subject to double taxation. To some degree, the negative impact of double taxation is mitigated by a maximum tax rate (the same that applies to long-term capital gain) on dividend distributions. For individuals in a tax bracket below 39.6 percent, the maximum tax rate is 15 percent. For individuals in the 39.6 percent tax bracket, the maximum tax rate is 20 percent.

The taxation of corporate liquidations is another example of double taxation. When a corporation liquidates, it is deemed to have sold all its assets to the shareholder(s) for fair market value.[11] So, to the extent there is a gain (fair market value of assets exceeds the tax basis), it is included in the gross income of the liquidating corporation. Then, the shareholder(s) is deemed to have sold the stock to the corporation in exchange for the assets (including money) distributed. To the extent the amount received exceeds a shareholder(s) tax basis in the stock, there would be capital gains recognition (whether short or long-term depends on the shareholder's(s) holding period). In the end, a corporate liquidation triggers double taxation.

Caution: **a Corporation Treated as a Personal Service Corporation:** If a corporation is deemed to be a "personal service corporation," it will be taxed at a 35 percent flat tax rate so the graduated corporate income tax rates are not available.[12] A personal service corporation is a corporation where substantially all of its activities involve the performance of services in the fields of health, law, engineering, architecture, accounting, actuarial science, performing arts, or consulting. Also, substantially all the stock must be owned directly by employees, retired employees, or their estates, or indirectly through partnerships, S corporations, or qualified personal service corporations.[13]

Caution: **Accumulated Earnings Tax (AET):** The accumulated earnings tax is a penalty tax imposed on a corporation that holds earnings in excess of its normal business needs. The rationale for the penalty is to prevent corporations from accumulating earnings that it might otherwise distribute as taxable dividends to its shareholders.[14] In determining the amount of accumulated earnings subject to the penalty tax, the corporation must demonstrate the amount it needs to retain to meet the reasonable needs of the business. In computing the penalty tax, that amount is considered to be the accumulated earnings credit meaning it will reduce the amount that would be subject to the tax.

For most corporations, the Code provides a minimum accumulated earnings credit of $250,000. For service corporations in the fields of health, law, engineering, architecture, accounting, actuarial science, performing arts, or consulting, the minimum accumulated earnings credit is $150,000. Because of the minimum accumulated earning credit, a corporation can accumulate up to $250,000 ($150,000 for service corporations) regardless of the needs of the business. On the other hand, if a corporation demonstrates, however, that it needs $2 million in retained earnings to run its business, its accumulated earnings credit would be $2 million.

The tax is 20 percent times the corporation's accumulated taxable income. Generally, accumulated taxable income is taxable income less federal income tax, dividends paid to shareholders and the accumulated earnings credit.[15]

Caution: **Personal Holding Company Tax:** Another corporate penalty tax is the personal holding company (PHC) tax.[16] The PHC tax is designed to keep shareholders from avoiding the individual income tax on certain types of income generated by property held inside a corporate entity. In other words, the motivation of the shareholders is to avoid personal income taxation on this type of income. The PHC tax is imposed on a corporation if it meets both a stock ownership test and a PHC income test.[17]

The stock ownership test is met if more than 50 percent of the value of the stock is owned, directly or indirectly, by no more than five shareholders. The PHC income test is met if 60 percent or more of the corporation's adjusted ordinary gross income is PHC income.

PHC income is generally defined to include:

- dividends, interest, royalties, and annuities;
- rents;
- mineral, oil, and gas royalties;
- copyright royalties;
- film rents;

- compensation from the use of corporate property by shareholders;
- personal service contracts; and
- income from estates and trusts.[18]

Similar to the AET tax rate, the PHC tax rate is 20 percent. The tax is imposed on the corporation's undistributed PHC income, which is generally PHC income of the corporation minus dividends paid to the shareholders.[19]

S CORPORATION

A subchapter "S" corporation (an "S corporation") is a corporation or an LLC that has specifically elected that status by filing Form 2553. Similar, but not identical to a partnership, the S corporation's income, deductions, capital gains and losses, charitable contributions, and credits are passed through to its shareholders.

Although S corporation status is a tax designation, for state law purposes, an S corporation is formed pursuant to state requirements of a regular corporation or LLC as is applicable. For tax purposes, an S corporation must be a domestic corporation organized under the laws of the United States or one of the individual states.[20]

The following types of entities are not eligible to become an S corporation:

- A financial institution that uses the reserve method of accounting
- An insurance company
- Corporations that elect to have credits for certain income from non-U.S. sources
- A current or former domestic international sales corporation[21]

An S corporation may only have one class of stock,[22] and each share must have equal distribution and liquidation rights. However, different shares may have different voting rights.[23] For example, shares could be issued that have no voting rights, or some shares may have twice (or three times) the number of votes as other shares. Generally, bona fide buy/sell agreements, agreements to restrict the transferability of shares, and redemption agreements do not create a second class of stock.[24] Providing a shareholder with reasonable employee benefits such as split-dollar life insurance or nonqualified deferred compensation will also not be considered as creating a second class of stock.

A C corporation and nonresident aliens may not be shareholders of an S corporation.[25] Permissible S corporation shareholders, include individuals, estates, or certain trusts. In addition, an S corporation has a shareholder limitation of no more than one hundred.[26] For this purpose, members of a family, as well as married couples, are considered one shareholder.[27] The types of trusts that may be shareholders of an S corporation include:

- a grantor trust whose owner is a U.S. citizen or resident;
- a trust that was a grantor trust before the owner's death may be a shareholder for two years after the death of the owner;
- a trust that has S corporation stock transferred to it may be a shareholder for two years after the transfer;
- a voting trust; or
- a qualified subchapter S trust (QSST) and an electing small business trust (ESBT).[28]

Assuming all requirements are met, by election of a beneficiary, a trust will be treated as a QSST.[29] A QSST is a trust with only one current income beneficiary (a citizen or U.S. resident) required to distribute all income in the year it is earned to the beneficiary. Additionally, it must not allow any distributions to anyone other than the beneficiary during the beneficiary's life. The beneficiary's income interest must terminate upon the earlier date of death or the termination of the trust. If the trust terminates during the lifetime of the income beneficiary, all trust's assets must be distributed to that beneficiary.

By election of the trustee, an ESBT is a trust in which all of the beneficiaries are individuals, estates, or certain charitable organizations. Trust income can be accumulated and/or sprinkled among the multiple beneficiaries. For S corporation eligibility purposes, each beneficiary of an ESBT is treated as a shareholder. This means that if a nonresident alien is a beneficiary or a potential beneficiary, the trust will be disqualified as an S corporation shareholder and cause the S corporation status to terminate. Similarly, if the number of beneficiaries or potential beneficiaries causes the S corporation to exceed the allowable number of shareholders, the trust will also cease to qualify.

Taxation of S Corporation Shareholders

Similar to a partnership, an S corporation is generally not subject to entity level tax.[30] Thus, the income, deduction, etc. of an S corporation passes through to its shareholders. Each shareholder's distributive share of such items are includible in gross income whether or not there is actual distribution. Shareholders take into account their shares of income, loss, deductions, and credit on a per-share, per-day basis.[31] However, unlike a partnership, special allocations are not permitted. In other words, each shareholder's distributive share must be in proportion to stock ownership. So, if Asher and Miranda are equal shareholders, their distributive shares must be equal. If they were 70-30 shareholders, Asher's distributive share would have to be 70 percent and Miranda's distributive share 30 percent.

Like separately stated partnership items, S corporation income or deductions that could directly affect the tax liability of the shareholder is passed through to the shareholder. Examples include capital gain income taxable at preferential rates as well as deductible charitable contributions made by an S corporation.[32]

The deductibility of pass through S corporation deductions is limited to the shareholder's basis in the stock. Basis is increased by shareholder contributions as well as his or her distributive share of income (including tax-exempt income). Basis is decreased (but not below zero) by (a) the distributive share of loss; (b) any non-deductible expense (that is not a capital expenses); and (c) shareholder distributions.[33] Deductions in excess of the basis in stock are carried forward indefinitely to future years until basis is increased by additional contributions and/or a distributive share of income.

Example: Asher, an S corporation shareholder, has a basis in his stock of $100. In 2019, Asher's distributive share of S corporation income is $20. In that same year, the S corporation distributes $10 to Asher. His basis in the stock is now $110 ($100 + $20 - $10). In 2020, the S corporation operates at a loss and Asher's distributive share of the loss is $65. As a result, Asher claims the $45 loss on his personal income tax return and reduces the basis in his stock to $45 ($110 – $65).

In 2021, the S corporation has another loss and Asher's distributive share of the loss is $55. Because Asher's distributive share of the loss is greater than his basis in the stock ($45), Asher's deduction is limited to $45. Therefore, the basis in Asher's stock is reduced to zero. The excess loss of $10 is carried forward indefinitely until his basis is increased by an additional contribution and/or a distributive share of income.

Distributions from an S corporation that do not exceed a shareholder's basis will not result in income to the shareholder. This is because a shareholder's basis is comprised of contributions and the distributive share of income. Thus, a shareholder who receives a distribution is deemed to recover basis. However, a distribution from an S corporation to a shareholder in excess of the basis in stock is taxable as capital gain.

Entity Level Taxation of an S Corporation

Built-In Gain

Although an S corporation is generally not subject to an entity level tax, an S corporation that had previously been a C corporation may be subject to an entity level tax on certain gains. If an S corporation disposes of property within five years after an election has been made, the gain attributable to pre-election appreciation of the property (built in gain that accrued during the period in which it was a C corporation) is taxed at the corporate level. The amount subject to tax is the gain that does not exceed the amount of taxable income imposed on the corporation if it were not an S corporation.[34] The rationale for this provision is to prevent former C corporations to avoid the corporate level tax on appreciated property by election S corporation status.

Tax on Passive Income

An entity level tax is imposed on excess "net passive income" of an S corporation. Passive investment income for this purpose is rents, royalties, dividends, interest, annuities, and proceeds from sales or exchanges of stock or securities. Passive investment income also does not include gross receipts derived in the ordinary course of business of lending or financing; dealing in property;

purchasing or discounting accounts receivable, notes, installment obligations, or servicing mortgages. Passive investment income does not include certain dividends from C corporations where the S corporation owns 80 percent or more of the C corporation.[35]

The tax is triggered in any year in which the corporation has earnings and profits and more than 25 percent of its gross receipts is generated by passive income.[36] All net passive income over that amount is taxed at the highest corporate rate (currently 35 percent) If an S corporation is subject to the passive income tax for three years in a row, its status as an S corporation will be lost on the first day of the fourth year.[37]

Advantages of S Corporation as an Entity Choice

Non-Tax Implications

As in a regular corporation, the shareholders of an S corporation enjoy limited liability and are not responsible for the debts and obligations of the corporation.

Tax Implications

Similar to a partnership, an S corporation is a pass through entity for income tax purposes. Therefore, unlike a C corporation, earnings are only taxed once. To the extent a shareholder has a positive basis, corporate distributions of earnings (dividends) are tax-free.

A major advantage an S corporation has as compared to a sole proprietorship or a partnership is no self-employment tax. So a shareholder's distributive share of S corporation income is subject only to income tax. Thus, it would seem that a shareholder who receives the entire distributive share of income is not subject to self-employment tax. However, if a shareholder who provides significant services to the S corporation is not paid a reasonable wage by the S corporation, there is the risk that the IRS would recharacterize all or some of such shareholder's distributive share of income as compensation. In that case, the recharacterized amount would be subject to FICA (social security and Medicare tax). To avoid this result, as long as a shareholder/employee's compensation is reasonable, the shareholder/employee can receive wages (subject to FICA) as well as self-employment free distributions.

Disadvantages of an S Corporation as an Entity Choice

Non-Tax Implications

Generally, because but for the tax election, an S corporation is in reality a state created corporation, the non-tax disadvantages are the same as those of a corporation taxed as a C corporation. For a discussion of those disadvantages, see the discussion in Disadvantages of a C Corporation as an Entity Choice, above.

Tax Implications

Perhaps the greatest tax disadvantage of an S corporation is its rigid rules that must be adhered to continuously throughout its existence. Included in those rules are the 100 maximum number of shareholders, one class of stock and the allowing of only specific types of shareholders (individuals, estates, certain trusts and tax-exempt organizations). In addition, special allocations are not permitted. Income and deductions must be allocated to shareholders based on the percentage of ownership.

Conversion to a C Corporation under the 2017 Tax Reform Act

Under prior law, if an S corporation converted to a C corporation, distributions of cash by the C corporation to the shareholders during the post-termination transition period were tax-free to the extent of the amount in the company's accumulated adjustment account. These distributions also reduced the shareholders' basis in the company's stock. The "post-termination transition period" was the one-year period after the S corporation election terminated.

The 2017 Tax Act provides that any accounting adjustments under IRC Section 481(a) that are required because of the revocation of the S corporation election of an "eligible terminated S corporation" (such as changing from the cash to accrual method of accounting) must be taken into account ratably during the six tax years beginning with the year of the change.[38]

An "eligible terminated S corporation" is defined as any C corporation which:

1. was an S corporation the day before the enactment of the 2017 Tax Act (i.e., December 22, 2017);

2. during the two-year period beginning on the date of enactment revokes its S corporation election under IRC Section 1362(a); and

3. where all of the owners of the S corporation on the date the election is revoked are the same owners (in identical proportions) as the owners on the date of the enactment of the 2017 Tax Act.[39]

Under the new rules, if there is a distribution of cash by an eligible terminated S corporation, the accumulated adjustments account will be allocated to that distribution, and the distribution will be chargeable to accumulated earnings and profits, in the same ratio as the amount of the accumulated adjustments account bears to the amount the accumulated earnings and profits.[40]

CHANGING ENTITY CLASSIFICATION

Changing a classification election is treated as a termination of the first entity for tax purposes and a transfer of the assets and liabilities to the new entity or the owners thereof.[41] Although a complete discussion is beyond the scope of this chapter, the following is a summary of the results:

- *Partnership to Corporation:* The partnership contributes all of its assets and liabilities to the corporation in exchange for stock. Immediately thereafter, the partnership liquidates and transfers the stock to the partners.

- *Corporation to Partnership:* The corporation liquidates and distributes all of its assets and liabilities to its shareholders. Immediately thereafter, the shareholders contribute the assets and liabilities to the newly-formed partnership.

- *Sole Proprietorship to Corporation:* The sole proprietor contributes all of the assets and liabilities of the business to the newly-formed corporation in exchange for the corporation's stock.

- *Corporation to Sole Proprietorship.* The corporation liquidates and distributes all of its assets and liabilities to its single owner.

FREQUENTLY ASKED QUESTIONS

Partnership

Question – What happens if a partner contributes property with a built-in loss to a partnership?

Answer – A partner may not shift a loss to other partners by contributing property with a built-in loss to a partnership. If the property is sold, the partner contributing property must be allocated the built-in loss.

Example: Albemarle contributes to a partnership property worth $25,000 with an adjusted basis in his hands of $50,000. If the property is ultimately sold for $25,000, the entire $25,000 loss is allocated to Albemarle.

Question – How are distributions from a partnership to a partner taxed if they exceed the partner's adjusted basis in the partnership?

Answer – Distributions of money or marketable securities in excess of the partner's basis in the partnership interest (often referred to as "outside basis") is taxable to the partner.[42] The income is generally treated as capital gain from the sale of the partnership interest on the date of the distribution. If property other than money (or marketable securities treated as money) is distributed to a partner, the partner generally does not recognize gain until he or she sells or otherwise disposes of the property.

Question – What are guaranteed payments and how are they treated for tax purposes?

Answer – Guaranteed payments are payments made by a partnership to a partner for services rendered to the partnership determined without regard to the income of the partnership. For example, a partner in a law firm might be guaranteed a base salary from the firm irrespective of the firm's profits, or a general partner in a real estate partnership might be guaranteed an annual management fee, regardless of the partnership's profits. A guaranteed payment is treated as a hybrid. For some purposes it is treated as a payment made to a non-partner; for other purposes it is treated similarly to a partner's distributive share. A guaranteed payment is taxable to a partner as ordinary income, regardless of the amount or character of the partnership's overall taxable income. Furthermore, the payment is deductible to the partners as an ordinary business expense under Code section 162.[43]

Question – How is health insurance coverage for partners taxed?

Answer – Generally, partners are treated as self-employed individuals, not employees, and the rules for personal health insurance apply. This means that partners can generally deduct 100 percent of amounts paid during a taxable year for insurance that provides medical care for the partner, spouse, and dependents during the tax year. The deduction is, however, limited to the amount of income earned from the partnership.[44] In addition, the deduction is not available to a partner for any calendar month in which he or she is eligible to participate in any subsidized health plan maintained by any employer of the partner or spouse.[45] This rule applies separately to traditional health insurance policies and long-term care insurance policies.

If a partnership pays health insurance premiums for a partner for services rendered by the partner in his capacity as a partner—and not as an employee—then the premium payments are considered to be "guaranteed payments" (see question above).[46] The partner is then taxable on the premium payments, and may or may not be able to deduct them on a personal return.

Limited Liability Companies

Question – What is an association, and how is it taxed under the "Check-the-Box" regulations?

Answer – Under the "Check-the-Box" regulations an association is an entity other than a corporation that is taxed as a C Corporation.[47] Some entities, such as LLCs or sole proprietorships, are classified as associations only as the result of an election. Other entities, such as "eligible foreign entities"—foreign entities that are not on the list of corporate equivalents in the regulations—in which all the members have limited liability, are classified as associations by default.

The term association is also used loosely to describe a variety of organizations, both incorporated and unincorporated. In this broader context, "association" does not imply any specific legal structure or tax status.

Corporations

Question – What are the income tax consequences that result from the creation of a corporation?

Answer – Corporations can generally be formed on a tax-free basis. The corporation will not recognize any gain (or loss) when it receives money or property in exchange for its own stock, whether the stock is newly issued or treasury stock.[48]

Also, generally, a shareholder who transfers money or property to a corporation in exchange for stock will not recognize gain or loss.[49] This rule applies to shareholders who in unison contribute property and receive the stock control 80 percent or more of the stock after the transaction.[50] If the persons who contribute property to the corporation receive additional property or money in the transaction (i.e., "boot"), some gain may be recognized.[51]

Question – How does tax reform impact the rollover of publicly traded securities gain into SSBICs?

Answer – The 2017 Tax Act repealed IRC Section 1044, which previously allowed taxpayers to roll over (and thus defer recognition of) certain capital gains from the sale of publicly traded securities if the amounts were used to purchase an interest in a specialized small business investment company (SSBIC). This repeal applies for tax years beginning after December 31, 2017.[52]

Question – Were the rules governing electing small business trusts (ESBTs) changed under tax reform?

Answer – The 2017 Tax Act expands the definition of a qualifying beneficiary under an electing small business trust (ESBT) to include nonresident aliens.[53] This provision is effective beginning January 1, 2018.

For tax years beginning after December 31, 2017, charitable deductions of an ESBT will be determined according to the rules that apply to individuals (rather than using the rules applicable to trusts and estates) except that deductions that are allowed for expenses paid in administering the trust that would not have been incurred but for the trust arrangement are allowed in determining adjusted gross income.[54]

Question – Was the technical termination of a partnership rule impacted by tax reform?

Answer – Under the 2017 Tax Act, the technical termination rule was repealed. Therefore, a partnership will be treated as though it is continuing even if more than 50 percent of the total capital and profits interest of the partnership are sold or exchanged. This provision applies for tax years beginning after 2017.[55]

CHAPTER ENDNOTES

1. IRC Sec. 761
2. Treas. Reg. §1.701-1(b)(2)(ii)(a).
3. IRC Sec. 741.
4. Treas. Reg. §301.7701-3(f)(2).
5. Treas. Reg. §301.7701-3(c)(1)(iv).
6. Treas. Reg. §301.7701-2(b).
7. Treas. Reg. §301.7701-2(c)(2)(iv).
8. Rev. Rul. 2004-41, C.B. 845.
9. IRC Sec. 170.
10. IRC Sec. 11(b)(1).
11. IRC Sec. 336(a).
12. IRC Sec. 11(b)(2).
13. IRC Sec. 448(d)(2).
14. IRC Sec. 531.
15. IRC Sec. 535.
16. IRC Sec. 541.
17. IRC Sec. 542(a).
18. IRC Sec. 543(a).
19. IRC Sec. 545(a).
20. IRC Sec. 1361(b)(1).
21. IRC Sec. 1361(b)(2).
22. IRC Sec. 1361(b)(1)(D).
23. IRC Sec. 1361(c)(4).
24. Treas. Reg. §1.1361-1(l)(2).
25. IRC Sec. 1361(b)(1).
26. IRC Sec. 1361(b)(1)(A).
27. IRC Sec. 1361(c)(1).
28. IRC Sec. 1361(c)(2).
29. IRC Sec. 1361(d).
30. IRC Sec. 1363(a).
31. IRC Sec. 1366(a).
32. IRC Sec. 1366(a)(1).
33. IRC Sec. 1367.
34. IRC Sec. 1374.
35. IRC Sec. 1375.
36. IRC Sec. 1362(d)(3)(A)(i).
37. IRC Sec.1362(d)(3).
38. IRC Sec. 481(d)(1).
39. IRC Sec. 481(d)(2).
40. IRC Sec. 1371(f).
41. Treas. Reg. §301.7701-3(g)(1).
42. IRC Sec. 731(a).
43. IRC Sec. 707(c).
44. IRC Sec. 162(l).
45. IRC Sec. 162(l)(2)(B).
46. Rev. Rul. 91-26, 1991-1 CB 184.
47. Treas. Reg. §§301.7701-2(b)(2), 301.7701-3.
48. IRC Sec. 1032(a).
49. IRC Sec. 351(e).
50. IRC Sec. 351(a).
51. IRC Sec. 368(c).
52. Former IRC Sec. 1044.
53. IRC Secs. 1361(c)(2)(B)(v), 1361(b)(1)(C).
54. IRC Sec. 641(c)(2)(E).
55. IRC Sec. 708(b)(1)(B) (repealed by the 2017 Tax Act).

COST RECOVERY CONCEPTS

CHAPTER 20

INTRODUCTION

Cost recovery is a term that refers to methods used by taxpayers to deduct the costs of business assets that generally must be deducted over a period of time, and not in the year that the assets were purchased. Cost recovery can also refer to amortization, which generally refers to deductions allowed for the acquisition of intangible property that has a limited useful life, but may be used in other situations.

WHEN IS IT INDICATED?

Depreciation is used when a taxpayer purchases certain capital assets. Generally, a taxpayer may not treat as an expense amounts that are paid for capital assets.[1] However, a taxpayer is allowed to take a deduction for the exhaustion, wear and tear, and obsolescence of property used in a trade or business or property held for the production of income.[2]

Only property with a limited useful life is subject to a deduction for depreciation. For that reason, land itself is not depreciable, although improvements to land can be depreciated. Also, inventory may not be depreciated.

TAX IMPLICATIONS

There are different methods that are used to depreciate property. The method that must be used depends on when the property was placed into service and the type of property it is, such as personal property or real estate.

Property is "placed into service" when it is first placed in a condition or state of readiness and availability for a specifically assigned function for use in a trade or business, for the production of income, or in a tax-exempt or personal activity.

Property Placed in Service Before 1981

Depreciable property that was placed in service before 1981 must be depreciated using the useful life of the property and its salvage value. The property, depending on its character (whether it is tangible or intangible, personal property, or residential or nonresidential real estate), may be depreciated using the straight line, 200, 150, or 125 percent declining balance, the sum of the years' digits, or any reasonable, consistently used method.

Accelerated Cost Recovery System

Generally, tangible property placed in service after 1980 must be depreciated using the Accelerated Cost Recovery System (ACRS). The ACRS was modified for property placed in service after 1986 (see Modified Accelerated Cost Recovery System below). The pre-1987 ACRS rules apply generally to property placed in service after 1980 and before 1987.

The pre-1987 ACRS deduction is determined by multiplying the taxpayer's unadjusted basis in the property by a prescribed recovery percentage. A taxpayer's unadjusted basis in an asset is the basis of the asset for purposes of determining gain. Basis is usually the cost of the asset, but the basis may be reduced by amounts elected for amortization or for expensing. Because land may not be depreciated, the basis of improved land must be allocated between the land and its improvements.

If property is used in an individual's trade or business as well as in a personal or tax-exempt activity during a taxable year, the depreciable basis is determined by multiplying the unadjusted basis, as figured above, by the percentage of time the property was used in the trade or business. For example, the unadjusted basis of a car driven 20,000 miles in a year, of which 15,000 miles were for business purposes, would be multiplied by 75 percent.

Each year, the property's basis is reduced by the amount of the depreciation deduction taken so that the adjusted basis of the property reflects accumulated depreciation deductions. If depreciation is not deducted, the basis must still be reduced by the amount of allowable depreciation, but this "missed" deduction may not be taken in a subsequent year.

Property is classified as three, five, ten, fifteen, eighteen, or nineteen-year property, and recovery percentages are prescribed for each classification. The following is the classification of property by recovery period:

3 years	autos, light trucks, research and development equipment
5 years	heavy-duty trucks, production line equipment, most office furniture, most other equipment except long-life public utility property and certain single purpose agricultural structures and facilities used for petroleum storage
10 years	certain intermediate-life public utility property, railroad tank cars, theme park structures, coal utilization property, manufactured residential homes, depreciable real estate with an average asset depreciation range guideline life of 12.5 years or less
15 years	certain long-life public utility property, low-income housing, and most real estate placed in service before March 16, 1984
18 years	most real estate placed in service after March 15, 1984 and before May 9, 1985
19 years	most real estate placed in service after May 8, 1985

In computing depreciation on personal property, salvage value is ignored and in the first year a full year's deduction is taken regardless of the month the property is placed in service. However, no ACRS deduction is allowed in the year of an early disposition of the property.

An alternative method of calculating depreciation is available under the ACRS. The taxpayer could have elected to calculate the ACRS deductions according to the straight line method using one of the recovery periods, below, for each class of recovery property. The election must have been made by the due date (including extensions) of the income tax return for the taxable year the property is placed in service. Once this alternative method has been elected, permission of the IRS is needed in order to change to the regular ACRS method.

Straight-Line Recovery Periods by Class of Property	
In the case of:	The individual may have elected a recovery period of:
3-year property	3, 5, or 12 years
5-year property	5, 12, or 25 years
10-year property	10, 25, or 35 years
15-year public utility property and low-income housing	15, 35, or 45 years
19-year property	19, 35, or 45 years

Note that during any taxable year, all personal property in a particular class which was placed in service during a particular year must have been depreciated using the same method. For real estate, however, the election may have been made on a property-by-property basis.

Modified Accelerated Cost Recovery System

Generally, the Accelerated Cost Recovery System (ACRS) was replaced with the Modified Accelerated Cost Recovery System (MACRS) for property placed in service after 1986. Faster depreciation than under ACRS was provided for certain property, new seven and twenty-year classes were created, and real estate was required to generally be depreciated over a much longer period than under the ACRS.[3]

The initial basis of the property is usually the cost of the property, which is then reduced by any available amortization or Section 179 expensing deductions (see below) and certain tax credits. The basis is then reduced each year by the amount of depreciation that is allowable. It is important to remember that even if depreciation is not claimed on depreciable property by a taxpayer, the basis is still reduced by the amount that could have been claimed.

The classification of property by recovery period and depreciation method is as follows:[4]

3 years 200% DB	class life of 4 years or less, certain horses, qualified rent-to-own property
5 years 200% DB	class life of more than 4 but less than 10 years, heavy trucks, buses, off-shore drilling equipment, most computer and data handling equipment, cattle, helicopters and noncommercial aircraft, automobiles and light trucks
7 years 200% DB	class life of 10 or more but less than 16 years, most office furnishings, most agricultural machinery and equipment, theme park structures, most railroad machinery, equipment and track, commercial aircraft, property without a class life
10 years 200% DB	class life of 16 or more but less than 20 years, vessels, barges and similar water transportation equipment, petroleum refining equipment
15 years 150% DB	class life of 20 or more but less than 25 years, industrial steam and electric generation/distribution systems, cement manufacturing equipment, commercial water transportation equipment (freight or passenger), nuclear power production plants, certain real property that is a retail motor fuels outlet
20 years 150% DB	class life of 25 years or more, certain farm buildings, railroad structures and improvements, telephone central office buildings, gas utility production plants and distribution facilities, but excluding real property with class life of 27.5 years or more
25 years straight line	water utility property
27.5 years straight line	residential rental property
39 years straight line	nonresidential real property (class life of 27.5 years or more)
50 years straight line	railroad grading or tunnel bore
DB stands for declining balance method switching to the straight line method at a time to maximize the deduction. 150 percent DB is substituted for 200 percent DB if three-, five-, seven-, or ten-year property is used in a farming business. An election can be made to use the straight line method instead of the declining balance method. Also, a taxpayer may elect to use the 150 percent declining balance method for three, five, seven, and ten-year property.	

The IRS has assigned "class lives" to most types of depreciable property, and Congress has also provided legislatively what class lives will be for certain property.

For certain property acquired after September 11, 2001, and before January 1, 2005, a depreciation "bonus" of 30 percent could be taken in the year the property was placed in service. Taxpayers could elect to not take this bonus depreciation. Also, for certain property acquired after May 5, 2003, and before January 1, 2005, bonus depreciation of 50 percent could be taken. For eligible property, taxpayers could elect 50 percent bonus depreciation, 30 percent bonus depreciation, or no bonus depreciation. Bonus depreciation is also allowed for property placed in service in 2008.[5]

In the year that depreciable property is acquired, the depreciation is limited to the portion of the year the property is held by the owner according to the following conventions. Residential rental property, nonresidential real property, and railroad grading or tunnel bore are treated as placed in service on the mid-point of the month in which the property is placed in service. Any other property is generally treated as placed in service on the mid-point of the year in which it was placed in service. There are similar rules regarding when property is considered to be disposed of by the taxpayer.[6]

The mid-quarter convention applies to property placed in service during the taxable year if the aggregate bases of property placed in service by the taxpayer during the last three months of the taxable year exceeds 40 percent of the aggregate bases of property placed in service during the taxable year. This is called "the 40 percent test." Regardless of whether the mid-year convention or the mid-quarter convention applies, no depreciation deduction is available for property placed in service and disposed of in the same year.

Property subject to the mid-month convention is treated as placed in service on the mid-point of the month without regard to whether the taxpayer has a short taxable year. The mid-quarter 40 percent test is also made without regard to the length of the taxable year. If property is placed in service in a taxable year that is three months or less, the mid-quarter convention applies regardless of when the property was placed in service, because 100 percent of property will have been placed in service in the last three months.[7]

In the case of a short taxable year and with respect to property to which the mid-year or mid-quarter convention applies, the recovery allowance is determined by multiplying the deduction that would have been allowable if the recovery year were not a short taxable year by a fraction, with the numerator equal to the number of months in the short taxable year and the denominator equal to twelve.

Alternative Depreciation System

An alternative depreciation system must be used for:

- tangible property that is used predominately outside the United States;
- tax-exempt use property;
- tax-exempt bond financed property;
- certain imported property covered by an executive order regarding countries engaging in unfair trade practices; and
- property for which the taxpayer makes an election to use the alternative system.

The election may be made with respect to each property in the case of nonresidential real property and residential rental property. For all other property, the election is made with respect to all property placed in service within a recovery class during a taxable year.[8]

The alternative depreciation deduction is determined using the straight line method and the applicable convention (mid-month, mid-quarter, or mid-year), over the following periods:

tax-exempt use property subject to a lease	longer of 125% of the lease term or period below
residential rental property and nonresidential real property	40 years
personal property with no class life	12 years
railroad grading or tunnel bore	50 years
all other property	the class life

Other Limitations

Depreciation deductions are also generally limited for certain property placed in service after June 18, 1984 if the business use of the property does not exceed 50 percent of its total use during the taxable year. This "listed property" includes any passenger automobile or certain other property used for transportation; any property of a type used for entertainment, recreation or amusement; certain computers, any cellular telephone; or other property specified by the IRS.[9]

If the business use of the listed property does not exceed 50 percent, depreciation under the pre-1987 ACRS and post-1986 MACRS is not allowed. For property placed in service after 1986, the amount of the depreciation is limited to the amount determined using the alternative depreciation system (described above).[10]

The depreciation of passenger automobiles that are purchased and leased is also subject to other limitations on the amount that can be taken as a depreciation deduction.

Depreciation Recapture

When depreciable property is sold, the seller often will realize more than his basis because of depreciation deductions that have been taken. Generally, this gain will be treated as a capital gain that may be subject to favorable tax rates while the gain is, at least in part, attributable to depreciation. To prevent a double benefit, the IRC requires that some of the gain that would otherwise generally be capital gain must be treated as ordinary income. In effect, it requires the seller to "recapture" some of the ordinary income that was offset in previous years by depreciation.[11] With respect to depreciable property other than real estate, the total amount of depreciation claimed is generally subject to the recapture rule under current law. With respect to real estate, the general rule under current law provides that property that has been depreciated under an accelerated method will be subject to recapture, while property that has been depreciated under the straight-line method will not. For residential real estate, the amount recaptured is the amount of depreciation claimed that is in excess of the amount that would have been allowable under the straight-line method. For nonresidential real estate that has been depreciated under an accelerated method, the entire amount of depreciation claimed is generally subject to recapture.

Cost Recovery for Intangible Assets

Generally, taxpayers are permitted depreciation deductions for certain intangible property. A depreciation deduction is allowed for certain computer software readily available to the general public, business interests and rights, and mortgage servicing rights.[12] Computer software eligible for this deduction is depreciated over a thirty-six-month period using the straight-line method. Other assets are depreciated under different schedules. The deduction generally is allowable for depreciable intangible property acquired after August 10, 1993, unless the taxpayer elects to take the deduction for such property acquired after July 25, 1991.

Intangible property for which a depreciation deduction is allowed includes:

(1) computer programs available for purchase by the general public that are designed to cause a computer to perform a desired function;

(2) a right under a contract or granted by a government entity that entitles the taxpayer to receive tangible property or services;

(3) a right under a contract or granted by a government agency if such right has a fixed duration of less than fifteen years, or if such right is fixed as to amount and would otherwise be recoverable under a method similar to a unit-of-production method;

(4) any interest in a patent or copyright; and

(5) any right to service indebtedness that is secured by residential real property.

Certain other intangible assets held for business or the production of income are eligible for amortization deductions over a 180-month period, in lieu of depreciation, under IRC Section 197. Assets that are eligible for 180-month amortization are not eligible for any other depreciation or amortization deduction. The taxpayer, must, of course, have a tax basis in such assets in order to amortize them. These assets include (among others) goodwill and going concern value, business books and records, operating systems, proprietary databases, and patents, copyrights, formulas, and similar items. Computer software eligible for thirty-six-month depreciation as described above cannot be amortized. The rules for amortization apply to intangible assets acquired by the taxpayer pursuant to a written contract that was in effect after August 10, 1993.

Section 179 Expensing

A taxpayer may elect to treat the cost of certain property as an expense in the year the property is placed in service. To qualify, the property must be eligible for depreciation or certain amortization provisions, it must generally be personal property (in other words, real estate is not eligible), and must have been acquired by purchase (from an unrelated person) for use in the active conduct of a trade or business. The property may not be an air conditioning or heating unit or "ineligible property." Ineligible property is generally property used outside the U.S., for lodging, by tax-exempt organizations, or by governments or foreign persons or entities. This election is not available to a trust or estate, and it may not be used for property held for the production of income.[13]

The aggregate cost that can be expensed when making this election is $25,000 for purchases made after 2010. These amounts are reduced by one dollar for each dollar of the cost of the above described property placed in service during the taxable year that exceeds $500,000 as indexed in 2007 through 2010, or $200,000 after 2010.[14]

The amount expensed is limited to the aggregate amount of income derived from the active conduct of any trade or business of the taxpayer. An amount that is not deductible because it exceeds the aggregate taxable income from any trade or business may be carried over and taken in a subsequent year.

The amount that may be carried over and taken in a subsequent year is the lesser of

(1) the amounts disallowed because of the taxable income limitation in all prior taxable years (reduced by any carryover deductions in previous taxable years); or

(2) the amount of unused expense allowance for such year. The amount of unused expense allowance is the excess of (1) the maximum cost of property that may be expensed taking into account the dollar and income limitations; or (2) the amount the taxpayer elects to expense. Married individuals filing separately are treated as one taxpayer for purposes of determining the amount that may be expensed and the total amount of the cost of all property eligible for expensing.

REPAIR REGULATIONS

On September 13, 2013, the IRS issued more than 200 pages of regulations that are intended to quell the controversy over the deduction/capitalization issue by providing a general framework for distinguishing capital expenditures from supplies, repairs, maintenance, and other deductible business expenses.[15]

The determination whether a particular expense is a deductible repair or maintenance expense or a depreciable capital expenditure generally requires an examination of the taxpayer's particular facts and circumstances. The subjective nature of the existing standards governing the determination—based on case law, the differing interpretations of various courts and on a number of IRS rulings—has resulted in considerable controversy between taxpayers and the IRS over many years.

The new rules—known as the "repair regulations"—also cover the retirement of depreciable property under Code section 167 (occurring when a depreciable asset is taken out of service with no salvage value) and provide accounting rules for property under the Modified Accelerated Cost Recovery System (MACRS) required by Code section 168. However, the repair regulations do not finalize the rules that address the definition of "disposition" for property subject to the section 168 MACRS.[16] Instead, revised regulations under section 168 were proposed with the final regulations.

Under Code section 263(a), certain business expenditures related to improving property must be capitalized and depreciated over the property's prescribed depreciable life. These expenditures include any amount:

1. paid out for new buildings or permanent improvements, or betterments made to increase the value of any property; or

2. expended in restoring property or in making good its exhaustion through a reserve for depreciation allowance.

Previous final rules issued under section 263(a) defined capital expenditures as including amounts paid to either (1) add to the value, or substantially prolong the useful life, of a taxpayer's property, or (2) adapt the property to a new or different use. However, those regulations also specified that amounts paid or incurred for incidental repairs and maintenance of property are not capital expenditures and may be currently deducted. Thus, there was confusion about how to classify many types of expenditures: was a taxpayer paying for something that "substantially prolonged the useful life" of the property, or undertaking "incidental repairs and maintenance"?

The final repair rules retain and modify many of the provisions contained in temporary and proposed regulations issued in 2011, and apply to taxable years beginning on or after January 1, 2014. However, taxpayers can choose to apply the final regs to taxable years beginning on or after January 1, 2012. The rules are divided into five basic parts:

- Regulation 1.162-3 provides rules for materials and supplies

- Regulation section 1.162-4 addresses repairs and maintenance

- Regulation section 1.263(a)-1 provides general rules for capital expenditures

- Regulation section 1.263(a)-2 provides rules for amounts paid for the acquisition or production of tangible property

- Regulation section 1.263(a)-3 provides rules for amounts paid for the improvement of tangible property

Materials and Supplies

While retaining the framework and many of the rules contained in the 2011 temporary regs, the final regulations expand the definition of materials and supplies to include property that has an acquisition or production cost of $200 or less (increased from $100 or less), clarify application of the optional method of accounting for rotable and temporary spare parts, and simplify the application of the de minimis safe harbor of Regulation section 1.263(a)-1(f) to materials and supplies. The final regs also define standby emergency spare parts and limit the application of the election to capitalize materials and supplies to only rotable, temporary, and standby emergency spare parts.

De minimis safe harbor. A taxpayer with an applicable financial statement may rely on the de minimis safe harbor and elect to currently deduct the cost of tangible property and materials and supplies only if the amount paid for the property does not exceed $5,000 per invoice, or per item as substantiated by the invoice.[17] An "applicable financial statement" is a statement filed with the SEC, audited by an independent CPA that is used for certain purposes, or a statement other than a tax return required to be provided to an agency of the federal or a state government (other than the IRS or the SEC).

The safe harbor also applies to a financial accounting procedure that expenses amounts paid for property with an economic useful life of twelve months or less as long as the amount per invoice (or item) does not exceed $5,000. Such amounts are deductible under the de minimis rule whether this financial accounting procedure applies in isolation or in combination with a financial accounting procedure for expensing amounts paid for property that does not exceed a specified dollar amount. Under either procedure, if the cost exceeds $5,000 per invoice (or item), then the amounts paid for the property will not fall within the de minimis safe harbor.

In addition, an anti-abuse rule is provided to aggregate costs that are improperly split among multiple invoices. The final regulations provide the IRS and the Treasury Department with the authority to change the safe harbor amount through published guidance.

The final regulations also include a de minimis rule for taxpayers without an applicable financial statement. Such taxpayers may rely on the de minimis safe harbor only if the amount paid for property does not exceed $500 per invoice (or item) as substantiated by the invoice.

Note that if a taxpayer meets the requirements for the safe harbor, which requires, in part, having written accounting procedures in place at the beginning of the taxable year and treating amounts paid for property as an expense in accordance with those procedures, then a change in the procedures, by itself, is not a change in accounting method.

However, the regulations specify that the de minimis safe harbor does not apply to:

1. amounts paid for property that is, or is intended to be included in inventory property;

2. amounts paid for land; or

3. amounts paid for rotable, temporary, and standby emergency spare parts that the taxpayer elects to capitalize and depreciate, or accounts for under the optional method of accounting for rotable parts pursuant to Regulation section 1.162-3(e).[18]

Repairs and Maintenance

The final regulations retain the rule from the 2011 temporary regulations providing that amounts paid for repairs and maintenance to tangible property are deductible if the amounts paid are not otherwise required to be capitalized under Regulation section 1.263(a)-3.

Routine maintenance safe harbor expanded. Under the 2011 temporary regs, the costs of performing certain routine maintenance activities for property other than a building or the structural components of a building were not required to be capitalized as an improvement. The final regulations extend the safe harbor to apply to buildings, provided the taxpayer reasonably expects to perform the relevant activities more than once during a ten-year period.

General Rules for Capital Expenditures

The new rules provide for the coordination with other provisions of the Internal Revenue Code, and state that nothing in the repair regulations changes the treatment of amounts that are specifically provided for in other Code provisions (other than Sections 162(a) and 212).[19] The Unicap rules under Code section 263A are cited as an example.

In addition to amounts paid to acquire, produce, or improve units of real or personal tangible property, the regulations cite examples of capital expenditures, including:

- amounts paid to facilitate the acquisition of a business or change the capital structure of a business entity; and

- amounts paid to acquire or create interests in land (such as easements, life estates, mineral interests, timber rights, or zoning variances).

Amounts Paid to Acquire or Produce Tangible Property

In general, the final regulations retain the rules from the 2011 temporary regulations with regard to expenses related to acquiring or producing tangible property. The new regulations continue the requirements to capitalize amounts paid to acquire or produce a unit of real or personal property, or to defend or perfect title to real or personal property. They also include rules for determining the extent to which taxpayers must capitalize transaction costs related to the acquisition of property.

The new rules also include the requirement from the 2011 regulations that taxpayers capitalize amounts paid to facilitate the acquisition or production of real or personal property and retain the list of "inherently facilitative costs" that generally must be capitalized as transaction costs.[20]

The final rules also clarify the meaning of "finders' fee" and "brokers' commission," and provide that if a real estate broker's commission is contingent on the successful closing of the acquisition of real property, the amount paid as the commission inherently facilitates the acquisition of the property acquired and, therefore, must be capitalized as part of the basis of such property.

Amounts Paid to Improve Property

For purposes of determining whether an amount improves, betters, or restores a unit of property and must be capitalized, the final repair rules generally define a "unit of property" as consisting of all the components of property that are functionally interdependent. Special rules are provided in the repair regs for determining the unit of property for buildings, plant property, and network assets and for determining the units of property for condominiums, cooperatives, and leased property, and the treatment of improvements (including leasehold improvements).

Restorations

The 2011 temporary regulations provided that an amount paid to restore (and therefore improve) a unit of property generally must be capitalized, if it meets one of six tests:

1. It is for the replacement of a component of a unit of property and the taxpayer has properly deducted a loss for that component (other than a casualty loss).

2. It is for the replacement of a component of a unit of property and the taxpayer has properly taken into account the adjusted basis of the component in realizing gain or loss resulting from the sale or exchange of the component.

3. It is for the repair of damage to a unit of property for which the taxpayer has properly taken a basis adjustment as a result of a casualty loss under Code section 165, or relating to a casualty event described in section 165 ("casualty loss rule").

4. It returns the unit of property to its ordinarily efficient operating condition if the property has deteriorated to a state of disrepair and is no longer functional for its intended use.

5. It results in the rebuilding of the unit of property to a like-new condition after the end of its class life.

6. It is for the replacement of a major component or a substantial structural part of the unit of property ("major component rule").

The repair regulations retain this basic rule, but clarify the definition of major component, and, more significantly, add a new definition for major components and substantial structural parts of buildings. The final regulations define a "major component" as a part or combination of parts that performs a discrete and critical function in the operation of the unit of property, and a "substantial structural part" as a part or combination of parts that comprises a large portion of the physical structure of the unit of property.

WHERE CAN I FIND OUT MORE?

IRS Publication 946, "How to Depreciate Property" has information about both depreciation and Section 179 expensing. It contains tables providing the appropriate percentages to calculate the depreciable property and has tables that list the appropriate class lives and recovery periods for property. It also provides a comprehensive example of a hypothetical business and how the business would calculate and report its depreciation.

IMMEDIATELY EXPENSING UNDER THE 2017 TAX ACT

The 2017 Tax Act allows full expensing for business owners with respect to property that is placed in service after September 27, 2017 and before January 1, 2023. Further, under the 2017 Tax Act, the requirement that the property be originally placed into service by the taxpayer is removed (i.e., tax reform permits accelerated expensing of used assets).[21]

The amount that may be expensed is reduced each year after January 1, 2023, as outlined in Figure 20.1.

Figure 20.1

ACCELERATED EXPENSING UNDER THE 2017 TAX REFORM ACT*			
Most types of property[22]		Certain types of property with longer production periods[23]	
Date placed in service	Expensing	Date placed in service	Expensing
9/21/17 to 12/31/22	100%	9-27-17 to 12/31/23	100%
1/1/23 to 12/31/23	80%	1/1/24 to 12/31/24	80%
1/1/24 to 12/31/24	60%	1/1/25 to 12/31/25	60%
1/1/25 to 12/31/25	40%	1/1/26 to 12/31/26	40%
1/1/26 to 12/31/26	20%	1/1/27 to 12/31/27	20%
1/1/27 and later	0%	1/1/28 and later	0%
Under a transition rule, the business may elect to apply a 50 percent depreciation allowance instead of the 100 percent allowance for the taxpayer's first tax year ending after September 27, 2017.[24]			

Used Property

The cost recovery amendments described above may be applied to used property if the property was not used by the taxpayer prior to the acquisition and all of the following are true:

1. The property was not acquired from certain related parties, including:

    a. The taxpayer's spouse, ancestors and descendants;

    b. An individual and a corporation more than 50 percent in value of the outstanding stock of which is owned, directly or indirectly, by or for the individual;

    c. A grantor and a fiduciary of any trust;

    d. A fiduciary of a trust and a fiduciary of another trust, if the same person is a grantor of both trusts;

    e. A fiduciary and a beneficiary of a trust;

    f. A fiduciary of a trust and a beneficiary of another trust, if the same person is a grantor of both trusts;

    g. A fiduciary of a trust and a corporation more than 50 percent in value of the outstanding stock of which is owned, directly or indirectly, by or for the trust or by or for a person who is a grantor of the trust;

    h. A person and an organization to which IRC Section 501 (relating to certain educational and charitable organizations which are exempt from tax) applies and which is controlled directly or indirectly by such person or (if such person is an individual) by members of the family of such individual;

    i. A corporation and a partnership if the same person owns more than 50 percent of the outstanding stock in the corporation or capital interest or profits of the partnership;

    j. An S corporation and another S corporation if the same person owns more than 50 percent of the outstanding stock of each corporation;

    k. An S corporation and a C corporation, if the same persons own more than 50 percent in value of the outstanding stock of each corporation;

    l. The executor and beneficiary of an estate;

    m. Two partnerships in which the same person owns more than 50 percent of the capital interests and profits; or

    n. A partnership and a person owning more than 50 percent of the capital interests and profits of the partnership;

2. The property was not acquired by one member of a controlled group from another member of that group;

3. The basis of the property in the hands of the person acquiring it is not determined in whole or part by reference to the adjusted basis of the property in the hands of the person from whom it was acquired or under IRC Section 1014(a) (basis of property acquired from a decedent); and

4. The cost of the property does not include the basis of the property as determined by reference to the basis of other property held by the taxpayer.[25]

Section 179 Expensing

IRC Section 179 generally allows a taxpayer to elect to expense (deduct) the cost of qualifying property instead of using depreciation to recover the cost over time. Under prior law, the most that a taxpayer could expense was $500,000 of the cost of the qualifying property that was placed in service during the year. However, that $500,000 amount was reduced (phased out) for by the amount by which the cost of the property placed in service during the year exceeded $2,000,000.

The 2017 Tax Act increased the maximum amount that can be expensed during the tax year to $1,000,000,[26] and increased the phase-out threshold amount from $2,000,000 to $2,500,000.[27] These amounts are indexed for inflation for tax years beginning after 2018.

The 2017 Tax Act also expanded the definition of qualified property[28] to include certain depreciable tangible property used primarily to provide lodging or in connection with providing lodging, and to include certain improvements to nonresidential real property that is placed in service after the date that the underlying property was first placed in service (roofs, heating, ventilation, air conditioning, fire protection and alarm systems and security systems).[29]

These provisions are effective for tax years beginning after December 31, 2017.

Section 280F Depreciation Limits

The 2017 Tax Act increased the IRC Section 280F depreciation limits that apply to certain passenger automobiles placed into service after December 31, 2017 as follows:

- First year: $10,000
- Second year: $16,000
- Third year: $9,600
- Fourth and later years: $5,760[30]

These rules apply to passenger automobiles for which additional first-year depreciation under IRC Section 168(k) is not claimed. The limits will be indexed for inflation for passenger automobiles that are placed in service after 2018.

Additionally, computer and peripheral equipment are removed from the definition of listed property to which the new rules apply (meaning that this property will not be subject to the heightened substantiation requirements that apply to listed property).[31]

These rules are effective for property placed into service after December 31, 2017 and for tax years ending after December 31, 2017.

FREQUENTLY ASKED QUESTIONS

Question – How do repairs to depreciable property affect the property's basis and therefore its depreciation deductions?

Answer – If a taxpayer creates depreciable property, the expense of creating the property may not be taken as a business expense, but instead the cost must be recovered using depreciation. In the same way, if improvements are made to depreciable property that slow down deterioration or prolong the life of the property, these improvements must also be depreciated and cannot be expensed. However, the cost of "incidental" repairs which do not materially add to the value of the property nor prolong the life of the property may be taken as a business expense in the year the expense is incurred.[32]

Question – What is depletion?

Answer – Depletion is another cost recovery method that excludes (by way of income tax deductions) from the proceeds of mineral operations the part of the proceeds that represents a tax-free return of an investor's capital. Depletion deductions compensate the owner of wasting mineral assets "for the part exhausted in production, so that when the minerals are gone, the owner's capital and his capital assets remain unimpaired."[33] There are two different types of depletion: cost depletion and percentage depletion. If a taxpayer is eligible to take both percentage depletion and cost depletion, the amount that results in the larger deduction must be taken.

Cost depletion is calculated under the following formula:[34]

$$\text{Cost Depletion} = \frac{\text{Basis of Property}}{\text{Units Remaining as of Tax Year}} \times \text{Units sold during year}$$

The Basis is the adjusted basis (including adjustments for previous depreciation) that would be used to determine the gain on the sale of the property. The Units Remaining is the units remaining at the end of the year plus the number of units sold during the year.

Percentage depletion is not based on the adjusted basis in the property, but instead uses a method where a specified percentage is multiplied by the investor's gross income from the property for that year.[18] The percentage rate will vary depending on the type of mineral or natural resource that is extracted. Certain taxpayers are not permitted to use percentage depletion, depending on the extracted natural resource and the classification of the taxpayer.

CHAPTER ENDNOTES

1. IRC Sec. 263(a).
2. IRC Sec. 167(a).
3. IRC Sec. 168.
4. IRC Secs. 168(c), 168(e); Rev. Proc. 87-56, 1987-2 CB 674.
5. IRC Sec. 168(k).
6. IRC Sec. 168(d).
7. Rev. Proc. 89-15, 1989-1 CB 816.
8. IRC Sec. 168(g).
9. IRC Sec. 280F.
10. IRC Secs. 1245, 1250.
11. IRC Sec. 167(f).
12. IRC Sec. 179.
13. Rev. Proc. 2008-66, 2008-45 IRB _____.
14. Treas. Reg. §1.162-4.
15. 78 Fed. Reg. 182 (September 19, 2013)
16. Treas. Reg. §§1.168(i)-1T to 1.168(i)-8T.
17. Teas. Reg. §1.263(a)-1(f).
18. Treas. Reg. §1.263(a)-1.
19. Treas. Reg. §1.263(a)-1.
20. Treas. Reg. §1.263(a)-2(f)(2)(ii).
21. IRC Sec. 168(k)(2)(A)(ii), 168(k)(2)(E)(ii).
22. IRC Sec. 168(k)(6)(A).
23. IRC Sec. 168(k)(6)(B).
24. IRC Sec. 168(k)(8).
25. IRC Secs. 168(k)(2)(E)(ii), 267(b), 707(b).
26. IRC Sec. 179(b)(1).
27. IRC Sec. 179(b)(2).
28. IRC Sec. 179(d)(1).
29. IRC Sec. 179(f)(2).
30. IRC Sec. 280F(a)(1)(A).
31. IRC Sec. 280F(d)(4)(A).
32. *Paragon Jewel Coal Co., Inc. v. Comm'r.*, 380 U.S. 624 (1965).
33. Treas. Reg. §1.611-2(a).
34. IRC Sec. 613.

BASIS

CHAPTER 21

INTRODUCTION

The concept of basis is an extremely important one in tax law. It is one of only a very small number of items that carries over from one year to the next when determining tax liability. For example, basis is used in determining:

1. gain or loss on the sale of an asset,
2. depreciation or amortization expense, and
3. deductibility of certain losses.

Basis is most commonly interpreted as the amount one pays for an asset. When that asset is sold, basis is subtracted from the amount received to determine the overall gain or loss realized. In this case, basis is the portion of the gross proceeds that is recovered income tax free upon the sale of an asset.

Example: Mark buys a plot of land for $10,000 using funds that he saved from working in a local restaurant. The $10,000 Mark paid for the land represents his basis in the land. A few months later, John offers to purchase the land from Mark for $25,000. To compute his reportable gain, Mark may subtract his basis from the amount he realizes in the sale. So Mark's gain would be $15,000, the $25,000 realized minus Mark's $10,000 basis. Without the basis rules, Mark would be taxed not only on the appreciation of the land, but also on his purchase price which came from savings which were already taxed when it was earned. So basis is a means by which the tax law prevents double taxation.

Because basis carries over from one year to the next and may be adjusted every year, it is one of the more complex and cumbersome burdens for taxpayers to comply with when preparing and filing their income tax returns. It is also an area that the Internal Revenue Service is likely to challenge upon the examination of a return. Maintaining complete, meticulous, and easily retrievable records of purchase payments and capital outlays is the best means of substantiating basis.

A STARTING POINT

As mentioned above, the starting point for determining basis is the amount that is paid in cash or other property for a particular asset. For example, Aaron Sterling, an investor, buys 100 shares of LISI, an information and analysis provider. Aaron's basis for his 100 shares of LISI will be the total price he paid. This includes any fees and commissions incurred as a result of the transaction. If the per share price at the time of purchase of the 100 shares is $50 and a $30 commission was paid on the transaction, Aaron's original basis is $5,030 (the total of the $5,000 cumulative share price plus the $30 commission).

When property other than (or in addition to) cash is used to acquire an asset, and the transaction does not qualify as a tax-free exchange, the basis of the property acquired is the sum of (a) any cash paid *plus* (b) the fair market value of any property transferred by the buyer. For instance, if Max Sterling purchased rental property for $10,000 in cash plus IBM stock worth $90,000, Max's original basis in the rental property would be $100,000 (the sum of the $10,000 cash he paid plus the $90,000 fair market value of the stock he transferred to the seller).

Typically, when an investor exchanges one property for another in an arm's length transaction, the market value of the property given up and the market value of the property received will be approximately equal. The fair market value of both properties will, as a practical matter, usually be ascertained by reference to the property whose value is most easily determined. In the example in the previous paragraph, it is easy to determine Max's basis in the rental property since Max paid for the property with cash ($10,000) and publicly traded IBM stock ($90,000), the value of which can easily be found.

When property is acquired subject to a mortgage or other debt, the basis of the property is not merely the amount of the investor's equity in the property. The basis is the total of the cash *and* the value of other property paid *plus* the amount of the debt assumed or incurred. For example, if Charlie Ratner buys a $1,000,000 apartment house, paying $250,000 in cash and borrowing the remaining $750,000, his basis in the property is the sum of the cash he's paid plus the debt he has assumed, (i.e., the full $1,000,000).

Basis is also used in depreciation calculations. The owner of property used in a trade or business that is subject to depreciation will use basis to determine the annual amount of expense. In the above example, Charlie's depreciable basis in the apartment house is $1,000,000 minus the amount of cost allocable to the land on which the building sits.

BASIS VARIATIONS

What complicates matters is the number of variations that exist for basis. Simply adding a word before "basis" changes the meaning within the tax law. What follows are examples of variations of the term "basis" and a short description of when the variation might be used.

Cost basis: "Cost basis" refers to the basis of property acquired by purchase. The cost of property includes amounts paid in cash, debt obligations assumed, or other property transferred by the buyer to the seller as part of the purchase price.[1]

Carry-over (or" transferred") basis: The donee (recipient) of a gift has a cost basis even though he or she may have paid nothing (see "transferred basis" and "stepped-up" basis, below).

Adjusted basis: The tax impact of certain transactions that occur after the initial purchase of a property may create the need for adjustments to the basis. Positive (upward) adjustments are made—and therefore basis is increased—when the owner makes additional investments or improvements with respect to the original property.[2] Downward adjustments are made—and therefore basis is reduced—when depreciation is claimed on property used in a trade or business.[3]

Unadjusted basis: "Unadjusted basis" is the amount of basis that can be claimed as cost recovery deductions (depreciation) over the duration of the recovery period (depreciable life) of the asset.[4] This term is used almost interchangeably with "depreciable basis" and is also used to identify a property's original cost basis.

Exchanged basis: "Exchanged basis" is basis that is determined in whole or in part by reference to other property held at any time by the taxpayer.[5] The most common application of this term is in the situation of a taxpayer who acquired property in what is called a "like-kind exchange" under Code section 1031. Prior to the enactment of Code section 7701(a)(42), "substituted basis" was used to describe what is now called "exchanged basis." In the context of a like-kind exchange, the exchanged basis starts with the taxpayer's adjusted basis in the relinquished property, and then (1) increases it by any gain recognized by the taxpayer in the exchange, and (2) decreases it by the value of any boot received.[6]

Transferred basis: As described more completely later in this chapter, "transferred basis" is basis that is determined in whole or in part by reference to the basis in the hands of the donor, grantor, or other transferor of property.[7] Prior to the enactment of Code section 7701(a)(43), this was usually referred to as "carryover basis." Many practitioners, and even some Code sections, continue to refer to transferred basis as carryover basis.

Stepped-up basis: Property received as an inheritance may obtain a "stepped-up" basis. If the decedent's property had a fair market value that exceeded its adjusted basis on the date of death, the property in the hands of the beneficiary receives a basis equal to the fair market value—that is, the basis gets a "step up" from the level it was at before the death occurred. For instance, if Dr. Rob Sterling purchased a home in Baltimore for $600,000 and it was worth $900,000 at the date of his death, Rob's heirs would compute any gain on a later sale using the stepped up $900,000 basis. (It is also possible for basis to be "stepped-down). These concepts will be explained more completely later in this chapter.

Negative basis: As a general rule, a taxpayer's basis is not permitted to be adjusted below zero. If negative basis were permitted, taxpayers could receive benefits for funds that were not actually spent on the asset. "Negative basis" is often used, even incorrectly, to describe situations in which a taxpayer's investment in a partnership or S corporation is reduced by losses in excess of their initial amount of capital. The impact of basis adjustments on flow-through entities will be discussed more completely later in this chapter.

BASIS FOR ALTERNATIVE MINIMUM TAX PURPOSES

The alternative minimum tax (AMT) is determined under a separate set of rules (See Chapter 10). Because certain items are treated differently for the purpose of computing a taxpayer's exposure to the AMT, there are times when it is possible for a taxpayer to have two or more adjusted basis figures for the same property.[8]

The most common difference in basis between the two tax systems is with adjusted basis for determining depreciation. Depreciation for certain property placed in service before January 1, 1999 was computed for AMT using different recovery methods and potentially longer lives. For assets placed in service after 1998, taxpayers must recompute depreciation using the same recovery period that they use for regular tax purposes but potentially a different recovery method.[9] As a result, upon the disposition of such an asset, the gain or loss for regular tax purposes will be different than what will be reported for the AMT. This disparity is due to the difference in the adjusted basis at the time of disposition.[10]

Corporate taxpayers that are subject to recomputing their depreciation using the allowable methods and lives for adjusted current earnings (ACE) may find that they have yet another set of adjusted basis numbers to track.[11]

Another area in which a taxpayer may have a different adjusted basis for regular tax and AMT purposes is with incentive stock options (ISOs). Although there is an exclusion from gross income for stock acquired by the exercise of ISOs, the exclusion is not permitted for the AMT.[12] As a result, the adjusted basis of the stock will be different.[13] This adjustment is more fully explained in Chapter 10 and Chapter 27.

USING BASIS TO DETERMINE DEDUCTIBLE LOSSES

The concept of basis is also applied to a taxpayer's investment in a pass-through entity, such as a partnership, limited liability company (LLC), or S corporation, to determine if losses from an entity are deductible. In a similar manner, individuals and certain C corporations must apply the at-risk limitation rules to activities that generate losses.[14] The at-risk rules are covered in detail in Chapter 23.

Partnerships (or LLCs Taxed as Partnerships)

A partner or LLC member (hereinafter referred to as "partner") typically determines the basis in their partnership interest (also known as the partner's "outside basis") starting with their initial investment in the partnership.[15] The starting point may be different if the partner acquired the partnership interest in any way other than as a direct purchase or contribution upon formation.

After the original cost basis is determined, the following adjustments are made each year to the partner's basis:

- Increases for the partner's distributive share of the partnership's taxable income[16]
- Increases for the partner's distributive share of the partnership's tax-exempt income[17]
- Increases for the partner's distributive share of the partnership's excess of depletion deductions over the basis of the depletable property[18]
- Reductions for distributions[19]
- Reductions for the partner's distributive share of partnership losses[20]
- Reductions for the partner's distributive share of partnership expenditures that are not capitalized and not deducted[21]
- Reductions for the partner's depletion deduction for partnership oil and gas property to the extent it does not exceed the proportionate share of the adjusted basis of the property

allocated to such partner under Code section 613A(c)(7)(D)[22]

As previously mentioned, in no situation is a partner's adjusted basis reduced below zero.[23] In the event that any of the above adjustments, if made in full, would decrease the partner's basis below zero, the adjustment is limited to the amount of available basis. In addition, the tax impact to the partner is also limited.

Example: John McFadden contributes $5,000 to a newly formed partnership. In the first year, John's distributive share of the partnership's taxable loss is $6,400. Under the basis rules, only $5,000 of that loss would be deductible by John. The remaining $1,400 loss is suspended. John could use that suspended loss to offset future income or it could become deductible if John's basis is otherwise increased in a future tax year.

Each partner's share of the partnership's liabilities is treated as additional basis for the partner's interest in the partnership. An increase in a partner's share of the partnership's liabilities is treated as if that partner had made an additional contribution to the partnership.[24] Any decrease in a partner's share of the partnership's liabilities is treated as a distribution made to the partner from the partnership.[25]

Example: Assume the same facts as above, except that John's share of the partnership's liabilities is $2,000. This would be treated as a contribution made by John to the firm for purposes of determining his basis. His basis would then be $7,000 ($5,000 plus $2,000) before the adjustment for the current year's loss. Since the adjustment for the current year loss is less than the available basis, all of the current year's loss would be deductible. John's adjusted basis at the end of the year is $600 ($7,000 minus $6,400).

One year later, John's partnership breaks even but is able to pay off all of its liabilities. John must adjust his basis for his share of the decrease in partnership liabilities. However, the $2,000 reduction of John's liabilities, which is treated as a distribution to John, exceeds his $600 adjusted basis by $1,400 ($600 – $2,000). Since John is not permitted to reduce his adjusted basis below zero and because he already received the tax benefit in the prior year for the additional $1,400 of losses supported by the liabilities, John would be required to report the $1,400 ($2,000 deemed distribution less $600 adjusted basis) as currently reportable income.

Shareholders in S Corporations

Determining a shareholder's basis in an S corporation is somewhat different from calculating a partner's basis. An S corporation shareholder may have two different adjusted basis numbers to track, one for his stock basis and one for his debt basis. Unlike a partner of a partnership, an S corporation shareholder does not adjust his basis for the partner's share of the S corporation's liabilities.

Typically, an S corporation shareholder's stock basis begins with the amount the shareholder paid for stock. The stock basis is then increased or decreased by the following adjustments:

- Increases for the shareholder's share of the S corporation's separately stated items of income[26]
- Increases for the shareholder's share of the S corporation's non-separately stated items of income[27]
- Increases for the shareholder's share of the S corporation's excess of depletion deductions over the basis of the depletable property[28]
- Reductions for distributions not included in the shareholder's gross income[29]
- Reductions for the shareholder's share of the S corporation's separately stated items of loss and deduction[30]
- Reductions for the shareholder's share of the S corporation's non-separately computed loss[31]
- Reductions for the shareholder's share of the S corporation's expenditures that are not capitalized and not deducted[32]

- Reductions for the shareholder's depletion deduction for S corporation oil and gas property to the extent it does not exceed the proportionate share of the adjusted basis of the property allocated to such shareholder under Code section 613A(c)(11)(B)[33]

As was the case with partnership basis, a shareholder's adjusted stock basis cannot be reduced below zero.[34] If a shareholder's stock basis is reduced to zero by losses and other adjustments of the S corporation, the shareholder may still be able to deduct the losses allocated to the shareholder assuming the shareholder has sufficient debt basis.

A shareholder may create debt basis by making a direct, bona fide loan to the S corporation. Note, however, that guarantees of S corporation debt or other indirect loans do not give a shareholder debt basis. Any unused portion of the reductions applicable to the shareholder's stock basis may be used to reduce the shareholder's debt basis.[35] Again, in no case can the shareholder's adjusted debt basis fall below zero.[36]

Once a shareholder reduces stock basis to zero and begins to reduce debt basis, any subsequent basis increases are first applied to restore the debt basis to the full amount of the outstanding loan.[37] Once the debt basis is fully restored, stock basis is increased from zero.

Example: Art Werner purchases a 50 percent interest in XYZ, Inc., an S corporation, for $10,000. In the first year, the company passes through a loss of $8,000 to Art. The $8,000 is deductible by Art because he has sufficient basis in his stock (subject to other limitations such as the passive activity rules). At the end of the first year, Art's adjusted stock basis is $2,000 ($10,000 original basis minus $8,000).

During the second year, Art directly loaned XYZ, Inc. $20,000 and guaranteed another loan of the S corporation for $50,000. Art's share of the second year loss was $27,000. Art will be able to deduct $22,000 of the $27,000 loss. First, Art's stock basis is reduced from $2,000 to zero. Second, Art reduces his debt basis from $20,000 to zero. Note that the guarantee of the S corporation loan does not give Mark any additional debt basis. The remaining $5,000 loss is suspended until Art has sufficient increases to his basis to cover it.

In the third year, XYZ, Inc. earned $150,000. Art's share is $75,000. Of the $75,000, $5,000 is offset by the suspended loss from the second year and is not reported by Art as income. The next $20,000 restores Art's debt basis and is reported as taxable income. The remaining $50,000 is also reported as income and increases Art's stock basis by this amount.

It is important to remember that an investor's ability to create basis through the use of debt is limited by the "at-risk" rules. These rules provide that losses are deductible only to the extent the investor is personally "at-risk." The at-risk rules are more fully covered in Chapter 23.

The at-risk rules limit deductions for borrowing that attempt to be characterized as "at-risk" for tax purposes when there is no actual economic risk to the investor. For instance, assume Janet Werner, a corporate executive, wants to purchase a $100,000 interest in an oil drilling venture. She intends to invest $20,000 of her own funds while borrowing the $80,000 balance. The bank providing the loan to Janet has agreed to make a "nonrecourse" loan to her. In other words, the bank will rely solely on the value of the property as its collateral for the debt. In the event Janet cannot repay the loan, the bank cannot look to Janet's other assets to cover the unpaid balance. Since the most Janet can lose on her investment is $20,000 in cash, her deductions will be limited to that $20,000 (plus the amount of income generated from the investment).

The at-risk rules cover essentially all investment activities except for real estate acquired before 1987. With respect to real estate subject to the at-risk rules, "qualified nonrecourse financing" is treated as an additional amount at-risk.

An investor is considered at-risk to the extent of:

1. cash invested, *plus*

2. the basis of property invested, *plus*

3. amounts borrowed for use in the investment that are secured by the investor's assets (other than the property used in the investment activity), *plus*

4. amounts borrowed to the extent the investor is personally liable for its repayment, *plus*

When the investment is made in partnership form:

1. the investor-partner's undistributed share of partnership income, *plus*

2. the investor-partner's proportionate share of partnership debt, to the extent he is personally liable for its repayment.

An investor is not considered "at-risk" with respect to nonrecourse debt (other than qualified nonrecourse financing, see above) used to finance the activity, or to finance the acquisition of property used in the activity.

Furthermore, an investor will not be considered "at risk" with respect to any other arrangement for the compensation or reimbursement of any economic loss.

Example: If Janet, in the example above, is able to obtain commercial insurance against the risk that the oil drilling fund will not return her original $20,000 cash investment, she would not even be considered "at-risk" on that amount.

Losses limited by the at-risk provisions are not lost; instead, these amounts may be carried over and deducted in subsequent years (but only if the investor's at-risk amount is sufficiently increased).

The benefit of previously deducted losses must be recaptured when the investor's at-risk amount is reduced below zero.

Example: Assume Tania's loss deductions from her interest in an oil drilling venture total $5,000 through the end of last year. Her basis in the venture at the end of last year (after the deductions) was $1,000. In the current year, Tania received $3,000 in cash distributions. Without any limitations for negative basis, that distribution would reduce Tania's basis by $3,000 to a figure of *minus* $2,000. But since an investor cannot have a negative basis in an investment for tax purposes, Tania must recapture the $2,000 of prior year deductible losses in order to bring her basis up to zero. In addition, Tania will not be able to deduct any losses from the venture in the current year because she has a zero basis.

BASIS OF PROPERTY ACQUIRED FROM A DECEDENT

Under current law, when an investor dies, the beneficiary of his property does not "carry over" the decedent's basis. Instead, the basis of property acquired from or passing from a decedent is the fair market value of the property as of the date of (a) the investor's death, or (b) the federal estate tax alternate valuation date if that date (typically six months after the date of death) is elected by the estate's executor.[38]

Therefore, if the value of an investment held until death increases from the date of its acquisition, the potential gain (or loss in the case of a decrease in value) is never recognized for income tax purposes.

An increase in the property's basis to its federal estate tax value is called a "step-up" in basis. Note that this "stepped-up basis" is obtained by the recipients of the property after the prior owner's death even though no one pays income tax on the intervening appreciation.

Example: Susan Smith purchased stock that cost $10,000. At the time of her death, the stock had a fair market value of $50,000. Her beneficiary would receive a $50,000 basis for the stock. The $40,000 appreciation in the value of the stock would never be subject to income taxes. If the beneficiary then sold the property for $65,000, his taxable gain would be only $15,000.

The alternate valuation method may be elected by an executor or administrator only if the election will decrease (a) the value of the gross estate and also (b) the amount of the federal estate tax imposed.[39] Generally, an election to use the alternate valuation date means that property will be included in the gross estate at its fair market value as of six months after the decedent's death.[40] However, if any property is distributed, sold, exchanged, or otherwise disposed of within six months after the decedent's death, the value of the property at that disposition date becomes the "alternate value."[41]

Example: Assume Les Brun, a widower, buys property for $10,000 and it is worth $50,000 at his death. Assume that his executor sells the asset for $45,000 three months after his death. If the alternate valuation date is elected, the valuation date for this property would be the date of its sale. Its basis becomes $45,000. The estate realizes no tax gain or loss because the $45,000 amount realized on the sale is equal to the property's $45,000 basis.

BASIS OF PROPERTY ACQUIRED BY GIFT

When property is acquired by lifetime gift and there is a gain on the sale by the donee, the general rule is that the property in the hands of the donee has the same basis (subject to an adjustment discussed below) it had in the hands of the donor.[42] The donee of the gift—the new owner—computes his basis by referring to the basis in the hands of the donor. In other words, the donor's basis is "transferred" and "carried over" to the donee so that gain will not escape tax but merely be deferred. Note that this is now technically defined as "transferred basis" under Code section 7701(a)(43) (although many practitioners continue to refer to this as "carry-over basis"). The gain remains deferred only until the donee disposes of the property in a taxable transaction.

Example: Assume that Jared purchases stock for $3,000. After it appreciates in value to $9,000, he gives it to Maria. The basis of the stock in Maria's hands for determining gain on a later sale by Maria is still $3,000. Therefore, if she sells it for $10,000, she has a $7,000 gain.

When the donor's basis is used, it is subject to an adjustment for any gift taxes paid on the net appreciation in the value of the gift (but not above the amount of the gift tax paid).[43] For instance, in the example in the paragraph above, if the gift tax were $1,500, the donee's basis would be the $3,000 carryover basis plus $1,000 adjustment, a total of $4,000.

The addition to basis is computed according to the following formula:

Filing status	2009	2008
Married filing jointly	$250,200	$239,950
Head of household	$208,500	$199,950
Unmarried	$166,800	$159,950
Married filing separately	$125,100	$119,975

In our example, the computation would be:

Married filing jointly	$110,000
Married filing separately	$55,000
All others	$75,000

The basis rule for determining loss on the sale of property acquired by gift is different from the rule for determining the amount of the gain on the sale. For purposes of determining the amount of a loss, the basis of the property in the hands of the donee is the lesser of (a) the donor's basis or (b) the fair market value of the property at the time of the gift.[44] The purpose of this special provision is to prevent investors from gaining a tax benefit by transferring property with a built-in loss to persons who could take advantage of tax losses.

Assume, for instance, that in the example above the value of the stock at the time of the gift was only $1,000. If Jared sold the stock, he would have a capital loss of $2,000 ($3,000 basis – $1,000 amount realized). If Jared had other capital losses of at least $3,000 but no capital gains, the additional $2,000 loss would be treated as a capital loss carryover for the year and would provide no immediate tax benefit to him. Were it not for the special provision, Jared might give the stock to his father who had capital gains. If his father were allowed to use Jared's $3,000 basis, his father could sell the stock, take a $2,000 loss, and obtain a current tax benefit from the loss that Jared himself could not have used. For this reason, the father, in determining his loss on the sale, must use as his basis the $1,000 fair market value of the property at the time of the gift since that is lower than Jared's $3,000 basis. If Jared's father sold the property for $900, he would only recognize a $100 loss on the sale ($900 proceeds less $1,000 basis). If Jared's father sold the property at a time when it was worth only $1,200 (or any other amount between the $1,000 fair market value at the date of the gift or the $3,000 transferred basis), no gain or loss would be recognized.

ALLOCATION OF BASIS

When the assets of a trade or business are acquired, the purchase price must be allocated among the acquired tangible and intangible assets using what is called the "residual allocation" method.[45] This process is extremely important to the acquiring taxpayer since the amounts allocated to each asset create the basis by which future depreciation and amortization expenses are determined.

The residual method uses a "class" system to identify the amount of the purchase price that is to be allocated to each asset. The purchase price is applied to the assets of each class in proportion to their relative fair market values. The asset classes are:[46]

Class I: Cash and general deposit accounts, including savings and checking accounts, but excluding certificates of deposit held in banks, savings and loan association and other depository institutions

Class II: Actively traded personal property, certificates of deposit and foreign currency

Class III: Accounts receivable and assets that the taxpayer marks-to-market at least annually

Class IV: Inventory or other property held primarily for sale to customers in the ordinary course of its trade or business

Class V: Assets not covered by any other class (typically the fixed assets of the business)

Class VI: Section 197 intangibles, except goodwill and going concern value

Class VII: Goodwill and going concern value

An independent appraisal of each asset being purchased is a recommended process in order to substantiate and document the allocation of the purchase price. Each of the amounts that are allocated may result in a potentially different tax treatment in the future for the acquirer. For instance, amounts allocated to fixed assets may be depreciable in the hands of the acquirer. In most cases, the taxpayer would then benefit from a relatively short recovery period (depending on the asset involved) and recoup a portion of the investment soon. Conversely, if more of the purchase price falls to goodwill, the acquirer may be faced with a much longer recovery period, if at all.

Example: ABC buys the assets of XYZ for $1,000,000. ABC acquires XYZ's accounts receivable valued at $200,000, inventory valued at $50,000, and fixed assets valued at $400,000. $200,000 of the purchase price is allocated to the accounts receivable and that amount becomes the basis for the receivables. Likewise, the inventory is allocated $50,000 of the purchase price and the fixed assets are allocated $400,000. The remaining amount of the purchase price, $350,000, is allocated to goodwill.

An allocation of basis is also required in circumstances when a taxpayer receives multiple types of property in a single transaction. The best example of this is improved real estate. The building, if used in a business or rental operation, would be eligible for depreciation, while the underlying land is not depreciable. Further, taxpayers may undergo a cost segregation study in order to determine if there are parts of a property that may be classified as depreciable property with a shorter life, thereby increasing the annual depreciation expense.

FREQUENTLY ASKED QUESTIONS

Question – How is a taxpayer's basis determined when selling a stock investment?

Answer – As previously discussed, the basis of one's stock investment is determined by the cost of the stock, plus any commissions paid. When a stock is sold and the investor sold less than their entire position in a given security, the stock is deemed to be sold using a first-in, first-out method (FIFO). FIFO is used whenever the investor does not or cannot specifically identify which shares of stock were sold.[47]

An investor may specifically identify the shares that were sold by delivering the shares to be sold to the broker. If the shares are held in street name by the broker, (1) the investor must identify to the broker at the time of the sale which shares are to be sold, and (2) the broker must confirm the share identification to the investor within a reasonable time after the sale.[48]

Beginning in 2011, brokers were required to comply with new cost basis reporting rules for their investors. Prior to this date, the only reporting requirement was for sales proceeds on the sale of securities. Following the schedule below, the information reports provided by brokers must also include the cost basis of the asset sold.

- **Beginning January 1, 2011**, brokers must report information on any common or preferred stock, exchange-traded funds (ETFs), American Depositary Receipts (ADRs) and Real Estate Investment Trusts (REITs).
- **Beginning January 1, 2012**, information about mutual funds and dividend reinvestment plans must also be recorded and reported.
- **Beginning January 1, 2013**, options, fixed income, and any other security otherwise not included in the previous tax years must be recorded by the brokerage and reported to the IRS.

The basis of security purchases prior to the above dates are not required to be reported by the brokers. So, for instance, the basis of a mutual fund purchased in June 2011 does not need to be reported by the broker when sold since the purchase occurred prior to the date of implementation.

Question – How is a taxpayer's basis determined when selling a mutual fund investment?

Answer – An investor's basis in a mutual fund starts with the original cost of the mutual fund shares, plus any commissions or fees paid. Basis is then increased by any amounts of reinvested income (typically taxable and tax-exempt dividend income and capital gain distributions). Basis may be reduced by distributions treated as return of capital. The sources of these basis adjustments are normally found on Form 1099-DIV or Form 2439, so it is imperative that these forms be maintained to properly maintain accurate basis records.

When less than the full amount of a mutual fund investment is sold, an investor has three choices for allocating basis to determine the capital gain or loss. The three methods are (1) FIFO, (2) specific identification, or (3) average basis. Like the rules for stocks, if the average basis method is not elected or specific identification is not used, basis should be determined on a FIFO basis.

An investor may elect to use the average basis method on a fund by fund basis. The election must be made in the first year that mutual fund shares from a given fund are sold. Every year after the election is made, a taxpayer is required to disclose the continued use of the method on all future sales of the same fund.

There are two average basis methods – single category and double category. The single category method is simply determined by the total basis of the mutual fund shares on the date of the sale divided by the total shares held immediately prior to the sale.[49] The holding period is determined on a FIFO basis. Note that many mutual fund companies provide single category average basis information to their shareholders each year along with their tax information statements.

When double category method is elected, a taxpayer is required to divide his mutual fund holding into short and long-term shares and the average basis for each of these lots are determined. From this point, the taxpayer may opt to sell out of the short or long-term position and use the appropriate average cost basis for those shares.[50] The use of the double category method is not widely used.

With the cost basis reporting requirements placed on the brokers (beginning in 2012 for mutual fund purchases), care must be taken to ensure that the correct cost basis is disclosed to the IRS on the Form 1099-B. Most brokers allow investors to select a cost basis method to be used in lieu of the broker's default method, which in most cases is single category average cost for purchases after the beginning reporting date.

Question – How is basis determined for a bond issued or purchased at a discount?

Answer – A bond issued at less than its stated redemption price is treated as a discounted bond. The amount of the discount is simply the difference between the redemption price and the issue price and is referred to as the original issue discount (OID). Over time, the holder of the bond is required to report the OID in their income and increase their basis in the bond by the same amount. If the bond is held to maturity, the full value of the bond will be paid and there will be no gain or loss (ignoring transaction costs) since the recognition of the full amount of the OID would have increased the taxpayer's basis to equal the face value of the bond.

If an OID bond is sold before its maturity, the bond's basis is determined by its original cost plus any OID previously recognized as income.[51]

A bond purchased at a discount on the secondary market is referred to as a market discount bond, and different rules apply. The amount of the market discount may be recognized in the bond holder's income on an annual basis by making an election on the bond holder's tax return in the year of the purchase.[52] If an election is not made, the market discount is recognized when the bond matures or is otherwise disposed of by the taxpayer (including via gift). Any gain on the bond is treated as ordinary income to the extent of the market discount.[53] The market discount rules do not apply to: (1) short-term obligations (such as T-bills) with fixed maturity dates one year or less from the date of issue; (2) tax-exempt obligations purchased before May 1, 1993; and (3) U.S. savings bonds.[54]

Question – How is basis determined for a bond issued or purchased at a premium?

Answer – If a debt instrument is purchased or issued at a price that is greater than the stated maturity amount, the bond holder is paying a premium. The amount of the premium paid on a taxable bond remains as part of the holder's basis of the bond until it is sold or redeemed unless an election is made to amortize the premium amount.[55] Tax-exempt bond holders are required to amortize the bond premium, even though no corresponding tax deduction results from the amortization. As amortization of a taxable or tax-exempt bond occurs, a bond holder's basis is reduced accordingly.[56]

Amortization of a taxable bond issued after September 28, 1987 is determined using the constant yield to maturity method and is reported as a reduction to the taxpayer's interest income each year (bond issued prior to that date may be amortized using any reasonable method).[57] However, the amount of the bond amortization may not be greater than the amount of interest being reported on that particular bond in any given year.[58]

Essentially, the election to amortize the premium paid on a taxable bond results in a tax deduction against a taxpayer's ordinary income through the reduction of taxable interest. If the election is not made, the taxpayer will report the bond premium by using a higher basis when the bond matures or is otherwise disposed of, resulting in an offset to their capital gain income and, usually, less of a tax benefit.

Note that for bonds with a call feature, the call date and amount must be used for the amortization calculation.[59]

Question – What is the basis of property converted from a nonbusiness use to a business use?

Answer – When property that is used personally is converted to business use, the property's basis is the lower of (1) the basis of the property when it was acquired for personal use, or (2) its fair market value at the time of the conversion.[60]

CHAPTER ENDNOTES

1. Treas. Reg. §1.1012-1(a).
2. IRC Sec. 1016(a)(1).
3. IRC Sec. 1016(a)(2).
4. IRC Sec. 168(b)(1).
5. IRC Sec. 7701(a)(42).
6. IRC Sec. 1031(d).
7. IRC Sec. 7701(a)(43).
8. Since so many states have decoupled from the federal tax depreciation system, especially with respect to the concept of "bonus" depreciation, many taxpayers are forced to maintain adjusted basis calculations for their fixed assets for state tax purposes.
9. IRC Sec. 56(a)(1).
10. IRC Sec. 56(a)(6).
11. IRC Sec. 56(g)(4)(A).
12. IRC Sec. 56(b)(3).
13. *Ibid.*
14. IRC Sec. 465(a)(1).
15. A partner's outside basis is defined as the partner's adjusted basis in the partnership interest. A partner's inside basis is defined as the partner's share of the partnership's adjusted basis in its assets.
16. IRC Sec. 705(a)(1)(A).
17. IRC Sec. 705(a)(1)(B).
18. IRC Sec. 705(a)(1)(C).
19. IRC Sec. 705(a)(2).
20. IRC Sec. 705(a)(2)(A).
21. IRC Sec. 705(a)(2)(B).

22. IRC Sec. 705(a)(3).
23. IRC Secs. 705(a)(2), 705(a)(3).
24. IRC Sec. 752(a).
25. IRC Sec. 752(b).
26. IRC Sec. 1367(a)(1)(A).
27. IRC Sec. 1367(a)(1)(B).
28. IRC Sec. 1367(a)(1)(C).
29. IRC Sec. 1367(a)(2)(A).
30. IRC Sec. 1367(a)(2)(B).
31. IRC Sec. 1367(a)(2)(C).
32. IRC Sec. 1367(a)(2)(D).
33. IRC Sec. 1367(a)(2)(E).
34. IRC Sec. 1367(a)(2).
35. IRC Sec. 1367(b)(2)(A).
36. *Ibid.*
37. IRC Sec. 1367(b)(2)(B).
38. IRC Sec. 1014(a).
39. IRC Sec. 2032(c).
40. IRC Sec. 2032(a)(1).
41. IRC Sec. 2032(a)(2).
42. IRC Sec. 1015(a).
43. IRC Sec. 1015(a).
44. IRC Sec. 1015(a).
45. IRC Sec. 1060(a).
46. Treas. Reg. §1.1060-1(c)(2).
47. Treas. Reg. §1.1012-1(c)(1).
48. Treas. Reg. §1.1012-1(c)(3).
49. Treas. Reg. §1.1012-1(e)(4).
50. Treas. Reg. §1.1012-1(e)(3).
51. IRC Sec. 1272(d)(2).
52. IRC Sec. 1278(b).
53. IRC Sec. 1276(a)(1).
54. IRC Sec. 1278(a)(1).
55. IRC Sec. 171(c).
56. IRC Sec. 1016(a)(5).
57. IRC Sec. 171(b)(3).
58. Treas. Reg. §1.171-2(a)(4).
59. IRC Sec. 171(b)(1)(B).
60. Treas. Reg. §1.165-9(b)(2) and §1.167(g)-1.

TAX BASIS PLANNING

CHAPTER 22

INCOME TAX PLANNING HAS REPLACED ESTATE TAX PLANNING FOR MOST TAXPAYERS

In today's tax environment, with an estate and gift tax exemption of $11,580,000 (in 2020)[1] the need for estate and gift tax planning is limited to a very small percentage of the population.[2] On the other hand, there are significantly more taxpayers including trusts and estates subject to income tax rates as high as 37 percent (potentially 40.8 percent if the NIIT is included).[3] For those taxpayers, effective income tax planning is paramount. So it is not surprising that practitioners have shifted the emphasis from estate and gift tax planning to income tax planning.

Perhaps one of the most valuable tax attributes that can save or cost the taxpayer a significant amount of tax is an asset's basis. Due to its importance in income tax planning, this chapter focuses on the different aspects of income tax basis planning. For example, basis is a vital component in determining gain or loss on the sale or exchange of an asset. To this point, the taxable gain with respect to the sale or exchange of an asset is the difference between the amount received and the asset's tax basis. So, the higher the basis, the lesser the amount of taxable gain. Similarly, the taxable loss, is the difference between the asset's tax basis and the amount received. In that case, the higher the basis, the greater the amount of taxable loss. In either scenario, a high basis saves income tax.

Depreciation is another aspect of basis. Since, depreciation is a deduction of an asset's tax basis over the applicable recovery period, a depreciable asset with a higher basis will generate more depreciation deductions than a depreciable asset with a low basis.

As alluded to above, because of the emerging dominance of income tax planning, estate and gift tax saving planning techniques have given way to planning techniques that save income tax. The following are examples of the refocusing of strategies:

- *Valuation.* When practitioners were more concerned with saving estate tax, low valuations of assets were coveted. Because estate tax is imposed on the value of assets, the lower the value, the lower the amount of estate tax. On the other hand, for income tax purposes, high basis is a positive. Upon the death of a decedent, the basis of the assets step up to fair market value meaning the higher the value the higher the basis. Since most estates are not subject to estate tax, higher valuations are no longer a negative.

Example: In 2010, Miranda Wright purchased land for $100,000 that she intends to leave to her cousin, Asher. Due to its location, the value of the land has increased significantly over the last six years. At the time of her death, the highest and lowest plausible valuations of the land were $2,500,000 and $1,800,000, respectively. However, even at the highest plausible valuation of the land, Miranda's taxable estate would be well below the estate tax exemption amount (subject to $0 estate tax). At a time when more estates were subject to estate tax, to save estate tax, Miranda's executor would have preferred the lowest plausible valuation. In this case, with no estate tax owing, assuming both valuations were equally credible, Miranda's executor would prefer the higher valuation of $2,500,000 so that Asher's basis in the land would be $2,500,000. Then, if Asher were to subsequently sale or exchange the land, any potential taxable gain would be lower and any potential taxable loss would be greater.

- *Trading Arguments.* Prior to the change in focus from estate planning to income tax planning, tax planners made successful valuation arguments that drove down the fair market value of assets to save estate tax. Now, because of the shift to income tax planning, there has been a role reversal, i.e., income tax planners seek higher valuations and the IRS seeks lower valuation. Ironically, the IRS will likely make the arguments planners used to make and vice versa.

- *Changing prior planning techniques* Due to the doubling of the estate tax exemption by the Tax Cuts and Jobs of 2017, taxpayers who previously adopted strategies to remove property from their estates will increasingly consider strategies that will pull appreciated property into the gross estate in order to receive a fair market value step up in basis.

Example: Miranda transfers marketable securities to a trust providing income to Asher for life with the remainder to pass to Ashley. If Miranda's goal is to prevent the trust corpus from being included in the gross estate, Miranda must not retain the right to income and/or the possession or enjoyment of the property as well as the ability to designate who can possess or enjoy the trust corpus or its income after the trust is created.[4] Assuming the inclusion of the trust corpus does not result in a taxable estate, if Miranda adopts this strategy, not only will she not save estate tax (there was none to save), it would prevent a stepped up basis of the trust corpus at her death. Therefore, Miranda should consider retaining some right in the trust that would pull the trust corpus into her gross estate. By doing so, the basis of the trust corpus would step up to fair market value without any estate tax cost.

- *Terminally Ill.* All possible tax basis planning techniques should be implemented expeditiously for those individuals facing a more imminent demise (i.e., terminally ill, chronically ill, those with a looming incapacity, and the elderly).

- *Documents.* Client estate planning documents must include greater flexibility to reduce income taxes in general including the ability to perform tax basis planning. One example might be to execute a General Power of Attorney which specifically permits the holder to convert an IRA into a ROTH IRA or make pre-mortem decisions that increase the heirs' tax basis (e.g., gifting assets with unrealized losses before death).

- *Lower Planning Thresholds.* Unlike estate tax planning that becomes relevant only if an estate is over the estate tax exemption amount, tax basis planning is relevant at virtually every income level. For example, assume a son of a chronically ill father has worked in the business (i.e., a sole proprietorship) for 30 years. Although all business assets have been depreciated to zero, they have a fair market value of $500,000. In transferring the business from father to son, an outright gift would be a bad choice because the father's zero basis in the business assets would carry over to the son. Instead, by testamentary devise, father should transfer the business to son, so that at father's death, the basis of the business assets would step up to fair market value. As a result, the zero basis would be transformed into a tax savings depreciable basis of $500,000 (date of death fair market value).

The following is a checklist of variables to be analyzed in developing a tax basis plan:

- Determine the current tax basis of each asset in the plan and whether it is depreciable or amortizable.

- Ascertain the current fair market value and, if possible to ascertain, the projected date of death fair market value of each asset in the plan.

- Factor in the health of the transferor. So if death is imminent, negative tax basis issues should be eliminated as expeditiously as possible. For example, if prior to death, an individual were to sell an asset with a low depreciated basis, some or all of the gain may be attributable to recapture and taxable at ordinary income tax rates. On the other hand, if passed by will, the date of death fair market value basis step up would eliminate any depreciation recapture income for the heirs. Also, a testamentary gift of an asset with a nominal basis (e.g., an artist's work product) can receive a significant stepped up basis.

- Be aware of the way the following aspects of state law in the transferor's state of domicile may impact the taxation or property rights of the transferor and potential transferees.
    - Relative income tax brackets
    - Estate and inheritance taxes
    - Community property issues
    - Spousal rights to elect against the assets of a deceased spouse
- Determine the relative federal income tax brackets of the transferor and potential transferees?
- Determine if it is likely that the transferor and/or the transferee will have taxable estates for state or federal tax purposes?
    - If so, determine whether there is sufficient liquidity to cover any state or federal estate taxes.
- Determine whether the transfer of any asset subject to a secured indebtedness to an individual or a trust will require a lender's approval.
- Ascertain whether there are existing trusts and/or estates that should be analyzed as a part of the plan?
    - Determine the basis and fair market value of assets in the estate or trust?
- Determine whether in the decedent's will there are any charitable bequests that do not reference specific assets (e.g., "I give $100,000 to my University.")?

BASIS RULES FOR LIFETIME GRATUITOUS TRANSFERS

Gifts are the most common type of gratuitous transfers and are often an integral part of income tax planning. With respect to a gift of an appreciated asset (fair market value is greater than the donor's basis), the donor's basis in lifetime gifts carries over to the donee.[5] However, with respect to a depreciated asset (donor's basis is great than the date of gift fair market value), for purposes of computing loss (i.e., the donee subsequently sells the gifted property), the donee's basis is the fair market value.

In effect, the unrealized gain of gifted property is taxable to the donee when sold. On the other hand, the unrealized loss of gifted property (the spread between the donor's basis and the fair market value of the gifted property) cannot be deducted by either the donor or the donee. Therefore, gifting an asset with an unrealized loss is generally not a good tax idea.

Example: Miranda Wrights gifts marketable stock worth $10,000 that she purchased for $14,000 to her son Asher. In turn, Asher sells it for $10,000. Because Asher's basis in the stock is the date of gift fair market value of $10,000 (rather than Miranda's $14,000 cost basis), there is no gain or loss. Thus, the unrealized $4,000 capital loss (attributable to Miranda's cost basis of $14,000) is effectively lost. On the other hand, if instead of gifting the stock, Miranda had sold the stock, she would have recognized the $4,000 loss. Then, she could have gifted $10,000 cash proceeds to Asher.

There are a number of nuances to gift transactions that merit discussion:

The No-Tax Window. As discussed above, the loss basis rules preclude the donee from deducting the donor's unrealized loss. However, if the donee sells the gifted asset for an amount greater than the donee's loss basis but less than the donor's original basis, what are the tax consequences to the donee? As illustrated in Scenario 2, below, the answer is neither a gain nor a loss is triggered on the sale.

There are three possible results with respect to the subsequent sale of a gift of property with an unrealized loss at the time of the gift. For purposes of the following three scenarios, assume that at the time of the gift, the donor's basis in the property was $200,000 and the fair market value was $100,000.

Scenario 1: Subsequent to the gift, the property appreciates in value and ultimately is worth $300,000. At that time, the donee sells the gifted property for that amount. Because the transaction triggers a gain rather than a loss, the donee's basis is the donor's original basis. So, in this case, the donee would recognize a gain of $100,000.

Scenario 2: Subsequent to the gift, the property appreciates from $100,000 to $150,000. At that time, the donee sells the gifted property for that amount. Because the selling price ($150,000) is greater than the *loss* basis, there obviously can be no loss. Similarly, because the selling price is less than the donor's basis, or $200,000 (the *gain* basis), there is no gain.

This is the No-Tax Window and is consistent with the purpose of the rule. In other words, the Internal Revenue Code does not allow a donor to "gift" an unrealized loss asset to a donee so that the donee can take a deduction for the donor's pre-gift loss. On the other hand, if the selling price of the asset is anywhere between the date of the gift's fair market value and the donor's original basis, the donee is not going to be penalized with a taxable gain. So, if a donee sells a *loss* gift for an amount between the date of the gift's fair market value and the donor's basis, it is recovered tax-free.

Scenario 3: Subsequent to the gift, the property depreciates to $80,000. At that time the donee sells the gifted property for that amount. In this scenario, using the loss basis of $80,000, the donee would recognize a $20,000 loss ($100,000 basis minus $80,000 sales price).

Liability in Excess of Basis. On occasion, gifted property is secured by a liability. So, if the donee assumes the liability from the donor, it is as if the donee purchased the gifted property for the amount of the secured liability. Therefore, if the amount of the secured liability exceeds the donor's basis in the gifted property, the donor would recognize taxable gain. Finally, to the extent the fair market value of the gifted property is *greater than* the secured liability, the transaction is treated as a part sale/part gift.[6]

Example: Miranda Wrights owns land with a fair market value of $200,000, a basis of $75,000 subject to a $125,000 secured liability. Miranda gifts the property to Asher subject to his assumption of the secured liability. As a result, the transaction is treated as a part sale/part gift. The sales part of the transaction triggers a taxable gain of $50,000 includible in Miranda's gross income ($125,000 minus $75,000). The gift part $75,000, or the difference between the fair market value of $200,000 and the consideration of $125,000 (the debt assumed by Asher). Asher's basis in the land is $125,000 ($75,000 increased by the amount of gain that Miranda recognized on the sales part of the transaction).

Practice Point: Interestingly, the IRS has never asserted that an heir's assumption of debt on devised property is taxable to the donor's estate. Death apparently eliminates the potential tax liability, even if the liability exceeds the fair market value of the inherited asset, i.e., the property's basis.

Basis Adjustments for Taxable Gifts. As a result of the unified estate and gift tax exemption, an individual would have to have gifted, in the aggregate, over his or her lifetime, more than the $5,000,000 plus the exemption amount before being subject to gift tax. For this reason, in the current environment, taxable gifts are rare. If a gift triggers a gift tax, however, the donee's basis in the gift is increased by a certain amount of the gift tax. Code section 1015(d)(6) provides as follows:

> "the increase in basis provided by this subsection with respect to any gift for the gift tax paid under chapter 12 shall be an amount (not in excess of the amount of tax so paid) which bears the same ratio to the amount of tax so paid as (i) *the net appreciation* in value of the gift, bears to (ii) *the amount of the gift*. Net appreciation... in value of any gift is the amount by which the fair market value of the gift exceeds the donor's adjusted basis immediately before the gift." (emphasis added)

Unknown Gift Basis. In many cases, the donee is unaware of the donor's basis in a gifted asset. This may be problematic because in most cases, the taxpayer has the burden of proving any positions taken on a tax return. However, section 1015(a) provides as follows:

"If the facts necessary to determine the basis in the hands of the donor or the last preceding owner are unknown to the donee, the Secretary shall, if possible, obtain such facts from such donor or last preceding owner, or any other person cognizant thereof. *If the Secretary finds it impossible to obtain such facts, the basis in the hands of such donor or last preceding owner shall be the fair market value of such property* as found by the Secretary as of the date or approximate date at which, according to the best information that the Secretary is able to obtain, such property was acquired by such donor or last preceding owner." (emphasis added). In *Caldwell & Co. v. CIR*,[7] the Sixth Circuit Court of Appeals ruled that if neither the donee nor the IRS could make a basis determination, then neither gain nor loss was recognized upon the sale of the gifted asset.

BASIS RULES FOR TESTAMENTARY TRANSFERS

General Rule. Essentially, Code section 1014 provides that the basis of property acquired from the decedent is the fair market value at the date of death. This means in the case of appreciated property, basis steps up and in the case of depreciated property, basis steps down. So, unlike gifts, the basis of property acquired from a decedent is always the fair market value. Effectively, for income tax purposes, unrealized gains and losses on assets in the decedent's gross estate are wiped out by death.

Exceptions and Nuances. There are number of exceptions to the general basis rule, including:

- *Income in Respect of Decedent.* Property characterized as income in respect of a decedent ("IRD") retains the decedent's tax basis in the property (see Chapter 17).[8]

- *Partnerships and LLCs.* The tax bases of "hot assets" held in a partnership or an LLC taxed as a partnership are not changed by death of a partner.[9]

- *S corporation IRD.* Code section 1367(b)(4) states as follows:

  (A) *In general.* If any person acquires stock in an S corporation by reason of the death of a decedent or by bequest, devise, or inheritance, section 691 shall be applied with respect to any item of income of the S corporation in the same manner as if the decedent had held directly his pro rata share of such item of income.

  (B) *Adjustments to basis.* The basis determined under section 1014 of any stock in an S corporation shall be reduced by the portion of the value of the stock which is attributable to items constituting income in respect of the decedent."

- *Employer Stock.* In a revenue ruling, the IRS ruled that "net unrealized appreciation" ("NUA") in employer stock distributed from a qualified retirement plan prior to the death of the participant does not receive a basis step-up.[10]

- *Alternate Valuation Date.* In the event an estate elects to value its assets on the alternate valuation date pursuant to Code section 2032, the basis of the assets are stepped up or stepped down by reference to the fair market values of those assets on that date.[11] In Revenue Ruling 62-223, the IRS ruled that any applicable depreciation from the date of death to the alternate valuation date reduces the asset's ultimate basis by the amount taken.

- *Special Use Valuation.* Code section 1014(a)(3) provides that if the estate elects a special use valuation pursuant to Code section 2032A, the special use value is the applicable asset's tax basis. Code section 1016(c)(1) provides that if a recapture tax is imposed pursuant to Code section 2032A(c)(1), then the basis of the asset is adjusted accordingly.

- *Conservation Easements.* Code section 1014(a)(4) provides that to the extent of the qualified conservation easement election made pursuant to Code section 2031(c), the tax basis is the decedent's basis in the asset.

- *Appreciated Property Gifted to the Decedent Within One Year of Death.* Pursuant to Code section 1014(e)(1), if appreciated property is gifted to the decedent within one year of the decedent's death and the asset is re-acquired by the donor or the donor's spouse as a result of the donee's death, there is no the step-up in basis.

- *Disc Stock.* Pursuant to Code section 1014(d), the basis of a decedent's interest in DISC stock is adjusted for unrealized dividends in the DISC.

PLANNING IDEAS AND TRAPS

Many individuals do not analyze the potential net-after-tax value of their gifts and bequests. However, that type of review should be a part of the planning.

Example: A donor with a son and a daughter makes the following gifts: The son receives 100 percent of an LLC. The LLC owns real property with a fair market value of $2 million and a basis of $300,000. Part of the unrealized gain is attributable to depreciation recapture income. The daughter receives $1.5 million in cash. Assume the son's combined state and federal capital gain rate and ordinary income tax rate is 30 percent and 45 percent, respectively. Immediately after the gift, son sells the property in the LLC. While the daughter might complain (due to the $500,000 discrepancy in the gifts), her gift nets a larger amount ($1.5 million) than the after tax amount of the son's gift. The son's net-after-tax value would be:

Sales Proceeds:	$2,000,000
Ordinary Income Tax Cost	–$315,000
Capital Gain Tax Cost	–$300,000
Net After-Tax-Value	$1,385,000

Fiduciary Trap: In situations similar to the above example, fiduciaries who exercise discretionary authority to distribute assets with different tax bases may be exposed to a beneficiary challenge, particularly if the after tax effect to a fiduciary family member is more beneficial than the after tax effect of other beneficiaries.

Gifting Loss Assets. If an asset has a significant unrealized loss that will step-down to fair market value at death, it would be better to make a lifetime gift of that asset to preserve at least a part of the tax benefit of the donor's basis.

Opportunity: Assume a terminally ill married client owns an asset with a basis of $500,000 and a fair market value of $200,000. If the client dies owning the asset, its basis will step down to fair market value effectively eliminating any tax benefit of the unrealized loss in the asset. In the alternative, the terminally ill client could make a gift of the asset to either:

(1) A spouse, unlike any other donee, assumes the donor's basis in the gifted asset for purposes of computing gain or loss. So, if the spouse subsequently sells the asset to the spouse for $200,000, the spouse would recognize the same $300,000 loss the donor would have recognized had he or she sold the asset during life.[12]

(2) To non-spousal family members or a trust for their benefit. Even though the donee would have a loss basis of $200,000, if the donee subsequently sells the asset for an amount between $200,000 and the donor's original basis of $500,000, the entire amount would be tax-free. See the No-Tax Window discussion earlier in the chapter.

Increasing the Value of Bequests. With a significant reduction in the number of taxable estates, the perspectives of the IRS and tax practitioners with respect to asset valuations has flipped. For a non-taxable estate, a tax practitioner favors higher property valuations to achieve the highest possible step up in basis. Importantly, higher valuations may trigger higher state death taxes that may at least partially offset the income tax benefits of a higher tax basis. Conversely, the IRS is likely to challenge techniques which create a higher value – probably using the arguments that tax practitioners successfully made when there were more taxable estates.

Opportunity: Assume that in 2018 besides other assets of $200,000, a terminally ill married client owns 40 percent of a business with a fair market value of $10 million. Assume the minority valuation discount is 30 percent. The client's sole heir owns the remaining 60 percent of the business. Based on the 30 percent discount, at the client's death, the fair market value of the 40 percent business interest would be $2.8 million ($4 million minus $1.2 million). Assume instead, that the client increases the percentage interest from 40 percent to 55 percent by purchasing a 15 percent minority interest from the heir for a $1.05 million note.

Because the client's increased 55 percent interest would not be subject to a minority discount, the interest would be worth at least $5.5 million. Adding the clients other assets ($200,000) and subtracting the note $1.05 million, the client would have a non-taxable estate of $4,875,000. On the other hand, the basis of her 55 percent interest would be stepped up to at least $5.5 million (perhaps more if a control premium is applied to the value). If after the client's death, the heir sold the business, the basis step-up would save at least $642,600 in capital gain taxes, assuming a 20 percent applicable capital gains rate and 3.8 percent net investment income tax rate.

Opportunity: Owners of a business entity should consider eliminating minority discounts with respect to any buy-out of an owner's interest in the business entity. Although such an arrangement may work if all ownership interests are minority interests, if there is a majority owner, it may raise the issue of whether the majority interest owner made an indirect gift to the minority interest owners.

Cross-Purchase Agreements. One of the particular oddities of the Tax Code is how two transactions that create the same economic result can be taxed differently.

Trap: Assume there are two owners of a C corporation. One of them dies, and his estate sells his 50 percent interest to the other shareholder for $500,000. In that transaction, the purchaser's tax basis in the corporation increases by $500,000. But assume the transaction was a corporate redemption for $500,000. Although both transactions result in the surviving shareholder owning 100 percent of the corporation, in the redemption, the surviving shareholder's tax basis is $500,000 less than it is in a cross-purchase. At a state and federal capital gain rate of 30 percent, if the surviving shareholder were to sell the stock to a third party, the difference in the form of the transaction could cost the surviving shareholder $150,000 in tax.

Choice of Entity. Upon the death of an owner, the basis of assets held in certain entities are subject to a basis step-up. So, if the decedent had an interest in such an entity, the basis of the decedent's share of those assets could potentially step-up to fair market value. For that reason, choice of entity should be part of the planning process. For example, if an individual decides to form a flow-through business entity, the choices include partnerships, LLCs and S corporations. If the entity is a partnership or an LLC taxed as a partnership, upon the death of a partner or member, subject to certain limitations, a date of death fair market value basis adjustment of the assets inside the business (in proportion to the partner's or member's interest in the entity) may be permitted (by making a Code section 754 election). There is, however, no similar provision available to shareholders of an S corporation.

Example: A decedent has a 99 percent interest in a general partnership that owns an asset worth $500,000 with a basis to the partnership (referred to as inside basis) of $1,000. Upon the decedent's death (assuming no valuation discounts) or "hot assets" owned by the partnership, a Code section 754 election is made so that the partnership inside basis attributable to the decedent partner's 99 percent interest would step up to its fair market value, or $495,000. So, if the partnership were to sale the asset for $500,000, no gain would flow-through to the decedent's heir (because with respect to the heir, the allocable amount of the sales proceeds of $495,000 is offset by the inside partnership basis of $495,000). On the other hand, if the same asset was held in an S corporation, there is no way, by election or otherwise, for a basis step up upon the death of the 99 percent shareholder.

Employer Stock and NUA. Pursuant to Code section 402(e)(4), a plan participant of a qualified plan who receives a lump sum distribution of employer stock includes only the retirement plan's cost basis in the stock as ordinary income. The *"net unrealized appreciation"* (often called "NUA") of the distributed employer stock is excluded from gross income.[13] Essentially, NUA is the excess of the fair market value of the employer stock over the retirement plan's basis in the stock. Upon the subsequent sale of the stock, the plan participant will recognize the NUA (as well as additional appreciation) as capital gain.

Tax Trap: Code section 402(e)(4)(B) requires a lump sum distribution for all NUA on employer securities to be excluded from the participant's gross income.[14]

Opportunity: Because upon the death of a plan participant, NUA is considered to be IRD, there is the potential for a significant gain to be recognized by the beneficiary or heir of the plan participant. To avoid the recognition of gain, during lifetime, if the stock is treated as "qualified appreciated stock" as defined in Code section 170(e)(5), the owner could make a charitable contribution of the stock. A donor can also make a charitable bequest of the NUA qualified appreciated stock to eliminate the IRD gain. Of course, this strategy assumes that the decedent has other assets to replace NUA stock that would otherwise pass to a non-charitable heir.

S Corporations and ESOPs. ESOPs (or other retirement plans) owning S corporation stock can create significant tax advantages and disadvantages for the plan participants. S corporation income allocated to the retirement plan is not subject to current income taxation. However, in Revenue Ruling 2003-27, the IRS ruled that S corporation stock held by an ESOP is subject to the same stock basis adjustments as any other shareholder including an upward basis adjustment of the ESOP's pro rata share of undistributed S corporation income. So, in computing the NUA with respect to a lump sum distribution of S corporation stock from an ESOP, the ESOP's basis in the stock includes any S corporation basis adjustments. Since the NUA is the difference between the fair market value of the stock and the ESOP's basis in the stock, there may be a small amount of NUA and a relatively large amount of ordinary income recognized by the participant.

> ***Tax Trap:*** As illustrated above, a plan participant of a retirement plan is not taxed on S corporation income during the time the stock is held in the plan. However, upon receiving a lump sum distribution of S corporation stock, because the plan participant must include the retirement plan's basis in the stock as ordinary income, the S corporation income that was not taxed during the time the stock was held in the retirement plan is effectively taxed in its totality at the time of the distribution. For this reason, the lump sum distribution of S corporation stock in a retirement could generate a substantial amount of ordinary income particularly if S corporation income has accumulated over many years, potentially increasing the plan participant's marginal tax rate upon distribution.

MARRIAGE, DIVORCE AND TAX BASIS

Divorce and Spousal Planning. The basis of marital assets should be considered in divorce property settlement negotiations. This is because assets of equal value may have disproportionate bases. The after-tax value of a high basis asset is likely to be much greater than the after-tax value of a low basis asset. However, because of the many nuances of tax law, family courts may be reluctant to get embroiled in speculative tax consequences.[15]

> *Example:* In a property settlement negotiation, one spouse has a choice between $900,000 in cash and stock with a fair market value of $1.1 million and a basis of $1,000. Assuming the recipient spouse would sell the stock, in spite of the $200,000 difference between the value of the stock and the cash, taking the cash is the better choice. Assuming the combined federal and state capital gains rate of the selling spouse is 23.8 percent, the sale of the stock will result in a tax cost of approximately $262,000, or a true net-after-tax value of only $838,000.

Spousal and Divorce Transfers. Transfers of property between spouses or former spouses incident to divorce are always treated as gifts. Unlike gifts however, the transferee spouse's basis in the transferred property is always the same as the transferor's basis. Thus, a transferee spouse who sells gifted property with an unrealized loss may claim the loss. For capital gain purposes, the holding period of the transferor spouse also carries over to the transferee spouse.

Liability in Excess of Basis. Unlike gift property subject to a liability, a transfer of property subject to a liability in excess of basis does not trigger gain[16] and the recipient spouse takes the transferor spouse's basis.[17] The unrealized gain (the difference between the amount of the liability and the property's basis) is simply deferred until the recipient spouse sells the property.

> ***Tax Trap:*** Assume a divorcing wife owns a tract of land with a fair market value of $2.1 million, a basis of $200,000 subject to a secured debt of $1.5 million and transfers the land to her husband. Anticipating the receipt of the $600,000 of equity in the property, husband immediately sells it to a third party subject to the liability for $600,000. Even though husband only received $600,000, he recognizes a gain of $1.9 million (because the amount realized also includes the $1.5 million liability assumed by the buyer). Assuming a state and federal effective income tax rate of 30 percent, husband total tax liability would be $570,000 netting him only $30,000 of the $600,000 of "equity" before payment of realtor commissions. Depending on the amount of the commission, husband might have to pay all or part of it from his own funds.

Tax Opportunity: In a non-divorce situation, assume wife is terminally ill and husband gifts the property described in the above example to her. In turn, wife who dies within a year of the gift, bequeaths the real property subject to the liability to a trust for the benefit of the couple's children. Because husband does not have any beneficial interest in the trust, the testamentary transfer of the property is not treated as coming back to him. Therefore, the property would not be subject to Code section 1014(e) (discussed earlier in this chapter) so that upon wife's death, the basis of the property would be stepped up to fair market value, i.e. $2.1 million. Subsequently, the trust sells the property subject to the liability for $600,000. Unlike the previous example, the trust would not recognize any gain and would net $600,000 (less closing costs and commissions) income tax-free.

PLANNING DOCUMENTS, ADVICE AND FLEXIBILITY

In an environment where basis planning is critical, having documents that allow flexibility to the individual, and, in some cases, third parties is paramount.

Powers of Attorney. Virtually every individual should have a well crafted and flexible general power of attorney authorizing the power holder to make broad and flexible decisions, including, but certainly not limited to:

- Ability to make gift advancements of bequests to individuals and charities the individual has provided for in the disposition documents. For example:
  - o Gifting an asset with an unrealized loss before the donor's death.
  - o Gifting a potential IRD asset to charity before death
- Allowing the power holder to change the client's domicile state for tax purposes.
- Allowing for changes in beneficiary designations of life insurance, retirement plans and IRAs (e.g., naming a donor advised fund to receive a large IRA).
- Permitting conversions of IRAs to ROTH IRAs during the client's life.

Disposition Documents. In drafting the relevant disposition documents, estate planning attorneys will increasingly provide greater flexibility for income tax planning, especially basis planning. For example, standard form Wills and Revocable Living Trusts should be drafted to include one or more of the following provisions that deal with basis issues:

- Contemplating the possible application of Code section 1014(e) to bequests by limiting the power or benefits of the original donor in appreciated property that was gifted to the decedent within a year of death.
- Making the fiduciary legally obligated to appraise non-readily marketable assets that are gifted or bequeathed. The obligation should probably include (for all gifted or bequeathed assets, whether readily marketable or not) providing each beneficiary with a statement of the tax basis and supporting detail, sufficient to withstand an IRS audit. The fees and costs associated with these tasks may be specially allocated to the beneficiaries who benefit from the reporting.
- Specifically recognizing any advancement of bequests made during the life of the decedent.
- Permitting the fiduciary to create sub-trusts designed to segregate assets with unique basis issues, such as appreciated property potentially subject to section 1014(e).
- Consider providing indemnities and releases of fiduciaries on decisions that potentially impact the tax basis of assets.
- Excluding fiduciaries from decisions on basis issues that directly benefit the fiduciary or immediate family members.

Client & Advisor Actions. Clients should be encouraged to deal with basis issues in their planning, including:

- Clients with multiple residences in different states should declare a domicile state. Domicile issues are generally fact specific and change over time (e.g., the decedent was in a nursing home in New Jersey for the last two years of his life). Properly documenting and periodically re-declaring residency can be an important part of tax planning.

- Clients should be encouraged to obtain detailed documentation of the basis of assets, store it in a safe place and provide the details and documents to their heirs and advisors.

- Advisors should consider drafting "CYA" letters outlining the facts they relied on in determining the basis of any asset. Consider having the donee/heirs confirm the facts by signing the letter, particularly when the facts are questionable.

Fiduciary Responsibilities. Consider the following questions in determining the scope of fiduciary responsibilities and authority?

- With so few estates being subject to a federal estate tax, do fiduciaries have a responsibility to appraise non-readily marketable property when there is clearly no state or federal estate tax due by the estate or concerns about a portability election? Can the fiduciary charge the cost of the appraisal to the donor's beneficial interest in the trust?

- Does the fiduciary have a responsibility to independently appraise non-readily marketable property that a donee passes back directly or indirectly to the donor within one year of the gift? Interestingly, two appraisals may be necessary for non-readily marketable property that may be subject to section 1014(e). One appraisal will determine the fair market value at the time of the gift to determine if the asset is *"appreciated property."* A second appraisal would determine the date of death value.

- Should a fiduciary or an advisor who provided an incorrect basis calculation be subject to a claim of an heir(s) who miscalculated tax liability based on the fiduciary's mistakes?

BASIS COMPLIANCE AND RECORD KEEPING ISSUES

There are a number of basis-related reporting and compliance requirements, including:

Estate Tax Basis Reporting. Prior to August 1, 2015, there were no statutory requirements requiring the estate tax return valuation of assets be consistent with the fair market value basis used by an heir for income tax purposes. Moreover, there was no requirement for an Executor to provide heirs with any tax basis information. As a result, many heirs made their own determination of the fair market value of testamentary gifted property that in many instances was higher than the value reported on the estate tax return. To eliminate this type of inconsistency, Code section 1014(f) was enacted pursuant to the Surface Transportation and Veterans Health Care Choice Improvement Act of 2015 providing as follows:

- Each beneficiary's basis in the inherited asset must be consistent with the value reported on any estate tax return – as is finally determined (e.g., if there is an audit that increases the value, basis is also adjusted).

- Per new Code section 6035(a), if a "Finally Determined Value" is not on the estate tax return, the Executor must file a Statement of Value with the IRS (copy to the beneficiaries).

- The new rules apply to property listed on an estate tax return filed after July 31, 2015. Note that it is the filing date, not the date of death that applies. The filing date has been delayed by the IRS until proposed regulations are issued.

- If the basis used by the beneficiary/heir is greater than the Finally Determined amount or the Statement Value, as is applicable, he or she may be subject to a 20 percent penalty with the statute of limitations extended to six years.

Caution: It is possible that the reported value and the concomitant tax basis may be adjusted in the course of an IRS audit, settlement with the IRS or a judicial decision. Because the adjustment could be made years after the estate tax return was filed, the affected heirs may be required to file amended tax returns.

Opportunity: Because very few estates are subject to estate tax, those focusing on income tax planning seek the highest valuation of assets to maximize tax basis. Since the purpose of Code section 1014(f) is consistency of basis (and no more), it does nothing to discourage that strategy perspective.

Trap: Code section 1014(f) fails to provide a means for heirs to challenge the Executor's Statement of Value. Because the IRS has a propensity to avoid third party conflicts, it is unlikely that a procedure for contesting value will be adopted in any future Regulations. Effectively, unless directly challenged by the IRS, the Executor's determination will be the one respected by the IRS. Although it is unlikely the IRS would challenge the Executor's Statement of Value in a non-taxable estate, the Executor may be subject to claims from heirs who disagree with the valuation.

Gift Tax Basis Reporting. Unless the donor voluntarily provides basis information to the beneficiary, there is no provision in the Internal Revenue Code that requires a donor to provide this information. On the other hand, a fiduciary duty may exist to provide this information.

Trust and Estate Basis Reporting. With respect to property distributions from an estate or trust, although Code section 6034A requires those entities to report on the recipient's Schedule K-1 the exact information as that set forth on the trust or estate's entity schedule K-1, there is no requirement to provide tax basis information.

Brokerage Statements. In the past, brokerage statements reporting the sales of a taxpayer's securities (i.e., stocks, bonds, etc.) did not include the taxpayer's basis in the stock. Therefore, unless the taxpayer maintained his or her own basis records, it was very difficult for the taxpayer to determine his or her basis in the securities. To solve this problem, the Emergency Economic Stabilization Act of 2008 (P.L. 110-343) added Code section 6045(g) requiring brokers to report the basis of "covered securities" to the account owner and the IRS. Failure to comply with the reporting responsibilities may be subject to the imposition of significant penalties.[18]

Taxpayer Penalties. Failure to properly report basis, when relevant, may result in the imposition of a number of potential penalties. For example, Code section 6662 provides for a 20 percent penalty for a *"substantial valuation misstatement,"* with the penalty increasing to 40 percent if there is a *"gross valuation misstatement."* Code section 6662(e) provides in part as follows:

> "there is a substantial valuation misstatement ... if the value of any property (or the adjusted basis of any property) claimed on any return of tax imposed by chapter 1 is 150 percent or more of the amount determined to be the correct amount of such valuation or adjusted basis (as the case may be)." Code section 6662(h)(2)(A)(i) increases the 150 percent to 200 percent to determine if a gross valuation misstatement occurred. In abusive cases, the IRS could apply Code section 6663 to impose a fraud penalty.

Appraisals. Obtaining appraisals of gifted or bequeathed assets that are not readily marketable is encouraged even if a gift or estate tax return is not required. The problem is how to establish the fair market value of an asset on the date it was gifted or bequeathed twenty years ago. Because of the importance of basis for income tax purposes, despite the cost and effort, obtaining appraisals is encouraged.

Specifically, Treasury Regulation section 301.6501(c)-1(f)(3) lists the information that should be contained in a gift appraisal. It is also advisable to review the appraisal requirements for charitable appraisals contained in Treasury Regulation section 1.170A-13(c)(3) and the definitions of qualified appraisals and qualified appraisers contained in Proposed Treasury Regulation section 1.170A-17.

It is important that the appraiser be seen as both independent and qualified. For example, see the definition of a "qualified appraiser" in Code section 170(f)(11)(E)(ii) and Treasury Regulation section 1.170A-13(c)(5) and in Proposed Treasury Regulation section 1.170A-17.

CONCLUSION

As income tax planning increases in importance, income tax basis planning is essential. Although a myriad of issues are discussed in this chapter, it is by no means intended to be exhaustive. In any event, there is no substitute for competent tax advice from a trusted and knowledgeable tax professional.

CHAPTER ENDNOTES

1. As permanently enacted pursuant to The American Taxpayer Relief Act of 2012 ("ATRA").
2. A Congressional Research Service Report estimated that less than 0.2 percent of all estates would be subject to an estate tax in 2013. For roughly 99.8 percent of US residents, income tax planning trumps federal estate tax avoidance. *"The Estate and Gift Tax Provisions of the American Taxpayer Relief Act of 2012,"* (issued on February 15, 2013).
3. In 2016, estates and trusts reach the highest bracket upon reaching taxable income of $12,400.
4. IRC Sec. 2036(a).
5. IRC Sec. 1015(a).

6. The assumption of the debt by the transferee is treated as a sale transaction. Treas. Reg. §1.1001- 2(a)(1) provides that "*... the amount realized from a sale or other disposition of property includes the amount of liabilities from which the transferor is discharged as a result of the sale or disposition.*"
7. *James E. Caldwell & Co. v. Comm'r*, 234 F.2d 660 (6th Cir. 1956), rev'g 24 T.C. 597 (1955).
8. See IRC Secs. 1014(c) and 691 and Chapter 17 in this book.
9. See IRC Sec. 751(a).
10. See Rev. Rul. 75-125.
11. IRC Sec. 1014(a)(2).
12. See IRC Sec. 1041.
13. For more information see: *Maldonado, "Basis Issues Complicate Qualified Plan Distributions of Employer Securities,"* Journal of Taxation, December 1992.
14. C.f., PLR 200434022.
15. *In re Marriage of Fonstein*, 17 Cal.3d 738 (1976), the California Supreme Court stated: "Regardless of the certainty that the tax liability will be incurred if in the future an asset is sold, liquidated or otherwise reduced to cash, the trial court is not required to speculate on or consider such tax consequences in the absence of proof that a taxable event has occurred during the marriage or will occur in connection with the division of the community property."
16. IRC Sec. 1041(e).
17. For a more detailed analysis of this issue, see *Boris Bittker & Lawrence Lokken, Federal Taxation of Income, Estates and Gifts*, ¶ 44.6 (2015); IRS PLR 9615026 (Apr. 12, 1996); IRS PLR 8644012 (Jul. 31, 1986); Treas. Reg. §1.041-1T(d) Q&A 12 (2015).
18. For more information, see: Soled, Goodman and Pochesci, *"Penalty Exposure for Incorrect Tax Basis Reporting on Information Returns,"* Journal of Taxation, August 2013 and Internal Revenue Bulletin 2010-47 (TD 9504, issued November 22, 2010), *"Basis Reporting by Securities Brokers and Basis Determination for Stock."*

PASSIVE ACTIVITIES AND AT-RISK RULES

CHAPTER 23

INTRODUCTION

The passive activities and at-risk rules provide hurdles that taxpayers must overcome in order for certain losses to offset other sources of income in a given year. The at-risk rules are applied after the basis limitation provisions discussed further in Chapter 21. If a taxpayer's loss passes the basis and at-risk limitation tests, the passive activity rules are applied. The at-risk rules focus on the taxpayer's investment (risk) in the venture, while the passive rules focus on the nature of the taxpayer's involvement in the venture. Losses may be suspended (i.e., can't be utilized in the current year but are not lost and may be used at a future date) at any or all of these levels.

Taxpayers often invest substantial amounts of money into ventures without being aware of the potential tax impact of these limitations. If a taxpayer expects losses from an investment to automatically offset their other sources of income, they may be in for a bad surprise.

This situation comes up very often with an investment in real estate. Since the depreciation on a property often outpaces the amortized principal in the early years, a property may throw off a positive cash flow but report a taxable loss. That taxable loss must meet the tests of each of the three limitation rules before the taxpayer can claim any of the loss as an offset to their taxable income.

The passive activity rules are also used to determine when trade or business and rental activities are subject to the Net Investment Income tax (NIIT). This determination now puts a greater importance on these rules in situations regardless of whether an activity is generating income or losses.

AT-RISK LIMITATION RULES

The at-risk limitation rules were added to the Internal Revenue Code with the Tax Reform Act of 1976. Prior to the addition of these rules, taxpayers were allowed to deduct losses from investment activities to the extent of their basis, which is determined by adding the taxpayer's:

1. actual cash investment;
2. adjustments from the results of operations;
3. liabilities the taxpayer is obligated to pay (recourse); and
4. costs financed through nonrecourse loans that the taxpayer will not be obligated to pay personally.

The enactment of the at-risk rules was the first major attempt by Congress to deal with the growing number of tax shelters. Tax shelters were a popular way for investors to take advantage of their ability to deduct losses up to their basis in the investment. The taxpayer's basis, however, was often increased by liabilities that the investor would never be called upon to pay in the event the business failed.

Initially, the at-risk rules were applied only to investments in five activities that were perceived to be the most abusive tax shelters. The five original activities subject to the at-risk limitation rules were:[1]

1. Farming
2. Exploring for or exploiting oil and gas resources

3. Holding, producing, or distributing motion picture films or videotapes

4. Equipment leasing

5. Exploring for or exploiting geothermal deposits

In 1978, the at-risk limitation rules were extended to all other investment activities except real estate. Finally, in 1986, the at-risk rules added real estate activities to the scope of activities covered by Code section 465.[2] The at-risk rules continue to apply under today's law and cover all investment activities.

INTRODUCTION TO THE PASSIVE ACTIVITY LOSS LIMITATION RULES

In a further effort to curb perceived abuses with the growing use of tax shelters, Congress enacted the passive activity loss (PAL) rules with the Tax Reform Act of 1986. At the time, tax shelters were being marketed to investors with the purpose of generating losses to offset high-income taxpayers' salaries and wages. Back in 1986, the highest marginal tax rate was 50 percent, so a great deal of tax savings was at stake.

Although the number of abusive tax shelters may have been reduced, in part, by these rules, they have cast a much wider net and many taxpayers who have not invested in tax shelters still have to deal with the PAL limitations each year when they file their tax return. The PAL rules are contained in Code section 469 and the corresponding regulations.

The PAL rules apply to any individual, estate, trust, certain closely held C corporations, and personal service corporations.[3] A passive activity can be practically any business or rental activity owned by a taxpayer directly or held by a taxpayer in a flow-through entity such as a partnership, limited liability company, or S corporation.

TAX IMPLICATIONS

At-Risk Rules

The at-risk limitations are applied to individual taxpayers and closely held corporations. Closely held corporations are defined as one having five or fewer shareholders owning more than 50 percent of the corporation's stock during the last half of the tax year.[4] For flow-through entities, such as partnerships, certain limited liability companies, and S corporations, these limitations are applied at the individual partner, member, or shareholder level.

The at-risk rules limit deductions for borrowing that attempts to be characterized as "at-risk" for tax purposes when there is no actual economic risk to the investor. For instance, assume Georgia wants to purchase a $100,000 interest in an oil drilling venture. She intends to invest $20,000 of her own funds while borrowing the $80,000 balance. The bank providing the loan to Georgia has agreed to make a "nonrecourse" loan to her. In other words, the bank will rely solely on the value of the property as its collateral for the debt. In the event Georgia cannot repay the loan, the bank cannot look to Georgia's other assets to cover the unpaid balance. Since the most Georgia can lose on her investment is $20,000 in cash, her deductions will be limited to that $20,000 (plus the amount of income generated from the investment).

The amount at-risk for a given activity is the combined total amount of money and the adjusted basis of other property contributed with respect to the activity and amounts borrowed with respect to the activity.[5] However, in order for an individual to be treated as at-risk for amounts borrowed by the entity owning the activity, the individual must be personally liable for the repayment of the borrowed amounts or pledge property outside the investment as security.[6] The courts have interpreted this to mean that the individual must have the ultimate liability for the repayment of the debt.

The at-risk rules cover essentially all investment activities (except for real estate acquired before 1987). With respect to real estate subject to the at-risk rules, "qualified nonrecourse financing" is treated as an additional amount at-risk. Qualified nonrecourse financing is any debt incurred that:

1. is borrowed for the holding of real property;

2. is borrowed from a "qualified person" (one in the business of lending money, such as a bank or savings and loan institution) or represents a loan from any federal, state, or local government or instrumentality thereof, or is guaranteed by any federal, state, or local government;

3. holds no person personally liable for repayment; and

4. is not convertible debt.[7]

An investor is considered at-risk to the extent of:

1. cash invested, *plus*
2. the basis of property invested, *plus*
3. amounts borrowed for use in the investment that are secured by the investor's assets (other than the property used in the investment activity), *plus*
4. amounts borrowed to the extent the investor is personally liable for its repayment (including qualified nonrecourse financing), *plus*

When the investment is made in partnership form —

1. the investor-partner's undistributed share of partnership income, *plus*
2. the investor-partner's proportionate share of partnership debt, to the extent he is personally liable for its repayment.

An investor is not considered "at-risk" with respect to nonrecourse debt (other than qualified nonrecourse financing, see above) used to finance the activity, or to finance the acquisition of property used in the activity, or with respect to any other arrangement for the compensation or reimbursement of any economic loss. For example, if Georgia is able to obtain commercial insurance against the risk that the oil drilling fund will not return her original $20,000 cash investment, she would not even be considered "at-risk" on that amount.

If a taxpayer does not have sufficient amounts at-risk in a given activity, the deductibility of the losses from that activity are limited to the amount at-risk. Any excess losses are carried forward to future years and may be utilized to offset future income from the activity or be deducted when the taxpayer adds amounts to the activity for which the taxpayer is deemed to be at-risk.

A taxpayer who previously deducted losses from an activity based upon amounts that were at-risk in a prior year may be required to recapture those losses if the amount that a taxpayer has at-risk falls in a future year.[8] This can happen if the taxpayer used a certain amount of liabilities as an amount at-risk to deduct losses to the full extent of the amount at-risk. If the subsequent principal repayments of the liability reduce the amount at-risk below zero, they would need to be recaptured in that year.

Taxpayers with losses from activities with amounts not at-risk are required by the IRS to complete and file with their tax return Form 6198, *At Risk Limitations*.[9]

Passive Activity Rules

In general, losses from passive activities are deductible in a given year to the extent the passive activity income exceeds the losses from passive activities. Passive activity losses in excess of passive activity income are suspended. Suspended passive activity losses are carried forward indefinitely to future years to offset future income from passive activities. PALs may not be used to offset other nonpassive income such as salaries, investment income, or capital gains. However, passive losses from one activity can generally be offset with passive income from a different activity.

Credits from passive activities are also disallowed unless there is net passive income in a given year. Like PALs, these credits are carried forward indefinitely to future years. There is no carryback provision for either PALs or passive activity credits.

Suspended losses, but not credits, may be utilized in the year in which an activity is completely or substantially disposed.

The IRS requires that taxpayers with passive activities complete and file with their tax return Form 8582, *Passive Activity Loss Limitations*. If credits from passive activities are being reported by a taxpayer in any year, Form 8582-CR, *Passive Activity Credit Limitations* should be used.

DETERMINING THE "ACTIVITY"

As you can see from the short introduction above, both the at-risk and passive loss rules use the term "activity." Unfortunately, what an activity is for purposes of the at-risk rules does not necessarily carry over to the PAL rules.

At-Risk Activities

The definition of an activity for the purposes of the at-risk limitation rules begins with the five original activities defined under Code section 465(c)(1). Each of the original five activities must be treated as a separate activity.[10] This has been interpreted to mean that any project that is covered under one of these activities must be accounted for separately under the at-risk rules. The only exception is for the leasing of tangible personal property by a partnership or S corporation. All leased assets placed in service in a single tax year are treated as a single activity.[11]

For activities other than the five original activities under Code section 465(c)(1), if the activities constitute a single trade or business, all the activities of that trade or business are aggregated if:[12]

1. the taxpayer actively participates in the management of the trade or business; or

2. the trade or business is carried on by a partnership or S corporation, and 65 percent or more of the losses for the tax year are allocable to persons who actively participate in the management of the trade or business.

The determination of an activity for purposes of the at-risk rules is very important since the losses of one activity that are limited by the at-risk rules may not be deducted using available at-risk amounts in another activity.

Passive Activities

A passive activity is (1) any activity that involves the conduct of a trade or business in which the taxpayer does not "materially participate" or (2) any rental activity.[13]

Since the definition of a "passive activity" includes the term "activity," one would expect to find a definition of "activity" somewhere. Unfortunately, taxpayers are not so lucky. An activity is based on a case by case "facts and circumstances" evaluation. The IRS has allowed any "reasonable method" to determine whether one or more trade or business activities constitute an appropriate "economic unit." Therefore, one or more trade or business activities may be grouped to represent an economic unit.

In order to group activities for the purpose of determining an appropriate economic unit, taxpayers must evaluate:[14]

1. the similarities and differences in types of business;

2. the extent of common control and ownership;

3. geographic location; and

4. interdependencies between or among the activities.

For example, taxpayers are generally allowed to aggregate activities in the same line of business into one activity without considering geographic location if the activities are commonly controlled by the same owners.

Example: A taxpayer owns an ice cream store and a shoe store in Pittsburgh, and an ice cream store and a shoe store in a Philadelphia shopping mall. There are four different possible combinations of the activities based on all the facts and circumstances:

1. One activity aggregating all four businesses

2. Two separate activities – a Pittsburgh activity and a Philadelphia activity

3. Two separate activities – an ice cream store activity and a shoe store activity

4. Four separate activities – one for each business

Certain activities may not be grouped. A rental activity that leases real property may not be grouped with a rental activity that leases personal property, unless the rentals are provided together.[15] Also, a rental activity may not be grouped with a trade or business activity unless the combination of the two activities represent an appropriate economic unit and:[16]

1. the rental activity is "insubstantial" in relation to the trade or business activity;

2. the business activity is "insubstantial" in relation to the rental activity; or

3. each owner of the trade or business activity has the same proportionate ownership in the rental activity.

Although "insubstantial" is not defined in the current regulations, prior temporary regulations accepted up to 20 percent of the total gross receipts of the combined activities to be considered insubstantial. However, this test is not valid under current rules which favor a stricter facts and circumstances test. As a result, the Service can challenge groupings even if the receipts of one of the activities are well below the 20 percent "insubstantial" level.

Example: A owns a building in which he operates a card store. The card store has two rental spaces. Gross receipts from the rental spaces are 15 percent of the total receipts of the combined activities. The rental activity may be insubstantial in relation to the combined activity, so the rental activity and business activity may possibly be grouped based on other subjective facts.

What is critically important is that the taxpayer makes a proper grouping election in the first year they wish to group activities. The regulations specifically exclude the ability to use the grouping rules solely to avoid a PAL problem.[17] In 2010, a revenue procedure was issued which describes how a grouping election should be made and what information needs to be included in the election.[18]

Married couples are considered as one taxpayer when applying the grouping rules. Therefore, if B owns a rental property and B's spouse, C, owns a retail store, the rental property and retail store may be grouped into one activity for the application of the PAL rules.

An activity is the unit of measurement for the PAL rules. Once the activity is determined, several tests are applied to determine whether the taxpayer's participation in the activity is passive or nonpassive. These tests include:

1. material participation (defined below);
2. active participation for rental real estate; and
3. if suspended losses of passive activities become available upon the complete disposition of an activity.

Once an activity group is created, the taxpayer may not change the groupings unless the combination of the activities is clearly inappropriate or a material change has occurred from when the initial grouping was made. Starting in 2013, there is an exception to this rule in which an individual or trust subject to NII tax is allowed a one-time "fresh start" regrouping which doesn't require a previous grouping to be inappropriate.[19] If the grouping is broken, disclosure must be made to the IRS.[20]

The IRS may regroup a taxpayer's activities if:[21]

1. the taxpayer's aggregation fails to reflect one or more appropriate economic units; and
2. one of the primary purposes of the taxpayer's grouping is to circumvent the PAL rules.

Since a group of activities is considered as one activity for the application of the PAL rules, suspended losses are only deductible upon the complete (or substantially complete) disposition of the group of activities.[22] This provision suggests that the taxpayer should group activities in the smallest possible units unless the goal of the grouped activities is to obtain a level of material participation.

APPLICATION TO NIIT

Provided that a taxpayer's income is above certain thresholds, the 3.8 percent NIIT applies to income that is generated from passive business activities as defined by the rules described above. The difference often comes down to whether the taxpayer materially participated in the business activities.

Importantly, not all activities related to the business count as "material participation." Activities that are undertaken in the capacity of an investor do not count as material participation. These generally are defined as activities that focus exclusively on the financial performance of the business, including reviewing and preparing summaries of the business finances for the investors own use.[23] In contrast, activities related to maintenance of equipment, supervision of employees, production of goods, or the provision of services to customers will typically count as material participation.

Example 1: William owns a chain of car washes in his town. The day-to-day operations are handled by a salaried manger, though William spends several hours per month reviewing the financial performance of each facility, and also spent a considerable amount of time summarizing the revenues generated by each car wash when he wanted to use them as collateral for a loan. Even though William may have spent a lot of time keeping a close eye on his businesses, these activities would still be viewed as activities undertaken in William's capacity as an investor and will not count as material participation in the business.

Example 2: Using the same facts above, except that William has a separate manager for each facility, and meets with each manger twice monthly to review staffing issues, conduct interviews with potential employees, and undertake cost-benefit analyses of equipment maintenance and upgrade possibilities. In this case, William most likely would be considered to be actively participating in his businesses, which could change how his income from the businesses is characterized for NIIT purposes.

If material participation is an important issue for the taxpayer for NIIT purposes, detailed contemporaneous records of those activities should be maintained.

FREQUENTLY ASKED QUESTIONS

At-Risk Limitations

Question – Do guarantees by a taxpayer of a partnership's debt increase the amount at-risk?

Answer – A guarantee of partnership debt does not increase the guarantor partner's amount at-risk unless the partner is actually required to make payments to the creditor.[24] The guarantor must have no right of action against any other party should payment be required under the terms of the guarantees.

Question – How are suspended at-risk losses carried forward?

Answer – If the at-risk rules prevent a taxpayer from deducting the full amount of a loss, the losses may be carried forward indefinitely. The losses may then be used to offset income in a future year from the same activity or when the taxpayer increases the amount at-risk in the activity. If the taxpayer recognizes a gain on the disposition of the activity, the gain could be offset by the suspended losses. However, unlike the passive rules, there is no automatic "freeing-up" of the losses on disposition.

Losses that are limited retain their character from year-to-year. That is, if a long-term capital loss is limited, the carryover will continue to be a long-term capital loss to be used when sufficient at-risk basis is generated. There are many instances where a taxpayer may have more than one type of loss limited by the at-risk rules. Although there is no formal ordering rule for deducting losses subject to the at-risk rules, the instructions to Form 6198 require a pro rata share of each type of loss limited by the at-risk rules be carried forward. Note that there was an ordering rule established by a proposed regulation in 1979.[25] However, the regulation has never been finalized. In fact, the instructions to Form 6198 contradict the proposed regulation.

Passive Activity Loss Limitations

Question – How does a taxpayer's participation in an activity impact the application of the PAL rules?

Answer – A taxpayer's participation determines whether the activity is treated as a passive activity or a nonpassive activity. To be a nonpassive activity, the taxpayer must "materially" participate in the activity.

Question – What is "material" participation?

Answer – Material participation is defined as a taxpayer's participation on a regular, continuous, and substantial basis.[26] The regulations under Code section 469 provide seven tests for material participation. A taxpayer that meets any one of the seven tests is deemed to be a material participant for that year. The tests must be applied on an annual basis to each activity of a taxpayer.

If a taxpayer materially participates in an activity that generates a loss in a given year, the loss may be used in that year to offset passive, portfolio, or nonpassive income. If a taxpayer is deemed not to be a material participant, any losses are generally treated as passive and are not deductible against any other source of income except income from other passive activities.

The seven tests for material participation are:[27]

1. The taxpayer participates in the activity for more than 500 hours during the year.

2. The taxpayer's participation in the activity constitutes substantially all of the participation by all individuals in the activity, including nonowners.

3. The taxpayer's participation is more than 100 hours during the year, and no other individual, including nonowners, participates more hours than the taxpayer.

4. The activity is a significant participation activity (the taxpayer participates more than 100 hours during the year) and the taxpayer's annual participation in all significant participation activities is more than 500 hours.

5. The taxpayer materially participated in the activity for any five tax years during the ten immediately preceding tax years.

6. If the activity is a personal service activity (one in the fields of health, law, engineering, architecture, accounting, actuarial science, performing arts, consulting, or any other trade or business in which capital is not a material income-producing factor), the taxpayer materially participated in the activity for any three tax years preceding the current year.

7. Based on all the facts and circumstances, the taxpayer participates on a regular, continuous and substantial basis during the year.[28]

There is reciprocity to the application of the material participation tests. If a taxpayer's spouse materially participates in an activity, the taxpayer is also considered to materially participate. In addition, participation of both spouses is combined to determine if the material participation tests are met regardless of whether a joint return is filed.

A close reading of the above tests show that the focus is on the quantity of hours, not the quality of the work performed. Any work performed by the taxpayer is considered participation for the purpose of these tests – unless (1) the work is not customarily done by the owner of an activity and (2) avoidance of PAL rules is a principal purpose.

Taxpayers must be able to substantiate their participation by reasonable means according to Treas. Reg. section 1.469-5T(f)(4). Under examination, the Internal Revenue Service tends to focus on contemporaneous documentation of hours spent in an activity in order to determine the level of participation. However, contemporaneous documentation is not required if the taxpayer can reasonably establish their participation by other means. Auditors will consider it difficult for someone who earns a salary reported on a Form W-2 to also have enough time to also spend 500 hours in a separate activity.

Taxpayers commonly use calendars, appointment books, phone records, e-mail logs, and automobile mileage logs to help support the level of participation. Some types of work do not count towards the required number of hours, including:

(1) Investor-type activities (unless the taxpayer is involved in the day-to-day management or operations), such as:

   a. studying or reviewing financial statements or reports;

   b. preparing or compiling summaries or analyses for the individual's own use; or

   c. monitoring finances or operations in a non-managerial capacity.

(2) Work not customarily done by an owner. This is asserted where the work is normally assigned to an employee, but was done by an owner in order to avoid the disallowance of losses under section 469.

(3) Services not integral to operations. The most common example of this limitation is travel time.

Question – Can a limited partner materially participate?

Answer – A limited partner cannot materially participate in an activity unless:[29]

1. the limited partner is also a general partner;
2. the limited partner participates more than 500 hours in the activity;
3. the limited partner materially participated for any five of the ten preceding years; or
4. the activity is a personal service activity and the limited partner participated for any three preceding years.

Note that limited liability company members are generally treated by the IRS as limited partners for the purpose of applying the material participation rules. However, as of this edition, no formal guidance has been issued by the IRS.

Question – How are the PAL rules applied to different types of income?

Answer – Income from a passive activity is divided into passive income and portfolio income. Portfolio income includes interest, dividends, and investment capital gains or losses and is fully reportable by a taxpayer without the application of the PAL rules. This split between passive and portfolio income is not found in most other areas of the tax law such as in the case of foreign income categorization in which most types of portfolio income are considered passive. Congress realized that such a split was necessary in the case of the passive rules to prevent taxpayers from creating passive (portfolio) investment companies whose income could be shielded by other types of passive income.

Passive losses are aggregated and applied against passive income in a given year. If the passive losses exceed the passive income for the year, the excess losses are allocated to the loss activities and are carried forward indefinitely.

Losses from publicly traded partnerships (PTPs) may only be used against income from that specific partnership. No grouping of PTPs is permitted, even if they operate in the same industry, such as oil and gas. As a result, losses from PTPs generally accumulate over time. Unless the PTP passes income through to the investors, a PTP may need to be disposed of in order to release the suspended losses and be used to offset other income.

Question – How are rental real estate activities treated under the PAL rules?

Answer – A rental real estate activity with active participation is separately categorized under the PAL rules. Up to $25,000 of losses from such activities (which are limited to those activities of natural persons) with active participation may be used to offset other nonpassive income.[30] This special loss allowance begins to be phased-out for joint filers with modified adjusted gross income (MAGI) over $100,000. The allowance is reduced 50 cents for every dollar of MAGI over $100,000.[31] Therefore, the special loss allowance is fully phased-out for married taxpayers in excess of $150,000.

Active participation is determined separately from material participation. In order to be considered an active participant, a taxpayer must make management decisions, such as approving tenants or setting policies, or arranging or performing other services, such as making repairs.[32] In addition, an active participant must be a 10 percent owner of the activity, by value, not including interests as a limited partner.[33]

Certain rental real estate activities are not considered as such under the PAL rules. These include rentals in which:[34]

1. the average period of use is seven days or less (e.g. a motel);
2. the average period of use is thirty days or less and significant personal services are provided (e.g. a hotel);
3. extraordinary personal services are provided;
4. rentals are incidental to nonrental activity;
5. the property is available for nonexclusive use (e.g. a golf course); or
6. the property is provided for use in a related entity with a nonrental activity.

Example: Roger owns a vacation property in New Jersey and rents it to individuals and families for an average of less than seven days (see number 1 above). As a result, the property is not automatically treated as a passive activity because it is not classified as a real estate activity. If Roger meets one or more of the material participation tests, the income or loss from the rental of the vacation property will not be treated as passive. Any loss from the rental will be fully deductible against his ordinary income.

Note, however, that since the activity is not treated as a rental real estate activity, the special "active" loss allowance described above is not available. Therefore, if Roger is not able to substantiate his material participation in the property, the loss would be passive with no offset from the special loss allowance. Ordinarily, this will occur in situations where the owner of the property uses a management company for the day-to-day rental operations. Since most of the material participation tests are based on hours devoted to the activity, the delegation of the management of the property will make it difficult, if not impossible, for a taxpayer to materially participate in such an activity.

Question – When do suspended losses for an activity become fully deductible?

Answer – Suspended losses of a passive activity become fully deductible in a complete, fully taxable disposition of the activity to an unrelated party.[35] The activity may also be considered as fully disposed if "substantially all" of the assets held by the activity are disposed. A discontinuation of operations or the retaining of the underlying assets is insufficient to be treated as a disposition.

Current year income or loss is then combined with the suspended losses of the activity. If the activity has a net loss in the year of disposition, the loss is treated as nonpassive if it exceeds income and gains from other passive activities. If the activity has net income in the year of disposition, the income is treated as passive and may be used to offset losses from other passive activities.

Question – What happens to suspended losses when there is not a complete, fully taxable disposition?

Answer – If an activity is disposed in a nontaxable or tax-deferred event, the suspended losses remain suspended and attach to the newly acquired property.

If an activity is sold through the use of an installment sale, the suspended loss is recognized each year in the same percentage as the gain on the sale.[36]

For dispositions of passive activities by gift, suspended losses are added to the donee's basis of the property. However, if the passive activity is subsequently sold at a loss by the donee, the basis for the loss is the lessor of the donee's basis including the suspended PAL or the fair market value on the date of the gift.[37] The result is that it may be better to dispose of the activity through a taxable transaction rather than by gift.

If a taxpayer dies with suspended PAL losses, the losses may be deducted on the decedent's final income tax return after being reduced by any step-up in the basis of the passive activity property.[38]

Question – In what circumstances are activities that are deemed to be passive recharacterized as nonpassive (NOPA rules)?

Answer – If property is rented to a nonpassive activity (the "self-rental" rules), if property is rented incidental to development activity, if a taxpayer significantly participates in an activity.

A taxpayer may not use net income from a property to offset other passive losses if the property is rented for use in a trade or business in which the taxpayer materially participates. Any income from self-rented property is treated as nonpassive. However, if the self-rented property generates a net loss, the loss is treated as passive since the rental activity would be deemed passive absent any other provisions.[39] Self-rentals, therefore, represent an area in which appropriately grouping the activities may be effective. However, since the regulations state income or loss is determined at each item of property (not necessarily the activity), a grouping that would still otherwise be considered passive, would not be effective for self-rented property purposes. Rental income from a property that which was rented less than twelve months before the disposition, and the taxpayer materially or significantly participated in the performance of services of enhancing the value of the property would be considered as nonpassive.[40]

An activity is considered a significant participation activity for a taxable year if it is a trade or business activity (not a rental activity) and the taxpayer participates in the activity for more than one hundred hours during the year. The income from all significant participation activities would be considered nonpassive to the extent it exceeds significant participation losses.[41]

Question – What are the special rules available to real estate professionals?

Answer – Real estate professionals treat otherwise passive rental real estate activities as nonpassive.[42] This provision, which was introduced in the early-1990s, gives such professionals the ability to convert passive rental real estate losses that they materially participate in and would otherwise be suspended into nonpassive losses that can be used to offset other sources of income.

In order to qualify as a real estate profession a taxpayer must meet the following requirements:

1. More than 50 percent of the personal services performed by the taxpayer are performed in real property trade or businesses in which the taxpayer materially participates.

2. The taxpayer must perform more than 750 hours in real property trade or businesses.[43]

A real property trade or business is one that involves real estate in one of the following activities:[44]

1. Development
2. Redevelopment
3. Construction
4. Reconstruction
5. Acquisition
6. Conversion
7. Rental
8. Operation
9. Management
10. Leasing
11. Brokerage

If a taxpayer meets these qualifications then they can make an election to treat all rental real estate activities as a single activity.[43] By making this affirmative election to combine rental real estate activities, the taxpayer treats all rental real estate interests as a single activity, including those held as a limited partner. Material participation is then determined for the activity as a whole. Absent this election, all rental activities are treated as separate activities and the taxpayer may be saddled with large suspended losses. Once the election to combine the rental real estate activities is made, it is irrevocable unless the facts and circumstances of the taxpayer materially change.

Question – How are losses from former passive activities handled?

Answer – Situations occur in which a taxpayer owns an activity that is properly classified as passive and, at some point in the future, the taxpayer is deemed to materially participate in the activity. Any suspended losses of the activity from the years in which the taxpayer treated the activity as passive are first deducted to the extent the taxpayer recognizes income form the same activity. Any remaining suspended losses from the former passive activity are treated as a normal PAL carryforward and may be used to offset passive income from other activities.

Question – Are there any specific rules for investments in hedge funds?

Answer – Certain taxpayers invest in partnerships that are not treated as a passive activity even though the taxpayer does not materially participate or invested as limited partner. Many hedge fund or other partnership Schedule K-1s report that the income or loss from the activity is neither passive nor portfolio under Treasury Regulation section 1.469-2T(d)(2). A partnership interest carrying this footnote on its Schedule K-1 is identifying the partnership as one that trades in stocks, bonds and securities for its own account (and those of its partners). Losses from such an activity should not be treated as being from a passive activity and, therefore, be deducted in full. Likewise, the income from such an activity cannot be used to offset other passive activity losses.

CHAPTER ENDNOTES

1. IRC Sec. 465(c)(1).
2. IRC Sec. 465(c)(3).
3. IRC Sec. 469(a)(2).
4. IRC Sec. 465(a)(1).
5. IRC Sec. 465(b)(1).
6. IRC Sec. 465(b)(2).
7. IRC Sec. 465(b)(6).
8. IRC Sec. 465(e).
9. IRS Ann. 84-14, 1984-6 IRB 22.
10. IRC Sec. 465(c)(2).
11. IRC Sec. 465(c)(2)(B)(i).
12. IRC Sec. 465(c)(3)(B).
13. IRC Secs. 469(c)(1)-(2).
14. Treas. Reg. §1.469-4.
15. Treas. Reg. §1.469-4(d)(2).
16. Treas. Reg. §1.469-4(d)(1).
17. Treas. Reg. §1.469-4.
18. Rev. Proc. 2010-13, 2010-4 IRB 329.
19. Treas. Reg. §1.469-11(b)(3)(iv).
20. Treas. Reg. §1.469-4(f).
21. Treas. Reg. §1.469-4(g).
22. Prop. Treas. Reg. §1.465-6(d).
23. Treas. Reg. §1.469-5T(f)(2)(ii)(B).
24. Prop. Treas. Reg. §1.465-38.
25. IRC Sec. 469(h).
26. Temp. Treas. Reg. §1.469-5T(a).
27. Treas. Reg. §1.469-5; Temp. Treas. Reg. §1.469-5T(a).
28. Temp. Treas. Reg. §1.469-5T(e).
29. IRC Sec. 469(i).
30. IRC Sec. 469(i)(3)(A).
31. Committee Report P.L. 99-514 (1986).
32. IRC Sec. 469(i)(6).
33. Treas. Reg. §1.469-1T(e)(3).
34. IRC Sec. 469(g).
35. IRC Sec. 469(g)(3).
36. IRC Sec. 469(j)(6).
37. IRC Sec. 469(g)(2).
38. Treas. Reg. §1.469-2(f)(6).
39. Treas. Reg. §1.469-2(f)(5).
40. Treas. Reg. §1.469-2T(f)(2).
41. IRC Sec. 469(c)(7)(A).
42. Treas. Reg. §1.469-9(g)(1).
43. IRC Sec. 469(c)(7)(B).
44. IRC Sec. 469(c)(7)(C).

MARRIAGE AND DIVORCE

CHAPTER 24

WHAT IS THE MARRIAGE PENALTY?

The "marriage penalty" is the anomaly of a married couple owing more tax than the combined total tax of two single individuals with the same amount of income. Although the marriage penalty manifests itself in many ways, the brunt of the penalty is attributable to the fact that tax rate brackets and the standard deduction for married couples were far less than twice what they were for single filers. Although since 2001, legislative changes to tax law has provided some relief, higher tax rates for some married couples as well as the phase-out of certain tax benefits at much lower income levels continue to perpetuate the marriage penalty for many taxpayers.

Tax Rates

For lower income taxpayers, one significant change that provided marriage penalty relief was to make the taxable income range of the 10 percent and 15 percent tax brackets for married couples filing jointly exactly twice the amount as the taxable income range of a single filer. For example, for tax year 2020, the 10 percent tax bracket for a married couple filing jointly is taxable income up to $19,750 or twice the taxable income of $9,875 for a single filer in that same tax bracket. Similarly, the new 12 percent bracket for a married couple filing jointly is taxable income over $19,750 but not over $80,250 or twice the taxable income range for a single filer of over $9,875 but not over $40,125.[1] Thus, for married taxpayers in those tax brackets, there is no marriage penalty.

Phase-outs

Simply stated, a "phase-out" occurs when a tax benefit is gradually reduced until it is significantly decreased and, in some instances, totally eliminated. For example, tax deductions such as itemized deductions and exemptions phase-out incrementally to the extent that a taxpayer's adjusted gross income exceeds an "applicable amount."

Phase-out of Itemized Deductions

In tax year 2016, for single taxpayers, the phase-out of certain itemized deductions begins with adjusted gross income in excess of the "applicable amount" of $259,400 as compared to adjusted gross income in excess of $311,300 for joint filers.[2] The phase-out reduces the amount of those itemized deductions by the lesser of 3 percent of the excess of adjusted gross income over the applicable amount or 80 percent of those deductions.[3]

Two unmarried individuals with a combined adjusted gross income of $518,800 ($259,400 each) would not be subject to any reduction of itemized deductions because neither taxpayer's adjusted gross income exceeded the applicable amount. On the other hand, if the same taxpayers were married, their combined adjusted gross income of $518,800 would exceed the applicable amount for joint filers of $311,300 by $207,500. As a result, in contrast to the single taxpayers who would suffer no loss of itemized deductions, the married couple could potentially lose up to $6,225 of itemized deductions (three percent of $207,500).

Standard Deduction

For 2020, the basic standard deduction for married taxpayers filing jointly is $24,800 or twice as much as $12,400 the standard deduction for a single taxpayer.[4] Thus, although the doubling of the standard deduction for joint filers would appear to mitigate the marriage penalty, the accelerated phase-out of itemized deductions

Figure 24.1

"MARRIAGE BONUS"		
Tax Benefit	*Single*	*Married Filing Jointly*
Exclusion of gain from sale of principal residence	Up to $250,000 of gain excluded	Up to $500,000 of gain excluded
Exclusion from gross income of employer provided health insurance	Exclusion does not extend to unmarried partner	Exclusion also includes health insurance provided to employee's spouse
"Averaging" high income of one spouse with lower income of other spouse	Unavailable	By filing a joint return, adding the lower income of one spouse to the higher income of the other spouse causes their combined income to be taxed at a lower overall rate than two unmarried single filers.
Earned Income Credit	A single non-working parent would not qualify for the credit due to the lack of earned income.	A non-working parent who is married to a spouse with low income would likely qualify for the credit.

(should they itemize rather than take the standard deduction) discussed above exacerbates the marriage penalty.

Deductions and Exemptions under the Tax Reform Act of 2017

The 2017 Tax Reform Act made significant changes to the way that deductions and exemptions are treated. In summary:

- The 2017 Tax Act suspends all miscellaneous itemized deductions for tax years beginning after December 31, 2017 and before January 1, 2026.[5]

- The 2017 Tax Act suspended the personal exemption for tax years beginning after December 31, 2017 and before December 31, 2025. In its place the standard deduction was increased to $12,000 for individuals and $24,000 for couples filing jointly ($12,400 and $24,800, respectively, in 2020).

See Chapter 7 for a more detail explanation of these changes.

MARRIAGE BONUS

In spite of the onerous effects of the marriage penalty, there are some positive tax advantages for married couples filing jointly. Figure 24.1 lists some of those tax advantages.

TAX IMPLICATIONS OF SAME-SEX MARRIAGE

As a result of the Supreme Court's decision in *Obergefell*,[6] the Federal government must recognize the validity of same-sex marriages in any state in which they are legal. This means that the IRS must apply the tax laws to married same-sex couples in the same way they are applied to heterosexual married couples. In light of the marriage penalty and marriage bonus discussed above, a same-sex couple should take into account the same tax and financial considerations that a heterosexual couple weighs in deciding whether to get married or remain single. Moreover, as discussed below, similar to heterosexual married couples, same-sex married couples should also consider whether it is prudent to file married separately rather than jointly.

Tax Implications of Filing Married Separately vs. Jointly

Married couples have the option of filing jointly or separately. Subject to the possible application of innocent spouse relief, married individuals are jointly and individually obligated to pay the tax, interest and penalties due on a joint return. The scope of responsibility can extend to an obligation to pay the tax for a spouse who did not properly report income and/or additional assessments of tax made by the IRS. For that reason, a spouse may choose to file a "separate" return if:

- he or she believes the other spouse is not reporting all of his or her income; or
- he or she does not want to be responsible for additional tax attributable to the lack of adequate withholding and/or sufficient estimated payments on the part of the other spouse.

On the flip side, there are many disadvantages inherent if filing married separately. Generally, there are many tax benefits that are either limited or simply not available for married individuals filing separately that will result in a much higher overall tax than would be owed if filing jointly.

Example: Samantha and Michelle are a married couple. In 2016, Samantha has a net capital loss of $3,000. Michelle, however, has no capital losses. If Samantha and Michelle file jointly, they will be able to deduct the entire $3,000 capital loss even though it is all attributable to Samantha. Conversely, if they file separately, Samantha will be able to deduct only $1,500 of the capital loss on her separate return and Michelle will not be able to deduct any part of the capital loss on her separate return.

Figure 24.2 sets forth a list of many of those limited or disallowed tax benefits.

Example: Asher and Ashley are a married couple. In 2020, the standard deduction for a married couple filing separately is $12,400 for

Figure 24.2

MARRIED FILING SEPARATELY VS. JOINTLY		
Tax Benefit	*Married Filing Jointly*	*Married Filing Separately*
Exclusion from Income of Employer's Dependent Care Assistance Program	$5,000	$2,500[7]
Deduction for Student Loan Interest or Tuition and Fees Deduction	Available	Not Allowed[8]
Income from Qualified U.S. Savings Bonds Used to Pay Higher Education Costs	Available	Not Allowed[9]
Exclusion of Social Security Benefit Payments	Some or All Excluded Based on Adjusted Gross Income	More Likely to be Taxed Up to 85 percent of the Benefits[10]
Rolling a Traditional IRA into a Roth IRA	Available	Not Allowed[11]
Child Care Credit Retirement Savings Contributions Itemized Deduction Personal Exemptions	Phase-out Do Not Begin Until Reach Higher Adjusted Gross Income Threshold	Phase-out Thresholds Are Half of Those for Married Filing Jointly
Credit for Expenses for Household and Dependent Care Services	Available	Not Allowed[12]
Earned Income Credit	Available	Not Allowed[13]
Standard Deduction or Itemized Deductions	One or the Other is Available. Joint filers generally deduct the higher of itemized deductions or standard deduction.	If one spouse itemizes the other spouse must itemize. See example below.[14]

each spouse. Asher has $15,000 of itemized deductions and Ashley has only $500 of itemized deductions. If Asher and Ashley each take the standard deduction, they would deduct $6,300 on their separate returns. On the other hand, if instead of taking the standard deduction, Asher chooses to itemize to take advantage of the $10,000 of itemized deductions. Because Asher itemized, Ashley will not be allowed to claim the $6,300 standard deduction. Instead, Ashley must also itemize limiting her deduction to $500. In this case they are better off taking the $24,800 standard deduction for a couple.

TAX IMPLICATIONS OF DIVORCE

As discussed below, the tax consequences with regard to child support and alimony are significant. Whereas the payment and receipt of child support from one spouse to the other has no tax consequences; the payor of alimony is entitled to a deduction and the payee must include it in income. There may also be significant tax consequences from the division of property that is part of every divorce decree.

Alimony

As stated above, alimony is deductible by the payor and includible in the gross income of the payee. However, simply labeling a payment as "alimony" does not mean it will be treated that way for tax purposes. Regardless of its designation by court order or agreement between divorcing spouses, to be treated as alimony for tax purposes, the requirements of Code section 71(b) must be met. Alimony is any payment in cash if:

- the payment is made to or on behalf of a spouse under a divorce or separation decree;
- the divorce decree is silent as to whether the payment as is not includible in gross income or allowable as a deduction. This means that if the parties do not want a payment to be treated as alimony, language in the instrument that states that it is not includible or deductible will negate its tax status as alimony;
- the payee spouse and the payor spouse are not members of the same household at the time of payment; and
- there is no liability to make this payment after the death of the payee spouse.

The requirement that alimony be paid in cash means it can only be made in cash, check or money order. Because of this limitation, a transfer of property or services to the payee spouse is not considered an alimony payment for tax purposes.[15]

The significance of payment not being treated as alimony has profound tax consequences.

Example: Pursuant to divorce decree, Asher is to pay Ashley $5,000 a month for five years as alimony. In the event of Ashley's death prior to the end of the term, Asher is obligated to continue to make those payments to Ashley's estate for the remaining duration. Under those circumstances, the payments would not be treated as alimony because Asher's obligation to make those payments continues following Ashley's death. As a result, for none of the years (including the years in which Ashley was alive), Asher will not be entitled to a deduction and Ashley will not be required to include those payments in gross income. Instead, the payments will be treated as a non-taxable "property settlement" with no tax consequences to either spouse.[16]

Front Loading Alimony

Because alimony payments are deductible to the payor spouse, there is the temptation to "front load" or make excessive payments in the early years of the alimony term to maximize deductions in those years. Then in later years, the payments are much less. So as a negotiation tactic, it is possible that in exchange for a larger up front deduction generated by a substantial initial payment, the payor spouse might agree to pay the payee spouse an overall larger amount of alimony. Conceptually, however, alimony is a mechanism to provide support to a spouse which means the payments should be relatively level over the payment period. So this type of front loading appears to be more like a disguised property settlement than an alimony arrangement.

In order to curb potential abuse, Code section 71(f) essentially recharacterizes "excessive payments" as non-alimony. Generally, excessive payments are the amounts that are disproportionate to amounts that would have been paid as alimony in a relatively level flow. Based on a formula beyond the scope of this chapter, all payments (including excessive payments) made in the first two years of the payment period are treated the same way as any alimony payments (i.e., deduction for payor and income for payee). In the third year, however, the Code reverses the deduction the payor received for the year one and year two excessive payments by requiring he or she to include those payments in gross income. Similarly, the Code reverses the inclusion by the payee spouse of excessive payment included in gross income by allowing a deduction for such payments. By doing so, the adjustment effectively converts the excessive payments into non-taxable non-deductible property settlement payments. Figure 24.3 provides an over-simplified table demonstrating the application of the front loading rules.

Alimony Payments under the 2017 Tax Reform Act

The 2017 Tax Act eliminated the previously existing above-the-line deduction for alimony for tax years beginning after 2018, and provides that alimony and separate maintenance payments are no longer included in the income of the recipient. This provision is effective for divorce or separation agreements that become effective after December 31, 2018, but also applies to divorce or separation agreements executed before that date that are subsequently modified and specify that the new provision will apply.[17] This means that the technique of front loading alimony payments described above is not available to clients under the new rules.

Under prior law, a taxpayer in a higher income tax bracket was essentially able to shift income to his or her former spouse (presumably in a lower tax bracket) through alimony payments. Certain specific requirements must be satisfied in order for a payment to be treated as alimony both under former and new law:

1. the payment is made in cash;

2. the divorce or separation instrument does not designate the payment as *not* includable or deductible as alimony;[18]

3. there is no liability to make the payments after the death of the recipient,[19] where the Tax Court held that "substitute" payments – i.e., post-death payments that would begin as a result of the death of the taxpayer's ex-wife, and would substitute for a continuation of the payments that terminated on her death, and that otherwise qualified as alimony – were not deductible alimony payments); and

4. if the individuals are legally separated under a decree of divorce or separate maintenance, the spouses are not members of the same household at the time the payment is made.

Figure 24.3

FRONT LOADING ALIMONY

	Year 1	Tax Consequences	Year 2	Tax Consequences	Year 3	Tax Consequences
Payor	Non-Excessive Alimony plus Excessive Alimony	Deduction	Non-Excessive Alimony plus Excessive Alimony	Deduction	Non-Excessive Alimony	Deduction
					Year 1 and Year 2 Excessive Alimony	Include in Gross Income
Payee	Non-Excessive Alimony plus Excessive Alimony	Include in Gross Income	Non-Excessive Alimony plus Excessive Alimony	Include in Gross Income	Non-Excessive Alimony	Include in Gross Income
					Year 1 and Year 2 Excessive Alimony	Deduction

Child Support

Unlike alimony, child support is not taxable to the recipient and not deductible by the payor.[20] This is because the paying of child support is the discharge of legal obligation inherent in parenthood. Similarly, the recipient spouse does not have income because he or she is obligated to use the payment for the support of the children. Consequently, with some planning, by increasing the amount of alimony payments and decreasing child support payments income can be shifted from a high income payor spouse to a low income payee spouse.

Example: Sam is in the 33 percent tax rate bracket and is willing to pay $9,000 of child support. His spouse, Jennifer, is in the 15 percent tax rate bracket and wants $11,000. Both can stay close to their goals and perhaps reach a compromise by treating the payments as alimony. Because Sam can deduct alimony payments, but not child support, he should be indifferent between paying $9,000 in child support and $13,433 ($9,000/(1-.33)) in alimony. If Jennifer receives $13,433 in alimony, she will have $11,418 ($13,433 × (1-.15)) cash after paying taxes. Reclassifying the payments from child support to alimony accomplishes both spouses' goals.

However, caution should be exercised with regard to alimony payments that appear to be "disguised" as child support. Pursuant to Code section 71(c), if part of a payment otherwise qualifying as alimony would be reduced on the happening of an event specified in the decree relating to a child attaining a certain age, marrying, dying, leaving school or the like, such part would be treated as child support rather than alimony. As these contingencies suggest, a reduction of "alimony" by a certain amount due to a child attaining the age of eighteen is more likely child support wrapped into an alimony payment. Not surprisingly, under those circumstances, the payor would not be entitled to a deduction and the payee would not be required to include in gross income that portion of the payment.

Example: Pursuant to their divorce decree, Asher is to pay Ashley $5,000 a month as alimony until their son Ben attains the age of eighteen. At that time, the alimony payment is to be reduced to $4,000 a month. Under those circumstances, only $4,000 of the $5,000 payment would be treated as alimony (deductible by Asher and included in gross income by Ashley). The other $1,000 payment that is to terminate when Ben attains the age of eighteen would be treated as child support.

Property Division

The division of property between divorcing spouses has no tax consequences. In other words, just as property flows freely between spouses during marriage without tax consequence, its division pursuant to a divorce is also tax free.[21] In fact, no gain or loss is recognized on the transfer of property from an individual to a spouse or a former spouse if the transfer is incident to the divorce. The transfer of property must occur within one year after the date on which the marriage ceases or must be related to the cessation of the marriage. In addition, the basis of property transferred from one spouse to another does not change.[22]

Example: Pursuant to the divorce decree, Jim transfers stock he owns to his spouse, Mary. The stock has a basis of $60,000 and a fair market value of $100,000. Jim recognizes no gain as a result of the transfer, and Mary takes his $60,000 basis in the property. If Mary sells the stock shortly after the divorce for $101,000, she will have $41,000 ($101,000 - 60,000) of taxable gain.

For negotiation purposes, any division of property should also take basis into consideration. This is because a property's basis as compared to the fair market value will determine whether the sale of the property would generate a taxable gain or loss. As illustrated by the example below, a division of property of equal value may be inequitable if there is a large disparity in the bases of the property.

Example: Asher and Ashley who are in the process of getting divorced have two properties with equal value. There is an antique car that Asher purchased for $100,000 which now has a fair market value of $200,000. In addition, there is a stock portfolio with a basis of $250,000 and a fair market value of $200,000. Although the values of the property are equal, the spouse who receives the antique care would recognize a $100,000 capital gain upon its sale to a third party. Thus, the amount of the after tax proceeds received would be less than $200,000. On the other hand, the spouse who receives the stock would recognize a $50,000 loss upon its sale to a third party. As a result, that spouse would receive the entire $200,000 tax-free as well as a potentially deductible loss that may reduce other taxable income. So if the parties intended a true equal split of property, they should also have taken into account the tax consequences of a subsequent sale.

Retirement Plans

Retirement plans such as pension and profit-sharing plans, Keogh plans of a self-employed individual, 401(k) plans, SIMPLE plans, and tax-deferred annuities are also available for tax-free division between spouses. Routinely, a negotiated or court ordered portion of a retirement plan is transferred into the name of the other spouse or child through a qualified domestic relations order (QDRO) issued by the family court.[23] QDROs provide an income stream from a qualified retirement plan to a spouse or child recipient.

If the beneficiary of the QDRO is the spouse, he or she is allowed to roll over the QDRO into an IRA.[24] Although distributions are subject to regular income tax, distributions from the QDRO prior to attaining the age of 59½ are not subject to the 10 percent early withdrawal penalty.[25]

Example: Ashley, who is forty years old, receives a distribution from the portion of her ex-spouse's retirement plan that was allocated to her through a QDRO. Although the distribution will be taxable to her, she is not subject to the 10 percent early withdrawal penalty. Thus, the benefits derived from a QDRO are (1) having access to funds allocated to her from in an ex-spouse's retirement account, and (2) receiving distributions without being subject to the 10 percent early withdrawal penalty.

Distributions from QDROs to children are treated differently. For example, distributions to a child are taxed to the participant rather than the child. Consequently, a QDRO to a child may not be rolled over into an IRA established for the child. However, distributions to or for the benefit of a child from the QDRO are not subject to the 10 percent early withdrawal penalty.

Finally, although individual retirement accounts can be divided tax-free, QDROs cannot be used as a division vehicle.[26] Usually, a portion of the IRA designated for the other spouse is rolled over to his or her existing or newly created IRA.

POST-DIVORCE TAX ISSUES

Filing as Head of Household

After a divorce, each spouse becomes a single filer. If there are children, however, it may be possible for one or both spouses to file as a head of household (HOH). Filing as a HOH is usually much more advantageous to filing as a single unmarried individual. In order to qualify, the taxpayer must meet the following requirements:

- Be considered unmarried on the last day of the tax year
- Pay more than half of the cost of maintaining the home
- Have a qualifying person (generally a minor child) live with the taxpayer for more than half the year[27]

The benefits of filing as HOH include:

- A higher standard deduction (in 2020, the standard deduction for HOH is $18,650 as compared to $12,400 for a single filer)[28]
- An extra personal exemption for each qualifying person
- Greater likelihood of qualifying for the earned income credit

Claiming a Child as a Dependent

Generally, the custodial parent is entitled to the exemption deduction for the child. By virtue of claiming the exemption, there are a whole host of other tax benefits potentially available to the claiming parent including:

- Child tax credit
- HOPE Scholarship credit
- Lifetime Learning Credit
- Head of Household filing status (discussed above)
- Dependent care credit
- Earned Income Credit

However, the custodial parent can essentially transfer the exemption to the noncustodial spouse by executing a Form 8332, *Release of Claim to Exemption for Child of Divorced or Separated Parents*.[29] If there are two or more children, the divorce decree may specify that one parent has custody of one child and the other parent has custody of the other. Under these circumstances, both parents may be able to file as HOH, claim a dependency exemption for the child as well as other child related tax credits.

PAYMENTS FOR TAX-RELATED DIVORCE LEGAL ADVICE

Each Spouse Pays His or Her Own Legal Fees

Generally, the legal expenses arising from a divorce are nondeductible, personal expenses. An exception to this rule allows a deduction for the portion of the legal fees that relates to tax advice or the production of income that may be part of the legal representation.[30] Tax-related issues encountered during divorce include gain from the property division, the taxability of alimony and child support, and distributions from retirement plans. Production of income issues includes attempts to obtain alimony or distributions from a qualified retirement plan. To take this deduction, however, the attorney must provide documentation that shows the portion of the legal fees related to tax advice or the production of income.

Example: Sue's legal fees from her divorce total $5,000. On his fee statement, there are tax advice related entries of $2,000. Legal fees related to tax advice are deductible as miscellaneous itemized deductions on Schedule A of Form 1040. The utility of the deduction, however, may be limited as miscellaneous itemized deductions are deductible to the extent that all of her miscellaneous itemized deductions exceed 2 percent of her adjusted gross income.

One Spouse Pays Legal Fees of Other Spouse

As stated above, legal fees related to divorce are generally considered to be personal non-deductible expenses. For that reason, one spouse who pays the legal fees of another spouse may not claim a deduction for those fees as a business expense. However, assuming it meets the requirements of Code section 71(b) discussed above, the payment of the fees on behalf of the other spouse could qualify as deductible alimony. In that case, the payee spouse would be required to include such fee payment in gross income. On the other hand, if the payee spouse is in a relatively low income bracket and the payor spouse is in a relatively high income tax bracket, the spouse who pays the other spouse's legal fees as an alimony payment could receive the benefit of the deduction with little or no tax detriment to the low tax bracket spouse who must include it in income.

FREQUENTLY ASKED QUESTIONS

Question – Why does a provision in the divorce decree that requires the payor spouse to continue to make payments to the payee's estate in the event of his or her death prior to the end of the payment term disqualify its treatment as alimony?

Answer – Alimony is intended to provide spousal support. This means the payments are intended to cover living expenses. Once a spouse dies, the need for support comes to an end. For this reason, payments required after the death of a spouse are more indicative of a property settlement rather than alimony support payments.

Question – How can the IRS ascertain whether the alimony deduction claimed by the payor spouse matches the amount included in the payee spouse's gross income?

Answer – Obviously, a payor spouse would like every payment made to a payee spouse to be deductible alimony. Conversely, a payee spouse would like every payment received to be non-taxable child support or a property settlement. With that temptation, a payor spouse might be inclined to overstate the alimony and a payee spouse might be inclined to understate the alimony. Under those circumstances, from the IRS perspective, this would create an unfavorable mismatch of over deduction and under inclusion. For that reason, it would behoove the IRS to have a means to ascertain that the payee and payor are at least imputing the same amount. This can be accomplished by cross referencing. On line 31a of Form 1040, the payor spouses enters the amount of alimony paid as an above-the-line deduction; and, on line 31b enters the social security number of the payee spouse. So by searching through the tax return data base, the IRS can cross check the return of the payee spouse to ascertain whether the amount deducted on line 31a of the payor's Form 1040 matches the amount of alimony income reported by payee spouse on line 11 of his or her Form 1040.

Question – Do payments to third parties, such as paying off an ex-spouse's credit cards, making the mortgage payment, or paying premiums for life insurance qualify as taxable/deductible alimony?

Answer – Yes, as long as the payments are in cash and on behalf of a spouse, they can be made to third parties instead of directly to the spouse. The key is that the payment cannot be for an item for which the payor has any personal liability. In other words, there is no alimony deduction for:

1. credit card payments with respect to a joint account;

2. mortgage payments on a home the payor owns even if he or she does live there; or

3. premium payments on life insurance if which the payor has an ownership interest in the policy.

Question – Should spouses who file separately coordinate their returns before filing?

Answer – Yes. Although in most instances married couples will pay less overall tax filing jointly, there are a number of couples who file separately. The reason may be lack of trust or a desire not to be responsible for the other spouse's tax deficiency. Or it can be that the couple just does not get along.

Example: The standard deduction for each spouse is $6,300. However, if one spouse itemizes the other spouse must also itemize. So if spouse A has $11,000 of itemized deductions and itemizes and spouse B has only $1,500 of itemized deductions, spouse B must also itemize. So in this case, spouse B's deduction shrinks from $6,300 to $1,500.

What if spouse B does not know that spouse A is itemizing or is unaware that if one spouse itemizes the other must as well? If in that case, spouse B claims the $6,300 standard deduction, it could result in an unwelcomed and unexpected notice from the IRS disallowing the standard deduction.

Also, if the spouses intend to split certain itemized deductions, each should be aware of what the other spouse intends to claim. The most common item is likely to be mortgage interest. It would be prudent for each spouse to include a statement with their returns indicating how much of the mortgage interest he or she is claiming of the total amount. However, in spite of this precaution, if the Form 1098 lists one spouse as the payor, it is certainly possible that the IRS will send the other spouse a notice proposing to disallow the mortgage interest deduction claimed on the return.

The bottom line is that married spouses who file separately may have a contentious relationship. That relationship will probably get worse if the return filed by one spouse causes IRS grief for the other spouse. Therefore, coordinating returns before filling is highly recommended.

CHAPTER ENDNOTES

1. Rev. Proc. 2013-35, 2013-47 IRB 537, Rev. Proc. 2015-53.
2. Rev. Proc. 2013-35, 2013-47 IRB 537, Rev. Proc. 2015-53.
3. IRC Sec. 68(a).
4. Rev. Proc. 2013-35, 2013-47 IRB 537, Rev. Proc. 2015-53.
5. IRC Secs. 67(g), 262A.
6. *Obergefell v. Hodges*, 135 S. Ct. 20171 (2015).
7. IRC Sec. 129(a)(2).

8. IRC Sec. 222(d)(4).
9. IRC Sec. 135(d)(3).
10. IRC Sec. 86(c)(1)(C).
11. IRS Publication 590.
12. IRC Sec. 21(e)(2).
13. IRC Sec. 32(d).
14. IRC Sec. 63(c)(6).
15. Treas. Reg. §1.71-1T.
16. IRC Sec. 1041.
17. The treatment of alimony was governed by former IRC Sec. 215.
18. See *Richardson v. Comm.*, 125 F.3d 551 (7th Cir. 1997), *aff'g* T.C. Memo 1995-554; see also Let. Rul. 200141036.
19. See, e.g., *Okerson v. Comm.*, 123 TC 258 (2004).
20. IRC Sec. 71(c).
21. IRC Sec. 1041.
22. IRC Sec. 1041(b)(2).
23. IRC Sec. 414(p).
24. IRC Sec. 402(e)(1)(B).
25. IRC Sec. 72(t)(2)(C).
26. IRC Sec. 408(d)(6).
27. IRC Sec. 2(b).
28. Rev. Proc. 2013-35, 2013-47 IRB 537, Rev. Proc. 2015-53
29. IRC Sec. 152(e)(2).
30. IRC Sec. 212.

TIMING OF INCOME AND DEDUCTIONS

CHAPTER 25

INTRODUCTION

A person who can control the timing of income and deductions may be able to save taxes or take advantage of the time value of money. The timing of income or deductions is generally done by shifting income or deductions to an earlier year or later year as needed. Some special tax provisions permit the shifting of income or deductions. In other instances, the ability to shift income or deductions is limited. Income and deductions are discussed in some detail in Chapters 3 and 7.

Taxes may be saved when income is shifted to a year in which tax rates are lower. Taxes may also be saved when deductions are shifted to a year in which tax rates are higher. Tax rates may be higher or lower based on changes in tax laws from year to year. They may also be higher or lower based on the amount of the individual's taxable income.

An individual can save taxes by controlling the amount of income or deductions in a year so that certain tax benefits can be achieved. For example, medical deductions are generally limited to the amount of medical expenses in excess of 7.5 percent of adjusted gross income. A person might be able to increase the amount of deductible medical expenses by shifting medical expenses and other deductions into a year while shifting income out of that same year.

If tax rates remain level, the time value of money can be used by accelerating deductions into an earlier year and deferring income into a later year. Paying taxes later rather than sooner allows the taxpayer to invest the deferred taxes and earn additional income. If tax rates are lower later, then taxes may also be saved. If tax rates are higher later, the value of deferring taxes must be weighed against the value of the increased taxes.

WHEN IS THE USE OF SUCH A DEVICE INDICATED?

1. *When Congress changes tax rates.* If tax rates go up, consider accelerating income and deferring deductions before the changes take full effect. If tax rates go down, consider deferring income and accelerating deductions before the changes take full effect.

2. *If the amount of a taxpayer's income fluctuates.* Income might fluctuate for a number of reasons or at certain times: because of a loss of a job or a change in jobs, because of the nature of the job (e.g., commissions are not level), because of general economic conditions (e.g., an upturn or a downturn), when a spouse starts or stops working, on account of disability, or at retirement. When income is high in a particular year, consider moving income out of and deductions into that year. When income is low in a particular year, consider moving income into and deductions out of that year.

3. *Even if the taxpayer's tax rates stay the same.* Consider deferring income and accelerating deductions to take advantage of the time value of money.

4. *When tax benefits are dependent on the amount of adjusted gross income.* Shifting income or deductions into or out of a year may save the benefit. For example, prior to 2015, a traditional IRA could be converted to a Roth IRA only if adjusted gross income does not exceed $100,000 for the year (see Chapter 31). Also, various tax provisions provide

for a phaseout of a tax benefit based on adjusted gross income, such as itemized deductions that are phased out at higher levels of income (see Chapter 4).

5. *When the taxpayer has high current income.* Retirement plans (see Chapter 31) permit income to be deferred to later in life, possibly when income and tax rates are lower. Installment sales (see Chapter 3) and like-kind exchanges (see Chapter 29) also permit income to be deferred to a later date. To some extent, tax shelters, such as real estate or oil and gas, permit deductions to be accelerated into earlier years.

WHAT ARE THE REQUIREMENTS?

1. A taxpayer who is using the accrual method of accounting (see Chapter 18) generally accrues income and deductions as economic performance occurs. For example, wages are generally treated as taxable when the work for which wages are paid is performed rather than when payment is made. And property taxes may be deductible in the year for which the taxes are owed rather than when paid. The ability to shift income is not as great as for a taxpayer using the cash method of accounting.

2. A taxpayer who is using the cash method of accounting (see Chapter 18) generally recognizes income as it is received and deductions as they are paid. Through control of when income is received or when deductions are paid, some flexibility to shift income or deductions is obtained. Certain taxpayers, including C corporations, partnerships with a C corporation as partner, and tax shelters, cannot use the cash method of accounting.

   Accelerating or deferring income or deductions is often simply a matter of moving the income or deduction from one year to the next year, or vice versa. It can be as simple as shifting income or deductions from January of one year to December of the preceding year, or from December of one year to January of the following year. For example, stock could be sold in December 2018 or January 2019, depending on whether the taxpayer would like to include the capital gain in income in 2018 or 2019. Similarly, a year-end bonus could be paid in either December of one year or January of the next year. Real estate taxes or medical expenses could be paid in December 2018 or January 2019, depending on whether the taxpayer would like to take the deduction in 2018 or 2019. Similarly, charitable contributions could be made in either December of one year or January of the next year.

3. The requirements for a number of special provisions for deferring income are discussed elsewhere in this book. These provisions generally provide deferral for a number of years. Retirement plans, including individual retirement accounts and qualified plans, may be used to defer income (see Chapter 31). Installment sales may be used to spread out income from the sale of assets over the years in which payments are received (see Chapter 3). A like-kind exchange of property can be used to postpone recognition of gain until the replacement property is sold (see Chapter 28). Sale of property to a charity in return for a charitable annuity or contribution of appreciated property to a charitable remainder trust can be used to obtain a current income tax charitable deduction while deferring recognition of gain from the property until later years (see Chapter 28). Nonqualified deferred compensation, discussed in *The Tools & Techniques of Employee Benefit and Retirement Planning*, is another way to defer income until a later year. Annuities, discussed in *The Tools & Techniques of Life Insurance Planning*, allow income to be deferred until annuity payments are received.

HOW IT IS DONE

Example 1: Robin expects to be in the 24 percent marginal tax rate bracket in 2018 and 2019. She will pay $2,400 of federal income tax on her $10,000 bonus whether it is paid on December 31, 2018 or January 1, 2019. By taking the bonus in January 2019, she has the use of the money for over a year before she pays tax on the income in April 2020. If she can earn 3 percent after-tax on the $2,400 in tax owed, the present value of the tax if paid in in April 2020 would be $2,382. The present value of the tax if paid in fifteen months in April 2020 would be $2,312. From a time value of money perspective, postponing the tax disbursement on the deferred income is advantageous.

If Robin's tax rate for 2019 will drop to 15 percent, as it might for someone who is retiring, the tax is reduced to $1,500 and the present value of the April 2020 payment is $1,445. Robin benefits from the reduced tax rate as well as the time value of money on the deferral.

On the contrary, if Robin's tax rate will increase to 37 percent because of an increase in compensation, the present value of the $3,700 of income tax owed in April 2020 would be $3,564. In this case, Robin should not defer the income to January 2019. The time value of money benefit from postponing the tax payment is less than the additional cost of paying tax at a higher rate.

Example 2: Sam expects to be in the 24 percent marginal tax rate bracket in 2018 and 2019. He will save $4,800 of federal income tax on a $20,000 charitable contribution whether it is paid on December 31, 2018 or January 1, 2019. By making the contribution in December 2018, he reduces his tax in April 2019 and has the use of the tax savings for over a year compared to making the contribution in January 2019. If he can earn 3 percent after-tax on the $4,800 in tax saved, the present value of saving the tax in three months in April 2018 is $4,764. The present value of reducing the tax in fifteen months in April 2020 is $4,624. From a time value of money perspective, accelerating the tax savings from a charitable contribution is advantageous.

If Sam's tax rate for 2019 drops to 15 percent, lowering the tax savings from the contribution to $3,000, the present value of making the charitable contribution in January 2019 and saving taxes in April 2020 drops to $2,890. In other words, the benefit of making the contribution in December 2019 is even greater because the tax savings are received sooner and at a higher marginal tax rate.

On the contrary, if Sam's tax rate will increase to 33 percent because of an increase in compensation, the present value of the $6,600 of income tax saved in April 2020 is $6,357. In this case, Sam should make the charitable contribution in January 2019. The additional benefit from saving tax at the higher marginal tax rate exceeds the benefit of making the contribution sooner.

TAX IMPLICATIONS

1. In general, income deferred to a later year reduces taxable income in the earlier year and increases taxable income in the year to which deferred. Income accelerated to an earlier year increases taxable income in such year and reduces taxable income in the later year.

2. In general, deductions accelerated to an earlier year reduce taxable income in such year and increase taxable income in the later year. Deductions deferred to a later year increase taxable income in the earlier year and decrease taxable income in the year to which deferred.

3. Certain tax provisions encourage the deferral of income. These include: annuities, retirement plans, installment sales, like-kind exchanges, and nonqualified deferred compensation.

4. Certain tax provisions encourage the acceleration of deductions. For example, accelerated depreciation is often permitted and a certain amount of otherwise depreciable property placed in service in a trade or business can be expensed in the year of purchase (see Chapter 20).

5. Various tax provisions restrict the acceleration of deductions. For example, prepaid interest or rent generally cannot be deducted until the expense is accrued or incurred. Investment interest expense is not deductible unless there is investment income to offset the deduction (see Chapter 7). Passive losses may not be deducted until there is passive income. A taxpayer may deduct losses with respect to certain activities only to the extent the taxpayer is at risk (see Chapter 22). Only a limited amount of net capital losses are deductible in any year; otherwise such losses must be offset by capital gains or carried over to another year (see Chapter 4).

6. The alternative minimum tax should also be considered when shifting income or deductions between years. This is discussed in detail in Chapter 10.

FREQUENTLY ASKED QUESTIONS

Question – What tax rate should be used to evaluate the benefit of deferring income to future years, the effective rate of tax to be paid on income for the year or the marginal rate of tax?

Answer – Either rate can be used, but the marginal tax rate approach is used more frequently. The effective rate of tax is equal to the amount of tax owed divided by the total income received during the year. The marginal rate of tax is the tax rate that will apply to the next dollar of taxable income to be received.

Assume a taxpayer is married with $125,000 of income in 2018. Taxable income after deductions is approximately $100,000. With $100,000 of taxable income, the marginal rate of tax is 22 percent, but tax owed is approximately $13,879 meaning an effective rate of tax of about 11 percent ($13,879/$125,000).

Marginal tax rates are used more frequently in planning because for a given level of income a planner can quickly project the amount of tax savings. For example, if a taxpayer is in the 22 percent marginal income tax rate bracket and contributes $15,000 to a 401(k) plan, the planner can readily predict that the 401(k) deferral will reduce income tax by $3,300.

The effective rate is useful for comparing the success of tax strategies from one year to the next. In a year a taxpayer contributes to a 401(k) plan, the effective rate of tax will decrease although the marginal rate may not. To illustrate, assume the above taxpayer with $125,000 of income contributed $15,000 of compensation to a 401(k). He would lower his taxable income to $85,000 ($100,000 – $15,000) and reduce his tax to about $10,579. His effective tax rate decreases from about 11 percent to about 8.5 percent ($10,579/125,000), but his marginal rate of tax remains 22 percent.

Question – When calculating the present value of tax savings, what investment rate should be used?

Answer – Excellent question for which there is no single correct answer. The investment rate differs from taxpayer to taxpayer. Conceptually, the taxpayer would use the after-tax rate of return of investments the taxpayer is investing in because the tax savings represents money that may be added to, or at least not withdrawn from, those investments to pay the government. For some investors, this rate may be the rate of return earned on risk-free investments, such as Treasury securities and certificates of deposit. For others, such as the owners of closely held businesses, the rate of return may far exceed investment returns available in the securities markets.

CONVERSION OF INCOME

CHAPTER 26

WHAT IS CONVERSION OF INCOME?

The federal income tax system is based upon two primary classifications of income: (1) ordinary and (2) capital. The technique of converting income from ordinary to capital can allow taxpayers to benefit from the reduced tax rates that capital income enjoys.

Long-term gains on the sale of capital assets have historically been granted preferential treatment. This is true under the current law, even after the passage of the American Taxpayer Relief Act of 2012 (ATRA)[1] and the Health Care and Education Reconciliation Act of 2010 (Reconciliation Act of 2010),[2] both of which increased taxes for some taxpayers.

ATRA introduced a new top tax rate for higher-income taxpayers and also a higher tax rate on capital gains for those taxpayers in the top tax bracket. The Reconciliation Act of 2010 added a new "net investment income tax (NIIT)" on investment income, which includes gain on the sale of certain capital assets for higher-income taxpayers.[3]

Under the current tax law in 2020, the highest ordinary income tax bracket is 37 percent. For most taxpayers, long-term capital gains are taxed at the capital gains tax rate of 15 percent (and for lower income taxpayers, the rate may be as low as 0 percent). For single taxpayers with AGIs above $518,400 ($622,050 for couples filing jointly), the capital gains rate increases from 15 to 20 percent. Additionally, the NIIT is 3.8 percent on long-term capital gains (such as on the sale of stock, bonds and mutual funds) for taxpayers who have modified adjusted gross income above certain thresholds ($200,000 for single taxpayers and $250,000 for married taxpayers filing a joint return). For higher-income taxpayers, the higher capital gains tax and the NIIT result in an overall tax rate of 23.8 percent.

Although somewhat diminished by recent tax increases, the preferential treatment for long-term capital gains persists and equates to a 17 percent differential in the maximum tax rates between ordinary income and certain capital gain income assuming that the NIIT is neutral regardless of income classification. The rate differential generates a great incentive for taxpayers to convert ordinary income into long-term capital gain.

However, there are times when proper planning dictates that ordinary, rather than capital treatment is preferable. For example, due to the long-term capital loss limitations discussed in Chapter 4, there is an incentive for taxpayers to report losses, not as capital losses but as a direct reduction to their ordinary income. Even if the capital loss limitations do not apply, a capital loss could be worth as little as fifteen cents on the dollar for taxpayers not in the highest income tax bracket compared with the 37 cents a taxpayer could potentially save if the transaction can properly be reported as an ordinary loss. Overall, taxpayers tend to focus on finding ways to treat gains as long-term capital and losses as ordinary income losses.

Taxpayers often focus on other ways to have certain forms of income treated in a manner that will result in lower taxation. Under current law, qualifying dividends are taxed at the same preferential rates applicable to long-term capital gains: a reduced rate of 15 percent for most taxpayers and possibly 0 percent for lower income taxpayers. For higher-income taxpayers, the rate is 20 percent plus the NIIT of 3.8 percent. The combined rate of 23.8 percent is still below the top tax rate of 37 percent. Consequently, it may be beneficial for a taxpayer to ensure that any dividends received will be eligible for treatment as qualifying dividends and taxed at lower rates.

CONVERTING ORDINARY INCOME INTO CAPITAL GAIN INCOME

With long-term capital gains and qualifying dividends being taxed at a rate of 15 percent for most taxpayers and 23.8 percent for higher-income taxpayers, it is easy to identify converting ordinary income into capital gain income as a beneficial tax planning strategy. The question then becomes – how can it be done?

First, start with the understanding that most people will be unable to convert their salary or wages into capital gain. It just cannot happen for most employees.

There are situations, however, in which executives may be able to structure a more complex compensation package that will result – at least partially – in long-term capital gain treatment.

That being said, the following is a list of techniques which will be addressed in this chapter for converting ordinary income to long-term capital gains and maximizing the use of these lower tax rates:

1. Holding securities for the required period to qualify as long-term capital gains
2. Using retirement plans to hold ordinary income or tax inefficient investments
3. Converting interest income into qualifying dividends
4. Structuring compensation packages

Holding Securities for the Required Period to Qualify as Long-Term Capital Gains

With capital gains tax rates currently at 15 percent for most taxpayers and 23.8 percent for higher-income earners, the easiest way to take advantage of these favorable tax rates is to ensure that capital assets are held for enough time to qualify for the long-term holding period. As discussed more completely in Chapter 4, Capital Gains and Losses, an asset must be a capital asset to be eligible for potential long-term capital gains treatment. A capital asset is any property except:

1. inventory;
2. depreciable or real property used in a taxpayer's trade or business;
3. specified literary or artistic property;
4. business accounts or notes receivable;
5. certain U.S. publications;
6. any hedging transaction clearly identified as such when acquired, originated, or entered into;
7. supplies of a type regularly used or consumed by the taxpayer in the ordinary course of a trade or business of the taxpayer; and
8. certain commodities derivative financial instruments held by a commodities derivatives dealer.[4]

Capital assets that are held for *more* than one year are treated as long-term. Any gain or loss on the sale of a capital asset held for more than one year is then a long-term capital gain or loss.[5] Unfortunately, in the quest for a lower tax rate, many taxpayers forget the inherent financial risks in holding certain capital assets too long.

In the late 1990s, the stock prices of many companies (especially internet-based technology companies that had been recently offered to the public) rose dramatically. Many taxpayers saw their wealth on paper soar to levels that they had not ever imagined. It was almost commonplace to see investments double or even quadruple in value in just a matter of months. With a large unrealized gain staring at them in the face and realizing that a tax would need to be paid on the gain when realized and recognized, a large portion of the taxpayers decided to wait until they met the one-year holding period to sell their stock. In early 2000, this would allow taxpayers to receive treatment under the maximum capital gains tax rate of 20 percent, compared to the highest marginal income tax rate of 37 percent.

With the bursting of the "Internet Bubble" in the early part of 2000, taxpayers saw their one-time wealth drop precipitously (or in some cases, practically vanish). Instead of generating a large short-term capital gain, on which ordinary income taxes would need to be paid, they often found themselves in a far worse position.

Example: Doug Davis bought 1,000 shares of NuTech, Inc. on April 15, 2018 (the date of its initial public offering) for $15,000. By late-December 2018, NuTech was trading above $95 per share. Since Doug is in the highest tax bracket (37 percent), he decides not to sell and recognize the $80,000 gain since the ordinary tax on the gain would wipe out $29,600 of the value, leaving him with a "mere" $50,400. Instead, Doug holds onto the stock into 2019 in order to reach the long-term holding period. The stock price tumbles during March of 2019 and Doug finally sells the stock in May 2019 for $3,000. Doug now has a $12,000 long-term capital loss that can only be used to reduce ordinary income by $3,000 (with the remainder carried forward for future years) unless he has other capital gains to offset. In retrospect, Doug would probably have preferred to keep his "mere" $50,400 after paying a $29,600 tax bill, rather than finishing with only $3,000 of stock proceeds and a $12,000 long-term capital loss.

There is a substantial tax benefit for holding a capital asset with an unrealized gain for the required period, particularly for individuals in higher marginal income tax brackets. However, this benefit must be weighed against the financial risks associated with the (potentially extreme) possible decline in the value of the asset during the time needed to meet the required holding period. This was evidenced once again with the drastic market declines in 2008.

As discussed in Chapter 4, Capital Gains and Losses, taxpayers may also control the taxation of their investment gains and losses by using the specific identification method when selling an investment. When multiple lots of the same asset are purchased, it may be beneficial to the taxpayer to treat something other than the first shares purchased as having been sold, to target shares eligible for long-term capital gains treatment or *non*-long-term capital loss (or ordinary loss) treatment.[6]

Using Retirement Plans to Hold Ordinary Income or Tax Inefficient Investments

Most qualified retirement plans allow for investments to grow on a tax deferred basis until amounts are withdrawn from the plan. Any interest, dividends, capital gains, or other sources of income earned within the retirement plan escape current taxation.[7]

When amounts generated by money that was never taxed are withdrawn from a retirement plan, the amount withdrawn is normally treated as ordinary income, regardless of the type of income that had been earned during the years.[8] For this reason, it is prudent for a taxpayer with an overall portfolio of retirement and non-retirement accounts to hold the income-producing assets within the retirement plan. Conversely, assets that will generate capital gain (or qualifying dividends subject to the 15 percent or 23.8 percent maximum tax rates) typically should be held outside of a retirement plan. By structuring assets in this manner, capital assets that will be eligible for long-term treatment once the holding period requirement is satisfied will enjoy the preferential tax rates and not be subject to ordinary income as retirement plan withdrawals, while income-producing assets (that would have been treated as ordinary income anyway) will continue to be treated as ordinary income when withdrawn from retirement accounts.

Example: Fred Bartons has $100,000 in his traditional individual retirement account (IRA) and $100,000 in a taxable brokerage account. No nondeductible contributions have been made to the traditional IRA. He owns two investments – a bond paying an uncompounded rate of 6 percent interest and a technology stock that increases in value by $10,000 each of the next five years. At the end of five years, Fred withdraws all of the funds from his IRA and sells all of his assets in the taxable brokerage account. His ordinary income tax rate is 35 percent and his capital gains tax rate is 15 percent. By holding the bond inside the IRA and the stock in his taxable account, he has $227,000, an additional $10,000, of wealth after taxes at the end of five years, as compared to holding the stock inside the IRA and the bond in his taxable account and having $217,000. (NOTE: Total taxes are calculated at the end of the period, although, in fact, tax on the bond interest would have been paid year by year; the result is the same in either case because the bond interest is assumed to be non-compounding.)

	IRA – Bond	Taxable – Stock	IRA – Stock	Taxable – Bond
Year 0	$100,000	$100,000	$100,000	$100,000
Year 1	$106,000	$110,000	$110,000	$106,000
Year 2	$112,000	$120,000	$120,000	$112,000
Year 3	$118,000	$130,000	$130,000	$118,000
Year 4	$124,000	$140,000	$140,000	$124,000
Year 5	$130,000	$150,000	$150,000	$130,000
Tax	($45,500)	($7,500)	($52,500)	($10,500)
Net	$84,500	$142,500	$97,500	$119,500
Total		$227,000		$217,000

Retirement plans are also an excellent choice for holding inefficient tax investments, such as many mutual funds. Mutual funds are required to distribute all of their interest and dividend earnings, as well as their recognized capital gains and losses each year. Therefore, unlike holding individual equity investments, mutual fund investors are often unable to control the timing of the recognition of various types of income from their investments. This is particularly applicable for capital gains and losses; an individual investor would likely have recognized interest and dividends paid even if held directly and not within a mutual fund.

This problem regarding the inability to control recognition of gains may be exacerbated if the mutual fund already has "nested" capital gains when acquired (capital gains recognized and pending distribution before the taxpayer purchases the fund). In this case, gains will be distributed to the taxpayer and consequently recognized, even though they are attributable to increases in the value of investments held before the taxpayer even owned the asset! On the other hand, some mutual funds may have nested capital *losses* and a taxpayer may be able to avoid recognition of gains after the fund is purchased because the gains will be offset by recognized but not used or distributed capital losses incurred before the taxpayer acquired the fund. This "nested" gains and losses effect can be further compounded if the underlying fund has substantial *unrealized* gains or losses on the underlying assets.

Many mutual funds are now being touted as "tax efficient" or "tax aware." Those who are considering investing in mutual funds outside of a retirement plan may benefit by reviewing these types of mutual funds since they typically will pay out less income that must be recognized and often completely avoid making any capital gain distributions each year. Alternatively, exchange traded funds, or "ETFs," may be a more tax efficient way to invest in certain market indices. Prior to the advent of ETFs, investors were commonly purchasing mutual funds that were tied to a given index. ETFs give investors the same basket of underlying investments, but trade like a stock, so they are better able to control the timing of the capital gains.

Converting Interest Income into Qualifying Dividends

Although qualifying dividends are taxed at a rate of 15 percent for most taxpayers and 23.8 percent for taxpayers in the top marginal tax bracket, interest and all other (non-qualifying) dividends are still taxed as ordinary income (subject to a maximum tax rate under current law of 37 percent plus the 3.8 percent NIIT for 2020).

Generally, qualifying dividends are dividends paid by domestic corporations and qualified foreign corporations (a foreign corporation's dividends would normally qualify provided the corporation was not in a country designated as a "tax haven").[9]

The focus of the current tax law is to reduce the impact of dividend double taxation by granting qualifying dividend treatment to any dividends paid out by entities that pay tax on income at the entity level (although the entity is not actually required to have *paid* tax on the specific income or dollars distributed for the dividend to receive preferential treatment). Certain types of payments or specific entities that make distributions do not receive qualifying dividend status. Dividends which do not qualify for the lower tax rate include:

1. Dividends paid by credit unions, mutual insurance companies, tax-exempt organizations, real estate investment trusts (REITs) (unless the REIT does not deduct distributions but instead pays tax at the REIT entity level), and employee stock ownership programs.[10]

2. Dividends paid on stock that was not held for more than sixty days during the 120-day

period beginning sixty days before the ex-dividend date (i.e., stock not purchased before the ex-dividend date will not be held on the record date—on which the corporation finalizes the list of shareholders who will receive the dividend. The ex-dividend date marks the deadline by which the investor must purchase the stock to receive the dividend. The ex-dividend date is usually two days before the record date, but may be as late as the day after the record date, depending upon the method of purchase and the brokerage account settlement requirements).[11]

3. Dividends paid on preferred stock that was not held for more than ninety days during the 180-day period beginning ninety days before the ex-dividend date.

4. Dividends that cause an obligation to make payments of property that is substantially similar to the stock or property that is paid as a dividend (e.g., a reciprocal dividend arrangement).[12]

Investors usually look to the expected after-tax yield on a prospective investment to determine whether it is worth the risk. With the lower tax rates on qualifying dividends, many solid blue-chip companies which have paid dividends on a consistent basis will provide, with the same dividend, a higher after-tax yield than they have in the past. This increased yield may justify the added risk of fluctuation in the stock price. Investors might consider shifting some of their funds from a lower-yielding fixed income investment into a dividend paying stock. This may be particularly applicable to the higher dividend payments often received from preferred stocks. However, it is *vital* to properly evaluate the (potentially *substantial*) increased risk of holding various types of dividend-paying equities instead of fixed income or guaranteed investments.

One potential downside to increasing one's qualified dividends is the impact on investment income for the purpose of deducting investment interest expense. Investment interest expense may be claimed as an itemized deduction to the extent the taxpayer has sufficient investment income. The tax law excludes dividends and capital gains that are subject to a tax rate that is other than a taxpayer's ordinary income tax rate from investment income. Therefore, qualified dividends are not considered to be investment income and certain margin interest may not be immediately deductible as a result.

Taxpayers may elect to treat some or all of their qualified dividends or long-term capital gains as investment income. The election essentially treats the specified amount as not subject to the preferential tax rate, but, rather, to the taxpayer's ordinary income tax rate. The investment interest expense then becomes deductible. The net result of the election is an acceleration of the deduction at a cost of forgoing the preferential tax rate. This election becomes economically feasible if the taxpayer would not otherwise generate sufficient investment income in the coming years.

Example: John Charrard incurs interest on his margin loan in the amount of $5,000. He has $100 of interest income and $10,000 of qualified dividends. Assuming he itemizes his deductions, he would be entitled to deduct $100 of his margin loan interest. The remaining $4,900 would be carried forward to future years until it can be utilized.

Alternatively, John could elect to treat $4,900 of his qualified dividends as investment income. The remaining $5,100 would still be taxed at 15 percent, but the elected amount would be taxed at his ordinary income tax rate. But the full $5,000 of margin loan interest could be deducted in the current year.

Structuring Compensation Packages

Certain highly paid executives may be able to structure compensation packages with their companies to convert compensation income that would otherwise be taxed as ordinary income into capital gain. Two of the more common compensation package items that foster potential capital gains treatment are restricted stock plans and incentive stock option awards. Incentive stock options are covered in detail in Chapter 27.

A company may grant stock to an employee subject to various restrictions. The granting of this stock is usually done at little or no cost to the employee. If the restrictions meet certain requirements, the employee may forgo recognizing compensation when the stock is received. Once the restrictions lapse, the employee would be taxed at that time based on the fair market value of the stock at that time as compensation received.

Stock that is issued to an employee is restricted stock only if the following two conditions are met:

1. The stock is subject to a substantial risk of forfeiture.[13]

2. The stock is not transferable.[14]

The stock is subject to a substantial risk of forfeiture only if there is a realistic expectation and requirement of future performance (or condition of refraining from a specified action or performance) of substantial services by the employee. For example, a requirement that stock is forfeited unless there is continued employment for X years would be a substantial risk of forfeiture; stock that is forfeited only upon being convicted of a crime does not meet the guidelines.[15] The non-transferability rule simply states that if the stock is allowed to be transferred to anyone other than the employer, the receiver of the stock would be forced to return the stock should the employee forfeit the right to the stock. The transferee must be subject to the same risk of forfeiture as the transferor.[16]

Once the stock, or any portion thereof, is no longer subject to restrictions, the stock award that is no longer restricted is recognized as compensation and taxed as ordinary income. The compensation is based on the excess of the stock's value on the date the restrictions lapse over the amount the executive paid for the stock.[17] The employee's holding period for the unrestricted stock would begin on this date (the date restrictions lapse) and any future appreciation after the restrictions lapse would be taxed as capital gain.

Example: Supurflous, Inc. issues 10,000 shares of stock to its new Chief Financial Officer, Gayle Conn, at no cost to her. The stock will vest in 2,000 share increments over the next five years. The vesting will only continue as long as Gayle remains employed by the Company. Under the terms of the stock agreement, she is not permitted to transfer the stock to anyone else. The stock would qualify as restricted stock and Gayle would not report any income upon receiving the shares from the Company. Once each fifth vests, the fair market value of that portion of the stock on that date would be treated as compensation to Gayle. If the stock price is $20 per share on the date that the first 20 percent of stock vests, Gayle would have taxable compensation of $40,000 (2,000 shares at $20 per share). Note that if Gayle was required to pay some portion of the cost of the stock as part of the transaction, only the excess of the stock's fair market value over the amount paid by Gayle would be considered taxable compensation.

Section 83(b) Elections

A planning opportunity exists for an employee to consider making an election under Code section 83(b) (an "83(b) election") to recognize income on the date the restricted stock is received, instead of waiting until the restrictions lapse. If an 83(b) election is made, the income element of the stock award is equal to the fair market value on the date of the award less the employee's cost. If an 83(b) election is made, the employee's holding period begins immediately and any future appreciation would be taxed as capital gain. The employee's basis in the stock under an 83(b) election is the fair market value of the stock when received (which would also equal the employee's cost plus the amount of compensation recognized under the 83(b) election).

Example: Gayle Conn decides to make an 83(b) election at the time the restricted stock is issued to her. At that time the stock is trading at $2 per share. Her 10,000 shares would generate compensation of $20,000 in the year of receipt. When the first 2,000 shares vest, the unrestricted stock would still be worth $40,000, as in the previous example, but, if she were to sell the shares, she would recognize a capital gain of $36,000 ($40,000 less 2,000 shares with a cost basis of $2 per share).

An 83(b) election must be made no later than thirty days (the "deadline" date) after the transfer of shares from the company to the employee.[18] Three copies of the election are required. One copy of the election must be filed with the Internal Revenue Service by the deadline date. A second copy must be attached to the employee's tax return for the year the stock is received. A third copy must be provided to the employer with an acknowledgement in writing being received in return.

There are a number of important considerations when evaluating whether an 83(b) election should be made. These include:

1. The employee does not receive any cash at the time of the stock award to pay the tax on the compensation recognized under an 83(b) election (unless separately provided by the employer as additional compensation).

2. If the restricted stock is forfeited after making an 83(b) election, only the amount of cash paid outright for the stock would be deductible by the employee. The compensation recognized and tax paid by making the 83(b) election is not deductible. Thus, in the example above, if Gayle made an 83(b) election and subsequently quit eleven months later, she would receive no stock whatsoever and would have no loss deduction available despite the fact that taxes had to be paid on the $20,000 of compensation ($7,000 of taxes paid at a 35 percent Federal tax rate) recognized because of the election. Consequently, the employee should be fairly comfortable that he or she will continue his/her performance of services through the date the restrictions on the stock will lapse.

3. If the stock price declines after an 83(b) election is made, the employee may actually recognize more income (the fair market value at issue) than he or she would have if an election were not made (the reduced fair market value when restrictions lapse).

4. If the stock has no value (or only a nominal value) at the time of the award, there is little or no downside to the employee by making an 83(b) election.

5. If the out-of-pocket cost to the employee is the fair market value of the stock at the time of the issuance (i.e., the employee pays the entire purchase price of the stock), no income is recognized by making an 83(b) election. This is because income recognition is only required to the extent that the fair market value of the stock granted exceeds the cost. However, by making the 83(b) election at no tax cost, all subsequent appreciation would be capital gain. Furthermore, even if the employee does in fact forfeit the stock, the loss will be deductible to the extent that the employee paid for the stock at issue.

6. If the stock price is expected to rise dramatically between the issuance date and when the restrictions are set to lapse, a large amount of income can be converted into capital gain by making an 83(b) election. This difference could potentially be so substantial (although stock price increases can never be certain) that the employee is willing to make an 83(b) election even when there is a high risk of forfeiture (without the subsequent loss deduction).

Example: Joseph Gantman paid $3 per share for the 15,000 shares of restricted stock issued by his employer. The restrictions on the stock were set to lapse in ten years as long as Joseph remained employed with the company. At the time of the transfer, the employer's stock was trading at $4 per share. Since Joseph believed the company's stock price would rise, he made an 83(b) election and recognized $15,000 of compensation in the year the restricted stock was issued. Five years later, Joseph is fired from his position with the company and the restricted stock is returned. Joseph may recognize a capital loss of $45,000 (15,000 shares at $3 per share cash paid at issue). Despite the fact that Joseph recognized $15,000 of compensation and paid taxes on it at the time the 83(b) election was made, no deduction is permitted for that portion of his loss.

Because some restricted stock grants extend out for many years, the employee is often virtually certain that the stock price of a solid and growing company will be higher in the future and that an 83(b) election would be beneficial. The primary issue becomes a determination by the employee about the likelihood of potential stock forfeiture.

CONVERTING CAPITAL LOSSES INTO ORDINARY LOSSES

While much of the focus of planning for the conversion of income revolves around making ordinary income eligible for long-term capital gains tax rates, there is some prudent planning that should be considered for converting capital losses into ordinary losses. Since certain losses may offset other sources of ordinary income on a dollar-for-dollar basis, the realization and recognition of these losses may save the taxpayer 39.6 percent or more of the amount of the taxpayer's loss on his/her tax bill.

ORDINARY LOSSES FOR SMALL BUSINESS STOCK

When stock (a capital asset) is sold at a loss or becomes worthless, the general rule is that the loss is a capital loss and is available to offset other capital gains in that year. If the capital losses exceed the capital gains, up to $3,000 of the net capital loss may be deducted against ordinary income in the current year. The balance is carried over to future years to offset capital gains in those years (also taking into account future capital losses). If there is a remaining net capital loss after including the loss carryforward and the future year's capital gains and losses, $3,000 of the net capital loss may again be deducted against ordinary income. This process may continue each year until the capital loss carryover is fully utilized.

Certain stock that is issued by a "small business corporation" as defined under Code section 1244 ("section 1244 stock") may receive preferential treatment in the event a loss is realized upon a sale or due to worthlessness. Specifically, a loss on section 1244 stock may be treated as an ordinary loss (instead of a capital loss). Section 1244 exists to encourage investors to put money into small businesses, despite the added risk associated with such investments, by providing more beneficial loss treatment in the event the business is not successful.

Only losses from the disposition of section 1244 stock are treated as ordinary. Gains from the sale of section 1244 stock continue to receive capital gain treatment (a rare "heads I win, tails you lose" for the taxpayer).

The section 1244 stock loss ordinary income deduction is limited to $50,000 per year ($100,000 for taxpayers filing a joint return).[19] If the loss from the sale or worthlessness of section 1244 stock exceeds this amount, the excess loss is still treated as a capital loss. Once the loss is characterized as a capital loss due to the imposition of the limitation, it remains a capital loss and is subject to the capital loss carryover rules. Consequently, taxpayers with section 1244 losses in excess of the annual limitations should consider selling the stock in multiple years to maximize the amount of losses that may be claimed as an ordinary deduction.

Section 1244 stock is identified as such (or determined later based upon available facts) at the time of issuance and must meet all of the following requirements:

1. The corporation is a "small business corporation."[20] A small business corporation is defined as one in which the amount of money and property received by the corporation for stock or as a contribution to capital does not exceed $1 million.[21] Once the corporation receives more than $1 million of capital, no additional section 1244 stock can be issued. However, the stock that was issued prior to the first million of capital was received will continue to be section 1244 stock. Special rules exist to designate which stock qualifies as section 1244 stock in the year the corporation's receipt of capital exceeds $1 million.[22]

2. The stock was issued to the taxpayer in exchange for cash or other property (excluding stock and securities).[23] Stock issued for services rendered by the taxpayer does not qualify. However, the taxpayer could receive the compensation in cash and pay for the stock with the cash received for the services provided.

3. The stock must have been issued directly to the owner of the stock. No person other than the person to whom the stock was issued may claim a loss under section 1244. In addition, the owner of the stock must be an individual or a partnership.[24] In the case of a partnership, a section 1244 loss is available only to those who were partners in the partnership on the date the stock was issued.

4. Stock must be either common stock or preferred stock issued after November 6, 1978. Securities convertible into common stock or common stock convertible into other securities does not qualify.[25]

In the year a loss is claimed, more than 50 percent of the corporation's gross receipts during the five most recent tax years must be from sources other than royalties, rents, dividends, interest, annuities, and sales or exchanges of stocks or securities.[26] In addition, the corporation must be an operating company during this period.[27] Corporations with cumulative deductions in excess of cumulative gross income during the previous five years are not subject to this gross receipts test.[28] If the corporation has not been in existence for at least five years, only the full years that the corporation has existed are considered. If the company existence is less than one year, the entire corporate life of the entity is considered.[29]

Example. Jackie Rhoads invests $150,000 into Qualford, Inc. Qualford's stock qualifies as section 1244 stock for Jackie. Six years after her investment, Qualford ceases operations, declares bankruptcy, and declares the stock to be worthless. If Jackie files a joint return, she and her husband may deduct $100,000 as an ordinary loss in the year the stock becomes worthless. The remaining $50,000 is a long-term capital loss available to offset their other capital gains.

Stock of an S corporation will usually be section 1244 stock in the hands of its owners. However, basis increases as a result of future contributions or reported flow-through income do not qualify as potential section 1244 losses.[30] The ratio of the original contributions to the total stock basis determines the portion that may be treated as a section 1244 loss.[31]

Example. Harry Townsend put $10,000 into his S corporation. He recognized $5,000 of income and put an additional $15,000 into the company over the years. His total basis is now $30,000. He sells his stock for $18,000, realizing a loss of $12,000 ($18,000 proceeds less $30,000 basis). Of this $12,000 loss, $4,000 is deductible as an ordinary loss from section 1244 stock ($10,000 ÷ $30,000 × $12,000). The remaining $8,000 is treated as a capital loss.

INVESTOR VS. TRADER STATUS

There is a segment of the population that spends so much time and effort investing in the stock market that their activity could be considered a profession. These individuals often attempt to profit from short-term swings in the market price of equities. The rise in the stock market in the late 90s coupled with the creation of "discount" brokers and online trading support made "day trading" a legitimate (although possibly short-lived) profession.

Taxpayers who trade securities for their own account will qualify either as an investor or trader for tax purposes. While the majority of people will be treated as investors, there are potentially large tax saving benefits for those who can qualify as a trader for tax purposes.

Investors typically buy securities and hold them for long-term appreciation. The time commitment involved, while it may be more than insignificant, does not rise to the level of being their main profession. When the securities are sold, the gain or loss is treated as a capital gain or loss. Expenses associated with their investing activity (excluding commissions which decrease the realized gain or loss[32]) are deductible as a miscellaneous itemized deduction subject to the 2 percent of adjusted gross income limitation,[33] and are not deductible at all for purposes of AMT calculations.[34] As a result, most, if not all, of an investor's expenses do not generate any substantial income tax savings. The reinstatement of the "Pease" limitation as part of the American Taxpayer Act of 2012, which limits certain itemized deductions including miscellaneous itemized deductions for higher-income earners, make this conclusion all but certain.[35] In contrast to investors, traders are treated as participating in the active conduct of a trade or business. As a result, the expenses of traders are treated as business expenses and are fully deductible from the trader's income in reporting his/her trading-business profits or losses. The expenses of a trader are reported on Schedule C of Form 1040, and the net income from the business on Schedule C is reported as an above-the-line item of income or loss when computing AGI. As a result, the expenses of a trader are typically transformed from an itemized deduction that rarely benefits many taxpayers to a bona fide offset to income (either directly reducing the trading-business income or flowing through as an above-the-line loss in computing AGI).

On the income side, the realized gain or loss of a trader still maintains its capital nature. Because the securities still generate capital gain or loss, traders remain subject to the $3,000 annual capital loss limitation and the wash sale rules under Code section 1091. Traders will often run afoul of the wash sale rules (even unintentionally or unknowingly) due to the high volume of trades that are made – often in the same security.

Maintaining capital gain or loss treatment is not usually valuable to taxpayers who want to qualify as a trader. Most, if not all of their trades will be either short-term gains or losses which, if taxed as a gain, will be subject to their marginal ordinary income tax rate. No benefit will be obtained from the more favorable long-term capital gain rate. So, traders have none of the upside where capital gains are involved, but still remain subject to the detriments to capital transactions (the annual loss limitation and the wash sale rules).

Traders may wish to consider making an election to "mark their security holdings to the market value" as of the end of the tax year.[36] The mark-to-market election forces the tax recognition of unrealized gains in the hands of a trader even though the security has not actually been sold. Since many traders operate as day traders, most open security positions are closed by the end of the trading day. As a result, traders do not generally have an inventory of securities that must be marked-to-market at the end of the year.

If the election is made, all gains and losses from the trading activity are treated as ordinary income or loss,[37] and are reported on Form 4797 instead of Form 1040, Schedule D. This applies even if the securities are not actually held on the last day of the year, as long as they would have qualified if they were still held.[38] Therefore, the annual $3,000 capital loss limitation and wash sale rules do not apply. The election is binding in the year it is made *and for all future years for the trader's business* and may not be revoked without the consent of the Internal Revenue Service.[39]

It is important to bear in mind that if the trader is generally very successful and most trades result in gains, then the mark-to-market election will guarantee that no security held for the trading business will *ever* be eligible for long-term capital gains treatment, even if the trader attempts to maintain particular securities with gains for the requisite holding period. Nonetheless, to the extent that most securities traders do not maintain positions for extended periods of time, the benefit of obtaining ordinary (rather than capital) loss treatment for all losses sustained throughout the taxable year generally weighs in favor of the mark-to-market election.

Traders fared well under the final regulations promulgated for the new net investment income tax (NIIT) regime under Code section 1411. As discussed fully in Chapter 13, the NIIT is a 3.8 percent surcharge on "net investment income" for taxpayers with modified adjusted gross income above certain levels. Net investment income includes (but is not limited to) interest, dividends, and capital gains. For NIIT purposes, interest and dividends for both investors and traders are treated the same: both are included in the calculation of net investment income. Regarding capital gains, the tax treatment is favorable for traders. The final regulations treat all trading gains and trading losses as capital gains and losses from the sale of property not used in an active trade or business.[40] That means that trading business gains and losses are able to offset investment capital gains and losses. Furthermore, the final regulations permit a section 475 trader to deduct excess losses from the trading business from other categories of income.[41]

Taxpayers may not simply declare themselves to be traders and avail themselves of the potentially more favorable rules. The tax court has ruled that "in determining whether an individual who manages his own investments is a trader, we consider the following nonexclusive factors: (a) the taxpayer's investment intent; (b) the nature of the income to be derived from the activity; and (c) the frequency, extent, and regularity of the taxpayer's securities transactions."[42]

Thus, a taxpayer is engaged in carrying on a trade or business as a securities trader only where both of the following are true: (a) the taxpayer's trading activity is substantial (must be frequent, regular, and continuous); and (b) the taxpayer seeks to catch the swings in the daily market movements, and profit from investments.[43] Factors such as the number of trades, the amount of time spent trading and researching potential trades, and the amount of time the securities are held all help to substantiate a taxpayer's classification as a trader.

Example: Bill Burns, a retired executive, lives on a $400,000 per year pension. To fill his time, he began trading stocks on a regular and frequent basis. In the first year, he incurred $20,000 of expenses and generated total losses of $50,000. His adjusted gross income for the year is expected to be approximately $500,000 (including other sources of income such as interest and dividends). The tax treatment of his "activity" will be dependent on whether he is an investor, trader, or a trader with a mark-to-market election. See Figure 26.1 for a summary of how his expenses and loss would be treated under each situation.

Figure 26.1

	INVESTOR	TRADER	MARK-TO-MARKET TRADER
Expenses	Itemized deduction subject to 2 percent of AGI limitation. With $500,000 of AGI, the first $10,000 of Bill's expenses would not be deductible (assuming no other itemized deductions). Further, the itemized deductions would be subject to the high income phase-out.	The full amount of expenses would be deductible on Form 1040, Schedule C as a business expense.	The full amount of expenses would be deductible on Form 1040, Schedule C as a business expense.
Loss	The $50,000 loss would be a capital loss available to offset other capital gains. If the losses are greater than the gains, $3,000 of the losses may be deducted from Bill's gross income. The remainder would be carried forward for future years.	The $50,000 loss would be a capital loss available to offset other capital gains. If the losses are greater than the gains, $3,000 of the losses may be deducted from Bill's gross income. The remainder would be carried forward for future years.	The full amount of the losses would be deductible from Bill's gross income as an ordinary loss.

CHAPTER ENDNOTES

1. P.L. 112-240 (2012).
2. P.L. 111-152 (2010).
3. IRC Sec. 1411. See Chapter 13 for more information about the NIIT.
4. IRC Sec. 1221.
5. IRC Sec. 1222(3).
6. Treas. Reg. §1.1223-1(i).
7. See IRC Sec. 408(e)(1).
8. See IRC Sec. 408(d)(1).
9. IRC Sec. 1(h)(11)(B)(i).
10. IRC Sec. 1(h)(11)(B)(ii).
11. IRC Sec. 1(h)(11)(B)(iii)(I).
12. IRC Sec. 1(h)(11)(B)(iii)(II).
13. IRC Sec. 83(c)(1).
14. IRC Sec. 83(c)(2).
15. Treas. Reg. §1.83-3(c)(2).
16. Treas. Reg. §1.83-3(a)(3).
17. IRC Sec. 83(a).
18. IRC Sec. 83(b)(2).
19. IRC Sec. 1244(b).
20. IRC Sec. 1244(c)(1)(A).
21. IRC Sec. 1244(c)(3)(A).
22. Treas. Reg. §1.1244(c)-2.
23. IRC Secs. 1244(c)(1)(B).
24. Treas. Reg. §1.1244(a)-1(b).
25. Treas. Reg. §1.1244(c)-1.
26. IRC Sec. 1244(c)(1)(C).
27. Treas. Reg. §1.1244(c)-1(e)(2).
28. IRC Sec. 1244(c)(2)(C).
29. IRC Sec. 1244(c)(2)(A).
30. IRC Sec. 1244(d)(1)(B).
31. Treas. Reg. §1.244(d)-2(a).
32. Treas. Reg. §1.263(a)-2(e).
33. IRC Sec. 67.
34. IRC Sec. 56(b)(1)(A)(i).
35. P.L. 112-240 (2012).
36. IRC Sec. 475(f).
37. IRC Sec. 475(d)(3)(A)(i).
38. IRC Sec. 475(d)(3)(A)(ii).
39. IRC Sec. 475(f)(3).
40. Treas. Reg. §1.1411-4(c).
41. Treas. Reg. §1.1411-4(f).
42. *Moller v. U.S.*, 52 AFTR2d 83-6333 (Nov. 18, 1983).
43. *Mayer, Frederick R.*, 32 Fed. Cl. 149, 74 AFTR 2d 94-6402 (Ct. Fed. Cl., 1994).

EQUITY BASED COMPENSATION PLANNING

CHAPTER 27

INTRODUCTION

Stock options are typically given to executives of publicly traded companies as an award for past performance or an incentive for future results. But they are also commonly granted to non-executive employees and used as incentive tools by larger non-publicly traded businesses as well.

A stock option is a right to purchase one share of stock at a specified price. Usually, stock options can be converted to stock only after a specified period of time has elapsed. Then, the exercise of the option must occur before the expiration of period of time specified in the option.

There are a number of key terms that need to be defined when discussing the taxation of stock options:

Grant – The transfer of the stock option by the company to the option holder. The date on which the employee receives the option is called the "grant date."

Strike Price – Also referred to as the "exercise price" or "option price," this is the predetermined price at which the option can be converted to stock.

Exercise – The transaction that converts the stock option into stock. The date on which the transaction occurs is known as the "exercise date."

Spread – The difference between the fair market value of the stock and the strike price of the stock option on the date of exercise. The spread also represents the potential compensation element of stock options that could be subject to taxation. The spread is sometimes referred to as the "bargain element."

Vesting – Some stock options may not be exercised immediately upon grant. Instead, the absolute and unconditional right to exercise the options may accrue or "vest" over a specified period of time. It is not uncommon, for example, for stock options to vest in equal amounts over four years. In that case, 25 percent of the stock options would become exercisable on each anniversary of the grant.

Vested – Refers to stock options that are currently exercisable.

In-the-money – Stock options with a strike price that is less than the current fair market value of the stock. If the reverse is true, an option is said to be "out-of-the-money" or "underwater."

For tax purposes, compensatory stock options are divided into two possible types. The type of stock option is determined as of the grant date and controls how the options will be taxed upon their exercise.

Nonqualified stock options (NQSOs). NQSOs are any stock option that does not qualify for special tax treatment under Code section 422. Taxation of these options occurs as of the exercise date. The spread between the exercise price and the stock price on the exercise date is taxed as additional compensation, subject to the taxpayer's ordinary income tax rate.

Incentive Stock Options (ISOs). Also referred to as statutory stock options, ISOs are covered by Code section 422. There are a number of stringent rules that must be adhered to, both by the company granting the options and the employee who receives the options. In general, the taxation of ISOs is deferred until the employee actually sells the stock. At that time, the employee is taxed at long-term capital gain rates on the difference between the selling price and the exercise price. But there are rules for alternative minimum tax ("AMT") purposes that could cause an acceleration, or pre-payment of tax in the year of exercise.

NONQUALIFIED STOCK OPTIONS

NQSOs are options that do not meet the requirements of Code Section 422, either intentionally or otherwise. There are generally no tax implications to the recipient of an NQSO on the grant date. The only exception is for publicly traded stock options. But it is extremely rare to find nonqualified employee stock options that trade in the public market. Note that employee stock options are different than puts and calls that commonly trade on publicly held companies.

NQSOs are a convenient and flexible way to award or encourage employees. There are no limits as to how many NQSOs may be granted, how the exercise price is determined, or the time limitation for expiration of the option. In fact, NQSOs are sometimes granted at an exercise price that is less than the fair market value of the stock on the grant date. These are referred to as "discounted stock options." But the deferred compensation rules of Code section 409A may cause such discounted stock options to be subject to tax upon grant (see further discussion of Code section 409A below).

The taxation of NQSOs typically occurs on the exercise date. At that point, the difference between the fair market value of the stock and the exercise price is recognized as additional compensation unless the stock is restricted (i.e. the stock is subject to a substantial risk of forfeiture and is not transferable). Payroll taxes must be withheld upon the exercise of NQSOs (federal, state, and local withholding, FICA, and FUTA). The spread is also included on the employee's Form W-2 wages in the year of exercise.

Employers benefit in two ways from the exercise of NQSOs. First, the company receives the gross exercise cost of the options. Second, the company is entitled to a tax deduction for the compensation element that is taxed to the employee.

Example: Balloons, Inc., Drew Freeney's employer, granted Drew an NQSO for 1,000 shares of stock of Balloons, Inc. The NQSO was exercisable immediately but was not publicly traded. The exercise price was $20 per share. When the stock hit $50 per share, Drew exercised the NQSO for all of the stock by paying Balloons, Inc. $20,000 (1,000 shares at $20 per share). As a result, he will recognize $30,000 of compensation (1,000 shares at $50 per share less his exercise cost of $20,000). Balloons, Inc. will report this $30,000 of compensation on Drew's Form W-2 for the year of exercise and will also claim a tax deduction for the same amount in the year of exercise. In addition, Drew must pay Balloons an amount sufficient to cover any required employee payroll taxes.

If, at the time a NQSO is exercised, the stock is deemed to be restricted, the taxation of the stock may be deferred until the restrictions lapse. As covered more fully in Chapter 26, Conversion of Income, if the stock is subject to a substantial risk of forfeiture and is not freely transferable by the employee, the stock is considered to be restricted stock.

Example: Using the same facts in the previous example, assume the stock option plan for Balloons, Inc. states that, although the NQSOs may be exercised at any time after grant, the stock will be forfeited if the employee leaves within five years of the date of grant and the stock is not transferable during that time. In that case, the taxation of the stock (and the company's deduction) would not occur until the restrictions lapse. On the fifth anniversary, if the stock is valued at $70 per share, Drew would be forced to recognize $50,000 of compensation income at that time ([$70 – $20] × 1,000). Drew's holding period for capital gain purposes begins on the date the restrictions lapse.

Diagram of Tax Consequences to the Employee

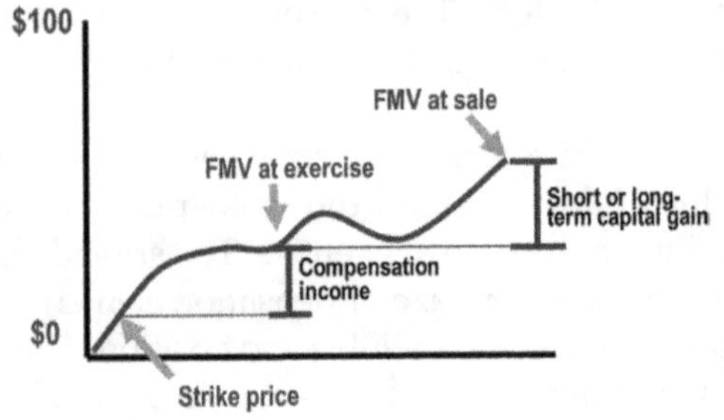

The employee does have the option to make a so called "Section 83(b) election." This would subject the stock to taxation at the time of exercise but enable the gain from that point to be capital gain. The mechanics of making Section 83(b) elections is covered in Chapter 26 Conversion of Income.

Example: Continuing with the same fact pattern, Drew feels very optimistic about both the growth potential of the stock and that he will be able to meet the terms of the restrictions. So he decides to make an 83(b) election despite the fact that the restrictions will not lapse for some time. The resulting compensation at the time of exercise will be subject to tax as a result of the 83(b) election. The holding period for the stock begins at the date of exercise, so all future appreciation will qualify for capital gain treatment once the stock becomes transferable.

Strategies for Exercising Nonqualified Stock Options

The benefit of an NQSO is that it gives the holder the benefit of any increase in value in the underlying stock without investing any money to get it. This means that, in effect, the holder receives two returns—one on the underlying stock and a second on the amount that would otherwise be paid to exercise the option. Assuming that the underlying stock is increasing in value, the longer the holder waits to exercise, the longer this advantage can be maintained. An important exception to the general rule would be high dividend stock. The holder of an NQSO does not receive dividends until the option is exercised, so if the stock pays high dividends, the holder may wish to exercise earlier.

Exercising nonqualified stock options generates taxable income to the extent of the difference between (a) the stock's fair market value and (b) the exercise cost. Therefore, it is equivalent to the employee receiving a cash bonus from the company and then the employee immediately using the bonus to purchase company stock. From this point, the taxpayer can opt to sell the stock or hold onto the resulting shares.

There are four common methods of funding the exercise cost of NQSOs:

1. *The employee pays the exercise cost and holds the stock.* If the employee believes that the stock has the potential to rise in the future, exercising NQSOs and holding the stock will begin the clock for long-term capital gain treatment. The exercise cost and resulting payroll taxes would need to be paid by the employee. The employee uses cash or other investments to pay the exercise price.

2. *Funds are borrowed to exercise NQSOs.* Borrowing money to cover the exercise cost and related payroll taxes may be a sound way to convert options to stock. The interest paid on such a loan will usually qualify as an investment interest expense that is potentially deductible by the employee.

3. *"Cashless" exercise.* NQSOs may be exercised and immediately sold for the fair market value of the stock. If the employee sells all of the stock, the exercise is the equivalent of a cash bonus. But in a sense, it is better than a real cash bonus since the timing of the taxable event is within the employee's control. A cashless exercise also occurs in situations where the employee sells only a sufficient number of shares to cover the exercise cost and the required payroll taxes.

Example: John Simms exercises 500 NQSOs with an exercise cost of $20 per share at a time when the stock is trading at $100 per share. In order to cover the exercise cost of $10,000 ($20 × 500), John immediately sells 100 shares ($100 × 100 = $10,000). The result is that John has 400 shares with a cost basis of $100.

Note that since options are exercised at an average fair market value, a cashless exercise may create a gain or loss since the sale of the stock would occur on the open market at the prevailing stock price.

4. *Exchanging existing shares to exercise NQSOs.* Instead of coming up with cash or borrowing funds to exercise NQSOs that the employee wishes to hold, existing shares of the company stock may be exchanged to cover the exercise cost and related payroll taxes. The exchange of existing shares for new shares in the same company is not taxable under Code section 1036.

Example: John Simms owns 100 shares with a basis of $10 per share outright. He exercises 500

NQSOs with an exercise cost of $ 20 per share at a time when the stock is trading at $100 per share. He exchanges the shares he owes outright to cover the $10,000 exercise cost ($100 × 100 = $20 × 500). 100 shares will have a cost basis of $10 per share—representing a carryover of the basis and holding period of the shares that were exchanged and not taxed. The remaining 400 shares will have a cost basis of $100 the taxable income recognized on the exercise of the 500 NQSOs. Note that John reaches the same tax result as in the previous example; however this option can yield a favorable result with ISOs.

INCENTIVE STOCK OPTIONS

A stock option can qualify as an ISO only if all of the requirements of Code section 422 are satisfied. As a general rule, the employee will not recognize any taxable income upon the grant or the exercise of an ISO. Instead, taxation will occur upon the ultimate sale of the stock acquired through the exercise of the ISO. So the timing of the taxable event is within the control of the employee. At that point, the resulting gain is normally taxed as a long-term capital gain.

Although no taxable income is recognized at the exercise of an ISO, the spread does create an adjustment item for alternative minimum tax (AMT) purposes. Since the AMT is often an unexpected (and costly) result of exercising ISOs, proper planning must be done to determine the amount and timing of ISO exercises.

Diagram of Tax Consequences to the Employee

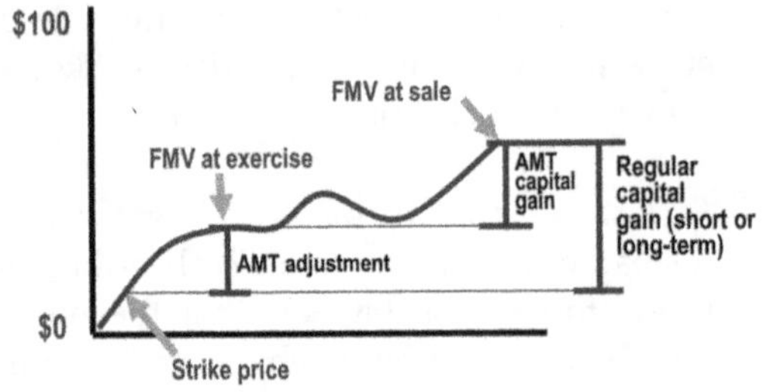

There are six requirements for an option to qualify as an ISO:

1. *Option plan must be approved by shareholders.* The stock option must be granted as part of a plan approved by the shareholders of the company. The number of shares available under the option plan and the eligible employees must be identified.[1]

2. *Expiration of options.* The options must be granted within ten years of the earlier of shareholder approval or adoption and exercised within ten years of the grant date.[2]

3. *Exercise price.* The exercise price of the option must equal or exceed the fair market value of the stock on the grant date.[3]

4. *Restrictions on transferability.* The options may not be transferred except upon the death of the employee. The employee can be the only eligible person to exercise an ISO.[4]

5. *Shareholder restrictions.* If an employee owns more than 10 percent of the company at the time the option is granted, the option price must be at least 110 percent of the stock's fair market value and the option must be exercised within five years of the grant date.[5]

6. *Limitation on grant.* The fair market value of the stock that can be obtained through the exercise of ISOs is limited to $100,000 per calendar year. The fair market value is determined as of the grant date. The applicable year is determined by the year in which the ISO is first exercisable. Any ISOs granted that exceed this limit are treated as NQSOs.[6] Note that this limitation is determined as of the grant date. It makes no difference when the options are ultimately exercised.

Example: Jones, Inc. grants Ted Johnson 10,000 ISOs with an exercise price of $50 per share. One-quarter of the ISOs vest over each of the next four years. Therefore, 2,500 ISOs with a total fair market value of $125,000 would be exercisable for the first time in each of the next four years. Only 2,000 of the options would qualify as ISOs (2,000 × $50 = $100,000). The remaining 500 options would be treated as NQSOs.

As previously mentioned, there is generally no income recognized by an employee upon the exercise of an ISO.[7] The exercise price of the ISO becomes the employee's basis in the stock and the holding period begins upon the exercise. Upon the sale of the stock in a "qualifying disposition," the taxpayer recognizes a long-term capital gain which is taxed at the more favorable capital gain rates. Unlike the rules for NQSOs, the issuing company does not receive a compensation deduction upon the exercise or ultimate sale of ISO stock in a qualifying disposition.

A qualifying disposition is one that occurs more than two years from the date of grant and more than one year from the date of exercise. In addition, the employee must have been continuously employed by the company that granted the ISO from the grant date up to three months before the exercise date (except in the case of death or disability).[8] Exchanges, gifts, and transfers of legal title are all considered dispositions for the purpose of this rule.

Example: Andy Williams is granted 1,000 ISOs on July 5, 2019. He exercises the options on July 6, 2020. He must hold the ISO stock until July 7, 2021 in order to sell the shares in a qualifying disposition.

Any disposition that is not a qualifying disposition is automatically considered to be a disqualifying disposition. If a disqualifying disposition of stock acquired by the exercise of an ISO occurs, the gain from the disposition is determined as follows:

1. Capital gain is recognized to the extent the selling price exceeds the fair market value on the date of exercise.

2. Ordinary income (treated as compensation) is recognized to the extent of the difference between the fair market value on the exercise date and the exercise cost. If the fair market value on the disposition date is less than the fair market value on the exercise date, the ordinary income is limited to the gain on the sale of the stock.

3. A capital loss is recognized only if the selling price is less than the exercise cost.

If a disqualifying disposition occurs, the ISO is essentially treated like a NQSO and the corporation would be entitled to a deduction for the ordinary income recognized by the employee.[9] Federal payroll taxes (FICA, FUTA, and federal income tax withholding) are not assessed on disqualifying dispositions.[10]

ISOs and the AMT

Although there is no income to be reported as a result of an exercise of ISOs for regular tax purposes, there are potential AMT implications. Generally, the spread that would be reported as compensation if the ISO were a NQSO is an addition to the employee's AMT income in the year of exercise.[11]

Since the spread is reported as income for AMT purposes, the employee has two different tax bases—one for regular taxes (equal to the exercise cost) and one for AMT (equal to the fair market value on the exercise date).

Example: Maria Shaunessy exercised 100 ISOs at a total cost of $5,000 in July. On the exercise date, the stock price was $75 per share. The total value of $7,500 (100 shares at $75 per share) less the exercise cost of $5,000 represents the spread that must be added to Maria's AMT income ($2,500). Maria's regular cost basis is the $5,000 exercise cost and her AMT cost basis is the $7,500 fair market value on the exercise date.

If the stock acquired through an ISO exercise is sold in a disqualifying disposition in the same year, no AMT adjustment is reported.[12]

Example: Using the same facts from the previous example, if Maria sells the stock for $8,500 in November of the same year, she would recognize a gain of $3,500. Of this amount $2,500 would be ordinary income ($7,500 – $5,000) and $1,000 would be a short-term capital gain. No AMT adjustment would be required.

Since the regular tax basis and AMT basis are different, the sale of stock acquired through ISOs in any other year represents an adjusted gain or loss for AMT purposes in the future year.

Example: Instead of selling the stock in November, Maria waits until January of the following year. The AMT adjustment of $2,500 would be reported in the year of exercise. In the year the ISO stock is sold, she would adjust her AMT income down by the $2,500 difference in the tax basis of the stock.

Warning: The $3,000 capital loss rules apply for AMT as well as for regular tax purposes. If the stock price declined from the date of the ISO exercise, it is possible that the amount of the negative adjustment will be limited to account for the $3,000 capital loss limitation.

Example: Jack Brown exercised 5,000 ISOs when the stock was trading at $100 per share. His total exercise cost was $10,000 and he reported a positive AMT adjustment of $490,000 and paid a large amount of AMT as a result. The stock price tumbled and Jack sold the stock in a qualifying disposition when it was trading at $40 per share. For regular tax purposes, Jack recognizes a long-term capital gain of $190,000 ([$40 × 5,000] – $10,000). For AMT purposes, Jack recognized a loss of $300,000 ($500,000 – $200,000). Since he has no other capital gains, his AMT loss is limited to $3,000. He will report an adjusted gain or loss of a negative $193,000 and carryover an AMT capital loss of $297,000 to future years.

Because of the potential AMT due in the year of exercise, combined with the capital loss limitations in future years, it may be wise to sell ISO stock that has declined since the exercise date in a disqualifying disposition in the same year as the year of exercise. It was not uncommon during the stock market's "Internet Bubble" to have an employee's AMT liability exceed the value of the stock when the tax was due. By selling stock in a disqualifying disposition, no AMT adjustment would need to be reported and the AMT can be minimized, if not eliminated. The net proceeds would then be used to pay the ordinary income tax due upon the disqualifying disposition.

The AMT adjustment created by the exercise of ISOs is a deferral item. As a result, any AMT that is paid may be recovered through the minimum tax credit ("MTC"). To the extent the AMT was generated by deferral items, a MTC is created. The MTC may generally be used in future years to offset a regular tax liability that exceeds the taxpayer's tentative minimum tax.

AMT paid as a result of ISO exercises is generally a prepayment of tax due to MTC and will be recovered when the ISO stock is sold or as time passes and the MTC is utilized. The MTC is covered more fully in Chapter 10.

STRATEGIES FOR EXERCISING INCENTIVE STOCK OPTIONS

The interplay of the AMT, MTC, and regular tax implications creates the need for long-term multi-year planning to determine the most tax efficient way to exercise ISOs. Of course the fluctuation in the stock price makes obtaining absolute tax efficiency impossible.

In addition to the strategies outlined earlier in this chapter for funding the exercise of NQSOs, which also apply to ISOs, the following are ISO strategies which should be considered:

Staggering ISO exercises. Many employees wait to exercise their ISOs until the expiration date is approaching under the assumption that they are deferring taxes. But it may be wise to exercise a certain number of ISOs each year to reduce the overall AMT impact.

Since the AMT is usually less than the regular tax liability for most taxpayers, there is a certain amount of ISO "spread" that can be absorbed each year without the imposition of the AMT. As a result, the employee (1) obtains ISO stock without paying any additional tax and (2) starts the clock running on the holding period needed for a qualifying disposition. After ISO stock is held for the requisite amount of time, the sale creates a negative adjustment, which then creates more room for additional ISOs to be exercised in the later years.

Example: Howard Washington projects that he is able to absorb $25,000 worth of AMT adjustments from the exercise of ISOs. He exercises 1,000 ISOs with a cost of $10 per share when the stock price is $35 per share. He reports the $25,000 adjustment but pays no AMT. Howard projects in the next year that he once again is able to absorb $25,000 of AMT adjustments. He also decides to sell the stock he acquired from the ISO exercise in the prior year (more than one year from the exercise date and two years from the grant date). The negative AMT adjustment of $25,000 will allow him to absorb a larger amount of positive AMT adjustments from current year ISO exercises. Note that due to capital gains tax rate differences, the amount that can be absorbed may be less than $50,000, the otherwise available AMT adjustment room and the negative AMT adjustment created by the sale.

Planning for restricted stock. If the stock that is acquired by an ISO is restricted, the AMT adjustment is not reported until the year in which the restrictions lapse. If the stock price rises between the exercise date and when the restrictions lapse, a larger AMT adjustment must be reported at that time.

As is the case for restricted stock acquired by the exercise of NQSOs, the employee has the option to make a Section 83(b) election at the time of exercise. The AMT adjustment would then be locked in based on the fair market value on the exercise date. The mechanics of making Section 83(b) elections is covered in Chapter 26, Conversion of Income.

Use of leverage to buy dividend paying stocks. Until ISOs are exercised and converted to stock, the employee has no right to any dividends. While there is a preferential tax rate for qualified dividends, it may make sense to exercise ISOs sooner, even if a loan were necessary to support the exercise cost.

Example: Six years ago, Nina Walsh was granted 10,000 ISOs with an exercise cost of $5 per share. The stock is now trading at $30 per share and pays an annual dividend of $1 per share. In order to exercise the ISOs, she would need to pay $50,000 (assume that she does not pay any AMT as a result of this exercise). Using an interest rate of 8 percent, her total interest on the loan would be $4,000 per year. The interest could be fully deductible against ordinary income as investment interest expense depending on Nina's investment income and other itemized deductions. Assuming her marginal tax bracket is 35 percent and the interest can be fully deducted, her total interest cost is $2,600, after taxes. Since she now owns the stock, she will receive $10,000 per year of dividends. Assuming her tax rate on qualified dividends is 15 percent, she will net $8,500 of dividend income, after taxes. As a result of this strategy, she is ahead $5,900 per year after taxes.

Exchanging stock for stock. A common practice is to use existing ISO stock to exercise more ISOs. Since ISO stock usually has an unrealized gain associated with the shares, this stock would achieve the maximum gain deferral. In order for the technique to work, the ISO stock that is being exchanged must have been held for the requisite amount of time to avoid the disqualifying disposition rules.

As mentioned earlier for the NQSO strategies, the number of shares used in the exchange retain the basis (for regular and AMT purposes) and holding period they had before the exchange. The additional shares acquired would have a regular tax cost equal to the amount of funds needed for the ISO exercise in excess of the value of the shares used in the exchange. The AMT basis for the new shares would be the fair market value of the new shares plus any additional amounts needed to fund the exercise cost.

Example: Mike Simms owns 100 shares of Palmer Corp. (acquired by ISO) with a regular tax basis of $10 per share and an AMT basis of $40 per share. He decides to exercise 500 ISOs he received from Palmer with an exercise cost of $20 per share. At the time of the exercise, the stock is trading at $100. Since the value of his existing shares equals his exercise cost of the ISOs ($10,000), he uses the existing shares to fund this cost. John will report an AMT adjustment of $40,000 ([$100 – $20] × 500). John will then have 500 shares of Palmer Corp. 100 of these shares will continue to have a cost of $10 per share for regular tax purposes and $40 per share for AMT purposes—representing a carryover of the basis and holding period of the shares that were exchanged and not taxed. The remaining 400 shares will have a cost basis of zero (John paid nothing for them) and an AMT basis of $40,000, the total fair market value of the additional shares acquired by the ISO exercise.

FREQUENTLY ASKED QUESTIONS

Question – How are commissions and fees incurred upon the sale of stock acquired by an option exercise treated?

Answer – Commissions and fees are added to the cost of the stock acquired. Therefore, even in the case of an option exercise and immediate sale of the stock, the employee may report a small capital loss as a result of these expenses.

Question – Do the states follow the federal rules for ISOs?

Answer – Certain states follow the federal rules and others do not. The laws of state of residency and the state in which the options were earned (if different) should be reviewed to determine how the options are treated. States which do not follow the federal ISO rules typically treat the options as NQSOs and subject them to tax in the year of exercise.

Question – How do the deferred compensation rules of Code section 409A apply to typical stock option plans?

Answer – Code section 409A was structured to tax certain plans that provide for the deferral of compensation into future years unless certain requirements were met. The requirements centered on the timing of the elections by the employee to defer compensation, how the deferred compensation plan was funded, and the ultimate distribution options to the employee.

NQSO plans are not subject to the 409A rules if the terms of the plan meet certain safe harbor guidelines as contained in the final 409A regulations:

1. The exercise price must not be less than the value of the stock on the date of the grant *and* the number of shares must be fixed on the original date of the grant.

2. The stock received on exercise is subject to tax under Code section 83.

3. The option does not include any feature for the deferral of compensation other than the deferral of income until the later of (a) the date of exercise or the disposition of the option, or (b) the time the stock first becomes substantially vested.[13]

If the plan fails to meet any one of these three provisions, the entire plan is tainted and taxation of the options would occur upon grant and potentially subject the employee to a 20 percent penalty on the deferred compensation.[14]

ISO plans are excluded from the Code section 409A rules.[15]

CHAPTER ENDNOTES

1. IRC Sec. 422(b)(1).
2. IRC Secs. 422(b)(2) and (3).
3. IRC Sec. 422(b)(4).
4. IRC Sec. 422(b)(5).
5. IRC Sec. 422(b)(6).
6. IRC Sec. 422(d).
7. IRC Sec. 422(a)(1).
8. IRC Sec. 422(a)(1).
9. IRC Sec. 421(b).
10. IRC Secs. 421(b), 3306(b)(19), and 3121(a)(22).
11. IRC Sec. 56(b)(3).
12. IRC Sec. 56(b)(3).
13. Treas. Reg. §1.409A-1(b)(5)(i)(A).
14. IRC Sec. 409A(a)(B).
15. Treas. Reg. §1.409A-1(b)(5)(ii).

Figure 27.1

COMPARISON OF NQSOs AND ISOs		
	Nonqualified Stock Options	**Incentive Stock Options**
Taxation at Grant	No tax consequences unless the option is publicly traded	No tax consequences
Number of Options	Unlimited	Only options on stock with an underlying value of $100,000, determined as of the grant date, may first be exercisable by an employee in any given calendar year.
Exercise Price	Can be set at any amount.	Cannot be lower than the fair market value of the stock on the grant date. If the employee is a 10 percent or greater shareholder, the exercise price must be at least 110 percent of the stock's fair market value on the grant date.
Taxation at Exercise	Difference between fair market value and exercise cost is taxable as ordinary income and is subject to payroll taxes. If the stock is restricted, taxation is deferred until restrictions lapse unless an 83(b) election is made by the employee.	No tax consequences for regular tax purposes. The difference between the fair market value and exercise cost is a positive AMT adjustment in the year of exercise unless the stock is sold in a disqualifying disposition in the same year.
Payroll Taxes	Must be collected upon exercise	Federal payroll taxes are not required upon the exercise or disqualifying disposition. Review state and local requirements.
Taxation at Disposition	Gain or loss on sale is recognized. Basis of stock is equal to the exercise cost and the amount of ordinary income reported on the exercise.	If the sale is a qualifying disposition, any gain is taxed as a long-term capital gain. The difference between the basis of the stock for regular tax and AMT purposes is a negative adjustment for determining AMT in the year of disposition. If the sale is a disqualifying disposition, the gain on the sale is ordinary income to the extent of the spread at the time of exercise. Any excess gain is capital gain.

DEDUCTIBLE CHARITABLE CONTRIBUTION PLANNING

CHAPTER 28

INTRODUCTION

The tax law encourages charitable giving by providing a tax deduction against both income and estate taxes. This allows people to be more generous than they would be otherwise. By understanding the nuances of the deductions, perhaps the charitably-inclined could afford to be even more generous.

A charitable contribution is a voluntary gift of a present interest in property to a qualified charity. Qualified charities include (but are not limited to): private foundations, religious organizations, units of government, nonprofit schools and hospitals, and other nonprofit organizations with a philanthropic purpose such as the American Red Cross or the Boys and Girls Club.

The charitably inclined can choose from many techniques to meet their goals and capture tax benefits. Most make outright or testamentary gifts of their entire interest in a piece of property. Others choose to make split-interest gifts (the gift is split between the charity and a non-charitable beneficiary) to meet a financial or estate planning goal. Still others, who want to maintain some control of the assets after donation, make gifts to organizations which later choose to support specific causes.

Despite the Tax Code's apparent goal to encourage charity, charitable contributions are limited in many ways. The amount deductible generally cannot exceed a percentage of the donor's income. The applicable percentage varies by whether the charitable organization is a public charity or private foundation and the type of property donated. Also, in certain instances, the value of the contribution is the taxpayer's basis in the property as opposed to its fair market value. Lastly, failing to substantiate the value of larger gifts, or overstating it, can lead to the strict denial of the deduction and significant penalties.

COMPARING THE INCOME, GIFT, AND ESTATE TAX CHARITABLE DEDUCTIONS

Charitable deductions under the gift and estate tax rules are similar to the income tax rules, but subtle distinctions do exist. For example, gifts to certain cemetery companies provide a donor with a current income tax charitable deduction, but such organizations are not mentioned by the gift tax or the estate tax rules.[1] In addition, although gifts to or for the use of possessions of the United States made exclusively for public purposes are deductible under Internal Revenue Code section 170(c), such gifts are not provided for in similar provisions of the gift and estate tax rules.

In certain cases, the estate and gift tax rules are more flexible than the income tax rules. First, unlike the income tax which is subject to the limitations discussed below, the estate and gift tax deductions can eliminate 100 percent of the gross amount subject to tax. Also, contributions to or for the use of any corporation organized and operated exclusively for religious, charitable, scientific, literary, or educational purposes do not have to be used within the United States to be deductible. Furthermore, the estate and gift tax rules allow deductions for contributions to or for the use of a fraternal society, order, or association without the requirement found in the income tax rules that such organizations be domestic. For gift tax purposes, nonresidents are subject to a separate set of rules that generally require that gifts be used within the United States or made to qualifying domestic corporations to be deductible. The distinctions noted above should be considered and the income, estate, and gift tax rules should each be examined to generally determine what types of organizations may receive charitable contributions.

WHAT IS A "QUALIFIED CHARITY"?

It is critical to determine to what type of organization a donor may make a contribution *and* also receive a charitable deduction for income tax purposes.[2] Charitable contributions to nonqualified organizations are *not* be deductible.

There is an important distinction between an *exempt* organization and an organization eligible to receive tax-deductible charitable contributions. An *exempt* organization is an organization that is exempt from federal income tax under Code Section 501.[3] Exempt organizations are commonly referred to as "501(c)(3) organizations because this is where the types of organizations eligible for exemption are listed in the Internal revenue Code. However, contributions to *exempt* organizations are *not* necessarily tax deductible. There are five types of organizations eligible to receive tax-deductible charitable contributions:

(1) **Charitable organizations**. A corporation, trust, community chest or fund, or foundation that satisfies all of the following requirements:

   a. Organized or created in (or under the laws of) the United States, any state, the District of Columbia, or a U.S. possession;

   b. Organized and operated *exclusively* for one or more of the following purposes:

      - religious, charitable, scientific, literary, or educational purposes,

      - to foster national or international amateur sports competition (so long as the organization's activities does not involve the provision of athletic facilities or equipment), *or*

      - for the prevention of cruelty to children or animals;

   c. No part of the organization's net earnings inure to the benefit of any private shareholder or individual; *and*

   d. The organization is not disqualified from tax exempt status due to its attempting to influence legislation, and the organization does not participate in activities considered a part of a political campaign on behalf of or against any candidate for public office.

(2) **Governmental units**. The United States, a state, a U.S. possession, a political subdivision of a state or possession, or the District of Columbia *if* the gift is made *exclusively* for public purposes.

(3) **War veterans' organizations**. If the gift is made to a domestic fraternal society, order or association organized in the U.S or a possession *if* no part of the organization's net earnings inures to the benefit of a private shareholder or individual.

(4) **Fraternal associations**. To qualify, the gift must be:

   a. made by an individual;

   b. made to a domestic fraternity society, order, or association operating under the lodge system; *and*

   c. used exclusively for religious, charitable, scientific, literary, or educational purposes, or for the prevention of cruelty to children or animals.

(5) Certain nonprofit cemetery companies.[4]

The organizations listed above are all eligible to receive tax-deductible charitable contributions. The IRS maintains the "Exempt Organizations Select Check," a publically available database of qualified charities.[5]

DEDUCTIBLE CHARITABLE CONTRIBUTIONS

For a charitable contribution to be deductible, the charity must receive some benefit from the donated property.[6] Here is a list of contributions that are *not* deductible.

- A contribution to a nonqualified organization (see "What is a Qualified Charity?")

- A contribution to a specific individual

- The portion of a contribution from which the donor receives, or expects to receive, a benefit

- The *value* of the donor's time or services

- The donor's personal expenses (however, nonpersonal, unreimbursed out-of-pocket expenses that are directly related to, and incurred in furtherance of, the services provided by the charitable organization are deductible as an additional charitable gift)

- Appraisal fees (although the fees may be deductible as a miscellaneous itemized deduction subject to the 2 percent of adjusted gross income (AGI) limitation)

- Certain contributions of partial interests in property

Moreover, a charitable contribution is made voluntarily and without receiving, or expecting to receive, anything of equal value.

If the donor pays more than "fair market value" (generally, the price at which property would change hands between a willing buyer and willing seller) to a qualified charitable organization for merchandise, goods, or services, the amount paid that is more than the value of the item can be a charitable contribution. In order for the excess amount to qualify, the donor must pay it with the intent of making a charitable contribution. A *quid pro quo* contribution is a payment made partly in consideration for goods or services. To determine whether such a payment qualifies as a charitable deduction, the IRS has adopted a 2-part test. To satisfy the test, a taxpayer must:

(1) intend to make a payment in excess of the fair market value of the goods or services received; *and*

(2) actually make a payment in an amount that exceeds the fair market value of the goods or services.[7]

If a donor receives a benefit as a result of making a contribution to a qualified organization, he can deduct only the amount of his contribution that is more than the value of the benefit he receives. The deduction must not exceed the *excess* of (1) the fair market value of the goods and services *over* (2) the fair market value of any goods or services provided in return.[8]

Example: Sally Smith pays $65 for a ticket to a charity dinner-dance, but the ticket itself has a fair market value of only $25. All of the proceeds will go to the charity and Sally knows that the value of the ticket is less than her payment. Sally's charitable contribution would be $40 – that is, the total payment ($65) minus the value of the benefit received by Sally ($25).

If a donor makes a payment to, or for the benefit of, a college or university and, as a result, receives the right to buy tickets to an athletic event in the athletic stadium of the college or university, the donor can deduct 80 percent of the payment as a charitable contribution.[9] However, if any part of the donor's payment is for tickets (rather than the right to buy tickets), that part is not deductible. In that case, the donor must subtract the price of the tickets from his payment. As a result, 80 percent of the remaining amount is a charitable contribution.

Example: Jack Jones pays $300 a year for membership in an athletic scholarship program maintained by State University. The only benefit of membership is that John has the right to buy one season ticket for a seat in a designated area of the stadium at the university's home football games. John can deduct $240 (80 percent of $300) as a charitable contribution.

Certain goods and services received in return for a charitable contribution may be *disregarded* for purposes of determining: (1) whether a taxpayer has made a charitable contribution; (2) the amount of any charitable contribution; and (3) whether any goods or services have been provided that must be substantiated or disclosed. These include:

- goods or services that have an insubstantial value under IRS guidelines (e.g., token items);

- certain membership benefits received for an annual payment of $75 or less (e.g., free or discounted admission to the organization's facilities or events; free or discounted parking; preferred access to goods or services; and discounts on the purchase of goods and services); *and*

- certain admission to events (i.e., admission, while the donor is a member, to events that are open only to members of the organization if the organization reasonably projects that the cost per person is not more than a specified amount).[10]

WHAT TYPES OF GIFT TECHNIQUES ARE AVAILABLE?

Although cash is the most common means of making a gift and makes the contribution easy for the donor and the charity, it is not necessarily the most advantageous for a donor from a tax perspective. For this reason, many advisors encourage clients to consider different techniques. The many options include:

- Outright Gifts
- Charitable IRA Distributions
- Testamentary Gifts
- Charitable Gift Annuities
- Pooled Income Funds
- Charitable Remainder Trusts
- Charitable Lead Trusts
- Donor Advised Funds
- Supporting Organizations
- Community Organizations
- Private Foundations
- Charitable Gifts of Life Insurance

Each technique is explained in detail below.

Outright Gifts

Most people are familiar with *outright gifts*. The simplest, most common type of outright gift is a cash contribution to charity. The value of a cash gift is inherently easy to determine, and proof of payment can be established easily. However, outright gifts can include non-cash assets such as securities, real estate, and other property.

Aside from the satisfaction of making a charitable gift, the donor also can benefit by:

- taking an immediate income tax deduction, generally for the fair market value of the gift, and
- removing assets from the gross estate (and, thus, reducing the amount of estate tax due in the future).

However, the charitable income tax deduction is limited in several ways. First, it is an itemized deduction and therefore provides no value to a taxpayer whose itemized deductions do not exceed the applicable standard deduction. Second, the amount of the charitable deduction available is limited to certain percentages of adjusted gross income.[11] Third, the charitable deduction is subject to the overall phase-out of itemized deductions for high income taxpayers.

Charitable IRA Distributions

Qualified Charitable Distributions (QCDs) allow an IRA owner to make a direct transfer of up to $100,000 from a pre-tax IRA tax free to a charity tax-free. QCDs have unique income tax benefits compared to other outright gifts.

It is very easy for a taxpayer to capture income tax benefits with a QCD because the limitations on deductibility do not apply. For example, the deductibility of charitable contributions is generally limited to 50 percent of a taxpayer's adjusted gross income, but this limitation does not apply to QCDs. Moreover, as an itemized deduction, the charitable deduction must exceed the taxpayer's standard deduction before it provides a tax benefit and is subject to the overall phase-out of itemized deduction. These limitations, however, do not apply to QCDs.

Moreover, a QCD counts toward an IRA owner's required minimum distributions (RMDs). By excluding an unneeded RMD from a taxpayer's gross income other savings are possible. For example, by excluding an RMD from income a smaller portion of a taxpayer's social security could be subject to taxation. Also, other means tested benefits might be available to a taxpayer with adjusted gross income below certain thresholds, such as lower Medicare Part B premiums.

Testamentary Charitable Gifts

Most charitable gifts are made by bequest or devise. A testimony charitable gift, or a charitable bequest or devise, is a charitable gift that is made by will, revocable during the life of the donor, and made after the donor's death. A testamentary gift can be made of any of the following:

- A specific amount
- A specific asset
- A percentage of the estate
- A residual amount

Charitable bequests can also reduce a donor's taxable estate.[12]

Example: Lisa died in 2020 with a gross estate of $17.7 million, but made a charitable bequest of $700,000. Without the charitable bequest (and assuming she did not use any of her unified credit), her estate would have owed federal estate taxes of $2,448,000 [($17,700,000 – $11,580,000) × 40%]. Because of her bequest of $700,000, the value of her estate was lowered for estate tax purposes from $17.7 million to $17.0 million, which lowered her federal estate tax bill to $2,168,000 [($17,700,000 – $700,000 – $11,180,000) × 40%].

Charitable Gift Annuities

A *charitable gift annuity* is a contract entered into between a charity and a donor in which the charity agrees to pay an annuity to the individual donor in return for an amount transferred by the individual to the charity. The result is that the charity receives a current gift and the donor/annuitant is provided with a predictable income stream for life.

A charitable gift annuity is basically the same as a commercial annuity. Like a commercial annuity, each payment that the annuitant receives is made up of a taxable interest portion and a tax-free return of principal. Whether the annuity offered by the charity provides a better return than a commercial annuity will vary.

The portion transferred to the charity that exceeds the actuarial value of the annuity, is considered a gift.[13] The present value of this gift is determined by reference to the tables contained in the estate tax regulations.[14] It is deductible from the taxable income of the donor at the time of contribution.

Pooled Income Funds

A *pooled income fund* is a trust maintained by a charity. Donors transfer property to the trust and receive units of participation equal to the donation's value. The donation is reinvested to generate income. The fund's income is payable to the donor, or the donor's designee, according to the number of units of participation held.[15] A simple analogy for a pooled income fund is a charitable mutual fund, since contributions to the fund from the different donors are commingled.

The income received by a noncharitable beneficiary is taxed like income received from any other complex trust. However, it will generally result in all of the distributions being taxed as ordinary income in the year received.[16]

The donor receives a current charitable deduction for the value of the remainder interest.[17] The charity, which maintains the pooled income fund, benefits from this arrangement by receiving the remainder at the death of the donor.[18]

Charitable Remainder Trusts

A *charitable remainder trust* (CRT) is an irrevocable trust created under IRC § 644. It provides for (1) payments to non-charitable beneficiar(ies) at least annually or on a more frequent basis and (2) a remainder interest in the trust property to be paid to a charity at a specific future time.[19] A CRT involves three key persons:

(1) The **donor**, who contributes an asset to the trust

(2) A **lead annuity or unitrust beneficiary**

(3) A **charitable beneficiary** of the remainder interest

The donor and the lead beneficiary can be and often are the same person.

CRTs are popular as a charitable giving technique because of the tax advantages. The donor receives a current income tax deduction, can contribute appreciated property to the trust without recognizing gain, and provide a stream of favorably taxed income to themselves or other person. It is very difficult to structure CRT as a mere tax-avoidance vehicle to increase the wealth of the donor's family. However, CRTs can maximize wealth transfer to charity and family, compared to other gifting options, by minimizing income and/or transfer tax liability.

Figure 28.1

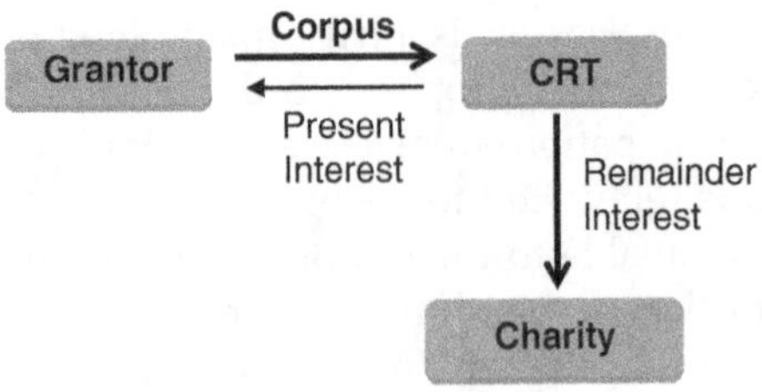

Charitable remainder trusts are designed in one of two basic variations, as explained below:

- Charitable Remainder Annuity Trusts (CRATs)
- Charitable Remainder Unitrusts (CRUTs)

Charitable Remainder Annuity Trusts

A *charitable remainder annuity trust* (CRAT) provides a non-charitable beneficiary a fixed payment at least annually. The payout percentage must be not less than 5 percent or more than 50 percent of the initial net fair market value of the trust.[20] The term of the annuity can be up to twenty years, over the life of the annuitant(s), the shorter of the two or the longer of the two.[21] The value of the remainder interest, determined using the interest rate provided by IRC Section 7520, must be at least 10 percent of the initial net fair market value of all property placed in the trust.[22] Typically, donors optimize the payments so the value of the remainder interest is close to the 10 percent minimum. These computations are made using the value of assets at the time of funding and therefore the trust cannot receive additional contributions.[23]

Charitable Remainder Unitrusts

A *charitable remainder unitrust* (CRUT) is similar to a CRAT. The principal difference is, however, the unitrust payout is variable and based on the value of the trust assets as of the annual valuation date. The lead interest in a CRUT takes one of four basic forms:

(1) **Standard CRUT**: The payout of the trust is a fixed percentage of not less than 5 percent or more than 50 percent of the net fair market value of the trust assets calculated at least annually.[24]

(2) **Net income unitrust**: The payout is the *lesser* of (1) the fixed percentage or (2) the actual income for the trust in that year (this type is also known as an "income only" unitrust).[25]

(3) **Net income with makeup unitrust (NIMCRUT)**: The payout is income-only, but the trust provides that to the extent income was less than the fixed percentage, deficiencies in past years are *made up* to if trust income exceeds the fixed percentage.[26]

(4) **Flip CRUT**: The payout is the lessor of income or the fixed percentage during the initial period and the fixed percentage in the remaining period.[27] Similar to a CRAT, the value of the remainder interest must be at least 10 percent of the net fair market value of the property as of the date it was contributed.[28] The term of the unitrust interest can be up to twenty years, over the life of the annuitant(s), the shorter of the two, or the longer of the two.

Charitable Lead Trusts

A *charitable lead trust* (CLT) is essentially the reverse of a charitable remainder trust. The charity receives the payment stream and the grantor retains a reversionary interest in the assets. The right to receive the reversionary interest can be transferred to another person in which case it would be referred to as a remainder interest.

As in the case of a CRT, a CLT can be either an annuity trust or a unitrust. A charitable lead annuity trust (CLAT) pays the charity a fixed amount of the trust's initial value each year, whereas a charitable lead unitrust (CLUT) pays the charity a fixed percentage of the value of the trust's assets revalued annually.[29]

The CLT can provide an estate tax benefit and income tax benefit to the donor's family. The value of reversionary interest for estate tax purposes is the value of the interest when the trust is formed. Because the assets can appreciate in value at a higher rate than the discount rate used to compute the value of the remainder interest, an estate tax-free transfer is possible. If the CLT is structured as a grantor trust (see Chapter 15), the grantor/donor is allowed an upfront income tax charitable deduction equal to the present value of the charity's interest.[30] If the CLT is not structured as a grantor trust, this deduction is not available to the donor, but the trust may be able to deduct the annuity or unitrust amounts as they are distributed to charity.

Figure 28.2

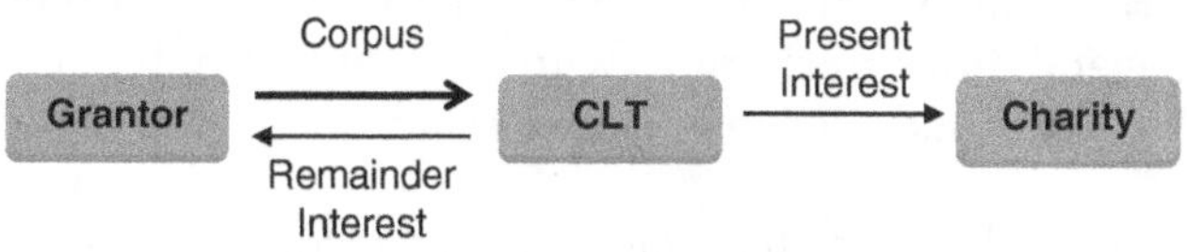

Donor Advised Funds

A *donor advised fund* provides a means by which a donor can make a deductible charitable contribution to a pool of assets and recommend how the contribution is used, but avoid the expense of a private foundation or supporting organization. Provided the donor does not have legal control over distributions, contributions qualify for a charitable deduction.[31] The basic types of donor funds are:

- **Donor Advised Funds:** This is a fast growing charitable tool. In brief, a donor enters into a written agreement with a sponsoring charity to establish an account to benefit the donor's causes. He then transfers cash or other assets to the account, receives an immediate charitable deduction, and over the next days, months, or years, requests that the sponsoring charity make grants to the donor's chosen charities. (Donor advised funds differ from pooled income funds in that they do not provide for a lifetime income stream to the donor or other beneficiary.) The donor receives regular statements from the sponsoring charity and, in some cases, may nominate an investment advisor or choose between a small number of investment funds.

  The sponsoring charity usually receives a small annual fee for managing the account and may provide services, ranging from performing due diligence on the donor's selected grants, to providing a list of worthy grant recipients which match the donor's goals and criteria.

- **Component Funds:** With this type of fund, a foundation establishes separate funds or trusts to receive and manage donors' contributions. If a donor's fund can qualify as a component fund, there are significant advantages. Even though the community foundation does not generally hold title to these component funds or trusts, a completed gift by the donor to such a trust is considered a donation to the community foundation.

Gifts of cash to a donor advised fund qualify for a current income tax charitable deduction up to 50 percent of the donor's adjusted gross income.[32] Furthermore, capital gain property is deductible up to 30 percent of the donor's adjusted gross income.

Donor advised funds are specifically defined as funds that:

1. are separately identified by reference to contributions of a donor or donors;

2. are owned and controlled by a sponsoring organization; and

3. allow the donor, or any person designated by the donor, advisory privileges with respect to the distribution or investment of amounts held in the fund by reason of the donor's status as a donor.[33]

A donor advised fund will not be treated as such if it makes distributions to only a single identified organization or governmental entity.[34] In addition, a donor advised fund may not make grants to individuals for travel, study, or similar purposes if certain conditions exist.[35]

Supporting Organizations

Supporting organizations and community foundations provide a great deal of flexibility for donors to structure charitable wishes. A *supporting organization* is a subcategory of public charity that, as its name implies, gives its founders and their descendants the opportunity to "support" favorite charitable causes by way of grants and distributions to public charities. One of the more common public charities supported are community foundations (see below). In general, these charitable giving vehicles allow the donor and descendants to charitably participate in the community for generations. Supporting organizations and community foundations work well together since the supporting organization can benefit from the community foundation's staff and accounting systems for their distribution and financial reporting needs.

Contributions to a supporting organization are generally treated just like contributions to any other public charity and, thus, qualify for the 50 percent contribution base limits.[36] Gifts of appreciated property to a supporting organization are generally deductible up to 30 percent of the donor's contribution base.[37]

Community Foundations

A *community foundation* is a 501(c)(3) grant-making organization which is a public charity for federal tax purposes. Community foundations must qualify as a "publicly supported" organization and satisfy one of two public support tests.

A community foundation has a board of directors or trustees whose main duty is to distribute funds for the use of charities in the community. A community foundation maintains separate trusts or funds, but these funds must be under the ultimate control of the governing body and treated as a single entity. Donors generally have two basic options for their funds. The first is to contribute to an unrestricted fund for community needs as determined by the board members. The second is several types of restricted accounts which may include a designated fund, a field of interest fund, a scholarship fund, an agency endowment fund, or a donor advised fund (see below).

Gifts of cash to a community foundation qualify for a current income tax charitable deduction up to 50 percent of the donor's contribution base.[38] Furthermore, capital gain property is deductible up to 30 percent of the donor's contribution base.[39]

Private Foundations

Standard Private Foundation

A *private foundation* (also referred to as a "family foundation") is a charitable organization generally established by an individual donor or a family who wishes to control, as much as possible, the use of their charitable contributions. Standard private foundations are the most common type. It allows the donor to memorialize his name or the name of a family member in perpetuity and passes on to future generations a charitable value system.

Standard private foundations generally don't engage in charitable activity, apply for any grants, or fundraise. Rather, it simply holds funds from which contributions are made to other charitable organizations. (This type of foundation is sometimes referred to as a "non-operating" foundation to distinguish it from a private "operating" foundation—see below.)

A private foundation can assist a donor who has a high-income-year to fund several years' worth of donations in one year. The foundation can then give grants to the donor's charities over the next several years. A private foundation can also help a donor make a gift to several different charities with an asset that is difficult to divide and donate (e.g., real estate).

Note, however, that standard private foundations are the most restrictive with respect to current income tax charitable deductions; they are also subject to a number of special taxes.[40] Also, cash contributions are only deductible up to 30 percent of the donor's contribution base. Gifts of long-term capital gain property are limited to 20 percent of the donor's adjusted gross income.[41]

Private Operating Foundations

A private "operating" foundation is a foundation that devotes most of its resources to the active conduct of charitable activities, rather than just making contributions to other charitable organizations.[42] Common examples include museums, libraries, and historic preservation sites. Of significance, certain exempt private operating foundation aren't subject to the IRC § 4940 tax on net investment income.

Another benefit is that the more liberal income tax deduction scheme for public charities also applies to private operating foundation donors. That is, contributions of cash up to 50 percent of adjusted gross income are deductible, rather than 30 percent. If property is contributed, donors may deduct the fair market value and up to 30 percent of adjusted gross income. By contrast, if the same donation was made to a standard private foundation, the deduction could exceed neither the donor's adjusted cost basis in the property nor 20 percent of the donor's adjusted gross income.

Charitable Gifts of Life Insurance

A charitable gift of life insurance is an easy way to make a significant gift to charity. It can be done in several ways. A donor can make a charity the beneficiary of a policy owned by the donor, donate a current policy, or have a charity purchase a new policy on the donor's life. The tax advantages of a charitable gift of life insurance depend on how the gift is structured. For instance, a donor may be able to receive a deduction for the value of premiums paid to maintain an existing or newly purchased policy, or for the value of a fully paid policy. Regardless, charitable gifts of life insurance can allow a donor to make a large gift in the future for a relatively small present outlay.

Figure 28.3

SIMPLE GIFTS		
TYPE OF GIFT	ADVANTAGES	DISADVANTAGES
Outright gifts	Donor can receive a current income tax deduction.	Assets are no longer available to the donor.
	Very simple.	
Testamentary Gifts	Charitable gift is revocable during life and can be drafted as a residual interest.	No current tax benefit.
		The gift may become a liability of an illiquid estate.
	Relatively inexpensive to include in a will.	Charitable bequests can add cost and time to administration.
		Income tax deduction is only allowed to the extent the contribution is made from the estate's income.

SPLIT-INTEREST GIFTS		
TYPE OF GIFT	ADVANTAGES	DISADVANTAGES
Charitable gift annuities	Combines a life annuity with a testamentary gift.	The annuity income is fixed.
	Donor receives a current income tax charitable deduction.	Risk the charity is not financially sound.
Pooled income funds	Income paid to the donor for life.	Income stream is unpredictable.
	Donation is tax deductible.	Income stream generally subject to ordinary income tax rates.
Charitable remainder trust (CRT)	Donor receives a current income tax deduction equal to the value of the remainder interest.	Expensive to create and administer.
	Income stream to non-charitable beneficiary can be taxed at favorable rates.	
Charitable lead trust (CLT)	Gift, estate, and generation skipping transfer tax savings are possible.	Expensive to create and administer.
	Income tax savings are possible.	Generally, can only provide a tax advantage if the grantor will have a taxable estate.

ENDOWMENT GIFTS		
TYPE OF GIFT	ADVANTAGES	DISADVANTAGES
Donor advised fund (DAF)	Inexpensive and easy compared to organizing a private or community foundation.	Donor has mere advisory privileges over the use of the gift.
	Favorable income tax deduction limits compared to private foundations.	
Supporting organization, community foundation	Less expensive to form and administer compared to a private foundation.	Donor has little control over investments and distributions.
	Favorable income tax deduction limits compared to private foundations.	
Private foundation	Donor can have some control over investments and distributions.	Very expensive to establish and maintain.
	Vehicle for the donor and his family to work together for a common charitable goal.	Maximum income tax deduction available in a given year is less than other options.

Figure 28.4

CHARITABLE INCOME TAX DEDUCTION LIMITS FOR GIFTS OF LIFE INSURANCE

- **Recently Issued Policy:** The deduction is equal to the lesser of
  - o the cost basis, or
  - o the fair market value of the contract. This is defined as the first premium paid.
- **Existing Life Policy in Premium Paying Mode:** The deduction is equal to the lesser of
  - o the cost basis, or
  - o the fair market value of the contract. This is defined as the interpolated terminal reserve plus unearned premium. This latter number is roughly equal to the cash surrender value but that is an approximation only.
- **Paid Up Life Insurance Policy:** The deduction is equal to the lesser of
  - o the cost basis, or
  - o the fair market value of the contract. This is defined as the replacement value of the contract. This latter number is equal to what the donor would have to pay for a new single premium policy with the same death benefit at his or her current age.

Definition of Cost Basis: In general, the cost basis is the sum of all premiums paid to date less 1) amounts surrendered or 2) dividends received in cash.

Policy Valuation: If requested, the insurance company will provide free of charge either 1) the interpolated terminal reserve plus unearned premium, or 2) the replacement cost for the policy on Form 712.

Source: *The Tools & Techniques of Charitable Planning* (2nd Edition), p. 100 (National Underwriter Company, 2007).

DEDUCTION LIMITS

Generally, contributions are limited to 50 percent of a taxpayer's adjusted gross income ("50 percent charities"). However, contributions to private charities are limited to 30 percent adjusted gross income ("30 percent charities"). Moreover, the deductibility of certain gifts of property are limited to 30 percent or 20 percent of adjusted gross income. Contributions that a taxpayer is unable to deduct in the current year due to an AGI limitation may be carried forward for up to five years (i.e. six tax returns).

Limits Based on Type of Charity

Public Charities

The charities listed below are frequently referred to as *public* charities. For 2018 and beyond a 60 percent limit (up from 50 percent in 2017) applies to the total of all charitable contributions that a donor makes during the tax year to public charities. This means that the donor's deduction for charitable contributions cannot be more than 60 percent of the donor's adjusted gross income for the year.[43] The following organizations are 60 percent limit charities:

- **Churches** and conventions and associations of churches;
- **Educational organizations** must be organizations with a regular faculty, curriculum, and student body;
- **Hospitals** and organizations that provide hospital or medical care, along with medical research organizations associated with those hospitals;
- **Organizations that benefit public colleges and universities** including organizations that are operated only to receive, hold, invest, and administer property and to make expenditures to or for the benefit of state and municipal colleges and universities, *and* that normally receive substantial support from the United States, or any state or their political subdivisions, or from the general public;
- **Governmental units** of federal, state, and local governments;[44]
- **Publicly-supported charities** can include corporations, trusts, community chests, funds, or foundations that normally receive a substantial part of their support from direct or indirect contributions from the general public, or from the federal state or local government;

- **Supporting organizations** that are organized and operated exclusively for the benefit of, to perform the functions of, or to carry out the purposes of one or more public charities);[45]

- **Donor advised funds** including a fund that has legal ownership and control of the donated assets immediately after the contribution. Donors may contribute to the fund and make nonbinding recommendations with regard to the ultimate distribution of the assets or how the assets are invested;[46] and

- **Certain private foundations.**[47]

Private Charities

Gifts made to or for the use of private charities (known as "30 percent charities") are limited to 30 percent of the donor's adjusted gross income. The 30 percent (private) charities include:

- standard private foundations (non-operating foundations) and

- veterans' groups, fraternal societies, and nonprofit cemeteries.[48]

To be deductible, a contribution to a 30 percent-type charity cannot exceed the *lesser* of (1) 30 percent of the donor's adjusted gross income, or (2) 50 percent of the donor's adjusted gross income *minus* the amount of charitable contributions allowable for 50 percent-type charities.

20 percent limit: The deduction for contributions of long-term capital gain property to most private foundations (i.e., family foundations) is limited to the *lesser* of (1) 20 percent of the donor's adjusted gross income; or (2) the 30 percent of adjusted gross income *minus* the amount of charitable contributions allowed for contributions to the 30 percent charities.

Limits Based on Type of Property

If a donor contributes property to a charitable organization, the amount of the donor's contribution is generally the fair market value of the property at the time of the contribution. "Fair market value" is defined as the price at which the property would exchange hands between a willing buyer and a willing seller, with neither party being under any compulsion to buy or sell, and both having reasonable knowledge of the facts.[49]

However, if a donor contributes property with a fair market value that is more than his adjusted (cost) basis in it, he may have to *reduce* the fair market value by the amount of "appreciation" (i.e., increase in value) when calculating his deduction. Different rules apply depending on whether the property is *long-term capital gain property* (see below) or *ordinary income property* (see below).

Long-Term Capital Gain Property

Special limitations apply with respect to charitable contributions of property that would generate long-term capital gain (LTCG) if sold at the time of the contribution. The term *capital gain property* means any capital asset whose sale at fair market value would have resulted in long-term capital gain.[50] Long-term capital gain property is any "capital asset" held for more than one year. "Capital assets" include stocks, Treasury bonds, and corporate bonds.[51]

The percentage limits affecting contributions of long-term capital gain property to public and private charities are as follows:

LTCG property donated to public charities: The deduction for contributions of long-term capital gain property to public charities is limited to the *lesser* of:

- 30 percent of the donor's adjusted gross income, *or*

- the unused portion of the 60 percent limitation.[52]

Although the deduction is generally limited to 30 percent, the donor has the benefit of deducting the full fair market value of the gift. The deduction for such gifts can be increased to the 60 percent limit if the donor elects to limit the amount of the deduction to his adjusted (cost) basis.[53]

LTCG property donated to private charities: Contributions of long-term capital gain property made to private charities (i.e., most private foundations) are subject to a different set of limitations. A donor's deduction to such organizations is limited to the *lesser* of:

- 20 percent of his adjusted gross income, or

- the unused portion of the 30 percent limitation described above.[54]

Ordinary Income Property

In the case of a charitable contribution of *ordinary income property* (i.e., property which, if sold, would result in ordinary income or short-term capital gain), the amount of the contribution is *reduced* by the amount of gain that would *not* have been long-term capital gain if the property had been sold at its fair market value at the time of contribution.[55] In other words, assuming the donor would not recognize any long-term capital gain if the property were sold, the donor's charitable deduction would be limited to his adjusted basis in the ordinary income property contributed.

Ordinary income property includes items such as:

- a work of art or manuscript created by the donor;
- letters or memorandums prepared by or for the donor;
- any capital asset held by the donor for one year or less (i.e., short-term capital gain property—see below); *and*
- Section 306 stock to the extent gain is treated as ordinary income on disposition.[56]

Short-term capital gain property is defined as any capital asset held by a donor for one year or less and can include such assets as Treasury bills, short-term corporate bonds, and stocks held for one year or less.[57]

Other Property Requiring Reduction in Value

Prior to the application of the percentage limitations, the value of two other types of gifts must be *reduced* by the amount of gain that would have been long-term capital gain if the property had been sold by the taxpayer at its fair market value as determined at the time of contribution. Simply put, the deduction is generally limited to the donor's adjusted (cost) basis in the property if:

- the donated property is appreciated *tangible personal property* that is put to an *unrelated* use by the charity; *or*[58]
- the appreciated property is contributed to, or for the use of, certain private non-operating foundations.[59]

Tangible personal property essentially means any property (other than land or buildings) that can be seen or touched. It includes furniture, books, jewelry, paintings, and cars.

In general, an item of donated property is considered to be a "related use" gift if it will be used in a manner that is consistent with the charity's charitable purpose(s). The term *unrelated use* means a use that is unrelated to the exempt purpose(s) or function(s) of the charitable organization.[60] For example, a donation of a valuable book collection to a library, which will display the collection in its archives and make the books available for reading by scholars and researchers, would fall into the "related use" category. A donation of office furniture to a charity that will use the gift to furnish its offices would also be a "related use" gift. On the other hand, a donation of a rare medieval manuscript to a modern art museum that sells the manuscript and uses the proceeds to purchase modern art would be an "unrelated use" gift.[61]

Special Rules for Donated Property

Publicly traded stock contributed to certain private foundations. Contributions to private nonoperating foundations (i.e., family foundations) of *qualified appreciated stock* can be accounted for at its full fair market value instead of the property's adjusted basis. *Qualified appreciated stock* is defined as corporate stock (1) for which market quotations are readily available, and (2) that would produce long-term capital gain for the donor if sold at the time of contribution. But note that the stock cannot be more than 10 percent of the value of the corporation's shares. A donation of publicly traded stock donated to a private family foundation (i.e., a 30 percent limit organization) is deductible up to 20 percent of the donor's adjusted gross income.[62]

Property that has decreased in value. If a donor contributes property that has *decreased* in value, the donor's deduction is limited to the property's fair market value.[63] A donor may not claim a deduction for the difference between the property's cost basis and its fair market value. In general, it is recommended that donors sell such property first, and then donate the cash to the intended charity.

Property subject to a debt. If the donor donates property subject to a debt (e.g., a mortgage), he must reduce the fair market value by any allowable deduction for the interest that he paid (or will pay) attributable to any period after the contribution.[64]

Future interests in tangible personal property. A donor cannot deduct the value of a contribution of a "future interest" in tangible personal property until all intervening interests in, and right to, the actual possession or enjoyment of the property have either expired or have been turned over to someone other than (1) the donor, (2) a related person, or (3) a related organization. A "future interest" is any interest that is to begin at some future time, regardless of whether it is designated as a future interest under state law.[65]

Summary

Deductibility of contributions to "60 percent Charities:"

Type of Property	Deductible Amount	Limitation
Cash	Fair market Value	60%
Ordinary income property	Lesser of Basis or Fair Market Value	60%
Long term capital gain property	Fair Market Value	30%
Tangible personal property charity uses	Fair Market Value	30%
Tangible personal property put to unrelated use	Lesser of Basis or Fair Market Value	60%

Deductibility of contributions to "30 percent Charities:"

Type of Property	Deductible Amount	Limitation
Cash	Fair market Value	30%
Ordinary income property	Lesser of Basis or Fair Market Value	30%
Long term capital gain property	Fair Market Value	20%
Tangible personal property charity uses	Fair Market Value	20%
Tangible personal property charity put to unrelated use	Lesser of Basis or Fair Market Value	30%

If more than one limit applies, the following summarizes how to deduct the contributions:

1. Contributions subject only to the 60 percent limit, up to 60 percent of your adjusted gross income.

2. Contributions subject to the 30 percent limit, up to the lesser of:

   a. 30 percent of adjusted gross income, or

   b. 60 percent of adjusted gross income minus your contributions to 60 percent limit organizations, including contributions of capital gain property subject to the special 30 percent limit.

3. Contributions of capital gain property subject to the special 30 percent limit, up to the lesser of:

   a. 30 percent of adjusted gross income, or

   b. 60 percent of adjusted gross income minus your other contributions to 60 percent limit organizations.

4. Contributions subject to the 20 percent limit, up to the lesser of:

   a. 20 percent of adjusted gross income,

   b. 30 percent of adjusted gross income minus your contributions subject to the 30 percent limit,

   c. 30 percent of adjusted gross income minus your contributions of capital gain property subject to the special 30 percent limit, or

   d. 60 percent of adjusted gross income minus the total of your contributions to 60 percent limit organizations and your contributions subject to the 30 percent limit.

5. Qualified conservation contributions (QCCs) subject to the special 60 percent limit, up to 60 percent of adjusted gross income minus any contributions in (1) through (4).

6. QCCs subject to the 100 percent limit for farmers and ranchers, up to 100 percent of adjusted gross income minus any contributions in (1) through (5).[66]

Example: Asher donates $100,000 of appreciated securities to his alma mater in 2016. The 30 percent limitation therefore applies. His adjusted gross income is approximately $160,000 in 2016 and therefore $48,000 ($160,000 × 30%) of the contribution is deductible currently. $52,000 ($100,000 – $48,000) carries forward to the next five tax years and remains subject to the 30 percent limitation.

In 2017, Asher has $170,000 of income and donates $20,000 in cash to an international relief effort, to which the 60 percent limitation applies. The $20,000 is deductible because it is less than the 60 percent limit of $102,000 ($170,000 × 60%). $51,000 ($170,000 × 30%) of the previous year's contribution carry-forward is also deductible (lesser of $51,000 or $102,000 – $20,000) and $1,000 ($52,000 – $51,000) carries over to 2018. Note that the total charitable deduction of $71,000 ($20,000 + $51,000) is less than the overall limit of $102,000 ($170,000 × 60%).

REQUIRED DOCUMENTATION & REPORTING

Generally, the deduction for a contribution is taken in the year the gift is made.[67] In order to deduct a charitable contribution, an individual donor must file Form 1040 *and* must itemize deductions on Schedule A. A charitable contribution will be allowed as a deduction only if *substantiated* (i.e., proven) in accordance with the regulations.[68]

All charitable contributions require written records in order to claim a deduction. For monetary gifts, no deduction is allowed for any contribution *unless* the donor maintains as a record of the contribution (i) a cancelled check., (ii) a receipt from the donee charitable organization showing the name of the donee, the date of the contribution, and the amount of the contribution., or (iii) other reliable written records showing the name of the donee, the date of the contribution, and the amount of the contribution.[69] For example, a cash gift to the Salvation Army made by dropping money into the jar hosted by a volunteer with a bell standing outside a mall during the holiday season is not deductible unless properly substantiated. For non-monetary gifts, no deduction is allowed for any contribution unless the donor maintains as a record of the contribution (i) The name of the donee, (ii) The date and location of the contribution, and (iii) a description of the property in detail reasonably sufficient under the circumstances.[70] However, a receipt is not required if the contribution is made in circumstances where it is impractical to obtain a receipt (e.g., by depositing property at a charity's unattended drop site).[71]

Contributions of $250 or More

Charitable contributions of $250 or more, whether in cash or property, also must be substantiated by a contemporaneous written acknowledgment of the contribution supplied by the charitable organization.[72] The acknowledgment must include the following information:

(i) The amount of cash contributed and a description (but not necessarily the value) of any property contributed.

(ii) A statement of whether the charitable organization provided any goods or services in consideration for the contribution.

(iii) If the donee organization provides any goods or services other than intangible religious benefits (as described in section 170(f)(8)), a description and good faith estimate of the value of those goods or services.

(iv) If the donee organization provides any intangible religious benefits, a statement to that effect.[73]

The acknowledgment is considered to be "contemporaneous" if it is obtained by the taxpayer on or before the earlier of:

(i) the date the taxpayer files the original return for the taxable year in which the contribution was made; or

(ii) the due date (including extensions) for filing the taxpayer's original return for that year.[74]

However, substantiation including the elements provided above in (i)-(iv) is not required if the information is reported by the charitable organization.[75]

Noncash Contributions Exceeding $500

If the claimed value of a noncash contribution exceeds $500, the taxpayer's records must also include the manner and approximate date the property donated was acquired and the cost or other basis, adjusted as provided by section 1016.[76] The taxpayer must also complete and attach to his tax return Form 8283 ("Noncash Charitable Contributions").

Contributions Exceeding $5,000

In addition to the requirements described above, individuals who claim a deduction for a charitable gift of property (except publicly traded securities) valued in excess of $5,000 ($10,000 for non-publicly traded stock) are required to do all of the following:

(1) obtain a qualified appraisal report;

(2) attach an appraisal summary (containing the information specified in regulations) to their return for the year in which the deduction is claimed; *and*

(3) maintain records of certain information related to the contribution.[77]

A qualified appraiser may *not* be any of the following:

- the taxpayer;
- a party to the transaction in which the taxpayer acquired the property;
- the charity;
- an employee of any of the above; or
- any other person who might appear not to be totally independent.[78]

The appraiser cannot base his fee on a percentage of the appraisal value, unless the fee is based on a sliding scale that is paid to a generally recognized association regulating appraisers.[79]

If the donor gives similar items of property (such as books, stamps, paintings, etc.) to the same charity during the taxable year, only one appraisal and summary is required. If similar items of property are given during the same taxable year to several charities, and the aggregate value of the donations exceeds $5,000, a separate appraisal and summary must be made for each donation.[80] The appraisal summary must be signed and dated by the charity as an acknowledgement of the donation.[81]

Taxpayers need not obtain a qualified appraisal of securities whose claimed value exceeds $5,000 if the donated property meets the definition of *publicly traded securities*, which are securities that are:

- listed on a stock exchange in which quotations are published on a daily basis; or
- regularly traded in a national or regional over-the-counter market for which published quotations are available.[82]

Penalties for Overvaluing Donated Property

If a taxpayer underpays his tax because of a *substantial valuation misstatement* of property donated to charity, he may be subject to a penalty of 20 percent of the underpayment attributable to the misstatement.[83] However, this penalty applies only if the underpayment attributable to the misstatement exceeds $5,000.[84] A "substantial valuation misstatement" exists if the value claimed is 150 percent or more of the amount determined to be correct.[85] If the value claimed is 200 percent or more of the amount determined to be correct, there is a "gross valuation misstatement," which is subject to a 40 percent underpayment penalty.[86]

An appraiser may be subject to a penalty if (1) the appraiser "knows, or reasonably should have known" that an appraisal would be used as part of a tax return and (2) the appraisal results in a substantial valuation misstatement or a gross valuation misstatement.[87] The amount of the penalty is the *lesser* of:

1. the greater of 10 percent of the amount of the underpayment attributable to the misstatement or $1,000; *or*
2. 125 percent of the gross income received by the appraiser from the preparation of the appraisal.[88]

A limited exception to the penalty exists if the value established in the appraisal by the appraiser was "more likely than not the proper value."[89]

CORPORATE CHARITABLE CONTRIBUTIONS

A corporation's total deduction for its charitable contributions may not exceed 10 percent of the corporation's taxable income. The corporation's taxable income, for this purpose, is computed without regard to charitable contributions, any capital or net loss carrybacks, and most of the special deductions for corporations.

WHERE CAN I FIND OUT MORE?

1. Leimberg, et al, *The Tools & Techniques of Charitable Planning*, 3rd Edition, The National Underwriter Company, 2014.

2. *Tax Facts on Investments*, The National Underwriter Company (updated annually).

FREQUENTLY ASKED QUESTIONS

Question – What factors should be considered when deciding between a charitable remainder annuity trust (CRAT) and a charitable remainder unitrust (CRUT)?

Answer – A CRAT offers the primary benefits of simplicity and certainty. With a CRAT, the retained interest is a fixed dollar amount. Therefore, since the amount is fixed, there is no need for an annual revaluation as with a CRUT. For that reason (i.e., no annual revaluation requirement), a CRAT will be considerably easier, and less expensive to administer than a CRUT, especially when there are hard-to-value assets being contributed to the trust.

A second consideration is the need (or desire) for a fixed return. With a CRAT, the annual payout is fixed. The annuity payment will not be reduced if the value of the trust decreases, unless the trust is completely liquidated by distributions.

A third consideration is the need for a hedge against inflation. While a CRAT offers the promise of a fixed annual return, this fixed annual payout can be a significant detriment in the event of inflation. For this reason, younger donors often prefer the flexible unitrust payment that is available with a CRUT, as opposed to the fixed payment guaranteed by a CRAT.

With a CRAT or a CRUT, the cash flow created from the trustee's investment of the entire amount of the proceeds from the tax-free sale of the contributed asset will be significantly more than the cash flow that would have been earned by the donor from the net after-tax proceeds had the contributed asset been sold. Furthermore, selling the contributed asset inside the CRAT or the CRUT and allowing the trustee to invest the proceeds in a diversified portfolio can diversify the donor's source of income.

Another consideration is whether additional contributions to the trust are contemplated. A donor can make multiple contributions to a single CRUT, but the *initial* contribution is the *only* contribution that can be made to a CRAT.[90]

Question – How is a charitable lead trust different from a charitable remainder trust?

Answer – While both are split-interest charitable trusts, there are significant differences between charitable lead trusts and charitable remainder trusts. The most obvious difference is that the lead and remainder beneficiary roles are reversed. In a lead trust, a charity is entitled to the annuity or unitrust interest and a noncharitable beneficiary is entitled to the remainder. Conversely, in a charitable remainder trust, the noncharitable beneficiary is entitled to the annuity or unitrust interest with a charitable beneficiary receiving the remainder interest.

Aside from the reversed trust interest roles, there are other differences. For example, charitable remainder trusts are tax-exempt entities, whereas charitable lead trusts are not. Additionally, charitable remainder trusts have minimum and maximum payout rates, as well as maximum term limits. Charitable lead trusts do not have these same requirements.[91]

Question – A taxpayer owns an asset that has appreciated rapidly since its acquisition. What are the implications if the asset has not been held for at least one year?

Answer – Donors of appreciated property are permitted to receive a charitable deduction equal to the fair market value of the asset provided that it has been held for at least one year (i.e. it qualifies for a long-term holding period). Consideration should be given to delaying the contribution of an asset that has significantly appreciated, but not met the long-term holding period requirement. If an asset is donated that has not been held for at least one year, the charitable contribution is limited to the taxpayer's basis in the asset.

Question – A taxpayer owns an asset that could be used by a charity, but is worth more than what the taxpayer would be willing to give. Can the taxpayer engage in a part-sale, part-gift transaction with a charity?

Answer – The part-sale, part-gift of property is covered by the bargain sale rules.[92] A bargain sale is split into transactions – one sale and one charitable contribution. The sale portion is subject to tax, generally as a capital gain. As a result, the tax basis of the property must be allocated between the two components of the transaction.

The tax basis allocated to the sale is determined by the proportion of the sales proceeds received in the transaction over the property's fair market value. This proportion is applied to the tax basis of the asset. The net sales proceeds in excess of the allocated tax basis represents the taxable gain.[93]

The difference between the fair market value of the property and the sales proceeds received is the charitable contribution amount.

Question – What are the special rules for conservation easements?

Answer – A conservation easement is a restriction placed on the use of a piece of real property. The land owner does not give up ownership or control of the land. Common conservation easements involve the saving of open space or a natural habitat, protecting historical value, or preserving property for outdoor recreation.

The amount of the deduction for a qualified conservation easement is normally determined by an appraiser, who ascertains the diminution of the property's fair market value as a result of the restrictions placed on the property. Since the land will normally constitute a donation of capital gain property, a conservation easement that is given to a public charity (a 50 percent charity) is limited to 30 percent of a taxpayer's AGI. For qualified conservation easements made after 2006, higher AGI limits and longer carryover may apply.

Question – How are donations of cars, boats, and airplanes treated?

Answer – For charitable donations of cars, boats, and airplanes exceeding $500 in value, the charitable deduction is determined, in part, by how the donated car, boat, or airplane is used by the charity.

If the charity sells the property without significantly using it or making material improvements, the deduction is limited to the proceeds received by the charity from the sale. The charity reports the proceeds received on a Form 1098-C, which is provided to the IRS and the donor of the property.

If the charity does significantly use the property or makes material improvements before ultimately selling it, the donor's deduction is determined by the fair market value of the property as of the date of the donation. The same rule would apply if the charity transfers the property to a needy individual. The charity will indicate such use, improvements, or transfer on Form 1098-C.

The taxpayer cannot deduct any amount for a donated car, boat, or airplane above $500 unless the charity provides acknowledgement on Form 1098-C. The charity is required to issue the form within thirty days of the sale or thirty days of meeting one of the other exceptions described above. The donor/taxpayer must attach Form 1098-C to his or her tax return for the year of the donation.

Question – When are donations made by credit card deductible?

Answer – The date of the charitable contribution is determined by when the charge is incurred. Therefore, if a taxpayer is looking to give money to a charity before the end of a particular taxable year, the donor may charge the donation to a favorite credit card (and get their frequent flyer miles!) even though the charge will not be paid until the following year.[94] However, if the taxpayer incurs interest or any other related charges as a result of using the credit card to fund the charitable gift, that amount is not deductible.

Question – What are the deduction rules for property that has declined in value?

Answer – If at all possible, taxpayers should not donate property used in a trade or business or held for investment that has declined in value. The charitable deduction is limited to the property's fair market value. The unrealized loss in the property is not considered to be an additional deduction either as a charitable contribution or as a capital loss.

Instead, the loss should be realized by selling the property for cash and, thereby, realizing the loss. Then, the taxpayer can donate the cash to the charity. The charity will realize the same amount as a donation, but the taxpayer will have a potentially deductible loss against their other sources of income.

Note that a loss on property held for personal use, such as the family car, is not deductible. So, all things being equal, nothing is lost by a taxpayer donating the family car instead of selling it first and donating the cash.

Question – How did the CARES Act change the rules for charitable contributions?

Answer – The CARES Act made several changes designed to encourage charitable giving during the COVID-19 outbreak. For the 2020 tax year, the CARES Act amended IRC Section 62(a), allowing taxpayers to reduce adjusted gross income (AGI) by $300 worth of charitable contributions made in 2020 even if they do not itemize. Under normal circumstances, taxpayers are only permitted to deduct cash contributions to charity to the extent those donations do not exceed 60 percent of AGI (10 percent for corporations). The CARES Act lifts the 60 percent AGI limit for 2020.

Cash contributions to public charities and certain private foundations in 2020 are not subject to the AGI limit. Individual taxpayers can offset their income for 2020 up to the full amount of their AGI, and additional charitable contributions can be carried over to offset income in a later year (the amounts are not refundable). The corporate AGI limit was raised to 25 percent (excess contributions also carry over to subsequent tax years).

CHAPTER ENDNOTES

1. IRC Secs. 2055(a), 2522(a).
2. Other charitable deductions include the gift tax charitable deduction and the estate tax charitable deduction. See the sidebar, above.
3. IRC Sec. 501(a).
4. IRC Sec. 170(c).
5. Available at: http://apps.irs.gov/app/eos/ePostSearch.do?searchChoice=revoked&dispatchMethod=selectSearch.
6. See *Winthrop v. Meisels*, 180 F.Supp. 29 (DC NY 1959), *aff'd*, 281 F.2d 694 (2nd Cir. 1960).
7. Treas. Reg. §1.170A-1(h)(1); *United States v. American Bar Endowment*, 477 U.S. 105 (1986).
8. Treas. Reg. §1.170A-1(h)(2).
9. IRC Sec. 170(l).
10. Treas. Reg. §§1.170A-1(h), 1.170A-13(f)(8); Rev. Proc. 2002-70, 2001-2 CB 845.
11. See IRC Sec. 170(b).
12. IRC Sec. 2055.
13. Treas. Reg. §1.170A-1(d).
14. Treas. Reg. §1.170A-1(d)(2). For gift annuities, the Section 7520 interest rate and the most current mortality tables are used to determine the value of the gift annuity. IRC Sec. 7520(a). The use of the Section 7520 rate for the month in which the gift was completed, or in either of the previous two months, is required. It is important to calculate the present values using the highest of these three Section 7520 rates. Generally speaking, the higher the Section 7520 rate, the lower is the value of the annuity and, consequently, the higher is the charitable deduction.
15. Treas. Reg. §1.642(c)-5(c)(2)(i).
16. Treas. Reg. §1.642(c)-5(a)(4).
17. In determining the amount of a charitable contribution to a pooled income fund for purpose of determining the allowable deduction, the value of the remainder interest is generally determined on the basis of the highest rate of return by the fund for any of the three taxable years immediately preceding the taxable year of the fund in which the transfer is made. If the fund has been in existence less than three years, the rate of return is deemed to be equal to the interest rate that is 1 percent less than the highest annual average of the monthly Section 7520 interest rates for the three years preceding the transfer. Generally, the higher the rate of return for the fund, the lower the present value of the charity's remainder interest, and the lower the current charitable deduction.
18. IRC Sec. 642(c)(5).
19. Treas. Reg. §1.664-1(a)(1)(i).
20. IRC Sec. 664(d)(1)(A).
21. IRC Sec. 664(d)(1)(A); Treas. Reg. §1.664-2(a)(5)(ii)(b)).
22. IRC Sec. 664(d)(1)(D).
23. Treas. Reg. §1.664-2(b).
24. IRC Sec. 664(d)(2)(A).
25. IRC Sec. 664(d)(3)(A).
26. IRC Sec. 664(d)(3)(B).
27. Treas. Reg. §1.664-3(c).
28. IRC Sec. 664(d)(2)(D).
29. IRC Sec. 170(f)(2)(b).
30. IRC Sec. 2522(c)(2). See also Treas. Reg. §§1.170A-6(c)(3), 20.2055-2(f)(2)(iv), 20.2055-2(f)(2)(v).
31. See Treas. Reg. §1.507-2(a)(8).
32. IRC Sec. 170(b)(1)(A).
33. IRC Sec. 4966(d)(2).
34. IRC Sec. 4966(d)(2)(B)(i).
35. IRC Sec. 4966(d)(2)(B)(ii).
36. IRC Sec. 170(b)(1)(A).
37. IRC Sec. 170(b)(1)(C).
38. IRC Sec. 170(b)(1)(A).
39. IRC Sec. 170(b)(1)(C).

40. IRC Secs. 4940-4945.
41. IRC Secs. 170(b)(1)(B), 170(b)(1)(D), 170(e)(5).
42. See IRC Sec. 4942(j)(3).
43. See "30 percent limit" below for the exception that applies to gifts of capital gain property for which the donor calculates his deduction using the fair market value without reduction for appreciation. Another exception to the 50 percent rule applies to gifts of capital gain property to public charities, which are limited instead to 30 percent.
44. Note that the gift must be made for *exclusively public purposes.*
45. IRC Secs. 170(b)(1), 170(c)(1), 170(c)(3), 509(a)(2), 509(a)(3).
46. Donor advised funds are specifically defined under I.R.C. Section 4966(c)(2) as a result of the Pension Protection Act of 2006.
47. Private foundations included in this group include private operating foundations, distributing (or conduit) foundations, and pooled fund foundations. A private operating foundation differs from a standard private foundation (i.e., family foundation) in that it must participate in charitable activities instead of just making contributions to other charitable organizations. Traditionally, these types of private foundations operate institutions such as museums, libraries, and historic preservation sites. Distributing foundations, like private operating foundations, must make a certain amount of distributions each year.
48. IRC Sec. 170(b)(1)(E).
49. Treas. Reg. §1.170A-1(c).
50. IRC Sec. 170(b)(1)(C)(iv).
51. IRC Sec. 1222(2).
52. IRC Sec. 170(b)(1)(C)(i).
53. IRC Sec. 170(b)(1)(C)(iii). This reduction must be made *before* the percentage limitations (explained above) are applied.
54. IRC Sec. 170(b)(1)(D).
55. IRC Sec. 170(e)(1)(A); Treas. Reg. §1.170A-4(a)(1).
56. Treas. Reg. § 1.170A-4(b)(1).
57. IRC Sec. 1222(1).
58. IRC Sec. 170(e)(1).
59. IRC Sec. 170(e)(1).
60. IRC Sec. 170(e)(1)(B).
61. See Treas. Reg. §1.170A-4(b)(3)(i).
62. IRC Sec. 170(e)(5).
63. Treas. Reg. §1.170A-1(c)(1).
64. Treas. Reg. §1.1011-2(a)(3); Rev. Rul. 81-163, 1981-1 CB 433.
65. Treas. Reg. §1.170A-5(a)(1).
66. IRS Publication 526.
67. IRC Sec. 170(a)(1). Different rules apply for future interests in tangible personal property, gifts of undivided present interest, and gifts of future interests in real property or intangible personal property. See IRC Sec. 170(a)(3); Treas. Reg. §1.170A-5.
68. IRC Sec. 170(a)(1).
69. IRC Sec. 170(f)(17); Treas. Reg. §1.170A-13(a)(1).
70. Treas. Reg. §1.170A-13(b)(1).
71. *Id.*
72. IRC Sec. 170(f)(8)(A); Treas. Reg. §1.170A-13(f).
73. IRC Sec. 170(f)(8)(B); Treas. Reg. §1.170A-13(f)(2).
74. IRC Sec. 170(f)(8)(C); Treas. Reg. §1.170A-13(f)(3).
75. IRC Sec. 170(f)(8)(D).
76. Treas. Reg. §1.170A-13(b)(3)(i).
77. Treas. Reg. §1.170A-13(c)(2).
78. Treas. Reg. §1.170A-13(c)(5)(iv).
79. Treas. Reg. §1.170A-13(c)(6).
80. Treas. Reg. §1.170A-13(c)(4)(iv)(B).
81. Treas. Reg. §1.170A-13(c)(4)(iii).
82. Treas. Reg. §1.170A-13(c)(7)(ix)(A).
83. IRC Secs. 6662(a), 6662(b)(3).
84. See IRC Sec. 6662(d).
85. IRC Sec. 6662(e)(1)(A).
86. IRC Sec. 6662(h)(2)(A)(i).
87. IRC Sec. 6695A(a)(1).
88. IRC Sec. 6659A(b).
89. IRC Sec. 6695A(c).
90. *The Tools & Techniques of Charitable Planning* (3rd Edition), p. 155 (National Underwriter Company, 2007).
91. *Ibid.*
92. Treas. Reg. §1.170A-4(c)(2)(ii).
93. IRC Sec. 1011(b).
94. Rev. Rul. 78-38.

LIKE-KIND EXCHANGES

CHAPTER 29

WHAT ARE LIKE-KIND EXCHANGES?

In general, when a taxpayer transfers property in exchange for cash or other property, the taxpayer must recognize gain or loss on the transfer.[1] However, there are several areas of the tax law that permit (or require) non-recognition of gains or losses in certain circumstances.

One of the more well-known non-recognition provisions is for like-kind exchanges. When a taxpayer transfers property to another party and, in exchange, receives property that is similar to what was given up, the taxpayer is essentially in the same economic position prior to the exchange. It is viewed as a continuation of the same investment. For that reason, there is no gain or loss recognized on property exchanged for other property that is of "like-kind."

As a result of the non-recognition of the gain or loss, the taxpayer's basis in the new property carries the basis of the transferred property, with certain adjustments. Therefore, the unreported gain or loss is not extinguished or forgotten but merely deferred into the future until the property received in the exchange is finally sold in a taxable transaction. The holding period of like-kind property relinquished in the exchange generally carries over (tacks on) to the holding period of the property that was received.

Transactions involving like-kind property may also include property not of a like-kind. The taxpayer not only receives the similar property but something else "to boot". This so-called "boot" may force the recognition of some or all of the otherwise deferred gain or loss.

Like-kind exchanges only apply to property held for productive use in a trade or business or for investment. Such exchanges are most commonly seen in transfers of real estate, automobiles, and business equipment (machines, computers, furniture, etc.).

As a result of the popularity of the non-recognition rule for like-kind exchanges, different techniques have emerged over the years to allow more taxpayers to participate in a variety of exchanges and meet the like-kind exchange requirements, such as:

- Multiparty exchanges – Like-kind exchanges involving more than two parties to the exchange;
- Deferred (or forward) exchanges – Like-kind exchanges involving the relinquishment of property prior to the receipt of replacement property; and
- Reverse exchanges – Like-kind exchanges involving the purchase of replacement property prior to the sale of the relinquished property.

Realizing that it is sometimes impossible to complete a like-kind exchange of properties at the exact same time, the like-kind exchange rules contain specific time periods during which like-kind property must be identified and obtained by the taxpayer.

Like-kind Exchange Rules under Tax Reform

The 2017 Tax Act limits the nonrecognition treatment provided under Code section 1031 to exchanges of real property that is not held primarily for sale.[2] This provision applies to exchanges occurring after December 31,

2017. An exception exists if either (1) the property involved in the exchange was disposed of on or before December 31, 2017, or (2) the property received in the exchange was received on or before December 31, 2017.[3]

The new rules also provide that real property located within the U.S. and foreign real property are not of a like-kind.[4]

This chapter analyzes the like-kind exchange rules under the old rules. Practitioners should be sure to establish exactly when the exchange occurred to make sure that the old rules apply.

GENERAL RULE FOR LIKE-KIND EXCHANGES

Code section 1031 sets forth the rules for like-kind exchanges of property. The rules, specify a number of requirements, each of which must be followed in order to ensure the applicability of the non-recognition provision. Code section 1031(a)(1) states:

> "No gain or loss shall be recognized on the exchange of property held for productive use in a trade or business or for investment if the property is exchanged for property of like kind which is to be held either for productive use in a trade or business or for investment."[5]

This general rule requiring non-recognition is mandatory, not elective. Therefore, taxpayers with losses built in to the property that will be exchanged would be wise to use the rules in reverse—that is, to ensure that the provisions of this tax law are *not* met.

Example: Stephanie Pressman owns an acre of land in the Philadelphia suburbs that she has held for investment purposes. She originally purchased the land for $50,000 and it is now worth $200,000. Jennifer Lansing owns an investment in five acres of land in rural West Virginia. Jennifer paid $250,000 for the land and it has a fair market value of $200,000. Stephanie and Jennifer agree to exchange their holdings. Stephanie's realized gain of $150,000 is deferred as part of the like-kind exchange, as is Jennifer's realized loss of $50,000. Stephanie will take the West Virginia property with a basis of $50,000 and Jennifer will receive the Philadelphia suburb property with a basis of $250,000. Jennifer could have recognized the $50,000 loss by ensuring that she did not meet the provisions of Code section 1031.

Non-Qualifying Property

The like-kind exchange provisions do not apply to certain types of property. Qualifying property does not include:

1. stock in trade or other property held primarily for sale,[6]
2. stocks, bonds or notes,[7]
3. other securities or evidences of indebtedness or interest,[8]
4. interests in a partnership[9] (unless the partnership has a valid election under Code section 761(a) in effect to be excluded from the application of the partnership rules of Subchapter K),[10]
5. certificates of trust or beneficial interests, or[11]
6. choses in action[12] (choses in action are defined by the Supreme Court as the "infinite variety of contracts, covenants, and promises, which confer on one party a right to recover a personal chattel or a sum of money from another.")[13]

Each party involved in an exchange does not need to treat the transaction as a like-kind exchange. One party could be required to treat the transaction as a like-kind exchange while another falls outside the rules for mandatory application.[14]

Example: Car Lot, Inc. is a dealer in passenger automobiles. Sebro, Inc. is a service business that is looking for a new car for its sole owner, John Sebro. Sebro purchases a new car from Car Lot, Inc. for $30,000. In exchange, Sebro trades-in a five-year old car that has an adjusted basis on Sebro's books of $5,000. Car Lot gives Sebro $8,000 on the trade and credits that amount against the $30,000 purchase price. Sebro pays $22,000 cash for the car. Since Car Lot is a dealer in passenger automobiles, the property is not qualifying property under Code section 1031(a)(2)(A).

However, Sebro is trading business property for business property and since the business has met the like-kind exchange rules, it is required to apply the like-kind exchange provisions and defer recognition of gain.

Property received will also not be considered as property of a like-kind if it is not identified on or before the day which is forty-five days after the date on which the taxpayer transfers the property relinquished in the exchange.[15] Furthermore, the replacement property must be received by the earlier of:

- the day which is 180 days after the date on which the taxpayer transferred the property relinquished in the exchange, or[16]
- the due date (including extensions) for the transferor's tax return for the taxable year in which the transfer of the relinquished property occurs.[17]

The regulations provide that the identification and replacement periods end at midnight of the 45th and 180th days following the relinquishment of the property, respectively.[18]

Example: On December 30, 2015, Highway Realty Partnership, a calendar year partnership, transfers an apartment building to Suburban Properties with the anticipation of having the transfer be treated as a like-kind exchange. In order to comply with the like-kind exchange time requirements, Highway Realty must identify the replacement property no later than midnight on February 14, 2016. The replacement property must be received no later than April 15, 2016, the due date of Highway Realty Partnership's tax return, unless the taxpayer requests an extension of time to file their 2015 tax return. In that case, Highway Realty has until midnight on June 29, 2016, to acquire the replacement property.

Like-Kind Property

So, what exactly is like-kind property? In general, property of a like-kind refers to the nature or character of the property and not to its grade or quality.[19] For example, a used car and a new car are like-kind property.

For the purposes of determining whether the like-kind requirement is satisfied, property can be categorized in three ways:

1. Depreciable tangible personal property
2. Other personal property
3. Real property

Depreciable Tangible Personal Property

Tangible personal property subject to depreciation is considered of a like-kind if the property in question is either of a like class or a like kind.[20] The regulations provide a safe harbor test for determining if property is of a like class. The test involves finding out if there are properties in the same "General Asset Class" or the same "Product Class."

The General Asset Classes are defined in Revenue Procedure 87-56[21] and contain a number of common properties that are used by businesses. The regulations provide that exchanged assets within one of the asset classes 00.11 through 00.28 and 00.4 of Rev. Proc. 87-56 are treated as like-kind property.[22] The following is a list of the General Asset Classes:

- Office furniture, fixtures, and equipment (asset class 00.11)
- Information systems (computers and peripheral equipment) (asset class 00.12)
- Data handling equipment, except computers (asset class 00.13)
- Airplanes (airframes and engines), except those used in commercial or contract carrying of passengers or freight, and all helicopters (airframes and engines) (asset class 00.21)
- Automobiles, taxis (asset class 00.22)
- Buses (asset class 00.23)
- Light general purpose trucks (asset class 00.241)
- Heavy general purpose trucks (asset class 00.242)

- Railroad cars and locomotives, except those owned by railroad transportation companies (asset class 00.25)

- Tractor units for use over-the-road (asset class 00.26)

- Trailers and trailer-mounted containers (asset class 00.27)

- Vessels, barges, tugs, and similar water-transportation equipment, except those used in marine construction (asset class 00.28)

- Industrial steam and electric generation and/or distribution systems (asset class 00.4)[23]

Exchanged property may alternatively be considered of a like-kind if it is in the same Product Class. The Product Class is a four-digit numerical code (the "SIC Code") contained within Division D of the Standard Industrial Classification Manual (the "SIC Manual"). If a property is listed in more than one product class, the property is treated as being listed in any one of those product classes. Note that four digit codes ending in "9" (miscellaneous categories) are not considered a product class for purposes of Code section 1031.[24]

A property may not be classified within more than one General Asset Class or one Product Class. The General Asset Class safe harbor is applied first. If a property is classified within a General Asset Class, it may not also be classified within a Product Class.[25]

Example: Barnum, Inc. trades-in a used BMW passenger car for a brand new Ford pick-up truck. The BMW is considered to be in General Asset Class 00.22 (automobiles) while the Ford is classified as General Asset Class 00.241 (light general purpose trucks). Since the two vehicles are classified within a General Asset Class, they may not also be classified within a Product Class.[26]

Other Personal Property

Since most properties that are exchanged are defined as depreciable tangible personal property or real estate, this is the least used of the three categories. Property that falls into this category includes primarily intangibles (such as patents or copyrights), and collectibles (such as stamps, gems, antiques or coins).

No like classes are provided for intangible personal property. The determination of whether intangible personal property is of a like-kind to other intangible personal property depends on the nature or character of the rights involved and also on the nature or character of the underlying property to which the intangible personal property relates.[27] The goodwill or going concern value of one business is not intangible personal property of a like-kind to the goodwill or going concern value of another business.[28]

Example: Bruce Mailer exchanges the copyright on one novel for the copyright on another novel. These properties are of a like-kind. However, exchanging a copyright on a novel for a copyright on a song is not an exchange of properties of a like-kind.[29]

Real Estate

Real estate is generally considered to be property of a like-kind with any other real estate property.

The regulations even provide an example of a like-kind exchange of real property in the city with a ranch or farm.[30] Also, unimproved real estate is of a like-kind with improved real estate.[31]

Example: Philadelphia Realty Partnership would like to exchange a suburban strip mall complex for an apartment building in the city. Since both properties qualify as real estate, they will be treated as properties of a like-kind.

A leasehold interest represents a lesser ownership than a fee interest in real estate. However, if the lease will exist for a sufficiently long enough period of time, it may be considered to be like-kind property with a fee simple interest. In order to meet the safe-harbor, the lease must last for at least thirty years (including all potential options to extend the term of the lease) to be considered as qualifying like-kind property.[32] A leasehold interest of less than thirty years may only be exchanged for another leasehold interest that extends less than thirty years.

An important point to consider is how international properties are treated under the like-kind exchange rules. Unfortunately for many taxpayers, real estate located in the United States is not considered to be property of a like-kind with property located outside the United States.[33]

Property Held for Productive Use in Trade or Business or for Investment

"Held for productive use in a trade or business or for investment" is not defined in the Code or in the regulations. However, in the past, the IRS has applied the definition of "property used in the trade or business" under Code section 1231(b) for purposes of the like-kind exchange rules. The taxpayer shoulders the burden of proving the property is held for use in a trade or business or for investment. The determination is made at the time of the exchange.

The inclusion of the words "held for" within the general rule for like-kind exchanges implies that there is a time element that may need to be satisfied in order for the like-kind exchange rules to apply. Although there is no holding period outlined in the law, it is clear that property acquired solely for the purpose of executing an exchange is not "held for productive use in a trade or business or for investment."[34]

Example: Phyllis owns a parcel of land (held for investment) that she contracts to sell to Joan. Phyllis agreed that if Joan could find suitable property of a like-kind, Phyllis would exchange her property for Joan's. Joan finds a property that Phyllis agrees to exchange for her land. Phyllis will recognize like-kind exchange treatment on the transaction, but Joan will not. Joan's acquisition of the property was done solely for the purpose of executing an exchange.

Recent commentary from the IRS Office of Chief Counsel provides some insight into what may constitute "held for productive use." In one instance, the IRS looked at aircraft held by a partnership that leased them to a related entity for the purposes of business travel and as a perk for senior executives. In an opinion that was counter to the field examiner's initial finding, the chief counsel's office declared that the aircraft were held for productive use even though the partnership that owned them did not show a profit.[35]

In another aircraft-related case, the chief Counsel's Office declared that aircraft were also held for productive use even though a low percentage of the aircraft's use was for business purposes, noting that types of use alone does not determine the purpose to which the property is being held.[36]

RECEIPT OF BOOT

Code section 1031 only applies to the like-kind property received in an exchange for other like-kind property. If the taxpayer, in addition to receiving like-kind property, receives money or other dissimilar property in the exchange ("boot", i.e., the taxpayer received the like-kind property and cash 'to boot'), gain will be recognized to the extent of (a) any money received plus (b) the fair market value of the boot received in the exchange.[37] However, in a classic "heads I win – tails you lose" ploy, the Code provides that if the transaction results in a loss to the taxpayer and boot is received in the exchange, the loss is not recognized.[38]

Like-kind exchanges rarely involve only property of a like-kind. The values of the exchanged properties will most likely not be identical, causing one party to "make-up" the difference by paying some cash, assuming some liabilities, or providing some other form of non-qualifying property (i.e., property that is not of a like-kind).

Example: Highpoint, Inc. and Crosstown, Inc. each own a piece of machinery (of a like-kind) used in their respective businesses. Highpoint's machine has an adjusted basis of $50,000 and a fair market value of $90,000. Crosstown's machine has an adjusted basis of $40,000 and a fair market value of $80,000. Highpoint agrees to accept Crosstown's machine plus $10,000 cash in exchange for their machine. Highpoint realizes a gain of $40,000 on the exchange ($80,000 value of Crosstown's machine plus $10,000 cash less the $50,000 adjusted basis of the relinquished machine). Highpoint must recognize $10,000 of the $40,000 realized gain because they received $10,000 of cash (boot). Crosstown realizes a gain of $40,000, but recognizes no gain – the gain is deferred since they met the like-kind exchange requirements and did not receive any non-qualifying property to boot.

When a liability is assumed (or property is taken subject to a liability) in an exchange, the liability is treated as boot received by the original debtor.[39] This is because, in the IRS view, the assumption of the original debtor's liability is equivalent to the new owner providing the original owner cash in the exchange to pay off the loan while simultaneously financing this cash by establishing a loan against the property received. This "implied cash transfer" is treated as boot received by the original debtor/owner.

Example: Longpoint Apartments owns a building with an adjusted basis of $500,000 that is valued at $1,700,000. The property currently has a mortgage of $1,000,000, leaving the owner with a net equity of $700,000. Longpoint exchanges the property with Shortfall Apartments, which owns an unencumbered building with a value of $700,000. The amount realized by Longpoint in the exchange is $1,700,000 ($700,000 value of property received plus $1,000,000 of liabilities assumed by Shortfall). The gain realized by Longpoint is $1,200,000 ($1,700,000 amount realized less $500,000 adjusted basis), of which the boot of $1,000,000 must be recognized as gain in the year of the transfer.

If an exchange involves the reciprocal assumption of liabilities, the amount of debt relief may be offset by the amount of liabilities assumed.[40] The amount of debt relief may also be offset by other forms of boot transferred in the exchange (e.g. cash).[41] However, other boot received may not offset boot given in the exchange.[42] Furthermore, it is notable that when the taxpayer *receives* boot, the amount treated as boot cannot be treated as boot in acknowledgment of any liabilities that were assumed, even though no boot was received if the cash were simply used to pay down the liability before the transfer.[43]

Example 1: LKE, Inc. transfers property subject to a $500,000 mortgage in exchange for property subject to a $400,000 mortgage. Since the liability transferred exceeds the liability assumed, the LKE would be in receipt of $100,000 of boot.

Example 2: Same facts as above except that LKE also transfers $100,000 of cash in the exchange. LKE's debt relief is completely offset by the liability assumed plus the cash transferred. Therefore, no boot is received in the transfer and LKE will not be required to report any gain.

Example 3: The other party to the transfer in the above example, ONO, Inc., has relinquished property subject to a $400,000 mortgage and received property subject to a $500,000 mortgage plus $100,000 of cash. ONO can fully offset the $400,000 of debt relief with the $500,000 of liabilities assumed. However, the $100,000 of cash received will still be treated as boot and may force ONO to recognize gain up to this amount on the exchange. Note that this treatment could be avoided by having LKE take the $100,000 of cash and pay down that amount of the liability immediately prior to the transfer. LKE and ONO would then each be assuming $400,000 of liabilities and no boot would be transferred to/from either party.

BASIS RULES

The basis of properties acquired in a like-kind exchange is identical to the basis of the property exchanged with the following adjustments:

- Decreased by the amount of money received.
- Increased by the amount of gain recognized on the like-kind property.
- Increased by the amount of boot transferred (money paid or the basis of the property transferred if other non-qualifying property besides cash was transferred).
- Increased by the amount of gain recognized on non-qualifying property transferred.
- Decreased by the amount of loss recognized on non-qualifying property transferred.[44]

Example: Using the facts included in the Highpoint/Crosstown example, Highpoint's basis in the new machine is $50,000 ($50,000 adjusted basis of relinquished property, reduced by $10,000 cash received, increased by $10,000 gain recognized). Therefore, if Highpoint sells the machine tomorrow for its $80,000 fair market value, the remaining $30,000 of deferred gain would be recognized.

A loss may be recognized in a like-kind exchange where the property transferred in the exchange includes property that is not like-kind.[45]

Example: Assume the facts from the previous example, except instead of using cash in the transaction Crosstown gives up a car with a fair market value of $10,000 and an adjusted basis of $30,000. Crosstown will recognize the $20,000 on the transfer of the car since it is not like-kind property. Crosstown's basis in the machinery will now be $50,000 ($40,000 adjusted basis in relinquished property, increased by the $30,000 basis of boot transferred, decreased by the $20,000 of loss recognized on non-qualifying boot transferred). Note that, for the purposes of the machinery, this is equivalent to the result if Crosstown simply transferred cash to achieve a basis of $50,000 ($40,000 adjusted basis in relinquished property, increased by $10,000 of boot transferred). However, in this situation Crosstown has been able to recognize the unrealized loss on the car as a part of the exchange.

If a taxpayer receives both like-kind property and property that is not like-kind, the basis is allocated first to the non-like-kind property to the extent of its fair market value, and then to the property that is of a like-kind, to the extent of the aggregate basis – the adjusted basis of the relinquished property, decreased by any money received or liabilities assumed, and increased (decreased) by any gain (loss) recognized on the exchange.[46]

Example: Continuing our Highpoint/Crosstown example, if Highpoint receives the car instead of cash, Highpoint will still realize a $40,000 gain on the exchange. Of this amount, $10,000 will be recognized as gain due to the receipt of the car as property not of a like-kind. The aggregate basis of the machine and the car is $60,000 ($50,000 adjusted basis of relinquished property, reduced by $0 cash received, increased by $10,000 gain recognized). The basis is then allocated first to the car, up to its fair market value of $10,000. The remaining $50,000 of basis is allocated to the machine, the like-kind property received in the exchange.

Expenses related to an exchange, such as brokerage fees and commissions, are treated the following way:

1. Deducted from the amount of gain or loss realized in the like-kind exchange
2. Offset against cash payments (boot) received
3. Included in the basis of the property received[47]

EXCHANGES BETWEEN RELATED PERSONS

The like-kind exchange rules provide a limitation on the application of the non-recognition provision in the situation where the parties to an exchange are related. The intention of Congress was to discourage such exchanges where the intent was to reduce or avoid gain recognition on subsequent sales, and to restrict "basis shifting."[48]

Under section 1031(f), if a taxpayer exchanges property with a related person in a transaction to which section 1031 originally applies and within two years of the date of the exchange, the taxpayer or the related party disposes of the property acquired in the exchange, the original gain or loss deferred from the original exchange must be recognized.[49] The gain or loss recognized is taken into account as of the date of the disposition of the property.[50]

Example: William Barson owns an apartment building with an adjusted basis of $300,000. His sister, Flora also owns an apartment building that was left to her by her late uncle. Her adjusted basis in the apartment building is $1,900,000. Both properties are valued at $2,000,000. Flora decides that she does not want to own and manage the property. William thinks that Flora's property has much more upside potential than his but if he were to sell his property, he would realize a $1,700,000 gain. The two decide to exchange properties. One year later, Flora realizes she can't take the stress of being a landlord anymore and sells her property for $2,000,000 and recognizes her $100,000 gain ($2,000,000 proceeds less $1,900,000 basis). By selling the property within two years of the exchange, she automatically triggers the gain to her brother, William, by application of Code section 1031(f). As a result, William will recognize the gain of $1,700,000 that was originally deferred under the like-kind exchange rules.

Of primary importance in the application of these related-party rules is the question of who is considered to be a related person. For purposes of this rule, a related person is defined in the same way as it is under Code section 267(b) and Code section 707(b)(1).[51] The most common application of the related person rule is where members of a family are involved in a transaction.[52] Members of a family include brothers, sisters (whether by the whole or half blood), spouse, ancestors (parents and grandparents) and lineal descendants (children and grandchildren).[53] However, nieces, nephews, aunts, uncles, in-laws, step-parents, step-children and step-grandchildren are not considered members of a family for this purpose.

Example: If William was Flora's nephew, the related party rules would not apply. Flora would recognize the gain on the sale of her property but would not trigger the gain recognition on William's property.

In addition, related parties under sections 267(b) and 707(b)(1) also include:

- A corporation and an individual that owns, directly or indirectly, by or for himself/herself, more than 50 percent of the value of the outstanding stock
- Two corporations that are members of the same controlled group
- A grantor and a fiduciary of any trust
- A fiduciary of a trust and a fiduciary of another trust, if the same person is a grantor of both trusts
- A fiduciary of a trust and a beneficiary of such trust
- A fiduciary of a trust and a beneficiary of another trust, if the same person is a grantor of both trusts
- A corporation and a fiduciary, if more than 50 percent of the value of the outstanding stock is owned, directly or indirectly, by or for the trust or by or for a person who is a grantor of the trust
- An organization to which section 501 applies and which is controlled directly or indirectly by such person or by members of the family of such individual
- A corporation and a partnership if the same persons own more than 50 percent in value of the outstanding stock of the corporation, and more than 50 percent of the capital interest, or the profits interest in the partnership
- A partnership and a person owning more than 50 percent of the capital interest, or the profits interest, in such partnership
- Two partnerships in which the same person owns, directly or indirectly, more than 50 percent of the capital interests or profit interests
- An S corporation and another S corporation if the same persons own more than 50 percent in value of the outstanding stock of each corporation
- An S corporation and a C corporation, if the same persons own more than 50 percent in value of the outstanding stock of each corporation
- Except in the case of a sale or exchange in satisfaction of a pecuniary bequest, an executor of an estate and a beneficiary of such estate

MULTIPARTY EXCHANGES

Like-kind exchanges frequently will involve more than two parties. Three and four parties to an exchange are not an uncommon occurrence.

Example: Lisa owns a building that Matt would like to purchase for cash. Lisa intends to use the proceeds to purchase another building and would prefer to structure the transaction as a like-kind exchange. Nate owns a building that Lisa would like to acquire. A like-kind exchange can be accomplished for Lisa in the following steps:

1. Matt purchases Nate's property for cash.

2. Matt and Lisa exchange their buildings in a transaction that qualifies as a like-kind exchange for Lisa.

Note that Matt would not receive like-kind exchange treatment on the transaction with Lisa since the property was acquired solely for the purpose of the exchange.

Although ultimately, in the final step, this transaction was structured as a basic like-kind exchange, if multiparty exchange structures were not permitted, the like-kind exchange rules would have much less applicability. The transferor of a property would be forced to not only find a person who would like to receive the property but also have property of a like-kind that the transferor wants in return.

FORWARD (DEFERRED) EXCHANGES

A forward (or deferred) exchange is one in which the taxpayer transfers the property now and receives replacement property at a later date. Section 1031 may still apply to such a transaction provided:

1. replacement property is identified within forty-five days of the transfer of the relinquished property ("the identification period"), and

2. replacement property is received by the earlier of the due date of the tax return (including extensions) for the year of the transfer or within 180 days of the transfer of the relinquished property ("the replacement period").

There are no extensions (aside from the tax return due date exception) to these time constraints. If the replacement property is either identified or received after the applicable respective time periods, the like-kind rules will not apply and gain or loss must be recognized on the transaction.[54]

Replacement property must be identified as such in either:

1. a written agreement covering the exchange that is signed by all parties before the end of the identification period; or

2. a written document signed by the taxpayer and hand delivered, mailed, faxed, or otherwise sent before the end of the identification period to:

   a. a person involved in the exchange (such as an intermediary, escrow agent or title company) other than the taxpayer, a related party, or the agent of the taxpayer; or to

   b. the person obligated to transfer the replacement property to the taxpayer (regardless of whether that person is a related party or an agent of the taxpayer).[55]

More than one property may be identified as replacement property. However, the maximum number of properties that may be identified is either three properties of any fair market value, or any number of properties, as long as the aggregate fair market value of the properties does not exceed 200 percent of the fair market value of the relinquished properties as of the date of the transfer.[56]

If more than the allowable number of properties is identified (i.e., neither of the prior paragraph requirements are satisfied), then no replacement properties will be treated as identified unless the replacement property is acquired before the end of the identification period, or identified before the end of the identification period and obtained before the end of the replacement period, the value of such property being at least 95 percent of the aggregate fair market value of all identified properties.[57]

The identification of a property as replacement property may be revoked before the end of the identification period in a written amendment to the original agreement that is sent to all parties to the agreement, or in an additional written document of revocation sent to the person to whom the original identification was sent.[58]

Replacement property will meet the time limitations if it is received before the end of the replacement period and is substantially similar to the identified property.[59]

Due to the complexities of transferring property before replacement property is identified, forward exchanges (as well as reverse exchanges, which will be discussed later) often involve more than two parties in the exchange. Taxpayers will frequently rely on "intermediaries" to ensure like-kind exchange treatment.

An intermediary will typically arrange to sell the taxpayer's property and purchase replacement property to exchange with the taxpayer. This arrangement will be treated as a like-kind exchange if the intermediary is a "qualified intermediary[60] and the taxpayer is not in constructive receipt of the proceeds on the sale of the relinquished property.

Avoiding Constructive Receipt

It is important in a deferred exchange that the taxpayer not be in constructive receipt of the proceeds of the sale during the process (i.e., after the sale but before the subsequent purchase).[61] A taxpayer is in constructive receipt of money or other property at the time that the taxpayer receives economic benefit from it, such as when it is credited to the taxpayer's account, set apart for the taxpayer, or otherwise made available so that the taxpayer may draw upon it at any time or may draw upon it at any time if notice of intention to draw is given.[62] The taxpayer avoids the constructive receipt rules as long as substantial restrictions must be placed on the taxpayer's control of the receipt of the funds or property, and continues to *not* be in constructive receipt unless and until the restrictions lapse, expire or are waived.[63]

Usually, an escrow account will be established to hold the proceeds from the sale of the relinquished property to meet the prior paragraph requirements for avoiding constructive receipt. If the escrow account is a "qualified escrow account," the taxpayer will not be in constructive receipt of the proceeds. A qualified escrow account is an escrow account wherein:

1. the escrow holder is not the taxpayer, a related party, or an agent of the taxpayer, and

2. the escrow agreement expressly limits the taxpayer's rights to receive, pledge, borrow, or otherwise obtain the benefits of the cash or cash equivalent held in the escrow account.[64]

A qualified trust may be used in place of a qualified escrow account provided the trust agreement expressly limits the taxpayer's rights to receive, pledge, borrow or otherwise obtain the benefits of the cash or cash equivalent held by the trustee, and the trustee is not the taxpayer, a related party, or an agent of the taxpayer.[65]

A qualified intermediary (QI) is not considered to be an agent of the taxpayer.[66] A QI is a person who:

1. is not the taxpayer, a related party, or already an agent of the taxpayer; and

2. enters into a written agreement with the taxpayer (the "exchange agreement") and, as required by the exchange agreement, acquires the relinquished property from the taxpayer, transfers the relinquished property, acquires the replacement property and transfers the replacement property to the taxpayer.[67]

Example: Albert Trammell wants to sell his office building. The adjusted basis of the building is $600,000 and it is worth $1,100,000. Lee Sheffield wants to buy Albert's office building. Linda Gomez wants to sell her apartment complex for $900,000. QI, Inc. is a qualified intermediary who is not a disqualified person (a related party or an agent of the taxpayer). The following steps fulfill the requirements necessary to ensure that Albert Trammell receives like-kind exchange treatment on the transaction:

Step 1 – On April 1, Albert enters into an agreement to sell his office building to Lee for $1,100,000. The closing is set for May 5. (Note: Lee does not care to or want to participate in a like-kind exchange).

Step 2 – On April 29, Albert enters into an exchange agreement with QI, Inc. The exchange agreement expressly limits his rights to receive, pledge, borrow or otherwise obtain the benefits of money or other property held by QI in a qualified escrow account. In the exchange agreement, Albert assigns to QI all of his rights in the agreement with Lee. Albert notifies Lee of the assignment to QI.

Step 3 – On May 5, Albert executes and delivers to Lee a deed conveying the office building to him. In return, Lee pays $1,100,000 to QI, Inc., which is placed into the qualified escrow account.

Step 4 – On June 10, Albert identifies Linda's apartment building as replacement property and delivers to QI, Inc. a written document that states the identification.

Step 5 – On July 17, Albert enters into an agreement with Linda to purchase the apartment building from Linda for $900,000. Albert then assigns his rights to QI and notifies Linda of the assignment in writing.

Step 6 – On August 21, QI pays $900,000 from the qualified escrow account to Linda who then transfers the deed conveying the apartment building to Albert. QI disburses the remaining $200,000 to Albert.

Result – Albert receives like-kind exchange treatment on the transfer of his office building to Lee in exchange for Linda's apartment building. His realized gain on the transfer is $500,000 ($1,100,000 amount realized less $600,000 adjusted basis). Since Albert received $200,000 of cash (boot), he will recognize $200,000 of the realized gain. His basis in the apartment building will be $600,000 (thus deferring the remaining $300,000 of gain while acquiring the replacement building worth $900,000).

REVERSE EXCHANGES

Forward or deferred exchanges refer to a transaction where a taxpayer relinquishes a property and subsequently identifies and receives replacement property. A reverse exchange, on the other hand, occurs in 'reverse' order - the replacement property is obtained before the relinquished property is transferred. Unfortunately, the regulations do not specifically cover this type of transaction.

Revenue Procedure 2000-37 added certain safe harbor procedures for reverse exchanges. In particular, a taxpayer who wishes to use a reverse exchange can employ an intermediary (similar to a qualified intermediary) in the form of an "exchange accommodation titleholder" (EAT). The EAT will not be treated as the taxpayer's agent.

In general, for a like-kind exchange to be effective, the taxpayer may not receive the replacement property before the relinquished property is transferred. However, if properly structured, an EAT, and not the taxpayer, will be considered the owner of the replacement property. The transfer of title by the EAT to the taxpayer will then be postponed until after the taxpayer transfers the relinquished property, completing the exchange.

The IRS will treat an EAT as the beneficial owner of the relinquished and replacement property if the property is held in a "Qualified Exchange Accommodation Arrangement" (QEAA). Property is held in a QEAA when each of the following five requirements are met:

1. *Ownership Requirement* – The EAT must possess qualified indicia of ownership of the transferred property during the time it is held by the EAT. The EAT must be a person other than the taxpayer or a disqualified person (a related party or an agent of the taxpayer). The EAT must be subject to federal income tax or be a partnership or S corporation owned more than 90 percent by persons subject to income tax.[68]

   Qualified indicia of ownership must be held by the EAT at all times from acquisition until ultimate transfer. Qualified indicia of ownership are either (1) legal title; (2) beneficial ownership under applicable principles of commercial law (e.g. a contract for deed); or (3) ownership of an interest in an entity that is disregarded as separate from its owner for federal income tax purposes, if the entity is the property's legal or beneficial owner.[69]

2. *Intent Requirement* – At the time the ownership is transferred to the EAT, the taxpayer must have a bona fide intent that the transferred property be held by the EAT as either replacement or relinquished property in an exchange that is intended to qualify for non-recognition of gain or loss under section 1031.[70]

3. *QEAA Requirement* – The taxpayer must enter into a written qualified exchange accommodation agreement with the EAT within five days following the transfer of property to the EAT. The terms of the agreement must specify that the EAT is holding the property for the benefit of the taxpayer in order to facilitate an exchange under section 1031 and Revenue Procedure 2000-37, that the EAT will be treated as the beneficial owner of the property for all federal income purposes, and that the income tax attributes of the property will be reported on the income tax returns of the taxpayer and the EAT as appropriate.[71]

4. *Identification of Relinquished Property Requirement* – Within the forty-five days following the transfer of qualified indicia of ownership of replacement property to the EAT, the taxpayer must identify relinquished property in a manner similar to the identification requirement under the rules for deferred exchanges.[72]

5. *Time of Transfer Requirement* – There are two separate 180 day time limits for the completion of the exchange. The first is that the length of time any one piece of property may be held in a QEAA by an EAT is 180 days regardless of whether it is the relinquished or replacement property.[73] Therefore, the longest time period that any relinquished or replacement property can be owned by the EAT is 180 days.

   The second time limit is a 180-day "combined time period" that the EAT may hold both replacement and relinquished property.

Example: Oceanside, Inc. enters into a reverse exchange by relinquishing property to an EAT. The EAT holds qualified indicia of ownership for 30 days during which time Oceanside identifies a like-kind replacement property and has the EAT obtain the property. The EAT transfers the replacement property to Oceanside (ostensibly completing the exchange for Oceanside), and now holds only the relinquished property. The EAT may continue to hold such property for up to 150 days before the relinquished property must be transferred to a new owner.

FREQUENTLY ASKED QUESTIONS

Question – How are like-kind exchanges reported for tax purposes?

Answer – Taxpayers involved in a like-kind exchange must complete and file Form 8824 in the year of the exchange.

Question – If a taxpayer acquires a property in a like-kind exchange and subsequently dies, is the deferred gain required to be recognized in the year of death?

Answer – No. The deferred gain would escape income tax just as if the taxpayer had held the relinquished property at the time of his death. Further, the property held at death would be entitled to a step-up in basis to its fair market value as of the date of the taxpayer's death.

Question – If a taxpayer acquires a property in a like-kind exchange and subsequently uses the property as a personal residence, can the gain exclusion rules of section 121 be used to effectively remove the deferred gain from taxation?

Answer – Yes, but with special rules. Ordinarily, a taxpayer must use and occupy a property as a personal residence for two of the last five years in order to avail themselves of the section 121 gain exclusion rules. However, a property that was acquired by a taxpayer who did not recognize gain under the like-kind exchange rules must hold the property for five years (in addition to meeting all of the other requirements of section 121) in order to qualify for the gain exclusion on the sale of a personal residence.

Question – When should the like-kind exchange rules be avoided?

Answer – Taxpayers may want to avoid the mandatory application of the like-kind exchange rules under the following circumstances:

- The property has an unrealized loss that would benefit the taxpayer by realizing the loss (this is normally the case with automobiles used in a trade or business).
- The taxpayer has losses in the current year (or carryovers into the current year) that can be utilized to absorb the gain on the sale of the property.
- The gain is passive under Section 469 and would be offset by current and suspended passive activity losses.
- The taxpayer anticipates that their personal tax rate will increase in future years and the payment of the tax on the gain in the current year would be more beneficial than if the gain were deferred.

Question – How might a taxpayer avoid the application of the like-kind exchange rules?

Answer – A desire to avoid the like-kind exchange rules often occurs with automobiles that are subject to luxury auto limitations. The luxury auto limitations slow down depreciation to a point that the actual value of the car may be declining more rapidly than the taxpayer can claim depreciation. As a result, a taxpayer who wants to purchase a new car would be wise to sell the used car to a third party and recognize the loss instead of trading in the used car in a transaction with the dealer of the new car.

There are many requirements for a like-kind exchange to occur. Willfully failing any of the requirements will create the opportunity to recognize gain or loss on the transaction.

Question – Do states follow the like-kind exchange rules?

Answer – Taxpayers need to review their individual state tax laws to determine if their state allows for the non-recognition of gain and loss on transactions involving like-kind property. While many do, some only classify transactions involving like-kind property in their state as a valid non-recognition event. For example, real estate in one state transferred for real estate in a neighboring state will generally qualify for like-kind treatment for federal purposes but may fail the state requirement since the new property is in a different state.

See Figures 29.1 and 29.2 for worksheets for single asset like-kind exchanges.

CHAPTER ENDNOTES

1. IRC Sec. 1001.
2. IRC Sec. 1031(a)(1).
3. IRC Sec. 1031(a)(2).
4. IRC Sec. 1031(h).
5. IRC Sec. 1031(a)(1).
6. IRC Sec. 1031(a)(2)(A).
7. IRC Sec. 1031(a)(2)(B).
8. IRC Sec. 1031(a)(2)(C).
9. IRC Sec. 1031(a)(2)(D).
10. IRC Sec. 1031(a)(2).
11. IRC Sec. 1031(a)(2)(E).
12. IRC Sec. 1031(a)(2)(F).
13. *Sheldon v. Sill*, 49 U.S. 441 (1850).
14. Rev. Rul. 75-292, 1975-2 CB 333.
15. IRC Sec. 1031(a)(3)(A).
16. IRC Sec. 1031(a)(3)(B)(i).
17. IRC Sec. 1031(a)(3)(B)(ii).
18. Treas. Reg. § 1.1031(a)-2(b)(1).
19. 1987-2 CB 674.
20. Treas. Reg. § 1.1031(a)-2(b)(2).
21. Treas. Reg. § 1.1031(a)-2(b)(2)(i) through (xiii).
22. Treas. Reg. § 1.1031(a)-2(b)(3).
23. Treas. Reg. § 1.1031(a)-2(b)(1).
24. See Priv. Ltr. Rul. 200241013.
25. Treas. Reg. § 1.1031(a)-2(c)(1).
26. Treas. Reg. § 1.1031(a)-2(c)(2).
27. Treas. Reg. § 1.1031(a)-2(c)(3) Examples (1) and (2).
28. Treas. Reg. § 1.1031(a)-1(c).
29. Treas. Reg. § 1.1031(a)-1(b).
30. Treas. Reg. §§ 1.1031(a)-1(c).
31. IRC Sec. 1031(h)(1).
32. Rev. Rul. 75-291, 1975-2 C.B. 332.
33. IRC Sec. 1031(b).
34. IRC Sec. 1031(c).
35. CCA 201601011 (Aug. 24, 2015).
36. CCA 201605017 (Oct. 19, 2015).
37. Treas. Reg. § 1.1031(d)-2.
38. Treas. Reg. § 1.1031(b)-1(c).
39. Treas. Reg. § 1.1031(d)-2.
40. Treas. Reg. § 1.1031(d)-2.
41. Treas. Reg. § 1.031(d)-2 Example (2)(b).
42. IRC Sec. 1031(d).
43. Treas. Reg. § 1.1031(d)-1(e).
44. IRC Sec. 1031(d).
45. Rev. Rul. 72-456, 1972-2 CB 468.
46. Senate Committee Print and Conference Committee Report to P.L. 101-239.
47. IRC Sec. 1031(f)(1).
48. *Id.*
49. IRC Sec. 1031(f)(3).
50. IRC Sec. 267(b)(1).
51. IRC Sec. 267(c)(4).
52. IRC Sec. 1031(a)(3).
53. Treas. Reg. § 1.1031(k)-1(c).
54. Treas. Reg. § 1.1031(k)-1(c)(4)(i).
55. Treas. Reg. § 1.1031(k)-1(c)(4)(ii).
56. Treas. Reg. § 1.1031(k)-1(c)(6).
57. Treas. Reg. § 1.1031(k)-1(d).
58. Treas. Reg. § 1.1031(k)-1(g)(4).
59. Treas. Reg. § 1.1031(k)-1(f)(1).

60. Treas. Reg. § 1.1031(k)-1(f)(2).
61. *Id.*
62. Treas. Reg. § 1.1031(k)-1(g)(3)(ii).
63. Treas. Reg. § 1.1031(k)-1(g)(3)(iii).
64. Treas. Reg. § 1.1031(k)-1(g)(4)(i).
65. Treas. Reg. § 1.1031(k)-1(g)(4)(iii).
66. Rev. Proc. 2000-37 § 4.02(1).
67. *Id.*
68. Rev. Proc. 2000-37 § 4.02(2).
69. Rev. Proc. 2000-37 § 4.02(3).
70. Rev. Proc. 2000-37 § 4.02(4).
71. Rev. Proc. 2000-37 § 4.02(5).
72. Rev. Proc. 2000-37 § 4.02(6).
73. IRC Sec. 121(d)(10).

Figure 29.1

DETERMINING GAIN OR LOSS		
1. Fair market value of qualifying property received	________	
2. Fair market value of other property (boot) received	+________	
3. Cash (boot) received	+________	
4. Net indebtedness relief associated with properties exchanged (net debt relief/boot)	+________	
5. Total consideration received (sum of lines 1 through 4)		________
6. Original cost or other basis of properties surrendered	________	
7. Accumulated depreciation of property surrendered	–________	
8. Adjusted basis (line 6 less line 7)		–________
9. Lesser of cash surrendered or line 4		–________
10. Gain or loss realized (line 5 less lines 8 and 9 – if a loss, skip next section)	________	
DETERMINING BOOT RECEIVED		
11. Indebtedness associated with property transferred (debt relief/boot)	________	
12. Indebtedness associated with property received	–________	
13. Cash surrendered	–________	
14. Fair market value of other property (boot) surrendered	–________	
15. Net boot received (line 11 less lines 12 through 14 but not less than zero)		________
16. Fair market value of other property (boot) received		+________
17. Cash received		+________
18. Boot received (sum of lines 15 through 17)		________
DETERMINING GAIN RECOGNIZED		
19. Gain recognized (Lesser of line 10 or 18)		________

Figure 29.2

DETERMINING BASIS OF PROPERTY RECEIVED			
1. Adjusted basis of qualifying property surrendered	______		
2. Adjusted basis of other property (boot) surrendered	+______		
3. Total adjusted basis of property surrendered (sum of lines 1 and 2)		______	
4. Cash surrendered and notes given		+______	
5. Indebtedness associated with property received		+______	
6. Gain recognized (line 19 from Figure 29.1)		+______	
7. Gain recognized on other property (boot) surrendered		+______	
8. (sum of lines 3 through 7)			______
9. Cash received			–______
10. Indebtedness associated with property surrendered			–______
11. Loss recognized on other property (boot) surrendered			–______
12. Aggregate basis of all properties received (line 8 less lines 9 through 11)			______
DETERMINING BASIS OF NON-RECOGNITION PROPERTY RECEIVED			
13. Aggregate basis of all properties received (from line 12)		______	
14. Fair market value of other property (boot) received		–______	
15. Basis of non-recognition property received (line 13 less line 14)		______	

PLANNING FOR THE SALE OR EXCHANGE OF ASSETS

CHAPTER 30

INTRODUCTION

When a taxpayer sells an asset, it could very well represent one of the single biggest sources of income the taxpayer will ever report in a lifetime. On the flip side, sales of assets often yield losses that—for income tax purposes—may be available to offset other sources of income the taxpayer will have to report. The planning techniques for the sale or exchange of assets can be summarized into three broad categories:

1. Planning for gain deferral

2. Planning for gain exclusion

3. Planning for loss recognition

As mentioned in Chapter 4, the appreciation (or depreciation) of an asset is not reportable in a taxpayer's income until the asset is sold. This ability to time and defer taxation of the asset's appreciation is a powerful tool. If a taxpayer were required to report a stock's (or any other appreciating assets) growth in value each year and pay tax on the appreciation, the ultimate value of the taxpayer's asset would be markedly diminished and the taxpayer could suffer liquidity problems because he would be taxed before actually receiving income to pay the tax.

Example: John Harrington bought 1,000 shares of LISI stock for $10 per share. His $10,000 investment appreciates 10 percent each of the next five years. If John had to pay a 15 percent tax on the appreciation each year (as opposed to paying tax on his gain when the property was ultimately sold), he might be forced to sell a portion of his investment. On the other hand, his investment would be worth $372.38 (approximately 2.5 percent) more at the end of the five years, if he could defer the taxation of the appreciation until the asset is sold.

Pay Tax on Appreciation				
	Beginning	**Appreciation**	**Tax**	**Ending**
Year 1	10,000.00	1,000.00	(150.00)	10,850.00
Year 2	10,850.00	1,085.00	(162.75)	11,772.25
Year 3	11,772.25	1,177.23	(176.58)	12,772.89
Year 4	12,772.89	1,277.29	(191.59)	13,858.59
Year 5	13,858.59	1,385.86	(207.88)	15,036.57
Defer Tax on Appreciation				
	Beginning	**Appreciation**	**Tax**	**Ending**
Year 1	10,000.00	1,000.00	–	11,000.00
Year 2	11,000.00	1,100.00	–	12,100.00
Year 3	12,100.00	1,210.00	–	13,310.00
Year 4	13,310.00	1,331.00	–	14,641.00
Year 5	14,641.00	1,464.10	(696.15)	15,408.95

Most of the time, taxpayers have control over when a taxable event such as a sale or exchange will occur and, therefore, also can time when gain or loss will be reported.

But there are situations in which a taxpayer has no such control and must report a gain or loss regardless of any action, or lack of action:

- Capital gain distributions by mutual funds

- Certain corporate acquisitions or mergers

- Cash received in lieu of fractional shares

- Gains or losses reported by flow-through entities such as S corporations, partnerships, or limited liability companies

Where the taxpayer does control the recognition of the gain or loss, there are a host of income tax planning techniques that can be implemented to possibly defer the gain into future years or possibly even exclude all or part of the gain from taxation altogether.

PLANNING FOR GAIN DEFERRAL

As noted in the previous example, deferring gain from one year to the next is a powerful income tax and financial planning tool. The ability to defer the payment of tax is in essence an interest free loan from Congress. The "magic" of compounding allows for much more wealth to be built by deferring the ultimate payment of taxes. But along with gain deferral come the risks associated with being in the market after a particular security or other asset has appreciated in value. For instance, when Internet stocks were booming in the late 1990s, many investors failed to sell at or near the market peak simply because of the tax consequences they would face. Unfortunately, too many investors rode the wave of Internet stocks up to the crest only to see their paper fortunes vanish.

There are a number of ways planners can help clients achieve a deferral of tax on appreciation:

- Specifically identifying the security being sold
- Electing to use one of the average cost methods for selling mutual funds
- Selling short against the box
- Buying or selling put and call options
- Negotiating an installment sale
- Entering into a like-kind exchange
- Electing involuntary conversion treatment
- Investing in a specialized small business investment company (SSBIC)
- Reinvesting the proceeds from the sale of qualified small business stock into another qualified small business stock
- The use of Opportunity Zones (see Chapter 4)

Identifying the Shares Involved in a Transaction

In many cases, a taxpayer may have purchased multiple lots of the same stock at different times. Each lot carries with it a different cost basis and beginning date for the holding period. When less than a taxpayer's entire investment is sold, the identification of which securities were sold can hold a great deal of significance in determining the amount of the gain or loss.

If the lot from which the shares were sold cannot be adequately identified, the earliest shares are deemed to be sold first.[1] This is the so-called first-in, first-out method (FIFO). But if the shares sold are adequately identified, the FIFO rule does not apply.[2]

Sometimes using the FIFO method will generate the smallest tax bill for the taxpayer. But it is more likely that the FIFO method will create the largest possible gain. When the FIFO method does not generate the smallest gain (or the largest loss), the taxpayer may benefit from specifically identifying the shares that were sold.

A common misconception is that taxpayers are permitted to use an average cost when stock is sold that was acquired at different times. This is not true. The average cost method is only available to sellers of mutual funds (as discussed later in this chapter). Sellers of stock or other securities may only use the FIFO or specific identification methods.

Note that brokers and investment firms are required to report to the Internal Revenue Service, not only the proceeds derived from the sale of securities, but also the cost basis and indicate whether the sale is short or long-term. See Chapter 21 for further information.

For those investors holding the stock certificate that they intend to sell, adequate identification is achieved by delivering the certificate that represents the shares being sold.[3]

If the shares being sold are held by a brokerage, bank or other investment company, the taxpayer must do two things in order to adequately identify the shares that are being sold:

1. At the time of the sale, the taxpayer specifies to the broker or other investment professional the specific security to be sold.

2. Within a reasonable time after the sale, the taxpayer receives written confirmation of the identification of the security that was sold.[4]

Example: Barbara Penney owns two lots of Weber Machines, Inc. stock. The first lot of one hundred shares was purchased twenty years ago for $500. The second lot of one hundred shares was purchased two years ago for $15,000. She wants to sell fifty shares and expects to receive $10,000. If she fails to specifically identify that she is selling fifty shares out of the second lot, she will recognize a gain of $9,750 (proceeds less half of the $500 basis). If she specifically identifies the shares from the second lot, her taxable gain will be only $2,500 (proceeds less half of the $15,000 basis).

In order to satisfy the first requirement, the taxpayer must give specific instructions as to which shares are being sold. This instruction is not required to be in writing. The shares being identified can be referred to by

- the date of purchase;
- the purchase price; or
- the lot itself (e.g. the shares purchased most recently).

This information will mean very little to the broker who will simply sell the number of shares as requested. But this information is precisely what must be confirmed in writing to the taxpayer in order to satisfy the second requirement of adequate identification.

If lots of an identical security are held in separate accounts, the identification of the shares sold is achieved by selling the shares out of the desired account.

Example: The older of Barbara Penney's two lots is held at AAA Financial while the newer lot is held at I-Trade. If she sells the fifty shares out of her I-Trade account, which should constitute adequate identification of the shares that are being sold. No written confirmation would be required.

Sales of Mutual Funds

Like sales of stock and other securities, the basis and holding period is applied to mutual funds on a FIFO basis. Taxpayers may achieve a more tax favored result by specifically identifying the shares of the mutual fund to be sold. The rules for specific identification of mutual fund shares are the same as for stock and securities.

In addition to the FIFO and specific identification methods, mutual fund owners can avail themselves of two other methods for determining cost basis and holding period. Both methods must be elected by the taxpayer on a fund-by-fund basis. Once an election is made with respect to a particular mutual fund, it is irrevocable without the consent of the IRS. The two methods are:

1. the single category average cost method; and

2. the double category average cost method.

Many mutual fund companies automatically calculate a mutual fund holder's gain or loss on the disposition of a portion of the mutual fund using the single category average cost method. This relieves the taxpayer of much of the burden of keeping track of all of the periodic investments as well as the dividend reinvestments that typically occur on a regular basis.

Taxpayers that elect to use the single category average cost method add the cost basis of all the shares held in the mutual fund and divide that total by the number of shares held. The average number is then used as the basis for the shares that were sold.[5]

For purposes of determining the taxpayer's holding period, mutual fund shares are deemed to be sold on a FIFO basis.[6] A quick way to determine if any of the shares that were sold during the year were short-term is to look at the number of shares that remain after the sale. If that number is greater than the number of shares acquired in the previous twelve months (the cut off for long-term holding period), then all of the shares sold should be considered as long-term. Otherwise, some of the shares sold may have a short-term holding period.

Example: Lisa Ramos bought shares in a mutual fund two years ago for $10,000. She has also added $500 per month to the mutual fund for the last twenty-four months. Last year, she also received a $500 dividend from the mutual fund which was reinvested. During the last two years, the mutual fund has done quite well and substantially increased in value. If Lisa uses the FIFO method of allocating basis to the shares that were sold, she would be using her lowest cost shares and generating the highest possible long-term capital gain. If she specifically identifies the more recent purchases as the shares that were sold, her gain would be minimized, but it would be treated as a short-term capital gain. By electing to use the single-category average cost method, Lisa receives the benefit of the mutual fund shares that have been purchased at a higher price by the corresponding increase in the overall average cost. She also treats the entire gain as a long-term capital gain since the holding period is determined on a FIFO basis.

The double category average cost method is an extension of the single category method. Taxpayers who elect to use the double category average cost method will need to calculate two averages. The first average cost is determined for all of the shares that meet the one-year holding period requirement for long-term treatment. Once that average cost number is obtained, the cost basis of the remaining shares are aggregated to determine the average cost for the short-term mutual fund shares.[7]

The second step to the double category average cost method is to identify whether the short-term or long-term shares are being sold. Since two average costs are calculated, it is possible to reduce the gain or report a loss if the short-term shares are sold first. In order to treat the short-term shares as being sold, the taxpayer must specifically identify (using the procedures described in the previous section) that the mutual fund shares being sold are the ones acquired within the last twelve months. Failure to specifically identify the shares being sold as from the short-term group will cause the shares to be treated as sold out of the long-term group first.[8]

Note that there are some flaws with the double category average cost method. First, it must be elected by the taxpayer with the filing of the tax return. This is generally long after the sale occurred. Second, in order to take advantage of selling out of the short-term group, the specific identification rules must be followed, which includes provisions for instructing the broker or mutual fund company *at the time of the sale.* Finally, if the election is made and the shares are not specifically identified as being sold out of the short-term group, the shares will be treated as sold out of the long-term group. The average cost of the long-term group will be less using the double category method than the average cost using the single category method in a rising market environment since the short-term shares will have a higher cost basis.

Figure 30.1

SINGLE-CATEGORY AVERAGING WORKSHEET		
1.	Beginning Basis	____________
2.	Cost of mutual fund share purchases	____________
3.	Reinvested dividends and distributions	____________
4.	Basis adjustments	____________
5.	Total basis (sum of lines 1 through 5)	____________
6.	Number of shares owned before sale	____________
7.	Average basis per share (divide line 5 by line 6)	____________
8.	Number of shares sold	____________
9.	Basis of shares sold (multiply line 7 by line 8)	____________
10.	Total basis before sale (from line 5)	____________
11.	Basis of shares sold (from line 11)	____________
12.	Ending basis	____________

Figure 30.2

DOUBLE-CATEGORY AVERAGING WORKSHEET		
1.	Beginning Basis	________
2.	Cost of mutual fund share purchases	________
3.	Reinvested dividends and distributions	________
4.	Basis adjustments	________
5.	Total basis (sum of lines 1 through 5)	________
6.	Number of shares owned before sale	________
7.	Basis of short-term shares owned before sale	________
8.	Number of short-term shares owned before sale	________
9.	Basis per short-term share (divide line 7 by line 8)	________
10.	Basis of long-term shares owned before sale	________
11.	Number of long-term shares owned before sale	________
12.	Basis per long-term share (divide line 10 by line 11)	________
13.	Number of shares sold	________
14.	Basis of shares sold (multiply line 13 by 9 or 12)	________
15.	Total basis before sale (from line 5)	________
16.	Basis of shares sold (from line 14)	________
17.	Ending basis	________

In order to elect an average cost method, a statement must be attached to the tax return for the first year in which the election is to apply. Once the election is made with respect to a particular mutual fund, it continues to apply until the mutual fund is completely disposed.

Selling Short Against the Box

A short sale is a transaction where an investor sells a stock that they do not own. Essentially what occurs is this: The investor "borrows" the shares from another investor and promises to "repay" the shares at a later time.

A short sale is opened at the time the investor receives the cash for the sale. The short position remains open until the investor closes the position by purchasing or delivering shares of the same stock to cover the short position. An investor who purchases shares to cover the open short position will realize a gain if the price of the stock has decreased and a loss if the price has increased—the exact opposite of traditional investing (buying "long").

If the investor currently owns a stock and opens a short position in the same security, the investor is "selling short against the box." The offsetting positions will ensure that the value of the investor's positions will remain constant. But if the long position has been held for less than one year at the time the short position is opened, or if a long position is acquired while a short position is opened:

1. any gain on the short sale will be treated as a short-term gain; and

2. the holding period for the long position begins when the short position is closed or when the stock is sold.[9]

Example: Ethan Dillworth owns 1,000 shares of Rose Petals, Inc. He initially purchased the shares for $15,000 and they have since grown in value to $60,000 (a $45,000 increase). In order to protect his gain, he decides to sell 1,000 shares short against the box. He opens the short position and receives $60,000 for the short sale. While both the long and short positions are open, his total gain of $45,000 is protected. If the stock falls to $40 per share, he would still have a $45,000 gain—$25,000 on the long position and $20,000 on the short position.

In the above example, the investor was able to protect his overall profit without having to recognize the inherent gain at the time the protective transaction, the short sale, was opened. However, the Taxpayer Relief Act of 1997 created the constructive sale rule to force the recognition of gain on certain transactions that have the effect of neutralizing an investor's potential for further fluctuations in value.

The constructive sale rule applies to transactions involving "appreciated financial positions" that remain open beyond a statutorily determined time. An appreciated financial position is any position with respect to any stock, debt instrument, or partnership interest if there would be gain were such position sold, assigned or otherwise terminated at its fair market value.[10] Therefore, if a short against the box position is opened at a time when the fair market value is less than the investor's basis, the constructive sale rules will not apply.

If the transaction does involve an appreciated financial position, the second test is to determine whether the open position was closed soon enough to avoid the application of the constructive sale rule. A constructive sale will not occur if:

1. the transaction is closed before the end of the thirtieth day after the close of the taxable year;

2. the taxpayer continues to hold the appreciated financial position throughout a sixty-day period beginning on the date the transaction was closed; and

3. the taxpayer does not, at any time during the sixty-day period, reduce his or her risk of loss with respect to the appreciated financial position (such as enter into another short against the box transaction).[11]

Example: Michelle Grattia opened a short against the box transaction on March 15 in order to protect a gain she has in her stock. She closes the short position by purchasing identical shares on January 20 of the following year. As long as she does not limit her risk of loss by opening another protective transaction, no constructive sale exists.

If a constructive sale occurs as a result of not complying with the three above requirements, the taxpayer will recognize the gain as if the position were sold at its fair market value on the date the protective transaction was opened.[12] This is true even though the taxpayer will not know that a constructive sale occurred in the prior year until as late as the end of March of the following year.

A constructive sale results in a deemed sale and immediate repurchase of the appreciated financial position.[13] In addition, the holding period of the appreciated financial position restarts as of the date of the constructive sale.[14] But since the short position is still open, the holding period will only restart upon the closing of the short position that created the constructive sale.[15]

Example: Linda Wellington owns 2,000 shares of stock in Dual Sound, Inc. with a cost basis of $10,000. She has held the stock for over two years. The stock is worth $30,000 when she opens a 2,000-share short position on December 12. On February 10 of the following year, she closes the short position by purchasing 2,000 shares on the open market. Since she failed to close the open short position by January 30, she is deemed to have made a constructive sale as of December 12. She must recognize the $20,000 long-term gain on her tax return. Her basis in the stock becomes $30,000 and the holding period will restart on February 10 when the short position is closed.

Buying or Selling Options

Options give investors the right to purchase or sell a certain number of shares of a particular stock at a stated price within a defined time period. A call option permits the option holder to buy the stock. A put option gives the option holder the right to sell the stock. Options trade on the open market and should not be confused with stock options that are granted by an employer to an employee. These types of stock options are covered in Chapter 27.

Of course for every option holder, there must be an option writer. The option writer is the one who will deliver the stock to the call holder if the call option is exercised or, in the case of a put option, will have the stock delivered to them if the put option is exercised by the put holder.

Each option controls one hundred shares of the underlying stock. An investor who purchases an option will pay a certain price or "premium" to acquire the right to buy or sell stock at a specified or "strike" price within a given time period.

Example: Alan Weiss purchases five call options on TripMaker, Inc. for $1,000 with a strike price of $50. The option expires one month later on August 21. If the company's stock price increases beyond $50 per share, the option is said to be "in the money" and may be exercised by Alan by paying $25,000 (five option contracts at $50 each multiplied by one hundred shares per contract). His total cost to acquire the shares would then be $26,000 ($25,000 stock cost plus $1,000 option cost).

If the option is not exercised by the end of the option contract period, the option is said to expire. The holder is treated as having sold the option as of the expiration date for no proceeds. The loss will be reported as short or long-term depending on the length of time the option was held.

The option may also be sold by the option holder to another party. Any gain or loss must be recognized on the transaction in accordance with the normal capital gain and loss rules.

Writers of put and call options receive the premiums that are paid by the option purchasers (after the various fees and commissions, of course). But no gain or loss is recognized by the option writer until the option is exercised, expires, or is otherwise closed.

Figure 30.3

TAX TREATMENT OF PUT AND CALL OPTIONS

Transaction	Option Holder	Option Writer
Call option is exercised	Basis of call option is added to the cost of the stock. Holding period for the stock begins on the date the option was exercised.	No gain or loss reported on option. Sales proceeds from sale of the stock combined with the proceeds on the sale of the option. Gain or loss from the sale of stock recognized on the date of the exercise.
Call option expires	Option treated as sold for $0 on the expiration date. Short or long-term loss recognized based on holding period of the option.	Short-term gain equal to the proceeds received from the writing of the option recognized on the expiration date. Gain cannot be long-term.
Call option position closed	Proceeds received less the premium paid are treated as a capital gain or loss. Holding period determines whether the gain or loss is long or short-term.	Short-term capital gain or loss recognized based on the difference between the initial amount received and the amount paid to close the transaction. Holding period of option cannot create a long-term gain or loss.
Put option exercised	No gain or loss reported on option. Amount received from the sale of the stock is reduced by the cost of the put option. Holding period of the stock determines long or short-term gain or loss.	No gain or loss reported on option. Basis of stock acquired reduced by the amount received for the put option.
Put option expires	Option treated as sold for $0 on the expiration date. Short or long-term loss recognized based on holding period of the option.	Short-term gain equal to the proceeds received from the writing of the option recognized on the expiration date. Gain cannot be long-term.
Put option position closed	Proceeds received less the premium paid are treated as a capital gain or loss. Holding period determines whether the gain or loss is long or short-term.	Short-term capital gain or loss recognized based on the difference between the initial amount received and the amount paid to close the transaction. Holding period of option cannot create a long-term gain or loss.

Options have the effect of hedging against further gains or losses in a particular stock. For this reason, it is possible to combine puts and call options to "collar" an open stock position and protect the inherent gain without having to sell the stock. Again, the constructive sale rules may apply.

It is clear that an investor who acquires only one-way protection is not treated as having made a constructive sale. For instance, an investor holding an appreciated financial position may purchase a put option to protect against a decline in the stock price. But the investor still may benefit from a further rise in the stock price and, in that case, would simply let the put option expire unexercised or sell the put option before the expiration date. Since only the downside is protected, a constructive sale is not deemed to have occurred.

Although regulations have not been issued on the use of stock options in the area of constructive sales, it is widely believed that buying a put option or writing a call option that is "deep in the money" may be equivalent to selling the stock short. For instance, if a put option is purchased with a strike price of $100 when the stock is trading at $60, the transaction may be treated like a short sale against the box, thereby forcing the application of the constructive sale rule.

If an investor combines put and call options and effectively limits the range of potential gain or loss, the "collar" will likely cause a constructive sale.

Example: Barry Hastings owns 1,000 shares of Kids World, Inc. with a value of $470,000 ($47 per share). Barry purchases ten put options with a strike price of $45 and writes ten call options with a strike price of $50. A collar this tight would be equivalent to a short sale and would likely be treated as a constructive sale.

The United States Treasury is expected to issue regulations dealing with just such a transaction. Commentators believe that a collar that has a spread of at least 20 percent around the current price should not cause a constructive sale. The length of time the collar may exist is also expected to be addressed by future regulations.

Example: If the Treasury does adopt a 20 percent spread rule, Barry (from the previous example) would be able to place a collar on his stock by using a spread of approximately $10. He could accomplish this by adjusting the strike price of the call option up to $55 or the put option down to $40.

Installment Sales

If the terms of the sale of real or personal property call for at least one payment to be made in a tax year later than the year of disposition, the installment sale rules may allow for a deferral of the taxation of the gain until the payment or payments are received.[16]

The taxation of an installment sale is determined by computing a gross profit percentage and applying this percentage to the payments that are received. The gross profit percentage will equal the total of all of the principal payments to be made by the buyer over the term of the installment sale, plus any liabilities assumed by the buyer, less the seller's adjusted basis in the property that was sold.

Each payment received under an installment sale agreement will typically consist of three parts:

1. Nontaxable recovery of basis

2. Capital gain

3. Interest

Interest is involved in any installment sale whether it is stated in the sales agreement or not. Agreements that fail to provide for interest (or do not provide for a rate of interest which is at least as high as the applicable federal rate) on the deferred payments will have imputed interest. Interest income is reportable by the seller of the property and thereby reduces the amount that is taxed at the more favorable capital gains rates. Likewise, the purchaser reports interest expense and should properly account for the true purchase price of the property.

When property is sold subject to an installment sale, and the parties to the contract later agree to change the stated purchase price, only the gross profit on remaining payments is recomputed.[17]

Example: 122 Downtown Associates contracts to sell a building on December 12, 2019.

Under the terms of the agreement, half of the purchase price is to be paid at the closing and the remaining half in June 2020. 122 Downtown Associates will realize a $100,000 gain upon the disposition. Without considering the application of other rules dealing with depreciation recapture or imputed interest, the taxpayer would recognize $50,000 of gain in 2019 and $50,000 of gain in 2020.

The application of the installment sale rules is automatic. Taxpayers who wish to recognize the entire gain in the year of disposition may elect out of the installment sale method of reporting by making such election on a timely filed return (including extensions) in the year of disposition.[18]

Installment sale reporting is not permitted for dispositions of:

1. real or personal property by dealers;[19]
2. personal property considered inventory;[20]
3. personal property under a revolving credit plan;[21] or
4. stock or securities traded on an established securities market.[22]

The installment sale method may not be used if the transaction generates a loss. Also, any portion of a sale which generates ordinary income due to the recapture of depreciation may not be deferred.[23] Installment sales are also covered in Chapter 3, Gross Income.

Like-kind Exchanges

When a taxpayer transfers property to another party and, in exchange, receives property that is similar to what was given up, the taxpayer is essentially in the same position prior to the exchange. It is viewed as a continuation of the same investment. For that reason, the tax law requires that no gain or loss be recognized on property exchanged for other property that is of "like-kind."

Like the rule for installment sales, the rule requiring non-recognition on like-kind exchanges is mandatory, not elective. Therefore, taxpayers with losses built in to the property that will be exchanged would be wise to use the rules in reverse—that is, to ensure that the provisions of this tax law are *not* met. Like-kind exchanges are fully covered in Chapter 29.

Electing Involuntary Conversion Treatment

When a taxpayer's property is destroyed, stolen, seized, condemned, or is under a threat of condemnation, an election is available under Code section 1033 that allows for gain deferral. In order to fully defer the gain, a taxpayer must purchase replacement property (or restore the original property) within a given time period. The replacement property must be similar or related in service or use to the original property that was subject to the involuntary conversion. In addition, the full amount realized must be reinvested in the replacement property. This amount usually is based on the insurance or condemnation proceeds received.

Gain must be recognized to the extent that the taxpayer receives unlike property or retains any portion of the amount realized, unless the replacement property was financed with new debt at the time of purchase.

The period of time permitted to restore or replace the original property begins on the date the property is disposed or the date of the threat or imminence of requisition or condemnation of the property, whichever is earlier.[24] The replacement period ends two years from the end of the tax year in which a gain is realized.[25] Longer replacement periods are in place for condemned real estate (three years), livestock (four years), a principal residence (four years), and property destroyed in the New York Liberty Zone (five years). An application for extension of time to replace property may be filed with the IRS based on reasonable cause.[26]

The taxpayer's basis in the new property will be the identical to the basis in the old property if all of the gain is deferred under these rules. Note that the involuntary conversion rules only apply to the deferral of gains. Losses are immediately recognized.

A taxpayer may replace involuntarily converted property with corporate stock that owns qualifying property.[27] Though rarely used, it is important to note that both the taxpayer's basis in the corporate stock and the corporation's basis in the assets must be reduced by the amount of gain deferred (cost of stock or fixed asset less gain deferral). This ensures the continued potential for double taxation which exists in a corporate environment.

Involuntary conversions stemming from presidentially declared disaster areas are granted additional relief under these rules. Replacement property may be any tangible property held for productive use in a trade or business.[28] It need not be similar in use or of a like-kind.

Specialized Small Business Investment Companies (SSBICs)

As a general rule, when an investor sells stock of a publicly traded company, gain must be recognized in the year of the sale. In 1993, an exception was created if taxpayer elects to rollover the sales proceeds into the purchase of common stock or a partnership interest in a specialized small business investment company (SSBIC) within a sixty-day period beginning on the date of the sale of the publicly traded securities. If the taxpayer fails to reinvest the entire amount of sales proceeds, gain is required to be recognized on any un-reinvested portion.[29]

A SSBIC is any partnership or corporation which is licensed by the Small Business Administration under Section 301(d) of the Small Business Investment Company Act of 1958.[30] SSBICs are few in number, often require large investments, and are typically very risky investments. A list of SSBICs can be found at www.sba.gov/inv/. But the lists include small business investment companies (SBIC) as well as *specialized* small business investment companies. Only those companies that are treated as SSBICs qualify for the rollover.

Only individuals and C corporations may defer gain by investing in a SSBIC. The rollover provisions are not available to estates, trusts, partnerships, LLCs, or S corporations.[31]

Individuals may defer up to $50,000 of gain per year not to exceed a lifetime maximum of $500,000.[32] For C corporations, the annual limit is $250,000 of gain, not to exceed $1,000,000 in all preceding years.[33]

The cost basis of an investment in a SSBIC must be reduced by any gain not recognized as a result of the election to rollover the gain.[34] But since 50 percent of the gain on the sale of an SSBIC investment may be excluded under Code section 1202, the basis is not reduced for the purpose of determining the gain eligible for exclusion.[35] That is, only the increase in value associated with the SSBIC is eligible for the exclusion, not the gain deferred under this election.

The election to defer recognition of the gain on the sale of publicly traded security must be made on Form 1040, Schedule D on or before the due date of the tax return for the year of the sale. The taxpayer must also attach a statement showing:

1. how the non-recognition was calculated;

2. the SSBIC in which the sales proceeds were invested;

3. the date the SSBIC stock or partnership interest was purchased; and

4. the basis of the SSBIC interest.[36]

Reinvesting Proceeds From the Sale of Qualified Small Business Stock into another Qualified Small Business Stock

All non-corporate taxpayers may elect to roll over a gain from the sale of "qualified small business stock" (QSBS) if:

1. the QSBS was held for more than six months; and

2. another QSBS is acquired during a sixty-day period following the date of sale.[37]

Like the rule for SSBIC rollovers, gain is only recognized to the extent that the amount realized on the initial sale exceeds the cost of the replacement QSBS.[38]

Qualified small business stock is stock originally issued after August 10, 1993 by a C corporation with aggregate gross assets of less than $50 million at any time from August 10, 1993 through the issuance of the stock.[39]

The business must also meet an active business requirement.[40] This requirement states that 80 percent or more of the business assets are used in one or more businesses other than certain excluded businesses.[41] Excluded businesses include certain personal service activities, banking and other financial services, farming, mineral extraction businesses, and hotels and restaurants.[42]

If a rollover occurs and the taxpayer elects the gain deferral treatment, the basis in the newly acquired QSBS is reduced by the amount of deferred gain.[43] The holding period for the newly acquired QSBS will include the holding period of the stock sold. But the newly acquired QSBS must be held for six months before another gain deferral may be elected.

Note that the definition of QSBS for purposes of the rollover of gain is identical to the definition of QSBS for purposes of the 50 percent gain exclusion, discussed below.

Example: Michael Rice invests $250,000 into Falcon Manufacturing Corp. on January 10, 2010. He sells the stock for $400,000 on July 26, 2020 realizing a $150,000 gain. On September 7, 2020 he purchases stock in Hale Manufacturing Corp. for $350,000. Both investments in Falcon and Hale qualify as QSBS. Michael must recognize $50,000 of the $150,000 gain since only $350,000 of the total sales proceeds was reinvested. He may elect to defer the remaining $100,000. If he does so, his basis in Hale would be $250,000. His holding period for determining long-term gain or loss on Hale will begin on January 10, 2020. But for the purpose of a further rollover under Code section 1045 or an exclusion of gain under Code section 1202, his holding period beings on September 7, 2020.

PLANNING FOR GAIN EXCLUSION

What is even better than deferring a gain into a future year? The answer is simple—excluding the gain from income forever. Obviously there are many fewer options that allow a taxpayer to perpetually exclude a gain from tax, but the following do exist and are discussed in detail below:

- Selling a personal residence
- Selling qualified small business stock held for more than five years (50 percent exclusion)
- Contributing appreciated property to charity

Selling a Personal Residence

The sale of a personal residence will often represent the single largest transaction a taxpayer will ever have. Since housing values have traditionally increased over time, the transaction is likely to result in a capital gain. Much of that gain may escape federal income taxation due to the special rules under Code section 121. The current rules are:

1. A taxpayer may exclude up to $250,000 of realized gain from the sale of a principal residence.[44]
2. Married taxpayers filing a joint return may exclude up to $500,000 of realized gain.[45]
3. The realized gain is determined by subtracting the taxpayer's adjusted basis (defined below) from the net selling price of the property.
4. If the transaction results in a net loss, the loss is not deductible.[46]

A principal residence is determined by all facts and circumstances available.[47] A residence may be a house, condominium, houseboat, trailer, cooperative apartment, etc.

Multiple Residences

If a taxpayer owns more than one residence, the determination of which residence is the principal residence is also made based on facts and circumstances.[48] The property used the majority of the time will generally be considered the principal residence. But other factors that are considered include:

- the taxpayer's place of employment;
- the principal place of abode of the taxpayer's family members;
- the address listed on the taxpayer's federal and state tax returns, driver's license, automobile registration, and voter's registration card;
- the taxpayer's mailing address for bills and correspondence;
- the location of the taxpayer's banks; and
- the location of religious organizations and recreational clubs with which the taxpayer is affiliated.[49]

In order to qualify for the gain exclusion, a taxpayer must meet the following three tests:

- *Ownership test* – the taxpayer must have owned the residence for at least two of the five years before the sale or exchange.[50]

- *Use test* – the taxpayer must have occupied the residence as a principal residence for periods adding up to two years within the five-year period ending on the date of the sale.[51]

- *One sale in two years test* – the taxpayer must not have used the exclusion for any residence sold or exchanged during the two-year period ending on the date of the current sale.[52]

For purposes of the use test, a short, temporary absence is generally counted as a period of use.[53] But a one-year sabbatical leave is not considered a short, temporary absence.[54]

Calculation of Basis

The calculation of a taxpayer's adjusted basis in a principal residence requires an analysis of the previous settlement sheet from the purchase of the principal residence that has now been sold. Certain items such as real estate taxes and points represent items of deduction in the year of purchase and should not be included in basis.

Any improvements that were made to the property during the period of ownership should also be added to the taxpayer's adjusted basis. But failure to maintain appropriate records could result in a larger gain being reported than necessary.

Example: Stacy Whitten, a single taxpayer, purchased her first home in 2008 for $200,000. A review of her settlement sheet from the purchase of that home shows closing costs of $4,000 that could be capitalized into the basis of her home. In 2012, she finished her basement at a cost of $10,000. Her total adjusted basis in her home is $214,000 when she sells her home in 2020. She receives $420,000 for her home and pays $16,000 of closing costs, including the sales commission. Her realized gain is $190,000. Since she qualifies for gain exclusion of up to $250,000, the entire gain is not taxed for federal income tax purposes.

Partial Gain Exclusion

Prior to May 7, 1997, gains were not excluded from income. Rather, there was a gain deferral subject to certain limitations. The gain deferral only applied if the proceeds were reinvested into a new residence. Note that there is no longer a requirement for the proceeds from the sale of a principal residence to be reinvested. This creates a potential windfall for taxpayers who decide to "trade down" into a smaller home.

Married taxpayers may exclude up to $500,000 of gain if:

1. either spouse owned the home for periods aggregating two years or more during the five-year period ending on the date of the sale;

2. both spouses used the home as a principal residence for periods totaling two years or more during the five–year period ending on the date of sale (including use before a marriage); and

3. neither spouse is ineligible for the exclusion because he or she had sold another home within the two-year period ending on the date of the sale to which the exclusion applied.[55]

If only one of the spouses, but not both, meet the second or third test, that spouse may still exclude up to $250,000 of gain on the joint return.

Taxpayers who fail to meet the ownership and use tests or the one sale in two years test may be eligible for a partial gain exclusion if the primary reason for selling the principal residence is due to:

1. a change of place of employment;

2. health; or

3. unforeseen circumstances.[56]

The partial exclusion is determined multiplying the maximum exclusion amount by a fraction. The denominator of which is 730 days or twenty-four months. The numerator of the fraction is the shorter of:

1. the lesser of the aggregate amount of time during the five-year period ending on the date of the sale that the taxpayer either (a) owned the residence or (b) used it as the principal residence; or

2. the amount of time elapsed since the taxpayer last used the maximum exclusion amount[57]

Example: Wayne and Wendy Right sold their home on October 1, 2019 and excluded $350,000 of gain. They bought a new house for $400,000 on the same date. As a result of a job transfer, Wayne and Wendy moved out of the house on February 1, 2020. They sold the house on June 1, 2020 for $450,000, realizing a $50,000 gain. Wayne and Wendy are entitled to a partial gain exclusion since the move was caused by a change in employment. They moved out of the house after 123 days. Based on the number of days between the sale of the former home and the sale of the home in question, the amount of time elapsed since the exclusion was last used is 243 days. The shorter of these two periods becomes the numerator of the fraction (123). Therefore, partial gain exclusion is $84,247 ($500,000 × 123 ÷ 730). Since the partial gain exclusion is greater than the gain realized, the entire gain is excluded from the Rights' income.

In order to qualify for the partial gain exclusion using the change of place of employment for a qualified individual, the change in place of employment must occur while the taxpayer owns and is using the property as a principal residence and the new place of employment is at least fifty miles farther from the residence sold than the former place of employment.[58] A qualified individual is the taxpayer, taxpayer's spouse, a co-owner of the property or other person whose principal place of abode is the same household as the taxpayer.[59]

If the move occurs for health reasons, the primary reason for the sale must be to obtain, provide, or facilitate the diagnosis, cure, mitigation, or treatment of a disease, illness or injury to a qualified individual.[60] A qualified individual includes those listed above as well as any of those individual's dependents and descendants of the taxpayer's grandparents.[61] A change in residence that is recommended by a physician qualifies as a health reason.[62]

An unforeseen circumstance is an event that the taxpayer does not anticipate before purchasing and occupying the residence.[63] The following events are deemed to be unforeseen circumstances under the temporary regulations:

1. The involuntary conversion of the property (e.g. destroyed by fire)

2. Natural or man-made disasters or acts of war or terrorism resulting in a casualty to the residence

3. A qualifying individual's (as defined under the change of employment test)

   a. death,

   b. cessation of employment resulting in unemployment compensation,

   c. change in employment status that results in the taxpayer's in ability to pay housing costs and reasonable basic living expenses for the taxpayer's household,

   d. divorce or legal separation, or

   e. multiple births from the same pregnancy

4. An event determined by the IRS to qualify as an unforeseen circumstance published in guidance of general applicability or in a ruling to a specific taxpayer[64]

Example: Lucy Swanson purchased her home and lived there three months before selling the property. Her major reason for selling the home was due to a neighbor who was extremely noisy and rude. Despite every attempt to improve the situation, she could not continue living in the house. The noisy neighbor is not an unforeseen circumstance that would qualify for a partial gain exclusion.

Beginning in 2009, gain from the sale of a principal residence may not be excluded for any period of time (hereinafter called "nonqualified use") where the taxpayer, the taxpayer's spouse, or the taxpayer's former spouse did not use the property as their principal residence. Gain is allocated between periods of qualified and nonqualified use based on the amount of time the property is used for each purpose. The amount of gain must be allocated to periods of nonqualified use based on the ratio of aggregate periods of nonqualified use over the total period of time the property was owned by the taxpayer.

This law change closed a well-known and regularly used loophole. Before the Housing Assistance Tax Act of 2008, taxpayers who owned a property as a vacation home could move into that property, use it as their primary residence for two years, and exclude up to $250,000 (or $500,000) of gain.

The new law does not apply to non-qualifying use prior to 2009. There are several exceptions to the definition of nonqualified use including leaving the home vacant and temporary absences due to change in employment, health, or unforeseen circumstances. In addition, the law allows a taxpayer a five-year period to sell the principal residence after having moved out of it, without having to count this time as nonqualified use.

Example 1: Matt Beregson bought a vacation home on January 1, 2012 and moved into it as his principal residence on January 1, 2018. On January 1, 2020, Matt sells the property. He meets the two-out-of-five-year requirement, but two years (2016 and 2017) are periods of nonqualified use. Therefore two-eighths (1/4) of the gain is not eligible for the exclusion.

Example 2: Jack Robinson buys a property on January 1, 2016 for $400,000 and uses it as a rental property for two years, claiming $20,000 of depreciation deductions. On January 1, 2018, Jack converts the property into his principal residence. Jack moves out of the property on January 13, 2020 and sells the property on January 1, 2021 for $700,000 for a gain of $320,000 ($700,000 less adjusted basis of $380,000). The $20,000 of gain attributable to the depreciation deductions is included in Jack's income regardless of the application of this rule. Of the remaining $300,000 gain, 40 percent (two of the five years the property is owned), or $120,000, is allocated to nonqualified use and is not eligible for the exclusion. Since the remaining gain of $180,000 is less than the maximum gain exclusion of $250,000 (assuming Jack is single), the remaining gain of $180,000 is excluded from income.

Selling Qualified Small Business Stock Held For More Than Five Years (50 Percent Exclusion)

As mentioned above, the sale of QSBS may be deferred if the proceeds are rolled over into another investment in QSBS. If QSBS is held for more than five years, a noncorporate taxpayer may exclude 50 percent of the gain from the sale of the stock.[65] The remaining half of the gain is taxed at a rate of 28 percent.[66] This generates an effective rate of 14 percent.

For alternative minimum tax purposes, 7 percent of the excluded gain must be added back to income in computing alternative minimum taxable income.[67] Special provisions have been added over the years that incorporate the following, higher, exclusion amounts:

- 75 percent gain exclusion for QSBS acquired after February 17, 2009 and on or before September 27, 2010[68]

- 100 percent gain exclusion for QSBS acquired after September 27, 2010 and on or before January 1, 2014[69]

The amount of gain eligible for the exclusion is limited on a per issuer basis. The excluded gain cannot exceed the greater of:

1. $10 million reduced by the taxpayer's aggregate prior year gains from stock of the same issuer; or

2. ten times the taxpayer's basis in his QSBS from such corporation disposed of during the year.[70]

Contributing Appreciated Property to Charity

Taxpayers often contribute various types of property to charity. Certain contributions of appreciated property may allow taxpayers to receive a double benefit—exclusion of capital gain coupled with a deduction for the fair market value of the property contributed. Note that this topic is covered more fully in Chapter 27, Charitable Contribution Planning and in the book, *Tools & Techniques of Charitable Planning* from The National Underwriter Company.

The most well documented technique involves the contribution of appreciated stock or securities to a public charity, donor advised fund, or private charity. If the stock or securities (or any other type of intangible personal property and real property) have been held for more than one year, the fair market value of the stock or securities on the date of the charitable contribution is allowed as a deduction. Since technically, the property has not been sold, no capital gain is recognized even though the donor receives a tax deduction.

Example: Donald McTish donates 100 shares of Abacab, Inc. when it is valued at $5,000. His basis in the stock is $3,000. Donald will report a charitable deduction (subject to adjusted gross income limitations) of $5,000. The $2,000 of appreciation is excluded from his income since the stock was not sold.

Had Donald sold the stock first and contributed the proceeds, the $2,000 would be taxed as a capital gain. Using a 15 percent capital gains tax rate, he would pay $300 of tax. If he contributed the full $5,000 of proceeds, his tax bill would still be $300 higher than it would have been had he contributed the stock directly to the charity.

If the property is used in a trade or business (Section 1231 property), the value of the donation must be reduced by the amount of ordinary income that would have been recaptured if the property were sold for its fair market value.[71]

Tangible personal property that has been held for more than one year may also receive a fair market value deduction. Again, the fair market value is reduced by any amount that would have been recaptured as ordinary income if the property were sold at its fair market value. But in order to receive the deduction for the fair market value, the donee's use of the property must be determined. If the property is used by the donee for anything other than its exempt purpose, the taxpayer's deduction is limited to the adjusted basis.

Example: A painting donated to a museum for public display is related to the museum's exempt purpose. If the painting were contributed to a school that sold the painting and used the proceeds for educational purposes, the donation would not be considered as used for the school's exempt purpose and would, thereby, limit the taxpayer's deduction.

Donations of capital gain property to public charities and donor advised funds ("50 percent charities") are limited to 30 percent of a taxpayer's adjusted gross income.[72] Donations of capital gain property to private foundations ("non-50 percent charities") are limited to 20 percent of a taxpayer's adjusted gross income.[73]

At the election of the taxpayer, a donation of capital gain property to a 50 percent charity may be limited to the taxpayer's adjusted basis. If the election is made, the donation may use the 50 percent of adjusted gross income limitation in place of the special 30 percent limitation.[74]

A taxpayer's deduction for donations of ordinary income and short-term capital gain property is limited to the taxpayer's basis in the property.[75]

Property that has decreased in value is still limited to its fair market value at the time of contribution.[76] Any loss is not deductible. Therefore, a taxpayer would generally be in better situation if the property were sold at a loss with a subsequent donation of the proceeds.

PLANNING FOR LOSS RECOGNITION

Almost as important as the planning that taxpayers should do for deferring or excluding the recognition of a gain is protecting the deductibility of a loss. As discussed in Chapter 4, if a taxpayer's losses exceed their gains in a given year, only $3,000 of the excess may be claimed currently against other sources of income. The balance of the net capital loss is carried over to future tax years to offset capital gains in those years. Therefore, large capital losses may take many years to recoup.

Example: Morris Branson was involved in an automobile accident in 2019. He received a lump sum disability payment of $100,000 in 2020. Against the advice of his team of financial planners, he invested the entire amount into a single Internet company stock. By the end of 2021, the investment was worth $500,000. Partly because he believed the stock would continue to rise and partly because he didn't want to pay approximately $80,000 in taxes, he held onto the stock into 2022. The value of Morris' stock dropped to $10,000 by the end of 2020. Morris sold the stock at that time. Morris has no other assets and does not anticipate recognizing any future capital gains. Under the current tax laws, Morris' $90,000 capital loss will take thirty years to recover by claiming $3,000 of the capital loss each year.

Although not much can be done given Morris' facts, there are planning opportunities—and one big trap—when losses are realized on an investment.

- Claiming a loss on worthless securities
- Deducting a loss from the sale of small business stock
- Planning around the wash sale rules (the trap)

Claiming a Loss on Worthless Securities

If a stock owned by an investor becomes worthless, a capital loss may be claimed as if the stock were sold on the last day of the year in which the stock became worthless.[77]

In order to support a claim that the investment has become worthless, it is necessary to show that there is no current value to the stock and no potential future value. This is often very difficult since, even though a company may halt the trading of its stock, declare bankruptcy, etc., the company may still have some value. This problem is further compounded by the requirement that the loss be claimed in the year the stock became worthless. It is often difficult to ascertain if a company has any value prior to the due date of a taxpayer's return. For this reason, taxpayers are given a seven-year period (four years longer than normal) to file an amended return in order to claim a loss on a worthless security.[78]

The best approach to deal with a security that is believed to be worthless is to enter into a transaction to sell the security. Some brokerage houses would be happy to purchase the stock for a nominal price simply to assist in the documentation of the sale. Note that a sale to a family member or other "related party" will not allow for the loss to be deductible by the taxpayer.

Example: Quincy Harris owns stock in Cool Technologies Corp. In November 2018, the company's stock is delisted. In January 2019, the company files for bankruptcy and subsequently ceases operations in April 2019. In June 2019, Cool Tech sends a letter to shareholders stating that the business has sold all of its assets and paid as much of their outstanding liabilities as they could in compliance with the bankruptcy court. No further payments to the shareholders will be made. Quincy can deduct the loss on the stock as of December 31, 2019, the last day of the year in which the company became completely worthless.

Deducting a Loss from the Sale of Small Business Stock

Taxpayers with losses in certain small business stock may benefit from the rules under Code section 1244. Losses on "1244 stock" may be deducted against the ordinary income up to an annual dollar limitation.[79] The loss may be triggered by a sale or exchange of the Section 1244 stock or by the worthlessness of the stock.

Section 1244 stock must meet the following requirements:

1. It must be common or preferred stock of a domestic corporation.
2. At the time of issuance the company must be a "small business corporation."
3. The stock must be issued in exchange for money or other property, but not stock or securities.
4. For the five years prior to the year of the loss (or since inception if in existence for less than five years), more than 50 percent of the corporation's aggregate gross receipts must have been derived from sources other than royalties, rents, dividends, interests, annuities, and sales or exchanges of stocks or securities.[80] This requirement does not apply if the corporation's allowable deductions exceed the gross income for the five-year period.[81]

A small business corporation is defined as one that has received less than $1 million of cash or other property in exchange for its stock.[82] Once the corporation has received $1 million, the corporation may identify which shares qualify as Section 1244 shares.

The ordinary loss for Section 1244 stock may only be claimed by an individual to whom the stock was originally issued. Shareholders that acquire otherwise qualifying Section 1244 stock through gift, inheritance or purchase are not eligible for Section 1244 treatment.[83]

The maximum amount a taxpayer may claim as a loss from the disposition or worthlessness of Section 1244 stock is limited to $50,000 per year for a single taxpayer or $100,000 for a married couple filing a joint return.[84] Section 1244 losses in excess of these annual limits are treated as capital losses.

Example: Bill Coleman started as business with his close friend Jack Haggarty. Each put $125,000 into the corporation. The business operated for a few years and then wound up operations. Both shareholders walked away with nothing. Assuming the stock qualifies as Section 1244 stock, Bill, who is married, may deduct $100,000 of the $125,000 loss as an ordinary loss. The remaining $25,000 is treated as a capital loss. Jack, who is single, is limited to a $50,000 ordinary loss and will treat the $75,000 balance as a capital loss.

An often overlooked situation involving Section 1244 stock involves stock of closely held S corporations. If a loss is sustained by an initial shareholder upon the disposition of the stock, the loss may qualify as an ordinary loss if the stock meets all of the Section 1244 requirements.

Planning Around the Wash Sale Rules

One area that can trap many taxpayers is the often misunderstood or forgotten wash sale rules. If a taxpayer sells stock or securities at a loss and, within a period beginning thirty days before the sale and ending thirty days after the sale, the taxpayer acquires or enters into a contract to acquire substantially identical stock or securities, the loss will not be allowed.[85] The "wash sale period" is therefore a sixty-one-day period covering thirty days before and after the sale. Note that the wash sale period covers sixty-one calendar days, not trading days.

In order for the wash sale rules to apply, there must be an investment in substantially identical securities. It has been widely accepted that stock of different companies are not substantially identical, even if they are in the same industry. So, a taxpayer could sell AT&T at a loss and purchase Verizon within the wash sale period. In fact, this is a technique that many financial planners tout to their clients. If the client does not want to be out of a particular investment because of a belief that a particular sector will increase in value, the wash sale rule may be avoided by simply investing in a similar company in the same industry.

Investors in mutual funds often run into wash sale issues where less than the entire mutual fund is sold. Dividend reinvestments are treated as purchases that may reduce the deductibility of a loss if they occur within the wash sale period. Like the theory for stocks, if a mutual fund investor wants to recognize a tax loss but still wants to be invested in the same asset class served by the mutual fund being sold, an investment in a similar mutual fund that has similar goals should not be deemed to be substantially identical. An exception may exist for index funds. Although there is no guidance one way or the other, it seems reasonable that an S&P 500 index fund from one mutual fund company is substantially identical to an S&P 500 index fund from another mutual fund company.

If the amount of stock or securities acquired within the wash sale period is less than the amount sold, then the loss is disallowed only with respect to the amount of the stock or securities acquired.[86]

Losses subject to the wash sale rules are added to the basis of the investment acquired during the wash sale period.[87] The holding period for the replacement investment includes the holding period of the original investment.

Example: Brian Mitchellson sold 500 shares of DotCom, Inc. at a loss of $10,000 on July 15. On August 10, Brian purchased another 500 shares of DotCom, Inc. for $40,000. Since Brian purchased substantially identical securities within thirty days after the sale, the loss is not deductible. Brian's basis for the new shares must be adjusted by the disallowed loss. His basis in the 500 shares purchased on August 10 becomes $50,000 and his holding period will include the holding period of the first sale.

Now that brokers are required to report basis on the sale of securities, they are also charged with identifying wash sales from transactions within the same account. While this does help taxpayers and the IRS report wash sales properly, these transactions have become much more difficult to find where the purchases or sales occur within different brokerage accounts.

FREQUENTLY ASKED QUESTIONS

Question – What is a taxpayer has a sale of a stock at a loss, followed by a repurchase of the same stock within the taxpayer's IRA, 401(k) or other retirement plan?

Answer – After many years of uncertainty, the IRS released Revenue Ruling 2008-5, which simply states that the wash sale rule applies to a taxpayer who sold stock for a loss and caused his IRA or Roth IRA to purchase substantially identical stock within thirty days after the sale. In order to avoid the wash sale rules, consider the following planning techniques:

1. Sell the stock at a loss followed by a repurchase thirty-one or more days after the sale.

2. Purchase replacement stock at least thirty-one days prior to the sale of the stock at a loss. This doubles the taxpayer's exposure to the stock for those thirty-one days and could require an outlay of cash that is not available to the taxpayer.

3. Purchase another stock that is likely to move similarly to the stock being sold at a loss. Obviously there is no guarantee that the replacement stock will move exactly like the loss stock. But after thirty-one days, the replacement stock can be sold and the original stock may be repurchased.

CHAPTER ENDNOTES

1. Treas. Reg. §1.1012-1(c)(1).
2. *Ibid.*
3. Treas. Reg. §1.1012-1(c)(2).
4. Treas. Reg. §1.1012-1(c)(3).
5. Treas. Reg. §1.1012-1(e)(4)(i).
6. Treas. Reg. §1.1012-1(e)(4)(ii).
7. Treas. Reg. §1.1012-1(e)(3)(i).
8. Treas. Reg. §1.1012-1(e)(3)(ii).
9. IRC Sec. 1233(b).
10. IRC Sec. 1259(b)(1).
11. IRC Sec. 1259(c)(3)(A).
12. IRC Sec. 1259(a)(1).
13. IRC Sec. 1259(a)(2)(A).
14. IRC Sec. 1259(a)(2)(B).
15. IRC Sec. 1233(b).
16. IRC Sec. 453(b)(1).
17. Rev. Rul. 72-570.
18. IRC Sec. 453(d).
19. IRC Sec. 453(b)(2)(A).
20. IRC Sec. 452(b)(2)(B).
21. IRC Sec. 453(k)(1).
22. IRC Sec. 453(k)(2).
23. IRC Sec. 453(i).
24. IRC Sec. 1033(a)(2)(B).
25. IRC Sec. 1033(a)(2)(B)(i).
26. Treas. Reg. §1.1033(a)-2(c)(3).
27. IRC Sec. 1033(a)(2).
28. IRC Sec. 1033(h)(2).
29. IRC Sec. 1044(a).
30. IRC Sec. 1044(c)(3).
31. IRC Sec. 1044(c)(4).
32. IRC Sec. 1044(b)(1).
33. IRC Sec. 1044(b)(2).
34. IRC Sec. 1044(d).
35. *Ibid.*
36. Treas. Reg. §1.1044(a)-1(b).
37. IRC Sec. 1045(a).
38. *Ibid.*
39. IRC Sec. 1202(d)(1).
40. IRC Sec. 1202(c)(2)(A).
41. IRC Sec. 1202(e)(1).
42. IRC Sec. 1202(e)(3).
43. IRC Sec. 1045(b)(3).
44. IRC Sec. 121(b)(1).
45. IRC Sec. 121(b)(2).
46. Treas. Reg. §1.165-9(a).
47. Treas. Reg. §1.121-1(b)(2).
48. *Ibid.*
49. *Ibid.*
50. IRC Sec. 121(a).
51. *Ibid.*
52. IRC Sec. 121(b)(3).
53. Treas. Reg. §1.121-1(c).
54. Treas. Reg. §1.121-1(c)(4), Example 4.
55. IRC Sec. 121(b)(2).
56. IRC Sec. 121(c).
57. IRC Sec. 121(c)(1)(A).
58. Temp. Treas. Reg. §1.121-3T(c)(2).
59. Temp. Treas. Reg. §1.121-3T(f).
60. Temp. Treas. Reg. §1.121-3T(d)(1).
61. Temp. Treas. Reg. §1.121-3T(f).
62. Temp. Treas. Reg. §1.121-3T(d)(2).
63. Temp. Treas. Reg. §1.121-3T(e).

64. Temp. Treas. Reg. §1.121-3T(e)(2).
65. IRC Sec. 1202(a)(1).
66. IRC Sec. 1(h)(4) and (7).
67. IRC Sec. 57(a)(7).
68. IRC Sec. 1202(a)(3).
69. IRC Sec. 1202(a)(4).
70. IRC Sec. 1202(b)(1).
71. IRC Sec. 170(b)(1)(C)(iv).
72. IRC Sec. 170(b)(1)(C)(i).
73. IRC Sec. 170(b)(1)(D).
74. IRC Sec. 170(b)(1)(C)(iii).
75. IRC Sec. 170(e)(1)(A).
76. Rev. Rul. 79-419.
77. IRC Sec. 165(g)(1).
78. IRC Sec. 6511(d)(1).
79. IRC Sec. 1244(a).
80. IRC Sec. 1244(c)(1).
81. IRC Sec. 1244(c)(2)(C).
82. IRC Sec. 1244(c)(3).
83. Treas. Reg. §1.1244(a)-1(b).
84. IRC Sec. 1244(b).
85. IRC Sec. 1091(a).
86. IRC Sec. 1091(b) and Treas. Reg. §1.1091-1(c).
87. IRC Sec. 1091(d).

RETIREMENT PLANNING

CHAPTER 31

INTRODUCTION

With the possible exception of an individual's home, an individual's most valuable asset may be an employer-sponsored qualified retirement plan such as a Section 401(k) plan, Section 403(b) arrangement or self-created traditional IRA or Roth IRA (collectively referred to as "Qualified Retirement Plans"). Since many individuals are participants or owners of Qualified Retirement Plan over the entire period of their employment (forty years or more), it is not unusual for these plans to be worth hundreds of thousands of dollars.

Generally, the advantages of Qualified Retirement Plans include the following.

- Growth and earnings are tax-deferred.
- An income tax deduction may be available when the plan or IRA is established.
- Tax rates may decrease before distributions (thus, the tax-deferred earnings are subject to a lower amount of tax).
- Qualified Retirement Plan assets are afforded additional protection in bankruptcy.

On the other hand, Qualified Retirement Plans are subject to complex rules that are fraught with tax traps for the unwitting individual. In many instances, the failure to comply with these rules may result in harsh adverse tax consequences to the individual and family members. Therefore, proper planning is essential.

For example, generally an individual who fails to take a minimum distribution (as explained below) from a Qualified Retirement Plan account beginning at age 70½ or an individual who takes a withdrawal from such account prior to reaching the age of 59½ may be subject to a substantial penalty. These two milestones are very important factors to consider when planning for retirement. When individuals retire before age 59½, planning to avoid the penalties that are imposed for premature distributions from Qualified Retirement Plans is an essential step in the planning process. Also, given the onerous penalty for failing to receive minimum required distributions once an individual reaches age 70½, it is imperative to make sure that the minimum required distribution rules are strictly followed.

Retirement plans that are started and owned by individuals are known as Individual Retirement Accounts (IRAs), and come in many different varieties. Retirement plans that are created by employers can be either defined benefit or defined contribution plans. Each type is discussed below.

TRADITIONAL IRA

A traditional IRA is a self-established Qualified Retirement Plan usually maintained by a bank or brokerage firm acting as trustee or custodian. An IRA provides the double tax benefit of deductible contributions and the tax-free growth of its earnings. Ultimately, distributions from IRAs are taxable to the owner of the IRA. Explained below are the rules regarding contributions and distributions.

Contributions

Subject to certain limitations, contributions to a traditional IRA are deductible. The amount of contributions, however, is not unlimited. Each year, the IRS sets a limit on the dollar amount an individual may contribute to a traditional IRA. For 2020, the contribution limit is the lesser of earned compensation or $6,000. Individuals over age fifty may contribute up to an additional $1,000, or a total contribution of up to $7,000. However, whether IRA contributions of those with an employer sponsored retirement plan are deductible is subject to phase out based on ***modified*** adjusted gross income.

Modified adjusted gross income is adjusted gross income computed by making the following adjustments[1] (to the extent they were included in the computation of adjusted gross income):

- Add back student loan interest deduction
- Add back tuition and fees deduction
- Add back IRA deductions (the amount that would be deductible but for the phase out)
- Subtract the taxable amount of social security benefits
- Add back domestic production activities deduction
- Add back excluded qualified saving bond interest
- Add back foreign earned income exclusion
- Add back exclusion of employer provided adoption benefits

Figure 31.1 sets forth the phase out of the IRA contribution deduction based on filing status and modified adjusted gross income.

One Spouse Participates in a Qualified Retirement Plan and the Other Spouse Does Not

If with respect to a married couple filing jointly, one spouse participates in a Qualified Retirement Plan and the other does not and modified adjusted gross income is less than $184,000, a full deduction up to the amount of the contribution limit is allowed. If modified adjusted gross income is between $184,000 and $194,000, the deduction phases out.

Coordination with Roth IRAs

If in addition to a traditional IRA, an individual has a Roth IRA (discussed below), the total amount of distributions to both accounts cannot exceed the lesser of $5,500 ($6,500 if the individual is age fifty or older) or earned compensation.

Figure 31.1

PHASE OUT OF IRA DEDUCTION FOR INDIVIDUALS WHO PARTICIPATE IN EMPLOYER SPONSORED QUALIFIED RETIREMENT PLANS

Filing Status	Modified Adjusted Gross Income	Amount of Deduction
Single or Head of Household	$61,000 or less	Full deduction of up to the amount of the contribution limit
	Greater than $61,000 but less than $71,000	Deduction phases out, i.e., the higher the modified adjusted gross income within this range, the lesser amount of deduction
	$71,000 or more	$0. Deduction totally phased out
Married Filing Jointly or Qualified Widow(er)	$98,000 or less	Full deduction of up to the amount of the contribution limit
	Greater than $98,000 but less than $118,000	Deduction phases out, i.e., the higher the modified gross income within this range, the lesser amount of deduction
	$118,000 or more	$0. Deduction totally phased out.
Married filing separately[2]	Less than $10,000	Deduction phases out, i.e., the higher the modified gross income within this range, the lesser amount of deduction
	$10,000 or more	$0. Deduction totally phased out.

Excess Contributions

Excess contributions to an IRA are subject to a 6 percent penalty per year as long as the excess amounts remain in the IRA. An excess contribution is:

- A contribution in excess of the contribution limit;
- A contribution into an IRA after an individual has attained the age of 70½; or
- Makes an improper rollover to an IRA.

However, the excess contribution penalty tax can be avoided if the individual withdraws the excess contribution by the due date of that year's Form 1040 (including extensions) as well as the income generated from those excess contributions.

Distributions

Generally, distributions from a traditional IRA are fully taxable and may not begin before age 59½ without the imposition of the premature disposition penalty. Exceptions to the premature disposition penalty are discussed later in this chapter. Once a taxpayer reaches age 70½, a minimum amount must be distributed from the IRA each year. The minimum required distribution rules are discussed in more detail later in the chapter.

SPOUSAL IRA

Provided a married couple files jointly, a separate spousal IRA can be established for a nonworking spouse or a spouse with earned compensation that is less than the contribution limit. In that case, the permissible contribution amount to a spousal IRA is the lesser of $5,500 ($6,500, if age fifty or older) or the total compensation included in gross income of the jointly filed return less a) the other spouse's contribution to a traditional IRA and b) any Roth IRA contributions made on behalf of the other spouse.[3]

Example: Miranda, a full time student with no income is married to Asher who is also a student. Both Miranda and Asher are under age fifty and file a joint income tax return. In 2020, Asher earns $9,000 from a part-time job as a waiter. Asher makes a contribution of $5,500 to his traditional IRA and creates a spousal IRA for Miranda. The maximum contribution to Miranda's spousal IRA is computed as follows:

The lesser of $5,500 or $4,500 ($9,000 (the couple's earned compensation) minus $5,500 (Asher's IRA contribution). Thus, the maximum 2020 contribution to Miranda's spousal IRA would be $4,500.

ROLLOVER IRA

In some instances, an individual may desire to move or "rollover" funds maintained in a Qualified Retirement Plan to a traditional IRA. This may occur when an individual separates from service or retires. A rollover IRA is established for this purpose. The IRA contribution limitation does not apply to rollovers meaning there is no limit to the amount that can be rolled over. Rollovers are discussed in more detail later in the chapter.

NONDEDUCTIBLE IRA

A nondeductible IRA is a traditional IRA in which the owner has made nondeductible contributions in addition to deductible contributions. So, a contribution that is nondeductible either because of the modified adjusted gross income limitation or because the individual or spouse is an active participant in an employer-sponsored Qualified Retirement Plan may nonetheless remain in the IRA. A nondeductible IRA contribution creates "basis" for the IRA owner. Thus, a portion of a distribution from a nondeductible IRA represents a nontaxable recovery of basis.

ROTH IRA

Because Roth IRAs are unlike any other type of Qualified Retirement Plan, all discussion regarding Roth IRAs are in this part of the chapter.

A Roth IRA is an IRA that is designated as a Roth IRA at the time it is established.[4] Unlike all other Qualified Retirement Plans, *all* contributions to a Roth IRA are not deductible,[5] but any "qualified distributions" are tax-free.

The contribution limitation of a Roth IRA is the regular IRA limitation for the year, including catch-up contributions, reduced by any deductible or nondeductible contributions to any traditional IRAs. Unlike a traditional IRA, provided the owner has earned income, contributions to a Roth IRA beyond age 70½ are allowed.[6]

Figure 31.2

PHASE OUT OF ROTH IRA CONTRIBUTION LIMITATION FOR INDIVIDUALS BASED ON FILING STATUS AND MODIFIED ADJUSTED GROSS INCOME

Filing Status	Modified Adjusted Gross Income	Amount of Permissible Contribution
Single or Head of Household.	Less than $117,000	Up to the contribution limit
	Equal to or greater than $117,000 but less than $132,000	Contribution limit phases out, i.e., the higher the modified adjusted gross income within this range, the lesser the permissible contribution amount
	$132,000 or more	$0. Contribution limit totally phased out
Married Filing Jointly or Qualified Widow(er)	Less than $184,000	Up to the contribution limit
	Equal to or greater than $184,000 but less than $194,000	Contribution limit phases out, i.e., the higher the modified gross income within this range, the lesser permissible contribution amount
	$194,000 or more	$0. Contribution limit totally phased out.
Married filing separately[7]	Less than $10,000	Contribution limit phases out, i.e., the higher the modified gross income within this range, the lesser permissible contribution amount
	$10,000 or more	$0. Contribution limit totally phased out.

Similar to a traditional IRA (discussed above) the contribution limitation of a Roth IRA is subject to phase out based on an individual's filing status and amount of modified adjusted gross income. Figure 31.2 sets forth the phase out of the Roth IRA contribution limitation based on filing status and modified adjusted gross income.

Tax-Free Qualified Distributions

Qualified distributions from a Roth IRA are entirely tax-free.[8] There are two requirements of a qualified distribution.

1. The distribution must be no earlier than the end of the five year taxable period beginning with the first taxable year for which the individual made a contribution to a Roth IRA; and

2. Beyond the five-year holding period, the distribution must be made:

   A. On or after the date on which the individual reaches age 59½;

   B. To a beneficiary (or the owner's estate) on or after the death of the owner;[9]

   C. Due to the owner's disability; or

   D. For a qualified special purpose distribution (first time homebuyer expenses up to $10,000) as defined in IRC Section 72(t)(2)(F).

Importantly, each Roth IRA owner has one five-year holding period that begins with the tax year for which he or she first made a contribution to a Roth IRA including a Roth IRA funded with assets of a converted traditional IRA (conversions discussed in more detail below). Therefore, to start the clock, the earlier an individual makes a Roth IRA contribution, the better.

Example: In the current year, Miranda Wright age fifty-three is contemplating retirement in seven years. She decides to roll over her 401(k) account into a traditional IRA. Then, upon her retirement, when she is in a lower income tax bracket, she intends to convert her traditional IRA into a Roth IRA. If she makes a contribution to a Roth IRA in the current year, the five-year holding period clock begins to run. This strategy has two advantages:

1. Seven years from now, when she converts her traditional IRA at time when she is in a lower tax bracket, her tax liability would be relatively low.

2. Additionally, with the expiration of the five-year holding period and being older than age 59½, all distributions from the Roth IRA would be tax-free.

Taxation of Nonqualified Distributions

Nonqualified distributions are taxable to the extent they exceed the account holder's basis. Basis is defined as an individual's after tax investment in an asset. In the case of a Roth IRA, basis is the sum of Roth IRA contributions (not deductible so made with after tax dollars) and the amount converted from a traditional IRA to a Roth IRA (conversions are discussed in more detail below). As to the latter, amounts converted from a traditional IRA to a Roth IRA are taxable upon conversion. Therefore, the taxable conversion amount is considered as basis.

Example. In 2019, Asher made a $1,000 contribution to a Roth IRA. In 2020, Asher converted a traditional IRA with an account value of $100,000 into his Roth IRA requiring the inclusion of that amount in gross income on his 2020 Form 1040. Asher's basis in his Roth IRA is $101,000 (the $1,000 contribution plus the $100,000 converted from his traditional IRA).

In addition to being subject to income tax, the account holder is also subject to the 10 percent premature distribution penalty with respect to the taxable portion of the nonqualified distributions. The taxation of nonqualified distributions is subject to an ordering rule by which the account holder is deemed to recover basis first. Only amounts exceeding the account holder's basis are taxable[10] (and potentially subject to the premature distribution penalty). For this purpose, all Roth IRAs are treated as a single Roth IRA and distributions are deemed to be made in the following order:

1. amounts contributed by the taxpayer, until all contributory assets are fully recovered (tax-free),

2. amounts converted to a Roth IRA, chronologically by tax year of conversion, until all conversion assets are fully recovered (tax-free), and

3. total earnings (taxable).[11]

Example: Two years ago, Jimmy Jones converted a $100,000 IRA to a Roth IRA. In the current year (prior to the expiration of the five-year holding period), Jimmy, age fifty-five, withdraws $40,000 from the Roth IRA. None of the exceptions to the premature distribution penalty apply. Since Jimmy was taxed at the time of the conversion of the traditional IRA to a Roth IRA, the $40,000 distribution is not included in gross income (otherwise it would be taxed twice). In addition, because the distribution was not taxable, there is also no 10 percent premature distribution penalty.

No Required Minimum Distributions

Unlike Qualified Retirement Plans, Roth IRAs are not subject to the lifetime minimum distribution requirements.[12] This applies to Roth IRAs created with regular contributions as well as converted funds. Thus, the owner has the ability to never take a lifetime distribution from the Roth IRA. This means the account can continue to grow tax-free until the owner's death.

However, at the owner's death, unless the owner's spouse is the sole beneficiary of the Roth IRA, required minimum distributions do apply. So, if the surviving spouse is not the sole beneficiary of the Roth IRA, the entire balance of the Roth IRA must be distributed by:

- December 31 of the year in which the fifth anniversary of the owner's death falls (if there is no designated beneficiary), or

- Over the life expectancy of the designated beneficiary starting no later than the December 31 of the year following the owner's death.[13]

Thus, designated beneficiaries of Roth IRAs may benefit from deferring the distributions by taking them out over their life expectancy. This allows for the Roth IRA balance to continue growing on a tax-free basis.

On the other hand, if the Roth IRA passes to the surviving spouse, he or she may treat the Roth IRA as his or her own (by rollover or otherwise) and like the deceased owner defer the application of the lifetime mandatory distribution rules until death.[14]

Conversions

Under current law, any taxpayer (regardless of level of income) is allowed to convert an eligible retirement plan to a Roth IRA.[15] As discussed above, the fundamental difference between a traditional IRA and a Roth IRA is the following:

- Roth IRA – No Deduction for Contributions – No Taxation with respect to Qualified distributions

- Traditional IRA – Deduction for Contributions – Taxation of Distributions

Depending on the circumstances, it may be desirable to convert a traditional IRA or other eligible retirement plan into a Roth IRA. For example, if an individual were to convert a traditional IRA to a Roth IRA, there are the following tax advantages:

- Comparatively, lower overall taxable income;

- Tax-free, rather than tax-deferred growth;

- No required minimum distributions at age 70½;

- Tax-free withdrawals for the owner's beneficiaries at death; and

- May be a factor in reducing or eliminating the 3.8 percent net investment income tax.

An individual contemplating a conversion should take into account the immediate and potentially full income taxation of the conversion funds.[16] Although, the converted IRA distributions are not subject to the 10 percent penalty for premature distributions,[17] the conversion may nonetheless result in a significant income tax liability. Therefore, if the resulting income tax is paid out of the converted funds, the bottom line amount ending up in the Roth IRA may be reduced significantly. On the other hand, if the individual is able to pay the tax from other funds, the entire amount of the converted traditional IRA funds would grow tax-free and not be subject to income tax when distributed.

Example: Miranda Wright is a single taxpayer in the combined 40 percent federal and state income tax bracket. Miranda has a traditional IRA with an account balance of $1,000,000. If Miranda converts her traditional IRA into a Roth IRA, the conversion would trigger a combined federal and state tax of $400,000. If the converted funds are Miranda's only source to pay the tax, the after tax amount of funds ending up in the Roth IRA would be reduced to 600,000. On the other hand, if Miranda is able to pay the tax with other funds, the entire $1,000,000 of converted funds would end up in the Roth IRA.

Timing a Roth IRA Conversion to the Owner's Advantage

As illustrated above, the conversion of a traditional IRA to a Roth IRA may trigger a significant tax liability. However, in a year in which the individual possess favorable tax attributes such as a charitable deduction carry-forward, investment tax credits, net operating losses, high basis nondeductible traditional IRA amounts, etc., it may be possible to minimize such tax.

Example: Assume the same facts as in the previous example, except in this case, Miranda has a $200,000 net operating loss and a $100,000 charitable deduction carry-over. Although the conversion triggers $1,000,000 of gross income, the combined $300,000 deduction results in net taxable income of $700,000. Based on a combined federal and state tax rate of 40 percent, the tax would be $280,000. So, if Miranda's has to pay the tax from the converted traditional IRA funds, $720,000 ($1,000,000 minus $280,000) would end up in the Roth IRA. Therefore, by using her other favorable tax attributes as an offset, Miranda minimizes her tax liability and maximizes the amount of converted funds ending up in the Roth IRA.

Re-characterizing a Roth IRA Conversion

It is possible that between the date of conversion and the due date of the income tax return, the value of the converted assets may decline in value. In that case, a portion of the tax generated by the conversion would be attributable to that lost value. Consequently, some or all of the benefit of the conversion may be minimized or completely lost. To reverse that result, an individual has a one-time opportunity to re-characterize (undo) the conversion. Provided the re-characterization occurs by the due date of the taxpayer's return, including extensions, for the year of the conversion (October 15th), the converted amount plus any earnings allocable to the converted amount may be returned (without adverse tax consequence) to the eligible retirement plan in a trustee-to-trustee transfer.[18]

Example: In 2019, Asher converts a traditional IRA worth $200,000 to a Roth IRA. As of October 1, 2020, the value of the funds had decreased to $150,000. If by October 15, 2020, Asher fails to re-characterize the Roth IRA back to a traditional IRA, he would include the full $200,000 in gross income. On the other hand, if by that date Asher does re-characterize the Roth IRA back to a traditional IRA, the conversion would be reversed without as if it had never occurred.

Reconverting a Re-characterized Roth IRA

A taxpayer who converts an eligible retirement plan to a Roth IRA and then re-characterizes the conversion has an opportunity to reconvert (i.e., undo the undoing). The deadline for reconverting is the later of:

1. the beginning of the tax year following the tax year for which the amount was converted to a Roth IRA, or
2. the end of the thirty-day period beginning on the day the original conversion is recharacterized.[19]

Roth IRA Conversions under the 2017 Tax Reform Act

The 2017 Tax Act modified the rules governing IRAs and Roth IRAs so that the previously existing recharacterization rules will no longer apply. Under prior law, if a taxpayer converted a portion of his or her traditional IRA funds to a Roth account, he or she had until October 15 of the following tax year to recharacterize (essentially, undo) the transaction and avoid the related tax liability. Taxpayers who converted Roth funds in 2017 have until October 15, 2018 to recharacterize the transaction.

However, under the 2017 Tax Act, if a taxpayer makes a Roth contribution, he or she is permitted to recharacterize the transaction as a contribution to a traditional IRA before the due date for his or her income tax return for the year.[20]

SEP-IRA

A simplified employee pension (SEP) IRA is an employer-sponsored arrangement that consists of a traditional IRA created for each employee with much higher contribution limits. In determining the annual contribution limit, a SEP-IRA is treated like a qualified profit sharing plan. Thus, an employer may contribute up to the lessor of (1) 25 percent of compensation or (2) $57,000 (for 2020). For this purpose, an employee's countable compensation is limited to $285,000 (for 2020).[21]

SIMPLE IRA

Generally, a SIMPLE IRA is a viable Qualified Retirement Plan for small businesses including a self-employed individual. The requirements of a SIMPLE IRA are as follows:

- Employer has one hundred or fewer employees
- Employer cannot have any other retirement plan
- Annual contributions by the employer are either a) a matching contribution of up to 3 percent of compensation (not limited by the annual compensation limit) or b) a 2 percent non-elective employer contribution for each eligible employee with compensation of up to $265,000.

- Elective employee contributions allowed
- Employee always 100 percent vested in his or her SIMPLE IRA account.

DEFINED CONTRIBUTION AND DEFINED BENEFIT PLANS

These are employer-sponsored Qualified Retirement Plans. For either type of Qualified Retirement Plan, the employer sponsor is entitled to an immediate deduction for contributions made to the plan each year. In addition, from the employee-participant's perspective, the earnings generated by the investment of the contributions grow tax-free as long as they are held by the plan.

Defined Contribution Plans

A defined contribution plan is funded by employee and/or employer contributions to an employee's individual account established for each participant. For the duration of a participant's participation in the plan, the earnings generated are not taxed. Because over time, the value of the account is subject to investment fluctuations, there is no guarantee to the participant of the amount of the future *benefit* ultimately received. At the time the participant is eligible to receive benefits, the benefit amount is based upon the account balance.

There are four basic types of defined contribution plans:

1. A **profit sharing plan** provides that the employer will determine, annually, how much will be contributed to the plan (based on profits or some other measure). However, there is no annual contribution requirement. Employer contributions are allocated among the participants' accounts based on a formula such as in proportion to compensation and/or other factors (such as years of service – or age).

2. A **401(k) plan** is a type of profit sharing plan that combines the employer contributions with elective salary deferrals made by the employee. In a traditional 401(k) plan, an employee is allowed to make pre-tax contributions. This means that although the deferred salary contributions are not taxed on the front end, the funds in the account are taxable when distributed. With the addition of a Roth 401(k) feature to the plan, however, employees are also allowed to make after-tax salary deferrals to their regular 401(k) account. Similar to a Roth IRA, the amounts contributed are not deductible (by virtue of being currently taxable to the participant). On the other hand, the distribution of the earnings on such contributions are tax-free when ultimately received.

   For 2020, the elective salary deferral is limited to $19,000 (including pre and after-tax deferrals). The catch up contribution limits which apply to those participants over age fifty also apply (an additional $6,000 in 2020).

3. **Money-purchase pension plan** – Unlike a profit sharing plan, a money purchase plan requires set annual contributions based upon the employees' compensation for the year. Each year the employer is required to make a contribution of a fixed percentage of each employee's compensation. For 2020, the amount of the contribution is limited to the lesser of 25 percent of compensation (up to $285,000) or $57,000.

4. **Target-benefit pension plan** – A target benefit pension plan is essentially a hybrid of a defined contribution and defined benefit plan. As the name suggests, a "target" benefit is determined by a formula (similar to a defined benefit plan). Based on actuarial valuations computed at the outset, a contribution allocated to a participant's account are commensurate with achieving that benefit. So to achieve the benefit goals, larger contributions are made with respect to older participants. However, because target benefit plans are considered to be defined contribution plans, they have the same limitation on contributions as money-purchase pension plans described above.

Defined Benefit Plans

Unlike a defined contribution plan, a "defined benefit" plan promises a specific and predicable monthly benefit payable to an employee at normal retirement age. The benefit is based on a formula that takes into account an employee's salary history, years of service and age. So, unlike a defined contribution plan, an employee's retirement benefit is not based on the plan's investment earnings. Therefore, the employer is obligated to fund the plan each year regardless of profitability or investment earnings. A defined benefit plan may offer up to the lesser of 100 percent of the participant's average compensation in the highest three years of service (usually at the end of the employee's career), or $230,000 (in 2020).[22] The amount of the employer's contribution is determined actuarially and must be funded each year regardless of the employer's profitability.

OTHER TYPES OF QUALIFIED RETIREMENT PLANS

Other arrangements that mimic qualified plans include Section 403(b) plans (for non-profit organizations and public school employees) and Section 457 plans (for government employees).

Deferred Annuities

A deferred annuity is another source of retirement income, but it is usually a personal investment and not typically associated with an employer/employee relationship. The investor makes a single large cash payment or a series of periodic payments to purchase the annuity. In return the annuity issuer agrees to pay a specified amount on a periodic basis beginning at some point in the future. The annuity payout may be for the life of the annuitant, for the joint lives of the annuitant and spouse, or for a fixed term. It may be immediate (i.e., it starts as soon as the payment is made for the contract with the insurer) or deferred for many years.

Once the annuity is purchased, the subsequent earnings accumulate on a tax deferred basis. No income from the annuity is taxed until the annuity begins or is otherwise cashed in.

An annuitant's investment in an annuity is recovered in equal tax-free amounts during the payment period. The excess of each payment (above the investment amount) is taxed at ordinary income rates. This means that part of each payment is considered a nontaxable recovery of capital (or basis) and part of each payment is considered income taxable at ordinary rates.

In general, the formula for determining the nontaxable portion of each year's annuity payment is:[23]

$$\frac{\text{Investment in the Contract}}{\text{Expected Return}}$$

This is called the "exclusion ratio." It is expressed as a percentage and applied to each annuity payment to find the portion of the payment that is excludable from gross income.[24]

For example, assume a seventy-year-old purchases an annuity for $12,000 (the investment in the annuity) with an expected return of $19,200. The exclusion ratio is 62.5 percent ($12,000 divided by $19,200). If the monthly payment he receives is $100, the portion that can be excluded from gross income is $62.50 (62.5 percent of $100). The $37.50 balance of each $100 monthly payment is taxed as ordinary income.[25]

The excludable portion of any annuity payment may not exceed the unrecovered investment in the contract (unless the annuity started before January 1, 1987). The "unrecovered investment in the contract" is the policy owner's premium cost (reduced by any dividends received in cash or used to reduce premiums and by the aggregate amount received under the contract on or after the annuity starting date to the extent it was excludable from income). This rule limits the total amount the policy owner can exclude from income to the total amount of his contribution. Once an annuitant outlives his or her actuarial life expectancy, 100 percent of each payment will be taxable.

"Premature" distributions (those made before certain dates listed below) are subject not only to the normal tax on ordinary income, but also to the 10 percent premature distribution penalty. The exceptions to this penalty are discussed in more detail later in this chapter.

If an annuity owner dies before the starting date of the annuity payments, the cash value of the contract must either be distributed within five years of death or used within one year of death to provide a life annuity or installment payments payable over a period not longer than the beneficiary's life expectancy. However, if the surviving spouse is the beneficiary; the distribution requirements are applied by treating the spouse as the owner of the annuity contract.

RETIREMENT PLAN DISTRIBUTION OPTIONS

The type of plan determines the rules and tax consequences that apply to distributions from the plan, as described below. This can be an important factor to consider when contemplating switching funds from one type of account to another.

Employer-sponsored Qualified Retirement Plans

Employer-sponsored retirement plans typically provide a number of alternative elective distribution options to an employee (or former employee) eligible to begin to receive benefits. In some cases, certain plans must offer a particular type of distribution options.

Defined benefit plans and money purchase pension plans are required to pay benefits in the form of a qualified joint and survivor annuity (QJSA) to retiring employees and a qualified preretirement survivor annuity (QPSA) to vested employees who die prior to retiring (unless, if married, with the employee's spouse consents, a different payment option, such as a lump sum, is elected). A QJSA is a life annuity based on the employee's life expectancy with a survivor annuity payable to the spouse, if married (or former spouse or child or dependent who is treated as surviving spouse under a QDRO – qualified domestic relations order). The amount payable to the surviving spouse must be no less than 50 percent or greater than 100 percent of the amount payable during the employee's lifetime. As a second alternative, by waiver of the QSJA (with the consent of the spouse), the plan must offer an elective qualified optional survivor annuity (QOSA). If per the QSJA, the spouse's survivor annuity is less than 75 percent of the employee's lifetime annuity, the QOSA must provide a spouse survivor annuity equal to 75 percent of the employee's lifetime annuity. Conversely, if per the QJSA, the spouse's survivor annuity is 75 percent or greater than the employee's lifetime annuity, the QOSA must provide a spouse survivor annuity of 50 percent of the employee's lifetime annuity.[26]

A QPSA is an annuity for the surviving spouse of a vested employee who dies prior to retiring or after separating from service but not retiring. Under these circumstances, the annuity must provide payments that would have been paid to the survivor pursuant to the QJSA offered by the plan if:

Scenario 1 – The date of the deceased employee's death occurred after attaining the plan's earliest retirement age. For purposes of determining the amount of annuity payments payable to the surviving spouse, it is as if:

- the employee actually retired on the day before death with
- a QJSA payable beginning on that date.

Scenario 2 – The date of the deceased employee's death occurred on or before he or she attained the plan's earliest retirement age. For purposes of determining the amount of annuity payments payable to the surviving spouse, it is as if:

- the employee separated from service on the date of death or on the actual date of separation if the employee had separated from service prior to his or her death;
- survived to the earliest retirement age;
- retired on the earliest retirement age with a QJSA payable beginning on that date; and
- died the next day.[27]

Defined contribution plans that are not money purchase pension plans may offer an annuity (payments guaranteed for a specified number of years, e.g., life annuity with 10 years guaranteed), installment payments or a lump sum as a form of benefit distribution. All of the benefit payment options must have the same actuarially equivalent value. If the employee chooses a lump sum distribution, he or she is allowed to roll over the distribution, tax-free, to the employee's own IRA or to a qualified plan maintained by the employee's new employer.

IRAs

The distribution options of IRA are much more flexible than the distribution options of employer sponsored Qualified Retirement Plans (discussed above). For example,

- IRA owners are not required to obtain spousal consent to a form of distribution. Additionally, IRAs are not subject to the QJSA/QPSA or QOSA requirements.
- Subject to the premature distribution penalty and minimum required distributions (discussed later in this chapter) distributions from IRAs can be in any form, at any time, and in any amount as the IRA owner desires.

Taxation of Retirement Plan Distributions

Unless a retirement distribution is rolled over to another eligible retirement plan, (i.e., funneled directly into another qualified plan or IRA), a distribution from any Qualified Retirement Plan is taxable as ordinary income in the taxable year in which it is received.[28]

If a Qualified Retirement Plan account includes nondeductible contributions (other than Roth IRA and Roth 401(k) contributions), it means the participant has funded the account, at least in part, with after tax dollars. Therefore, that portion of the account balance represents the taxpayer's basis that is recovered tax-free when distributions are made.[29] However, for income tax purposes, basis is not recovered first (before the distributions become 100 percent taxable). Instead, each distribution will consist of both a taxable and nontaxable portion.

Computation of Nontaxable Portion of a Distribution from an IRA

For purposes of computing the nontaxable portion of a distribution from an IRA, all the taxpayer's IRAs are aggregated (including those without any nondeductible contributions). The following is the formula for computing the nontaxable portion of a distribution from a nondeductible IRA (see discussion above):

$$\frac{\text{All Nondeductible Contributions}}{\text{Balance of all IRAs (including any current year withdrawals)}} \times \text{Amount Distributed} = \text{Nontaxable Portion of Distribution}$$

Example: In 2020, Thomas Hewer, age sixty, withdrew $20,000 from one of his IRAs. Over the years, he had made $20,000 of nondeductible contributions to that IRA. As of the end of the year, his three IRAs (including the $20,000 withdrawal) have an aggregate value of $200,000. Applying the above formula, of the $20,000 distribution, only $2,000 will be a tax-free recovery of basis.

$$\left[\frac{\$20{,}000}{(\$200{,}000)}\right] \times \$20{,}000 = \$2{,}000$$

Taxation of Non-Lump Sum Distributions from Qualified Retirement Plans

The taxation of a non-lump sum distribution from a Qualified Retirement Plan depends on whether the distribution is in the form an annuity. If the distribution is a periodic payment in a systematic liquidation of the participant's benefit and assuming that the employee has made nondeductible contributions, the annuity rules of Code section 72 apply to determine the taxability of the benefit.[30]

Taxation of Payments from a Qualified Retirement Plan in the Form of an Annuity

Applying the rules of Code section 72, if annuity payments are made from a qualified plan, the tax-free portion of the distribution (the employee's basis for nondeductible contributions) is recovered evenly over a specified number of payments.

For example, if the annuity is payable over two or more lives, the nontaxable portion of each monthly payment (or exclusion ratio) is determined by dividing the employee's cost basis by the number of payments as shown in the table below:[31]

If the combined ages of the annuitants are:	Number of Payments
Not more than 110	410
More than 110 but not more than 120	360
More than 120 but not more than 130	310
More than 130 but not more than 140	260
More than 140	210

The amount of the annuity payment that represents the recovery of the employee's basis is determined by multiplying the exclusion ratio by each payment. The exclusion ratio is applied until the employee's basis is completely recovered. Thereafter, subsequent payments are totally taxable. If the participant dies prior to the full recovery of basis, a deduction in the amount of the unrecovered basis is allowed on the participant's final return.

Lump Sum Distributions

A lump sum distribution (LSD) is a distribution, or series of distributions, of a participant's entire balance in a qualified plan or IRA paid out in a single tax year. The taxable amount of the LSD is the total value of the distribution less the participant's basis (usually compromised of after-tax contributions). Generally, a

LSD is taxed in the year of receipt. Since a LSD may be substantial, care must be taken in deciding whether to elect it as a distribution option to prevent all or part of it being taxed unnecessarily at the highest income tax rate.

In the event an employee is changing employment, LSDs can be rolled over (see below) into another eligible retirement plan or into an IRA so as to continue the tax deferral. On the other hand, if the participant has a net operating loss or other credits or carryovers that may otherwise expire, it may be wise to elect to receive a LSD so as to minimize the amount of taxable income by using those deductions and credits to offset a potentially substantial taxable distribution.

Rollovers

As discussed throughout this chapter, tax-free rollovers of distributions from qualified plans, IRA and other retirement plans allow the continuation of the tax deferral of the earnings generated by these plans. Generally, an "eligible rollover distribution" is rolled over to an "eligible retirement plan." However, if the individual fails to transfer the eligible rollover distribution to an eligible retirement plan no later than the sixtieth day following the day of receipt, such amount would be included in gross income subject to tax. Rollovers from qualified plans do not need to be converted to cash prior to completing the rollover. Stock, bonds, mutual fund shares or other noncash property may be rolled over without being sold.[32]

Participant receives a distribution from a Qualified Retirement Plan. If the participant receives a distribution from a Qualified Retirement Plan, it must be rolled over to an eligible retirement plan within sixty days after the funds are received.[33] The sixty-day period begins on the day after the distribution is received. If the sixtieth day falls on a weekend or legal holiday, the next business day will be considered the last day for the rollover to occur.[34]

An *eligible retirement plan* generally includes any of the following:

1. a traditional IRA,
2. a qualified pension, profit sharing or stock bonus plan,
3. an eligible Section 457 governmental plan (if certain separate accounting requirements are met), and
4. a Section 403(b) plan.[35]

An eligible rollover distribution is any distribution to a participant of all or part of his or her account balance in a Qualified Retirement Plan that is not:

1. part of a series of substantially equal periodic payments made at least annually over (a) the life or life expectancy of the participant or the joint life expectancies of the participant and designated beneficiary or (b) a specified period of ten years or more – the test is applied at the beginning of the payout period,
2. a minimum required distribution
3. the nontaxable portion of a distribution unless made to a traditional IRA or a qualified plan and certain requirements are met,
4. the excess 401(k) annual additions of elective deferrals that are returned due to Code Section 415 limitations,
5. corrective distributions of excess contributions, deferrals or aggregate contributions along with the income allocable to the corrective distributions under a 401(k) plan,
6. distributions to a beneficiary other than a surviving spouse or a current or former spouse under a qualified domestic relations order,
7. hardship distributions, or
8. deemed distributions of plan loans.[36]

The downside of an eligible rollover distribution paid directly to the participant is the 20 percent federal income tax withholding.[37] Additionally, state income tax withholding may be required. On the other hand, if the distribution is rolled over directly to the eligible retirement plan, there is no withholding requirement. A direct rollover may be in the form of a trustee-to-trustee transfer accomplished through a wire transfer or a check made payable to the trustee.[38]

Temporary Use of Rollover Distributions

Due to a temporary lack of funds, some participants use all or part of an eligible rollover intending to replenish those funds prior to the expiration of the sixty-day period. In that case, the participant risks adverse tax consequences should he or she be unable to roll over the full amount of the distribution within that period. To the extent the participant fails to roll over all or part of the distribution into a new IRA, the amount of the shortfall would be treated as a distribution subject to income tax and potentially a 10 percent premature distribution penalty if the participant is under the age of 59½.

Example: Joanne Risler, age forty-five, decided to take a distribution from her IRA account to purchase a new car costing $24,000. Because Joanne realized the trustee would withhold 20 percent in federal income tax, or $6,000, she requested a gross distribution of $30,000. Anticipating the receipt of a $30,000 bonus within the next two months, she was sure she would be able to roll over $30,000 into a new IRA within the sixty-day period. Pursuant to her request, Joanne received a check for $24,000 from her IRA account which she used to purchase the car. Subsequently, due to the withholding of a variety of items from her $30,000 bonus, she netted only $20,000. In order to complete a full rollover, Joanne must raise another $10,000 from other sources. Since Joanne is under age 59½, if she does not make up the difference within the sixty-day period, the $10,000 would be taxable in the year of distribution and also subject to a 10 percent premature distribution penalty.

Limitation of Number of Rollovers

An individual is limited to only one rollover from an IRA in any 365-day period.[39] The 365-day period begins on the date of the first IRA withdrawal. However, trustee-to-trustee transfers and direct transfers to and from Qualified Retirement Plans are excluded from the one-year rule.[40] The rationale for this rule is to prevent individuals from taking a series of short term loans from IRAs tax-free by being able to roll over the amount distributed to another IRA within the sixty-day period.

Example.

- On March 1, Sarah Parker withdraws $10,000 from her IRA at ABC Bank. This is the first time Sarah ever made a withdrawal from any IRA or other Qualified Retirement Plan.
- On April 29, Sarah rolls over that withdrawal by depositing $10,000 into another IRA at First National Bank.
- On July 3, she rolls over her account balance from a Qualified Retirement Plan maintained by her former employer into a rollover IRA at Finest Investments.
- On July 29, Sarah directs a trustee-to-trustee rollover of the balance in her rollover at Finest Investments to an IRA at Prudent Bank.
- On February 3 of the following year, Sarah withdraws $10,000 from her IRA at First National Bank.
- On February 20, Sarah rolls over the February 3 withdrawal by depositing $10,000 into another IRA at Prudent Bank.

The first rollover by Sarah, the plan to IRA rollover and the trustee-to-trustee rollovers are all permissible. This is because the first withdrawal on March 1 was rolled over by Sarah within sixty-days and there was no other withdrawal from a Qualified Retirement Plan within 365 days prior to that withdrawal. The next two withdrawals were permissible because direct plan to IRA transfers and trustee-to-trustee transfers are not subject to the 365 day rule. However, the February 3 withdrawal from Sarah's IRA at First National Bank is taxable because it occurred less than 365 days from her March 1 withdrawal. Therefore, the $10,000 withdrawal will be taxable in the year of distribution and potentially subject to the 10 percent premature distribution penalty.

Previously, the one rollover in a 365 day period rule was applied to each IRA separately. Therefore, an individual with two IRAs could withdraw and rollover funds from each IRA within the same 365 day period. Beginning in 2015, the IRS announced that only one rollover will be permitted in the 365 day period regardless of the number of IRAs an individual owns.[41] This policy change does not impact the type of rollovers that have never been subject to the 365 day rule (such as direct trustee-to-trustee transfers, etc.).

Pros and Cons of Rollovers from Employer-Sponsored Qualified Retirement Plans to an IRA

There are several good reasons not to roll over a distribution from an employer- sponsored Qualified Retirement Plan to an IRA. This is because, as detailed below, the participant has more flexibility with funds in such a plan than he or she would have if those funds were in an IRA:

1. Taxpayers may borrow from qualified plans (provided the plan permits participant loans), but not IRAs.

2. Life insurance can be purchased within a qualified plan, but not an IRA.

3. If the employee separates from service after age fifty-five, distributions taken from an employer sponsored Qualified Retirement Plan are not subject to the premature distribution penalty. Conversely, the IRA premature distribution penalty applies until the account holder reaches age 59½ unless an exception to the penalty applies.

4. Employer-sponsored Qualified Retirement Plans provide broader federal creditor protection in the case of malpractice, bankruptcy, divorce, business, or creditor problems.

On the other hand, a rollover from a qualified plan into an IRA will preserve the ability to roll over the funds back into a qualified plan in the future. The future rollover into a qualified plan preserves the benefits listed above.

Example. On March 1, 2020, Sally Rhodes receives a distribution of $250,000, the entire balance of her 401(k) account with a former employer. Although Sally does not yet have a new job, she plans to retire at fifty-five, at which time she would need to tap into her retirement funds. Since she is unemployed, she does not have a new Qualified Retirement Plan in which to roll over her 401(k) account balance. Thus, within sixty days of receiving the 401(k) distribution, Sally rolls it over into a newly created IRA. Then, when she begins her new job, she can roll over the amount in the IRA to her new employer's Qualified Retirement Plan. By doing so, if Sally does retire at age fifty-five, she can receive distributions without incurring the 10 percent premature distribution penalty.

Sixty-day Rollover Waiver

Individuals who fail to meet the sixty-day rollover deadline may nonetheless apply for relief pursuant to IRC Section 408(d)(3)(I). If relief is granted, the IRS will waive the sixty-day rollover requirement. According to this Code section, the IRS may grant the waiver, if failing to do so would be against equity or good conscience, including casualty, disaster, or other events beyond the reasonable control of the individual.

In determining whether to grant a waiver, the IRS will consider all relevant facts and circumstances, including:

1. errors committed by a financial institution;

2. inability to complete a rollover due to death, disability, hospitalization, incarceration, restrictions imposed by a foreign country or postal error;

3. the use of the amount distributed (for example, in the case of payment by check, whether the check was cashed); and

4. the time elapsed since the distribution occurred.

Automatic waivers of the sixty-day rule are granted for failed rollovers caused by errors made by financial institutions.

Distributions of Employer Securities

Large publicly traded corporations often use company stock to fund matching contributions to their employees' retirement plans. In many instances, employees are allowed to direct the plan administrator to purchase company stock as an investment option (sometimes using employer contributed funds and sometimes using employee nondeductible contributed funds). As a result, a participant's account may own a substantial amount of company stock.

Although it may be contrary to prudent asset allocation judgment, the accumulation of company stock receives preferential tax treatment when the stock is included in a lump sum distribution (LSD). Specifically, an employee is not taxed on the net unrealized appreciation (NUA) of employer securities received as part of a LSD.[42] NUA is the excess of the fair market value of the employer securities received on the distribution date over the aggregate cost or other basis of such securities to the plan. In most cases, the basis in the stock is the amount the plan administrator paid to purchase the stock for the participant. Only the basis of the shares is taxable to the employee.

Upon the subsequent sale of the employer stock, the recognized gain is treated as long-term capital gain (subject to the maximum capital gains tax rate) to the extent it is attributable to the untaxed NUA. Any additional gain is treated as long or short-term based on the employer's post-distribution hold period.[43]

Importantly, if the employer securities are sold within the plan prior to the LSD, the favorable tax treatment for the NUA is lost. Likewise, if the entire LSD, including the company stock is rolled over into an IRA or other retirement plan, the favorable tax treatment of the company stock is lost.

Finally, if the company stock is not rolled over, although the preferential tax treatment described above would be preserved, the 10 percent penalty for premature distributions will apply if the employee receives the LSD before age 59½. However, it the company stock is not rolled over, the tax and penalty are imposed on the basis of the company stock, not the fair market value.

Example. At age forty-five, Rich Davidson leaves his job and receives an LSD from his employer's 401(k) plan. The distribution consists of $300,000 in cash and $150,000 of company stock, with a basis of $60,000 and a NUA of $90,000. To avoid tax on the $300,000 cash distribution, Rich rolls over that portion of the LSD into an IRA. He keeps the stock and includes $60,000 (the plan's basis in the stock) in gross income in addition to paying a 10 percent premature distribution penalty ($6,000). Subsequently, Rich sells the stock. Of the recognized gain, $90,000 (the NUA) will be taxed as long-term capital gain. Any additional gains will be treated as long or short-term based upon his holding period from the date of distribution.

If a taxpayer receives company stock that has a built in loss or is worthless, special rules may apply. If the participant receives worthless stock in which the taxpayer has basis (i.e., the stock was purchased with nondeductible contributions), an ordinary loss may be claimed as a miscellaneous itemized deduction subject to the 2 percent floor.[44]

On the other hand, if the employee company stock is not worthless, but is worth less than the employee's nondeductible contributions (employee's rather than the plan's basis), the loss would be recognized only if the stock was sold or exchanged.[45] The loss will be either long or short-term depending on the holding period beginning on the date of distribution.[46]

DISTRIBUTION RELATED PENALTIES

In some instances, a premature distribution or the failure to take a required distribution may result in a penalty to the participant.

Premature Distributions

In addition to regular income tax, a participant who receives a distribution from an employer sponsored Qualified Retirement Plan and an IRA (including a Roth IRA) prior to attaining the age of 59½ is also potentially subject to a penalty tax on a premature distribution.[47] The penalty is 10 percent of the taxable amount of the premature distribution.[48] The penalty does not apply to the nontaxable portion of the distribution or the amount that is rolled over into another IRA or qualified plan within the prescribed time periods.

Note: The penalty is increased to 25 percent for the first two years an employee participates in a SIMPLE IRA plan.[49]

Example 1. Sam Sneed, age thirty-five, withdraws $2,000 from his IRA to pay for damages to his car. Because Sam never made nondeductible contributions to the IRA, he has no basis. Therefore, in the year of distribution, Sam includes $2,000 in gross income and pays an additional $200 premature distribution penalty.

Example 2. Assume that $800 of the $2,000 distribution was the recovery of Sam's basis. As a result, in the year of distribution, Sam would include $1,200 in gross income and pay an additional $120 premature distribution penalty.

The following are premature distributions that are not subject to the 10 percent penalty:

- Made on or after the death of the owner.[50]

- Made on account of the disability of the owner.[51]

- Part of a series of substantially equal periodic payments over the life of the owner or the lives of the owner and a designated beneficiary.[52] For non-IRA type retirement accounts, this exception applies only after the employee separates from service.[53] See further discussion below.

- Used to pay medical expenses that exceed 10 percent (7.5 percent, if under sixty-five) of the taxpayer's adjusted gross income (without regard to whether the employee/owner itemizes deductions for that taxable year).[54]

- From a qualified plan and made to an employee following separation from service after reaching age fifty-five (does not apply to IRAs).

- From a qualified plan and paid to an alternate payee pursuant to a qualified domestic relations order (does not apply to IRAs).

- From an IRA and used to pay the health insurance premiums of an unemployed owner who has received unemployment compensation for at least twelve consecutive weeks in the year of the distribution or in the previous year (this exception does not apply to qualified plan distributions).[55]

- From an IRA and used to fund higher education expenses, which may include graduate school, for the taxpayer, spouse, children or grandchildren (this exception does not apply to qualified plan distributions).[56] Qualified higher education expenses include tuition, fees, books, supplies, required equipment and room and board.[57]

- From an IRA and used for a first-time home purchase, up to a $10,000 lifetime cap (this exception does not apply to qualified plan distributions).[58] In order to use this exception, a qualified first time homebuyer must use the distribution within 120 days to fund the costs of acquiring, constructing or reconstructing a residence, including any usual or reasonable settlement, financing or other closing costs.[59] An individual is a first time homebuyer if the individual, and, if married, his or her spouse had no present ownership interest in a principal residence during the two-year period ending on the date of acquisition of the principal residence.[60] The distribution may be used to fund the first time home purchase of the owner, the owner's spouse, or any child, grandchild or ancestor (including their spouses) of the owner.

Substantially Equal Periodic Payments

The premature distribution penalty exception for substantially equal periodic payments (SEPP) is very useful if the taxpayer has a recurring annual need for funds prior to reaching age 59½. This commonly occurs when a taxpayer retires early and virtually all of the taxpayer's wealth is tied up in retirement plan accounts.

To avoid the penalty, SEPPs must be made at least annually and must continue until *the later of*:

1. the date the individual turns age 59½, or

2. the close of the five-year period beginning with the date the initial payment was received.[61]

The amount of the SEPP cannot be altered before the later of the two above dates (except on account of death or disability). If payments are altered, all of the prior payments under the SEPP are retroactively taxed as if a SEPP did not exist. The tax is payable in the first year the modification is made. Interest will also be assessed beginning on the date the tax would have been paid had a SEPP not been in place and ending on the date the actual payment is made.[62]

SEPPs may be calculated using one of three methods:

1. *Life Expectancy Method* – The annual payment is determined in a manner similar to the minimum required distribution rules. The account balance as of December 31 of the year prior to the distribution year is divided by a life expectancy factor using one of the following three tables:

   - Uniform Lifetime Table
   - Single Life Expectancy Table
   - Joint Life Expectancy Table, if there is a designated beneficiary

   Since the account balance will change each year, the amount of the SEPP will vary from year to year. This is the only permissible variation in the amount of the SEPP. This method generally produces the smallest amount payable under a SEPP and offers the least amount of control since the investment performance of the retirement account will have a material impact on the future required distribution.

2. *Fixed Amortization Method* – The annual payment is determined by amortizing the account balance at the beginning of the SEPP over the life expectancy at a chosen interest rate. The owner's life expectancy or joint life expectancy of the owner and designated beneficiary is determined using one of the three tables listed in the life expectancy method. The interest rate factor must not exceed a "reasonable interest rate." Any interest rate that does not exceed 120 percent of the federal mid-term rate for either of the two months immediately preceding the beginning of the SEPP is considered reasonable.[63] Once the amortized amount is determined, the SEPP is not recalculated. The same amount is distributed each period.

3. *Fixed Annuitization Method* – The annual payment is determined by dividing the account balance by an annuity factor using a mortality table and a reasonable interest rate, as defined above.[64] Like the fixed amortization method, the amount of the SEPP will not change from period to period.

For those taxpayers who start a SEPP and use either the fixed amortization or fixed annuitization methods, a one-time change is allowed to the life expectancy method, in any year after a SEPP begins.[65] Once the change is made to the life expectancy method, that SEPP may not be changed back to either of the other methods. No other modification to the SEPP is permitted.

There is some question as to whether the SEPP can incorporate a cost-of-living adjustment each year and not violate the SEPP. Revenue Ruling 2002-62 clearly states that, if a SEPP is modified prior to the time period at which a SEPP ends, "all payments in the series lose the shelter of the exemption, and the penalty applies, retroactively and with interest, to all pre-age 59½ distributions."

A *modification* occurs when there is (i) any addition to the account balance other than gains or losses, (ii) any nontaxable transfer of a portion of the account balance to another retirement plan, or (iii) a rollover by the taxpayer of the amount received, resulting in such amount not being taxable. Of course, a modification would also occur if the taxpayer took out more or less than the SEPP mandates. However, various letter rulings issued by the IRS (in years prior to the release of Revenue Ruling 2002-62) have allowed for cost of living adjustments and other modifications. Revenue Ruling 2002-62 does not specifically address modifications of this type.[66]

Significantly, SEPPs apply to each retirement plan of the taxpayer, rather than the aggregate of all plans.[67] Therefore, if a taxpayer has a large IRA from which to set up a SEPP, it may be better to divide the IRA into two or more IRAs before beginning the SEPP. Only one of the IRAs will pay the SEPP distributions. Thereafter, if additional funds are needed on an annual basis, one or more of the other IRAs can begin making SEPP distributions as well.

When determining how to set up a SEPP, it is best to work from the desired end result, backwards.

1. Determine how much is needed on an annual basis from the SEPP.

2. Perform calculations to determine how much of an account balance is needed to produce the desired level of distributions.

3. Separate the account into at least one SEPP account and one non-SEPP account.

When determining how to set up the SEPP, consider the following:

- The life expectancy method will generally produce smaller SEPP distributions and will not be known for the next year until the end of the current year.
- A higher reasonable interest rate will result in a larger payment under the annuitization and amortization methods.
- A smaller payment can be determined using a designated beneficiary and a joint life expectancy.
- The SEPP should be set up with only the amount of the account balance needed to support the desired distribution. Protect the ability to have future SEPPs by dividing the account balance into more than one account.

Example. Harvey Wilson is fifty-five years old and recently retired. He wishes to set up the largest SEPP possible using his $250,000 IRA. At the time the SEPP would begin, the reasonable interest rate is 4.50 percent and Harvey's single life expectancy is 29.6 years. Based on this information, the SEPP can be established using one of the following three methods:

a. Life expectancy method = $703.83 per month

b. Amortization method = $1,287.33 per month

c. Annuitization method = $1,277.42 per month

The amortization method provides the largest benefit to Harvey. If Harvey requires something less than $1,287.33 per month, it may be beneficial to divide his IRA into two accounts. So, if Harvey needs $1,000 per month, he can set up two IRAs, one with $194,200 and the other with $55,800. Using the amortization method, the larger account will generate the necessary $1,000 monthly payment.

Minimum Required Distributions

During Owner's Lifetime

The earnings generated in a retirement account are tax deferred during the period in which they are held in the account. To prevent the indefinite deferral of income tax, the minimum required distribution (RMD) rules[68] force retirement account owners to receive taxable distributions. RMDs must begin by the owner's required beginning date (RBD).

Note that the minimum distribution rules discussed in this section apply to qualified plans, 403(b) tax sheltered annuities, section 457 plans and traditional IRAs. The owners of Roth IRAs are not subject to the lifetime RMD rules. Minimum distributions from Roth IRAs are required only upon the death of the account owner.[69]

RMDs must begin no later than the participant's or account owner's required beginning date (RBD).[70] Once distributions begin, they must continue each year in minimum required amounts.

Under the SECURE Act, the RBD for qualified plan participants is April 1 of the year following the year in which the individual attains age 72, rather than age 70½ starting in 2020. However, employees who continue to work for the employer sponsoring the qualified plan after age 72 and who own 5 percent or less of the employer may defer taking distributions until they actually retire (provided the plan permits it).[71]

Taxpayers who were required to begin RMDs under the old 70½ rule will must continue to make RMDs even if they have not yet reached age 72. See Chapter 37 for more details. Also, under the new COVID-19 legislation, RMDs are not required for the 2020 tax year. See Chapter 38 for more details.

The RBD for IRA owners and for qualified plan participants who own more than 5 percent of the business is April 1 of the year following the year in which they turn age seventy-two, even if they have not retired.

Section 403(b) plans generally follow the same rules as qualified plans, except that all participants who work beyond age seventy-two may defer starting distributions until April 1 of the year after the year they retire. However, some 403(b) plan participants may be permitted to defer distributions of pre-1987 account balances until they reach age seventy-five.

RMDs are calculated each year independently of any other year without any carryover. So, if during 2018, a taxpayer receives $5,000 more than her RMD for 2018, she may not apply the excess to reduce her RMD in any other year.[72]

Determining the RMD

The RMD for a year is determined by dividing the account balance, determined as of the last valuation date in the preceding year, by the owner's life expectancy. The account balance is determined as of the last valuation date in the preceding calendar year.[73] No adjustments are made to the account balance for contributions or distributions occurring after that date.

Example: In 2020, Fred Lubert turned age 72. Using his account balance on December 31, 2019, his first RMD is $20,000. Since he turned age 70½ in 2020, he must receive that distribution by April 1, 2021. As of December 31, 2020, he did not receive his first RMD. Although his account balance as of December 31, 2019 is used to determine his 2020 RMD, the account balance is not reduced by the undistributed RMD payable by April 1, 2021 (that could have been paid prior to December 31).

Determining Life Expectancy

Distributions during the life of a retirement account owner must begin no later than the owner's RBD and must be distributed over a period no longer than:

1. the owner's life expectancy,
2. the life expectancies of the owner and a designated beneficiary, or
3. a fixed period that does not extend beyond such life expectancies.[74]

The final regulations provide that the RMD can be calculated by using the factor found in the Uniform Lifetime Table based on the owner's age at the end of the applicable distribution calendar year.[75] This table may be used regardless of the age of the designated beneficiary or if there is no designated beneficiary.

The only exception to the use of the Uniform Lifetime Table is if the designated beneficiary is a spouse who is more than ten years younger than the participant/owner. In that case, the Joint and Last Survivor Table may be used.[76]

Example: Alex Weston is seventy-five years old, his wife Renee is sixty-two and his son Todd is forty. Alex has three IRAs. One names his wife as the designated beneficiary, the second names Todd and the third names his estate. During his lifetime, the applicable life expectancy factors to be used to determine Alex's RMDs are:

Beneficiary	Table Used	Account Balance	Life Expectancy	RMD
Renee	Joint and Last Survivor	$800,000	25.0	$32,000
Todd	Uniform Lifetime	$300,000	22.9	$13,100
Estate	Uniform Lifetime	$250,000	22.9	$10,917

For each qualified plan and IRA, RMDs must be determined separately. The RMD for a qualified plan must be distributed from that qualified plan.[77] On the other hand, if an individual has more than one IRA, the RMDs for each IRA may be distributed from any one or more of the owner's IRAs.

Example: Adam Coultier is seventy-three years old. The RMD from his qualified plan is $8,000. His two IRAs require RMDs of $5,000 and $16,000. To satisfy the RMD with respect to the qualified plan, Adam must receive at least an $8,000 distribution that plan. For the IRAs, he may receive the RMDs out of each of the IRAs or receive the total amount of the RMDs ($21,000) out of one of the IRAs.

RMDs are calculated each year through the year of the owner's death using the Uniform Lifetime Table (or the Joint and Last Survivor Table if the participant/owner is married to a spouse more than ten years younger than the participant/owner). This rule applies regardless of who is the beneficiary of the participant/owner's retirement arrangement.

Special Rules for Surviving Spouses

If the decedent's spouse is the sole beneficiary of the decedent's IRA, he or she has the following options:

- Treat the decedent's IRA as his or her own by designating himself or herself as the owner.
- Treat the decedent's IRA as his or her own by rolling it over into a traditional IRA (or some other eligible retirement plan).
- Treat himself or herself as the beneficiary of the decedent's IRA.

If the surviving spouse elects to treat the IRA as his or her own IRA, then the normal IRA rules will apply. This means that distributions to a surviving spouse under age 59½ may be subject to the 10 percent premature distribution penalty. On the other hand, RMDs will not start until the surviving spouse reaches the age of 70½.

In the alternative, if the surviving spouse elects to treat himself or herself as the beneficiary of the decedent's IRA, RMDs are made over the surviving spouse's life expectancy. Those distributions must begin by December 31 of (i) the year the decedent would have attained the age of 70½, or (ii) the year after the decedent's year of death.

Example: Upon the death of his wife, Miranda Wrights at age forty-nine, Asher, also age forty-nine, elects to treat her IRA as an inherited IRA naming himself as the beneficiary. By doing so, any distribution Asher receives prior to attaining age 59½ would not be subject to the 10 percent premature distribution penalty. Additionally, RMDs would not begin until the year in which Miranda would have attained the age of 70½. So by making this election, until that year, Asher has the flexibility of taking penalty-free distributions as he sees fit allowing the undistributed funds to continue to grow tax-free.

After the Owner's Death

Owner Dies after His or Her RBD

If an owner dies after his or her RBD, like any other year, the RMD for the year of death must be calculated and distributed. Beginning with the year following the year of death, distributions must continue at the same pace as they were before the death of the account owner;[78] however, final regulations require payouts to be determined based upon the life expectancy of the "designated beneficiary" of the account. For this purpose, the designated beneficiary is determined as of September 30 of the year following the year of the owner's death. The required distribution periods are based on the type of beneficiary, as follows:

- *No designated beneficiary* – If no designated beneficiary is named (e.g., the account is payable to the owner's estate, a nonqualifying trust, or a charity), the account owner's single life expectancy as of his or her birthday in the year of death is determined by using the Single Life Table.[79] The life expectancy is the divisor for the purpose of calculating the RMD and is reduced by one in each subsequent year.
- *Nonspouse designated beneficiary* – The beneficiary's single life expectancy is determined in the year following the year of the owner's death by using the Single Life Table. However, if the owner's single life expectancy is longer (i.e. the owner was younger than the beneficiary), that life expectancy may be used. The life expectancy is the divisor for the purpose of calculating the RMD and is reduced by one in each subsequent year.
- *Spouse is sole designated beneficiary* – The spouse's life expectancy is determined using the Single Life Table based on the spouse's age at the end of the calendar year for each RMD. This life expectancy is determined each year, so the spouse's life expectancy will be reduced by something less than one each

year. If the owner's single life expectancy is longer, that factor may be used and reduced by one each subsequent year. Upon the death of the spouse, RMDs can be made over his or her remaining single life expectancy determined in the year of death and reduced by one each year thereafter. If the spouse is not the sole beneficiary, the rules for no designated beneficiary or non-spousal beneficiaries applies depending on who the other beneficiary is.

Owner Dies before His or Her RBD

If the account owner dies before his or her RBD or if the account is a Roth IRA, the general rule is that the entire account balance must be distributed on or before December 31 of the year which includes the fifth anniversary of the owner's death (the "five-year rule").[80] An exception to the five-year rule applies if there is a non-spouse designated beneficiary and distributions begin by December 31 of the year after the year in which the owner died. In this case, distributions may be made over the beneficiary's life expectancy.

If the decedent's spouse is the sole beneficiary of the decedent's IRA, he or she has the following options:

- Treat the decedent's IRA as his or her own by designating himself or herself as the owner.
- Treat the decedent's IRA as his or her own by rolling it over into a traditional IRA (or some other eligible retirement plan).
- Treat himself or herself as the beneficiary of the decedent's IRA.

If the surviving spouse elects to treat the IRA as his or her own IRA, then the normal IRA rules will apply. This means that distributions to a surviving spouse under age 59½ may be subject to the 10 percent premature distribution penalty. On the other hand, RMDs will not start until the surviving spouse reaches the age of 70½.

In the alternative, if the surviving spouse elects to treat himself or herself as the beneficiary of the decedent's IRA, RMDs are made over the surviving spouse's life expectancy. Those distributions must begin by December 31 of (i) the year the decedent would have attained the age of 70½, or (ii) the year after the decedent's year of death.

Example: John Ashworth died at the age of forty-seven leaving $750,000 in his IRA wife his wife Andrea (age forty-six) named as the beneficiary. Other than the IRA, the couple has no other assets and Andrea does not work. If Andrea rolls over the IRA into her IRA or elects to treat it as her own, any distribution she would receive prior to reaching age 59½ would likely be subject to the premature distribution penalty (unless one of the exceptions applied). Instead, if she leaves the IRA in John's name and takes distributions as the beneficiary of a decedent's IRA, the premature distribution penalty does not apply.

IRA Trusts

Although most IRA account holders name individuals as the beneficiaries of their IRAs, in some instances, naming a trust as the beneficiary may be a better alternative. This is because once an individual becomes the owner of the account, the original owner has no control over the disposition of the funds in the IRA. Conversely, a trust can provide at least some level of asset protection from the beneficiary's creditors as well as a mechanism to provide for successor beneficiaries.

The regulations provide special rules permitting an IRA owner to designate a trust as the beneficiary of his or her IRA. In setting up such a trust, there are four basic requirements:

1. The trust is valid under state law.
2. The trust is irrevocable or will, by its terms, become irrevocable upon the death of the account owner.
3. The trust beneficiaries are identifiable from the trust document.
4. A copy of the trust document is provided to the trustee or administrator, or the owner agrees to provide a copy of the trust instrument to the plan upon request.[81]

There are two types of IRA trusts – Conduit Trust and Accumulation Trust.

Conduit Trust. A conduit trust requires the trustee to distribute the RMD from the IRA to the conduit beneficiary (based on life expectancy). The trust document may also allow the trustee to make discretionary distributions in excess of the RMD to the beneficiary. In other words, the trust document could authorize such distributions for the health, education, maintenance and support of the beneficiary.

If there are multiple beneficiaries, the RMD will be determined based on the life expectancy of the oldest beneficiary. In that case, all distributions the trustee receives from the IRA (RMD and all other distributions) must be distributed to one or more of the conduit beneficiaries. Accumulations are not permitted in a conduit trust.

Accumulation Trust. Unlike a conduit trust, an accumulation trust allows for the accumulation of RMDs within the trust. This means that the trustee is not required to distribute all or part of the IRA funds it receives. The applicable distribution period upon which RMD is based is the life expectancy of the oldest individual living at the time of the account owner's death and is either (1) a current beneficiary, i.e., entitled to receive a distribution from the trust or (2) a remainder beneficiary, i.e., entitled to receive a distribution from the trust upon its termination.

Penalty for Failure to Make RMDs

Failure to pay any portion of an RMD by the due date of the distribution is subject to a penalty equal to 50 percent of the unpaid amount.[82] However, the IRS may waive the penalty by demonstrating that the unpaid amount was due to reasonable error and steps are being taken to distribute the proper amount.[83] The IRS is more likely to waive the penalty in instances in which the error is attributable to the plan administrator or financial institution holding the individual's retirement account.

Example: Aaron Hastings failed to make a proper request to receive his 2020 $25,000 RMD. As a result, no distribution was received. Therefore, a penalty of $12,500 (50 percent of $25,000) would be imposed unless he can show that the lack of a distribution was due to a reasonable error and took steps to assure that the RMD is distributed to him. In this case, it is unlikely that the IRS would waive the penalty because Aaron simply failed to make a timely request for the RMD.

Qualified Charitable Distributions of RMD

Now permanent, each year, an individual age 70½ or older required to take RMD can direct the custodian of his or her IRA (excluding an inherited IRA, a SEP-IRA or a Simple IRA) to make that distribution (capped at $100,000) to one or more qualifying charitable organization(s).[84] Although there is no charitable deduction, the consequences of the distributions received by charity are even better than if the individual had actually received the deduction. Some of the advantages include the following:

- Subject to the $100,000 cap, the individual would meet his or her minimum required distribution.
- The amount distributed is not taxable to the individual.
- The amount distributed is not included in gross income meaning the individual is more likely to limit the amount of taxable social security and not to lose a portion of deductible itemized deductions as well as numerous other tax benefits that are affected by higher amounts of adjusted gross income.

Stated differently, although the individual is not entitled to a charitable contribution deduction, the exclusion of the amount contributed from gross income is better than a charitable deduction. In the end, the exclusion of the RMD (that is distributed to charity) from gross income is the equivalent of an above the line charitable deduction with all the tax benefits such a deduction creates for the individual.

FREQUENTLY ASKED QUESTIONS

Question – What changes to the hardship distribution and retirement plan loan rules were enacted under the 2017 Tax Act?

Answer – The 2017 Tax Act modified the plan loan rules for tax years beginning after 2017. Under prior law, if a loan from a qualified plan (including 403(b) and 457(b) plans) had not been repaid when the participant left employment or the plan was terminated (among other reasons), the outstanding loan balance would be offset against his or her account balance and would become taxable if not rolled over to another retirement account within sixty days.

Under the 2017 Tax Act, the sixty-day deadline is extended to the participant's tax filing deadline for the tax year in which the offset occurs if the amount is treated as distributed from the participant's qualified 401(k) plan, 403(b) plan or 457(b) plan because either (1) the plan was terminated or (2) because the participant failed to meet the loan repayment terms because of a separation from employment (if the plan provides that the accrued unpaid loan amount must be offset at this time).

This extended time period does not apply to loans that have already been deemed taxable distributions (whether because the loan installment payment remained unpaid beyond the applicable cure period or because the loan's terms did not comply with the IRC requirements).

Question – When are contributions to retirement plans required to be funded?

Answer – The funding deadline for IRAs (including Roth IRAs) is April 15 of the year following the year for which the contribution is intended. Qualified plan funding (other than salary deferrals which must be deposited within thirty days by the employer) must be completed by the extended due date of the tax return on which the deduction will be claimed, generally October 15.

Question – Are amounts rolled over or converted from a traditional IRA to a Roth IRA subject to a 10 percent penalty tax if the owner is less than 59½ years of age at the time of the rollover?

Answer – Although a conversion is not subject to the 10 percent early withdrawal penalty when the conversion occurs, it may be subject to the penalty if withdrawals from the Roth IRA occur within five years of the conversion and the reason for the withdrawal does not qualify as one of the exceptions to the Section 72(t) 10 percent penalty tax.

If a portion of the distribution is categorized as a taxable conversion asset under the ordering rules and the distribution occurs within five taxable years of the taxable year of the conversion, the portion of the distribution attributable to amounts that were includable in income due to the conversion is subject to the 10 percent penalty tax. If the distribution occurs after the five-year period, the penalty tax does not apply.

Question – Who benefits from an eligible retirement plan to Roth IRA conversion?

Answer – Roth IRAs have their greatest attraction to those people who do not need to withdraw any funds from their retirement plans during life, especially those individuals who expect to live well beyond the average life expectancy due to their sex, genetic heritage and/or health. A retirement plan participant approaching age seventy-two is generally required to take distributions that will substantially diminish, if not eliminate, the account over a long life span.

Converting to a Roth IRA just before death should be considered when benefits will otherwise have to be paid out just after death since such conversion may permit the longer post-death deferral of distributions.

For estate planning purposes, if retirement plan must be used to fund the credit shelter trust, part of the advantage of escaping estate taxes is mitigated by the necessity of the trust to pay income taxes out of its principal; in many cases the tax rate on such taxable income will be higher for the trust than for any of the beneficiaries. While this can be corrected by a withdrawal from the retirement plan of a sufficient amount (grossed-up by the income tax), this requires the loss of continued deferral inside the retirement plan. With the Roth IRA conversion, the income taxes are removed from the estate but the deferral of taxes continues and the credit shelter pays no income taxes on the receipt of distributions from the Roth IRA.

Question – Can the owner of a Roth IRA change his designated beneficiary after reaching the age of 70½?

Answer – The Roth IRA participant is permitted to change his "designated beneficiary" after age 70½, and have that change be effective for determining minimum required distributions after his death. The new designated beneficiary's life expectancy at the date of the owner's death will be used for determining the amount of the required distributions.

CHAPTER ENDNOTES

1. IRC Sec. 219(g)(3).
2. If a married individual filing separately did not live with the other spouse at any time during the year, the IRA deduction phase out table for a single individual is applied.
3. IRC Sec. 219(c).
4. IRC Secs. 408A(b), 7701(a)(37).
5. IRC Sec. 408A(c)(1).
6. IRC Sec. 408A(c)(4).
7. If a married individual filing separately did not live with the other spouse at any time during the year, the Roth IRA contribution phase out table for a single individual is applied.
8. IRC Sec. 408A(d)(1).
9. IRC Sec. 408A(d)(2)(A)(i).
10. IRC Sec. 408A(d)(4)(B)(I).
11. IRC Sec. 408A(d)(4)(B)(I).
12. IRC Sec. 408A(c)(5)(A).
13. IRC Sec. 401(a)(9)(B)(iii).
14. IRC Sec. 401(a)(9)(B).
15. IRC Sec. 408(d)(3)(C).
16. IRC Sec. 408A(d)(3)(A)(i).
17. IRC Sec. 408A(d)(3)(A)(ii).
18. IRC Sec. 408A(d)(6) and (7).
19. Treas. Reg. §1.408A-5, Q&A-9(a)(1).
20. IRC Sec. 408A(d)(6)(B)(iii).
21. IRC Sec. 401(a)(17).
22. IRC Sec. 415(b)(1)(A).
23. IRC Sec. 72(b)(1).
24. Treas. Reg. §1.72-4(a)(2).
25. Treas. Reg. §1.72-4(d)(2). Note, however, that if the annuity starting date is after December 31, 1986, the excludable amount is limited to the investment in the contract. Once that amount is recovered, all future annuity payments are fully subject to ordinary income tax. IRC Sec. 72(b)(2).
26. Notice 2008-30, A-8, 2008-12 IRB.
27. Treas. Reg. §1.401(a)-20, A-18.
28. IRC Secs. 72 and 408(d)(1).
29. IRC Secs. 72(e) and 408(d).
30. IRC Secs. 402(a) and 403(a)(1). Special tables are used for joint life expectancies and separate computations may be necessary to determine expected return in some situations, such as where there is a period certain guarantee.
31. IRC Sec. 72(d)(B)(iv).
32. IRC Sec. 402(c).
33. IRC Sec. 402(c)(3).
34. IRC Sec. 7503.
35. IRC Sec. 402(c)(8)(B).
36. IRC Sec. 402(c)(4).
37. IRC Sec. 3405(c).
38. Treas. Reg. §1.401(a)(31)-1, Q-3.
39. IRC Sec. 408(d)(3)(B).
40. Rev. Rul. 78-406, 1978-2 CB 157.
41. Announcement 2014-15 referencing the decision in *Bobrow v. Comm'r.*, T.C. Memo. 2014-21.
42. IRC Sec. 402(e)(4)(B).
43. Treas. Reg. §1.402(a)-1(b)(1)(i)(b).
44. Rev. Rul. 72-328, 1972-2 CB 224.
45. Rev. Rul. 72-15, 1972-1 CB 114.
46. Let. Rul. 8724049.
47. IRC Sec. 72(t)(2)(A)(i).
48. IRC Sec. 72(t)(1).
49. IRC Sec. 72(t)(6).
50. IRC Sec. 72(t)(2)(A)(ii).
51. IRC Sec. 72(t)(2)(A)(iii).
52. IRC Sec. 72(t)(2)(A)(iv).
53. IRC Sec. 72(t)(3)(B).
54. IRC Sec. 72(t)(2)(B).
55. IRC Sec. 72(t)(2)(D).
56. IRC Secs. 72(t)(2)(E), 72(t)(7)(A).
57. IRC Sec. 529(e)(3).
58. IRC Sec. 72(t)(2)(F).
59. IRC Sec. 72(t)(8)(C).
60. IRC Sec. 72(t)(8)(D)(i) A longer period is provided in the event the individual had owned a principal residence outside the United States or was a member of the Armed Forces.
61. IRC Sec. 72(t)(4).
62. IRC Sec. 72(t)(4)(A)(ii)(II).
63. Rev. Rul. 2002-62, 2002-42 IRB 710.
64. Rev. Rul. 2002-62, 2002-42 IRB 710. The mortality table appears in Appendix B of the Revenue Ruling.
65. Rev. Rul. 2002-62, 2002-42 IRB 710.
66. The IRS interprets Revenue Ruling 2002-62 to permit a one-time modification in the method used. See "Retirement Plans FAQs Regarding Substantially Equal Periodic Payments," Question 8, available at: http://www.irs.gov/Retirement-Plans/Retirement-Plans-FAQs-regarding-Substantially-Equal-Periodic-Payments.
67. Let. Rul. 9050030.
68. RMD computations can be performed on Steve Leimberg's RMD Calculator (Leimberg.com or (610) 924-0515).
69. IRC Sec. 408A(c)(5).
70. IRC Sec. 401(a)(9)(A).
71. IRC Sec. 401(a)(9)(C).
72. Treas. Reg. §1.401(a)(9)-5, Q&A-2.
73. Treas. Reg. §1.401(a)(9)-5, Q&A-3.

74. IRC Sec. 401(a)(9)(A).
75. Treas. Reg. §1.401(a)(9)-5, Q&A-4.
76. The Joint and Last Survivor Table can be found in Treas. Reg. §1.401(a)(9)-9.
77. Treas. Reg. §1.401(a)(9)-8, Q&A-1.
78. IRC Sec. 401(a)(9)(B).
79. The Single Life Table can be found in Treas. Reg. §1.401(a)(9)-9.
80. IRC Sec. 401(a)(9)(B)(ii).
81. Treas. Reg. §1.401(a)(9)-4, Q&A-3 and 5.
82. IRC Sec. 4974.
83. Treas. Reg. §54.4974-2, Q&A-7.
84. IRC Sec. 408(d)(8)(A).

INCOME ISSUES IN WEALTH TRANSFER PLANNING

CHAPTER 32

INTRODUCTION

Income tax issues in wealth transfer planning can be summarized into four categories: (1) basis management, (2) income shifting, (3) grantor trust status, and (4) "statutory tax shelters". Basis management is important to minimize a family's future income tax obligations. Maintaining a grantor trust, as opposed to a non-grantor trust, can increase wealth transfer. Finally, understanding "statutory tax shelters" can yield significant benefits; these include qualified tuition programs, grantor retained annuity trusts, the exclusion of gain for the sale a principal residence and qualified personal residence trusts.

Wealth transfer planning has been significantly changed by the passage of the 2017 tax reform legislation, which essentially doubled the estate tax exemption. (This chapter is primarily written using the old set of rules for explanatory purposes; see "Wealth Transfer Planning under the 2017 Tax Reforms" below for details about the changes that begin in 2018.) However, wealth transfer planning is, almost by definition, a long-term process, and most parts of the tax reform legislation are scheduled to sunset in ten years. While practitioners should be aware of the new rules, they should also be prepared for those rules to change in the future.

BASIS MANAGEMENT

Basis management in estate planning primarily involves Code sections 1014 and 1015. Code section 1014 generally provides that the basis in property acquired by a decedent equals the fair market value of the property at the time of the decedent's death. Many call this provision the basis "step-up" at death; however it's important to recognize it can also cause a "step-down" in basis. Code section 1015 generally provides that basis in property acquired by gift is the same as the donor's basis, which is commonly called carry-over basis.

Estate Tax Basics

To recognize the importance of this distinction, a basic understanding of the estate tax is required. In 2016, the estate tax rate is a flat 40 percent and each individual has a $5,450,000 exemption from it. No one who dies with assets valued less than that threshold owes estate tax and only the portion of assets which exceed the threshold are subject to estate tax. In order to prevent taxpayers from giving away all their assets before death to avoid the estate tax there is a gift tax which is assessed at the same rate.

It is possible to make a tax-free gift, however. In 2016, a taxpayer can give up to $14,000 to another without incurring gift tax – this is called annual exclusion gifting. Over time, and if a number of beneficiaries are available, such gifts can amount to significant estate tax savings.

Example: Don and his wife Carol expect to have a taxable estate. They have two children and six grandchildren. Every year, Don and Carol both make annual exclusion gifts to their children, the children's spouses and to all the grandchildren. This makes a total of twenty annual exclusion gifts with a total value of $280,000 (2 × 10 × $14,000). The following chart shows the amounts removed from the gross estate and the resulting tax savings given the current 40 percent estate tax rate if they make the annual exclusion gifts for various time periods. Assume that the annual gift tax exclusion amount remains at $14,000 per year/per donee and that the assets transferred produce a total return of six percent.

Years	Total Transfer	Tax Savings
5	1,578,386	631,354
10	3,690,623	1,476,249
15	6,517,272	2,606,909
20	10,299,966	4,119,986
25	15,362,063	6,144,825

Moreover, donors can basically allocate their estate tax exemption of $5,450,000 to gifts in order to make them tax-free – this is called lifetime exemption gifting. This however, reduces the amount exempt from the estate tax at the giver's death.

Lifetime exemption gifts are the foundation of most estate tax minimization plans. This is because gifting appreciating assets directly, or in trust, to younger generations of the family removes any appreciation from the older generation's taxable estate. Put another way, the value is frozen for estate tax purposes on the day of the gift.

Example: Don and Carol each give $5,450,000 to a trust for the benefit of their children and grandchildren. They use their lifetime exemptions to make the gift tax-free. The following chart shows the amounts removed from the gross estate and the resulting tax savings given the current 40 percent estate tax rate depending on how long they live after making the gift. Assume that the estate tax exemption remains $5,450,000 and that the assets transferred produce a total return of six percent.

Years	Amount in Trust	Less Exemption	Amount Outside Estate	Tax Savings
	14,586,659	(10,900,000)	3,686,659	1,474,664
10	19,520,240	(10,900,000)	8,620,240	3,448,096
15	26,122,484	(10,900,000)	15,222,484	6,088,994
20	34,957,777	(10,900,000)	24,057,777	9,623,111
25	46,781,391	(10,900,000)	35,881,391	14,352,556

In recent years however, the estate tax exemption increased significantly, the estate tax rate decreased, and income tax rates increased. This combination reduces or eliminates the efficacy of making lifetime gifts because of Code sections 1014 and 1015. For example, in 2004 the top estate tax rate was 48 percent, the estate tax exemption was $1,500,000 and the maximum capital gain tax rate was 15 percent. Therefore, at that time taxpayers were prudent to gift property, live with a Section 1015 carryover basis and forgo the Section 1014 step-up because the difference between the rates was significant. However, currently the maximum capital gain rate is 23.8 percent and the maximum estate tax rate is 40 percent which is less than half the 2004 rate differential [48% – 15% = 33% > 40% – 23.8% = 16.2%]. Moreover, with a much higher estate tax exemption, many fewer taxpayers are confident that estate tax will apply at their death [$5,450,000 > $1,500,000].

Carryover vs. Adjusted Basis

The basis adjustment at death is a significant incentive to transfer appreciated property by testamentary as opposed to inter vivos gift. However, inter vivos gifts remain common place for taxpayers with very large estates because reducing transfer tax usually remains more important than a basis increase. The basic tradeoffs between Code sections 1014 and 1015 are best understood with an example.

Example: The Taylors own a car wash equipment manufacturing business worth $5,000,000. However, their adjusted basis is only $2,000,000. If they were to sell the business, the average tax rate which would apply to the gain is 25 percent. If they give the business to their daughter now it will have a built-in income tax liability of $750,000 [($5,000,000 – $2,000,000) × 25%]. However, if they make a testamentary gift of the business, the step-up in basis eliminates the income tax liability.

For those who expect to owe estate tax, waiting to make testamentary dispositions increases their estate tax liability if their property is appreciating. It is therefore an incentive to make transfer tax-free gifts and forgo the basis step-up.

Example: The Taylors determine the business will be worth at least $12,000,000 before their death and, based on the value of their other assets, the estate tax will be assessed against the value of the business. If they give the business to their daughter now, using lifetime exemption gifts, they will owe no gift tax and will shift $7,000,000 [$12,000,000 – $5,000,000] of appreciation out of their taxable estate saving $2,800,000 [$7,000,000 × 40%] of estate tax. However, the family will forgo the basis step-up and the elimination of $2,500,000 [$12,000,000 – $2,000,000] of future income tax liability.

For those who might receive a step-down in basis at death, the math is significantly different.

Example: Just before contemplating their estate plan, the Taylors invest an additional $4,000,000 in the business, which makes their total basis $6,000,000 [$2,000,000 + $4,000,000]. However, it is yet to translate into additional revenue and therefore the appraised value of the business remains $5,000,000. The Taylors do not want to sell the business, however if they make a testamentary disposition of the business at its current value. Code section 1014 will require a step-down in basis at an income tax cost of $250,000 [(6,000,000 – $5,000,000) × 25%]. It therefore may be prudent to make an inter vivos gift to their daughter.

Code section 1015 however, in order to prevent loss shifting, requires the recipient of property with a built-in loss to take "split-basis." If such property further decreases in value, the recipient's basis equals the fair market value at the time of the gift. If the property increases in value to an amount greater than the donor's basis, the recipient's basis equals the donor's basis. Moreover, if the value of the property is greater than the donor's basis, but less than the fair market value at the time of the gift the recipient recognizes neither gain nor loss.

Example: The Taylors gift the business when it's worth $5,000,000 and their basis is $6,000,000. If the daughter sells it for $4,500,000 she will recognize a loss of $500,000 [4,500,000 – $5,000,000]. If she sells it for $5,500,000 she will recognize neither gain nor loss. If she sells if for $6,500,000 she will recognize a gain of $500,000 [$6,500,000 – 6,000,000]. By gifting the assets before death the Taylors preserve basis which is significant if the asset recovers in value. If they died holding the asset, Code section 1014 causes $1,000,000 [$6,000,000 – $5,000,000] of basis to be permanently lost.

INCOME SHIFTING

Due to the progressive rate tax system, shifting income from parents and grandparents to younger less wealthy generations can reduce a family's overall income tax burden. For example, a grandparent might have a marginal tax rate of 50 percent and a grandchild might have a marginal tax rate of 15 percent. In such a situation, income shifting could increase the amount of additional wealth the family can accumulate by 35 percent.

Example: Jonathan gives $10,000 of corporate bonds with a 6 percent yield to his grandson James, age twenty-five, using an annual exclusion gift. Jonathan's investments generate a lot of income and he lives in New York so his marginal tax rate is 50 percent. He loses $300 [$600 × 50%] of the $600 [$10,000 × 6%] yield to taxation. Whereas James is attending graduate school in Florida so his marginal tax rate is only 15 percent. He will only pay $90 [$600 × 15%] of income tax on the yield.

A significant, but surmountable, limitation on this strategy is the "kiddie tax." It generally requires a child's unearned income to be subject to the parent's tax rate and applies to a child who is under eighteen or a full-time student under 24.[1] Shifting investment income to persons in younger generations will often not provide income tax savings due to the kiddie tax. Nevertheless, there are many potential beneficiaries to whom the kiddie tax would not apply.

Despite the kiddie tax largely limiting the beneficiaries of income shifting arrangements to those perhaps in their mid-twenties or older, there is usually significant concern regarding transferring excessive responsibility to immature family members. To alleviate such concerns, a structure called a family limited partnership (FLP) is often used. The older generation funds an LLC with some of the family's assets, retains units with voting rights and gifts units without voting rights to younger generations outright or in trust.

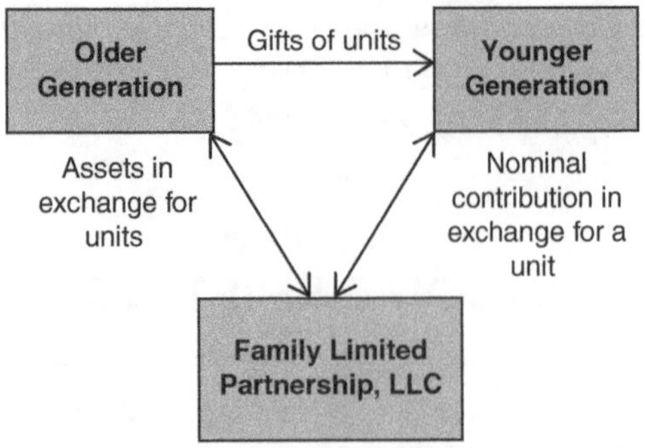

Usually, the older generation owns 98-99 percent of partnership initially. Then, over time, the older generation gives non-voting partnership units to the younger generation. The goal is usually for the older generation to retain only a nominal number of voting units sufficient to control the partnership while the majority of the wealth and income flows to the younger generation.[2]

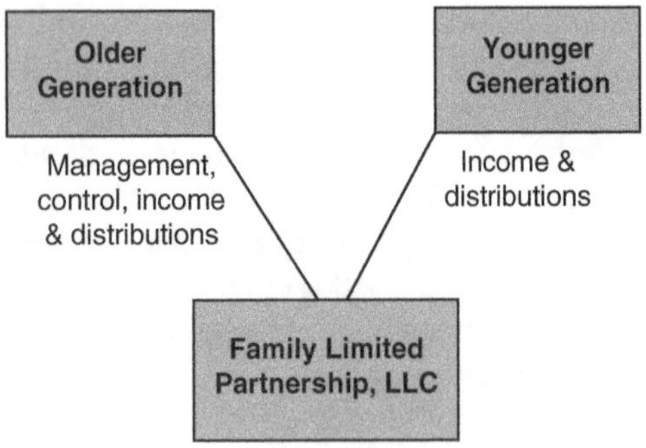

GRANTOR TRUST STATUS

After managing basis, perhaps the most important income tax aspect of estate planning is the strategic use of grantor trusts. Establishing these trusts has a number of tax advantages for certain families. However, one of the most important aspects is the grantor can pay the income tax owed by a grantor trust without incurring additional gift tax.[3]

Generally, any transfer to a trust is either an annual exclusion gift, a lifetime exemption gift, or a taxable gift. Tax-free transfers using the first two options are capped and taxable gifts are usually avoided because accelerating payment is rarely advantageous. However, those who form grantor trusts can uniquely make an additional gift tax-free transfer to trust – the grantor can pay the trust's income tax. The best way to understand this advantage is to continue the example.

Example: The Taylors transfer their business and other marketable securities to trust. These assets generate $700,000 of taxable income which is taxed at a 40 percent average rate. A non-grantor trust pays $280,000 (40% of $700,000) of income tax and is able to accumulate an additional $420,000 ($700,000 – $280,000) annually outside the Taylors' taxable estate. However, a grantor trust accumulates $700,000 annually outside of the Taylor's taxable estate if the Taylors pay the income tax directly. This saves the family an additional $112,000 (40% of $280,000) of transfer tax annually.

Another advantage is the ability of the grantor to swap assets with a grantor trust. Such a swap is not a taxable event provided the assets are of equal value and the assets retain a carryover basis. Swaps are commonly used near-death to greatest effect in order to move low basis property from a trust to the grantors in order to capture a basis step-up. However, they can also be used to preserve losses, management income, and shift the family's highest appreciating assets into trust.

Example: Mr. and Mrs. Taylors' bond portfolio has a fair market value of $5,000,000 and a basis in the same amount. The bond portfolio is far in excess of their needs because their health is failing. The Taylor's can filter the marketable securities portfolio transferred to trust years ago and identify $5,000,000 of significantly appreciated equity positions; the aggregate basis is $3,000,000. If the Taylor's swap these assets, the step-up in basis at the Taylor's death eliminates a $2,000,000 ($5,000,000 – $3,000,000) built-in-gain.

"STATUTORY TAX SHELTERS"

"Statutory tax shelters" for the purposes of this chapter can be defined as any tax benefit Congress explicitly included in the Tax Code which encourages taxpayers to structure their affairs in a certain manner. While there are many such incentives, three provisions are commonly employed by estate planners: Qualified Tuition Programs (QTPs or 529 Plans), Grantor Retained Trusts, and Qualified Personal Residence Trusts (QPRTs).

Qualified Tuition Programs

Qualified tuition programs provide an income tax free savings account for higher education expenses.[4] Funds in the account grow income tax free as are distributions made for qualified education expenses. Qualified tuition programs are an excellent vehicle for many families to save for college. In fact many of these accounts accumulate greater funds than the student needs.

Fortunately, it's possible to change the beneficiary of overfunded QTP accounts. In order to preserve the tax advantage, understanding and planning for this is important. There is no income tax consequence if the new beneficiary is a member of the family of the old beneficiary,[5] which is defined as:

- a spouse;
- a first cousin;
- a child or a descendant of a child, including their spouses;
- a brother, sister, stepbrother, or stepsister, including their spouses;
- a father, mother, or an ancestor of either, including their spouses;
- a stepfather or stepmother, including their spouses;
- a son or daughter of a brother or sister, including their spouses; or
- a brother or sister of the father or mother of the taxpayer, including their spouses.[6]

Grantor Retained Trusts

Grantor Retained Trusts are a structure provided by statute which is used to secure favorable valuations for estate and gift taxes.[7] There are three varieties: Grantor Retained Annuity Trusts (GRATs), Grantor Retained Unitrusts (GRUTs), and Grantor Retained Income Trusts (GRITs). For all three, the grantor retains a right to a series of payments and the other beneficiary of the trust the remainder. The amount of the transfer to trust subject to gift tax is determined by subtracting the present value of the retained interest from the gift. Therefore, to the extent the estimated value of the retained interest deviates from the actual performance of the assets in trust, an estate tax advantage can be realized.

Grantor Retained Annuity Trusts (GRATs) are a common, simple and effective estate tax planning technique. The grantor transfers property to a trust and receives a term annuity paid at least annually. The present value of the annuity payments is calculated using an IRS published discount rate called the 7250 rate. Usually, the trust is structured so the calculated value of the annuity to be repaid to the grantor equals the amount transferred to the trust thereby eliminating any present estate or gift tax consequence. However, if the 7520 rate is less than the rate of appreciation of the assets in trust that differential passes to the remainder beneficiary estate and gift tax free. Moreover, a GRAT can be structured to eliminate the risk of poor asset performance creating an estate tax disadvantage.

Grantor Retained Income Trusts (GRITs) can be very effective, but are fairly uncommon. Instead of a payment which might include principal, the grantor only retains an income interest with a GRIT. If the trust's assets are invested in growth assets, as opposed to income producing assets, the Tax Code overvalues the retained interest and allows a greater portion of the remainder to transfer gift and estate tax-free. The GRIT therefore can be extremely efficient. However, in 1990 Congress believing this to be abusive prohibited the remainder beneficiary from being a member of the grantor's family—making the GRIT quite uncommon.

Grantor Retained Unitrusts (GRUTs) are the least common type. This is because it is the least efficient at reducing the grantor's estate tax obligation. The GRUT pays a percentage of the amount in trust to the grantor. Relative to the GRAT or GRIT this makes it far more difficult for a GRUT to build-up a remainder interest because the grantor's interest increases as the remainderman's interest increases.

The income tax consequences of each variant are extremely similar. These trusts follow the same rules as all grantor trusts: all income is taxable to the grantor; although it is possible to swap assets with the trust, and the payments to the grantor have no income tax consequences. After payments to the grantor end, the trust terminates and the remainder is paid to the beneficiary without income tax consequence.

Assets contributed to and distributed from these trusts generally follow the carry-over basis rules. However, there is a notable exception. If the grantor fails to outlive the term of the retained interest, the assets in the trust are included in the grantor's estate and will receive a basis adjustment. The most common example of this is when the grantor fails to outlive the term of the GRAT annuity. Importantly, such inclusion in the grantor's estate eliminates any estate tax benefit generated by the GRAT.

Qualified Personal Residence Trusts

Qualified Personal Residence Trusts (QPRTs) are a structure that can be used to transfer a taxpayer's house out of an estate. The grantor transfers their home to a trust, retains the right to live in it rent free for a period of years and thereafter rents it from the trust. This is beneficial from a valuation prospective because the initial rent-free period reduces the value of the remainder interest and therefore the estate and gift tax consequences.

The QPRT is a grantor trust which terminates after the rental period. The house is then transferred to the remainderman either directly or more often in further trust. During the initial period the grantors pay all of the usual expenses of maintaining the residence personally without income tax consequences. After the initial period, the grantors pay rent to the remainderman who recognizes it as income, but i is able to deduct the expenses of maintaining the home as well as depreciate the value of the home over time.

The QPRT takes a carryover basis in the house. Unless the house declined in value, the grantors lose two benefits by transferring it to a QPRT. First, the adjustment in basis at death will be unavailable if the grantors survive the rental period. Second, the trust will not be able to take advantage of the exclusion of gain under Code section 121 from the sale of a principal residence.

WEALTH TRANSFER PLANNING UNDER THE 2017 TAX REFORMS

The 2017 Tax Act doubled the transfer tax exemption to $10 million per individual (as indexed for inflation, the amount is $11.58 million, or $23.16 million per married couple, for 2020). The rules permitting a step-up in basis were retained and the estate and GST taxes were not repealed.

The 2017 Tax Act doubled the transfer tax exemption to $10 million per individual (as indexed for inflation, the amount is $11.58 million, or $23.16 million per married couple, for 2020).

Tax reform did not change the maximum gift tax rate, as originally proposed, so that a maximum rate of 40 percent will continue to apply to non-exempt gifts. Further, the $15,000 (as indexed for inflation) annual gift tax exclusion remains in place for 2020.

The 2017 Tax Act roughly doubled the transfer tax exemption (as indexed for inflation, the amount is $11.58 million, or $23.16 million per married couple, for 2020). The rules permitting a step-up in basis were retained and the estate and GST taxes were not repealed.

CHAPTER ENDNOTES

1. IRC Sec. 1(g)(2).
2. IRC Sec. 704(e).
3. Rev. Rul. 2004-64.
4. IRC Sec. 529.
5. IRC Sec. 529(c)(3)(C)(II).
6. IRC Sec. 529(e)(2).
7. IRC Sec. 2702.

INCOME TAX PLANNING FOR CLIENTS WITH SHORTENED LIFE EXPECTANCIES

CHAPTER 33

This chapter will focus on income tax planning issues for clients who are facing a looming demise—primarily the terminally or chronically ill. Many of the issues in this chapter also apply to those facing incapacity, such as dementia or Alzheimer's.

PRELIMINARY REVIEW

The starting point for planning for a client with a shortened lifespan is to quickly gather all of the relevant information about the client's assets and planning efforts to date, including (but certainly not limited to):

- Reviewing the client's existing documents and making sure they:
  - o clearly reflect the client's wishes;
  - o minimize points of conflict (e.g., don't use Co-Fiduciaries who despise each other);
  - o minimize the income taxes paid by the client, heirs, estate and/or trusts;
  - o provide flexibility, including the ability to change the estate plan during the life of the client;
  - o designate the correct decision makers (e.g., Power Holders, Personal Representatives, Trustees); and
  - o provide legal protection to the people who will be making legal decisions for the client.
- Check the client's beneficiary designations, pay on death designations and ownership of assets to make sure assets are not passing in unexpected or tax-costly ways (e.g., not naming a beneficiary of an IRA, passing a retirement plan to the estate; jointly held accounts with dad's third wife).
- Determine if a spouse, particularly a second or third spouse is entitled to claim an elective share against the client's estate and determine if there are methods under applicable state law to reduce that elective share, particularly if the dying spouse wants the assets to pass to a person(s) other than the surviving spouse. Be careful of potential conflicts of interest (e.g., previous representation of both spouses).
- Obtain a current list of the client's assets and any assets held in trusts and estates that are commonly controlled by the client or other family members.
  - o Prepare an analysis of how assets will pass under the documents and discuss that analysis with the client.
  - o Determine the tax basis of all assets and look for planning opportunities.
- Review the client's federal and state income tax returns and determine whether there are tax carry-forwards (e.g., net operating losses, capital loss carry forwards, and charitable deduction carry-forwards) that will expire with the client's passing. Additionally, evaluate tax matters for the most recent period for which an income tax return has not yet been filed.

- Determine the relative income tax brackets and estate tax inclusion of the client, any trusts, any spouse and heirs.

CAUTIONS

Here are a few words of caution that every advisor should consider when working with clients with a limited life expectancy:

- Before implementing any income tax savings strategy, always have a competent tax advisor run the numbers to make sure the anticipated tax benefits are not reduced or eliminated by other tax consequences.
- Always examine the relevant section(s) of the Internal Revenue Code, Treasury Regulations and revenue rulings to make sure there are not limitations or exclusions to the general rules outlined in this chapter.
- Analyze which tax benefits may be lost by implementing the proposed strategy (e.g., a loss of step up in basis at death if assets are gifted during life).
- Most planning strategies create unintended consequences. Make sure you are aware of those consequences and alert the client.
- Be careful in adopting a strategy for which there is little governing law to support it. Avoid approaches based on the premise that *"if there is nothing that says we can't take this approach, it must be allowed."* Always remember that the taxpayer carries the burden of proving tax positions.
- Just because the client says something is true does not mean that it is. Clients at this stage of life are often confused or incorrect in their memories. Always obtain the supporting documents (e.g., copies of the actual beneficiary designations) as a part of the planning.
- Be careful to understand who you represent and avoid the inherent conflicts of interest, which often arise when a family member is facing imminent death or incapacity.
- Document your engagement and recommendations. If your client chooses not to adopt your recommendations, document that decision in writing. Remember that clients will probably not be able to confirm what you discussed with them.
- Understand that for most clients and their families, pre-mortem tax planning is not remotely their highest priority. Even excellent tax related recommendations may be ignored or delayed.

INCOME TAX CONSQUENCES OF GIFTING BY THE TERMINALLY ILL

In general, the donee assumes the donor's tax basis in a gifted asset. Therefore, upon a subsequent sale of an appreciated asset (i.e., the date of gift's fair market value exceeds the donor's basis), the donee (rather than the donor) will be taxed on that gain. For estate tax purposes, however, gifting appreciated assets removes them from the taxable estate and potentially saves estate tax. On the other hand, if the donor holds the appreciated assets until death, the tax basis of the appreciated assets step up to fair market value so as to purge all pre-death appreciation. As a result, upon the subsequent sale by the heirs, there should be little or no income tax.

In the case of a gift by a terminally ill person, death is likely to be proximate to the time of the gift. Therefore, the final decision of whether to gift or hold such assets is extremely time sensitive.

So is it better for a terminally ill person to gift appreciated assets so as to remove them from the taxable estate (shifting the income taxation from the donor to the donee but saving estate tax) or to hold such assets until death to take advantage of the basis step up (saving income tax)?

In other words, do the estate tax savings of making lifetime gifts outweigh the income tax savings of a date of death fair market value basis step up?

In recent times, the difference between the estate tax rate and the income tax rate (including capital gains taxes) has significantly shrunk. Therefore, in the case of a taxable estate, the estate tax savings may be offset by the income tax liability and vice versa. So, it may not make that much difference either way. However, this would not be the case with respect to high basis assets (with little or no appreciation). Due to the high basis, the subsequent sale of the asset by the donee would likely trigger a small amount of income tax.

An even better strategy is to take advantage of the annual gift tax exclusion in the making of gifts of high basis assets. This is because an annual exclusion gift ($15,000 per donee in 2020) reduces the donor's estate without reducing the estate tax exemption amount. For example, a donor who made twenty annual exclusion gifts to children, children's spouses and grandchildren would reduce the estate by $3000,000 (20 times $15,000). Yet, because all the gifts were equal to the annual exclusion, there would be no decrease in the donor's estate and gift tax exemption. Moreover, if the gifts were of high basis assets, there would likely be little or no tax generated by the sale of the assets by the donees.

Conversely, if the donor's estate is non-taxable, there would be no estate tax even if the donor retained the asset. In this instance, retaining a low basis asset until death would be the better choice, because at no estate tax cost, the tax basis of the inherited asset would step up to the date of death's fair market value. So, upon the subsequent sale of such assets by the heirs, there would be little or no income tax triggered.

GIFTS OF APPRECIATED ASSETS (IN EXCESS OF THE ANNUAL EXCLUSION AMOUNT) BY DONOR WITH TAXABLE ESTATE

As discussed above, the donee assumes the donor's tax basis in gifted property. This raises the question of whether a donor who has an asset with a significant unrealized gain and a taxable estate should a) sell the asset, gift the proceeds to the donee and pay the resulting income tax out of the donor's other assets; b) make a lifetime gift of the asset to a donee, who in turn will sell the asset and pay the tax; or c) hold the asset until death and receive a fair market value basis step-up that will eliminate all taxable unrealized appreciation.

Example: A donor is contemplating whether to a) gift $2.1 million in marketable securities (with a basis of $100,000) to her children; b) sell the stock, pay the tax with other funds and gift the $2.1 million of cash to her children; or c) hold the stock until her death. Both the donor and her children have an effective state and federal capital gain tax rate of 30 percent.

Scenario 1: Donor sells the stock and gifts the $2.1 million proceeds to her children.

Here, donor would have a gain of $2 million ($2.1 million minus $100,000 basis), triggering a tax of $600,000 (30 percent of $2 million) that she pays from her other funds. For estate tax purposes, the $600,000 tax payment reduces her estate. For federal estate tax purposes, at a 40 percent federal estate tax rate, there would be an estate tax savings of $240,000 (40 percent of $600,000 of tax removed from the estate). So, the estate tax savings effectively offsets a portion of the income tax. As illustrated below, it would cost the donor $2,460,000 to make this $2.1 million gift to donees.

COST OF GIFT TO DONOR			
Amount of Gift	**Income Tax Triggered by Sale**	**Estate Tax Savings Attributable to Donor's Income Tax**	**Net Cost of Gift to Donor**
$2,100,000	$600,000	$240,000	$2,460,000
GIFT TO DONEE			
Amount of Gift	**Income Tax Payable by Donee**		**Net Tax-Free Gift**
$2,100,000	$0 (Donee received money)		$2,100,000

Scenario 2: Donor gifts the stock to children who in turn sell the stock.

On the subsequent sale, because the children would assume donor's basis in the stock, they would recognize the $2 million gain. Then, after paying the $600,000 of income tax, the children would net $1.5 million rather than the $2.1 million value of stock. Stated differently, it would cost the donor $2.1 million to make a $1.5 million net gift to her children.

COST OF GIFT TO DONOR		
Amount of Gift	**Income Tax**	**Net Cost to Donor**
$2,100,000	$0 (Donor did not sell the stock)	$2,100,000
GIFT TO DONEE		
Amount of Gift	**Income Tax Triggered by Sale**	**Net Tax-Free Gift**
$2,100,000	$600,000	$1,500,000

Scenario 3: Donor leaves the stock to children at her death.

In this instance, at donor's death, her tax basis in the stock would step up to fair market value. As a result, if the children were to immediately sell the stock, there would be no taxable gain.

COST OF TESTAMENTARY GIFT TO DONOR		
Amount of Gift	**Income Tax**	**Net Cost to Donor**
$2,100,000	$0	$2,100,000
TESTAMENTARY GIFT TO DONEE		
Amount of Gift	**Income Tax Triggered by Sale**	**Net Tax-Free Testamentary Gift**
$2,100,000	$0 (No gain generated because sales price $2.1 would be equal to stepped up tax basis also $2.1)	$2,100,000

INCOME TAX CONSEQUENCES OF GIFTS OF DEPRECIATED ASSETS

There are special basis rules that apply to gifts of depreciated assets (e.g., the donor's tax basis in the gifted asset is greater than the fair market value). If at the time of the gift, the donor's tax basis in the gifted asset is greater than its fair market value, the donee's tax basis for computing loss is the fair market value of the asset.[1]

Example: Asher gifts a tract of land with a fair market value of $200,000 and a tax basis of $500,000 to his friend Miranda Wright. Subsequently, the land further depreciates at which time Miranda sells the land for $100,000. Because at the time of the gift, the fair market value of the land was greater than Asher's tax basis, Miranda's basis for computing loss is the $200,000 fair market value. Therefore, Miranda will recognize a $100,000 loss ($200,000 basis minus $100,000 sales price). Effectively, the pre-gift depreciation ($300,000 the amount by which the land depreciated in Asher's hands) that is expunged from Miranda's basis is not deductible by her.

On the other hand, if instead of gifting the land, Asher sells the land for $100,000, he would recognize a loss of $400,000 ($500,000 basis minus $100,000 sales proceeds). By selling the depreciated asset rather than gifting it, Asher can take advantage of the entire loss. After the sale, Asher could gift the proceeds from the sale to Miranda.

Finally, upon death, the tax basis of depreciated assets *step down* to fair market value.[2] So, in the above example, if instead of selling or gifting the land, Asher had devised it to Miranda, the tax basis in the land would be $200,000 (date of death value).

Opportunity: In certain instances, despite not being able to deduct the pre-gift loss, gifting depreciated assets can be more advantageous than devising such assets. For example, a terminally ill client could gift the asset to either:

(1) *A spouse.* Unlike a gift to any other person, regardless of whether an asset has appreciated or depreciated in the hands of the donor spouse, the donee spouse always assumes the tax basis of the donor spouse.[3] So, if the spouse subsequently sells the asset, the spouse will receive the same gain or loss as the donor would have received had the donor sold it during life.[4]

(2) *To non-spousal family members or a trust for their benefit.* Although the tax basis of a non-spouse donee in depreciated property is the date of gift fair market value, there is another special rule that may be of some benefit. If the donee sells the asset for an

amount that is greater than the date of gift fair market value ($200,000) but less or equal to the *donor's* basis ($500,000), there is no gain or loss.[5] In other words, although the donee cannot claim any pre-gift depreciation, the donee may recover up to the full amount of the donor's tax basis tax-free.

Example: Miranda Wright sells the gifted tract of land she received from Asher for $450,000. At the time of the gift, the fair market value of the land was $200,000 and Asher's tax basis was $500,000. Although Miranda is not allowed to deduct what would have been Asher's $50,000 loss, there is no tax on any of the $450,000. This is because the amount Miranda received is less than Asher's basis. So, even though Miranda is not allowed to claim Asher's loss, she is allowed to recover his original basis tax-free.

INCOME TAX CONSEQUENCES OF GIFTING TO THE TERMINALLY ILL

Dealing with IRC Section 1014(e)

Gifting assets to a terminally ill individual may result in unintended tax consequences. Pursuant to Code section 1014(e), the basis of property acquired by a decedent within one year of death that is essentially reacquired from the decedent by the donor *does not* step up to fair market value.

Example: In 2019, Miranda Wright gifts land worth $500,000 with a tax basis of $200,000 to Asher. As a result, Asher's basis in the gifted land is $200,000. In January 2020, less than a year after the gift, Asher dies leaving the land to Miranda. Because Miranda reacquired the land she had gifted to Asher within one year of his death, her tax basis in the land is $200,000 (Asher's basis) rather than $500,000, the date of death fair market value.

The rationale for this rule is to prevent individuals from making gifts to dying individuals in order to reacquire the same property at death with a stepped up tax basis.[6]

On the under hand, under the right circumstances, gifting property to a terminally ill family member may be advantageous for tax purposes.

Opportunity: Assume a client owns a tract of land that has a fair market value of $2.1 million, a basis of $200,000 and secured debt of $1.5 million. If the client sells the property, the recognized gain is $1.9 million. After paying off the $1.5 million mortgage and paying federal and state tax of $570,000 (assuming a state and federal effective income tax rate of 30 percent), the client would receive $30,000.

But instead of selling the land and assuming client's husband is terminally ill, the client gifts the land directly to the husband. Even though the secured liability ($1.5 million) exceeds the tax basis of the asset ($200,000), the gift of the land by wife to husband is not considered a part-gift part sale (that would normally trigger taxable gain to a non-spouse donor). Thus, the gift is entirely income tax-free,[7] In turn, husband transfers the land to a revocable trust for the benefit of the couple's children. By not providing any beneficial interest in the trust to the donor/wife, IRC section 1014(e) does not apply (because the gifted property would not be deemed to be reacquired by the donor spouse). Therefore, upon husband's death, because assets in a revocable trust are includible in the grantor's gross estate, the tax basis of the land would step up to $2.1 million. Assuming the trust immediately sells the land, there would be no taxable gain. As a result, after paying off the $1.5 million mortgage, the trust would net $600,000.

In the alternative, if wife did have a beneficial interest in her husband's revocable trust and if husband dies within a year of the gift, wife could disclaim any interest to that trust to avoid the application of section 1014(e). By making a qualified disclaimer, it is as if wife predeceased husband so that she did not reacquire property gifted to her husband within a year of his death.

Opportunity: There are other simple ways to avoid the application of IRC section 1014(e). For example, assume a donor creates a grantor trust with the transfer of $1.0 million in cash. The sole lifetime beneficiary of the trust is the grantor/spouse's dying spouse who is given a testamentary power of appointment. The donee/spouse exercises that power in favor of the donor or a trust for the donor's benefit. While the dying spouse is still alive, the grantor spouse sells the property to the trust for $1.0 million. At the date of donee/spouse's death, the property has a fair market value of $2.0 million. As a result (unless the IRS successfully argues the application of the step transaction doctrine):

- The sale by the donor/grantor to the grantor trust is not taxable to the donor/grantor.[8]

- Code section 1014(e) would not apply because the gift to the trust was cash and cash is not "appreciated" and because the donor spouse did not retain any powers over the trust to cause it to be an incomplete gift.

- Because the dying spouse possessed a general power of appointment he or she is considered the owner of the trust property, so the trust corpus (including the purchased property) would be included in the donee/spouse's estate pursuant to Code section 2041(a)(2).

- Because the trust corpus is included in the dying spouse's gross estate, pursuant to Code section 1014(b)(9), the tax basis of the trust property would step up to fair market value (in this case $2.0 million).

INCOME TAX BENEFITS OF CHARITABLE GIVING

Many clients make testamentary charitable bequests. However, for income tax purposes, the estate does not generally receive any income tax benefit, except the possible avoidance of any IRD that is allocated to the charitable bequest.[9]

Opportunity: Because an individual rather than the estate is more likely to enjoy the income tax benefits of charitable contributions, consider making the charitable gift before the client's death with a corresponding charitable income tax deduction. Part of this plan might include accelerating income (e.g., receiving a work bonus while alive rather than after death when it would constitute IRD taxable to the estate) into the client's last tax year so as to use the charitable deduction to offset the accelerated income. For example, making a $50,000 lifetime charitable contribution in lieu of a $50,000 charitable bequest could save the decedent up to $21,700 in federal income taxes (i.e., $50,000 times a 43.4 percent top federal income tax rate).

Trap: Make sure the dispositive documents are changed to remove the charitable bequests. Otherwise, the charity might have an additional claim against the estate. In the alternative, have the charity acknowledge that the gift is an advancement of the bequest.

Trap: Make sure the client can take full advantage of the charitable income tax deduction, because charitable deduction limitations and/or itemized deduction limits could reduce the tax benefit.

Opportunity: In the event the client decides to make charitable bequests (rather than or in addition to lifetime gifts), consider providing in the disposition documents (such as a Will or Revocable Trust) that the bequests are funded with assets in which there is IRD (e.g., retirement plan and/or IRA accounts). By doing so, the IRD income would be offset by the charitable deduction effectively eliminating the income tax cost incurred by heirs.

Opportunity: Code section 408(d)(8)(F) permits certain individuals over age 70½ to direct the payment of their required minimum distributions of up to $100,000 to qualified charities. There are two tax advantages to this type of charitable contribution. First, the amount distributed to charity is not included in gross income (in other words, the amount contributed is offset by the charitable contribution). Therefore, it potentially minimizes the impact of a high amount of adjusted gross income has on the phase out of certain tax benefits. Second, the amount of the charitable contribution is not subject to the various code sections that limit charitable deductions. Third, if an IRA is comprised of non-deductible contributions and deductible contributions, the amounts passing to charity first come from taxable funds, effectively preserving the tax-free savings of the non-deductible contributions.[10]

Trap: The above provision does not apply to contributions to donor-advised funds and supporting organizations. Clients wanting to retain some control over their charitable gifts must consider the tax impact of avoiding this limitation.

TAKING ADVANTAGE OF LOSS CARRY-FORWARDS

Income tax planning for a client with a limited life expectancy begins with an examination of the most recent federal income tax returns, and other transactions not yet reflected on an income tax return as well any unrealized losses in the client's current assets.

Any of the decedent's unused tax loss carry-forwards (e.g., capital losses that were not used in previous years, net operating loss carryforwards and charitable deduction carryforwards) cannot be used by the estate or heirs.[11] Instead, they simply vanish at death. Moreover, if the decedent spouse was the sole source of a loss or deduction carryforward and a joint return was filed, the surviving spouse may not claim the loss except on the final joint return.

Opportunity: There are at least three ways to use expiring losses.

- o First, the client (or persons holding a general power of attorney) could accelerate the client's income to be offset by any expiring losses.
- o Second, assuming a joint return is filed, a surviving spouse might take pre-mortem actions to create taxable income to offset the soon-to-expire losses on the couple's last tax return(s).
- o Third, assuming a joint return is filed in the decedent's year of death, a surviving spouse could take year-of-death, postmortem steps (e.g., accelerating income) to offset the losses.[12] For example, assume the deceased Husband has a $400,000 NOL from his failing business and the Wife has a $400,000 traditional IRA. In the year of death, the Wife could convert $400,000 traditional IRA into a ROTH IRA to take advantage of the expiring NOL.

Opportunity: Code section 402(e)(4)(B) permits a plan participant to elect the taxation of the Net Unrealized Appreciation ("NUA")[13] in employer stock in his or her retirement plan in the year of distribution. Assume, a terminally ill plan participant has a NOL carry-forward that will expire at the participant's death. By making the election, the NOL could be used to reduce or eliminate the amount of the taxable NUA.

Opportunity: Generally the accrued interest earned on series E and EE saving bonds are not taxed until received. However, by election of the executor (or surviving spouse), per Code section 454(a), such accrued interest would be includible as gross income in the decedent's last tax year.[14] As a result, it would create taxable income to be offset by expiring tax carryforwards.

DECEDENT'S FINAL RETURN

Because so few estates are subject to estate tax, maximizing income tax deductions to be claimed on the decedent's final return (particularly, if there is a surviving spouse) has become a more important part of estate planning.

Opportunity: Below are a number of deductions that may be available for a decedent's final return:

- o Unamortized mortgage loan costs.[15]
- o The entire standard deduction, notwithstanding the point in the year in which the decedent died (i.e., there is no partial year proration in the year of death).[16]
- o The decedent's final medical expenses provided they are paid within one year of death.[17]
- o If an individual with a lifetime annuity dies before recovering their investment in the annuity contract, the unrecovered basis may be deductible on the decedent's final return.[18]

TAX PLANNING FOR RETIREMENT PLANS

Many clients with high valued retirement plans have not focused on the tax consequences to their named beneficiaries.

Opportunity: Clients with taxable estates who are in relatively low income tax brackets should consider taking lifetime distributions from retirement plans, paying the income tax and then gifting or bequeathing the money. For example, assume a terminally ill mother has an IRA with a $15,000 account balance. Assume she is in the 10 percent income tax bracket and her only child is in the combined state and federal 50 percent income tax bracket. If she withdraws the entire $15,000 account balance, her tax would be $1,500. If she pays the tax from other funds and gifts the proceeds to her child, it would save the child $6,000 (i.e., $15,000 times 40 percent) in income taxes.

Opportunity: Terminally ill clients should consider a Roth IRA conversion of existing IRAs and retirement plan accounts. The tax triggered by the conversion paid by the client will reduce the taxable estate while the heirs will enjoy the tax-free growth of the Roth IRA over their life expectancy. For example, assume a terminally ill client with a $500,000 IRA converts it into a Roth IRA. Ultimately, the Roth IRA will pass to the client's heirs who will be able to take tax-free withdrawals.[19] Although the conversion triggers an immediate income tax cost to the IRA owner, the tax is not paid from the Roth IRA account. Assuming the client has a taxable estate, the payment of the income tax is the equivalent of an estate tax deduction.

Trap: Be careful in advising a surviving spouse below age 59½ to automatically roll over the deceased spouse's IRA into the surviving spouse's IRA account. If the spouse does so, the IRA is treated as his or her IRA, not an inherited IRA. Therefore, withdrawals taken prior to age 59½ may be subject to the 10 percent premature withdrawal.[20] On the other hand, if the surviving spouse treats it as an inherited IRA, withdrawals at any age are not subject to the penalty.

Opportunity: Consider naming a qualified trust as the beneficiary of an inherited IRA[21] to provide asset protection to the beneficiary of the trust (who will receive distributions from the trust). In the *Clark v. Rameker* decision,[22] the U.S. Supreme Court unanimously ruled that an inherited IRA (meaning one in which an individual was the owner) did not have the bankruptcy protection as does an ERISA retirement account or a taxpayer's own IRA. Note, some state statutes may offer some partial protections for IRAs and other retirement benefits.[23]

Advisors should encourage clients to make sure the plan administrator has acknowledged receipt of the last retirement plan and IRA beneficiary designation made by the account holder. Always discuss the pros and cons of each beneficiary designation with clients as a part of the estate planning process.

Trap: Clients may directly or indirectly (e.g., by failure to name a primary or contingent beneficiary) cause their estates to be the beneficiary of their IRA. This mistake can be costly because:

- o The beneficiary is the estate, the heirs lose the right to "stretch" distributions from the IRA over their life expectancies. For a Roth IRA, all funds must be withdrawn within five years of the decedent's death. However, for a traditional IRA, if the owner died *after* April 1 of the year the deceased would have turned 70½, distributions can be taken out over what would have been the deceased account owner's remaining life expectancy.
- o The IRA funds become a part of the estate subject to the claims of creditors of the estate.
- o If a creditor forces withdrawals from the IRA to cover debts, the estate is subject to and liable for any income taxes and/or penalties resulting from the withdrawal.
- o In some states, the lack of a specific beneficiary may result in their inclusion in the amount of the estate subject to a spousal elective share claim.

Eliminating a Spousal Interest. Remarried clients should consider whether to eliminate their current spouse's right to their retirement assets. Generally, beneficiary designation changes in an ERISA retirement plan require written spousal approval.[24] However, this is not the case with respect to IRAs.[25] In *Charles Schwab v. Debickero*,[26] after retirement, a husband rolled a 401(k) into an IRA naming his children from a prior marriage as the beneficiaries. Husband died and his wife argued that because her husband had rolled his 401(k) into the IRA, she should receive the same protections that his ERISA plan had provided to her. The Ninth Circuit disagreed: "*Thus, under both section 401(a) and the accompanying regulations, there is no basis for imposing on the Schwab IRA the automatic survivor annuity requirements of section 401(a)(11) and overriding the beneficiary designations rightfully made by Wilson in establishing the account.*"

Opportunity; If a client who has children and/or grandchildren from a prior marriage and wants to limit their current spouse's control and/or benefit of an ERISA plan, he or she should consider rolling it into an IRA.

Trap: Check the elective share rules in the couple's domicile state to make sure there are no direct or indirect statutory rights to the IRA inuring to the surviving spouse.[27] If there is such a potential claim, request the spouse to waive rights making sure the waiver is in total compliance with any statutory requirements. For example, the state may require "fair disclosure" to the waiving spouse of the impact of the waiver.

ESTATE BASIS PLANNING PROVIDES INCOME TAX SAVINGS TO BENEFICIARIES

Due to the increasingly higher estate tax exemption amounts that result in fewer taxable estates, pre-mortem basis planning (in the absence of a taxable estate tax) takes on a new significance. While in the era of more taxable estates, the primary focus in estate tax driven valuations was to minimize the value of the bequeathed or gifted asset, now, higher valuations of assets subject to a step up to fair market value is now the focus. Ironically, estate planners and the IRS have reversed roles. As a result, practitioners are now more likely to adopt the IRS valuation arguments (*"dad retained too much control over the FLP so, under 2036, the entire value of the FLP is includible in his taxable estate"*). Alternatively, the IRS is apt to use tax practitioners' previous arguments to support a lower value.

Opportunity: Because most individuals will not have a taxable estate, it is prudent to change strategies designed to discount the value of assets includible in an individual's gross estate. Assume Mom is terminally ill and has a 33 percent membership interest in an LLC that owns a farm and an apartment building worth $2.0 million and $1.0 million, respectively. Prior to Mom's death, the LLC members vote to liquidate the LLC and distribute the $1.0 million apartment building to her and the $2.0 million farm to the other LLC members. If, alternatively, the LLC had not been liquidated, an appraisal of Mom's 33 percent membership interest would have included a 40 percent minority interest discount, or a total value of $600,000 (i.e., $3.0 million times 33 percent ownership interest times a 40 percent discount). Therefore, upon her death, the basis of her LLC membership interest would be $600,000. On the other hand, because Mom received the apartment building valued at $1.0 million for her 33 percent interest, at her death, the tax basis of the apartment building would be the non-discounted $1.0 million. Consequently, this higher basis in the apartment building will provide a greater depreciation deduction for the heirs and a lower taxable gain if the apartment is sold.

Opportunity: Several decades ago, Dad created an FLP. Over the years, Dad has gifted limited partnership units to family members. Under current case law, pursuant to Code section 2036, Dad's control over the FLP would cause the gifted units to be included in his gross estate. Assume Dad's total estate including the current value of the gifted units is well below his available estate tax exemption. In preparing the federal estate tax return, the advisor should assert that Dad's retained control causes the gifted units to be included in his taxable estate. Why? Because the basis of the gifted FLP units will step-up to Dad's date of death fair market value and with a Code section 754 election, the basis of the assets in the FLP can also step-up.

SAVING INCOME TAX BY ELIMINATING INCOME IN RESPECT OF A DECEDENT

Generally, income in respect of a decedent (IRD) is gross income that a decedent was entitled to but did not actually receive as of the time of death. For that reason, a cash method decedent taxpayer (most taxpayers are) would not report that income on the last return. Ultimately, the entity (trust or estate) or heirs who do receive the IRD include it in gross income. For example, the untaxed account balance of an IRA is IRD. See Chapter 17 for a full discussion of IRD.

Given the current higher income tax rates, especially on trust and estate taxable income, the receipt of IRD can result in significant income tax. For planning purposes, if a client's estate is expected to receive IRD, it is prudent to examine ways to reduce its impact. For example:

- Making lifetime charitable gifts from an IRD asset such as an IRA (e.g., a section 408(d)(8)(F) transfer of an IRA directly to charity) to reduce the amount of IRD income that would be taxable to the decedent's estate or heirs.

- Because the highest tax bracket of trusts and estates is reached at a relatively modest amount of income, income accumulated in an estate or trust is likely to be highly taxed. To mitigate this result:

  o Determining if it is advisable to distribute IRD assets to heirs promptly after the owner's death to heirs who are in lower marginal income tax brackets, recognizing that such distributions may not be the best choice for immature beneficiaries.

  o Accelerating income to a terminally ill client so it is reportable prior to death to take advantage of lower marginal income tax rates (e.g., making a Roth conversion before death).

Caution: Not all IRD is bad. For example, an heir who inherits an IRA is permitted to "stretch" minimum required distributions over his or her life expectancy. The amount not distributed remains in the IRA. For younger beneficiaries, the compounding effect of the assets growing tax-free inside the IRS or retirement plan can create a substantial benefit. See the discussion of "stretch IRAs" in Chapter 17.

ESTATE AND TRUST INCOME TAXES

As noted in Chapter 16, the income tax rate for trusts and estates can be extremely high, even when the trust or estate has a nominal amount of taxable income.

Opportunity: Among the issues that the planner should be cognizant of and potentially change before the client passes away are:

o Do trusts permit discretionary spraying of income among a class of heirs (e.g., "all my descendants")? If there is only one income beneficiary of the trust, the ability to reduce income taxes by spraying income among a number of heirs in lower tax brackets is lost. Note that certain kinds of trusts mandate only one lifetime income beneficiary (e.g., marital trusts and certain trusts owning S corporation stock).

o Determine if the investment of the assets of any trusts or inheritable assets can be converted to capital gain driven assets as opposed to ordinary income investments to reduce the trust's income tax cost of accumulating income and/or the income tax cost to heirs who receive trust distributions.

o Does the terminally ill client (or anyone else) hold a power of appointment to change the terms of a trust without sufficient flexibility to reduce the income taxes on heirs?

o Is there any requirement that the trust accumulate income? If so, the income tax cost of such accumulations should be quantified and perhaps convert assets to capital gain driven investments subject to a lower income tax cost.

o Identify the discretionary distribution powers of the trustees and determine whether those powers can be used to cause the basis of assets in those trusts to step up to fair market value upon the death of the terminally ill client.

o Make sure that any trust that will hold S corporation stock is a qualified trust. If it is a trust that is not a qualified S corporation trust, then the trust's ownership of stock could result in the termination of the S corporation status for all shareholders.

Opportunity: A trust, by its terms, may provide broad trustee distribution powers to the client, yet, upon death, not be included in his or her estate. If the trust owns assets with significant unrealized gains and if it does not create exposure to a state or federal death tax, consider making discretionary principal distributions of appreciated assets to the dying client. Upon the client's death, the basis of those assets will step up to fair market value. Leave the assets with unrealized losses in the trust to avoid a step-down in basis.

Trap: In the above example, if the trust making the distribution is a grantor trust and, upon the dying client's death, the distributed asset will pass directly or indirectly back to the grantor, section 1014(e) might deny a step-up in basis. In that case, to avoid the loss of the basis step up, it might be possible for the grantor to renounce any grantor powers before the distribution is made.

When the surviving spouse dies with assets in a qualified marital trust, the assets are included in the spouse's estate, and the basis becomes the asset's date-of-death fair market value.

Opportunity: A terminally ill client is the beneficiary of a marital trust with substantial unrealized losses in the trust assets. Upon the client's death, the assets will step down to their lower fair market value. However, if the trust sells the assets before the spousal/beneficiary's death, the losses can be preserved for remainder beneficiaries.[28]

Opportunity: The income taxation of grantors, trusts, and beneficiaries varies widely from state to state. Even though the tax rate in most states is relatively low, the long-term imposition of a state income tax can amount to substantial tax dollars, especially in states that do not provide any tax break for capital gains. Consequently, clients who are creating trusts (especially trusts that are intended to accumulate dollars) should consider establishing the trusts in a jurisdiction that minimizes state and local income taxes.

Perspective: Early in the process of planning for a terminally ill client, all of the client's existing documents should be examined to see if changes are necessary to provide for flexibility and a lower post-mortem tax cost, particularly if the client should become incapacitated before the planning is completed (e.g., broad powers in the client's general power of attorney).

THE CLIENT'S ESTATE PLANNING DOCUMENTS

To facilitate the planning discussed in this chapter for an individual in early or anticipated incapacity, drafting flexible and general powers of attorney ("GPOA") and revocable "living" trusts can play an essential role.

General Powers of Attorney. As Americans live longer, incapacity is becoming a growing issue. Guardianship is an expensive and time consuming process that can often be replaced by a well-drafted General Power of Attorney (GPOA).

Opportunity: Clients and their advisors should be spending more time discussing the terms of their GPOA. Among the terms clients should consider in their GPOA are:

- Permitting the advancement of personal and charitable bequests if the remaining assets are sufficient to support it. The document may require an acknowledgement/waiver from the recipient acknowledging that the distribution is in lieu of comparable bequests under the client's dispositive documents.
- Even if the state statute provides that the GPOA survives incapacity of the principal (i.e., it is "durable"), include survival language in the document so that there is no question of enforceability in those states that require durable language in GPOAs.
- To ensure that the death of the named power holder does not force the grantor's family into a guardianship for the incapacitated individual, name one or more successor power holders (i.e., spouses should not be the sole power holders of the other).
- Provide the power holder specific authority to sign and file any state or federal tax returns (listing the years) on behalf of the maker.
- Serving as the GPOA holder of an incapacitated person can be very time consuming. Consider providing specific language in the GPOA regarding holder compensation and payment of reasonable expenses.

Trap: Practitioners should be careful about how broadly the power is granted to the holder of a GPOA.

- If the agent is permitted to make unfettered gifts to herself or to satisfy her obligations, the GPOA may be construed as a General Power of Appointment causing the principal's assets to be included in the power holder's estate.[29]
- Specifically provide that the principal has no powers over any life insurance on the agent's life (i.e., an incapacitated spouse owns life insurance on the life of the other spouse who holds the Power of Attorney) to avoid having the policy included in the agent's estate pursuant

to Code section 2042.[30] Give that power to a different power holder who is not the insured.

Trap: A January 26, 2015 New York Times article noted that it has become "routine" for nursing homes to attempt to gain guardianship over residents to use that power to pay nursing home bills.[31] Moreover, other family members may attempt to gain control of an incapacitated person if they disagree with the actions of the person holding the GPOA. In some states, appointment of a guardian revokes or limits the agent holding the GPOA (for example, Florida,[32] Texas,[33] Virginia,[34] and Washington[35]). To minimize this risk, provide in the GPOA the identity of the person who should be named as guardian over the person and assets of the signer of the document.

Caution: As if the variation of the rules governing GPOAs were not complicated enough, for Americans living overseas, there are vast differences from foreign country to foreign country governing the use of powers of attorney and Medical Directives. So clients moving overseas should consult local counsel in their new country of domicile in executing Medical Directives and GPOAs.

Documenting Residency. Determining the residency of a client is extremely important. Many clients have multiple homes in different states or clients with limited life expectancy have been moved to another state to be closer to their family members. The residency of the client can create significant tax and dispositional issues (e.g., moving an incapacitated married client from Georgia to Florida can significantly increase the rights of the surviving spouse, such as a spouse from a second marriage).[36] As a part of their engagement, advisors should evaluate the estate and income tax consequences of the client's tax domicile and the local requirements of any estate planning documents that were previously executed in another state. Part of this work should include properly documenting the client's domicile.

Other Documents. As noted throughout this chapter, all of the client's estate planning documents, beneficiary designations, account ownerships, tax returns and other documentation need to be thoroughly reviewed as a part of this process, with appropriate changes being made while the client still has the capacity to make decisions.

CONCLUSION

Understandably, for an individual facing imminent incapacity and/or a looming death, tax planning is a low priority for the individual and the family. Considering feelings of loss and sadness, income tax planning can be perceived as unseemly when incapacity or death sits outside the door. But the unfortunate reality is that it is not the deceased who will suffer the legacy of poor planning, it is the survivors.

CHAPTER ENDNOTES

1. IRC Sec. 1015(a).
2. IRC Sec. 1014.
3. IRC Sec. 1041(b).
4. See IRC Sec. 1041.
5. See IRC Sec. 1015(a). See Chapter 22 on Tax Basis Planning.
6. For more information, see: Scroggin, "*Understanding Section 1014(e) and Tax Basis Planning*," LISI Estate Planning Newsletter #2192 (February 6, 2014).
7. See IRC Sec. 1041(e). See PLR 9615026 and Treas. Reg. §1.1041-1T(d), Question 12.
8. See Rev. Rul. 85-13.
9. For an excellent overview of the rules governing charitable giving, see Horwood, "Imagine the Possibilities: Opportunities for Non-Cash Donors," BNA Estates, Gifts and Trusts Journal, January 12, 2012. The article provides an excellent overview of the rules governing charitable deductions of non-cash assets and includes a helpful table.
10. IRC Sec. 408(d)(8)(D) (2015).
11. See Rev. Rul. 74-175, 1974-1 CB 52.
12. See IRC Sec. 6013(a).
13. See Chapter 17 on IRD for a discussion of NUA.
14. See: Rev. Rul. 68-145, 1968-1 C.B. 203.
15. Rev Rul. 86-67, 1986-1 C.B. 238.
16. U.S. Dep't of Treasury, Internal Revenue Serv., Publication 559, *Survivors, Executors, and Administrators 5 (2015).*
17. IRC Sec. 213(c) (2015).
18. IRC Sec. 72(b)(3)(A) (2015).
19. For more information, see Keebler, "Roth Conversions in 2012: Now's the Time to Convert," LISI Employee Benefits and Retirement Planning Newsletter #591 (January 19, 2012).
20. *See* IRC Sec. 72(t) (2015); *Sears v. Comm'r,* 100 T.C.M. (CCH) 6 (2010); *Gee v. Comm'r,* 127 T.C. 1 (2006); Bob Keebler & Michelle Ward, *Sears v. Commissioner: Spousal Rollover Trap,* Emp. Benefits & Retirement Plan. Newsletter (LISI), No. 543, Oct. 12, 2010.

21. For more information and drafting considerations, see Mary Vandenack, *Reconsidering the Design of Trusts Used as IRA and Qualified Account Beneficiaries Post-Clark*, Asset Protection Plan. Newsletter (LISI), No. 252, July 7, 2014; Ed Morrow, *Clark v. Rameker: Supreme Court Holds that Inherited IRAs Are Not Protected in Bankruptcy, Are Spousal Inherited IRAs and Even Rollover IRAs Threatened As Well?* Asset Protection Plan. Newsletter (LISI), No. 248, June 16, 2014.
22. 134 S. Ct. 2242 (2014).
23. Ed Morrow, *50 State Exemption Chart on IRAs, Non-ERISA 403(b) Plans & Roth Variants*, Asset Protection Plan. Newsletter (LISI), No. 256, Aug. 7, 2014.
24. 29 U.S.C.A. §1055(c)(2)(A) (West 2015).
25. 29 U.S.C.A. §§1051-1061 (West 2015).
26. 593 F.3d 916 (9th Cir. 2010).
27. *C.f.*, Fla. Stat. Ann. §732.2035(7) (West 2015).
28. See: IRC Sec. 642(h) (2015).
29. For more detailed analysis of this issue, see Andrew H. Hook, *Durable Powers of Attorney*, 859-3rd Tax Mgmt. (BNA), at Art. XIII.C.2.a; Peter B. Tiernan, *Agent's Powers in a Durable Power of Attorney Can Result in Unexpected Tax*, 32 Est. Plan. 34 (Dec. 2005).
30. *See* Rev. Rul. 84-179, 1984-2 C.B. 195.
31. Nina Bernstein, *To Collect Debts, Nursing Homes Are Seizing Control over Patients*, N.Y. Times, Jan. 26, 2015, http://www.nytimes.com/2015/01/26/nyregion/to-collect-debts-nursing-home-seizing-control-over-patients.html.
32. Fla. Stat. Ann. §709.2109(1)(c) (West 2015).
33. Tex. Prob. Code Ann. §485 (West 2015).
34. Va. Code Ann. §64.2-1606 (West 2015).
35. Wash. Rev. Code Ann. §11.94.010(1) (2015).
36. See: Scroggin, "*What can go Wrong with Spousal Rights in Remarriage*," Estate Planning Journal, February 2016.

DISCHARGE OF DEBT INCOME

CHAPTER 34

INTRODUCTION

Many taxpayers are astonished when they receive a Form 1099-C indicating that they must report on their tax return income from the discharge or cancellation of debt, be it because of a forgiven credit card balance or a bank loan discharged in the aftermath of a foreclosure or some other discharge of a debt. This shock and angst is typically heightened by the taxpayer's lack of cash to pay the tax. After all, how can an individual who has just lost her house through a foreclosure or short sale find the funds to pay a potentially large tax bill? Moreover, taxing such a financially devastated individual seems unfair and counterintuitive to the notion that items of gross income are "accessions to wealth, clearly realized."[1]

Yet, there is a sound reason to treat discharge of debt as taxable income. Lenders—including credit card companies and vendors—provide a borrower with an economic benefit. This benefit is not treated as currently taxable income because of the corresponding obligation to repay the benefit.[2] The cancellation of that repayment obligation essentially voids the tax-free characterization of the previously enjoyed economic benefit. Consequently, the discharge of the obligation to pay causes a previously non-taxable economic benefit to become taxable.

Whether it is apparent to the taxpayer or not, from an economic benefit perspective the discharge of an individual's debt is equivalent to that person receiving money. Any amount of money received by a taxpayer may—or may not—be taxable depending on the context in which it is received. For example, money received for services performed by the taxpayer is included in gross income as compensation,[3] and money received for the use of property is included in gross income as rent.[4] On the other hand, money received as a gift is excluded from gross income.[5] The discharge of a taxpayer's debt is economically equivalent to receipt of money. So the tax treatment of a discharge of debt depends very much on the circumstances in which the discharge occurs.

Once the taxpayer is relieved of the obligation to repay the underlying debt, the taxpayer must then include the forgiven amount in gross income. Under most circumstances, the Internal Revenue Code explicitly includes a discharge of debt in gross income. Code section 61(a)(12) includes a discharge of debt in the taxpayer's gross income if:

1. the taxpayer and the creditor have a pure debtor-creditor relationship; and
2. a debtor's legally enforceable obligation to repay the debt is forgiven by the creditor for no consideration.

For example, if a bank forgives a customer's loan, the balance of the loan when it was forgiven is includible in the customer's gross income pursuant to section 61(a)(12) because the customer and the bank have a pure debtor-creditor relationship and the bank forgave a legally enforceable repayment obligation for no consideration. On the other hand, if the debtor and the creditor have some other relationship, that relationship may alter how the taxpayer is to include the discharged debt in gross income.

Example: Garry Gizmo borrows $10,000 from his employer to purchase a car. The loan is evidenced by a promissory note bearing market interest which is due and payable on the one year anniversary of the loan. On the maturity date, Gary's employer forgives the loan. In this case, unlike a borrower and a conventional lender, Gary and his boss have an employee-employer relationship. For this reason, rather than characterize the forgiven debt as section 61(a)(12) income, it is treated as compensation income under Code section 61(a)(1).[6]

We can think of the example above as if Gary's employer had actually paid him $10,000 in compensation that he in turn used to repay the loan. Obviously, if that had occurred, there would be no discharge because the loan would have been paid in full. The only difference between the two scenarios is whether any money changed hands. For tax purposes, regardless of how the transaction is structured, the employee is deemed to have received taxable wages and not discharge of debt income because of his employment relationship with the "lender."[7]

In addition to a pure debtor-creditor relationship between the parties, Code section 61(a)(12) requires that the debt be discharged for no consideration. If the debt is satisfied by the transfer of money or some other valuable good, the transaction is not considered a discharge of the debt, and is not included as section 61(a)(12) income.

Example: Patty Portrait borrows $10,000 from Gene Gallery. When the loan becomes due, Patty lacks the funds to pay it. In lieu of payment, Gene agrees to accept a painting Patty purchased several years ago for $5,000, which is now worth $10,000. Although Patty and Gene have a pure debtor-creditor relationship, Patty is essentially selling the painting to Gene for an amount equal to the outstanding debt. In the alternative, Gene could purchase the painting from Patty for $10,000 that she in turn could pay to Gene to satisfy the loan.

Similar to the previous example, even though no money actually changed hands, there is no forgiven debt. Instead, the transaction is treated as a sale of the painting. Patty's income (likely capital gain) is the difference between the fair market value of the painting—$10,000, which also happens to be the loan balance—and her basis of $5,000. Here, Patty realizes a $5,000 gain that is included in gross income under Code section 61(a)(3), rather than section 61(a)(12).[8]

WHEN CAN A DISCHARGE OF DEBT BE EXCLUDED FROM GROSS INCOME?

Sometimes items that are normally included in gross income are nonetheless excluded by a specific section of the Code. Such is the case with respect to Code section 61(a)(12) discharge of debt income. Under certain circumstances, Code section 108 excludes a discharge of debt from a taxpayer's gross income. The exclusion can apply to any type of liability, including loans, lines of credit, and credit card debt. The discharge can occur as the result of a creditor write-off, foreclosure, short sale, deed in lieu of foreclosure, or abandonment. However, this exclusion only applies to a discharge of debt that is otherwise required to be included in gross income under Code section 61(a)(12).

Types of Indebtedness

There are two important—and related—ways to categorize any debt. First, all debt is either "secured" or "unsecured." The second distinction is between "recourse" versus "nonrecourse" indebtedness.

Secured versus Unsecured

Debt is "secured" if the borrower pledges specific property as collateral against the loan. As a hedge against a potential default, many lenders insist on securing a loan with specific property owned by the borrower that is pledged as collateral. By doing so, payment of a defaulted loan is assured to the extent of the value of the secured property. Common types of secured loans include home mortgages and car loans. If the borrower fails to repay the loan according to schedule, the lender may take possession of the collateral (the house or the car) and use the proceeds from its sale to repay the loan.

If no collateral is offered, then the loan is "unsecured."

Recourse versus Nonrecourse

In a "recourse" debt, the borrower's obligation to repay a recourse debt is unconditional. This means that in the event of default, the lender may legally pursue collection against not only the assets purchased by borrowed money but *all* of the borrower's assets, even if the loan is secured by collateral.[9] Recourse debt may be either secured or unsecured, depending on whether the borrower pledged any of the property as collateral against the loan.

The main difference between a recourse and "nonrecourse" debt is that in nonrecourse debt, the lender cannot attach other assets of the borrower. Stated another way, the borrower has no *personal* obligation to repay a defaulted loan, and the lender's only remedy is repossession of the collateral. To protect the lender, at the time that the loan is completed the value of the collateral property is usually at least equal to the amount of the nonrecourse loan. As long as the borrower conforms to the terms of the loan, the borrower retains ownership of the secured property. Unlike recourse debt, nonrecourse debt is *always* secured by the borrower's property pledged as collateral.

Example: Barry Businessman borrows $200,000 from Second Bank. The loan is nonrecourse and secured by a warehouse with a fair market value of $200,000. Several years later, the value of the warehouse has decreased to $100,000. So instead of paying the $200,000 loan to retain the warehouse worth $100,000, Barry decides to default on the loan. In a foreclosure action, the warehouse is transferred to Second Bank extinguishing Barry's obligation to repay the remaining balance of $100,000 ($200,000 minus $100,000 the fair market value of the warehouse). As a result, Second Bank absorbs the $100,000 loss.

Which Types of Debt Can Be Excluded from a Taxpayer's Gross Income?

To qualify for the exclusion from a gross income under Code section 108, a discharged debt must satisfy two conditions: First, the discharge must be of "indebtedness of the taxpayer." While this sounds simple, the definition of the term is quite specific, mandating that the discharged debt must be either:

- recourse indebtedness of the taxpayer; or
- debt that is secured by the taxpayer's property.

Because recourse indebtedness can also be secured debt, it is not uncommon for the discharge of a recourse debt to satisfy the first condition of section 108 in both ways.

If the debt meets the first condition of Code section 108, the next step is to determine if the discharge falls into one of several categories that qualify for exclusion from the taxpayer's gross income. The categories are listed below:

1. *Bankruptcy exclusion:* Any discharge that occurs in a bankruptcy case—regardless of amount—is excluded from gross income.[10]

2. *Insolvency exclusion:* A discharge that occurs when the taxpayer is insolvent—defined as when the taxpayer's liabilities exceed the fair market value of assets[11]—is excluded to the extent that the debtor was insolvent prior to the discharge.[12]

3. *Qualified farm indebtedness exclusion:* A discharge of "qualified farm indebtedness" (subject to certain limitations beyond the scope of this chapter) can be excluded from gross income. "Qualified farm indebtedness" is debt that is directly in connected with a business in which 50 percent or more of the aggregate gross receipts for the three years preceding the taxable year of the discharge is attributable to farming.[13]

4. *Qualified real property business indebtedness exclusion:* Discharged debt that is "qualified real property business indebtedness" can be excluded from gross income (subject to certain limitations discussed later in this chapter) if the debt was incurred for the purposes of acquiring, building ,or substantially improving real property that is used in a trade or business.[14] This exclusion is not available to C corporations.

5. *Qualified principal residence indebtedness exclusion:* A discharge of debt related to a taxpayer's principal residence can be excluded (subject to certain limitations beyond the scope of this chapter) if the discharge occurred before January 1, 2014. The debt must have been incurred to acquire, build, or make substantial improvements or renovations to the taxpayer's principal residence.[15]

6. *Student loan exclusion:* A discharge of student loans that occurs because the borrower worked for a certain period of time for a particular type of employer (such as public interest work) can be excluded from gross income.[16]

7. *Discharged debt that would have been deductible if paid:* If a taxpayer could have deducted some portion of the payments toward a debt (e.g. interest payments on a business loan), then the discharged debt will not be included in the taxpayer's gross income. This exclusion only applies to the amount of the debt that would have been tax deductible had it been paid.[17] This type of discharge still carries consequences for the taxpayer's gross income: rather than being included as income, the discharge means that the taxpayer will not enjoy the benefit of the deduction.

8. *Discharge of purchase money debt:* "Purchase money debt" is money that is lent by a seller to a buyer to facilitate a purchase. The code treats a discharge of this type of debt as a reduction in the purchase price, and it is therefore excluded from the buyer/borrower's gross income. This exclusion applies even when the buyer is not in bankruptcy or insolvent.[18]

In many instances, it is possible that the discharge of debt may qualify for more than one category of exclusion under Code section 108. For example, a debtor who files bankruptcy may also be insolvent. If a discharge of debt qualifies for more than one of the section 108 exclusion categories, Figure 34.1 sets forth which of the exclusions would take precedence.[19]

The following example contains a step-by-step analysis of whether and to what extent a discharge of debt section 61(a)(12) would be excluded from gross income under section 108.

Example: Molly Cule, a sole proprietor, takes out $100,000 in recourse debt from First Bank to fund working capital in her business. A year later when the loan becomes due, Molly defaults. Although Molly owns attachable assets, First Bank forgives the loan without pursuing a legal collection action against her. At the time of the discharge the amount of Molly's liabilities are $140,000 (including the $100,000 loan), and the fair market value of Molly's single asset—a construction crane used in her business—is $90,000. Thus, prior to the discharge, Molly is insolvent with a negative net worth of $50,000—the amount by which her liabilities ($140,000) exceeds the fair market value of her cumulative assets ($90,000).

Step 1 – Is there section 61(a)(12) discharge of debt income? Recall that section 108 exclusions only apply to discharges of debt that would otherwise be considered gross income under Code section 61(a)(12). Here, Molly's discharge meets the section 61(a)(12) requirements because:

1. Molly and First Bank have a pure debtor-creditor relationship; and

2. First Bank forgave a legally enforceable debt for no consideration.

Figure 34.1

If a discharge of debt qualifies for all the following section 108(a)(1) exclusions:	**The exclusion that takes precedence is:**
• Bankruptcy exclusion • Insolvency exclusion • Qualified farm indebtedness exclusion • Qualified real property business indebtedness exclusion • Qualified principal residence indebtedness exclusion	Bankruptcy exclusion
• Insolvency exclusion • Qualified farm indebtedness exclusion • Qualified real property business indebtedness exclusion	Insolvency exclusion
• Insolvency exclusion • Qualified principal residence indebtedness exclusion	Qualified principal residence indebtedness exclusion

Thus, Molly has $100,000 of discharge of debt income tentatively included in gross income under section 61(a)(12).

Step 2 – Is the discharged debt considered "indebtedness of the taxpayer?" Molly's loan is not secured by her property, but it is a recourse loan. Upon her default, First Bank decided to forgive the $100,000 loan balance rather than pursue a legal collection action against Molly to attach her assets. Because the bank could have pursued all of Molly's assets, the $100,000 discharged loan meets the first requirement of section 108 by being a recourse loan.

Step 3 – Does the discharge fall into one of the exclusion categories found in section 108? Recall that immediately before the discharge Molly was insolvent to the extent of $50,000. Thus, the insolvency exclusion applies to Molly's $100,000 loan discharge. Also, though Molly was insolvent at the time of discharge, there is no indication that the discharge occurred pursuant to a bankruptcy, and none of the other section 108(a)(1) exclusions are applicable. Thus, the only exclusion applicable is the insolvency exclusion.

Step 4 – How much of the discharged debt is excluded from gross income under the applicable section 108 exclusion? Not all of the section 108 exclusions exclude the entire discharge of debt from gross income. Here, the insolvency exclusion is limited to the extent the taxpayer was insolvent prior to the discharge. Prior to the discharge Molly was insolvent by $50,000. After the $100,000 discharge, however, Molly became solvent by $50,000 ($90,000 asset minus the remaining liabilities of $40,000).

Thus, Molly's insolvency exclusion is limited to $50,000 of the $100,000 in discharged debt—the amount by which she was insolvent prior to the discharge. The remaining $50,000 of discharged debt made her solvent and increased her net worth from zero to $50,000. After applying the insolvency exclusion, Molly would include $50,000 in gross income under section 61(a)(12) from the discharge of the First Bank loan.

DISCHARGES OF DEBT IN FORECLOSURE-TYPE TRANSACTIONS

By their very nature, foreclosures, short sales, and deeds in lieu of foreclosure (collectively known as "foreclosure-type transactions") often involve discharges of debt. The question is whether the discharge qualifies as gross income under section 61(a)(12) and is therefore potentially excludible under section 108. The answer to this question depends greatly on whether the discharged debt was recourse or nonrecourse. Most of this section will discuss discharges of debt in foreclosure-type transactions under the assumption that the discharge applies to recourse debt. The rules for nonrecourse debt in foreclosure transactions are more complicated, and will be discussed separately.

At the outset, it is important to note that the Code treats foreclosures,[20] short sales, and deeds in lieu of foreclosure[21] as sales for tax purposes. This treatment means that in addition to potentially reporting income from a discharge of debt, a taxpayer must also calculate the gain or loss from the sale.

If the sale price of the underlying property is equal to or greater than the taxpayer's cost basis, the difference between the sale price and the taxpayer's cost basis for the property is considered "gain" on the sale of property (even though the taxpayer may not actually see any of that money), and is included in gross income under Code section 61(a)(3), rather than section 61(a)(12). Recall that section 108 exclusions are only available for discharges of debt income that fall under section 61(a)(12). Accordingly, the amount of discharge of debt income that falls under section 61(a)(12)—and is therefore potentially excludable under section 108—is limited to the amount by which the debt on the property that is forgiven exceeds the sale price.

It is also possible for the sale price to be less than the taxpayer's cost basis in the property. In that case, the difference between the sale price and basis is realized as a loss under Code section 165. When realizing a loss on the sale of the property, the discharge of debt income is still limited to the amount by which the balance of the loan exceeds the sale price of the property.

An important issue that often arises in foreclosure-type transactions is that a discharge of the debt is not guaranteed. If the sale price of the underlying property is less than the amount of discharged debt, the creditor can either pursue a legal collection action against the debtor to satisfy the remaining balance of the debt, or simply forgive the remaining balance of the debt. The treatment of this remaining balance varies according to state law, and is often subject to the lender's discretion or an agreement that the borrower may have reached with the lender prior to the sale. Sometimes the debt left over after the sale is forgiven. In other instances, the lender will continue to pursue the borrower (and all legal assets) for the balance of the loan.

Nonrecourse Debt

The most significant difference between recourse and nonrecourse debt is the absence of personal liability in the event of default. Unlike recourse liability discussed above, *all* gain realized from a foreclosure-type transaction involving a nonrecourse loan is treated as income under Code section 61(a)(3). This is because the discharge of the nonrecourse debt occurs through a transfer of the underlying secured property, which is treated as a sale. Although the resulting "gain" extinguishes the debtor's obligation to repay the balance of the loan, it is not considered discharge of debt income under Code section 61(a)(12). Regardless of whether the amount of the outstanding debt is more or less than the sale price of the underlying property, foreclosure-type transactions involving nonrecourse debt can *never* produce income under Code section 61(a)(12), and thus the income can *never* be excluded under Code section 108, even if the balance of the loan exceeds the sale price of the property.[22]

Example: Molly Cule purchases a commercial office building for $100,000. The purchase price is financed entirely with a $100,000 nonrecourse loan from First Bank secured by the building. Several years later, when the principal balance of the loan is still $100,000, Molly defaults. Consequently, First Bank forecloses on the property. At the time of the foreclosure, as a result of $40,000 of depreciation deductions, Molly's basis in the building is $60,000. The property sells for $80,000 at auction.

After the $80,000 in sale proceeds are applied to the loan, an unpaid balance of $20,000 remains. If the loan had been recourse, First Bank could have pursued a legal collection action against Molly to satisfy the balance. If First Bank chose not to do so, there would be $20,000 of discharge of debt income. Here, the remaining nonrecourse debt is simply extinguished upon the transfer of the secured property to the creditor.

In this transaction, Molly realizes $40,000 of section 61(a)(3) income. (It may be useful to think of this as $20,000 in "gain" from the sale, and $20,000 of income from the discharge of debt that falls under section 61(a)(3), rather than section 61(a)(12) because it is non-recourse debt.) Because Molly has no section 61(a)(12) income, none of the $40,000 is subject to exclusion under section 108.

Many may wonder how a nonrecourse debtor, such as Molly in the example above, can have "income" from the discharge of nonrecourse debt that she has no personal obligation *to repay*. The answer relates back to the economic benefit of the initial borrowing. By virtue of the nonrecourse loan, the borrower enjoyed the economic benefit of acquiring the property. The only reason the borrowed funds were not included in gross income was due to the obligation to repay the loan.[23] When the borrower defaults on the loan, the transfer of the property to the lender extinguishes that obligation and the previously enjoyed (but originally untaxed) economic benefit of the borrowed funds becomes taxable income.

REFINANCING TRANSACTIONS

The treatment of discharged debt in refinancing transactions (including refinancing, restructuring, and partial forgiveness of debt) is treated similarly to discharges in foreclosure-type transactions, with one important difference.

As discussed above, income realized from discharge of *nonrecourse* debt via a transfer of the underlying secured property to the creditor (as is deemed to occur in a foreclosure-type transaction) is never treated as Code section 61(a)(12) income. However, if a creditor forgives a portion of nonrecourse debt and allows the debtor to retain the secured property (as is the case in a refinancing transaction), the discharge is not treated as a sale. This means that income from the discharge is reported under Code section 61(a)(12) rather than 61(a)(3), and is potentially excludable from the taxpayer's gross income under Code section 108.[24] The analysis of discharged debt in refinancing transaction proceeds in much the same way is it does in a foreclosure-type transaction involving recourse debt.

Example: Molly Cule borrows $100,000 from First Bank through a nonrecourse note. The loan is secured by a parcel of undeveloped land with a fair market value of $100,000 held by Molly as an investment. Subsequently, the fair market value of the land decreases to $80,000. Because the loan is "upside down," Molly offers First Bank a deed in lieu of foreclosure. In response, First Bank offers to reduce the amount of loan from $100,000 to $80,000—allowing Molly to retain the property—and Molly agrees. As a result, Molly has $20,000 of section 61(a)(12) income because 1) Molly and First Bank have a pure debtor-creditor relationship; 2) First Bank forgave the debt for no economic consideration; and 3) in order to retain ownership of the land, Molly is obligated to repay the reduced loan balance of $80,000.

Unlike a foreclosure-type transaction involving nonrecourse debt in which the obligation to repay is extinguished, a reduction of nonrecourse debt on property retained by the debtor does not extinguish the liability. For that reason, a partial forgiveness of nonrecourse liability triggers discharge of debt income. Similar to the discharge of recourse debt, the reduction of nonrecourse debt is eligible for potential exclusion pursuant to Code section 108. Figure 34.2 summarizes the differences in how discharges of recourse and nonrecourse debt are treated under the Code.

QUALIFIED REAL PROPERTY BUSINESS INDEBTEDNESS EXCLUSION

Often, business owners obtain secured loans in order to acquire and/or substantially improve the real property used in their trade or business. Occasionally, some or all of the debt is forgiven, resulting in discharge of debt income that may be excluded from gross income pursuant to the qualified real property business indebtedness (QRPBI) exclusion under Code section 108.[25] For a financially distressed business owner, taking advantage of this exclusion may be a less onerous alternative to filing bankruptcy.

QRPBI can be generated in a foreclosure-type transaction or in a refinancing transaction. As discussed above, in a foreclosure-type transaction, only the discharge of recourse indebtedness can qualify for the exclusion.[26] On the other hand, in a refinancing transaction in which the debtor retains the secured property, the discharge of both recourse and nonrecourse indebtedness can qualify for the exclusion.

For the most part, the QRPBI exclusion functions the same as the other types of section 108 exclusions discussed above. However, it is subject to two additional limitations.

First, the amount excluded cannot exceed the difference between the outstanding total balance of the

Figure 34.2

FORECLOSURE-TYPE TRANSACTIONS		
Amount of Discharge	**Recourse Debt**	**Nonrecourse Debt**
Sale price of secured property equal or greater than outstanding balance of debt	Treated as a sale resulting in either section 61(a)(3) income or section 165 loss	Treated as a sale resulting in either section 61(a)(3) income or section 165 loss
Sale price of secured property is less than the outstanding balance of debt	Treated as two transactions: • a sale to the extent of the sale price of the secured property, resulting in either section 61(a)(3) income or section 165 loss • a discharge of debt to extent outstanding balance of debt exceeds the sale price of secured property	Treated as a sale resulting in either section 61(a)(3) income or section 165 loss regardless of the amount of the debt
REFINANCING TRANSACTIONS		
Amount of Discharge	**Recourse Debt**	**Nonrecourse Debt**
Any amount forgiven	Treated as discharge of debt income under section 61(a)(12)	Treated as discharge of debt income under section 61(a)(12)

loan (prior to the discharge) and the fair market value of the property, as reduced by any other qualified real property business indebtedness. In other words, start with the outstanding balance of the loan which is to be forgiven (in whole or in part). Subtract from that balance the fair market value of the property. Then subtract the outstanding balance of any other loans that qualify as "real property business indebtedness" and are secured by the same property. Whatever amount remains after the subtractions is the upper limit of the QRPBI exclusion.

The second limitation on the QRPBI exclusion is simpler, at least in concept: in addition to the first limitation, the QRPBI exclusion also cannot exceed the aggregate bases of the taxpayer's depreciable property.[27] Obviously, calculating this limit on the QRPBI exclusion can be more or less complicated depending on the amount of depreciable property owned by the taxpayer.

Finally, it should be noted that the requirement to reduce other tax attributes (discussed in more detail below) does not apply to the QRPBI exclusion. Instead, Code section 108(c)(1)(A) requires the taxpayer to reduce the basis of the qualified business real property by the amount of the QRPBI exclusion when it is taken. Importantly, if the QRPBI exclusion is taken in the context of a foreclosure-type transaction, the newly reduced basis is used when calculating the amount of gain or loss from the sale.

HOW DOES EXCLUDING DISCHARGE OF DEBT INCOME AFFECT OTHER DEDUCTIONS AND CREDITS?

Once the type and amount of Code section 108 exclusion has been determined, the exclusion is allowed unconditionally. However, taking advantage of the bankruptcy, insolvency, or qualified farm indebtedness exclusions may affect the taxpayer's other deductions and credits. If a taxpayer has certain "tax attributes," section 108(b) requires a reduction of those tax attributes in an amount equal to the excluded discharge of debt income. A "tax attribute" is an item that reduces a taxpayer's tax liability. In other words, although section 108 is an exclusion section (and, thus, a tax attribute in its own right), there is a mandatory trade-off of some of the taxpayer's other tax attributes. If a taxpayer has a significant amount of certain tax attributes at the time of the discharge, the immediate tax benefit of the section 108 exclusion of discharge of debt income may be offset by the loss of other tax benefits.

Examples of tax attributes that are subject to reduction include a net operating loss, capital loss carryover, certain tax credits, and basis. Tax attributes that relate to deductions are treated differently than those that area related to credits. Deduction-related attributes (including basis) are reduced by one dollar for each dollar of excluded discharge of debt income.[28] Attributes related to credits are reduced by 34.3 cents for each dollar of excluded discharge of debt income.[29]

The adjustment of other tax attributes is the last step in a complex analysis of whether income from a discharge of debt can—and should— be excluded from a taxpayer's gross income under section 108. Figure 34.3 summarizes the steps that need to be taken to complete that analysis.

FREQUENTLY ASKED QUESTIONS

Question – Does the bankruptcy exclusion or the insolvency exclusion provide greater tax advantages?

Answer – Obviously, the decision to file for bankruptcy should not be taken lightly. However, looking at the issue purely from a tax perspective, the bankruptcy exclusion provides far greater tax advantages for several reasons.

First, *all* debt discharged in a bankruptcy proceeding is excludible from gross income. The insolvency exclusion is limited to the extent of the taxpayer's pre-discharge insolvency, which is almost always less than the amount that would be discharged in a bankruptcy case. When using the insolvency exclusion, the amount of the discharge that creates positive net worth for the taxpayer is not excludable from gross income under section 108.

Example: Barry Businessman has liabilities totaling $550,000 and assets with an aggregate fair market value of $250,000. Thus, Barry is insolvent with a negative net worth of $300,000. A number of Barry's creditors decide to forgive a total of $340,000 of Barry's indebtedness.

If the discharge occurs outside of bankruptcy, the discharge would qualify for the insolvency

Figure 34.3

REQUIREMENTS FOR EXCLUSION OF DISCHARGE OF DEBT INCOME UNDER CODE SECTION 108	
Analysis	**Requirements**
Step 1: Is there section 61(a)(12) discharge of debt income?	• Pure debtor-creditor relationship • Debt discharged for no consideration
Step 2: Is debt discharged "indebtedness of the taxpayer?"	• All recourse debt • All debt secured by the taxpayer's property
Step 3: Is it the right kind of discharge?	• Bankruptcy • Insolvency • Qualified farm indebtedness • Qualified business real property indebtedness • Qualified principal residence indebtedness (prior to January 1, 2014 • Discharged debt that would have been deductible if actually paid • Certain student loan forgiveness • Purchased money price adjustment
Step 3A: If more than one of the exclusions apply, which takes precedence?	• Bankruptcy over all others • insolvency over all the others except bankruptcy and qualified principal residence
Step 4: How much of the discharge debt is excluded from gross income?	• Bankruptcy—no limitation • Insolvency—to the extent of taxpayer's pre-discharge insolvency • Qualified farm indebtedness —subject to certain limitations beyond the scope of this chapter • Qualified real property business indebtedness—subject to certain limitations discussed above • Qualified principal residence indebtedness—subject to certain limitations beyond the scope of this chapter • Discharged debt would have been deductible if actually paid—no limitation • Certain student loan forgiveness—no limitation • Purchase money price adjustment—no limitation
Step 5: Is a reduction of other tax attributes required?	• Required for bankruptcy, insolvency and qualified farm indebtedness exclusions
Step 6: If a reduction of tax attributes are required, which method is most favorable?	• Can use reduction schedules in either section 108(b)(2) or 108(b)(5)

exclusion. As a result, the exclusion would be limited to $300,000—the amount of Barry's pre-discharge insolvency. The rest of the discharged amount ($40,000) would be taxable as section 61(a)(12) income.

Conversely, if the discharge occurs through bankruptcy, the entire amount of discharged liability ($340,000) would be excluded from gross income pursuant to the Bankruptcy Exclusion. Thus, even though the discharge made Barry solvent, there is no limitation of the exclusion amount.

Second, establishing a taxpayer's insolvency may be problematic. This is because the value of all the taxpayer's assets—even those that would be exempt from creditors' claims in a bankruptcy proceeding—are included.[30] Examples of types of property that are exempt from creditors' claims in a bankruptcy proceeding, but are nonetheless considered in determining insolvency, include:[31]

- Qualified retirement accounts
- IRA accounts

- Whole life insurance policies
- Real property

Thus, the value of otherwise exempt assets may substantially reduce—if not totally eliminate—a taxpayer's insolvency, leaving little or no exclusion to apply to any discharge of debt income. To avoid potential taxation, it may be prudent for a taxpayer in that position to file bankruptcy (if he or she was inclined to do so) as a way to exclude the entire amount of discharged debt income pursuant to the bankruptcy exclusion.

Question – Section 108(f) provides a student loan exclusion with regard to the discharge of all or part of a student loan. Is a taxpayer who qualifies for that exclusion required to reduce his or her tax attributes pursuant to Code section 108(b)(2) or Code section 108(b)(5)?

Answer – No. The mandatory reduction of tax attributes specifically applies to the bankruptcy, insolvency, and qualified farm indebtedness exclusions,[32] but not the student loan exclusion in Code section 108(f).

Question – How does tax reform impact an individual's ability to discharge student loan debt?

Answer – Under the 2017 Tax Act, income resulting from the discharge of student loan debt because of the death or permanent and total disability of the borrower is not included in taxable income.[33] This provision is effective for loans that are discharged after December 31, 2017.

CHAPTER ENDNOTES

1. *Comm'r. v. Glenshaw Glass*, 348 US 426, 431 (1955).
2. *Comm'r. v. Rail Joint Co.*, 61 F.2d 751 (2d Cir. 1932).
3. IRC Sec. 61(a)(1).
4. IRC Sec. 61(a)(5).
5. IRC Sec. 102(a).
6. Treas. Reg. §1.61-12(a).
7. The employer would be entitled to a corresponding deduction pursuant to Code section 162.
8. For Gene, there would be no tax consequences since the repayment of the principal of a loan is not a taxable event to the lender. In essence, Gene has simply purchased a painting for $10,000. Had Gene also recovered interest, he would have to report that interest as income.
9. Though procedures vary by state, generally a lender must pursue the lender's property that was pledged as collateral first. If the sale of the repossessed collateral does not fully repay the balance of a recourse loan, the lender may then pursue the borrower's other property. There are also limits on which assets may be pursued by a creditor, and how much of those assets may be claimed. These limits also vary from state to state, as well.
10. IRC Secs. 108(a)(1)(A) and 108(d)(2).
11. IRC Secs. 108(a)(1)(B) and 108(d)(3).
12. IRC Secs. 108(a)(3).
13. IRC Secs. 108(a)(1)(C).
14. IRC Secs. 108(a)(1)(D) and 108(c).
15. IRC Secs. 108(a)(1)(E) and 108(h).
16. IRC Sec. 108(f).
17. IRC Sec. 108(e)(2).
18. IRC Sec. 108(e)(5).
19. IRC Sec. 108(a)(2).
20. *Helvering v. Hammel*, 311 U.S. 504 (1941).
21. *Freeland v. Comm'r.*, 74 T.C. 970 (1980).
22. Treas. Reg. §1.1001-2(c), Example 7; *Comm'r. v. Tufts*, 461 U.S. 300 (1983).
23. *Comm'r. v. Tufts*, 461 U.S. 300 (1983).
24. Rev. Rul. 91-31, 1991-1 C.B. 19.
25. IRC Sec. 108(a)(1)(D).
26. IRC Sec. 61(a)(12) income is a prerequisite for any section 108 exclusion since the discharge of nonrecourse indebtedness in a foreclosure-type transaction is treated as section 61(a)(3) income, the QRPBI exclusion would not apply.
27. IRC Sec. 108(c)(2)(B).
28. IRC Sec. 108(b)(3)(A).
29. IRC Sec. 108(b)(3)(B).
30. *Carlson v. Comm'r.*, 116 T.C. 87 (2001).
31. The types—and the amounts of those types—of property that are exempt from creditors in a bankruptcy proceeding varies depending on the circumstances of the debtor and state law.
32. IRC Sec. 108(b)(1).
33. IRC Sec. 108(f)(5).

IRS INCOME TAX AUDITS

CHAPTER 35

An impending IRS audit can be a daunting experience. Generally, an audit means that the IRS is questioning one or more items reported on a tax return(s). In the worst case scenario, the taxpayer may face a substantial increase in tax plus interest and penalties. Even worse, if the audit involves the understatement of income, the examining revenue agent may refer the case to the Criminal Investigation Division of the IRS. Such a referral may lead to criminal prosecution by the U.S. attorney.

Often, in response to an audit letter from the IRS, a taxpayer will ask "Why me?" This may not be obvious to the preparer, but responding timely and fully is critical to the process. This chapter discusses the mechanics of IRS income tax audits, including sources for preparation, conduct during the exam, issue resolution, and potential outcomes of the audit.

INTRODUCTION

Tax compliance does not end with the filing of the income tax return. A taxpayer who receives an audit letter from the IRS is well advised to contact a tax professional with expertise in the underlying issues. Upon being retained by the taxpayer, the tax professional should give the matter immediate attention. There are three basic types of audits conducted by the Examination Division of the IRS with standard IRS notification letters that differ depending on the type of audit.

TYPES OF AUDITS

Correspondence Audits – CP-2000 Notice

Of all IRS audits, a correspondence audit is the least intrusive because it is conducted entirely by mail or fax communication to and from the IRS. In fact, many taxpayers may have no idea they are being audited. The audit begins with a "letter" to the taxpayer called a CP-2000 notice. In the notice, items of income paid to the taxpayer (i.e., nonemployee compensation) and deductible items paid by the taxpayer (i.e., mortgage interest) reported by third parties to the IRS are compared to the corresponding amounts the taxpayer reported on the income tax return. If the amounts do not match, the IRS will recompute the taxpayer's taxable income and tax based on the third party amounts (the IRS will presume those amounts are accurate). (See Internal Revenue Manual 4.10.10 "Standard Paragraphs and Explanation of Adjustments").

Example: Miranda Wright a sole proprietor reported $50,000 of nonemployee compensation she received from Asher, one of her major customers. According to the Form 1099 filed by Asher to the IRS (Miranda should have received a copy), Miranda was paid $60,000. Due to the discrepancy between the amount Miranda reported on her return and the amount Asher reported on Form 1009, the IRS sends Miranda a CP-2000 notice. Presuming the amount reported on the Form 1099 is correct, taxable income and tax liability are recomputed.

If the taxpayer wishes to challenge the IRS recomputation (i.e., the taxpayer can prove the Form 1099 sent by the third party is incorrect), the taxpayer has thirty days to mail or fax an appropriate response. In the event the notice includes multiple items the taxpayer wishes to dispute, the taxpayer's response should include all supporting documents with a cover letter indexed to those documents. If the examiner reviewing the taxpayer's response agrees with the taxpayer, no changes will be made to the taxpayer's income tax return.

On the other hand, if the taxpayer agrees to some but not all of the adjustments, the taxpayer can concede some and dispute others. If in the latter instance, after reviewing the taxpayer's response, the examiner agrees with the taxpayer, a new report will be issued recomputing the taxpayer's taxable income and tax liability based on the agreed upon adjustments.

If the taxpayer agrees to all of the adjustments, the taxpayer should sign the CP-2000 notice and return it to the IRS with payment of the tax owing, plus interest and any applicable penalties.

In many instances, after responding to the CP-2000, the taxpayer is frustrated by not receiving a timely response from the IRS. Sometimes, the taxpayer's response is either never delivered or is delivered late to the IRS. So, if the taxpayer responds by mail, the CP-2000 should be sent by certified mail requiring a signature. If the taxpayer responds by fax, the taxpayer should retain the fax confirmation of receipt.

If a response is not received by the IRS within thirty days, the IRS will close the case and formalize a proposed assessment of the taxpayer's recomputed tax liability as set forth on the CP-2000 notice. Next, the IRS will mail the taxpayer a Statutory Notice of Deficiency (often referred to as a "Ninety-Day Letter") allowing the taxpayer to file a petition to the Tax Court challenging the proposed assessment within ninety days of the date of the letter. For an extended explanation of a Ninety-Day Letter, see the discussion "Resolution of An Audit", below.

Office Audit

Unlike a correspondence audit, an office audit is conducted at a local IRS office. By mailed notice, the IRS sets a time and date when the taxpayer or representative is to appear for the audit. In addition to setting the time and date, the notice will also specify the issues to be examined by the IRS. Depending on the scope of the audit, the IRS may request all relevant records for the year(s) under examination (such as bank statements, cancelled checks, etc.) plus the last month of the previous year and first month of the subsequent year. In addition, the IRS may request a copy of one or more prior year's or subsequent year's tax returns. Typically, office audits are of very small businesses and wage earners.

Field Audit

Generally, for larger businesses and/or more complex issues, it may be impractical for the taxpayer to bring all requested records to an IRS office. Therefore, for the convenience of the taxpayer and the revenue agent, a field audit is conducted at the taxpayer's home, business office, or tax professional's office. This kind of audit is usually more comprehensive and time consuming than an office audit. Similar to an office audit, the audit notification notice will set forth the date and time the IRS intends to conduct the audit (allowing the taxpayer to request a different date and time) as well as listing which of the taxpayer records the revenue agent intends to review. Depending on the complexity of the issues being audited, a revenue agent may spend days or weeks conducting the audit.

THE BEGINNING OF AN AUDIT

Regardless of the type of audit, the taxpayer should consider retaining a tax professional to handle the matter. However, a tax professional will not be allowed to represent a taxpayer before the IRS, unless the taxpayer executes a Form 2848 – Power of Attorney (POA) naming the tax professional(s) as representative. The authority granted is limited to the type of tax (usually income) and the tax periods (usually tax years) listed on the Form 2848. If the tax professional represents a married couple (whether they filed a joint return or a separate return), each spouse must execute a separate Form 2848. Once the IRS receives the Form 2848, the POA can then deal with the IRS directly.

Depending on the type of audit, the level of preparation required by the tax professional may vary. Generally, the tax professional should first review the applicable tax return(s), including all documentation and information that was used in their preparation. Additionally, if the audit is issue based (i.e., whether a certain type of expense is deductible), the tax professional should research the relevant areas of tax law. Anticipating and preparing for the revenue agent's likely questions could shorten the time between the first appointment and the final resolution.

RESOLUTION OF THE AUDIT

Generally, early resolution of an audit is better for the taxpayer. To this point, once the revenue agent issues the audit report, unless there are unusual circumstances, no further adjustments (unfavorable to the taxpayer) will likely be made. On the other hand, if the revenue agent has to make repeated requests for missing documentation that expands the time frame of the audit, the time lag would provide the revenue agent the opportunity to review other issues (potentially detrimental to the taxpayer).

If in the course of an office audit or field audit a revenue agent wants to review additional documentation, the agent will issue an Information Document Request, Form 4564, listing the additional requested documentation, a deadline for submission, and whether another appointment (presumably to discuss the documentation) is necessary.

In the course of an audit, it is not uncommon for the taxpayer or tax professional to resolve issues by negotiation. Through a process of "give and take," the IRS may concede a certain issue(s) in exchange for the taxpayer conceding another issue.

Example: There are two issues with respect to the audit of Asher's income tax return. Asher, a sole proprietor, inspects aircraft for certain small commercial airlines. On Schedule C, Asher deducted $20,000 of office supplies purchased at Walmart. Asher purchased all of his personal items and office supplies at Walmart without documenting how much on a particular receipt was business or personal. In addition, Asher took depreciation deductions of his car based on his assertion that 70 percent of his mileage was for business. Initially, the revenue agent sought to disallow the entire office supply deduction and recompute Asher's depreciation deduction based upon 60 percent of business use. In negotiating these issues with the revenue agent, the POA, Miranda Wright, conceded the depreciation issue. In turn, the revenue agent disallowed only 20 percent of the office supply deduction (allowing Asher a $16,000 deduction).

At the end of the audit, the revenue officer will either: 1) propose adjustments to the taxpayer's return(s) (some of which may have been negotiated as illustrated by the above example); or 2) accept the taxpayer's return as filed with no adjustments. Obviously, an increase of income and/or decrease of deductions will result in a proposed assessment of additional tax (plus interest and penalties). If the taxpayer agrees with the proposed changes, the taxpayer or the POA signs the audit report, Form 4549. If at that time, the taxpayer is unable to pay the tax liability (including interest and penalties), an online installment payment can be arranged provided the liability can be paid in full within one year. Otherwise, the taxpayer will have to deal with the Collection Division to negotiate a payment arrangement.

On the other hand, if the taxpayer does not agree and does not sign Form 4549, within a few weeks after the closing conference with the revenue agent (or supervisor), the taxpayer will receive a package from the IRS containing the following:

- A "thirty-day letter" notifying the taxpayer of the right to appeal the proposed changes within thirty days
- A copy of the audit report explaining the revenue agent's proposed changes
- An agreement or waiver form (providing the taxpayer with another opportunity to accept the IRS's proposed changes when Form 870 is used for agreement)
- A copy of Publication 5 (Appeal Rights)

Thirty-Day Letter. Accompanying the thirty-day letter, there is a computation report setting forth proposed adjustments to the taxpayer's tax return. If the taxpayer decides not to pursue a further challenge, the taxpayer signs and returns the agreement form. At that point, the case is closed and the IRS assessment of tax, interest, and penalties would become final. If the taxpayer does not sign off within thirty days from the date of the letter, the taxpayer can submit a request to have the case heard by the IRS Office of Appeals. In the event the taxpayer does not make a timely appeal to the Office of Appeals, the IRS will send the taxpayer a Ninety-Day Letter (see below).

IRS Office of Appeals. The appeal discussed above is heard by the local Office of Appeals (which is separate and independent from the local IRS office and the only level of appeal within the IRS). Appeal conferences are informal and conducted by correspondence, telephone, or at a personal conference. Short of litigation, this is the last chance for the taxpayer and the IRS to resolve their differences. In the event the taxpayer and the Office of Appeals are unable to resolve the dispute, the

IRS will then send the taxpayer a Ninety-Day Letter (see below).[1]

Ninety-Day Letter. If the individual fails to respond to the Thirty-Day Letter or fails to resolve the dispute with Appeals, the IRS will send the taxpayer a Ninety-Day Letter (Statutory Notice of Deficiency). The letter explains that the taxpayer has ninety days from the date of the notice to challenge the IRS's proposed assessment by filing a petition with the Tax Court.[2] By filing a petition, the taxpayer has the opportunity to protest the IRS's proposed assessment before the Tax Court without having to pay the proposed tax.

If the taxpayer does not have a strong case, or if the IRS proposed assessment is correct, filing a petition with the Tax Court would likely be a waste of time and money. Under these circumstances, the taxpayer should consider simply paying the assessed liability or execute an installment payment arrangement with the IRS. On the other hand, if the taxpayer believes he or she can prevail in a Tax Court proceeding, depending on the amount in controversy, the taxpayer may be able to take advantage of the less formal (and possibly less expensive) small tax case procedure.[3] The failure to file a timely petition will result in an enforceable assessment of tax (plus interest and penalties) against the taxpayer.

Mitigating the Impact of Interest and Penalties

During the period in which a taxpayer disputes an IRS proposed assessment of tax, interest on the tax and proposed penalties continue to accrue. So, if the resolution of the case from the end of the audit through the date the Tax Court issues a decision spans a number of years, interest continues to accrue. Thus, if the taxpayer ultimately loses the case, it is possible for the overall tax liability to have increased substantially over that period.

If the taxpayer decides to file a Tax Court petition but is fearful of the imposition of additional interest by not prevailing, the additional accrual of interest can be stopped or reduced by sending a *deposit* to the IRS to cover all, or part, of the potential assessment. A deposit is different from a payment in that (1) a deposit can be returned to the taxpayer without filing a claim for a refund, and (2) a deposit does not earn interest. Most importantly, because the taxpayer cannot litigate a case in Tax Court if the tax is paid, a deposit does not disqualify the taxpayer from pursuing the case in that forum.

Example: In the aftermath of an audit of her 2017 income tax return, Mary filed a timely petition with the Tax Court on February 1, 2020. At that time, Mary's overall liability (tax, interest and penalties) was $25,000. If on March 17, 2020, the Tax Court decides the case against her, interest accruing over that period would be added to the assessment. On the other hand, if Miranda was able to make a deposit of $25,000, she would owe nothing more even though she lost the case. Also, if she was to prevail she would be entitled to a $25,000 refund.

Taxpayer does not file petition in Tax Court. If the taxpayer does not file a timely petition with the Tax Court, but desires to challenge the IRS's position, the only option is to do the following:

- Pay the tax to the IRS.
- File a claim for refund with the IRS.
- Wait for up to six months for a response from the IRS.
- If the IRS denies the taxpayer's claim or fails to respond within six months, sue for a refund in United States District Court (in the district in which the taxpayer resides) or United States Court of Federal Claims.

AUDITS INVOLVING A SIGNIFICANT AMOUNT OF UNDERREPORTED INCOME

Audits involving a significant amount of underreported income can be problematic for the taxpayer. For example, the normal statute of limitations for the assessment of tax by the IRS is the later of three years from the due date of the return or the date on which it was actually filed. On the other hand, if the taxpayer has underreported more than 25 percent of gross income reported on the return, the statute of limitations is extended to six years. Moreover, if the underreporting is due to fraud, there is no statute of limitations; and, even worse, the case may be referred to the IRS

Criminal Investigation Division. Such a referral could lead to criminal prosecution by the U.S. Attorney.

How to Determine the Percentage of Underreported Income

Federal income tax is imposed on gross income. Internal Revenue Code section 61(a) defines gross income as "all income from whatever source derived" followed by fifteen specific types of gross income. See Chapter 3 for a discussion of gross income. Ascertaining how much gross income was omitted from the return is crucial in the determination of whether the taxpayer has underreported more than 25 percent.

In many instances, an omission of gross income is straightforward as it is due to the failure to include an amount reported on a Form W-2 (wage income) or a Form 1099 (nonemployee compensation). However, there are two important rules to note with respect to certain income types in determining the amount of underreported income. The first rule is that gross business income, or gross income reported on Schedule C of Form 1040, is gross receipts minus cost of goods sold.[4]

Example: In 2020, Asher reports Schedule C gross receipts of $200,000 and cost of goods sold of $50,000. Therefore, Asher's Schedule C gross business income is $150,000. In addition, Asher has dividend income of $1,000. So gross income reported on Asher's return is $151,000 ($150,000 + $1,000). Therefore, if Asher omitted more than $37,750 of gross income (25 percent of $151,000) from his 2020 Form 1040, the six-year underreporting statute of limitations would apply. In reviewing Asher's bank statements before the audit, the tax professional discovers a May 1 deposit of $50,000 that was not included on Asher's Schedule C. If Asher had included that deposit, his gross business income would have been $200,000 rather than $150,000. Therefore, Asher's underreporting of the $50,000 deposit is well over the 25 percent threshold. Unless Asher can document that the $50,000 was attributable to a nontaxable source (loan proceeds, a gift, a transfer from another account, etc.), the six-year statute of limitations would apply. In addition, if audited, the revenue agent might conclude that Asher had committed civil and/or criminal tax fraud. In the latter case, the revenue agent might refer the manner to the Criminal Investigation Division of the IRS.

Before meeting with the IRS, the tax professional should perform an analysis of the taxpayer's bank deposits to determine the source of any unreported income; and, if it should have been included in gross income. So, if Asher can document the $50,000 deposit as the proceeds of a loan, there would be no underreporting and no fraud. On the other hand, if Asher had inadvertently failed to include the $50,000 (i.e., it was income) and everything else reported on the return is fully supported, whether the case is referred to Criminal Investigation Division for possible criminal prosecution will be a judgment call by the revenue agent. In making this decision, the revenue agent may extend the audit to the prior and/or subsequent years to see if similar omissions of income recurred in multiple tax years.

As to an assertion of tax fraud, intent usually requires a pattern of conduct consistent with fraud. If the mistake is limited to one tax year, no pattern of fraudulent conduct can be established. In that case, the revenue agent may propose a tax increase adjustment without imposing the civil fraud penalty or referring the case to the Criminal Investigation Division. Similarly, Asher's defense could be the omission of the $50,000 deposit (assuming it should have been included in gross income) was the result of unusual circumstances. For example, perhaps Asher was in poor health possibly bedridden for a period of time and his friend, Miranda Wright made the bank deposit but did not report it to the bookkeeper.

The second rule applies to the sale or exchange of property reported on Schedule D of Form 1040. Under previous law, an underreporting of gross income occurred only if the taxpayer understated the amount realized or the gross proceeds from the sale or exchange of property.[5] Therefore, if the taxpayer understated "taxable income" by overstating the basis of the sold or exchanged property, there was no underreporting of gross income. Effective for returns filed after July 31, 2015, however, the Code was amended so that an overstatement of basis is deemed to result in an understatement of gross income.[6]

Example: Asher reports Schedule C gross receipts of $200,000 and cost of goods sold of $50,000. Therefore, Asher's Schedule C gross business income is $150,000. He also reported $1,000 of dividend income. Finally, on Schedule D, Asher reported the sale of ABC stock at no gain or loss (gross proceeds $75,000 less basis $75,000). So gross income reported on Asher's return is $151,000 ($150,000 + $1,000 + $0). Thus, if Asher omitted more than $37,750 of gross income (25 percent of $151,000), the six-year underreporting statute of limitations would apply. In reviewing Asher's stock records, the revenue agent discovered that Asher's basis in ABC stock was $25,000. Therefore, he overstated his basis by $50,000 and understated his taxable income by $50,000 ($75,000 gross proceeds less correct basis of $25,000). Under prior law, there would be no underreporting because the increase in taxable income was the result of overstatement of basis (i.e., Asher properly reported gross proceeds of $75,000). However, under current law, the $50,000 increase in taxable income resulting from the overstatement of basis is deemed to be an understatement of gross income and would trigger the six-year statute of limitations.

Addressing a significant underreporting audit may involve a variety of different issues. Those issues include:

- **Verifying Amounts Reported on Form 1099s Were Included in Gross Income.** Many audits such as a correspondence audit involving a CP-2000 Notice are based on third party information provided to the IRS, such as nonemployee compensation paid to an independent contractor on Form 1099. If a sole proprietor taxpayer has received numerous Form 1099s setting forth payments for services provided that those payments would likely have been aggregated and reported on the total amount on Schedule C. In the event the IRS questions whether any or all of the amounts reported on the various Form 1099s have been included in the taxpayer's income, their inclusion in total Schedule C gross receipts should be easily verified by providing a spreadsheet. If certain amounts are not included in gross receipts, the revenue agent will make an adjustment to increase income unless the tax professional can show why it is not reportable.

- **Common Types of Underreported Income and How the IRS Quantifies It.** Common types of underreported income include illegal income from selling drugs, guns, etc. or not reporting cash receipts from a business. On the other hand, borrowed funds and gifts are not taxable. However, the burden of proving funds were received via loan or gift is on the taxpayer.

If the IRS suspects that a taxpayer has unreported income (other than borrowed funds or gifts accounted for by the taxpayer), how is it quantified? Often, if the revenue agent can establish a likelihood of underreported or unreported income, he or she will employ the indirect method to compute the underreported amount. There are various indirect methods such as the fully developed cash T, percentage mark-up, net worth analysis, source and application of funds, or bank deposit and cash expenditures analysis. Depending on the circumstances, the computations under these methods may be complicated. Set forth below are the formulas for the bank deposit and cash expenditure method and the source and application of funds method.

- **Bank Deposit and Cash Expenditure Method.** Under this method, the premise is that all money received by a taxpayer is either spent or deposited in a bank account. Therefore, cash expenditures are presumed to have been paid with unreported taxable funds unless the taxpayer can document a nontaxable source for the cash.

Step 1 – Start with all deposits into business and personal bank accounts.

Step 2 – Add all expenditures (business, personal, and capital) paid for in cash.

Step 3 – Add the increase of cash on hand (difference between cash at the beginning of the tax year and the end of the tax year).

Step 4 – Decrease by the amount of nontaxable receipts (transfers between accounts, loan proceeds, and gifts).

Step 5 – The application of Steps 1 through 4 results in the amount of corrected gross receipts.

Step 6 – Decrease the Step 5 amount by the gross receipts claimed on the return.

Step 7 – The Step 6 amount is the amount of unreported income.

- **Source and Application of Funds Method.** Pursuant to this method, if the taxpayer's total expenditures exceed declared income plus income from nontaxable sources, the excess amount of expenditures is presumed to have been paid from unreported or underreported income. For this purpose, examples of sources of funds include declared income (wages, dividends, interest, etc.) and nontaxable income (gifts and loan proceeds). Applications of funds include the payment of business and personal expenses, purchases, etc.

Example: Miranda Wright has the following amount of income and expenditures:

Sources	
Dividends:	$5,000
Interest:	$5,000
Schedule C Gross Receipts:	$50,000
Total:	$60,000
Applications	
Schedule C Expenses:	$32,000
Personal Living Expenses:	$50,000
Total:	$82,000

Because the sum of the applications ($82,000) exceeded Miranda's income from taxable sources ($60,000), the difference ($22,000) is deemed to be understated taxable income.

WHICH DIVISION OF THE IRS CONDUCTS THE AUDITS?

Small Businesses

Office and field audits for individual taxpayers who file complicated 1040s, Schedules C, E, F or Form 2106, as well as small businesses with assets under $10,000,000 and who file a Form 1120, 1065 or 1120S are conducted by the Small Business and Self-Employed Division of the IRS. In a typical field audit, a revenue agent may travel to the taxpayer's place of business and work from there. The agent may decide to tour the business to understand what the taxpayer does and how the income and expenses are recorded.

A taxpayer's method and types of internal control can help determine the scope of the examination. For example, a Mom and Pop business often blends business with personal transactions so that the revenue agent is compelled to verify income through an indirect method. As a part of the audit process, the revenue agent will seek to determine how the taxpayers supported their life style. Often the question is how the taxpayer pays personal bills and the source of cash to pay out of pocket expenses. If the taxpayer appears to report adequate income, the revenue agent will likely focus on small amounts of income that may have been reported on Form 1099s and from casual sales and expenses. If the revenue agent identifies personal expenses and capital items, the agent will disallow them as being nondeductible. Depending on the results of examination, the revenue agent may want to review related returns, such as a Form 1120S or Form 1065 and possibly audit those returns.

Large Businesses

The Large Business and International Division of the IRS deals with corporations, subchapter S corporations, and partnerships with assets greater than $10 million. Usually, this type of business employs a significant number of employees, engages in activities that involve complicated tax law issues and/or conducts business globally. Because this type of taxpayer is more likely to be audited by the IRS, it tends to have dedicated internal staff to interact with revenue agents during an audit. These field audits are likely to be lengthy requiring a revenue agent to be assigned to the audit location for a long period of time. (See Publication 5125, LB&I examination Process related Internal Revenue Manual 4.46 LB7I Guide for Quality Examinations.)

PARTNERSHIP AUDITS

With the enactment of the Bipartisan Budget Act of 2015, the rules for auditing partnerships and LLCs taxed as partnerships changed. The new rules are effective for tax years beginning on or after January 1, 2018. Under the current rules enacted by TEFRA (Tax Equity and Fiscal Responsibility Act of 1982), partnership audit adjustments are allocated to and collected from the individual partners.

Current Rules for Partnership Audits

Partnerships with More Than Ten Partners (or Ten or Fewer Partners if any Partner is a Partnership or Trust)

The partnership must designate one partner to act as the "tax matters partner" to specifically deal with the IRS. IRS audit adjustment of certain "partnership items" determined at the partnership level pass through to the individual partners. Therefore, the individual partners are responsible for the payment of any additional tax (plus interest and penalties).

Partnership with Ten or Fewer Partners

Assuming all partners are individual (other than a nonresident alien), each partner is subject to the same audit procedures that apply to regular individual taxpayers. However, by election, the partnership may choose to be subject to the procedure described in the previous paragraph.

Electing Large Partnerships of at Least One Hundred Partners

Eligible partnerships may elect to be treated as an electing large partnership (ELP) subject to a unified audit procedure. Audit adjustments with respect to examined returns are reflected on each effected partner's current year return not on an amended return. Although this audit procedure was intended to make audits of large partnerships less burdensome, few large partnerships make the election.

New Partnership Audit Rules Effective on or after January 1, 2018

Default Audit Procedure Rule

Effective for tax years beginning on or after January 1, 2018, there is a new default audit procedure that applies to all partnerships unless a partnership is eligible to elect out. In operation, all adjustments of partnership items of income, gain, loss, deduction, credit, and partners' distributive shares of a year under review ("reviewed year") will be made at the partnership level. If there are adjustments, the partnership will be responsible for the "imputed underpayment of tax," interest, and penalties. The imputed underpayment is computed by netting the adjustments of income, gain, loss, and deduction. In the netting process, all positive adjustments (income or gain) and negative adjustments (deduction or loss) are netted without regard to character (capital or ordinary). In other words, all income, gain, deduction, or loss are treated as if they were of the same character. If the netting yields a net positive, that amount is multiplied by the highest tax rate in effect for the reviewed year. Currently, the highest tax rate is 39.6 percent.

Although the imputed underpayment amount may be harsh and overstating the underlying tax liability of the partners, that amount may be reduced based on any of the following:

- Partner(s) file amended returns and pay the tax owing for the reviewed year
- Partnership demonstrates that partnership items are allocable to tax-exempt entities
- Partnership demonstrates that partnership items are allocable to a corporate partner taxable at a lower income tax rate
- Partnership demonstrates that long-term capital gains and/or qualified dividends are allocable to an individual taxable at the applicable lower tax rate

So assuming the partners and the partnership take the applicable mitigating steps, the imputed underpayment of tax should be adjusted to the proper amount of the collective tax liability of all partners.

Alternative Rule

As an alternative rule, a partnership receiving a notice "final partnership administrative adjustment" may opt out of the default audit procedure rule. So, by election (referred to as the "push-out election"), instead of a partnership level tax, the responsibility for the additional tax triggered by the adjustments for the reviewed year would be passed through to the partners. Procedurally, the partnership would issue adjusted Schedule K-1s to the partners who would be responsible to pay his or her or its share of the additional tax. Also, it is possible that certain partnership item adjustments in the reviewed year will trigger adjustments in a prior or subsequent year. If that occurs, the additional tax triggered by those adjustments would also be reported and paid by the partners on their adjustment year returns.

AUDIT TRIGGERED BY FAILURE TO FILE RETURNS

Some taxpayers may believe that not filing income tax returns is a viable way to avoid the IRS "radar." In other words, if a taxpayer simply does not file a return, there is nothing for the IRS to audit and/or assess against the taxpayer. The fallacy with this strategy is that as a collection agency, the IRS is not inclined to wait for a habitually delinquent taxpayer to file tax returns.

Generally, if a taxpayer has failed to file a return for four or five years (although it could be fewer years), the IRS may prepare a "Substitute for Return(s)" with respect to a taxpayer's unfiled income tax returns. In preparing such returns, the IRS inputs the income reported to the IRS from third parties (i.e., Form W-2s and Form 1099s). If the taxpayer is married, the return is prepared as married filing separately taking the standard deduction and one personal exemption. So, if the taxpayer had itemized deductions or other tax credits or deductions that may have reduced tax liability, they are not taken into account. Therefore, a substitute for return is likely to overstate the taxpayer's liability. Importantly, the substitute for return does not start the running of the statute of limitations. Finally, depending upon the amount of income and tax, the failure to file can lead to a referral to the Criminal Investigation Division based on an intent to evade taxes. Any claim of failing to file for health reasons should be well documented.

A taxpayer receiving a notice of a substitute for return should retain a responsible tax preparer to prepare the missing tax returns. On occasion, the taxpayer may not have received the notice of a substitute for return and only finds out in the course of an IRS collection action. Under this circumstance, the IRS will allow the taxpayer to file a return to replace the substitute for return.

> *Example:* Miranda received a notice of levy of her bank account. For the past two years she did not file income tax returns and had either ignored numerous IRS notices or did not receive them. The notice of levy includes the name and telephone number of an IRS contact person. Asher, Miranda's POA, contacts that revenue officer and discovers that the IRS had prepared substitute for returns for those two unfiled years. Believing the tax liability computed on those substitute for returns is overstated, Asher requests a release of the levy with a reasonable amount of time to prepare correct returns including all of Miranda's deductible expenses.

WHERE CAN I FIND OUT MORE?

1. IRS.gov Publications
   - Publication 1: Your Rights as a Taxpayer
   - Publication 5: Your Appeal Rights and How to Prepare a Protest if you Don't Agree
   - Publication 17: Your Federal Income Tax for Individuals
   - Publication 334: Tax Guide for Small Business
   - Publication 556 (Rev. September 2013): Examination of Returns, Appeal Rights, and Claims for Refund
   - Publication 594: The IRS Collection Process
2. https://www.irs.gov/Businesses/Small-Businesses-&-Self-Employed/A-Z-Index-for-Business (If this link is broken, try irs.gov and use the search box for your topic, including lines of business and Audit Technique Guides for insight on types of business and types of taxpayers such as partnerships.)
3. Internal Revenue Manual (IRM), Part 4.10 Examination Techniques, includes Information Document Requests, Form 4564, Correspondence Audits etc.
4. Powers of Attorney Form 2848, 2848 instructions and IRM 4.10.3.2.1.1.
5. IRS Videos including Your Guide to an IRS Audit at http://www.irsvideos.gov/audit/.
6. Weekly updates from the IRS e-News for Tax Professionals.

FREQUENTLY ASKED QUESTIONS

Question – Why should I furnish copies of returns of non-audit tax years to a revenue agent when requested?

Answer – Generally, it is to the taxpayer's advantage to furnish the requested returns. Depending on the issues relevant to the audit, the revenue agent may want to review the returns of prior and/or subsequent years to see how a particular item was reported in those years. Although the revenue agent can obtain copies from the IRS Service Center, it could take months to retrieve. Usually, it is to the taxpayer's advantage for an audit to be completed sooner rather than later so that no new issues are raised. In any case, if upon review of those returns, the revenue agent determines no further examination is required (i.e., the audit is not extended to other tax years), no other action will be required.

Question – What are the consequences to the taxpayer for not reporting all income?

Answer – Minimally, if the taxpayer's return is audited, there will be an adjustment resulting in additional tax, interest and penalties. Beyond that, if the revenue agent discovers a large omission of income, the agent may refer the case to the Criminal Investigation Division for a potential criminal fraud prosecution. The burden of proof in proving fraud is on the government. So, if the taxpayer's defense is "I gave everything to my preparer and the tax preparer must have made a mistake," the tax preparer who prepared the return may have a conflict of interest. In that case, the taxpayer should consider retaining an attorney specializing in fraud.

Question – Does a taxpayer who is audited as a result of information provided to the IRS by an informant have the right to know of the referral?

Answer – The IRS is not required to inform the POA or the taxpayer of the source of any information they may use to start an examination. However, any information provided by an informant must be independently verified and support any adjustments made to the taxpayer's tax liability. So, if the informant's claim has no basis in fact, no change will be made. On the other hand, if the informant claims the taxpayer diverted income and the IRS can independently verify it, adjustments will be made accordingly.

Question – How does the POA revoke a Power of Attorney (Form 2848)?

Answer – A POA may seek revocation of a Power of Attorney for a variety of reasons. For example, at times, individuals are no longer able to afford representation and the POA does not work for free. In other instances, the taxpayer may be unable or unwilling to provide the information the POA needs in order to deal effectively with the IRS. To revoke the Power of Attorney, the instructions to do so are on Form 2848.

Question – Under what circumstances should a taxpayer represented by a tax professional *not* attend a meeting with the IRS?

Answer – In many instances, a taxpayer's presence is quite helpful. The taxpayer has total knowledge of the business and should be competent to explain various transactions and records. If relevant, the taxpayer can explain how and why certain business decisions were made. On the other hand, if a taxpayer is openly hostile to the IRS this can work against a speedy resolution. Also, if a taxpayer is likely to offer more information than asked or if in poor health, not being present may be advisable.

Question – How does the IRS contact taxpayers and when should a taxpayer be suspicious if the taxpayer receives a call from the "IRS"?

Answer – The IRS does not call taxpayers to request name or social security numbers because it already has this information. Scams in which the caller purports to be the "IRS" requesting this type of information or threatening harsh collection action keep mutating. The taxpayer should never fall for these scams. Such scams are included in the IRS website's Twelve Deadly Sins.

The IRS does, however, send letters regarding audits, Earned Income Credits and Identify Theft. Letter 5071C requires that the taxpayer verify individual identities before issuing the tax refund. If the taxpayer ignores the letter, no refund will be issued. In any event, the tax practitioner should advise their clients to contact them whenever they receive correspondence from the IRS or any tax authority.

CHAPTER ENDNOTES

1. If the taxpayer believes IRS personnel is abusing authority, the taxpayer has the right to contact an office called the Taxpayer Advocate to address this concern.
2. The ninety-day letter will state the last day a petition can be filed, i.e., the last day of the ninety-day period.

3. Publication 556 states "**Small tax case procedure.** If the amount in your case is $50,000 or less for any one tax year or period, you can request that your case be handled under the small tax case procedure. If the Tax Court approves, you can present your case to the Tax Court for a decision that is final and that you cannot appeal. You can get more information regarding the small tax case procedure and other Tax Court matters from the United States Tax Court, 400 Second Street, N.W., Washington, DC 20217. More information can be found on the Tax Court's website at www.ustaxcourt.gov."
4. IRC Sec. 6501(e)(1)(B)(i).
5. *U.S. v. Home Concrete & Supply, LLC*, 132 S. Ct. 1836 (2012).
6. IRC Sec. 6501(e)(1)(B)(ii) as added by Section 2005 of the Surface Transportation and Veterans Health Care Choice Improvement Act of 2015.

WORKING WITH THE IRS

CHAPTER 36

INTRODUCTION

Given a choice, most taxpayers would prefer not dealing with the IRS on any level. However, in some instances, a taxpayer may achieve a better overall result by reaching out to the IRS. In this chapter, several ways of reaching out to the IRS are explored, including submitting a private letter ruling request, participating in Fast Track Mediation and Fast Track Settlement as a means to resolve ongoing disputes with the IRS, as well as tips on how to obtain relief from onerous IRS penalties.

PRIVATE LETTER RULINGS

Overview

In spite of the voluminous Internal Revenue Code, Treasury Regulations, Revenue Rulings, Revenue Procedures, and the like, in many instances a taxpayer may be uncertain as to the tax consequences of a particular transaction either contemplated or already consummated. So, in those instances, particularly if adverse tax consequences could result in a significant tax liability, the taxpayer should consider requesting a private letter ruling from the IRS. Also, should the taxpayer make a procedural mistake, such as a late S corporation filing or some other mistake that may be corrected pursuant to Treasury Regulation section 301.9100, the taxpayer may be compelled to submit a request for a private letter ruling in order to get relief from the IRS.

Submitting a private letter request is much more than a written request for relief. For this reason, each calendar year, in the first issued revenue procedure, the IRS sets forth in great detail the requirements for a private letter ruling submission. It also includes a sample format for a private letter request that can be used as a template.

Framing the Pertinent Issues in a Private Letter Ruling Request

Sequentially, in the private letter ruling request, the taxpayer must first set forth the pertinent facts of the transaction. Next, the taxpayer identifies the issues and requests the IRS to rule on the tax consequences of the transaction (hoping for a favorable decision).

Example: Miranda Wright, the surviving spouse of Asher who died intestate, requested a private letter ruling based on the following facts: The sole beneficiary of Asher's IRA (somebody other than Miranda) predeceased Asher. Unfortunately, according to the policy of the service provider of the IRA, because Asher failed to name a contingent beneficiary (such as Miranda), Asher's estate (Miranda being the sole heir and administrator) became the beneficiary of the IRA. If Asher had named Miranda as the contingent beneficiary, however, as his surviving spouse, she could have elected to designate the IRA as her own. In that case, Miranda could roll it over, tax-free, to another IRA. On the other hand, as the sole heir of Asher's estate (not treated in the same way as a surviving spouse), it would be considered an inherited IRA not eligible for rollover. In any event, Miranda elected to treat the IRA as her own (as if she had been a surviving spouse contingent beneficiary) and directed the service provider to re-designate the account in her name, accordingly. In a private letter ruling request, Miranda asked the IRS to validate her election as a surviving spouse for tax purposes.[1]

The taxpayer can rely on a favorable ruling from the IRS, So, if a taxpayer is subsequently audited and the issue is raised by the revenue agent, the IRS will honor the ruling.

Example: In the above example, after receiving a favorable ruling from the IRS, Miranda rolls the IRA directly into one of her IRAs. In a subsequent audit, the revenue agent takes the positon that a tax-free rollover is not allowed with respect to an inherited IRA. In defending her position, Miranda produces the favorable private letter ruling in which the IRS validated her election as a surviving spouse. The revenue agent honors the ruling and concedes the issue in Miranda's favor.

The Consequences of a Private Letter Ruling

Although, as illustrated by the last example, the recipient taxpayer of a private letter ruling may rely on it, other taxpayers cannot. In fact, even with a favorable ruling, there is no absolute guarantee as to the tax consequences. This is because the IRS can revoke or modify a previously issued private letter ruling if the IRS determines that the ruling was incorrect or not consistent with the current position of the IRS. In most cases, however, a revocation or modification is prospective. Retroactive revocations are usually not issued by the IRS provided:

1. there has been no misstatement or omission of material facts;
2. the facts at the time of the transaction are not materially different from the facts on which the letter ruling was based;
3. there has been no change in the applicable law;
4. the letter ruling was originally issued for a proposed transaction; and
5. the taxpayer directly involved in the letter ruling acted in good faith in relying on the ruling and revoking the ruling would be to the detriment of the taxpayer.

If the taxpayer meets all of these conditions, the ruling will not be retroactively revoked or affected by the issuance of subsequent regulations.

Example: In PLR 9233053,[2] the IRS ruled that the creation of a charitable remainder trust to fulfill a legally enforceable charitable pledge was not an act of self-dealing by the donor. Subsequently, the IRS revoked that ruling[3] but deferred the effective date of the revocation until the termination of the trust and distribution of all its assets. By virtue of an essentially prospective revocation, the distribution of the trust assets to satisfy the donor's enforceable pledge did not trigger the self-dealing excise tax.

Finally, if the IRS decides to rule against the taxpayer's position, the taxpayer will be notified in advance. In that case, the taxpayer can either accept the ruling or withdraw the request. However, even if the taxpayer withdraws the request, the IRS will forward the file to the taxpayer's local IRS office.

The Proper Procedural Submission of a Private Letter Ruling Request

As detailed in the first revenue procedure issued by the IRS each calendar year, the requesting taxpayer must attach copies of all pertinent documents to the request. Additionally, the submission must include the complete factual details of the transaction as well as any related relevant facts, names and addresses, and the social security or tax identification number of the taxpayer. Beyond that, the taxpayer must address the history of the issue, analysis, detail of any similar or pending request, as well as any supporting and/or contrary authority for the taxpayer's position. Original signatures of the taxpayer, a penalty of perjury statement, and signatures of an authorized representative, if there is one, are required. Importantly, Appendix C of the revenue procedure is a multi-page checklist of over fifty questions that must be answered. The completed checklist must be included on the top of the package to be submitted to the IRS along with the applicable user fee. Although the user fee tends to be hefty, there are provisions for reduced user fees for low income taxpayers.

What Happens During the Period in Which the Private Letter Request is Under Consideration

Obviously, there is a time lag between the submission of the private letter ruling request and the IRS ruling. During this period, the taxpayer must report relevant developments to the IRS, such as an audit examination of a pertinent return to which the request relates or the requirement of filing a return that is the focus of the private letter ruling. Also, the taxpayer may request a telephone or in person conference. Any informal opinion expressed by the IRS during such a conference is not binding. As mentioned above, if the IRS indicates the likelihood of an adverse opinion, the taxpayer may withdraw the request. If the IRS requests additional information, the taxpayer has twenty-one days to provide it unless the IRS grants an extension. Failure to provide additional information in a timely fashion may result in the request being closed with no private letter ruling issued.

The Consequences of Not Following IRS Procedure May Require the Submission of a Private Letter Ruling for Relief

In general, the IRS provides taxpayers with detailed procedural steps with respect to making elections and the like in revenue procedures. So, if a taxpayer fails to follows those steps, the IRS would likely not honor the election. In that case, the taxpayer's only recourse may be the submission of a private letter ruling for relief.

Example: In order for a surviving spouse to take advantage of a deceased spouse's unused estate tax exemption, an estate tax return must be filed (even if a return would not otherwise be required). For deaths occurring in 2011 and 2012, many estates had not filed returns for purposes of seeking portability. Moreover, in the wake of *United States v. Windsor*,[4] portability became available to married same sex couples. So to provide relief, in Rev. Proc. 2014-18,[5] the IRS allowed estates to qualify for portability with the filing of a Form 706 stating on top of the return "FILED PURSUANT TO REV. PROC. 2014-18 TO ELECT PORTABILITY UNDER SECTION 2010(c)(5)(A)" on or before December 31, 2014.

However, a number of otherwise eligible taxpayers timely filed the Form 706 (likely using a tax preparation software program) and inadvertently failed to handwrite that statement on the top of the return. Thus, because those filers failed to comply with terms of the revenue procedure, the IRS did not accept those returns. The IRS did, however, send a form letter advising those filers to seek Treas. Reg. §301.9100-3 relief by submitting a private letter ruling request.

Use and Reliance of Private Letter Rulings by Other Taxpayers

All private letter rulings are published and are accessible by the general public. However, all taxpayer identifying information is deleted to ensure the privacy of the requesting taxpayer. Although the holding of a private letter ruling is non-binding to any taxpayer other than the recipient taxpayer, practitioners often view the holdings as an indication of the IRS position on a certain issue. This is particularly true with respect to an issue that has not been addressed in case law or other binding authority and there are numerous private letter rulings with similar facts and similar results. Because of the nonbinding effect of a private letter ruling, however, practitioners who rely on the IRS holdings do so at their own peril.

Last Word on Private Letter Rulings

In deciding to submit a private letter ruling, the following considerations should be taken into account:

- Tax practitioner fees
- User fees
- Likelihood of favorable ruling
- Amount of potential tax liability or tax savings
- Time lag between submission and receipt of the IRS ruling

As detailed in this chapter, submitting a private letter request can be a time consuming and complicated process. Therefore, to make a proper submission, a taxpayer may be compelled to hire a tax practitioner.

Professional fees added to the user fee could be an expensive proposition. In addition, a taxpayer should weigh the likelihood of a favorable ruling with the amount of the potential tax liability or tax savings at stake. Finally, with IRS budget cuts and dwindling personnel hours devoted to private letter rulings, there may be a significant time lag between the submission and receipt of the ruling. During that time lag, there is always the possibility of a change in the Code and/or regulations or the IRS taking a position on an issue that precludes a favorable ruling. Based on these considerations, submitting a private letter request may be a risky proposition that in the end is not cost effective, particularly if it results in an adverse ruling.

On the other hand, if a taxpayer decides to seek a private letter ruling involving a complex issue, the taxpayer should hire a competent tax professional and be diligent in following the submission requirements set forth in the revenue procedure (including the attachment of all required documents) so as to prevent any unnecessary delays. Although there are no guarantees, an organized well-written ruling request supported with legal authority as well as persuasive arguments distinguishing relevant negative authority can make the difference between a positive and a negative ruling.

FAST TRACK MEDIATION – COLLECTION DISPUTES

Fast Track Mediation (FTM) is a nonbinding voluntary process for the taxpayer and the IRS to resolve a dispute. In fact, the IRS goal is to achieve resolution within forty days. However, before the taxpayer's case can be considered for FTM, the taxpayer must attempt to resolve all issues by working cooperatively with the IRS revenue officer. If the parties are unable to reach an agreement, the taxpayer should have a conference with the officer's manager. If after that, no agreement is reached, the taxpayer may pursue FTM.

To begin the process, the taxpayer must submit a completed Form 13369 and a written statement detailing his or her position with respect to the disputed issues to the revenue officer. After the application is accepted, a trained mediator from the IRS Office of Appeals is assigned to attempt to mediate an agreement between IRS Collection and the taxpayer. Importantly, every step of the procedure is voluntary for both parties, so no decision can be imposed on the taxpayer or the IRS.

If the parties are able to resolve their disputes through FTM, both the taxpayer and the IRS benefit. From the taxpayer's perspective, it is a relatively speedy and less costly way to resolve an IRS dispute. From the IRS' perspective, it is an effective alternative to a drawn out dispute with a taxpayer.

There are a number of cases and issues that cannot be mediated through FTM:

- Cases considered in the Collection Appeal Program
- Cases considered by an IRS campus case
- Frivolous issues of the type usually raised by tax protestors and other cases and issues set forth in Rev. Proc. 2003-41[6]

Finally, participating in FTM does preclude the availability of other dispute resolution options, including a hearing before Appeals or a conference with an IRS manager. So, if the dispute is not resolved through FTM, the taxpayer may pursue any of the otherwise available appeal rights.

Example: Vera, age thirty-five, a compliant taxpayer, has a history of upwardly progressive positions. She is a single mother providing all support for her daughter born in 2011. In 2018, Vera suffers a heart attack, loses her job, and is faced with a significant amount of medical bills. To pay her medical bills, Vera sells stock and recognizes a taxable gain. In 2019, Vera files a timely 2018 income tax return but is unable to pay the $45,000 of income tax due. Due to bad health, Vera is unable to resume full time employment now or in the future. Through a tax professional, she files an Offer in Compromise proposing to pay $500 to settle the $45,000 tax liability. Being unable to work due to her medical condition, Vera is compelled to borrow money from her parents to make home mortgage and car payments. Her home mortgage payments are larger than the IRS local standard because she is unable to refinance and the home has been modified for her physical needs. She would have to borrow the $500 offer amount from her parents.

The Offer in Compromise officer rejects Vera's offer because she contends that Vera could pay the entire $45,000 tax liability by cashing in her $10,000 IRA, borrow additional funds by obtaining a second mortgage on her home and from her one credit card, and surrendering her $10,000 whole life insurance policy. Vera contends she is unable to take these actions without threatening the security of her home and daughter. Upon the rejection of her Offer, she applies for FTM. An Offer in Compromise of this type is included in Revenue Procedure 2014-63, and the tax advisor prepares a request to mediate to which the IRS agrees.

Both sides meet with the mediator, and in the face-to-face meetings, with additional substantiation, the IRS agrees that Vera is entitled to an increase in the local guideline for housing. The mediator suggests that an appropriate offer would be larger than $500 but smaller than $45,000. Finally, the IRS and Vera agree that given her inability to work and continuing child care, $1000 would be an acceptable offer.

FAST TRACK SETTLEMENT – RESOLVING DISPUTES DURING AN AUDIT

Fast Track Settlement (FTS) is a program to assist taxpayers and the IRS to resolve disputes during an audit. Similar to FTM, FTS is voluntary and nonbinding unless the parties agree to a final resolution. To be considered for FTS, the taxpayer must have worked cooperatively with the revenue agent, followed by a conference with the manager in attempting to resolve the disputed issues. To apply for FTS, the taxpayer must complete Form 14017 with a written statement detailing the taxpayer's position on the disputed issues. The goal is to resolve the dispute within sixty days of the IRS receipt of the application.

FTS is conducted by a mediator assigned from the IRS Office of Appeals to assist the parties in resolving the disputed issues. In addition to mediation, the Appeals mediator may offer settlement proposals. Since FTS is nonbinding, the taxpayer or the IRS can reject any settlement proposal.

If FTS does not result in the resolution of the disputed issues, the taxpayer may pursue all other available dispute resolution options and appeal rights, including protesting a hearing before Appeals or a conference with an IRS manager. If the taxpayer and the IRS do resolve their disputes, potential litigation is avoided in a cost efficient manner.

FTS is not available with respect to the following types of cases:

- Collection cases
- Correspondence audit cases in which no specific IRS personnel has been assigned
- Frivolous issues of the type usually raised by tax protestors
- Other specific issues set forth in Announcement 2011-5

ABATEMENT OF IRS PENALTIES

The assessment of a penalty computed as a percentage of the delinquent tax can be devastating. In some instances, however, abatement of penalties is possible. For example, with the filing of the appropriate return or form, a taxpayer subject to a failure-to-file, failure-to-pay, or failure-to-deposit penalty may request that the IRS not assess the applicable penalty. With respect to an assessed penalty, the taxpayer can submit a written request for penalty abatement to the IRS. Finally, if the taxpayer has paid the penalty, the taxpayer can submit Form 843, Claim for Refund and Request for Abatement provided it is filed within three years of the return due date of filing date, or within two years of the date that the penalty was paid.[7] The denial of a penalty in whole or in part can be appealed for reconsideration.[8]

Penalty relief can be granted based on reasonable cause, statutory exceptions, administrative relief and the correction of an IRS error.

Reasonable Cause: In a penalty abatement letter to the IRS, a taxpayer seeking penalty abatement for reasonable cause must explain why the failure to timely file and/or pay the tax liability is excusable under the particular circumstances. Some examples of reasonable cause are:

- Serious medical condition
- Being out of the country

- Incarcerated
- Destruction or theft of documents
- Death of a close family member

Essentially, the taxpayer should demonstrate why it was impossible to timely comply. Depending on the underlying reason for untimely compliance, the penalty abatement letter should include pictures of a flood, insurance claims, a death certificate, or hospital records as proof. Obviously, the payment of the tax in full (including interest) is indicative of the taxpayer's good faith.

Statutory Exceptions: Due to a natural disaster or a catastrophic event (a major hurricane, a devastating fire, etc.), Congress may provide specific statutory exceptions of penalty relief to affected taxpayers.

Administrative Relief: The First Time Abatement (FTA)[9] is an example of an administrative waiver that provides penalty relief for qualified taxpayers. The applicable penalties are failure to file, failure to pay, and/or failure to deposit taxes. To qualify for this relief, all the following must be true:

- The taxpayer was not previously required to file a return or was not subject to penalties for the three tax years prior to the tax year of the penalty.
- All returns or extensions have been filed.
- Tax has either been paid or an arrangement to pay has been made.

Correction of IRS Error: The IRS is required to abate any portion of any penalty due to erroneous written advice by an officer or employee of the IRS acting in an official capacity.[10] If appropriate, the IRS will consider abatement with respect to taxpayer reliance on erroneous oral advice. In making this determination, the IRS will consider whether the taxpayer relying on this advice exercised ordinary business care and prudence, the relationship between the taxpayer's situation, advice and the penalty; the taxpayer's prior tax history and experience with tax requirements, and whether correct information was provided in written material given to the taxpayer.

Limited Abatement for Relying on the Advice of a Tax Advisor: The only penalty that may be abated due to the erroneous advice of a tax advisor is the accuracy-related penalty based on reasonable cause. As to the failure to file, pay, or deposit penalties, the taxpayer is deemed responsible.

However, it is possible (determined on a case by case basis) that a taxpayer who relied on the erroneous advice of a tax advisor on a substantive tax issue may be eligible for relief from other penalties. In the Internal Revenue Manual, there is an example of a taxpayer who relied on an advisor's opinion that employees were "contract labor."[11] Although the IRS disagreed, it abated the penalty because the employer researched all relevant IRS publications and provided clear and complete information of the duties of the workers to the tax advisor who provided an erroneous opinion.

FREQUENTLY ASKED QUESTIONS

Question – Is statutory interest on a delinquent tax liability a penalty and how is it computed?

Answer – Technically, statutory interest is not a penalty. Essentially, it compensates the government for not having the use of the tax funds during the time the tax is delinquent. The interest rate as determined quarterly is the federal short term rate plus 3 percent interest compounded daily.

Question – What are the penalty rates for the failure to pay and the failure to file?

Answer – The failure to pay penalty is one-half of one percent for each month, or part of a month, up to a maximum of 25 percent of the amount of unpaid tax. The failure to file penalty is 5 percent of the tax owed for each month or part of a month up to a maximum of 25 percent of the unpaid tax. Although it is possible for both penalties to be imposed concurrently, there is a maximum of 25 percent of the unpaid tax.

Question – What factors do the IRS take into account in deciding whether to abate a penalty based on a showing of reasonable cause?

Answer – Essentially, the IRS considers whether the taxpayer exercised ordinary business care and prudence, but due to circumstances or events beyond the taxpayer's control was unable to comply in a timely manner. Also taken into account is when the excusing event occurred and how long after the event did the taxpayer comply. For example, if a family member died several months prior to the due date of the return and the return was filed a year after the due date, penalty relief may not be appropriate. Yet another consideration is whether the taxpayer could have anticipated the event that caused the non-compliance and whether the taxpayer could have reasonably been in compliance. Finally, even if the taxpayer has a plausible reasonable cause excuse, there is no guarantee of abatement. The IRS has a Penalty Appeal Online Self-help Tool[12] which may be of help.

Question – How can the taxpayer be sure that the IRS has calculated interest and penalties correctly?

Answer – It is important to compute the amount of penalties and interest proposed by the IRS, which are occasionally in error. Commercial software is available to compare and check the IRS calculations and indicate savings if abatement is procured.

CHAPTER ENDNOTES

1. Based on PLR 201612001 (March 18, 2016).
2. May 22, 1992.
3. PLR 9714010 (December 20, 1996).
4. 570 U.S. 12 (2013).
5. 2014-7 IRB 513.
6. 2003-1 C.B. 1047.
7. IRC Sec. 6511 (a).
8. Internal Revenue Manual 20.1.1.3.5.1.
9. Internal Revenue Manual, Penalty Handbook 20.1.1.3.6.1.
10. IRC Sec. 6404(f).
11. Internal Revenue Manual, Penalty Handbook, 20.1.1.3.3.4.3 Example section 2.
12. https://www.irs.gov/Individuals/PENALTY-APPEAL-Online-Self-Help-Tool-.

THE SECURE ACT

CHAPTER 37

As a part of the year-end budget package at the end of 2019, Congress passed the long-awaited SECURE Act.[1] The SECURE Act contains a number of provisions that will impact nearly every American. Some of the highlights include:

- Changes to the rules governing qualified plan contributions and required minimum distributions (RMDs).
- Creating of a fiduciary safe harbor for employers who would like to select the annuity provider to use in qualified plans.
- New rules for inherited qualified plans.
- New rules that are designed to encourage the use of multiple employer plans (MEPs).
- Incentives for small business employers to adopt qualified plans, including auto-enrollment features.

These and other aspects of the SECURE Act are discussed in greater detail below.

REQUIRED MINIMUM DISTRIBUTION RULES

The SECURE Act increased the required beginning date from age 70½ to age 72. This means that taxpayers who reach age seventy-two in 2020 will be required to take their first RMD by April 1, 2021, (and their second RMD, for the 2021 tax year, by December 31, 2021). Qualified plan participants who are not 5 percent owners can continue to rely on the "still working" exception to delay RMDs from 401(k) plans.

The SECURE Act does not provide retroactive relief. Taxpayers who reached age 70½ in 2019 will continue to be subject to the old rules—meaning that they will be required to take their first RMD by April 1, 2020.

Note that there has been no corresponding change to the age at which taxpayers can make qualified charitable distributions (QCDs) from IRAs. However, because the primary value of the QCD lies in reducing the taxpayer's RMD obligation, clients who had planned on making a QCD but have yet to reach age seventy-two may wish to wait.

Also, while the IRS proposed updated life expectancy tables late in 2019, those tables assume a required beginning date of 70½. It remains unclear whether the IRS will update these tables to reflect the new age 72 RBD.

Potential Downside to Delaying RMDs

Clients with sizeable IRA or 401(k) balances should evaluate whether pushing back their RMD obligations is a positive strategy. Waiting to take RMDs could lead to higher overall RMDs, potentially pushing the client into a higher tax bracket in retirement without smart tax planning.

Converting traditional defined contribution funds to a Roth over time (or even purchasing a qualified longevity annuity contract, or QLAC, within the retirement account) could help clients avoid this scenario.

IRA CONTRIBUTION RULES

Under the SECURE Act, contributions to traditional retirement accounts are now permitted at any age (previously, taxpayers were not permitted to contribute to traditional retirement accounts after age 71½). The previously applicable "earned income" limitation on eligibility to contribute continues to apply, meaning that the taxpayer (or spouse) must have earned income for the year in order to contribute.

Taxpayers who make both post-70½ (deductible) IRA contributions and take qualified charitable distributions (QCDs) are also subject to an anti-abuse rule. Future QCDs are reduced by the total amount of deductible post-70½ IRA contributions that have not offset another QCD, although the amount cannot be reduced below zero.[2] Amounts that cannot be treated as a pre-tax QCD can be treated as an itemized deduction for the taxpayer.

The SECURE Act also modified the definition of compensation so that certain stipends provided to graduate students can be counted as compensation for IRA contribution purposes after December 31, 2019. Similarly, qualified foster care payments (excluded from income) can be treated as compensation for plan years effective after December 31, 2015, (retroactively) for defined contribution plans and after 2019 for IRAs.[3]

LIFETIME INCOME OR ANNUITY OPTIONS WITHIN A RETIREMENT ACCOUNT

Prior to enactment of the SECURE Act, 401(k) plan sponsors rarely offered an annuity-within-the-401(k) option even though they were allowed to provide clients with these lifetime income options—primarily because sponsors and employers were reluctant to take on more fiduciary responsibility than they already had.

The SECURE Act alleviated some of this concern by creating a fiduciary safe harbor for selecting the annuity provider.[4] If the employer/plan sponsor satisfies the requirements below, that fiduciary will not be held responsible for the inability of the insurance company providing the annuity to satisfy future financial obligations under the contract.

Plan sponsors can now satisfy their fiduciary obligations in choosing the annuity provider by conducting an objective, thorough and analytical search *at the outset* to evaluate annuity providers. The sponsor must also evaluate the insurance carrier's financial capability to satisfy the annuity obligations, as well engage in a cost-benefit analysis with respect to the annuity offering (the sponsor is permitted to rely upon a written representation from the insurance company demonstrating the carrier's financial standing). The written representation must state that the insurance company:

- is properly licensed;
- has met state licensing requirements for both the year in question and seven prior years;
- will undergo financial examination at least once every five years; and
- will notify the plan fiduciary of any changes in status.[5]

From this information, to qualify under the safe harbor, the plan sponsor must draw the conclusion that the carrier is financially capable and that the contract cost is reasonable—in other words, the plan sponsor must have no reason to believe the representations are false. The plan sponsor must also obtain updated written representations at least once a year.

The plan sponsor must determine that the cost of the annuity option is reasonable in relation to the benefits and features provided by the annuity. There is no requirement that the plan sponsor choose the least expensive annuity option.[6]

While this provision is expected to make it easier for plan sponsors to offer annuity options without fear of added fiduciary liability, the SECURE Act also makes the annuity portable once the plan participant has chosen the lifetime income option. Effective for tax years beginning after December 31, 2019, the annuity can be transferred in a direct trustee-to-trustee transfer between qualified plans (or between a qualified plan and an IRA) if the lifetime income option is removed from the original plan's investment options.[7] The option will be available to participants beginning ninety days prior to elimination of the annuity option from their current plan's investment options (i.e., the portability window remains open for ninety days).[8]

The SECURE Act also gives clients more information that can allow them to evaluate how the annuity option could work for them. Effective twelve months after the Department of Labor issues guidance, defined contribution plans will be required to provide participants with lifetime income estimates. The DOL is directed to issue guidance no later than December 20, 2020. Practically, these estimates will take the form of an annual disclosure containing an estimate of the monthly income the participant could receive as annuity based upon the participant's account balances. Plans must provide this statement at least annually even if the plan does not offer an annuity option.

Selecting an Annuity Option as a Retirement Plan Investment

For most clients, the biggest draw of the annuity within a 401(k) option will be obtaining the peace of mind associated with lifetime income guarantees. However, while an annuity option will likely be attractive for many clients, it remains important to fully evaluate the annuity option once it becomes more broadly available. Annuity options generally pay out a guaranteed amount each month regardless of how long the client lives. Annuities can also protect the client's principal 401(k) balance from market downturns.

However, clients also need to evaluate the potentially higher fees that can accompany the annuity option. Clients should be advised to evaluate both the fees associated with the specific annuity options (noting that fee structures can vary) along with the potential surrender charges that will apply for clients who change their minds.

As with early 401(k) withdrawals, early annuity withdrawals can also generate a 10 percent tax penalty. Interest provision can also vary—in some cases, the annuity will have a fixed "floor" interest rate below which the client's earnings cannot drop. On the other hand, the annuity will likely also have a "cap" which earned interest cannot exceed even if the markets perform exceptionally well.

Plan sponsors should be aware that the spousal benefit and spousal consent rules were not changed by the SECURE Act. This means that married participants who select an annuity benefit must either choose a benefit that provides a spousal survivor benefit or obtain spousal consent to select an alternate benefit.

NEW RULES FOR INHERITED QUALIFIED PLANS

In previous years, as retirement accounts have grown in value, the idea of using the account to provide a tax-preferred legacy to future generations had grown in popularity. To offset some of the cost of the SECURE Act, Congress limited the value of the stretch for most taxpayers who do not qualify as "eligible designated beneficiaries" (see below). Under prior law, non-spouse beneficiaries could take distributions from the inherited IRA either over a five-year period or using the beneficiary's life expectancy. Also, the rules for taking distributions differed depending upon whether the original owner died before or after the required beginning date.

After enactment of the SECURE Act, distribution rules for beneficiaries are the same regardless of when the original account owner died.[9]

Under the new law, most non-spouse account beneficiaries will be required to take distributions over a ten-year period.[10] However, the law also eliminates the requirement that inherited account beneficiaries must take a distribution each year. Practically, this means that all beneficiaries can stretch the tax deferral potential of the inherited account over ten years, taking the entire value as a distribution at that point. The law did not change the rules applicable to surviving spouses who inherit the account.

The new limitations on the stretch treatment of defined contribution plans and IRAs applies for most clients beginning in 2020. Collectively bargained plans, 403(b) plans, 457 plans and other governmental plans will not be impacted until 2022. If the taxpayer has already annuitized the funds irrevocably, the new rules do not apply and the annuity contract terms will govern distributions.

Exceptions exist for a newly created class of beneficiaries called "eligible designated beneficiaries". Eligible designated beneficiaries who are not required to use the "ten-year rule" for distributions (so that the pre-SECURE Act rules apply) include:[11]

- Surviving spouses,
- Disabled beneficiaries,
- Chronically ill beneficiaries,

- The account owner's children who have not reached "the age of majority", and
- Individuals who are not more than ten years younger than the original account owner.

Whether an individual is an eligible designated beneficiary is determined as of the date of the original account owner's death.[12]

A child who inherits a retirement account will take required distributions under the old rules (i.e., using the child's life expectancy) until reaching the age of majority. Once the child reaches age eighteen,[13] the child becomes subject to the ten-year rule beginning at that point, rather than beginning with the account owner's death.[14] Note that only the account owner's minor children qualify as eligible designated beneficiaries. Grandchildren and other minor children become subject to the ten-year rule beginning with the original account owner's death regardless of their age.

"Disabled beneficiaries" for this purpose are those defined in IRC Section 72(m)(7). Disabled beneficiaries include those who are unable to engage in any substantial gainful activity by reason of any medically determinable physical or mental impairment which can be expected to result in death or to be of long-continued and indefinite duration.

"Chronically ill beneficiaries" include those who are unable to perform (without substantial assistance) at least two activities of daily living for a period of ninety days due to a loss of a functional capacity or those who require substantial supervision to protect them from threats to health and safety because of severe cognitive impairment.[15]

A trust may be used to secure payments from the inherited account over the life expectancy of a disabled or chronically ill beneficiary.

Upon the death of the eligible designated beneficiary, the ten-year rule applies regardless of whether that individual's beneficiary is also an eligible designated beneficiary.[16]

The SECURE Act rules apply for tax years beginning after December 31, 2019 and apply to all defined contribution-type plans (the rules governing distributions from Roth IRAs were not changed).

Trusts as Beneficiaries

Often, taxpayers have named trusts—known as "see-through" or "look-through" trusts—as retirement account beneficiaries for a variety of planning reasons. Under pre-SECURE Act law, if the trust was properly drafted, the trust beneficiary's life expectancy could be used in determining required distributions from the inherited account. Where the trust has a beneficiary who is not an individual, or who is not identifiable from the trust terms, the trust will fail as a look-through trust and the five-year distribution rule will apply (under both pre- and post-SECURE Act law).

Post-SECURE Act, an existing trust strategy may be disadvantageous for a number of reasons. First, the taxpayer must review the terms of the trust itself. In many cases, these types of trusts were drafted as "conduit trusts" to provide that the required minimum distribution would be distributed from the IRA to the trust each year (and then, often, passed immediately out of the trust to the actual beneficiary). Because there is no longer a required minimum distribution requirement for inherited accounts until ten years have passed, without changing the trust terms, the beneficiary could automatically be subject to tax on the entire account balance in year ten under the terms of many conduit trusts (because year ten is the only year in which a required minimum distribution exists—i.e., the entire remaining account balance).

Further, the funds will pass to the account beneficiary much more quickly than the account owner may have intended with the use of a conduit trust. Many clients may wish to evaluate alternative structures (such as accumulation-type trusts) to ensure that the IRA funds remain controlled by a trustee with sound investment management skills, rather than distributed to a potentially irresponsible beneficiary.

The impact of a trust with discretionary distribution terms—"accumulation trusts", where much of the IRA balance remains within the trust after distribution from the IRA—also need to be examined to determine the potential tax consequences. Clients, of course, should be aware that trusts are subject to much higher tax rates that may apply to the accumulated assets, but for some, this might be a valid trade-off.

Clients should note that if the trust in question does not qualify as a see-through trust, the previously applicable distribution rules will apply (i.e., the IRA will be treated as though it has no designated beneficiary, so the new ten-year rule that applies to designated beneficiaries will not apply). In other words, the IRA would have to be distributed under the old five-year rule or, in some cases, over the life expectancy of the original account owner depending upon the owner's age at death. If the account is treated as not having a designated beneficiary, such as in the case where an estate or charity is named beneficiary—that could actually provide for a longer stretch, depending upon the original account owner's age at death (absent IRS guidance to the contrary).

Pending future IRS guidance, flexibility will be key for many clients looking to maximize the stretch under the new rules. Trust provisions can (absent future guidance) be drafted to provide for a "flip" between options depending upon the client's age at death.

Notably, if the client has established a see-through trust and the beneficiary of that trust is disabled or chronically ill, and so an eligible designated beneficiary, the old life expectancy rules will continue to apply. It remains unclear whether this will be the case with spouses, minor children and it is expected that the IRS and Treasury will release additional guidance on the use of trusts as IRA beneficiaries generally.

Alternative Planning Strategies

Clients who had relied upon the availability of the stretch IRA rules should be advised about alternative planning strategies if they do not plan to spend their IRA funds (or are worried that they will not get the chance to spend those funds) during retirement. For some, this could be as simple as naming a spouse as beneficiary rather than a child or grandchild (the spouse retains the ability to stretch the tax benefits of the IRA over his or her lifetime). Others might wish to increase the number of IRA beneficiaries to spread (and potentially minimize) the tax hit over the ten-year distribution period.

Executing a series of Roth conversions over time can provide clients with a source of tax-free income to leave to beneficiaries if the tax benefits of the stretch IRA were the client's primary concern.

Some clients might be more attracted to the qualified charitable distribution (QCD) strategy, which allows them to give to charity instead of adding to their taxable income with IRA RMDs after their required beginning date has passed. Each account owner who has reached age 70½ can transfer up to $100,000 per year to a qualified charity in a trustee-to-trustee transfer, eliminating or reducing their tax obligation and simultaneously reducing the overall IRA balance.

Others might be more inclined to explore alternative trust strategies to pass their accumulated retirement funds onto children or grandchildren on a tax-preferred basis for the beneficiaries. Combining life insurance with a trust is one potential option. Clients can direct their RMDs into a trust to fund purchase of a life insurance policy (with the trust as beneficiary of the policy, and the client's heirs as beneficiary of the trust itself).

The RMDs transferred into the trust can be used to pay the insurance premiums. When the policy death benefits are eventually distributed to the trust, the benefit will be tax-free to the beneficiaries and the trust (unlike the distributions that the beneficiaries would have to take from the IRA, which would be fully taxable to the beneficiaries).

MULTIPLE EMPLOYER PLANS

The SECURE Act fundamentally changed the nature of multiple employer plans (MEPs) by removing both the "common nexus" requirement[17] and the "one bad apple" rule.[18]

The common nexus requirement restricted the MEP option to small business employers with a relatively strong connection—whether operating in the same industry or same geographic location. Although final regulations issued last summer relaxed the common nexus rule, the SECURE Act goes even further. Under the SECURE Act, even employers that do not operate in the same industry or in the same location can join together in an "open MEP" that can be administered by a pooled plan provider (generally, a financial services firm).[19] The pooled plan provider must be named by the plan as a fiduciary, as plan administrator and responsible for all administrative duties. The pooled plan provider must also register with the Treasury secretary as such.[20]

Use of the pooled plan provider to act as both plan administrator and a fiduciary with respect to the plan is intended to ease both the administrative burden and fear of fiduciary liability for small business owners. However, each employer participating in a plan with a pooled plan provider will be treated as plan sponsor with respect to the portion of the plan attributable to employees and beneficiaries of that employer.[21]

Eliminating the one bad apple rule shields participating employers from fiduciary liability if one member of the MEP violates the MEP rules or otherwise fails to satisfy applicable fiduciary duties. Under the one bad apple rule, the entire MEP could be disqualified based upon the actions of only one employer that participated in the plan—based upon the assumption that the MEP is to be treated a single unified plan.

The SECURE Act provides that if one employer's actions would disqualify the plan, only that employer's portion of the MEP will be disqualified. Under the new rules, in the case of one participating employer's failure to act in accordance with the qualification rules:

(1) the assets of the plan attributable to employees of the employer will be transferred to a plan maintained only by that employer (or successor), to an eligible retirement plan under Section 402(c)(8)(B) for each person whose account is transferred (unless the Treasury determines that it is in the best interests of the participant for the assets to remain in the plan), and

(2) the employer (and not the plan in which the failure occurred) will be held liable for any liabilities with respect to such plan attributable to the employees of the employer.[22]

The SECURE Act directs the Treasury to issue additional guidance on many of these issues (including model plan language). Before this guidance is released, however, the law directs that employers and pooled plan providers will not be treated as failing to meet a requirement if they make a good faith, reasonable effort in interpreting the new provisions.

The new MEP rules become effective beginning in plan years after 2020.

Considering MEPs for 2021 and Beyond

While the introduction of open MEPs, effective beginning in 2021, is an exciting change for small business clients, some industry experts still consider the administrative costs of the MEP to be high compared to those of larger employers. One SECURE Act change that allows unrelated employers to file a single Form 5500 (filed by the plan administrator) could help ease that cost burden.

Additionally, the employer continues to bear fiduciary responsibility with respect to selecting and monitoring the pooled plan provider. Pooled plan providers can outsource investment decisions to another fiduciary (likely, outsourcing will to be to a fiduciary known as a "3(38) fiduciary"). This arrangement does spread the costs of investment advice among the MEP participants to reduce expenses, but the extent of the employer's fiduciary exposure still remains unclear under the law.

Employers may also wish to consider the extent of the investment options that will be available under the MEP format. It is possible that some plans will provide investment options that are much more limited than the 401(k) and retirement savings options that are already established and available to small business clients. Offering only a limited selection of investments may reduce fiduciary monitoring responsibilities for the client, but could also hinder the performance of their retirement funds.

INCENTIVES FOR SMALL BUSINESS EMPLOYERS

The SECURE Act expands the retirement plan start-up credit for small businesses who are eligible. The credit available under IRC Section 45E, available for three tax years, is increased to the greater of (a) $500 or (b) the lesser of (i) $250 per employee of the eligible employer who is not a highly-compensated employee and who is eligible to participate in the eligible employer plan maintained by the employer or (ii) $5,000.[23]

Eligible small employers (under IRC Section 408(p)(2)(C)(1)) who provide an eligible auto-enrollment feature[24] are eligible for an additional $500 per year credit (for the first three years the auto-enrollment feature is offered).[25]

The credit for auto-enrollment can be claimed even if a new auto-enrollment feature is added to an existing plan.

Limits on Auto-enrollment

Generally, employers are permitted to provide automatic enrollment features that automatically enroll and contribute a portion of employees' income to their retirement plan. Under pre-SECURE Act law, the most employers could automatically defer as a plan default was 10 percent of an employee's compensation. The SECURE Act increases that default percentage to

15 percent for tax years beginning after 2019 for any year after the first plan year when the employee's compensation is automatically deferred into the plan.[26]

Expand Access to 401(k)s for Part-time Employees

Under prior law, employers were permitted to exclude workers who performed fewer than 1,000 hours of service per year from participation in the employer-sponsored 401(k) (this rule still stands, as modified by the SECURE Act's additional eligibility requirement).

The SECURE Act modified this rule in order to expand access for certain part-time employees. Under the new law, employees who perform at least 500 hours of service for at least three consecutive years (and are at least twenty-one years old[27]) also must be allowed to participate in the employer-sponsored 401(k).[28] These long-term, part-time employees may, however, be excluded from coverage and nondiscrimination testing requirements.[29] The new rule also does not apply to employees covered under collectively bargained plans.[30]

In other words, under the new law, employees must be eligible to participate in a 401(k) upon the earlier of (1) the plan's eligibility requirements as established under pre-SECURE Act law, or (2) the end of the first period of three consecutive twelve-month periods where the employee has provided at least 500 hours of service. Plans are permitted to allow part-time employees to participate earlier, however.

While the SECURE Act rule requires employers to allow certain long-term, part-time employees to participate in the 401(k), it does not require employers to contribute on behalf of those employees (although employers are free to do so). The law only requires that these employees be permitted to make their own contributions to the 401(k).

The new applies to 401(k) plans, but absent future guidance to the contrary, does not change the rules for part-time participants in 403(b) plans. Part-time employees will not be eligible to participate under the new rules until 2024. However, employers should act in advance to create a method for tracking employee hours this year (as hours will begin to be counted in 2021 for calendar-year plans).

This SECURE Act provision becomes effective for plan years beginning after December 31, 2020. However, twelve-month periods beginning before January 1, 2021 are not taken into account for purposes of determining whether an employee qualifies.

Qualified Plan Loans

The SECURE Act prohibits qualified plans from making plan loans through credit cards and similar arrangements.[31] This new rule applies immediately (i.e., as of the date of enactment of the SECURE Act, December 20, 2019).

Timing Rules for Adopting a Retirement Plan Change

The SECURE Act now allows employers to adopt retirement plans that are funded entirely by the employer after the end of the year. Plans such as stock bonus plans, pension plans, and profit sharing plans may be adopted up to the due date for filing the employer's tax return for the year (including extensions). The employer now has the option of electing to treat that plan as though it was adopted the last day of the prior tax year.[32] This provision is effective for tax years beginning after December 31, 2019. For many small business clients, this means that they can adopt the plan by September 15 and reduce their tax liability through contributions for the prior tax year.

Cash balance plans can be offered in addition to traditional 401(k) plans, so that clients can also contribute up to $57,000 to the 401(k) in 2020. For small business owners in service businesses, this can be beneficial because the larger pre-tax contribution limits that apply to cash balance plans can reduce the client's taxable income to qualify for the new 20 percent tax deduction under Section 199A. Like 401(k) plans, contributions to cash balance plans reduce taxable income, so maximizing contributions to both types of accounts can prove valuable to the small service business client in order to qualify under 199A. Clients should pay close attention to the cash balance plan contribution rules, which may make these plans attractive primarily to business owners with few or no employees. See Chapter 5 for more information on the Qualified Business Income Deduction.

Clients seeking to take advantage of the new timing rule should remember that the IRS considers a plan to be "adopted" when a plan document has been signed.

401(k) Safe Harbor Rules

The safe harbor 401(k) plan rules generally provide that the plan will be deemed to satisfy the extensive nondiscrimination rules to which 401(k)s are subject so long as the employer guarantees that it will make certain matching or nonelective contributions for employees. However, notice and timing requirements have historically made these safe harbor plans less attractive for many business owners. Prior to the SECURE Act, plan sponsors were limited in their ability to implement safe harbor provisions mid-year. Practically, notice requirements that had to be sent prior to the beginning of a plan year meant that employers had to implement safe harbor provisions at the beginning of the plan year.

Under the new law, plan sponsors are permitted to amend their 401(k) plan documents to provide for safe harbor nonelective contributions:

1. no later than thirty days prior to the end of the plan year; or

2. if the employer contribution is at least 4 percent of employee compensation, after thirty days prior to the end of the plan year and before the last day for distributing excess contributions to the plan (usually, by the end of the next plan year).[33]

Further, under the SECURE Act, the notice requirements for safe harbor nonelective contributions of at least 3 percent of employer compensation has been eliminated (notice requirements for plans that provide only for an employer match remain in place). For more information on safe harbor plans.

Nondiscrimination Testing for Closed Defined Benefit Plans

The SECURE Act made changes that would make it easier for certain sponsors of closed defined benefit plans to satisfy their nondiscrimination testing requirements.[34]

Many employers who have closed defined benefit plans to new participants have continued to allow groups of "grandfathered" employees to earn benefits under the closed defined benefit plans. Because of this, many of these plans have had difficulties meeting the applicable nondiscrimination requirements as more of these grandfathered employees become "highly compensated" over time. For a number of years, the IRS has released relief from the nondiscrimination rules for closed defined benefit plans. The SECURE Act essentially codifies a number of these relief provisions.

Generally, a defined benefit plan cannot discriminate in favor of highly compensated employees with respect to any plan benefit, right or feature. Under the SECURE Act, defined benefit plans will be treated as passing nondiscrimination testing with respect to benefits, rights and features if:

1. the plan passes nondiscrimination testing in the plan year during which the plan closure takes place, and the two subsequent plan years;

2. the plan was not amended after closure to discriminate in favor of highly compensated employees, either by modifying the closed class or the benefits, rights and features provided to that class; and

3. the plan was closed before April 5, 2017, or there was no substantial increase in value of either coverage or value of the benefits, rights and features for the five-year period before the plan was closed.[35]

A plan is treated as having had a "substantial increase" in coverage or value of the benefits, rights, or features during the applicable five-year period only if, during that period:

"(i) the number of participants covered by such benefits, rights, or features on the date the five-year period ends is more than 50 percent greater than the number of such participants on the first day of the plan year in which the period began, or

"(ii) the benefits, rights, and features have been modified by plan amendments in such a way that, as of the date the class is closed, the value of the benefits, rights, and features to the closed class as a whole is substantially greater than the value as of the first day of such five-year period, solely as a result of the amendments."[36]

Additionally, closed defined benefit plans can be aggregated with the employer's defined contribution plans for purposes of compliance testing if:

1. the defined benefit plan provides benefits to a closed group of participants;

2. the defined benefit plan passes nondiscrimination and coverage testing in the plan year during which the plan closure takes place, and the two subsequent plan years;

3. no amendments that discriminate in favor of highly compensated employees were made after the plan closed; and

4. the plan was closed before April 5, 2017 or there was no "substantial increase" in value of either coverage or value of the benefits, rights and features for the five-year period before the plan was closed (see above).[37]

If the defined benefit plan is aggregated with a plan that provides matching contributions, the defined benefit plan must also be aggregated with the portion of the DC plan that provides elective deferrals and the matching contributions must be treated in the same way as nonelective contributions for purposes of nondiscrimination and coverage testing.[38]

The nondiscrimination relief is effective immediately, but plans have the option of applying this relief retroactively to plan years beginning after December 31, 2013.

FORM 5500 RULES

Prior to the passage of the SECURE Act, the IRS could assess a penalty of up to $25 per day with a cap of $15,000 per year for taxpayers who filed Form 5500 late. Effective for years beginning after December 31, 2019, the SECURE Act increased the penalty to $250 per day for late filers and up to $150,000 per plan year (note that an additional DOL penalty, not impacted by the SECURE Act, exceeds $2,000 per day with no annual cap).[39] Penalties for failure to timely file a Form W-4P withholding notice also increased, to $100 per failure and up to $50,000 per year. The penalty for failure to timely file Form 5310-A (notice of plan merger, spin-off or asset transfer) increased to $250 per day up to $150,000 per year.

Filing a Single Form 5500 for a Group of Plans

The SECURE Act now allows certain related defined contribution plans and individual account plans[40] to file a single Form 5500. To be eligible, the plans must share:

- The same trustee,
- One or more of the same named fiduciaries,
- The same administrator,
- Plan years beginning on the same date, and
- The same investments or investment options for participants and beneficiaries.[41]

SECTION 529 PLANS

The year-end legislative package containing the SECURE Act, which primarily impacts retirement-related provisions, also expands upon the permissible uses of Section 529 plan dollars. The 2017 tax reform legislation provided that 529 plan funds can be used to fund up to $10,000 in private elementary, secondary and religious school tuition. The SECURE Act further expands the definition of qualified higher education expenses.

Under the SECURE Act, up to $10,000 in 529 plans can be used to repay the designated plan beneficiary's student loans (or student loans of the beneficiary's siblings).[42] The $10,000 limit is a cumulative, lifetime limit, meaning that the amount is reduced by any distributions treated as qualified higher education expenses under the new provisions in prior years. However, amounts treated as a qualified education expense with respect to a sibling's student loan repayments are not counted with respect to amounts available for the designated plan beneficiary. The available deduction for student loan interest for a taxpayer is reduced in any taxable year by the amount of distributions treated as qualified higher education expenses under IRC Section 529(c)(9) with respect to loans that would be includible in gross income under Section 529(c)(3)(A) if not for the new rule.[43]

Additionally, up to $10,000 in expenses associated with the beneficiary's participation in registered apprenticeship programs can be treated as qualified education expenses.[44]

The SECURE Act's expansion of 529 programs applies retroactively, for tax years beginning after December 31, 2018.

FREQUENTLY ASKED QUESTIONS

Question – Does the SECURE Act create any new exceptions to the 401(k) early withdrawal penalty?

Answer – Yes. The SECURE Act now allows penalty-free withdrawals to cover expenses related to the birth or adoption of a child.[45] Penalty-free withdrawals of up to $5,000 can be made for up to one year following the birth or legal adoption of the child. Adopted children generally include children under age eighteen, but can also include someone who has reached age eighteen but is physically or mentally disabled and incapable of self-support.[46]

Although the withdrawal will be free from penalty, ordinary income tax rates will apply to the amount withdrawn.

The new provision applies on a per-person basis, meaning that *each* parent can take a $5,000 penalty-free distribution absent future guidance to the contrary. Further, the new rule also appears to permit a $5,000 penalty-free withdrawal per birth or adoption, so that parents can take advantage of the rule for multiple births or adoptions.

This provision is optional for plan sponsors. If permitted, the participant will be entitled to repay all or a portion of the amount withdrawn to a qualified retirement plan in which the participant participates (even if it is a different plan) if the recipient plan provisions provide for repayment.[47] If permitted, the qualified plan re-contribution will be treated as an eligible rollover made in a trustee-to-trustee transfer within sixty days of the distribution.

Question – Did the 2019 year-end legislative package make any changes to the "kiddie tax" rules?

Answer – Yes. Under the new law, the changes made by the 2017 tax reform legislation with respect to the kiddie tax rules were repealed.[48]

Under the 2017 tax reform legislation, the unearned income of minors was to be taxed based upon the rates applicable to trusts and estates, and the earned income to be taxed at the rates applicable to single filers. Prior to tax reform, income subject to the kiddie tax rules (i.e., the unearned income of minors) was taxed at the parent's income tax rate.

The repeal of the 2017 kiddie tax changes is effective beginning in 2020. However, taxpayers have the option of electing to have either set of rules apply retroactively, in 2018 and 2019.[49] The new law also eliminated the reduced AMT exemption amount for minors subject to the kiddie tax (retroactively, to 2018). Because of this unexpected change, clients whose children have unearned income may wish to compare the tax results under both sets of rules to determine which will result in the lowest tax liability.

CHAPTER ENDNOTES

1. While the SECURE Act had originally been filed as a separate bill in 2019, it was ultimately passed as part of the Further Consolidated Appropriations Act, 2020; Pub. L. 116-94 (Dec. 20, 2019).
2. IRC Sec. 408(d)(8)(A).
3. SECURE Act, Sec. 106, Sec. 116.
4. New ERISA Sec. 404(e).
5. ERISA Sec. 404(e)(2).
6. ERISA Sec. 404(e)(3).
7. IRC Sec. 401(a)(38).
8. IRC Sec. 401(k)(2)(B)(i)(VI).
9. IRC Sec. 401(a)(9)(H)(i)(II).
10. IRC Sec. 401(a)(9)(H)(i)(I).
11. IRC Sec. 401(a)(9)(E)(ii).
12. IRC Sec. 401(a)(9)(E)(ii) (flush language).
13. What constitutes the "age of majority" is defined by state law, which is 18 is most states, but 21 in others.
14. IRC Sec. 401(a)(9)(E)(iii).
15. I.e., the standard of IRC Sect. 7702B(c)(2).
16. IRC Sec. 401(a)(9)(H)(iii).
17. ERISA, Sec. 3(2).
18. IRC Sec. 413(e)(1)(B).
19. IRC Sec. 413(e)
20. IRC Sec. 413(e)(3).
21. IRC Sec. 413(e)(3)(D).
22. IRC Sec. 413(e)(2).
23. IRC Sec. 45E(b)(1).
24. As defined by IRC Sec. 414(w)(3).
25. IRC Sec. 45T.

26. IRC Sec. 401(k)(13)(C)(iii).
27. IRC Sec. 401(k)(15)(A).
28. IRC Sec. 401(k)(2)(D).
29. IRC Sec. 401(k)(15)(B).
30. IRC Sec. 401(k)(15)(C).
31. IRC Sec. 72(p)(2)(D).
32. IRC Sec. 401(b)(2).
33. IRC Sec. 401(k)(12)(F)
34. IRC Sec. 401(o).
35. IRC Sec. 401(o)(1)(A), (C).
36. IRC Sec. 401(o)(1)(D).
37. IRC Sec. 401(o)(1)(B).
38. IRC Sec. 401(o)(1)(B)(ii).
39. IRC Sec. 6652(e).
40. As defined under IRC Sec. 414(i) or ERISA Section 3(34).
41. SECURE Act, Sec. 202.
42. IRC Sec. 529(c)(9).
43. IRC Sec. 221(e)(1).
44. IRC Sec. 529(c)(8).
45. IRC Sec. 72(t)(2)(H).
46. IRC Sec. 72(t)(2)(H)(iii)(II).
47. IRC Sec. 72(t)(2)(H)(v).
48. SECURE Act Sec. 501, striking IRC Sec. 1(j)(4).
49. SECURE Act Sec. 501(c).

COVID-19 LEGISLATION

CHAPTER 38

In the spring of 2020 the United States began to deal with impact of the spread of the COVD-19 virus nationwide. The virus has proven to be extremely contagious and brings with it a risk of death and serious complication that exceeds what it is typically seen with other types of infections like the annual flu. In response to this new threat to public health, most states imposed public health directives requiring schools and many businesses to close, and to allow employees to work remotely from home if possible.

The economic consequences of these orders have been severe, with unemployment quickly reaching rates not seen since the 1930s. In an attempt to ease the economic shock, Congress passed several pieces of COVID-19 legislation and related administrative developments. Many of the changes contained in this legislation make significant changes to current tax rules. Some of these changes will be unique for the year 2020, and others will have lasting impacts. The changes outlined below cover:

- The Families First Coronavirus Response Act;
- The CARES Act;
- IRS Notices related to the new legislation; and
- IRS and DOL FAQs that help taxpayers understand how the new rules will be implemented.

It is anticipated that there will be additional legislation passed in 2020, and the changes already enacted will continue to result in new regulations, administrative interpretations, and litigation. Planners should remain cognizant of the newest changes to offer the best possible advice for their clients in the short and long term.

FAMILIES FIRST CORONAVIRUS RESPONSE ACT

The Families First Coronavirus Response Act applies to private employers with fewer than 500 employees (and government employers), and makes several key changes to paid time off laws. The bill: (1) provides 80 hours' additional paid sick leave for employees (prorated for part-time workers) and (2) expands FMLA protections. The additional paid sick leave is capped at $511 per day (total of $5,110) for employees who cannot go to work or telecommute because they (1) are experiencing COVID-19 symptoms and seeking a diagnosis, or (2) are subject to government-mandated quarantine or a recommendation to self-quarantine.

The additional paid sick leave is capped at 2/3 of the employee's pay rate, subject to a maximum of $200 per day or $2,000 total if the employee (1) is caring for or assisting someone subject to quarantine, (2) caring for a child whose school or care provider is unavailable or (3) experiencing "substantially similar conditions" specified by HHS.

Calculating Sick Pay for Part-Time and Variable Hour Workers

With respect to the FMLA extension, the rate of pay for part-time employees is based upon the number of hours they would normally be scheduled to work. For employees with variable schedules, pay is based upon a number equal to the average number of hours that the employee was scheduled per day over the six-month period ending on the date on which the employee takes such leave, including hours for which the employee took leave of any type or (2) if the employee did not work over such period, the reasonable expectation of the employee at the time of hiring of the average number of hours per day that the employee would normally be scheduled to work. As of now, the law provides that leave may not be carried over into 2021.

Concurrent Use of FFCRA Leave

The FFCRA implemented a new paid sick leave law and expanded FMLA leave options for employees impacted by COVID-19. Many employers have independent policies in place that provide employees with leave options, and the DOL regulations raised questions about when the employer can require the employee to use that leave prior to, or concurrently with, FFCRA leave.

Employers cannot require employees to concurrently use leave during the first two weeks of paid sick leave for non-childcare related reasons. Employers can, under some circumstances, require use of employee leave concurrently with expanded FMLA leave for childcare reasons.

Employers are only eligible for tax credits with respect to leave paid out under the new law. If the employer requires the employee to use otherwise available employer-paid leave, the tax credit is unavailable with respect to that portion of the employee's pay.

Employee Rights After FFCRA Leave

Employers are generally prohibited from retaliating against employees to take paid sick leave or expanded FMLA leave under the FFCRA. However, the law does not protect employees from layoffs or furloughs undertaken for other reasons, such as the general economic downturn.

Exceptions exist for key employees and very small employers with fewer than twenty-five employees. The exception allows employers to refuse returning the employee to work in the same position if the employee took leave for childcare-related reasons, and all four of the following hardship conditions exist:

1. the position no longer exists due to economic or operating conditions that affect employment and due to COVID-19 related reasons during the period of leave;
2. the employer makes reasonable efforts to restore the employee to the same or an equivalent position;
3. the employer makes reasonable efforts to contact the employee if an equivalent position becomes available; and
4. the employer continues to make reasonable efforts to contact the employee for one year beginning either on the date the leave related to COVID-19 reasons concludes, or the date twelve weeks after the leave began, whichever is earlier.

FFCRA Exemption for Very Small Businesses

Generally, business owners with fewer than fifty employees can claim an exemption from the paid sick leave and expanded FMLA law if they can show that payment would jeopardize their business as a going concern. DOL FAQ have provided new details, which substantially narrow the availability of the exemption. To qualify, the employee must be taking leave to care for children because of COVID-19 and must satisfy one of three possible criteria to demonstrate that paid leave would jeopardize the business. The three conditions are:

1. providing leave would result in the small business expenses and financial obligations exceeding available business revenues, causing the business to stop operating at minimal capacity;
2. absence of the employee requesting leave would result in a substantial risk to the financial health or operational capabilities of the small business because of their specialized skills, knowledge of the business, or responsibilities; or
3. there are not sufficient workers who are able, willing, and qualified, and who will be available at the time and place needed, to perform the labor or services provided by the employee requesting paid leave, and these labor or services are needed for the small business to operate at a minimal capacity.

Tax Relief for Small Business Owners

The new law contains a tax credit to help small business owners subject to the new paid sick leave and expanded FMLA requirements. The tax credit is computed each quarter, and allows as a credit (1) the amount of qualified paid sick leave wages paid in weeks one-two, and (2) qualified FMLA wages paid (in the remaining ten weeks) during the quarter.

The credit is taken against the employer portion of the Social Security tax. Amounts in excess of the employer Social Security taxes due will be refunded as a credit (in the same manner as though the employer had overpaid Social Security taxes during the quarter). The Act also provides a tax credit for qualified health plan expenses that are allocable to periods when the paid sick leave or family leave wages are paid.

CARES ACT

RMDs Suspended for 2020, Penalty Waived for Coronavirus Distributions

The CARES Act suspended the required minimum distribution (RMD) rules for 2020—a suspension that applies to all 401(k), 403(b), and certain 457(b) deferred compensation plans maintained by the government, as well as IRAs. The law also contains a provision waiving the 10 percent early distribution penalty that applies to retirement account withdrawals. The relief generally mirrors the relief commonly granted in more localized natural disaster situations.

The Act allows employees to take up to $100,000 in distributions from an employer-sponsored retirement plan (401(k), 403(b) or defined benefit plan) or an IRA without becoming subject to the penalty. Unless the participant elects otherwise, inclusion of the distribution in income is spread over three years, beginning with the tax year of distribution. The Act also provides a repayment option, where the participant has the option of repaying the distribution over the three-taxable year period beginning with the tax year of distribution. In this case, the distribution will be treated as an eligible rollover made in a trustee-to-trustee transfer within the sixty-day window.

Qualified Plan Loans

The CARES Act relaxed the rules to provide relief for qualified plan participants with existing plan loans. If a participant had an existing plan loan with a repayment obligation falling between March 27 and December 31, 2020, that repayment obligation was extended for one year. Any subsequent repayment obligations are to be adjusted to reflect this extension. For plan participants who are "qualifying individuals," the plan loan limits were increased to the greater of $100,000 or 100 percent of the vested balance in the participant's account.

NOL Relief for Struggling Businesses

The CARES Act allows corporations to carry back net operating losses (NOLs) incurred in 2018, 2019, and 2020 for five years (excluding offset to untaxed foreign earnings transition tax). Post-tax reform, these NOLs could only be carried forward. For tax years beginning prior to January 1, 2021, businesses can offset 100 percent of taxable income with NOL carryovers and carrybacks (the 80 percent taxable income limitation was lifted).

With respect to partnerships and pass-through entities, the CARES Act amended the effective date for the new excess business loss rules created by the 2017 tax reform legislation. The new rules will only apply beginning in 2021 (rather than 2018). Pass-through taxpayers who have filed a return reflecting excess business losses will presumably be entitled to refund by filing an amended return, absent guidance to the contrary.

Expanded Charitable Donation Deduction for 2020

The CARES Act made several changes designed to encourage charitable giving during the COVID-19 outbreak. For the 2020 tax year, the CARES Act amended IRC Section 62(a), allowing taxpayers to reduce adjusted gross income (AGI) by $300 worth of charitable contributions made in 2020 even if they do not itemize.

Under normal circumstances, taxpayers are only permitted to deduct cash contributions to charity to the extent those donations do not exceed 60 percent of AGI (10 percent for corporations). The CARES Act lifts the 60 percent AGI limit for 2020. Cash contributions to public charities and certain private foundations in 2020 are not subject to the AGI limit. Individual taxpayers can offset their income for 2020 up to the full amount of their AGI, and additional charitable contributions can be carried over to offset income in a later year (the amounts are not refundable). The corporate AGI limit was raised to 25 percent (excess contributions also carry over to subsequent tax years).

Penalty-Free Payroll Tax Deferral

The CARES Act allows both employers and independent contractors to defer payment of employer payroll taxes without penalty. Importantly, employers with fewer than 500 employees are entitled to withhold payroll taxes as an advance repayment of the tax credit for paid sick leave and expanded FMLA leave under the FFCRA.

Under the CARES Act payroll tax deferral, employers are permitted to defer the employer portion of the payroll tax on wages paid through December 31, 2020 for up to two years. Payroll taxes are generally due in two installments under CARES: 50 percent by December 31, 2021 and the remaining 50 percent by December 31, 2022. Economic hardship is presumed, meaning the employer does not have to produce documentation establishing that COVID-19 impacted the business. Payroll tax deferral options apparently apply to all employers, regardless of size. However, employers who have loans forgiven under the CARES Act Payroll Protection Loan program are not eligible for the deferral.

Employee Retention Tax Credit

The CARES Act creates a new refundable tax credit designed to help employers who retain employees during the COVID-19 health crisis. The credit is taken against employment taxes and is equal to 50 percent of the first $10,000 of qualified wages paid to the employee. The credit is available for calendar quarters where either (1) operations were either fully or partially suspended because of a government-issued order relating to COVID-19 or (2) the business' gross receipts declined by more than 50 percent when compared to the same calendar quarter in 2019.

Business Interest Elections

The IRS gives businesses substantial flexibility in making and revoking elections related to business interest expense deduction under the CARES Act. A taxpayer may elect under Section163(j)(10)(A)(iii) not to apply the 50 percent ATI limitation for a 2019 or 2020 taxable year (2020 only for partnerships). A taxpayer permitted to make the election makes the election not to apply the 50 percent ATI limitation by timely filing a federal income tax return or Form 1065 (or amendments) using the 30 percent ATI limitation. No formal statement is required to make the election. The taxpayer can then later revoke that election by filing an amended return or form. Similarly, to use 2019 ATI for 2020, the taxpayer merely files using 2019 ATI (and can then later revoke that election by filing a timely amended return or form).

Bonus Depreciation Fix: Amended Returns for Partnerships

The CARES Act provided retroactive relief to partnerships on multiple fronts, including by fixing the so-called "retail glitch" to allow businesses to take advantage of 100 percent bonus depreciation on qualified improvement property through 2022. Existing law may have prevented partnerships from filing amended Forms 1065 and Schedules K-1. Instead, partnerships would have been required to file an administrative adjustment request, so that partners would not have received relief until filing returns for the current tax year.

Retroactive use of Prior Year Corporate AMT Credits

The 2017 Tax Act generally repealed the corporate AMT, but also permitted corporations to continue claiming a minimum credit for prior year AMT paid. The credit can generally be carried forward to offset corporate tax liability in a later year. The CARES Act eliminates certain limitations that applied to the carryover provision, so that corporations can claim refunds for their unused AMT credits for the first tax year that began in 2018 (i.e., the corporation can take the entire amount of the refundable credit for 2018). The corporation must submit the application for refund before December 31, 2020 and, for convenience, the IRS has institutes a fax procedure for both AMT credit and NOL refund purposes.

Telehealth Coverage and HDHP/HSA Eligibility

In response to the evolving COVID-19 pandemic, the CARES Act further expands the pre-deductible services high deductible health plans (HDHPs) may offer. HDHPs are now permitted to cover the cost of telehealth services without cost to participants before the HDHP deductible has been satisfied. HDHPs providing telehealth coverage do not jeopardize their status as HDHPs. Plan members similarly retain the right to fund HSAs after taking advantage of cost-free telehealth services. Under normal rules, HDHPs cannot waive costs for anything other than certain preventative services without jeopardizing HDHP status. Remote health services can be provided under a safe harbor rule through December 31, 2021.

2019 TAX CERTAINTY AND DISASTER RELIEF ACT

The 2019 Tax Certainty and Disaster Relief Act extended the rules governing qualified disaster distributions from retirement accounts, discussed below for victims of disasters that occurred in 2018 through sixty days after enactment of the bill (December 20, 2019). The distribution itself must be made within 180 days after enactment of the law to qualify.

Qualified disaster areas generally include any area the President declares as such. However, to prevent a double benefit, the term "qualified disaster area" does not include the California wildfire disaster area, as defined in the 2018 Bipartisan Budget Act.

In general, the benefits of taking a distribution under the SECURE Act's expansion of the disaster relief option are:

- The taxpayer is exempt from the penalty on early distributions,
- The taxpayer is exempt from withholding requirements on the distribution,
- The taxpayer can elect to treat the distribution as having been distributed over a three-year period (or within the single year of distribution, and
- The taxpayer is able to repay the distribution within three years of receiving the distribution.
- Individuals affected by a qualified disaster qualify for relaxed rules on loans from qualified plans. The plan administrator may increase the regular $50,000 limit on plan loans to $100,000 and the 50 percent of vested benefit limit to 100 percent.

IRS NOTICES

Notice 2020-15: HDHPs Can Pay Coronavirus Costs

The IRS announced that high deductible health plans are permitted to cover the costs associated with the coronavirus. HDHPs can cover coronavirus-related testing and equipment needed to treat the virus. Generally, HDHPs are prohibited from covering certain non-specified expenses before the covered individual's deductible has been met. Certain preventative care expenses are excepted from this rule. HDHPs will not jeopardize their status if they pay coronavirus-related expenses before the insured has met the deductible, and the insured will remain HSA-eligible. The guidance applies only to HSA-eligible HDHPs.

Notice 2020-18: 90-Day Extension of the Federal Tax Payment Deadline

In response to the coronavirus pandemic, the IRS has announced that it will extend the tax payment deadline from April 15, 2020 to July 15, 2020. Interest and penalties during this period will also be waived. The April 15 filing deadline was also extended to July 15, although in separate guidance. Individuals and pass-through business entities owing up to $1 million in federal tax are eligible for the relief, as are corporations owing up to $10 million in federal tax. Individuals who do not anticipate being able to file by July 15 should be aware of their option for requesting a six-month filing extension to October 15. The extension is available by filing Form 4868.

Notice 2020-23: IRS Expands COVID-19 Extensions

Notice 2020-23 provides expanded relief for taxpayers with a filing or payment obligation arising after April 1, 2020 and before July 15, 2020. Specifically, deadlines are extended to July 15, 2020 for actions required with respect to:

1. estate and trust income tax payments and return filings;
2. estate and generation-skipping transfer tax payments and return filings on Form 706 and related forms;

3. gift and generation-skipping transfer tax payments and return filings on Form 709 and related forms; and

4. estate tax payments of principal or interest due as a result of an election made under IRC sections 6166, 6161, or 6163 and annual recertification requirements under section 6166.

Similarly, taxpayers who faced deadlines with respect to Tax Court actions between April 1 and July 15 have their deadlines postponed until July 15.

Revenue Procedure 2020-23 also allows partnerships to file amended returns and issue revised Schedules K-1 for 2018 and 2019 to take advantage of retroactive CARES Act relief (and, absent further guidance, even if they are not taking advantage of CARES Act relief). The relief applies for 2018 and 2019 as long as the original Forms 1065 and Schedules K-1 were filed/issued before April 13, 2020 (the date Rev. Proc. 2020-23 was released).

Partnerships can file amended Form 1065 and Schedule K-1 (electronically or by mail), by checking the Form 1065 "amended return" box and writing "FILED PURSUANT TO REV PROC 2020-23" at the top. The same statement must be included in a statement attached to amended Schedules K-1 sent to partners. The amended returns must be filed/furnished to partners by September 30, 2020.

IRS AND DOL FAQS

COVID-19 Filing, Payment Extensions

The IRS FAQ clarifies that the filing and payment extensions (from April 15 to July 15) apply regardless of whether the taxpayer is actually sick or quarantined because of COVID-19. For fiscal year taxpayers with 2019 returns due April 15, the deadline is extended to July 15 regardless of whether April 15 is an original or extended filing deadline. Taxpayers facing filing or payment deadlines that are not April 15 must note that their deadlines have not generally been extended.

The relief also does not apply to payroll or excise tax payments (deposit dates remain unchanged, but employers may be eligible for the new paid sick leave tax credit, see Tax Facts Q 8550). Taxpayers do not have to do anything to take advantage of the extension—they simply file their returns and make required payments by the new July 15 deadline. Taxpayers who filed and schedule a payment for April 15 must, however, take action to reschedule their payment for July 15 if they wish (by contacting the credit or debit card company if the payment was scheduled directly with the card issuer).

Counting Employees for COVID-19 Paid Sick Leave & FMLA Expansion Purposes

A new DOL FAQ provides that an employer is subject to the expanded paid sick leave and FMLA rules if the employer has fewer than 500 full-time and part-time employees. Employees on leave and temporary employees should be included, while independent contractors are not included in the count. Each corporation is usually a single employer. When a corporation has an ownership interest in another corporation, the two are separate employers unless they are joint employers for Fair Labor Standards Act purposes. Joint employer status is based on a facts and circumstances analysis, and is generally the case when (1) one employer employs the employee, but another benefits from the work or (2) one employer employs an employee for one set of hours in a workweek, and another employer employs the same employee for a separate set of hours in the same workweek.

Extension of COBRA Election Period

Under normal circumstances, an individual has sixty days from the date when a COBRA qualifying event occurs to elect COBRA coverage (or make a new COBRA election). In light of the COVID-19 outbreak, the IRS and DOL have announced an extension of this sixty-day window. The sixty-day election window is essentially paused for relevant time periods that include March 1, 2020. The clock is stopped and will not resume ticking until the end of the "outbreak period". The outbreak period is defined as the window of time beginning March 1, 2020 and ending sixty days after the date that the COVID-19 national emergency is declared ended. The forty-five-day payment clock and thirty-day grace period for late COBRA payments are also paused.

AFTER-TAX EQUIVALENTS OF TAX-EXEMPT YIELDS

APPENDIX A

TAX EXEMPT YIELDS

Bracket	10%	12%	22%	24%	32%	35%	37%
1.0	1.11	1.14	1.28	1.32	1.47	1.54	1.59
1.1	1.22	1.25	1.41	1.45	1.62	1.69	1.75
1.2	1.33	1.36	1.54	1.58	1.76	1.85	1.90
1.3	1.44	1.48	1.67	1.71	1.91	2.00	2.06
1.4	1.56	1.59	1.79	1.84	2.06	2.15	2.22
1.5	1.67	1.70	1.92	1.97	2.21	2.31	2.38
1.6	1.78	1.82	2.05	2.11	2.35	2.46	2.54
1.7	1.89	1.93	2.18	2.24	2.50	2.62	2.70
1.8	2.00	2.05	2.31	2.37	2.65	2.77	2.86
1.9	2.11	2.16	2.44	2.50	2.79	2.92	3.02
2.0	2.22	2.27	2.56	2.63	2.94	3.08	3.17
2.1	2.33	2.39	2.69	2.76	3.09	3.23	3.33
2.2	2.44	2.50	2.82	2.89	3.24	3.38	3.49
2.3	2.56	2.61	2.95	3.03	3.38	3.54	3.65
2.4	2.67	2.73	3.08	3.16	3.53	3.69	3.81
2.5	2.78	2.84	3.21	3.29	3.68	3.85	3.97
2.6	2.89	2.95	3.33	3.42	3.82	4.00	4.13
2.7	3.00	3.07	3.46	3.55	3.97	4.15	4.29
2.8	3.11	3.18	3.59	3.68	4.12	4.31	4.44
2.9	3.22	3.30	3.72	3.82	4.26	4.46	4.60
3.0	3.33	3.41	3.85	3.95	4.41	4.62	4.76
3.1	3.44	3.52	3.97	4.08	4.56	4.77	4.92
3.2	3.56	3.64	4.10	4.21	4.71	4.92	5.08
3.3	3.67	3.75	4.23	4.34	4.85	5.08	5.24
3.4	3.78	3.86	4.36	4.47	5.00	5.23	5.40
3.5	3.89	3.98	4.49	4.61	5.15	5.38	5.56
3.6	4.00	4.09	4.62	4.74	5.29	5.54	5.71

TAX EXEMPT YIELDS	Bracket	10%	12%	22%	24%	32%	35%	37%
	3.7	4.11	4.20	4.74	4.87	5.44	5.69	5.87
	3.8	4.22	4.32	4.87	5.00	5.59	5.85	6.03
	3.9	4.33	4.43	5.00	5.13	5.74	6.00	6.19
	4.0	4.44	4.55	5.13	5.26	5.88	6.15	6.35
	4.1	4.56	4.66	5.26	5.39	6.03	6.31	6.51
	4.2	4.67	4.77	5.38	5.53	6.18	6.46	6.67
	4.3	4.78	4.89	5.51	5.66	6.32	6.62	6.83
	4.4	4.89	5.00	5.64	5.79	6.47	6.77	6.98
	4.5	5.00	5.11	5.77	5.92	6.62	6.92	7.14
	4.6	5.11	5.23	5.90	6.05	6.76	7.08	7.30
	4.7	5.22	5.34	6.03	6.18	6.91	7.23	7.46
	4.8	5.33	5.45	6.15	6.32	7.06	7.38	7.62
	4.9	5.44	5.57	6.28	6.45	7.21	7.54	7.78
	5.0	5.56	5.68	6.41	6.58	7.35	7.69	7.94
	5.1	5.67	5.80	6.54	6.71	7.50	7.85	8.10
	5.2	5.78	5.91	6.67	6.84	7.65	8.00	8.25
	5.3	5.89	6.02	6.79	6.97	7.79	8.15	8.41
	5.4	6.00	6.14	6.92	7.11	7.94	8.31	8.57
	5.5	6.11	6.25	7.05	7.24	8.09	8.46	8.73
	5.6	6.22	6.36	7.18	7.37	8.24	8.62	8.89
	5.7	6.33	6.48	7.31	7.50	8.38	8.77	9.05
	5.8	6.44	6.59	7.44	7.63	8.53	8.92	9.21
	5.9	6.56	6.70	7.56	7.76	8.68	9.08	9.37
	6.0	6.67	6.82	7.69	7.89	8.82	9.23	9.52

SUGGESTED CHARITABLE GIFT ANNUITY RATES–SINGLE LIFE

APPENDIX B

Approved by the American Council on Gift Annuities on April 24, 2018 Rates effective as of July 1, 2018			
Age	**Rate**	**Age**	**Rate**
5-15	3.0	67-68	5.3
16-20	3.1	69	5.4
21-24	3.2	70	5.6
25-28	3.3	71	5.7
29-34	3.4	72	5.8
35-38	3.5	73	5.9
39-41	3.6	74	6.1
42-44	3.7	75	6.2
45-47	3.8	76	6.4
48-49	3.9	77	6.6
50-51	4.0	78	6.8
52-53	4.1	79	7.1
54	4.2	80	7.3
55-56	4.3	81	7.5
57	4.4	82	7.7
58	4.5	83	7.9
59	4.6	84	8.1
60-61	4.7	85	8.3
62	4.8	86	8.5
63	4.9	87	8.7
64	5.0	88	8.9
65	5.1	89	9.2
66	5.2	90+	9.5

Approved by the American Council on Gift Annuities on April 24, 2018
Rates effective as of July 1, 2018

WARNING: These annuity rates, for both immediate and deferred annuities and for both single life and two lives, should not be used if the gift portion, based on IRS tables and the applicable discount rate, is not more than 10 percent of the amount paid for the annuity.

NOTES:

1. The rates are for ages at the nearest birthday.
2. For immediate gift annuities, these rates will result in a charitable deduction of at least 10 percent if the CFMR [IRC Sec. 7520 interest rate] is 2.8 percent or higher, whatever the payment frequency. If the CFMR is less than 2.8 percent, the deduction will be less than 10 percent when annuitants are below certain ages.
3. For deferred gift annuities with longer deferral periods, the rates may not pass the 10 percent test when the CFMR is low.
4. To avoid adverse tax consequences, the charity should reduce the gift annuity rate to whatever level is necessary to generate a charitable deduction in excess of 10 percent.

Source: American Council on Gift Annuities

GROUP TERM LIFE INSURANCE

APPENDIX C

General. In general, the cost of up to $50,000 of group-term life insurance coverage provided to an employee by his employer is *not* includable in the employee's gross income. However, the employee must include in his income the cost of employer-provided insurance that exceeds $50,000 of coverage, and then reduce that amount by any amount the employee paid toward the purchase of the insurance.[1]

If the individual's employer provided *more than* $50,000 of coverage, the amount included in the employee's income is reported as part of his wages in Box 1 of Form W-2. It is also shown in Box 12 with code C.[2]

Group-term life insurance is term life insurance protection (i.e., insurance that covers the insured person for a fixed period of time) that:

1. provides a general death benefit that is excluded from gross income under Code section 101(a);
2. is provided to a group of employees;
3. is provided under a policy carried by the employer; and
4. provides an amount of insurance to each employee based on a formula that prevents individual selection.[3]

If a group-term life insurance policy includes "permanent" benefits (i.e., a paid-up or cash surrender value), the employee must include in his income, as wages, the cost of the permanent benefits *minus* the amount the employee paid for them. The employer should tell the employee the amount to include in his income.[4]

Entire cost excluded. Under the following exceptions to the general rule, an employee will *not* be taxed on the cost of group-term life insurance over and above the $50,000 exclusion amount if:

- The employee is permanently and totally disabled and has ended his employment;[5]
- The individual's employer is the beneficiary (directly or indirectly) of the policy for the entire period the insurance is in force during the tax year;[6] or
- A charitable organization to which contributions are deductible is the only beneficiary of the policy for the entire period the insurance is in force during the tax year.[7]

Entire cost taxed. Under the following circumstances, the $50,000 exclusion amount will not apply, requiring the employee to be taxed on the entire cost of group-term life insurance. The $50,000 exclusion occurs if either of the following circumstances applies:

- The individual's employer through a qualified employees' trust, such as a pension trust or a qualified annuity plan, provides the insurance;[8] or
- The individual is a key employee and his employer's plan discriminates in favor of key employees.[9]

Calculating the cost. To figure the taxable cost for each month of coverage, the employee should multiply the number of thousands of dollars of insurance coverage for the month (less $50,000, figured to the nearest tenth) by the cost from the table below. The employee's age on the last day of the tax year should be used.[10] The employee should prorate the cost from the table if less than a full month of coverage is involved.[11]

Table I – Uniform premiums for $1,000 of group term life insurance protection* (effective for group term life insurance provided after June 30, 1999)	
5-Year Age Bracket	*Cost per $1,000 of protection for 1-month period*
Under 25	$0.05
25 to 29	0.06
30 to 34	0.08
35 to 39	0.09
40 to 44	0.10
45 to 49	0.15
50 to 54	0.23
55 to 59	0.43
60 to 64	0.66
65 to 69	1.27
70 and above	2.06
*In using the above table, the age of the employee is his attained age on the last day of his taxable year. Reg. §1.79-3(d)(2).	

If the employee pays any part of the cost of the insurance, his entire payment reduces, dollar-for-dollar, the amount the employee would otherwise include in his income. However, an employee *cannot* reduce the amount that is includable in his income by:

- Payments for coverage in a different tax year;
- Payments for coverage through a cafeteria plan (unless the payments are after-tax contributions); or
- Payments for coverage not taxed to him because of the exceptions discussed above.[12]

Example: For example, assume that an employee, age fifty-two, is provided with $150,000 of group term life insurance coverage in each month of the taxable year 2014. His employer pays the entire premium. As seen in the calculation below, the excess coverage for each month of the taxable year is $100,000 ($150,000 – $50,000). The cost of the group term insurance is $276, which is arrived at by multiplying the Table I rate of $0.23 for age fifty-two by twelve months to obtain a yearly rate of $2.76, and then multiplying this rate by one hundred to obtain $276, the cost for $100,000 of coverage.

Cost of Group Term Life Insurance in Excess of $50,000	
Employee's Date of Birth:	January 1, 1955 (Age: 52)
End Employer's Taxable Year:	Calendar
Employee's Contribution:	$0
Employee's Tax Bracket:	28.00%
Level Amount of Group Insurance:	$150,000
Cost of Group Term Insurance:	$276
Estimated Tax on Term Group Insurance:	$78

Assume further that the employee contributes $0.15 per month per $1,000 of insurance. The employee's total contribution for the year would amount to $180, which is calculated by multiply the $0.15 by twelve months and then by one hundred. The $180 is subtracted from the cost of $276 to arrive at a figure of $96, which the employee must include in income.

The "price" of excess coverage, as computed above, is not, of course, the tax payable but the amount to be included in the employee's gross income. Thus, in the first example, if the employee's marginal tax bracket is 28 percent, he is obtaining $150,000 of group term coverage for a price of $78 (28 percent of $276) for the taxable year.

ENDNOTES

1. IRC Sec. 79(a).
2. See IRC Sec. 6052(a); Treas. Reg. §§1.6052-1, 1.6052-2.

3. Treas. Reg. §1.79-1(a).
4. Treas. Reg. §1.79-1(d).
5. IRC Secs. 79(b)(1); 72(m)(7).
6. IRC Sec. 79(b)(2)(A).
7. IRC Sec. 79(b)(b)(2)(B).
8. IRC Sec. 79(b)(3); Treas. Reg. §1.79-2(d)(1).
9. IRC Sec. 79(d)(1).
10. Treas. Reg. §1.79-3(d)(2).
11. See IRC Sec.79(c); Treas. Reg. §1.79-3
12. Treas. Reg. §1.79-3(f)(2).

INCOME TAX RATE SCHEDULES

APPENDIX D

TAXABLE YEARS BEGINNING IN 2020

SINGLE INDIVIDUALS					JOINT RETURNS AND SURVIVING SPOUSES				
Taxable Income			*Tax on Lower Amount*	*Tax Rate on Excess*	*Taxable Income*			*Tax on Lower Amount*	*Tax Rate on Excess*
$-0-	to	$9,875	$-0-	10%	$-0-	to	$19,750	$-0-	10%
9,875	to	40,125	987.50	12%	19,750	to	80,250	1,975.00	12%
40,125	to	85,525	4,617.50	22%	80,250	to	171,050	9,235.00	22%
85,525	to	163,300	14,605.50	24%	171,050	to	326,600	29,211.00	24%
163,300	to	207,350	33,271.50	32%	326,600	to	414,700	66,543.00	32%
207,350	to	518,400	47,367.50	35%	414,700	to	622,050	94,735.00	35%
518,400	to	......	156,235.00	37%	622,050	to	......	167,307.50	37%

MARRIED FILING SEPARATELY					HEAD OF HOUSEHOLD				
Taxable Income			*Tax on Lower Amount*	*Tax Rate on Excess*	*Taxable Income*			*Tax on Lower Amount*	*Tax Rate on Excess*
$0	to	$9,875	$-0-	10%	$-0-	to	$14,100	$-0-	10%
9,875	to	40,125	987.50	12%	14,100	to	53,700	1,410.00	12%
40,125	to	85,525	4,617.50	22%	53,700	to	85,500	6,162.00	22%
85,525	to	163,300	14,605.50	24%	85,500	to	163,300	13,158.00	24%
163,300	to	207,350	33,271.50	32%	163,300	to	207,350	31,830.00	32%
207,350	to	311,025	47,367.50	35%	207,350	to	518,400	45,926.00	35%
311,025		......	83,653.75	37%	518,400	to	......	154,793.50	37%

TAX RATE SCHEDULE FOR ESTATES AND TRUST				
Taxable Income			*Tax on Lower Amount*	*Tax Rate on Excess*
$-0-	to	$2,600	$-0-	10%
2,600	to	9,450	260.00	24%
9,450	to	12,950	1,904.00	35%
12,950	to	......	3,129.00	37%

TAXABLE YEARS BEGINNING IN 2019

SINGLE INDIVIDUALS					JOINT RETURNS AND SURVIVING SPOUSES				
Taxable Income			*Tax on Lower Amount*	*Tax Rate on Excess*	*Taxable Income*			*Tax on Lower Amount*	*Tax Rate on Excess*
$-0-	to	$9,700	$-0-	10%	$-0-	to	$19,400	$-0-	10%
9,700	to	39,475	970.00	12%	19,400	to	78,950	1,940.00	12%
39,475	to	84,200	4,543.00	22%	78,950	to	168,400	9,086.00	22%
84,200	to	160,725	14,382.50	24%	168,400	to	321,450	28,765.00	24%
160,725	to	204,100	32,748.50	32%	321,450	to	408,200	65,497.00	32%
204,100	to	510,300	46,628.50	35%	408,200	to	612,350	93,257.00	35%
510,300	to	......	153,798.50	37%	612,350	to	......	164,709.50	37%

MARRIED FILING SEPARATELY					HEAD OF HOUSEHOLD				
Taxable Income			*Tax on Lower Amount*	*Tax Rate on Excess*	*Taxable Income*			*Tax on Lower Amount*	*Tax Rate on Excess*
$-0-	to	$9,700	$-0	10%	$-0-	to	$13,850	$-0-	10%
9,700	to	39,475	970.00	12%	13,850	to	52,850	1,385.00	12%
39,475	to	84,200	4,543.00	22%	52,850	to	84,200	6,065.00	22%
84,200	to	160,725	14,382.50	24%	84,200	to	160,700	12,962.00	24%
160,725	to	204,100	32,748.50	32%	160,700	to	204,100	31,322.00	32%
204,100	to	306,175	46,628.50	35%	204,100	to	510,300	45,210.00	35%
306,175		......	82,354.75	37%	510,300	to	......	152,380.00	37%

TAX RATE SCHEDULE FOR ESTATES AND TRUSTS				
Taxable Income			*Tax on Lower Amount*	*Tax Rate on Excess*
$-0-	to	$2,600	$-0-	10%
2,600	to	9,300	260.00	24%
9,300	to	12,750	1,868.00	35%
12,750	to	......	3,075.00	37%

INNOCENT SPOUSE RULES

APPENDIX E

Married taxpayers typically choose to file a joint tax return because this filing status provides certain benefits. If married taxpayers file a joint tax return, both are jointly and individually responsible for the tax and any interest or penalty due on the joint return even if they later divorce.[1] This is true even if a divorce decree states that a former spouse will be responsible for any amounts due on previously filed joint returns. One spouse may be held responsible for all the tax due even if the other spouse earned all the income.

However, in some cases, based on the innocent spouse rules, a spouse may be relieved of some or all of his or her joint and several liability for tax, interest, and penalties assessed on a joint tax return.[2] The three types of relief are as follows:

- ***Innocent spouse relief*** for additional tax owed by a spouse because his or her spouse (or former spouse) failed to report income or claimed improper deductions or credits;
- ***Separation of liability relief*** provides for the allocation of any item giving rise to a deficiency on a joint return to the spouse responsible for the deficiency as if the responsible spouse had reported such item on a separate return.[2] In other words, it shifts the joint liability for the deficiency to the responsible spouse;[3] and
- ***Equitable relief*** may apply when a spouse does not qualify for innocent spouse relief or separation of liability relief with regard to an unpaid tax or deficiency.[4]

INNOCENT SPOUSE RELIEF

A spouse must meet all of the following conditions to qualify for innocent spouse relief:

- The spouse must have filed a joint return that has an understatement of tax directly related to his or her spouse's erroneous items. Any income omitted from the joint return is an erroneous item. Deductions, credits, and property bases (for computing taxable gain or loss) are erroneous items if they are incorrectly reported on the joint return.
- The spouse establishes that at the time he or she signed the joint return, he or she did not know, and had no reason to know, that there was an understatement of tax.
- Taking into account all the facts and circumstances, it would be unfair to hold the spouse liable for the understatement of tax; and
- The spouse requests relief no later than two years after the date the IRS first attempted to collect the tax from him or her.[5]

SEPARATION OF LIABILITY RELIEF

To qualify for separation of liability relief, the following conditions must be satisfied:

- A joint return was filed.
- At the time of the election, the spouse requesting the relief was separated or divorced (or widowed) or had not been a member of the same household at any time during the twelve-month period ending on the date of the request for relief.

- The requesting spouse sought relief within two years of the first IRS collection activity.

- At the time of the signing of the joint return, the requesting spouse had no actual knowledge of the non-requesting spouse's item giving rise to the deficiency.[6]

EQUITABLE RELIEF

A spouse who does not qualify for innocent spouse relief or separation of liability relief, may qualify for equitable relief from joint and several liability. Unlike the latter two forms of relief, equitable relief covers underpayment of tax attributable to the other spouse in addition to an income tax deficiency. Rev. Proc. 2013-34[7] sets forth a three-step procedure to determine whether equitable relief is warranted.

First, the following threshold requirements must be met:

1. The requesting spouse filed a join return for the tax year in question.

2. The requesting spouse does not qualify for innocent spouse relief or separation of liability relief.

3. The claim for relief is timely filed.[8]

4. There were no assets transferred between the spouses as part of a fraudulent scheme by the spouses.

5. The non-requesting spouse did not transfer disqualified assets to the requesting spouse.[9]

6. The requesting spouse did not knowingly participate in the filing of a fraudulent joint return.

7. Absent certain exceptions, the tax liability from which the requesting spouse seeks relief is attributable to an item of the non-requesting spouse that resulted in a deficiency or an underpayment of tax.

Second, in order to qualify for streamlined relief, the following three conditions must be met:

1. The spouse requesting the relief was separated or divorced (or widowed) or had not been a member of the same household at any time during the twelve-month period ending on the date of the request for relief.

2. The spouse requesting relief would suffer economic hardship[10] is relief was not granted.

3. The spouse requesting relief did not know and or have reason to know that there was a deficiency with regard to the originally filed return, or, in the case of an underpayment, did not know or have reason to know that the non-requesting spouse would or could not pay the tax liability reported on the joint return.

Finally, if the requesting spouse fails to qualify for streamlined relief, equitable relief may be available if taking into account all of the facts and circumstances, it would be inequitable to hold the requesting spouse responsible for the deficiency or underpayment. Rev. Proc. 2013-34 lists the following non-exclusive list of factors to be considered in determining whether equitable relief is warranted. In doing so, the IRS "grades" the factors as weighing in favor of relief, against relief or neutral:

1. Whether the requesting spouse was married to the non-requesting spouse at the time the IRS made its determination regarding the deficiency or underpayment.

2. Economic hardship, i.e., the ability of the requesting spouse to pay reasonable living expenses if relief is not granted.

3. Lack of actual knowledge or reason to know of deficiency or whether the non-requesting spouse would not or could not pay the tax liability (that was ultimately not paid) at the time or within a reasonable amount of time after filing the return.[11]

4. Legal obligation by the requesting or non-requesting spouse to pay the outstanding tax liability as evidenced by a divorce decree or other legally binding agreement.

5. Whether the requesting spouse received a significant benefit from the unpaid tax or deficiency. A significant benefit goes beyond normal support and encompasses a lavish lifestyle. The revenue procedure further provides that if the amount of the unpaid tax or deficiency is small so that

neither spouse received a significant benefit, this factor is considered to be neutral. However, in a recent decision, the Tax Court rejected the revenue procedure's characterization of that factor being graded neutral – holding that the lack of a significant benefit from a relatively small deficiency should weigh in favor of relief for the requesting spouse.[12]

6. Whether the requesting spouse has made a good faith effort to comply with the income tax laws in the taxable years following the taxable year or years to which the relief relates.

7. The state of the requesting spouse's mental or physical health at the time the return or returns were filed.

HOW IT IS DONE

In order to request innocent spouse relief, separation of liability relief, or equitable relief, the requesting spouse must:

- file Form 8857 (Request for Innocent Spouse Relief) or a written statement containing the same information required on Form 8857, and

- sign Form 8857, or the written statement, under penalties of perjury.[13]

If a spouse requests relief from joint liability, the IRS is required to notify the non-requesting spouse to allow him or her to oppose the request by providing the IRS with relevant information.[14] If the IRS denies the spouse's request for relief, he or she may challenge the denial by filing a petition for review by the Tax Court.[15] In that event, the Tax Court must provide the non-requesting spouse notice of the proceeding and allow him or her to become a party in opposition to the request for relief.[16]

Spouses living in community property states (Arizona, California, Idaho, Louisiana, Nevada, New Mexico, Texas, Washington and Wisconsin) who file separate returns are also eligible for innocent spouse relief.[17]

Finally, it is possible that as part of the relief granted, the requesting spouse may be entitled to refund or tax credit with respect to amounts he or she paid to the IRS. This relief, however, is not available to spouse's requesting separation of liability relief.[18]

INJURED SPOUSE RELIEF

The IRS has the authority to apply a taxpayer's income tax refund from one tax year against outstanding income tax liabilities from other tax years.[19] As a result, if one spouse has an outstanding tax liability that he or she is solely responsible to pay, it may create a dilemma if the couple files a joint return. If such a joint return generates a refund, the IRS will generally apply the entire refund to the outstanding tax liability of the responsible spouse[20]—thus depriving the non-responsible spouse of his or her share of the refund. However, if the non-responsible spouse files an "injured spouse" claim, the IRS is required to pay over his or her share of the refund.[21] In order to make the claim, the injured spouse files a Form 8379 either with the originally filed joint return or separately.

ENDNOTES

1. IRC Sec. 6013(d)(3); IRS Publication 971.
2. *Howerter v. Comm'r.*, T.C. Summary Opinion 2014-15 (February 19, 2014).
3. IRC Sec. 6015(c).
4. IRC Sec. 6015(f).
5. IRC Sec. 6015(b).
6. IRC Sec. 6015(c), 6015(c)(3); Treas. Reg. §1.6015-3.
7. 2013-43 I.R.B. 397, superseding Rev. Proc. 2003-2 C.B. 296.
8. If the relief is of joint and several tax liability, the claim must be made within the ten-year collection statute of limitation period. Rev. Proc. 2013-34, §4.01(3)(a). If the relief is a claim for a tax credit or refund, the claim must be made by the later of three years from the date the return was filed or two years from the date of payment. Rev. Proc. 2013-34, §4.01(3)(b).
9. A "disqualifying asset" is an asset transferred from the non-requesting spouse (the one who purportedly should be responsible for the tax) to the requesting spouse for the principal purpose of tax avoidance. IRC Sec. 6015(c)(4)(B).
10. Economic hardship such that the requesting spouse would lack the means necessary for basic living expenses.
11. With regard to knowledge of whether the tax liability could or would be paid, the revenue procedure provides that if the requesting spouse was abused by the non-requesting spouse or the non-requesting spouse maintained control of the household finances by restricting the requesting spouse's access to that information; and, because of the abuse or financial control, the requesting spouse was not able to question the payment of the tax reported for fear of the non-requesting spouse's retaliation, this factor would weigh in favor of relief even if the requesting spouse knew or had reason to know of the non-requesting spouse's intent or ability to pay the taxes.
12. *Howerter v. Comm'r.*, T.C. Summary Opinion 2014-15 (February 19, 2014).
13. Treas. Reg. §1.6015-5.
14. IRC Sec. 6015(h)(2); Treas. Reg. §1.6015-6.

15. IRC Sec. 6015(e).
16. IRC Sec. 6015(e)(4).
17. IRC Sec. 66(c); Treas. Reg. §1.66-4, Rev. Proc. 2013-34, 2013-43 I.R.B. 397 superseding Rev. Proc. 2003-61, 2003-2 C.B. 296.
18. IRC Sec. 6015(g)(3).
19. IRC Sec. 6402(b).
20. Rev. Rul. 84-171, 1984-2 C.B. 310.
21. IRM 25.15.1.2.5; Treas. Reg. §§31.285.2(f) and (g).

INDEX

A

B

C

D

I

J

K

L

M

N

P

S

T

U

W